D1484701

How to Prepare for
FLORIDA REAL ESTATE EXAMS

Salesperson, Broker, Appraiser

by

J. Bruce Lindeman, Ph.D.
Professor of Real Estate
University of Arkansas
at Little Rock

Jack P. Friedman, Ph.D., CPA, MAI
Author and Consultant, Dallas, Texas
Former Laguarta Professor of Real Estate
Department of Finance/Real Estate Research Center
Texas A&M University

BARRON'S

© Copyright 1997 by Barron's Educational Series, Inc.

All rights reserved.
No part of this book may be reproduced
in any form, by photostat, microfilm, xerography,
or any other means, or incorporated into any
information retrieval system, electronic or
mechanical, without the written permission
of the copyright owner.

All inquiries should be addressed to:
Barron's Educational Series, Inc.
250 Wireless Boulevard
Hauppauge, New York 11788

Library of Congress Catalog Card No. 96-45154

International Standard Book No. 0-8120-9809-9

Library of Congress Cataloging-in-Publication Data

Lindeman, J. Bruce (John Bruce)
    How to prepare for Florida real estate exams : salesperson,
  broker, appraiser / by J. Bruce Lindeman, Jack P. Friedman.
        p.   cm.
    ISBN 0-8120-9809-9
    1. Real estate agents—Licenses—Florida. 2. Real property—Florida—
  Examinations, questions, etc.   I. Friedman, Jack P.   II. Title.
  KFF282.R4L56   1997
  346.75904'3'076—dc21   95-45154
                                                        CIP

PRINTED IN THE UNITED STATES OF AMERICA

98765

CONTENTS

Illustrations

Tables

PREFACE

In recent years, legal, social, economic, and financial matters affecting Florida real estate have become more complex, creating greater educational needs for those who are engaged in the real estate business. In Florida today, a salesperson, broker, or appraiser cannot survive solely on a pleasant disposition and a neat appearance. Real estate workers must be aware of and obey federal, state, and local regulations. They need in-depth knowledge of each property being brokered, including its physical surroundings and its economic, legal, social, and political environment.

In recognition of these needs, Florida has adopted more stringent standards for the licensure of real estate brokers and salespersons. These standards include more education, and more rigorous examinations. Population mobility, the need for licensure reciprocity, increased federal regulation, and greater communication and cooperation between state license law officials have all led to greater uniformity in real estate licensing standards. Also, as of 1993, real estate appraisers had to be state certified. Appraisers (both experienced workers and new entrants) now must take qualifying examinations that can lead to three levels. As a result, the appraisal section of the book now serves the needs of those desiring preparation for appraiser certification or licensing as well as those who seek sales or broker licenses.

This book was written as an introduction to real estate, taking into consideration real estate complexities, the need for more knowledge, and the trend toward uniformity among states. It is primarily intended to serve those seeking to meet licensure requirements, but it may also satisfy the needs of persons wanting to know more about real property law, contracts, finance, brokerage, ethics, leasing, appraisal, mathematics, fair housing, truth in lending, and other such topics. For the person just wanting to buy or sell a home, the glossary may serve as a reference for greater understanding of the transaction. It alone can prevent misunderstandings that are costly in terms of time and money.

A careful reading of any document is crucial to understanding it. Many people have unfortunately lost money by failing to read and understand contracts before signing them. Similarly, a careful reading of this book will be helpful toward understanding the complex subject—real estate—it concerns. Questions have been included at the end of each chapter and comprehensive exams at the end of the book so that you can test your understanding of the material presented, both chapter by chapter and at the end. Though your instructor can be of valuable assistance, the knowledge that you gain will approximate the effort that you expend.

Should you become actively engaged in the real estate business, we wish you success. We hope that all your dealings will be honest and fair. Only in this way can the real estate business become recognized as a profession.

We are grateful to the many people who have aided us in preparing this book, especially Suzanne Barnhill and Max Reed. The Florida Association of Realtors gave us permission to reproduce their Listing Contract and Contract for Sale and Purchase. Attorneys' Title Insurance Fund, Inc. of Orlando, Florida allowed us to reproduce their Warranty Deed form. We thank both of them. We thank our families for their patience and dedicate this book to them.

J. Bruce Lindeman
Jack P. Friedman

PART I: INTRODUCTION TO REAL ESTATE

Chapter 1/*How to Use This Book*

If you are reading this book, you are probably interested in employment in the real estate field in Florida. Real estate is a fast-growing, exciting field that offers almost unlimited income potential to a person who is willing to work hard and to learn the special features of this very interesting business.

If you want to enter the real estate business as a salesperson, broker, or appraiser, then, among other requirements, you will have to take and pass an examination. Potential real estate salespeople and real estate brokers take *licensing* examinations in order to get sales or brokerage licenses. A person whose ambition is real estate appraisal takes a *certification* examination in order to become a certified appraiser. In either case, taking the exam is only one step (you also need educational preparation, for example), but it is a very important one. This book is designed to help you to succeed in taking that important step. To fulfill this purpose, the book has a number of important features that enhance its usefulness to you:

1. This book can be used to study for any licensing or certification examination offered in Florida.
2. Special emphasis is given to the topics that license applicants find most troublesome on examinations:
   a. Arithmetic and real estate math
   b. Contracts
   c. Closing statements (for broker applicants)
3. Hundreds of sample questions are included at the ends of chapters, covering all the materials discussed.
4. There are *ten* complete model examinations for you to practice on: two for the salesperson exam, two for the broker's exam, one for each of the three appraisal certification exams, and three supplemental exams for broker applicants, covering listings, sale contracts, and settlement. All in all, well over 2,000 practice questions are provided in the text and examinations combined!
5. A full and complete glossary is included, along with instructions as to the best study strategy for getting the most out of it.
6. Chapter 23, the final chapter before the model tests, describes the *strategy* and *techniques* of taking examinations so that you can be sure to get every point possible.

TOPICS

This book is divided into 23 chapters of text, the sample examinations (Chapter 24), and a final chapter of answers and explanations. Each chapter covers a specific topic. Some are long; others, short. However, it should be remembered that the material in most of the chapters complements the material in the others. This is especially true in Part III, "Real Estate Contracts." The first chapter of Part III (Chapter 6, "Introduction to Contracts") discusses all the things you should know that apply to all of the separate contracts with which you must be familiar. Each of the other chapters in Part III is devoted to one or more types or parts of real estate contracts. For each of these chapters, all the general material in Chapter 6 applies to what you are learning. Chapter 7 discusses land description. Chapters 8 through 12 point out the specific characteristics of each type of real estate contract; these characteristics are in addition to all those mentioned in Chapter 6. Chapters 14 and 15 cover appraisal. No matter what exam you're studying for, you should study Chapter 14, but if you aren't preparing for an appraisal certification exam, you can skip Chapter 15.

SAMPLE QUESTIONS AND EXAMINATIONS

Most chapters are followed by sample questions covering the material contained in the chapter and written in the format most frequently encountered on licensing examinations. You can use these questions to test yourself on what you have read.

When you have finished studying the material in the book, you can take the model examinations in Chapter 24. These will enable you to check your retention of the material you have read and will give you some experience in taking real estate examinations in a format similar to the licensing examination. Each exam has time limits as indicated.

You should not take all the examinations at once. Rather, take one, and then correct it, using the key in Chapter 26. The questions you got wrong will pinpoint the areas in which you need further study. Do this additional studying, and then take the second examination. Once again, use the questions you missed to guide you to still further study. For questions involving mathematics, the answer explanations in Chapter 26 should help you to understand why you missed each question you got wrong and to avoid making the same mistake again. Then take the third examination, once again using the few questions you miss as guides for final study before taking the licensing examination itself.

If you are applying for a broker's license, you will also find the supplemental examinations on closing statements (settlement statements) and on contracts helpful. If your state uses the rectangular survey, there is also an applicable practice exam.

TAKING EXAMINATIONS

Chapter 23 has been specially prepared to give you all the knowledge available concerning the *techniques* of taking examinations. This chapter will tell you all you must know about how to prepare for an examination, how to approach it, and how to get the highest score possible. *Be sure to read Chapter 23!* It provides valuable guidelines for taking the licensing examination and will introduce you to the kind of examination you can expect to encounter.

Applying to Take the Examination

All real estate licensing is administered by the Division of Real Estate (DRE) of the Florida Department of Business and Professional Regulation (DBPR). To get information about examinations, and applications to take them, write or call the Division of Real Estate offices in Orlando:

> Division of Real Estate
> 400 West Robinson Street
> P.O. Box 1900
> Orlando, FL 32802-1900
> (407) 245-0810

Examinations are given every month at testing sites in Miami and Orlando. Also, every two months the examinations are given in Panama City.

Both the salesperson's and broker's examinations contain 100 questions; applicants are allowed 2 1/2 hours to take the examinations. Appraiser examinations are of varying lengths.

When you send in your application, you must also include two 2- × 2-inch photographs suitable for identification purposes, and a set of your fingerprints (obtained at a local law enforcement office). You must also submit the application fee:

> Salesperson—$185
> Broker—$195
> Appraiser—$430

These fees cover the examination, registration of the license, and the license fees for the first license period (two years).

Requirements

Applicants must show that they have had the required experience (if any), and have met required education standards:

Salesperson applicants must complete a 63-hour course in Real Estate Fundamentals, called Course I, before taking the examination. No real estate experience is necessary.

Broker applicants must complete an additional 72-hour course (Course II), and must have been active real estate salespersons for at least twelve months during the five years preceding the application. Also, one cannot take Course II until one has accumulated at least six months of experience as an active salesperson.

Licensed appraiser applicants must have completed an approved 75-hour course, and show that they have had two years experience in the appraisal field.

Certified Residential Appraiser applicants must have completed 120 hours of approved coursework, and have two years of appraisal experience.

Certified General Appraiser applicants need 165 hours of coursework, and two years experience, which must include at least one year of experience in nonresidential appraisal.

Salesperson and broker applicants also should order (from DRE, for $10.00) a copy of the *Florida Real Estate Commission Handbook*. It contains the Florida Real Estate License Law (Chapter 475 of the Florida Statutes, as amended), the rules and regulations of the Florida Real Estate Commission, and reprints of several other bodies of regulation governing the real estate business. It is required that this book be used in required prelicensing courses in Florida, so you may already have it. However, if it has been some time since you took the course (or if you haven't taken it yet), you should get an updated copy. Be sure to read it carefully; it should be used along with this book, because the Florida real estate exams assume that you have read, and know, the *Handbook*.

Studying for the Examination

1. Assemble all the study materials you will need. They include:
   a. This book
   b. The *Handbook*
2. Now begin studying. Start with Chapter 2 in this book, "Definitions of Real Estate Terms." Read it carefully, making sure you take note of all the terms. Don't try to understand them all at this point; just become slightly familiar with them.
3. Proceed through the chapters in the order they appear in the book. When you get to Chapter 5 ("Florida Real Estate License Law"), have your copy of the License Law handy to refer to.
4. When you have read this book through to Chapter 23 and have answered all the questions at the end of each chapter, take a sample examination in your field of interest and correct it. Note your weak areas, to be concentrated upon in later study.
5. Now that you have covered general real estate principles and your state's special materials, take another practice examination. Repeat this step as often as necessary.
6. Real Estate Broker applicants should take the supplemental examinations in Chapter 25.

Now you should be ready to take, and PASS, your chosen real estate examination. Be sure to schedule your studying so that you finish up only a day or two before the actual examination; in this way, all the material you have learned will be fresh in your mind.

Chapter 2/*Definitions of Real Estate Terms*

On the following pages is a glossary of real estate terminology. It is quite extensive and probably covers all the terms you might be expected to be familiar with when you take a licensing examination. We suggest that you begin your preparation for the examination by carefully reading over this glossary. This may seem a boring and tedious thing to do, but it will have many advantages. The main benefit is that it will acquaint you with some important terminology used in the real estate business. Once you have studied these terms, the remaining material in this book will be much easier for you to absorb; you will already have at least a minimal familiarity with most of what you read. In fact, the purpose of the rest of the book is to show you how all the many items defined in the glossary relate to one another in the real estate business.

The best way to study the glossary is to go over it once fairly quickly. Don't skip anything, but don't study it intensely, either. A while later, begin to go over the terms much more carefully, absorbing each definition as it is given. Make sure not to skip over anything: many real estate terms may look familiar because they are composed of familiar words. More likely than not, however, you will find that the *real estate meaning* is *not* the one you are used to. This is one of the more serious problems that many people have with the real estate licensing examinations: you must learn terminology and be able to understand and use the special meanings that many words have in a real estate context.

Once you have spent a good amount of time on the terminology, go on through the rest of the book, using the glossary for reference whenever you need to. Later, as the time for the examination approaches, you will find it very helpful to go over the glossary again. It will be a sort of thumbnail review for you to read the terms once again, after you have studied the rest of the book. This will be of considerable help in your final preparation for the examination, especially since you will often encounter strictly definitional questions such as "The term *fee simple* means most nearly——."

Note that italic type within a definition calls attention to important terms that are defined elsewhere as separate entries. Small caps also denote cross references.

Glossary

AAA TENANT / *See* TRIPLE-A TENANT.

ABSTRACT OF TITLE / A summary of all of the recorded instruments and proceedings that affect the title to property.

Importance: A person going to buy real estate or lend money on it wants assurance of ownership. Usually an attorney or title insurance company prepares an abstract of title, based on documents in the county courthouse, to be certain of ownership; and only if title is good or marketable does that person buy or make the loan. Typically, *title insurance* is also acquired.

ABUTTING / Adjoining or meeting. *See also* ADJACENT.

ACCELERATION CLAUSE / A provision in a loan giving the lender the right to declare the entire amount immediately due and payable upon the violation of a different loan provision, such as failure to make payments on time.

Importance: Without an acceleration clause, a missed payment is just that—one overdue payment. The acceleration clause means the entire loan is due, and the real estate may be foreclosed on.

ACCEPTANCE / The act of agreeing to accept an offer.

Importance: To have a valid contract there must be an offer and an acceptance. The acceptance may be from either party to the other: for example, buyer/seller; landlord/tenant.

ACCESS RIGHT / The right of an owner to get to and from his/her property.

Importance: Property may be or may become encircled by other property. The access right gives an easement by necessity, which allows the owner of landlocked property to cross over adjacent property to reach a street.

ACCESSION / Additions to property as a result of annexing fixtures or alluvial deposits.

ACCRETION / Addition to land through processes of nature, such as deposits of soil carried by streams. *See* ALLUVIUM.

ACRE / A measure of land: 43,560 square feet.

ACTION TO QUIET TITLE / *See* QUIET TITLE SUIT.

ACTUAL EVICTION / Expulsion of a tenant from the property.

ADJACENT / Lying near but not necessarily in actual contact with.

Importance: When describing the physical proximity of property, the word includes touching property and other nearby parcels; for example, property across the street.

ADJOINING / Contiguous; attaching; in actual contact with.

Importance: In describing the proximity of land, adjoining property is actually touching.

ADJUSTABLE RATE MORTGAGE (ARM) / A mortgage loan with an interest rate that is allowed to vary during the life of the loan; usually there are *caps* on the amounts by which the interest rate can change annually and over the life of the loan.

Importance: ARMs are often a viable alternative to fixed rate mortgages, and are especially desirable to the borrower who expects that rates will decline. Often the initial rate is lower than that on a fixed-rate mortgage, and there are caps on the ceiling rate that can be charged if interest rates rise.

ADMINISTRATOR / A person appointed by a court to administer the estate of a deceased individual who left no will.

Importance: If a person dies leaving a will, an executor is usually named to carry out the provisions of the will. When there is no *executor*, an administrator is appointed by the court. The administrator receives a fee.

ADMINISTRATOR'S DEED / A deed conveying the property of a person who died without a will (intestate).

Importance: If a person owned real estate and died without leaving a will, the administrator will give a deed. However, the administrator does not want the potential liability associated with a general warranty deed, so an administrator's deed is used.

ADULT / A person who has attained the age of majority.

Importance: In Florida, a person who is 18 years of age is considered an adult. Also, some persons who are married or are in military service may be considered adults though not yet 18. A contract with a minor can be *disaffirmed* by the minor or by that person shortly after he/she becomes an adult.

AD VALOREM / According to valuation.

Importance: Used in describing a property tax rate. *See also* AD VALOREM TAX.

AD VALOREM TAX / A tax based on the value of the thing being taxed. **Example:** If the effective tax rate is 1 percent, the tax will be $1 per $100 of property value.

Importance: In Florida there are several taxing jurisdictions that levy ad valorem taxes. Tax districts include the city, county, and town, or village.

ADVERSE POSSESSION / A means of acquiring title to real estate when an occupant has been in actual, open, notorious, exclusive, and continuous occupancy of the property for the period required by state law, which is a minimum of 10 years in Florida.

Importance: A person can gain title to real estate (or lose title) by acting in a certain way for long enough. In Florida, this process may take 10 or more years, depending on the circumstances.

AFFIDAVIT / A statement or declaration in writing, sworn to or affirmed before some officer who is authorized to administer an oath or affirmation.

Importance: Some statements must be in the form of an affidavit before they can be recorded. For example, a contractor's lien must be in affidavit form to be perfected.

AFFIRM / To confirm; to ratify; to verify.

AGENCY / The legal relationship between a principal and his/her *agent* arising from a contract in which the principal employs the agent to perform certain acts on the principal's behalf.

Importance: The law of agency governs the rights and obligations of a broker to the principal and of a licensed real estate salesperson to the broker.

AGENT / A person who undertakes to transact some business or to manage some affair for another, with the authority of the latter. **Example:** An owner employs a broker to act as his agent in selling real property; the broker in turn employs salespersons to act as her agents to sell the same property.

Importance: An agent has certain duties to the principal, including loyalty. The agent is to act in the best interest of the principal, even when such action is not in the agent's best interest.

AGREEMENT OF SALE / A written agreement between seller and purchaser in which the purchaser agrees to buy certain real estate, and the seller agrees to sell, upon the terms and conditions of the agreement. Also called *offer and acceptance; contract of sale.*

Importance: When you are buying or selling property, your rights and obligations are described in this document. Offer this document or accept it only when you are satisfied that it contains what you will agree to in a final transaction.

AIR RIGHTS / The right to use, control, or occupy the space above a designated property. **Example:** The Met Life Building in New York City is built on air rights above the Grand Central Railroad Station.

Importance: Most property ownership rights include air rights up to the skies; however, air rights may be limited to a certain height, or, conversely, air rights may be the only property owned, having a floor that begins a stated number of feet above the ground.

ALIENATION / Transferring property to another, as the transfer of property and possession of lands, by gift or by sale, from one person to another.

Importance: In Florida, property may be transferred by voluntary alienation, as in a sale for cash, or involuntarily, as in a condemnation.

ALLUVIUM (ALLUVION) / Soil deposited by accretion; usually considered to belong to the owner of the land to which it is added.

AMENITIES / In appraising, the nonmonetary benefits derived from property ownership. **Examples:** pride of home ownership; accessibility to good public schools, parks, and cultural facilities.

Importance: Ownership of real estate may add to one's self-esteem and community involvement.

AMORTIZATION / A gradual paying off of a debt by periodic installments.

Importance: Most mortgages require the payment of interest plus at least some amortization of principal, so that the loan is eventually retired by the amortization payments.

AMORTIZATION TERM / The time required to retire a debt through periodic payments; also known as the *full amortization term.* Many mortgage loans have an amortization term of 15, 20, 25, or 30 years. Some have an amortization schedule as a 30-year loan, but require a *balloon payment* in 5, 10, or 15 years.

Importance: Both the lender and the borrower are assured that the loan will be retired through regular payments without the need to refinance.

ANNUAL PERCENTAGE RATE (APR) / The cost of credit, expressed as an annual interest rate that must be shown in consumer loan documents, as specified by the Federal Reserve's *Regulation Z,* which implements the federal Truth In Lending Act.

ANNUITY / A series of equal or nearly equal periodic payments or receipts. **Example:** The receipt of $100 per year for the next five years constitutes a $100 five-year annuity.

ANTICIPATION, PRINCIPLE OF / In real estate appraisal, the principle that the value of a property today is the present value of the sum of anticipated future benefits.

Importance: The anticipation principle serves as the basis for the *income approach* to appraisal.

ANTITRUST LAWS / Federal and state acts to protect trade and commerce from monopolies and restrictions.

APPORTIONMENT / (1) *Prorating* property expenses, such as taxes and insurance, between buyer and seller. (2) The partitioning of property into individual parcels by tenants in common.

APPRAISAL / An opinion or estimate of the value of a property.

Importance: If a buyer is unfamiliar with the value of real estate in an area, it is prudent to require that, as a condition of the agreement of sale, the property be appraised for an amount at least equal to the price being paid. Also, lenders require an appraisal of property as a requirement for making a loan. The borrower will pay the appraisal fee.

APPRAISAL APPROACH / One of three methods used in estimating the value of property: *income approach, sales comparison approach,* and *cost approach.* See each.

Importance: Having three separate methods to estimate the value of property will add confidence to an appraiser's value estimate. However, not all approaches are applicable for all properties.

APPRAISAL BY SUMMATION / *See* COST APPROACH.

APPRAISAL DATE / In an *appraisal report,* the date to which the value applies; distinguished from *report date.*

Importance: Because market conditions change, the appraisal date establishes the conditions for which the value is estimated.

APPRAISAL FOUNDATION / An organization that came into existence in the late 1980s in an effort to encourage uniform requirements for appraisal qualifications and reporting standards. *See also* UNIFORM STANDARDS OF PROFESSIONAL APPRAISAL PRACTICE.

APPRAISAL INSTITUTE / An organization of professional appraisers that was formed in 1991 by the merger of the American Institute of Real Estate Appraisers and the Society of Real Estate Appraisers. It offers *MAI* and *SRA* designations.

APPRAISAL REPORT / A document that describes the findings of an appraisal engagement. Reports may be presented in the following formats: oral, letter, form, or narrative, and may be self-contained, summary, or restricted. *See* UNIFORM STANDARDS OF PROFESSIONAL APPRAISAL PRACTICE.

APPRAISER / A person qualified to estimate the value of real property.

In Florida, one may be an assistant appraiser or residential licensee, a certified residential appraiser, or certified general appraiser.

APPRECIATION / An increase in the value of property.

Importance: Appreciation is one of the most significant benefits from real estate ownership. Gains from inflation as well as real income are included.

APPURTENANCE / Something that is outside the property itself but is considered a part of the property and adds to its greater enjoyment, such as the right to cross another's land (i.e., a *right-of-way* or *easement*).

Importance: The right to use another's land for a special purpose can materially affect the value of the subject property.

ARM / *See* ADJUSTABLE RATE MORTGAGE.

ARM'S LENGTH TRANSACTION / The "typical, normal transaction," in which all parties have reasonable knowledge of the facts pertinent to the transaction, are under no pressure or duress to transact, and are ready, willing, and able to transact.

ASA / A senior professional designation offered by the American Society of Appraisers. The ASA designation is awarded upon meeting rigorous requirements that include extensive experience, education, and approved sample reports.

AS IS / Without guarantees as to condition, as in a sale.

ASSESSED VALUATION / A valuation placed upon property by a public officer or a board, as a basis for taxation.

Importance: The assessed value of a property is typically a reasonable estimate by the tax assessor, who must periodically review all property in the jurisdiction. By contrast, an appraisal of a single property is more likely to approximate its market value.

ASSESSMENT / A charge against real estate made by a government to cover the cost of an improvement, such as a street or sewer line. *See also* ASSESSED VALUATION.

Importance: Property buyers and owners need to recognize that they may have to pay assessments for municipal improvements that affect their property. Frequently, the owner has little or no influence on the decision.

ASSESSMENT RATIO / The ratio of assessed value to market value. **Example:** A county requires a 40 percent assessment ratio on all property to be taxed. Property with a $100,000 value is therefore assessed at $40,000 (40 percent of $100,000), and the tax rate is applied to $40,000.

ASSESSOR / An official who has the responsibility of placing an assessed value on property.

Importance: The assessor estimates the value of each piece of real estate in the tax jurisdiction, but does not fix the tax rate or amount.

ASSIGNEE / The person to whom an agreement or contract is sold or transferred.

Importance: This legal term refers to the person who receives the contract.

ASSIGNMENT / The method or manner by which a right or contract is transferred from one person to another.

Importance: Contracts for the sale of real estate are generally assignable, except when financing must be arranged or certain conditions are imposed on a party. In a lease, an assignment gives all the rights of the original tenant to the new tenant.

ASSIGNOR / A party who assigns or transfers an agreement or contract to another.

Importance: Although many contracts can be assigned, the assignor is not necessarily relieved of the obligation. For example, debts cannot be assigned. Another party can assume a debt, but the original borrower remains liable.

ASSUMPTION OF MORTGAGE / The purchase of mortgaged property whereby the buyer accepts liability for the debt that continues to exist. The seller remains liable to the lender unless the lender agrees to release him/her.

Importance: When entering an agreement for the purchase or sale of real estate, the financing should be checked to determine whether the mortgage is assumable. If the mortgage carries favorable terms and is assumable, this fact will add value to the transaction.

ATTACHMENT / Legal seizure of property to force payment of a debt.

Importance: Property can be taken as security for a debt provided that such action has court approval.

ATTEST / To witness to; to witness by observation and signature.

Importance: Certain documents must be attested to as a condition for recording at the county courthouse.

ATTORNEY-IN-FACT / A person who is authorized to act for another under a power of attorney, which may be general or limited in scope.

Importance: A person may give another the right to act for him/her in some or all matters (*power of attorney*). The designated person, called an attorney-in-fact, need not be an attorney at law.

AVULSION / The sudden removal of land from one owner to another that occurs when a river abruptly changes its channel.

Importance: If a stream or river is a boundary line, the boundary may change with the addition or removal of land.

BALANCE, PRINCIPLE OF / In real estate appraisal, the principle that there is an optimal mix of inputs that, when combined with land, will result in the greatest land value. Inputs, or *factors of production*, include labor, capital, and entrepreneurship.

BALLOON PAYMENT / The final payment on a loan, when that payment is greater than the preceding installment payments and satisfies the note in full. **Example:** A debt requires interest-only payments annually for 5 years, at the end of which time the balance of the principal (a balloon payment) is due.

Importance: In arranging financing for real estate, if a balloon is involved the borrower will need to plan for the large balance that will come due.

BARGAIN AND SALE DEED / A deed that conveys real estate, generally lacking a warranty. The *grantor* will thus claim to have ownership but will not defend against all claims. This is the type of deed commonly used in Florida; the grantee usually acquires title insurance to guard against title flaws.

Importance: Sometimes a property owner does not wish to offer a *warranty deed*, but will give more assurance than is offered by a *quitclaim deed*. A bargain and sale deed is a compromise between those two.

BASE AND MERIDIAN / Imaginary lines used by surveyors to find and describe the location of land.

Importance: In states that use a rectangular or government survey method, these lines are similar to latitude and longitude.

BASE LINE / Part of the *government rectangular survey* method of land description. The base line is the major east-west line to which all north-south measurements refer.

BENEFICIARY / The person who receives or is to receive the benefits resulting from certain acts.

BEQUEATH / To give or hand down personal property by a will.

BEQUEST / Personal property that is given by the terms of a will.

BILATERAL CONTRACT / A contract under which each party promises performance. *Contrast* UNLATERAL CONTRACT.

BILL OF ASSURANCE / Recorded restrictions affecting a subdivision and a part of all deeds to lots therein.

BILL OF SALE / A written instrument that passes title of personal property from a seller to a buyer.

Importance: A real estate sales agreement is prepared on an agreement of sale. A bill of sale is used when furniture and portable appliances are sold.

BINDER / An agreement, accompanied by a deposit, for the purchase of real estate, as evidence of good faith on the part of the purchaser.

Importance: This is a pre-contract agreement that may or may not be legally enforceable. It provides the terms to be in the contract.

BLANKET MORTGAGE / A single *mortgage* that includes more than one parcel of real estate as security.

Importance: When one piece of property is insufficient collateral for a loan, the borrower may be able to satisfy the requirement by putting up more property as security. It is a good idea to negotiate release clauses whereby each parcel can be released from the mortgage when a portion of the loan is paid off, without having to pay off the entire loan.

BOARD OF DIRECTORS / People selected by stockholders to control the business of the corporation.

BONA FIDE / In good faith; without fraud. **Example:** A purchaser pays for property without knowledge of any title defects. In a bona fide sale the seller accepts consideration without notice of any reason against the sale.

Importance: An act in good faith is open, sincere, and honest.

BOND / A certificate that serves as evidence of a debt. *See also* MORTGAGE.

Importance: There are many types of bonds that may be used in real estate. A *mortgage bond* is secured by a mortgage on property. A *completion bond* (also called *performance bond*) is usually issued by a bonding company to assure completion of construction if a contractor fails.

BOOT / Nonrealty included to balance the value of the realty exchanged.

BOY / Abbreviation for "beginning of year."

Importance: In most leases, rent is due in the beginning of each period. If a commercial lease requires annual payments, rent is due in the beginning of the year (BOY).

BROKER / A person who is licensed by the state of Florida to act for property owners in real estate transactions, within the scope of state law.

Importance: In Florida, a person must be licensed as a broker to act in a real estate transaction for another. A licensed real estate salesperson must be sponsored by a broker who accepts responsibility for the salesperson's acts. A broker is regulated by the law of agency, which requires the broker to act in the best interest of the principal.

BROKERAGE / The business of being a *broker*.

Importance: Parties are brought together in a real estate transaction, such as a sale, lease, rental, or exchange.

BUILDING CAPITALIZATION RATE / In appraisal, the *capitalization rate* is used to convert an *income stream* into one lump-sum value. The rate for the building may differ from that for the land because the building is a wasting asset.

BUILDING CODES / Regulations established by local governments and describing the minimum structural requirements for buildings, including foundation, roofing, plumbing, electrical, and other specifications for safety and sanitation.

Importance: Work on real estate must be in compliance with the building codes, or it will not pass the required inspections.

BUILDING INSPECTION / Inspection of property as it proceeds under construction to assure that it meets building codes: foundation, plumbing, electrical wiring, roofing, materials. Also, periodic inspection of existing public buildings for health and safety considerations.

BUILDING LINE / A line fixed at a certain distance from the front and/or sides of a lot, beyond which the building may not project.

Importance: When situating improvements on a lot, it is important to observe the building line. Often, one must check with the city to ascertain exactly where this line is.

BUILDING LOAN AGREEMENT / See CONSTRUCTION LOAN.

BUILDING PERMIT / Permission granted by a local government to build a specific structure at a particular site.

BUNDLE OF RIGHTS THEORY / The theory that ownership of realty implies rights, such as occupancy, use and enjoyment, and the right to sell, bequeath, give, or lease all or part of these rights.

Importance: In a real estate transaction, knowing what one has or is acquiring is vital, because some of the bundle of rights may be missing.

BUYDOWN / Payment of discount points at loan origination in order to secure a lower interest rate; the rate may be bought down for only a few years or for the life of the loan.

Importance: When offered low rate financing on property being bought, one should determine whether the buydown applies to just the first few years or the full term of the loan.

CANCELLATION CLAUSE / A provision in a contract that gives the right to terminate obligations upon the occurrence of certain specified conditions or events.

Importance: A cancellation clause in a lease may allow the landlord to break the lease upon sale of the building. A lessor may need a cancellation clause if he/she plans to sell the building; the buyer may have another use for it.

CAP / A limit on the amount by which the interest rate on an *adjustable rate mortgage* may be changed; usually there are annual caps and lifetime caps.

Importance: Without caps, interest rates of adjustable rate mortgages can increase without limit. Also, abbreviation for income *capitalization*.

CAPITALIZATION / A process whereby anticipated future income is converted to one lump sum capital value.

Importance: Rental property evaluation is enhanced by the capitalization process. Income is divided by a *capitalization rate* to estimate value, using the following formula:

$$\text{Property Value} = \frac{\text{Rental Income less Operating Expenses}}{\text{Capitalization Rate}}$$

CAPITALIZATION RATE / A rate of return used to convert anticipated future income into a capital value. The capitalization rate includes interest and principal recovery.

Importance: *See also* CAPITALIZATION.

CAPITALIZED INCOME / The value estimated by the process of converting an *income stream* into a lump-sum amount; also called *capitalized value*.

CARRYING CHARGES / Expenses necessary for holding property, such as taxes and interest on idle property or property under construction.

Importance: When considering nonrental real estate as an investment, carrying charges should be taken into account.

CASH FLOW / Periodic amounts accruing from an investment after all cash expenses, payments, and taxes have been deducted.

CASH-ON-CASH / *See* EQUITY DIVIDEND.

CAVEAT EMPTOR / "Let the buyer beware." The buyer must examine the goods or property and buy at his/her own risk.

Importance: This was once an accepted condition of sale. Home buyers in some states have much more protection now, as sellers and brokers are required to disclose problems or face possible penalties.

CAVEATS / Warnings, often in writing to a potential buyer, to be careful.

CCIM / *See* CERTIFIED COMMERCIAL INVESTMENT MEMBER.

CC&Rs / Covenants, conditions, and restrictions. These are limitations on land use, usually in a deed, imposed in a subdivision. Protects homeowners by preventing certain uses and assuring uniformity.

CEASE AND DESIST / Order by a court or administrative agency prohibiting a person or business from continuing an activity.

Used in real estate brokerage to prevent antitrust behavior among firms, or in illegal discrimination.

CENSUS TRACT / Geographical area mapped by the U.S. government for which demographic information is available. This information may be used by retailers, real estate developers, and brokers to estimate consumer purchasing power in a market area.

CERTIFICATE OF NO DEFENSE / *See* ESTOPPEL CERTIFICATE.

CERTIFICATE OF OCCUPANCY / A document issued by a local government to a developer, builder, builder-owner, etc., permitting a new structure to be occupied by members of the public. Issuance of the certificate generally indicates that the building is in compliance with public health and *building codes*.

CERTIFICATE OF REASONABLE VALUE / The appraisal document required for a VA-guaranteed home loan.

CERTIFICATE OF REDEMPTION / Document provided by county tax collectors showing that all past-due property taxes have been paid.

CERTIFIED COMMERCIAL INVESTMENT MEMBER (CCIM) / A designation awarded by the Realtors National Marketing Institute, which is affiliated with the *National Association of Realtors®*.

CERTIFIED GENERAL APPRAISER / A person qualified to appraise any property, under appraiser certification law recently adopted by most states. At least 2 years of general appraisal experience, 165 hours of education, and a passing grade on a state examination are usually required.

CERTIFIED PROPERTY MANAGER (CPM) / A member of the Institute of Real Estate Management, an organization affiliated with the *National Association of Realtors®*.

CERTIFIED RESIDENTIAL APPRAISER / A person qualified to appraise residences and up to four units of housing, under appraiser certification law. Standards call for less education, less experience, and a less comprehensive examination than are required for a certified general appraiser.

CERTIFIED RESIDENTIAL BROKER (CRB) / A designation awarded by the Realtors National Marketing Institute, which is affiliated with the *National Association of Realtors®*.

CHAIN / A unit of land measurement, 66 feet in length.

Importance: In surveying, land descriptions sometimes use the chain.

CHAIN OF TITLE / A history of *conveyances* and *encumbrances* affecting a title from the time the original patent was granted, or as far back as records are available. *See also* ABSTRACT OF TITLE.

CHATTEL / Personal property, including autos and household goods and fixtures.

Importance: Many laws have different applications, depending on whether a property is real estate or chattels. It can be important to know the type of property.

CHATTEL MORTGAGE / A pledge of personal property as security for a debt.

CLEAR TITLE / A title free and clear of all *encumbrances*.

Importance: When buying or selling real estate, it is essential to know whether the title is encumbered or clear. If it is not clear, the effect of the encumbrances on the value or use of the real estate must be checked.

CLIENT / The person who employs a broker, lawyer, accountant, appraiser, and so on.

Importance: The law describes certain relationships that a professional has with a client. In a real estate transaction it is essential to know exactly what that relationship is. *See also* AGENCY.

CLOSING / (1) The act of transferring ownership of a property from seller to buyer in accordance with a sales contract. (2) The time when a closing takes place.

CLOSING DATE / The date on which the seller delivers the deed and the buyer pays for the property; also called *settlement date*.

Importance: The *agreement of sale* will reflect when closing is to take place. A buyer or seller may be considered to have defaulted on a contract if unable to close by the agreed-upon date.

CLOSING STATEMENT / An accounting of funds from a real estate sale, made to both the seller and the buyer separately. Florida requires the broker to furnish accurate closing statements to all clients to any transaction in which he/she is an agent.

Importance: This statement shows the accounting, which should be consistent with the agreement of sale. If an error is suspected in the closing statement, the closing should not take place.

CLOUD ON THE TITLE / An outstanding claim or *encumbrance* that, if valid, will affect or impair the owner's title.

Importance: A cloud on title can restrict use and affect ownership. This should be cleared before closing. An attorney or title company should be consulted for assurance of title.

COLLATERAL / Property pledged as security for a debt.

COLOR OF TITLE / That which appears to be good title but is not.

Importance: A person can be fooled by believing he/she is receiving good title. An attorney or title company's input is essential.

COMMERCIAL PROPERTY / Property designed for use by retail, wholesale, office, hotel, and service users.

Importance: Nearly all cities and towns have zoning that restricts the location of commercial property.

COMMINGLE / To mingle or mix, as by the deposit of another's money in a broker's personal account.

Importance: Brokers generally must maintain all *earnest money* in an account that is separate from their personal funds.

COMMISSION / (1) The amount earned by real estate brokers for their services; (2) the official body that enforces real estate license laws.

Importance: (1) Commissions are the way real estate brokers earn money. (2) The Florida Real Estate Commission licenses brokers and salespersons and may suspend a license for certain behavior.

COMMITMENT / A pledge or promise; a firm agreement.

Importance: When financing is needed to buy property, a commitment from a lender must be obtained. The loan terms are noted in the commitment, which may include an interest rate lock-in.

COMMON ELEMENTS / Generally, in a *condominium* development, land or a tract of land considered to be the property of the development in which all owners can enjoy use.

Importance: Owners of condominiums share in the use of and payment for common areas, such as walkways, recreational facilities, and ponds. A homeowner's association typically manages the common area.

COMMON LAW / The body of law that has grown out of legal customs and practices that developed in England. Common law prevails unless superseded by other law.

COMMUNITY PROPERTY / Property accumulated through joint efforts of husband and wife and owned by them in equal shares. The doctrine now exists in Arizona, California, Idaho, Louisiana, Nevada, New Mexico, Texas, and the state of Washington.

Importance: Husband and wife must agree to all real estate transactions involving community property.

COMPARATIVE MARKET ANALYSIS (CMA) / An estimate of the value of property using only a few indicators taken from sales of comparable properties, such as price per square foot.

Importance: Real estate brokers and agents, because they are not state-certified appraisers, may not perform appraisals, so they estimate the value of a subject property using a CMA in order to serve their clients.

COMPARATIVE SALES APPROACH / *See* SALES COMPARISON APPROACH.

COMPARATIVE UNIT METHOD / An appraisal technique to establish relevant units as a guide to appraising the subject property. **Examples:** (1) Parking garages are compared per space. (2) Bowling centers are compared per lane. (3) Land may be sold per square foot or per front foot.

COMPLETION BOND / A legal instrument used to guarantee the completion of a development according to specifications. More encompassing than a performance bond, which assures that one party will perform under a contract under condition(s) that the other party performs, the completion bond assures production of the development without reference to any contract and without the requirement of payment to the contractor.

COMPOUND INTEREST / Interest paid on the original principal and also on the unpaid interest that has accumulated. **Example:** $100 deposited in a 5 percent savings account earns $5 interest the first year. If this interest is not withdrawn, the account's second-year earnings are 5 percent of $105, or $5.25.

Importance: Compound interest is the cornerstone of all financial computations, including monthly mortgage payments and remaining balances.

COMPS / An appraisal term, short for "comparables"; that is, comparable properties.

CONDEMNATION / (1) The taking of private property for public use, with just compensation to the owner, under *eminent domain*; used by governments to acquire land for streets, parks, schools, and by utilities to acquire necessary property; (2) declaring a structure unfit for use.

Importance: All property is subject to condemnation, though the government must show need. The amount of compensation can be disputed.

CONDITION(S) / Provision(s) in a contract that some or all terms of the contract must be met or the contract need not be consummated. **Examples:**
- Buyer must obtain certain financing.
- House must be appraised at a certain amount.
- City must give occupancy permit.
- Seller must pay for certain repairs.

CONDITIONAL SALES CONTRACT / A contract for the sale of property stating that the seller retains title until the conditions of the contract have been fulfilled.

Importance: Generally, buyers have less of an interest under this type of contract than is conveyed by the receipt of a deed at closing.

CONDOMINIUM / A system of ownership of individual units in a multiunit structure, combined with joint ownership of commonly used property (sidewalks, hallways, stairs). *See also* COMMON ELEMENTS.

Importance: A condominium can be mortgaged by its individual owner, who must pay assessments for common area maintenance.

CONFORMING LOAN / A mortgage loan that is eligible for purchase by FNMA or FHLMC.

CONFORMITY PRINCIPLE / An appraisal principle that holds that property values tend to be maximized when the neighborhood is reasonably homogeneous in social and economic activity.

CONSENT DECREE / A judgment whereby the defendant agrees to stop the activity that was asserted to be illegal, without admitting wrongdoing or guilt.

CONSIDERATION / Anything of value given to induce entering into a contract; it may be money, personal services, love and affection.

Importance: A contract must have some consideration to be legally binding.

CONSTANT / *See* CONSTANT PAYMENT LOAN.

CONSTANT PAYMENT LOAN / A loan on which equal payments are made periodically so that the debt is paid off when the last payment is made.

Importance: Although each periodic payment is the same, the portion that is interest declines over time, whereas the principal portion increases.

CONSTRUCTION LOAN / A loan used to build on real estate.

Importance: Many construction lenders require, among other things, that the builder obtain a commitment for a permanent loan before they will issue a construction loan. Commercial banks are the most common source of construction loans. The rate is often the prime rate plus 2 percent plus 1 or more discount points. The loan is advanced in stages as the project is completed.

CONSTRUCTIVE EVICTION / An eviction existing when, through the fault of the landlord, physical conditions of the property render it unfit for the purpose for which it was leased.

CONSTRUCTIVE NOTICE / The legal presumption that everyone has knowledge of a fact when that fact is a matter of public record. **Example:** A buys land from B, believing that B is the owner. However, B was a huckster; C owned the property. Because C's deed had been properly recorded, A had constructive notice of C's ownership and cannot claim ownership against C.

CONTIGUOUS / Actually touching; contiguous properties have a common boundary. *See also* ADJOINING.

CONTINGENCY CLAUSE / *See* CONDITION(S).

CONTRACT / An agreement between competent parties to do or not to do certain things for a consideration.

Importance: A valid contract is enforceable in a court of law. All contracts for real estate must be in writing to be enforceable, except leases for less than 1 year.

CONTRACT FOR DEED / *See* LAND CONTRACT.

CONTRACT FOR SALE / *See* AGREEMENT OF SALE.

CONVENTIONAL LOAN / A mortgage loan other than one guaranteed by the *Veterans Administration* or insured by the *Federal Housing Administration*.

Importance: Conventional loans generally require a larger down payment than others, although the required down payment for conventional loans can be decreased with private mortgage insurance.

CONVERTIBLE ARM / An *adjustable rate mortgage* that offers the borrower the option to convert payments to a fixed-rate schedule at a specified point within the term of the loan. Conversion is made for a nominal fee, and the interest rate on the fixed-rate loan is determined by a rule specified in the ARM loan agreement.

CONVEY / To deed or transfer title to another.

Importance: This term is used to imply a sale or transfer of ownership.

CONVEYANCE / (1) The transfer of the title of real estate from one to another; (2) the means or medium by which title of real estate is transferred.

Importance: This term usually refers to use of a deed, but can also be used for a lease, mortgage, assignment, encumbrance.

COOPERATIVE / A type of corporate ownership of real property whereby stockholders of the corporation are entitled to use a certain dwelling unit or other units of space.

Importance: Special income tax laws allow the tenant stockholders to deduct on their tax returns the housing interest and property taxes paid by the corporation.

CORPOREAL / Visible or tangible. Corporeal rights in real estate include such things as the right of occupancy under a lease.

COST APPROACH / One of the three appraisal methods of estimating value. The estimated current cost of reproducing the existing improvements, less the estimated depreciation, added to the value of the land, gives the appraised value; also called *appraisal by summation*.

Importance: Most properties sell for market value. The cost approach is useful for proposed construction or for estimating the amount of insurance needed.

COUNTEROFFER / Rejection of an offer to buy or sell, with a simultaneous substitute offer.

COVENANTS / Promises written into deeds and other instruments and agreeing to do or not to do certain acts, or requiring or preventing certain uses of the property.

Importance: When buying real estate, it is prudent to determine whether any of the covenants would inhibit or prevent a proposed use of the property.

CPM / *See* CERTIFIED PROPERTY MANAGER.

CRB / *See* CERTIFIED RESIDENTIAL BROKER.

CUL-DE-SAC / A street with an intersection at one end and a closed turning area at the other. Often valued in the design of residential subdivisions for the privacy provided to the homes on the street.

CURABLE DEPRECIATION / *Depreciation* or deterioration that can be corrected at a cost less than the value that will be added.

Importance: It is economically profitable to correct curable depreciation.

DAMAGES / The amount recoverable by a person who has been injured in any manner, including physical harm, property damage, or violated rights, through the act or default of another.

Importance: Damages may be awarded for compensation and as a punitive measure, to punish someone for certain acts.

DATE OF APPRAISAL / *See* APPRAISAL DATE.

DEBT/EQUITY RATIO / The relationship of these two components of *purchase capital*. **Example:** Mortgage = $75,000; equity = $25,000. Therefore, the debt/equity ratio is 3:1. This is equivalent to a 75 percent *loan-to-value ratio* loan.

DECREE / An order issued by a person in authority; a court order or decision.

Importance: A decree may be final or interlocutory (preliminary).

DEDICATION / The gift of land by its owner for a public use and the acceptance of it by a unit of government. **Example:** Streets in a subdivision, land for a park, or a site for a school.

DEDICATION BY DEED / *See* DEDICATION; DEED.

DEED / A written document, properly signed and delivered, that conveys title to real property. *See also* BARGAIN AND SALE DEED, GENERAL WARRANTY DEED, QUITCLAIM DEED, SPECIAL WARRANTY DEED.

DEED IN LIEU OF FORECLOSURE / A deed that conveys a defaulting borrower's realty to a lender, thus avoiding foreclosure proceedings.

DEED OF TRUST / *See* TRUST DEED.

DEED RESTRICTION / A clause in a deed that limits the use of land. **Example:** A deed may stipulate that alcoholic beverages are not to be sold on the land for 20 years.

Importance: A buyer should check that deed restrictions will not inhibit an intended use of property; a seller should consider whether he/she wants to restrict the use of land.

DEFAULT / (1) Failure to fulfill a duty or promise, or to discharge an obligation; (2) omission or failure to perform any acts.

Importance: Upon default, the defaulting party may be liable to the other party(ies).

DEFEASANCE / A clause in a mortgage that gives the borrower the right to redeem his/her property after he/she has defaulted, usually by paying the full indebtedness and fees incurred. **Example:** A late payment on a mortgage or other *default* doesn't necessarily cause the borrower to lose the property. Defeasance may allow redemption, though the loan and fees may have to be paid.

DEFENDANT / The party sued in an action at law.

DEFERRED PAYMENTS / Money payments to be made at some future date.

DEFICIENCY JUDGMENT / A court order stating that the borrower still owes money when the security for a loan does not entirely satisfy a defaulted debt.

Importance: When property is foreclosed on, the amount realized by the sale of the collateral may not satisfy the debt. The lender may be able to get a deficiency judgment to recover the balance owed.

DELIVERY / Transfer of the possession of a thing from one person to another.

Importance: In a real estate transaction there should be delivery of a deed. For example, if an owner dies without giving a deed to a relative while alive, a verbal promise to give the property is inadequate.

DEMOGRAPHY / The study of population characteristics of people in an area, including age, sex, income.

DEPRECIATION / (1) In appraisal, a loss of value in real property due to age, physical deterioration, or functional or economic obsolescence; (2) in accounting, the allocation of the cost of an asset over its economic useful life.

Importance: It should be recognized that the value of real estate may decline; also, that one can reduce income taxes by claiming depreciation as a tax expense.

DEPRESSION / Economic conditions causing a severe decline in business activity, reflecting high unemployment, excess supply, public fear.

DESIGNATED REAL ESTATE INSTRUCTOR (DREI) / A *real estate* teacher, typically of licensing preparation courses, who has been designated by the *Real Estate Educators Association*. **Example:** To qualify as a DREI, Don had to demonstrate classroom teaching techniques to a panel of teachers, who judged his effectiveness. Don also offered experience and expertise in real estate law.

DEVISE / A gift of real estate by will or last testament.

DEVISEE / A person who inherits real estate through a will.

DIRECT CAPITALIZATION / The value estimated by dividing *net operating income* by an overall *capitalization rate* to estimate value. *See also* CAPITALIZATION. **Example:**

Gross income	$100,000
Operating expenses	−40,000
Net operating income	$ 60,000
Capitalization rate	0.12
Value estimate	$500,000

DIRECT SALES COMPARISON APPROACH / *See* SALES COMPARISON APPROACH.

DIRECTIONAL GROWTH / The location or direction toward which a city is growing.

Importance: An investor can often make a profit by purchasing land in the path of a city's growth.

DISCHARGE IN BANKRUPTCY / The release of a bankrupt party from the obligation to repay debts that were, or might have been, proved in bankruptcy proceedings.

DISCOUNTED PRESENT VALUE / *See* DISCOUNTING.

DISCOUNTING / The process of estimating the present value of an *income stream* by reducing expected *cash flow* to reflect the *time value of money*. Discounting is the opposite of compounding; mathematically they are reciprocals.

DISCOUNT POINTS / Amounts paid to the lender (usually by the seller) at the time of origination of a loan, to account for the difference between the market interest rate and the lower face rate of the note (often required when FHA or VA financing is used).

Importance: Discount points must be paid in cash at closing. Buyer and seller should agree, at the time they prepare an agreement of sale, as to who is to pay the points, or what the limits are on the number of points to be paid.

DISPOSSESS PROCEEDINGS / The legal process by a landlord to remove a tenant and regain possession of property.

Importance: If a tenant breaches a lease, the landlord will want to regain possession of the property.

DISTRIBUTEE / A person receiving or entitled to receive land as the representative of the former owner; an heir.

DOCUMENTARY EVIDENCE / Evidence in the form of written or printed papers.

Importance: Documentary evidence generally carries more weight than oral evidence.

DOWER / Under common law, the legal right of a wife or child to part of a deceased husband's or father's property. Not used in Florida.

Importance: Dower has been generally abolished or severely altered in most states. *Community property* applies in some states, though not Florida.

DREI / *See* DESIGNATED REAL ESTATE INSTRUCTOR.

DUAL AGENT / An agent who represents more than one party to a transaction.

DUE DILIGENCE / A study that precedes the purchase of property, considering the physical, financial, legal, and social characteristics.

DURESS / Unlawful constraint exercised upon a person whereby he/she is forced to do some act against his/her will. **Example:** "Your signature or your brains will be on this contract."

Importance: A person who signs a contract or performs another act under duress need not go through with the agreement.

EARNEST MONEY / A deposit made by a purchaser of real estate as evidence of his/her good faith.

Importance: Earnest money should accompany an offer to buy property. Generally, a broker, attorney, or title company deposits the money in a separate account, beyond the control of the principals, until the contract is completed.

EASEMENT / The right, privilege, or interest that one party has in the land of another. **Example:** The right of public utility companies to lay their lines across others' property.

Importance: Easements allow utility service without requiring the public utility to buy the land. However, a potential real estate purchaser should determine exact locations of all easements to be sure they won't interfere with planned land uses.

ECONOMIC DEPRECIATION / Loss of value from all causes outside the property itself. **Example:** An expensive private home may drop in value when a sanitary landfill is placed nearby.

ECONOMIC LIFE / The remaining period for which real estate improvements are expected to generate more income than operating expenses cost.

Importance: As land improvements age, they tend to command less rent (in real terms) while maintenance costs rise. The economic life is the expected life of positive contributions to value by buildings or other land improvements.

ECONOMIC OBSOLESCENCE / *See* ECONOMIC DEPRECIATION.

EFFECTIVE GROSS INCOME / For income-producing property, *potential gross income*, less a vacancy and collection allowance, plus miscellaneous income. *See also* GROSS INCOME. **Example:** An office building rents for $12 per square foot and contains 100,000 leasable square feet. A 5 percent vacancy and collection allowance is expected. A small concession stand provides $1,000 of annual revenue.

Potential gross income:
$12 × 100,000 = $1,200,000
Less: Vacancy
   and collection
   allowance @ 5%   −60,000
Add: Miscellaneous
   income   +1,000
Effective gross
   income $1,141,000

EJECTMENT / An action to regain possession of *real property*, and to obtain damages for unlawful possession.

Importance: Ejectment allows a rightful owner to remove a squatter or trespasser.

EMINENT DOMAIN / The right of the government or a public utility to acquire property for necessary public use by *condemnation*; the owner must be fairly compensated.

Importance: Governments or those with governmental authority can acquire property they need under the federal Fifth Amendment and state constitutions. As to the amount paid, the parties are entitled to a "day in court."

ENCROACHMENT / A building, a part of a building, or an obstruction that physically intrudes upon, overlaps, or trespasses upon the property of another.

Importance: A *survey* is often required as part of a real estate contract, to determine whether there are any encroachments on the property.

ENCUMBRANCE / Any right to or interest in land that diminishes its value. Included are outstanding mortgage loans, unpaid taxes, easements, deed restrictions, mechanics' liens, leases, and deed restrictions.

ENDORSEMENT / The act of signing one's name on the back of a check or note, with or without further qualification; also, the signature itself.

ENVIRONMENTAL ASSESSMENT / A study of the property and area to determine health hazards:

Phase I. To identify the presence of hazards (e.g., asbestos, radon, PCBs, leaking underground storage tanks).

Phase II. To estimate the cost of remediation or clean-up.

Phase III. To remediate the environmental contamination.

ENVIRONMENTAL IMPACT REPORT (or STATEMENT) / Describes probable effects on the environment of a proposed development; may be required by a local government to assure the absence of damage to the environment.

EOY / Abbreviation for "end of year."

Importance: Most mortgage loans call for payments at the end of each period. If the loan requires annual payments, a payment would be due at the end of the year (EOY).

EQUITABLE TITLE / The interest held by one who has agreed to purchase but has not yet closed the transaction.

EQUITY / The interest or value that the owner has in real estate over and above the liens against it. **Example:** If a property has a market value of $10,000, but there is a $7,500 mortgage loan on it, the owner's equity is $2,500.

EQUITY DIVIDEND / The annual *cash flow* that an equity investor receives; same as *cash-on-cash* return.

EQUITY OF REDEMPTION / The right of a real estate owner to reclaim property after default, but before foreclosure proceedings, by payment of the debt, interest, and costs. *See also* DEFEASANCE.

EQUITY YIELD RATE / The rate of return on the *equity* portion of an investment, taking into account periodic *cash flow* and the proceeds from resale. The timing and amounts of *cash flow* after debt service are considered, but not income taxes.

EROSION / The gradual wearing away of land through process of nature, as by streams and winds.

Importance: Planting vegetation can often prevent soil erosion.

ESCALATOR MORTGAGE / *See* ADJUSTABLE RATE MORTGAGE.

ESCHEAT / The reversion of property to the state of Florida in the event that the owner dies without leaving a will and has no legal heirs.

Importance: In the absence of a will, the assets of a person who has no legal heirs will escheat to the state of Florida.

ESCROW / An agreement between two or more parties providing that certain instruments or property be placed with a third party for safekeeping, pending the fulfillment or performance of some act or condition.

Importance: It is prudent to place money or property in escrow rather than to give it to the other principal of a pending transaction.

ESCROW ACCOUNT / *See* TRUST ACCOUNT.

ESCROW AGENT / A neutral third party (such as a lawyer, broker, or title company) who is trusted by buyer and seller to close a transaction. The buyer and seller give instructions with conditions that must be met in order to close.

ESTATE / The degree, quantity, nature, and extent of interest a person has in real or personal property.

ESTATE AT SUFFERANCE / The wrongful occupancy of property by a tenant after his/her lease has expired.

ESTATE AT WILL / The occupation of real estate by a tenant for an indefinite period, terminable by one or both parties at will.

ESTATE FOR LIFE / An interest in property that terminates upon the death of a specified person. *See also* LIFE ESTATE.

ESTATE FOR YEARS / An interest in land that allows possession for a definite and limited time.

ESTATE IN REVERSION / An estate left by a *grantor* for him/herself, to begin after the termination of some particular estate granted by him/her. **Example:** A landlord's estate in reversion becomes his/hers to possess when the lease expires.

ESTOPPEL CERTIFICATE / A document by which, for example, the mortgagor (borrower) certifies that the mortgage debt is a lien for the amount stated. He/she is thereafter prevented from claiming that the balance due differed from the amount stated. Estoppels apply also to leases.

Importance: The buyer of property on which there is a mortgage or lease should get estoppels to be sure the terms of those agreements are as expected. The right to get estoppel certificates may be written into the lease or mortgage.

ET AL. / Abbreviation of *et alii* ("and others").

ET UX. / Abbreviation of *et uxor* ("and wife").

EVALUATION / A study of the potential uses of a property, but not to determine its present value.

Importance: Evaluations include studies as to the market for and the marketability of a property, feasibility, *highest and best use*, land use, and supply and demand.

EVICTION / A legal proceeding by a lessor (landlord) to recover possession of property.

Importance: Eviction allows a landlord to regain property when a tenant does not uphold the lease. A legal process must be followed.

EVICTION, PARTIAL / A legal proceeding whereby the possessor of the property is deprived of a portion thereof.

EXCESS RENT / The amount by which the *rent* under an existing *lease* exceeds the rental rate on comparable existing space.

Importance: Should the lease expire or the tenant break the lease, the new rental rate will probably be at (lower) market rates.

EXCHANGE / Under Section 1031 of the Internal Revenue Code, like-kind property used in a trade or business or held as an investment, can be exchanged tax free. *See also* BOOT.

EXCLUSIONARY ZONING / Zoning laws of a community that would serve to prohibit low and moderate-income housing; considered to be illegal.

EXCLUSIVE AGENCY LISTING / An employment contract giving only one broker the right to sell the property for a specified time and also allowing the owner to sell the property him/herself without paying a commission.

Importance: This is sometimes arranged when an owner wants to continue personal selling efforts while employing a broker. Acceptable to some brokers for some properties.

EXCLUSIVE RIGHT TO SELL LISTING / An employment contract giving the broker the right to collect a commission if the property is sold by anyone, including the owner, during the term of the agreement, and often beyond the term to someone the broker introduced. *Compare* EXCLUSIVE AGENCY LISTING; *contrast with* OPEN LISTING.

EXECUTE / (1) To make out a contract; (2) to perform a contract fully.

Importance: In real estate, unsigned contracts are generally meaningless.

EXECUTED CONTRACT / A contract all terms and conditions of which have been fulfilled.

Importance: When executed, a contract is enforceable.

EXECUTOR / A person designated in a will to carry out its provisions concerning the disposition of the estate.

Importance: The person making a will should name an executor or co-executor who is trustworthy and capable of carrying out the terms of the will. If there is no will and no executor, the court appoints an *administrator*.

EXECUTRIX / A woman who performs the duties of an executor.

EXPENSE RATIO / A comparison of *operating expenses* to *potential gross income*. This ratio can be compared over time and with that of other properties to determine the relative operating efficiency of the property considered. **Example:** An apartment complex generates potential gross income of $1,000,000 annually, and incurs operating expenses of $400,000 over the same time period. The expense ratio of 40 percent can be compared to its historical rate and the same ratios competitive properties. The comparison may disclose reasons for differences that can be used to bolster the property's efficiency.

FACTORS OF PRODUCTION / In economics, land, labor, and capital.

FAIR HOUSING LAW / A federal law that forbids discrimination on the basis of race, color, sex, religion, handicap, familial status, or national origin, in the selling or renting of homes and apartments.

FDIC / *See* FEDERAL DEPOSIT INSURANCE CORPORATION.

FEDERAL DEPOSIT INSURANCE CORPORATION (FDIC) / A U.S. government agency that insures depositors' accounts in commercial banks and savings and loan associations.

Importance: Federal insurance, up to $100,000 per account, provides depositor confidence in the banking system and in the individual bank. Banks and savings and loan associations add liquidity to the real estate market.

FEDERAL HOUSING ADMINISTRATION (FHA) / A U.S. government agency that insures to lenders the repayment of real estate loans.

Importance: The FHA is instrumental in assuring that financing is available for housing for low and moderate income levels. Programs include single-family homes, condos, apartments, nursing homes, even new towns.

FEDERAL NATIONAL MORTGAGE ASSOCIATION (FNMA) / A U.S. government-sponsored corporation that buys and sells existing residential mortgages; known as Fanny Mae.

Importance: FNMA significantly increases liquidity in the mortgage market. Without FNMA, it might be difficult for lenders who originate loans to find buyers for those loans. FNMA has standardized the loan submission and approval process, and has brought the mortgage finance business on a par with other national credit markets.

FEDERAL SAVINGS AND LOAN INSURANCE CORPORATION (FSLIC) / A U.S. government agency that once insured deposits in federal savings and loan institutions. *See also* FDIC.

FEDERALLY RELATED TRANSACTION / A real estate transaction that is overseen by a federal agency including the Federal Reserve Board, Federal Deposit Insurance Corporation, Office of Comptroller of Currency, Office of Thrift Supervision, National Credit Union Association, and Resolution Trust Corporation.

Importance: A real estate appraiser used in a federally related transaction must be state licensed or certified.

FEE SIMPLE OR FEE ABSOLUTE / Absolute ownership of real property; the owner is entitled to the entire property with unconditional power of disposition during his/her life, and the property descends to his/her heirs and legal representatives upon his/her death intestate.

Importance: When buying real estate, the seller can give only the rights he/she has. A buyer should determine whether complete ownership in fee simple will be received.

FHA / *See* FEDERAL HOUSING ADMINISTRATION.

FHA LOAN / A mortgage loan insured by the FHA.

Importance: FHA loans generally reduce the required down payment to 3 percent (sometimes less) but require FHA mortgage insurance, in addition to interest, at 0.5 percent annually.

FIDUCIARY / (1) A person who, on behalf of or for the benefit of another, transacts business or handles money or property not his/her own. (2) founded on trust; the nature of trust.

Importance: A fiduciary, or a person in such capacity, must act in the best interest of the party who has placed trust.

FILTERING DOWN / The process whereby, over time, a housing unit or neighborhood is occupied by progressively lower-income residents.

FINAL VALUE ESTIMATE / In an *appraisal* of *real estate*, the appraiser's value conclusion. **Example:** An appraiser has determined these three amounts of value based on each appraisal approach:

Cost approach	$600,000
Sales comparison approach	$575,000
Income approach	$560,000

She then reconciles these amounts, decides which is most relevant, and offers a final value estimate. If the income approach is considered most indicative of purchaser behavior, the amount may be $560,000 to $570,000, depending on the relative weight assigned to each approach.

FINANCIAL FEASIBILITY / The ability of a proposed land use or change of land use to justify itself from an economic point of view.

Importance: Financial feasibility is one test of the *highest and best use* of land, but not the only test. Nor does the financial feasibility of a project necessarily make it the most rewarding use of land.

FINANCING LEASE / A lease wherein lessee becomes lessor to the operating tenant.

FIRST MORTGAGE / A mortgage that has priority as a *lien* over all other mortgages.

Importance: Generally, the first mortgage is the one recorded first. When a first mortgage is retired, existing mortgages of lower priority will move up. In case of foreclosure, the first mortgage will be satisfied before other mortgages.

FIXED EXPENSES / In the operation of *real estate*, expenses that remain the same regardless of occupancy. *Contrast* VARIABLE EXPENSES. **Examples:** Insurance and interest expenses are expected to be the same, whether or not a building is occupied, so they are fixed expenses. By contrast, the costs of utilities and office cleaning will vary with occupancy.

FIXTURES / Personal property attached to the land or improvements so as to become part of the real estate.

Importance: When buying or selling real estate,

it is best to specifically identify which appliances remain and which do not. Otherwise, fixtures remain with the property.

FLOOR LOAN / The minimum that a lender is willing to advance on a *permanent mortgage*. An additional principal amount will be loaned upon attainment of a certain occupancy rate.

FNMA / *See* FEDERAL NATIONAL MORTGAGE ASSOCIATION.

FORBEARANCE / A policy of restraint in taking legal action to remedy a *default* or other breach of contract, generally in the hope that the default will be cured, given additional time.

FORECLOSURE / A legal procedure whereby property pledged as security for a debt is sold to pay a defaulted debt.

Importance: Foreclosure gives a lender the right to sell property that was pledged for a debt. All parties to a mortgage contract should recognize its consequences.

FORFEITURE / Loss of money or anything else of value because of failure to perform under contract.

FRAUD / The intentional use of deception to purposely cheat or deceive another person, causing him/her to suffer loss.

Importance: Fraud, intentionally deceiving another, is far worse than misrepresentation, which is an incorrect or untrue statement. Consequently, punishment for fraud is more severe.

FREEHOLD / An interest in real estate without a predetermined time span. **Example:** A fee simple or a life estate.

FRONT FOOT / A standard measurement of land, applied at the frontage of its street line.

Importance: This measure is used for city lots of generally uniform depth. Prices are often quoted as the number of dollars per front foot.

FSLIC / *See* FEDERAL SAVINGS AND LOAN INSURANCE CORPORATION.

FULL AMORTIZATION TERM / *See* AMORTIZATION TERM.

FULLY AMORTIZED LOAN / A loan having payments of *interest* and *principal* that are sufficient to liquidate the loan over its term; self-liquidating. *See also* AMORTIZATION TERM.

FUNCTIONAL DEPRECIATION / Loss of value from all causes within the property, except those due to physical deterioration. **Example:** A poor floor plan or outdated plumbing fixtures.

FUNCTIONAL OBSOLESCENCE / *See* FUNCTIONAL DEPRECIATION.

FUTURE VALUE OF ONE / *See* COMPOUND INTEREST.

GAAP / Generally Accepted Accounting Principles, the set of rules considered standard and acceptable by certified public accountants. Accounting deductions are required for real estate depreciation, even for assets that appreciate in value.

GABLE ROOF / A pitched roof with sloping sides.

GAMBREL ROOF / A double pitched roof having a steep lower slope with a flatter slope above.

GAP MORTGAGE / A loan that fills the difference between the *floor loan* and the full amount of the *permanent mortgage*.

GENERAL WARRANTY DEED / A deed in which the *grantor* agrees to protect the *grantee* against any other claim to title of the property and also provides other promises. *See also* WARRANTY DEED.

Importance: This is the best type of deed to receive.

GIFT DEED / A deed for which the consideration is love and affection, and no material consideration is involved.

Importance: A gift deed is frequently used to transfer real estate to a relative.

GI LOAN / Home loans guaranteed by the U.S. Veterans Administration (VA) under the Servicemen's Readjustment Act of 1944 and later; also known as a *VA loan*. The VA guarantees restitution to the lender in the event of default.

Importance: The VA guarantees 60 percent of the loan, up to $36,000. Lenders are assured of no losses, provided the property's market value decline is less than $36,000; consequently, most lenders do not require a down payment.

GLA / *See* GROSS LEASABLE AREA.

GNMA / GOVERNMENT NATIONAL MORTGAGE ASSOCIATION (GINNIE MAE)

GOVERNMENT RECTANGULAR SURVEY / A rectangular system of land survey that divides a district into 24-mile-square tracts from the *meridian* (north-south line) and the *base line* (east-west line). The tracts are divided into 6-mile-square parts called townships, which are in turn divided into 36 tracts, each 1 mile square, called sections.

Importance: This system is still used in several western states. For urban or suburban purposes the *lot and block number* and/or *metes and bounds* methods predominate.

GRACE PERIOD / Additional time allowed to perform an act or make a payment before a *default* occurs.

Importance: Many mortgage contracts have a grace period before a late payment is considered a default. It is usually wise to solve the problem before the grace period expires.

GRADE / (1) Ground level at the foundation of a building; (2) the degree of slope on land (e.g., a 2 percent grade means that the elevation rises 2 feet for every 100 linear feet).

Importance: The grade of land should be checked to determine whether it suits a planned use of the land.

GRADED LEASE / *See* GRADUATED LEASE.

GRADIENT / The slope, or rate of increase or decrease in elevation, of a surface; usually expressed as a percentage. *See also* GRADE.

GRADUATED LEASE / A lease that provides for graduated changes in the amount of rent at stated intervals; seldom used in short-term leases.

Importance: Graduated leases allow rent changes automatically, so that there is no need to revise the entire lease just to change the rent. These are often long-term leases that suit both landlord and tenant.

GRANT / A technical term used in deeds of conveyance of property to indicate a transfer.

GRANTEE / The party to whom the title to real property is conveyed; the buyer.

GRANTOR / The person who conveys real estate by deed; the seller or donor.

GRI / A graduate of the Realtors® Institute, which is affiliated with the *National Association of Realtors®*.

Importance: The GRI designation indicates that a real estate salesperson or broker has gone beyond the minimum educational requirements.

GRM / *See* GROSS RENT MULTIPLIER.

GROSS INCOME / Total income from property before any expenses are deducted. Gross income may be further described as *potential*, which assumes neither vacancy nor collection losses, or *effective*, which is net of vacancy and collection losses.

GROSS LEASABLE AREA (GLA) / The floor area that can be used by a *tenant*; generally measured from the center of joint partitions to outside wall surfaces. *Contrast* NET LEASABLE AREA.

GROSS LEASE / A lease of property whereby the landlord (lessor) is responsible for paying all property expenses, such as taxes, insurance, utilities, and repairs. *Contrast* NET LEASE.

Importance: Landlord and tenant agree in writing as to who pays each operating expense. Otherwise there is strong likelihood for disagreement and litigation.

GROSS POSSIBLE RENT / *See* POTENTIAL GROSS INCOME.

GROSS RENT MULTIPLIER (GRM) / The sales price divided by the rental rate. **Example:** The sales price is $40,000; the gross monthly rent is $400; the GRM = $40,000/$400 = 100. It may also be expressed as an annual figure (8.333), that is, the number of years of rent equaling the purchase price.

Importance: In many investment situations the price is set based on a multiple of the rent level.

GROUND LEASE / An agreement for the rent of land only, often for a long term, at the expiration of which all of the real estate belongs to the landowner.

Importance: Sometimes land can be purchased or leased separately from buildings, thus splitting ownership into components that are more desirable. A property buyer or lessee must be mindful of the lease terms and the effect of such a lease on using or financing the property.

GROUND RENT / The rent earned by leased land.

Importance: Ground leases may be net or gross. In a net lease the *tenant* pays expenses, such as insurance and real estate taxes.

GUARDIAN / A person appointed by a court to administer the affairs of an individual who is not capable of administering his/her own affairs.

Importance: An *incompetent* cannot enter a valid contract. It is important to deal with the person's guardian.

HABENDUM CLAUSE / The "to have and to hold" clause that defines or limits the quantity of the estate granted in the deed. **Example:** "To have and to hold for one's lifetime" creates a life estate.

HEIRS AND ASSIGNS / Terminology used in deeds and wills to provide that the recipient receive a *fee simple* estate in lands rather than a lesser interest.

Importance: These words give the recipient complete ownership, not just an estate for a limited duration of time.

HEREDITAMENTS / Any property that may be inherited, whether real or personal, tangible or intangible.

HIGHEST AND BEST USE / The legally and physically possible use that, at the time of *appraisal*, is most likely to produce the greatest net return to the land and/or buildings over a given time period.

Importance: To realize the full value of land, the improvements built on it must represent its highest and best use.

HIP ROOF / A pitched roof formed by four walls sloped in different directions. The two longer sides of the roof form a ridge at the top.

HISTORIC DISTRICT / A designated area where the buildings are considered to have some significant historic character. Such designation makes the area eligible for certain federal assistance programs and protects the area from clearance in conjunction with federally sponsored programs.

HOLDER IN DUE COURSE / A person who has taken a note, check, or similar asset (1) before it was overdue, (2) in good faith and for value, and (3) without knowledge that it had been previously dishonored and without notice of any defect at the time it was negotiated to him/her.

Importance: A holder in due course is an innocent buyer of paper (a debt).

HOLDOVER TENANT / A tenant who remains in possession of leased property after the expiration of the lease term.

Importance: A holdover tenant has a *tenancy at sufferance*. The landlord may dictate the terms of occupancy.

HOME EQUITY LOAN / A loan secured by a second mortgage on one's principal residence, generally to be used for some nonhousing expenditure.

HOMESTEAD / The status provided to a homeowner's principal residence. Protects the home against judgments up to specified amounts.

Importance: In Florida, the owner can continue possession and enjoyment of a home against the wishes of creditors.

HOMESTEAD EXEMPTION / A reduction of $25,000 from the tax value of a home, for ad valorem taxes of a city, county, or school district.

HUD / Abbreviation for U.S. Department of Housing and Urban Development.

HYPOTHECATE / To pledge a thing as security without having to give up possession of it.

Importance: The word *hypothecate* comes (through Late Latin and French) from a Greek word meaning "to put down as a deposit" and has the same meaning as the French-derived word *mortgage*.

ILLIQUIDITY / Inadequate cash to meet obligations. Real estate is considered an illiquid investment because of the time and effort required to convert it to cash.

IMPLIED AGENCY / Occurs when the words and actions of the parties indicate that there is an agency relationship.

IMPROVEMENT RATIO / The value of *improvements* relative to the value of unimproved land. **Example:** Land worth $250,000 was improved with a $750,000 building. The improvement ratio is $750,000/$250,000 or 3:1.

IMPROVEMENTS / Additions to raw land that tend to increase value, such as buildings, streets, sewers.

Importance: An improvement is anything except the raw land. *See also* HIGHEST AND BEST USE.

INCHOATE / (1) Recently or just begun; (2) unfinished, begun but not completed. **Examples:** In real estate, this term can apply to *dower* or *curtesy* rights prior to the death of a spouse, instruments that are supposed to be recorded, and interests that can ripen into a vested estate.

INCOME / The money or other benefit coming from the use of something. Gross sales or income is the full amount received; net income is the remainder after subtracting expenses. Many persons in real estate prefer to use *cash flow* as the measure of income, whereas those in accounting prefer *net income*.

INCOME APPROACH / One of the three appraisal methods used in arriving at an estimate of the market value of property; the value of the property is the present worth of the income it is expected to produce during its remaining life.

Importance: Annual income for rental property can be capitalized into value to estimate the property's worth.

INCOME MULTIPLIER / The relationship of price to income. *See also* GROSS RENT MULTIPLIER.

INCOME PROPERTY / Property whose ownership appeal is that it produces income. **Examples:** Office buildings, shopping centers, rental apartments, hotels.

INCOME STREAM / A regular flow of money generated by a business or investment.

INCOMPETENT / A person who is unable to manage his/her own affairs by reason of insanity, imbecility, or feeblemindedness.

Importance: When conducting business with an incompetent, his/her guardian's consent is required.

INCURABLE DEPRECIATION / (1) A defect that cannot be cured or is not financially practical to cure; (2) a defect in the "bone structure" of a building.

Importance: When appraising real estate using the *cost approach*, incurable depreciation is separated from curable to indicate the actual loss in value sustained by the property.

INDENTURE / A written agreement made between two or more persons having different interests.

Importance: Indentures are used in mortgages, deeds, and bonds. They describe the terms of the agreement.

INDEPENDENT CONTRACTOR / A contractor who is self-employed for tax purposes. When real estate salespeople are self-employed, the broker is not required to withhold taxes.

INDEPENDENT FEE APPRAISER / A person who estimates the value of property but has no interest in the property and is not associated with a lending association or other investor.

INDEX / (1) A statistic that indicates some current economic or financial condition. Indexes are often used to make adjustments in wage rates, rental rates, loan interest rates, and pension benefits set by long-term contracts. (2) To adjust contract terms according to an index.

INDEX LEASE / A lease in which rentals are tied to an agreed upon index of costs. **Example:** Rentals are to increase along with the Consumer Price Index.

Importance: An index lease can provide fairness to both parties in a long-term leasing arrangement.

INDUSTRIAL PROPERTY / Property used for industrial purposes, such as factories and power plants.

Importance: Land to be used for industrial purposes must be zoned for that purpose.

INFLATION / A loss in the purchasing power of money; an increase in the general price level. Inflation is generally measured by the Consumer Price Index, published by the Bureau of Labor Statistics.

Importance: Real estate is considered a hedge against inflation because it tends to be long lasting and holds its value in real terms. As the value of the dollar drops, real estate tends to command more dollars. For example, a home purchased in 1967 for $50,000 was resold in 1976 for $100,000 and in 1995 for $200,000. The home did nothing to cause its price to change; inflation caused the house to command more dollars.

INFRASTRUCTURE / The basic public works of a city or subdivision, including roads, bridges, sewer and water systems, drainage systems, and essential public utilities.

INJUNCTION / A writ or order issued by a court to restrain one or more parties to a suit or a proceeding from performing an act that is deemed inequitable or unjust in regard to the rights of some other party or parties in the suit or proceeding.

Importance: An injunction can prevent a wrongdoing while the legal process continues, that is, before a final judgment is made about the rights of the parties.

IN REM / Latin for "against the thing." A proceeding against *realty* directly, as distinguished from a proceeding against a person (used in taking land for nonpayment of taxes, and so on). By contrast, *in personam* means "against the person."

INSTALLMENTS / Parts of the same debt, payable at successive periods as agreed; payments made to reduce a mortgage.

Importance: Many debts are paid in installments that include interest for a recent period plus some amount for *amortization*.

INSTALLMENT TO AMORTIZE ONE DOLLAR / A mathematically computed factor, derived from *compound interest* functions, that offers the level periodic payment required to retire a $1.00 loan within a certain time frame. The periodic installment must exceed the periodic interest rate. *See also* AMORTIZATION; AMORTIZATION TERM.

INSTRUMENT / A written legal document, created to effect the rights and liabilities of the parties to it. **Examples:** Deed, will, lease.

INSURABLE TITLE / A title that can be insured by a title insurance company.

Importance: When acquiring real estate, a buyer should determine whether the title is insurable. If not, there are probably valid claims that will affect his/her use or ownership.

INSURANCE COVERAGE / Total amount and type of insurance carried.

Importance: It is conservative to retain insurance coverage based on the replacement value or cost of one's valuables.

INTANGIBLE VALUE / Value that cannot be seen or touched. **Example:** The goodwill of an established business.

INTER VIVOS TRUST / A trust set up during one's lifetime.

INTEREST / (1) Money paid for the use of money; (2) the type and extent of ownership.

INTEREST RATE / (1) The percentage of a sum of money charged for its use; (2) the rate of return on an investment.

Importance: The loan interest rate is an important ingredient in determining the periodic installment payment.

INTERPLEADER / A proceeding initiated by a neutral third party to determine the rights of rival claimants to property or a transaction.

Importance: An escrow agent can call for an interpleader when there is a dispute between the buyer and seller.

INTESTACY / *See* INTESTATE.

INTESTATE / A person who dies leaving no will or a defective will. His/her property goes to his/her legal heirs.

Importance: Florida law determines inheritance rules for intestates. If there are no heirs, the property *escheats* to the state.

INVESTMENT PROPERTY / Property that is owned for its income-generating capacity or expected resale value. **Example:** Apartments, office buildings, undeveloped land.

INVESTMENT VALUE / The estimated value of a certain real estate investment to a particular individual or institutional investor; may be greater or less than *market value*, depending on the investor's particular situation.

INVOLUNTARY ALIENATION / A loss of property for nonpayment of debts such as taxes or mortgage foreclosure.

INVOLUNTARY LIEN / A lien imposed against property without the consent of the owner (unpaid taxes, special assessments).

Importance: A lien can be created without any action by the landowner.

IRREVOCABLE / Incapable of being recalled or revoked; unchangeable, unalterable.

JEOPARDY / Peril, danger, risk. **Example:** Property pledged as security for a delinquent loan is in jeopardy of *foreclosure*.

JOINT TENANCY / Ownership of realty by two or more persons, each of whom has an undivided interest with *right of survivorship*. **Example:** A and B own land in joint tenancy. Each owns half of the entire (undivided) property. Upon A's death, B will own the entire property, or vice versa.

JOINT VENTURE / An agreement between two or more parties who invest in a single business or property.

JUDGMENT / A court decree stating that one individual is indebted to another and fixing the amount of the indebtedness.

Importance: A judgment is a final determination of the matter, decided by a court.

JUDGMENT CREDITOR / A person who has received a court decree or judgment for money due to him/her.

JUDGMENT DEBTOR / A person against whom a judgment has been issued by a court for money owed.

JUDGMENT LIEN / The claim upon the property of a debtor resulting from a judgment. **Example:** A won't pay his debt to B. After establishing the debt in court, B may be allowed by the court to put a lien on A's real estate.

JUDICIAL FORECLOSURE / Procedure used when a trustee or mortgagee requests court supervision of a foreclosure action.

JUNIOR LIEN / *See* JUNIOR MORTGAGE.

JUNIOR MORTGAGE / A *mortgage* whose claim against the property will be satisfied only after prior mortgages have been sold; also called *junior lien*.

Importance: A junior (second, third) mortgage has value as long as the borrower continues payments or the property's value is in excess of the mortgage debts.

LACHES / Delay or negligence in asserting one's legal rights.

Importance: If a person does not act in a reasonable time to assert his/her rights, he/she may be barred from doing so because of the delay.

LAND / The surface of the earth; any part of the surface of the earth. (Note: Legal definitions often distinguish land from water.)

LAND CONTRACT / A real estate installment selling arrangement whereby the buyer may use, occupy, and enjoy land, but no *deed* is given by the seller (so no title passes) until all or a specified part of the sale price has been paid.

Importance: In comparison to a deed, a land contract is easier to foreclose should the buyer fail to make the payments.

LAND LEASE / Only the ground is covered by the lease. *See also* GROUND LEASE.

LANDLORD / A person who rents property to another; a *lessor*.

LANDMARK / A fixed object serving as a boundary mark for a tract of land.

Importance: In surveying, a landmark serves as a reference point.

LAND PATENT / *See* PATENT.

LAND, TENEMENTS, AND HEREDITAMENTS / A phrase used in early English law to express all sorts of *real estate*.

Importance: This is the most comprehensive description of real estate.

LEASE / A contract in which, for a consideration called *rent*, one who is entitled to the possession of real property (the *lessor*) transfers those rights to another (the *lessee*) for a specified period of time.

Importance: A lease is an essential agreement, allowing an owner to transfer possession to a user for a limited amount of time.

LEASED FEE / The landlord's ownership interest in a *property* that is under *lease*. *Contrast* LEASEHOLD.

LEASEHOLD / The interest or estate on which a *lessee* (tenant) of real estate has his/her lease.

Importance: A leasehold can be quite valuable when the tenant's rent is below the market rate and the lease is for a long term.

LEASEHOLD IMPROVEMENTS / Fixtures, attached to *real estate*, that are generally acquired or installed by the tenant. Upon expiration of the *lease*, the tenant can generally remove them, provided that removal does not damage the property and is not in conflict with the lease. **Examples:** Cabinets, light fixtures, window treatments of a retail store in a leased building.

LEASEHOLD VALUE / The value of a tenant's interest in a *lease*, especially when the *rent* is below market level and the lease has a long remaining term.

LEASE WITH OPTION TO PURCHASE / A lease that gives the lessee (tenant) the right to purchase the property at an agreed upon price under certain conditions.

Importance: Because the option allows but does not compel the purchase, it gives the tenant time to consider acquisition.

LEGAL DESCRIPTION / Legally acceptable identification of real estate by the (1) *government rectangular survey*, (2) *metes and bounds*, or (3) *lot and block number* method.

LESSEE / A person to whom property is rented under a *lease*; a tenant.

LESSOR / A person who rents property to another under a *lease*; a landlord.

LEVEL ANNUITY / *See* ANNUITY.

LEVERAGE / The use of borrowed funds to increase purchasing power and, ideally, to increase the profitability of an investment.

Importance: If the property increases in value or yields financial benefits at a rate above the borrowed money interest rate, leverage is favorable, also called positive. But if the rate of property benefits is less than the interest rate, the investor's losses are increased.

LICENSE / (1) Permission; (2) a privilege or right granted by the state of Florida to an individual to operate as a real estate broker, salesperson, or appraiser.

Importance: (1) License allows a person to use property for a limited time. (2) In Florida, a person must be licensed as a broker (or salesperson) to receive payment for a sale, lease, or other transaction.

LICENSED APPRAISER / In Florida, an *appraiser* who meets certain state requirements, but can appraise only residential units of not more than $1 million. *See also* CERTIFIED GENERAL APPRAISER; CERTIFIED RESIDENTIAL APPRAISER.

LICENSEE / A person who holds a real estate license.

Importance: In Florida, only licensees are entitled to receive compensation for assisting with a real estate transaction. Education and the passing of examinations are requirements of licensing.

LIEN / A charge against property making it security for the payment of a debt, judgment, mortgage, or taxes; a lien is a type of *encumbrance*.

Importance: A lien makes the property collateral for a debt. Some liens may allow the property to be sold to satisfy the debt.

LIFE ESTATE / A freehold interest in land that expires upon the death of the owner or some other specified person.

Importance: A person with a life estate may use the property, but not abuse it, for as long as he/she lives. Then it reverts to the *remainderman*.

LIFE TENANT / A person who is allowed to use property for his/her lifetime or for the lifetime of another designated person. *See also* LIFE ESTATE.

LIQUIDATED DAMAGES / An amount agreed upon in a contract that one party will pay the other in the event of a breach of the contract.

LIS PENDENS / Latin for "suit pending"; recorded notice that a suit has been filed, the outcome of which may affect title to a certain land.

Importance: Title to the property under consideration may be in jeopardy.

LISTING / (1) A written employment contract between a *principal* and an *agent* authorizing the agent to perform services for the principal involving the latter's property; (2) a record of property for sale by a broker who has been authorized by the owner to sell; (3) the property so listed. *See also* EXCLUSIVE AGENCY LISTING, EXCLUSIVE RIGHT TO SELL LISTING, NET LISTING, OPEN LISTING.

LITIGATION / The act of carrying on a lawsuit.

LITTORAL / Part of the shore zone of a large body of water.

Importance: Littoral rights differ from *riparian rights*, which pertain to a river or stream.

LOAN CONSTANT / *See* MORTGAGE CONSTANT.

LOAN-TO-VALUE RATIO (LTV) / The ratio obtained by dividing the mortgage principal by the property value.

Importance: Lenders typically provide loans with a stated maximum loan-to-value-ratio. For conventional home loans it is typically 80 percent. In many cases it can be increased to 95 percent if mortgage insurance is purchased. VA and FHA loans may offer higher ratios.

LOCK-IN / An agreement to maintain a certain price or rate for a certain period of time.

Importance: In many *mortgage* commitments the lender agrees to lock in the interest rate for a certain period, such as 60 days. Sometimes a lock-in is provided only upon payment of a *commitment* fee.

LOT AND BLOCK NUMBER / A land description method that refers to a recorded plat. **Example:** Lot 6, Block F of the Sunnybrook Estates, District 2 of Rover County, Florida.

LOT LINE / A line bounding a lot as described in a survey of the property.

Importance: Lot lines mark boundaries. There may also be building *setback* requirements, or *building lines*, within a lot.

LTV / *See* LOAN-TO-VALUE RATIO.

MAI / A member of the *Appraisal Institute*, which is affiliated with the *National Association of Realtors*®.

Importance: The MAI designation is one of the most coveted in real estate. Many appraisals of large commercial properties are done by MAIs.

MAJORITY / The age at which a person is no longer a minor and is fully able to conduct his/her own affairs; in Florida, majority is 18.

Importance: A contract with a minor is voidable by the minor.

MARGIN / A constant amount added to the value of the *index* for the purpose of adjusting the interest rate on an *adjustable rate mortgage*.

MARGINAL PROPERTY / Property that is barely profitable to use. **Example:** The sale of cotton that has been efficiently raised yields $100, but the cotton cost $99.99 to raise. The land is therefore considered marginal land.

MARKETABILITY STUDY / An analysis, for a specific client, of the probable sales of a specific type of real estate product.

MARKETABLE TITLE / A title that a court will consider so free from defect that it will enforce its acceptance by a purchaser; similar to *insurable title*.

MARKET APPROACH / *See* SALES COMPARISON APPROACH.

MARKET DATA APPROACH / *See* SALES COMPARISON APPROACH.

MARKET PRICE / The actual price paid in a market transaction; a historical fact.

Importance: *Market value* is a theoretical concept, whereas market price has actually occurred.

MARKET STUDY / *See* MARKET ANALYSIS.

MARKET VALUE / The highest price a buyer, willing but not compelled to buy, will pay, and the lowest price a seller, willing but not compelled to sell, will accept. Many conditions are assumed to exist.

Importance: In theory, property would sell for its market value.

MASS APPRAISING / An effort, typically used by tax *assessors*, to determine the salient characteristics of properties in a given submarket, to allow an approximation of value for each. Sophisticated statistical techniques are used frequently in mass appraising.

MATERIAL FACT / A fact that is germane to a particular situation; one that participants in the situation may reasonably be expected to consider.

Importance: In a contract, a material fact is one without which the contract would not have been made.

MECHANIC'S LIEN / A lien given by law upon a building or other improvement upon land, and upon the land itself, as security for the payment for labor done upon, and materials furnished for, the improvement.

Importance: A mechanic's lien protects persons who helped build or supply materials.

MEETING OF THE MINDS / Agreement by all parties to a contract to its terms and substance.

Importance: When there is a meeting of the minds, the contract is not based on secret intentions of one party that were withheld from another.

MERIDIAN / North-south line used in government rectangular survey.

METES AND BOUNDS / A land description method that relates the boundary lines of land, setting forth all the boundary lines together with their terminal points and angles.

Importance: A person can follow a metes and bounds description on a plat or on the ground.

MILL / One tenth of a cent; used in expressing tax rates on a per dollar basis. **Example:** A tax rate of 60 mills means that taxes are 6 cents per dollar of assessed valuation.

MINERAL RIGHTS / The privilege of gaining income from the sale of oil, gas, and other valuable resources found on land.

MINOR / A person under an age specified by law (18 in Florida).

Importance: Real estate contracts entered into with minors are voidable by the minor.

MISREPRESENTATION / An untrue statement, whether deliberate or unintentional. It may be a form of nondisclosure where there is a duty to disclose or the planned creation of a false appearance. Where there is misrepresentation of *material fact,* the person injured may sue for *damages* or rescind the contract.

MONUMENT / A fixed object and point designated by surveyors to establish land locations. **Examples:** Posts, pillars, stone markers, unique trees, stones, pipes, watercourses.

MORATORIUM / A time period during which a certain activity is not allowed.

MORTGAGE / A written instrument that creates a lien upon real estate as security for the payment of a specified debt.

Importance: The mortgage allows a defaulted debt to be satisfied by forcing a sale of the property.

MORTGAGE BANKER / One who originates, sells, and services *mortgage* loans. Most loans are insured or guaranteed by a government agency or private mortgage insurer.

MORTGAGE BROKER / One who, for a fee, places loans with investors but does not service such loans.

MORTGAGE COMMITMENT / An agreement between a lender and a borrower to lend money at a future date, subject to the conditions described in the agreement.

Importance: The terms of the commitment are important, especially the interest rate *lock-in*, if there is one.

MORTGAGE CONSTANT / The percentage ratio between the annual mortgage payment and the original amount of the debt.

MORTGAGEE / A person who holds a *lien* on or *title* to property as security for a debt.

Importance: The mortgagee receives the lien; the *mortgagor* receives the loan.

MORTGAGOR / A person who pledges his/her property as security for a loan. *See also* MORTGAGEE.

MOST PROBABLE SELLING PRICE / A property's most likely selling price when not all the conditions required for a *market value* estimate are relevant. **Example:** An appraiser estimated a property's most likely sales price at $100,000, assuming a sale within 20 days, whereas its market value of $120,000 might require up to 6 months to realize.

MULTIPLE LISTING / An arrangement among a group of real estate *brokers*; they agree in advance to provide information about some or all of their listings to the others and also agree that commissions on sales of such listings will be split between listing and selling brokers.

MULTIPLIER / A factor, used as a guide, applied by multiplication to derive or estimate an important value. **Examples:** (1) A *gross rent multiplier* of 6 means that property renting for $12,000 per year can be sold for six times that amount, or $72,000. (2) A population multiplier of 2 means that, for each job added, two people will be added to a city's population.

NAR / *See* NATIONAL ASSOCIATION OF REALTORS®.

**NATIONAL ASSOCIATION OF REALTORS®
(NAR)** / An organization devoted to encouraging
professionalism in real estate activities.

Importance: The NAR has strong lobbyists that
protect the interest of the real estate community,
especially of homeowners. It also has affiliates related to appraising, counseling, and managing real
estate.

NEGATIVE AMORTIZATION / An increase in
the outstanding balance of a loan resulting from the
failure of periodic debt service payments to cover
required interest charged on the loan. Generally occurs under indexed loans for which the applicable
interest rate may be increased without increasing
the monthly payments. *Negative amortization* will
occur if the indexed interest rate is increased.

NET INCOME / In real estate this term is now *net
operating income*. In accounting, net income is
the actual earnings, after deducting all expenses,
including interest and depreciation, from gross
sales.

NET LEASABLE AREA (NLA) / For office and
retail properties, the portion used exclusively by the
tenant; generally excludes hallways, restrooms, and
other common areas.

Importance: The rent per square foot may be
judged consistently between buildings when it is
based on this space measurement.

NET LEASE / A lease whereby, in addition to the
rent stipulated, the lessee (tenant) pays such things
as taxes, insurance, and maintenance. The landlord's rent receipt is thereby net of those expenses.

Importance: The responsibility for maintenance
costs is shifted to the lessee; the lessor is a passive
investor.

NET LISTING / A listing in which the broker's
commission is the excess of the sale price over an
agreed upon (net) price to the seller. Discouraged
in Florida. **Example:** A house is listed for sale at
$100,000 net. The broker's commission is $1 if it
sells for $100,001. But if it sells for $150,000, the
broker receives $50,000.

NET OPERATING INCOME (NOI) / Income
from property or business after operating expenses
have been deducted, but before deducting income
taxes and financing expenses (interest and principal
payments).

NLA / *See* NET LEASABLE AREA.

NOI / *See* NET OPERATING INCOME.

NONCONFORMING USE / A use that violates
zoning ordinances or codes but is allowed to continue because it began before the zoning restriction
was enacted.

Importance: This allows a prior use to continue,
but puts restrictions on future uses of the property.

NONRECOURSE / Carrying no personal liability.
Lenders may take the property pledged as collateral
to satisfy a debt, but have no *recourse* to other assets
of the borrower.

NOTARY PUBLIC / An officer who is authorized
to take acknowledgments to certain types of documents, such as *deeds*, *contracts*, and *mortgages*, and
before whom affidavits may be sworn.

Importance: Most documents must be notarized
as a condition of being recorded.

NOTE / A written instrument that acknowledges a
debt and promises to pay.

Importance: A note is enforceable in a court of law.
Collateral for the note may be sold to satisfy the debt.

NOTICE TO QUIT / A notice to a tenant to vacate
rented property.

Importance: The tenant is permitted to complete
the term of the lease, except in cases of *tenancy at
will* or *tenancy at sufferance*.

NOVATION / Substitution of a revised agreement
for an existing one, with the consent of all parties involved. Technically, anytime parties to an existing
contract agree to change it, the revised document is
a *novation*.

NULL AND VOID / Having no legal validity.

OBLIGEE / The person in whose favor an obligation is entered into.

OBLIGOR / The person who binds him/herself to
another; one who has engaged to perform some
obligation; one who makes a bond.

OBSOLESCENCE / (1) A loss in value due to reduced desirability and usefulness of a structure because its design and construction have become
obsolete; (2) loss due to a structure's becoming
old-fashioned, not in keeping with modern needs,
with consequent loss of income.

Importance: Obsolescence can cause a loss in
value just as *physical deterioration* does.

OFFER AND ACCEPTANCE / *See* AGREEMENT
OF SALE.

OPEN-END MORTGAGE / A mortgage under
which the mortgagor (borrower) may secure additional funds from the mortgagee (lender), usually stip-
ulating a ceiling amount that can be borrowed.

Importance: A development in real estate finance is a line-of-credit home equity loan. This
works the same as an open-end mortgage.

OPEN LISTING / A listing given to any number
of brokers without liability to compensate any except the one who first secures a buyer ready, will-

ing, and able to meet the terms of the listing or secures the seller's acceptance of another offer. The sale of the property automatically terminates all open listings.

OPEN MORTGAGE / A mortgage that has matured or is overdue and is therefore open to foreclosure at any time.

OPERATING EXPENSE RATIO / A mathematical relationship derived by dividing *operating expenses* by *potential gross income*.

Importance: A comparison of rents for properties would be incomplete without also comparing operating expenses. Apartments generally have operating expense ratios between 30 and 50 percent; this may be exceeded when the lessor pays utilities or the apartments are in low-rent areas. Office buildings often have higher operating expense ratios (40 and 60 percent) because more intensive management and maintenance, such as cleaning services, are provided.

OPERATING EXPENSES / Amounts paid to maintain property, such as repairs, insurance, property taxes, but not including financing costs or depreciation.

OPERATING LEASE / A lease between the lessee and a sublessee who actually occupies and uses the property.

Importance: In an operating lease the lessee runs the property; by contrast, in a *financing lease* the lessee becomes lessor to the operating tenant.

OPERATING STATEMENTS / Financial reports on the cash flow of a property.

OPTION / The right, but not the obligation, to purchase or lease a property upon specified terms within a specified period. **Example:** The right to buy certain land within 90 days at $5,000 per acre. The property becomes reserved for that time period.

ORAL CONTRACT / An unwritten agreement. With few exceptions, oral agreements for the sale or use of real estate are unenforceable in Florida.

Importance: When dealing with real estate, agreements should be in writing.

ORIGINAL EQUITY / The amount of cash initially invested by the underlying *real estate* owner; distinguished from sweat equity or payments made after loan is made.

OVERAGE / *See* PERCENTAGE RENT.

OVERALL CAPITALIZATION RATE (OVERALL RATE OF RETURN) / The rate obtained by dividing *net operating income* by the purchase price of the property.

Importance: Rates of return from properties may be compared to each other; or the rate may be divided into income to estimate property value.

OWNERSHIP RIGHTS TO REALTY / Possession, enjoyment, control, and disposition.

PACKAGE MORTGAGE / A mortgage arrangement whereby the principal amount loaned is increased to include *personalty* (e.g., appliances) as well as *realty*; both realty and personalty serve as collateral.

PARCEL / A piece of property under one ownership; a lot in a subdivision.

PARTIALLY AMORTIZED LOAN / A loan that requires some payments toward *principal* but does not fully retire the debt, thereby requiring a *balloon payment*. *See also* AMORTIZATION.

PARTIAL OR FRACTIONAL INTEREST / The ownership of some, but not all, the rights in *real estate*. **Examples:** (1) *leasehold;* (2) *easement;* (3) *hunting rights.*

PARTITION / The division of real property between those who own it in undivided shares. **Example:** A and B own land as tenants in common until they partition it. Thereafter, each owns a particular tract of land.

PARTNERSHIP / An agreement between two or more entities to go into business or invest. Either partner may bind the other, within the scope of the partnership. Each partner is liable for all the partnership's debts. A partnership normally pays no taxes but merely files an information return. The individual partners pay personal income tax on their share of income.

PARTY WALL / A wall built along the line separating two properties, lying partly on each. Either owner has the right to use the wall and has an *easement* over that part of the adjoining owner's land covered by the wall.

PATENT / Conveyance of title to government land; also called a *land patent*.

PAYMENT CAP / A contractual limit on the percentage amount of adjustment allowed in the monthly payment for an *adjustable rate mortgage* at any one adjustment period. Generally it does not affect the interest rate charged. If the allowable payment does not cover interest due on the principal at the adjusted rate of interest, *negative amortization* will occur.

PERCENTAGE LEASE / A lease of property in which the rental is based on a percentage of the volume of sales made upon the leased premises. It usually provides for minimum rental and is regularly used for retailers who are tenants.

Importance: The retailer pays additional rent only if sales are high; the shopping center owner has an incentive to make an attractive shopping area.

PERCENTAGE RENT / The rent payable under a *percentage lease*; also called *overage*. Typically, the percentage applies to sales in excess of a pre-established base amount of the dollar sales volume.

Importance: Percentage rent provides incentive to a landlord for making a store or shopping area appeal to the market.

PERIODIC ESTATE / A lease, such as from month-to-month or year-to-year. Also known as periodic tenancy.

PERMANENT MORTGAGE / A mortgage for a long period of time (more than 10 years).

Importance: A permanent mortgage usually replaces construction or interim financing, and provides steady interest income plus *amortization* payments to the lender. For the borrower it means that there is no need to seek new financing.

PERSONAL LIABILITY / An individual's responsibility for a debt. Most mortgage loans on real estate are *recourse* (i.e., the lender can look to the property and the borrower for repayment). *Contrast* NONRECOURSE.

PERSONALTY / Personal property; that is, all property that is not *realty*.

Importance: Many laws and terms that apply to real property are not the same as those for personalty. When dealing with both types, appropriate law and terminology must be applied.

PHYSICAL DEPRECIATION (DETERIORATION) / The loss of value from all causes of age and action of the elements. **Examples:** Faded paint, broken window, hole in plaster, collapsed porch railing, sagging frame.

PLANNED UNIT DEVELOPMENT (PUD) / A zoning or land-use category for large tracts that allows several different densities and forms of land use, planned as a single well-integrated unit.

PLAT / A plan or map of a certain piece or certain pieces of land. **Examples:** A subdivision plat or a plat of one lot.

PLAT BOOK / A public record containing maps of land showing the division of the land into streets, blocks, and lots and indicating the measurements of the individual parcels.

Importance: The tax assessor's office, usually in a city or county, maintains a plat book that is open for public inspection.

PLOTTAGE / Increment in the value of a plot of land that has been enlarged by assembling smaller plots into one ownership.

Importance: Combining several small tracts into one ownership can provide a large enough land area for a more profitable use than would be possible

otherwise. However, it is often difficult to get several owners to sell, as some hold out for a high price.

PMI / Abbreviation for private mortgage insurance.

POCKET CARD / Identification required for *salespersons* and *brokers* in Florida.

Importance: Issued by the state licensing agency, it identifies its holder as a licensee and must be carried at all times.

POINTS / Fees paid to induce lenders to make a *mortgage* loan. Each point equals one percent of the loan principal. Points have the effect of reducing the amount of money advanced by the lender, thus increasing the effective interest rate.

POLICE POWER / The right of any political body to enact laws and enforce them for the order, safety, health, morals, and general welfare of the public.

Importance: Government authorities get the power of *eminent domain* through their police power.

POTENTIAL GROSS INCOME / The theoretical amount of money that would be collected in a year if all units in a rental building were fully occupied all year; also called *gross possible rent*.

POWER OF ATTORNEY / An instrument authorizing a person to act as the agent of the person granting it.

Importance: By using a power of attorney, one can designate a specific person to do everything or just certain limited activities.

PREMISES / Land and tenements; an estate: the subject matter of a *conveyance*.

PREPAYMENT CLAUSE / A clause in a mortgage that gives a mortgagor (borrower) the privilege of paying the mortgage indebtedness before it becomes due.

Importance: Sometimes a penalty must be paid if prepayment is made, but payment of *interest* that is not yet due is waived.

PRESERVATION DISTRICT / A zoning designation to protect and maintain wildlife, park land, scenic areas, or historic districts.

PRICE FIXING / Illegal effort by competing businesses to maintain the same price, such as the commission rate on the sale of real estate.

PRIMARY LEASE / A lease between the owner and a tenant who, in turn, has sublet all or part of his/her interest.

Importance: The tenant in the primary lease is still responsible to the landlord, even though the subtenant(s) occupy the space.

PRINCIPAL / (1) The employer of an *agent* or *broker*; the broker's or agent's client; (2) the amount of money raised by a mortgage or other loan, as distinct from the interest paid on it.

PROBATE (PROVE) / To establish the validity of the will of a deceased person.

Importance: Probate relates not only to the validity of a will but also to matters and proceedings of estate administration.

PROBATE COURT / *See* SURROGATE'S COURT.

PROCURING CAUSE / A legal term that means the cause resulting in accomplishing a goal. Used in real estate to determine whether a broker is entitled to a commission.

PROJECTION PERIOD / The time duration for estimating future *cash flows* and the resale proceeds from a proposed real estate investment.

PROMISSORY NOTE / A promise to pay a specified sum to a specified person under specified terms.

PROPERTY / (1) The rights that one individual has in lands or goods to the exclusion of all others; (2) rights gained from the ownership of wealth. *See also* PERSONALTY; REAL PROPERTY.

PROPERTY LINE / The recorded boundary of a plot of land.

Importance: A *survey* is performed in order to establish property lines and describe them on a *plat*.

PROPERTY MANAGEMENT / The operation of property as a business, including rental, rent collection, maintenance.

Importance: Property managers remove the daily burden from real estate investors, thus allowing them to be free from daily business operations.

PROPRIETORSHIP / Ownership of a business, including income-producing real estate, by an individual, as contrasted with a partnership or corporation.

PRORATE / To allocate between seller and buyer their proportionate shares of an obligation paid or due; for example, to prorate real property taxes or insurance.

Importance: Many items of expense are prorated between buyer and seller, to the date of closing.

PURCHASE CAPITAL / The amount of money used to purchase real estate, regardless of the source.

PURCHASE CONTRACT / *See* AGREEMENT OF SALE.

PURCHASE MONEY MORTGAGE / A mortgage given by a grantee (buyer) to a grantor (seller) in part payment of the purchase price of real estate.

Importance: Institutional lenders are often unable or unwilling to finance certain types of property, so the seller must accept a purchase money mortgage to facilitate a sale.

QUIET ENJOYMENT / The right of an owner, or any other person legally entitled to possession, to the use of property without interference.

Importance: No interference should be caused by a landlord to a tenant who is in compliance with a lease.

QUIET TITLE SUIT / A suit in court to remove a defect, cloud, or suspicion regarding the legal rights of an owner to a certain parcel of *real property*.

Importance: A potential claimant is told to bring forward his/her claim so its validity can be judged. If it is not valid, the claimant must stop interference with the owner.

QUITCLAIM DEED / A deed that conveys only the *grantor's* rights or interest in real estate, without stating their nature and with no warranties of ownership.

Importance: This deed is often used to remove a possible cloud from the title.

RANGE LINES / In the *government rectangular survey* method of land description, lines parallel to the principal *meridian*, marking off the land into 6-mile strips known as ranges; they are numbered east or west of the principal meridian. *See also* BASE AND MERIDIAN.

RATE OF INTEREST / *See* INTEREST RATE.

REAL ESTATE / Land and all attachments that are of a permanent nature.

Importance: Real estate is distinguished from personal property. At one time real estate was the sole source of wealth and achieved a special place in the law because of its importance.

REAL ESTATE EDUCATORS ASSOCIATION / A professional organization composed primarily of persons who teach *real estate* in junior colleges and proprietary license preparation schools.

REAL ESTATE INVESTMENT TRUST (REIT) / A *real estate* mutual fund, allowed by income tax laws to avoid the corporate tax if 95 percent of its income is distributed. It sells shares of ownership and must invest in real estate or mortgages.

Importance: A REIT allows small investors to participate in the ownership of large, potentially profitable, real estate projects.

REAL ESTATE SETTLEMENT PROCEDURES ACT (RESPA) / A law that states how *mortgage* lenders must treat those who apply for federally funded real estate loans on property with 1–4 dwelling units. Intended to provide borrowers with more knowledge when they comparison shop for mortgage money.

REAL PROPERTY / The right to use real estate, as (1) *fee simple* estate, (2) *life estate*, or (3) *leasehold* estate; sometimes also defined as *real estate*.

REALTOR® / A professional in real estate who subscribes to a strict code of ethics as a member of the local and Florida boards and of the *National Association of Realtors*®.

Importance: Fewer than half of those licensed to sell real estate are REALTORS®. In many areas a person must be a REALTOR® to participate in the predominant *multiple listing* service.

REALTY / The property rights to real estate.

REAPPRAISAL LEASE / A lease whereby the rental level is periodically reviewed and reset by independent appraisers.

Importance: Landlord and tenant can agree on a long-term lease knowing that the rent will be fair throughout the term because of the reappraisal clauses in the lease.

RECESSION / Economic slowdown; officially declared after two consecutive quarters of reduced gross domestic product.

RECISION / *See* RESCISSION.

RECORDING / The act of entering *instruments* affecting the title to real property in a book of public record.

Importance: Recording in this manner gives public notice of the facts recorded.

RECOURSE / The ability of a lender to claim money from a borrower in *default*, in addition to the property pledged as *collateral*.

REDLINING / An illegal practice of a lender refusing to make home loans in certain areas. The term is derived from a lender circling, with a red pencil on a map, areas where the institution will not lend.

Importance: If home loans will not be made in a certain area, property values will plummet and neighborhoods deteriorate rapidly. Redlining is an illegal discriminatory practice.

REDUCTION CERTIFICATE / A document in which the mortgagee (lender) acknowledges the sum due on the mortgage loan.

Importance: This is used when mortgaged property is sold and the buyer assumes the debt.

REGISTERED APPRAISER / In Florida, the entry-level appraiser designation.

REGULATION Z / Implementation by the Federal Reserve of the federal Truth-in-Lending Act; it specifies how the *annual percentage rate* of a loan is calculated and expressed in consumer loan documents.

REGULATORY TAKING / A series of government limits to property use that constitutes a condemnation of property.

REIT / *See* REAL ESTATE INVESTMENT TRUST.

RELEASE / The act by which some claim or interest is surrendered.

RELEASE CLAUSE / A clause in a mortgage that gives the owner of the property the privilege of paying off a portion of the indebtedness, thus freeing a part of the property from the mortgage.

Importance: Release clauses are frequently used when a mortgage covers more than one property (*blanket mortgage*), so that a particular parcel can be released upon some payment.

RELICTION / Gradual subsidence of waters, leaving dry land.

Importance: Ownership of land beneath a lake, for example, can become more important as reliction occurs.

REMAINDER / An estate that takes effect after the termination of a prior estate, such as a *life estate*.

Importance: The *remainderman* owns the property outright upon the death of the *life tenant*.

REMAINDERMAN / The person who is to receive possession of a property after the death of a *life tenant*.

Importance: Many people wish to allow a surviving spouse to occupy property for the rest of his/her life, with a child as the remainderman.

RENT / The compensation paid for the use of real estate.

Importance: Rent is the most important portion of a lease and may be paid in money, services, or other valuables.

RENT MULTIPLIER / *See* GROSS RENT MULTIPLIER.

RENT ROLL / A list of tenants, generally with the lease, rent amount, and expiration date for each tenant.

REPLACEMENT COST / The cost of erecting a building to take the place of or serve the functions of a previous structure.

Importance: Replacement cost often sets the upper limit on value; it is often used for insurance purposes.

REPORT DATE / In an appraisal, usually the date of the last property inspection.

REPRODUCTION COST / The normal cost of exact duplication of a property as of a certain date. Note: Replacement requires the same functional utility for a property, whereas a reproduction is an exact duplicate, using the same materials and craftsmanship.

RESALE PRICE / In a projection of real estate investment performance, the selling price that it is assumed a property could fetch at the end of the projection period. *See also* RESALE PROCEEDS.

RESALE PROCEEDS / Net case remaining to investor after sale of investment property and paying mortgage payoff and selling costs.

RESCISSION / The act of cancelling or terminating a contract. Rescission is allowed when the contract was induced by fraud, duress, misrepresentation, or mistake. *Regulation Z* allows one to rescind certain credit transactions within three business days (not applicable to first mortgages on a home). Purchasers of certain land that must be registered with the Department of Housing and Urban Development may rescind within three business days.

RESIDENTIAL SALES COUNCIL / An affiliate of the Realtors National Marketing Institute of the *National Association of Realtors®* that provides educational and promotional materials for members, most of whom are involved in residential real estate sales or brokerage.

RESTRAINT ON ALIENATION / A legal situation that would, if allowed to be enforced, prevent property from being sold easily. Restraints on alienation are against public policy so they cannot be enforced by law.

RESTRICTION / A limitation placed upon the use of property, contained in the deed or other written *instrument* in the chain of title.

Importance: If buying property with restrictions, the buyer should determine its suitability for the uses he/she requires.

RESTRICTIVE COVENANT / *See* RESTRICTION

REVERSION / The right of a lessor to possess leased property upon the termination of a lease.

Importance: A lease is valid for an established term, after which the lessor receives the reversion.

REVERSIONARY INTEREST / The interest a person has in property upon the termination of the preceding estate.

Importance: A lessor's interest in leased property is a reversionary interest.

REVOCATION / The recalling of a power of authority conferred, as a revocation of a power of attorney, a license, an agency.

Importance: A person with the authority to convey may also have authority to revoke, with reason.

RIDER / An amendment or attachment to a contract.

RIGHT OF SURVIVORSHIP / The right of a surviving joint tenant to acquire the interest of a deceased joint owner; the distinguishing feature of *joint tenancy* and *tenancy by the entireties*.

Importance: The right of survivorship is often used where the joint tenants are closely related.

RIGHT-OF-WAY / (1) The right to use a particular path for access or passage; a type of easement; (2) the areas of subdivisions dedicated to government for use as streets, roads, and other public access to lots.

RIPARIAN OWNER / A person who owns land bounding upon a lake, river, or other body of water.

RIPARIAN RIGHTS / Rights pertaining to the use of water on, under, or adjacent to one's land.

Importance: In most states, riparian rights do not permit property owners to alter the flow of water to their downstream neighbors.

SALE-LEASEBACK / The simultaneous purchase of property and leasing back to the seller. The lease portion of the transaction is generally long-term. The seller-lessee in the transaction is converted from an owner to a tenant.

SALES COMPARISON APPROACH / One of three appraisal approaches; also called *market approach* and *market data approach*. Value is estimated by analyzing sales prices of similar properties (comparables) recently sold.

Importance: Virtually all appraisals of homes, and many appraisals of other properties rely most heavily on the sales comparison approach. Two other approaches are *cost* and *income*.

SALES CONTRACT / A contract by which the buyer and seller agree to the terms of sale.

Importance: This document also called *agreement of sale* and *contract for sale and purchse* stipulates the rights and responsibilities of buyers and sellers.

SALESPERSON / A person who is licensed to deal in real estate or perform any other act enumerated by Florida real estate license law, while in the employ of a *broker* licensed by the state.

Importance: A salesperson's license is required for anyone to sell another's property. The salesperson must have a sponsoring broker.

SALES PRICE / The amount of money required to be paid for real estate according to a contract, or previously paid.

SALVAGE VALUE / The estimated value that an asset will have at the end of its useful life.

Importance: Real estate improvements, though long lasting, have a limited useful life at the end of which there may be salvage or scrap value.

SANDWICH LEASE / A lease held by a lessee who sublets all or part of his/her interest, thereby becoming a lessor. Typically, the sandwich lease-holder is neither the owner nor the user of the property.

Importance: The sandwich lessee tries to profit from income tax advantages or the rent differential between the other leases.

SATISFACTION OF MORTGAGE / *See* SATIS-FACTION PIECE.

SATISFACTION PIECE / An *instrument* for recording and acknowledging final payment of a mortgage loan.

Importance: After a loan has been paid off, the borrower should record a satisfaction of mortgage or satisfaction piece.

SECTION (of Land) / One square mile in the *government rectangular survey*. There are 36 sections in a 6-mile-square township.

SECURITY INSTRUMENT / An interest in real estate that allows the property to be sold upon a default on the obligation for which the security interest was created. The security interest is more specifically described as a *mortgage* or a *trust deed*.

SEIZIN / The possession of realty by a person who claims to own a *fee simple estate* or a *life estate* or other salable interest.

Importance: Seizin is a covenant needed to transfer ownership to another.

SENIOR RESIDENTIAL APPRAISER (SRA) / A designation awarded by the Appraisal Institute.

Importance: Many of the most qualified residential appraisers have this designation.

SEPARATE PROPERTY / Property acquired by either spouse prior to marriage or by gift or devise after marriage, as distinct from *community property*.

Importance: In community property states, property that is separate before marriage can remain that way; property acquired during marriage by joint effort is community property.

SETBACK / The distance from the curb or other established line within which no buildings may be erected. *Compare* BUILDING LINE.

Importance: Setbacks must be observed; if they are violated during construction, the property may have to be razed.

SETTLEMENT STATEMENT / *See* CLOSING STATEMENT.

SEVERALTY / The ownership of *real property* by an individual as an individual.

Importance: Severalty is distinguished from joint ownership, whereby two or more persons are owners.

SPECIAL ASSESSMENT / An *assessment* made against a property to pay for a public improvement by which the assessed property is supposed to be especially benefited.

Importance: A municipality may install a new sewer line or sidewalk; each owner along the path may be charged a special assessment, in addition to a regular tax.

SPECIAL-PURPOSE PROPERTY / A building with limited uses and marketability, such as a church, theater, school, public utility.

SPECIAL WARRANTY DEED / A deed in which the *grantor* limits the title warranty given to the *grantee* to anyone claiming by, from, through, or under him/her; the grantor. The grantor does not warrant against title defects arising from conditions that existed before he/she owned the property.

Importance: The seller does not guarantee title against all claims—just those while he/she was the owner.

SPECIFIC PERFORMANCE / A legal action in which the court requires a party to a contract to perform the terms of the contract when he/she has refused to fulfill his/her obligations.

Importance: This action is used in real estate because each parcel of land is unique; consequently a contract concerning one parcel cannot be transferred or applied to another.

SPOT ZONING / The act of rezoning a parcel of land for a different use from all surrounding parcels, in particular where the rezoning creates a use that is incompatible with surrounding land uses.

SRA / *See* SENIOR RESIDENTIAL APPRAISER.

STAGFLATION / A term coined in the 1970s to describe an economic situation of stagnant economic condition with inflation.

STATE-CERTIFIED APPRAISER / *See* CERTIFIED GENERAL APPRAISER; CERTIFIED RESIDENTIAL APPRAISER.

STATUTE / A law established by an act of a legislature.

Importance: Statutes are written laws; laws are also made through judicial interpretation and government administration.

STATUTE OF FRAUDS / A Florida law that provides that certain contracts must be in writing in order to be enforceable; applies to deeds, mortgages, and other real estate contracts.

Importance: The statute of frauds requires that contracts involving real estate be in writing.

STATUTE OF LIMITATIONS / A certain statutory period after which a claimant is barred from enforcing his/her claim by suit.

Importance: If a practice continues beyond the statute of limitations the person who is adversely affected may be barred from trying to prevent it.

STATUTORY DEDICATION / The owners of a subdivision or other property file a plat that results in a grant of public property, such as the streets in a development.

STEP-UP LEASE / *See* GRADUATED LEASE.

STIPULATIONS / The terms within a written *contract*.

STRAIGHT-LINE DEPRECIATION / Equal annual reductions in the book value of property; used in accounting for replacement and tax purposes.

Importance: Straight-line provides less depreciation in the early years of an asset than does an accelerated method. Most taxpayers prefer accelerated depreciation because it minimizes current taxes. However, for financial reporting purposes, most companies prefer straight-line because it provides a higher net income.

SUBAGENCY / The relationship under which a sales agent tries to sell a property listed with another agent. This situation is common under a *multiple listing* service (MLS). A listing contract is taken by a listing broker and entered into the MLS, from which any member broker may sell the property. The listing broker and the selling broker split the commission.

SUBDIVIDING / The division of a tract of land into smaller tracts.

Importance: Subdividing allows raw acreage to be developed with streets, utilities, and other amenities added, resulting in lots ready for houses to be built.

SUBDIVISION / A tract of land divided into lots or plots suitable for home building purposes. Some states and localities require that a subdivision *plat* be recorded.

SUBJECT TO MORTGAGE / A method of taking title to mortgaged real property without being personally responsible for the payment of any portion of the amount due. The buyer must make payments in order to keep the property; however, if he/she fails to do so, only his/her equity in that property is lost.

SUBLEASE / A lease from a lessee to another lessee. The new lessee is a sublessee or subtenant. *See also* SANDWICH LEASE.

SUBLET / *See* SUBLEASE.

SUBORDINATE MORTGAGE / One having a lower priority to another; the subordinate mortgage has a claim in foreclosure only after satisfaction of mortgage(s) with priority.

SUBORDINATED GROUND LEASE / A lease used when the *mortgage* has priority over the *ground lease*.

Importance: In case of a *default*, the unsubordinated interest has a prior claim to the subordinated interest.

SUBORDINATION CLAUSE / A clause or document that permits a mortgage recorded at a later date to take priority over an existing mortgage.

Importance: Ordinarily a second mortgage automatically moves up to become a first *lien* when the first mortgage is retired. If the second mortgage has a subordination clause, it will remain a second mortgage when a first mortgage is refinanced.

SUBSURFACE RIGHTS / *Same as* MINERAL RIGHTS.

SURETY / A person who guarantees the performance of another; a guarantor.

Importance: The surety becomes liable for the contract, just like the original principal. The surety is called when the principal fails to perform some duty.

SURRENDER / The cancellation of a lease before its expiration by mutual consent of the lessor and the lessee.

Importance: Surrender occurs only when both parties agree to it.

SURROGATE'S COURT (PROBATE COURT) / A court having jurisdiction over the proof of wills and the settling of estates and of citations.

SURVEY / (1) The process by which a parcel of land is measured and its area ascertained; (2) the blueprint showing the measurements, boundaries, and area.

Importance: A survey is needed to determine exact boundaries and any *easements* or *encroachments*.

TAX / A charge levied upon persons or things by a government.

Importance: Many different types of taxes affect real estate. Most local governments levy an *ad valorem tax* based on the property value. The federal government has an income tax, but rental property owners may deduct operating expense, interest, and depreciation expense, thereby reducing their taxable income.

TAX SALE / The sale of property after a period of nonpayment of taxes.

Importance: Unpaid taxes become a *lien*. Property may be sold for the nonpayment of taxes.

TEASER RATE / An unusually low interest rate offered for the first few months or year of a mortgage loan; used as an enticement to potential borrowers.

Importance: When comparing interest rates on loans offered, a buyer should determine future rate adjustments, as the initial rate may be discovered to be a teaser.

TENANCY AT SUFFERANCE / Tenancy established when a lawful tenant remains in possession of property after expiration of a lease.

Importance: The tenant at sufferance has no estate or title; the landlord may oust the tenant at any time.

TENANCY AT WILL / A license to use or occupy lands and tenements at the will of the owner.

Importance: There is no fixed length of possession. The tenant may leave or may be put out at any time.

TENANCY BY THE ENTIRETIES / An estate that exists only between husband and wife, with equal right of possession and enjoyment during their joint lives and with the *right of survivorship;* that is, when one dies, the property goes to the surviving tenant.

TENANCY IN COMMON / An ownership of realty by two or more persons, each of whom has an undivided interest, without the *right of survivorship*. Upon the death of one of the owners, his/her ownership share is inherited by the party or parties designated in his/her will.

TENANCY IN SEVERALTY / Ownership of real property by an individual as an individual; ownership by one person.

Importance: Tenancy in severalty is distinguished from *joint tenancy* and/or *tenancy in common,* whereby two or more persons are owners.

TENANT / A person who is given possession of real estate for a fixed period or at will. *See also* LEASE.

TENEMENTS / (1) Everything of a permanent nature; (2) anything attached to the soil. In common usage a tenement is a run-down apartment building.

TERMITES / Insects that bore into wood and destroy it.

Importance: Termite inspections by reputable pest control companies are often required in a real estate transaction. In some places it is customary to require a seller to post a termite bond as assurance that the foundation has been properly treated.

TERMS / Conditions and arrangements specified in a contract.

Importance: Anything lawful may be included in a contract and becomes part of its terms.

TESTAMENT / A will.

TESTAMENTARY TRUST / Created by a will, which comes into effect only after the testator's death.

TESTATE / Having made a valid will. *Contrast* INTESTATE.

TESTATOR / A man who makes a will.

TESTATRIX / A woman who makes a will.

"TIME IS OF THE ESSENCE" / A phrase that, when inserted in a contract, requires that all references to specific dates and times of day concerning performance be interpreted exactly.

TIME VALUE OF MONEY / The concept that money available now is worth more than the same amount in the future because of its potential earning capacity.

TITLE / Evidence that the owner of land is in lawful possession thereof; evidence of ownership. The word is often clarified or qualified by an adjective, such as *absolute, good, clear, marketable, defective, legal.*

TITLE ABSTRACT / *See* ABSTRACT OF TITLE.

TITLE INSURANCE / An insurance policy that protects the holder from any loss sustained by reason of defects in the title.

Importance: The premium is paid once and is good only until ownership changes.

TITLE SEARCH / An examination of the public records to determine the ownership and *encumbrances* affecting real property.

Importance: A title search is typically performed before *title insurance* is issued. If the search shows a title risk, the policy may contain an exception or may not be issued.

TOPOGRAPHY / The state of the surface of the land; may be rolling, rough, flat.

Importance: The topography may affect the way land can be developed, including potential uses.

TORT / A wrongful act that is not a crime but that renders the perpetrator liable to the victim for damages.

TOWNSHIP / A 6-mile-square tract delineated by *government rectangular survey*.

TRACT / A *parcel* of land, generally held for *subdividing;* a *subdivision.*

TRADE FIXTURES / Articles placed in rented buildings by the tenant to help carry out trade or business. The tenant may remove the fixtures before the expiration of the lease, but, if the tenant fails to do so shortly after the lease expires, the fixtures become the landlord's property.

TRADING UP / Buying a larger, more expensive property.

TRANSFER DEVELOPMENT RIGHTS / A type of *zoning ordinance* that allows owners of property zoned for low-density development or conservation use to sell development rights to other property owners. The development rights purchased permit the landowners to develop their parcels at a higher density than otherwise allowed. The system is designed to provide for low-density uses, such as historic preservation, without unduly penalizing some landowners.

TRIPLE-A TENANT / A tenant with an excellent credit record; also called *AAA tenant*. **Example:** The U.S. Postal Service and the American Telephone and Telegraph Company are examples of triple-A tenants because they are unlikely to *default* on a lease.

TRIPLE NET LEASE / A lease whereby the tenant pays all expenses of operations, including property taxes, insurance, utilities, maintenance, and repair.

TRUST ACCOUNT / A bank account separate and apart and physically segregated from a broker's own funds, in which the broker is required by state law to deposit all money collected for clients; called an *escrow account* in some states.

TRUST DEED / A *conveyance* of real estate to a third person to be held for the benefit of another; commonly used in some states in place of mortgages that conditionally convey title to the lender.

TRUSTEE / A person who holds property in trust for another to secure performance of an obligation; the neutral party in a *trust deed* transaction.

TRUSTEE'S DEED / The deed received by the purchaser at a foreclosure sale; issued by the *trustee* acting under a *trust deed*.

TRUSTOR / The person who conveys property to a trustee, to be held in behalf of a *beneficiary;* in a *trust deed* arrangement, the *trustor* is the owner of real estate and the *beneficiary* is the lender.

UNDIVIDED INTEREST / An ownership right to use and possession of a property that is shared among co-owners, with no one co-owner having exclusive rights to any portion of the property. *Compare with* PARTITION.

UNEARNED INCREMENT / An increase in the value of real estate due to no effort on the part of the owner; often due to an increase in population.

Importance: *Appreciation* of land in the path of growth is considered an unearned increment because the landowners did nothing to cause it.

UNIFORM COMMERCIAL CODE (UCC) / A group of laws to standardize the state laws that are applicable to commercial transactions. Few of the laws have relevance to real estate.

UNIFORM RESIDENTIAL APPRAISAL REPORT (URAR) / A standard form for reporting the *appraisal* of a dwelling.

Importance: This form is required for use by the major secondary mortgage purchasers. It provides numerous checklists and appropriate definitions and certifications that are preprinted on the form.

UNIFORM RESIDENTIAL LANDLORD AND TENANT ACT (URLTA) / A model law governing residential leasing practice and leases, adopted wholly or in part by about 15 states.

UNIFORM STANDARDS OF PROFESSIONAL APPRAISAL PRACTICE (USPAP) / Standards promulgated by the *Appraisal Foundation* that set forth the requirements for research and reporting with which a professional appraiser is to comply.

UNILATERAL CONTRACT / An obligation given by one party contingent on the performance of another party, but without obligating the second party to perform. *Compare with* BILATERAL CONTRACT.

UNITY / Four unities are required to create a joint tenancy: interest, possession, time, and title. In other words, the joint tenants must have an equal interest arising from the same conveyance, the same undivided possession, and the same use during the same time.

URAR / *See* UNIFORM RESIDENTIAL APPRAISAL REPORT.

URBAN PROPERTY / City property; closely settled property.

Importance: Urban property is more valuable than rural or suburban land because of its greater business activity.

URLTA / *See* UNIFORM RESIDENTIAL LANDLORD AND TENANT ACT.

USPAP / *See* UNIFORM STANDARDS OF PROFESSIONAL APPRAISAL PRACTICE.

USURY / A rate of interest higher than that permitted by law.

Importance: Florida usury laws have different ceiling interest rates applying to each type of loan. Penalties are severe for usury rates.

VALID / (1) Having force, or binding force; (2) legally sufficient and authorized by law.

Importance: A valid contract can be enforced in court.

VA LOAN / *See* GI LOAN.

VALUATION / (1) Estimated worth or price; (2) valuing by appraisal.

Importance: Valuation is the process of estimating the worth of an object.

VALUE / (1) The worth of all the rights arising from ownership; (2) the quantity of one thing that will be given in exchange for another.

Importance: Price is the historic amount that was

paid; value is an estimate of what something is worth. Often value is qualified as to a specific type: market, user, assessed, insurable, speculative.

VARIABLE EXPENSES / Property operating costs that increase with occupancy.

VENDEE / A purchaser; a buyer.

VENDEE'S LIEN / A *lien* against property under a *contract of sale*, to secure the deposit paid by a purchaser.

VENDOR / A seller.

VERIFICATION / Sworn statements before a duly qualified officer as to the correctness of the contents of an *instrument*.

VICARIOUS LIABILITY / The responsibility of one person for the acts of another.

VIOLATION / An act, a deed, or conditions contrary to law or the permissible use of real property.
Importance: When there is a violation of a law or contract, the perpetrator may be liable for damages and/or penalties.

VOID / Having no force or effect; unenforceable.

VOIDABLE / Capable of being voided, but not void unless action is taken to void. **Example:** Contracts to real estate entered into by minors are voidable only by the minors.

VOLUNTARY ALIENATION / Legal term describing a sale or gift made by the seller or donor of his/her own free will.

WAIVER / The voluntary renunciation, abandonment, or surrender of some claim, right, or privilege.
Importance: A person may waive a right when that right is not especially important to him/her in the overall transaction.

WARRANTY / A promise or representation contained in a *contract*.
Importance: Usually a seller's warranty pertains to the quality, character, or title of goods that are sold.

WARRANTY DEED / A deed that contains a covenant that the *grantor* will protect the *grantee* against any and all claims; usually contains covenants assuring good title, freedom from *encumbrances*, and *quiet enjoyment*. *See also* GENERAL WARRANTY DEED; SPECIAL WARRANTY DEED.

WASTE / Often found in a mortgage or lease contract, this term refers to property abuse, destruction, or damage, (beyond normal wear and tear).

The possessor causes unreasonable injury to the holders of other interests in the land, house, garden, or other property. The injured party may attempt to terminate the contract or sue for damages.

WATER TABLE / The distance from the surface of the ground to a depth at which natural groundwater is found.
Importance: The water table may affect the type of buildings that are possible on a parcel of land, and the ability to get well water.

WETLANDS / Land, such as a marsh or swamp, normally saturated with water.

WILL / The disposition of one's property to take effect after death.
Importance: If a person dies without a will (*intestate*), the property goes to his/her heirs at law. If a person dies intestate without heirs, the property *escheats* to the state of Florida.

WITHOUT RECOURSE / Words used in endorsing a note or bill to denote that the future holder is not to look to the debtor personally in the event of nonpayment: the creditor has recourse only to the property and the borrower is held harmless after foreclosure.
Importance: In *default*, the borrower can lose the property mortgaged, but no other property. There can be no *deficiency judgment*.

WRAPAROUND MORTGAGE / A mortgage that includes in its balance an underlying mortgage. Instead of having distinct and separate first and second mortgages, a wraparound mortgage includes both. For example, suppose there is an existing first mortgage of $100,000 at eight percent interest. A second mortgage can be arranged for $50,000 at 12 percent interest. Instead of getting that second mortgage, the borrower arranges a wraparound for $150,000 at ten percent. The first mortgage of $100,000 stays intact. The borrower pays the wraparound lender one payment on the $150,000 wraparound, and the wraparound lender remits the payment on the first mortgage to the first mortgage lender.

ZONE / An area set off by the proper authorities for specific use, subject to certain restrictions or restraints. Changing the zoning of property usually requires approval by the city council.

ZONING ORDINANCE / An act of city, county, or other authorities specifying the type of use to which property may be put in specific areas. **Examples:** residential, commercial, industrial.

Chapter 3/*Fundamentals of Florida Real Estate Law*

Introduction

This is the first chapter of subject matter material. Much of what is mentioned in this chapter will be discussed in greater detail in future chapters. Here, however, we are going to summarize Florida real estate law in its entirety, with the exception of license and contract law.

The subject matter of this chapter is a very fertile source of license examination questions, particularly since it concerns things that the average layperson knows little or nothing about. In this manner the examining authorities can make sure that successful licensing applicants have, indeed, studied the laws and customs of the real estate business and know enough about it to be worthy of public trust.

Property

Property refers to the legal rights to use and enjoy any thing. Strictly speaking, the term *property* does not refer to the things themselves, but to the legal rights that a society allows someone with regard to the use of and enjoyment of these things. In practice, however, we tend to use the word *property* to mean the things themselves, so we don't think it odd for someone to say, "That car is my property." To be absolutely proper, however, he should be saying, "The *rights* to use and enjoy that car are my property."

That may sound like nitpicking, and perhaps it is. When you are speaking of legal matters, though, it is essential to be precise and clear, or you can land in serious trouble. If a contract is drawn up vaguely, or if the description of a piece of land is inexact, the preparer can be held responsible for problems caused by the ambiguity.

Property is divided into two kinds: *real property* and *personal property*. Respectively, these are also known as *realty* and *personalty*. Realty is the property rights to real estate; personalty is the property rights to everything else.

Both realty and personalty can divided into the *tangible* and *intangible*. When we speak of realty, these things are referred to as *corporeal* and *incorporeal*. Corporeal property is the right to use, own, and enjoy real estate directly. The term *incorporeal* concerns the right to use property that actually belongs to another; examples are easements, rights-of-way, or mere permission to use someone else's property.

Real estate is defined as *land and everything permanently attached to it*. A "permanent attachment" is (a) anything that grows on the land, (b) anything that is built upon the land (including roads, fences, etc., as well as buildings), and (c) fixtures. *Fixtures* are items that may appear to be personal property but are considered to be part of the land also. Fixtures may include window air conditioners, major appliances, draperies, and other items of that nature. There is no cut-and-dried definition of a fixture, so many of the court disputes concerning real estate contracts involve misunderstandings concerning what are and aren't fixtures.

Many objects can be either realty or personalty, depending on how they are used. A brick is personalty until it is mortared into place on the wall of a building, at which time it becomes realty. A tree is realty when it is growing, but it becomes personalty when it is cut down. Fixtures are the "gray area," where an argument can be made either way as to the nature of the item. Florida courts decide such a problem based upon the answers to these questions:.

1. The *intent* of the person(s) who put it there. This is the most important criterion; if the court can determine what the intent was (Was it *meant* to remain as a part of the real estate?), then usually there is no need to inquire further.

    Often, however, it is difficult or impossible to determine for sure just what the original intent was, because whoever put it there is long gone, dead, or can't be found. Then the court will consider the following tests:

2. How it is *attached* to the property. The more "permanently" it is attached, the more likely it is to be a fixture. A window air conditioner inserted in a hole put into the wall for the purpose of containing it is more likely to be a fixture than if it just sits in a window and is easily removed.

3. Relationship to the land's expected use. The more it is *adapted* to the use of the land, the more likely it is to be a fixture.

4. Agreement of the parties: if buyer and seller agree that it is a fixture, then it is—no matter what it may be. The way to avoid dispute is to write into the purchase contract the nature (fixture or personal property) of anything that may be at all doubtful.

Estates in Land

The collection of rights that someone may have in real estate can be called an *estate* if it is large enough. Estates are divided into two groups: *freehold* and *nonfreehold*. The basic difference is that a freehold estate is of uncertain duration because it extends for at least one specified individual's lifetime, and we never know just how long that will be. The divisions of freehold estates are *inheritable* and *noninheritable*. Nonfreehold estates involve various kinds of leases. Leases are contracted for specific periods of time, so it is known exactly when these kinds of estates will cease to exist.

Inheritable estates are called *fee simple* estates. Basically these give their owners absolute rights to do whatever they want with the land involved, subject only to the general law, such as zoning and building codes. Most important, as far as the law is concerned, is the right to *dispose* of the estate in any legal manner: by selling it, by giving it away, or by willing it to someone.

Noninheritable estates are called *life estates*. In a life estate arrangement the owner, called the *life tenant*, has the right to use, occupy, and enjoy the property so long as he lives, but upon his death the ownership of the property goes to a predetermined person referred to as the *remainderman*. When the life tenant dies, if the remainderman is not the original grantor, it is called an *estate in remainder*. Since the life tenant has rights to the property only so long as he lives, he can transfer to others only those rights. Consequently he may sell his interest to someone, but that person will have to relinquish the property upon the original life tenant's death. The same would happen if the life tenant leased the property to someone and died before the lease expired. Furthermore, the life tenant is considered to be the custodian of the property for the remainderman: he cannot allow the property to deteriorate beyond ordinary wear and tear, because he must protect the remainderman's interest in it.

Nonfreehold estates are leases for specific terms. The lessee, or tenant, has the right (unless she contracts to give it up) to assign or otherwise dispose of her leasehold rights if she has a *leasehold estate*. Furthermore, she has the right to use, occupy, and enjoy the real estate during the period of her lease.

An estate in land requires that its owner have the following rights: the right to *possess* the land, the right to *use* the land, and the right to *dispose* of his estate to someone else. Possession means, basically, just that: the right to occupy the land and make use of it, and to exclude everyone else from the land. A person who has *some* rights to use land, but not all possessory rights, is said to have an *interest* in land. An interest occurs when a person has a month-to-month lease that either party can terminate at any time (*tenancy at will*) because no specific duration is mentioned. An interest also occurs when *license to use* is involved; here there is mere permission, and not even a contractual arrangement. This might occur if someone asked permission to come onto your land one afternoon to go fishing.

Creation of Estates in Land

Estates in land are created in the following ways: by *will, descent, voluntary alienation, involuntary alienation,* and *adverse possession.* (*Alienation* is a legal term which means "passing property to another.") One receives an estate *by will* if he inherits it by virtue of being *so designated in someone's will.* One receives an estate *by descent* if he is *designated by law* as the recipient of some property of a deceased person. This occurs if the person dies *intestate* (with no will); every state has laws governing the disposition of such property.

Voluntary alienation is the most common means whereby a person receives estates in land. This term refers to voluntary exchanges, sales, and gifts, wherein the one who gives up the property does so willingly. *Involuntary alienation* occurs where the owner of an estate is forced, in a legal manner, to give up some or all of her rights by the action of law. This most commonly occurs in the case of bankruptcy or of having some other kind of legal judgment entered against one, such as a foreclosure or failure to pay property taxes. Involuntary alienation also occurs by eminent domain (see page 42) and by adverse possession.

Adverse possession is a special means of acquiring ownership. All states have statutes permitting adverse possession, which is the right of a person who has used another's land actually to receive a legal claim to that land, in fee simple. The ancient idea behind this is that, if the true owner is so uninterested in his land that he does nothing during this period of time to prevent someone else from putting it to use, the community is better off by letting this other person actually have the full rights to the land. Adverse possession cannot be acquired overnight; Florida requires 7 years to establish these rights. The adverse possession must be *open, notorious, continuous,* and *hostile.* This means that the claimant, during the required time period, must have acted completely as if the property were his own, including defending his "rights" against encroachment by others and being perfectly open in his actions. He must also have paid the property taxes during this time. The adverse possession must continue throughout the statutory period; a person can't use someone else's land for the summer of 1965 and later for the summer of 1995 and then claim that he has been using it for 30 years. Further, no tenant can claim against his landlord, because every time a tenant pays rent he legally acknowledges that the person receiving payment is the true owner. Nor may one claim against the government, on the theory that one is already the nominal "owner" of public property. *Easements* (see page 40) also can be acquired by adverse possession; they are called *easements by prescription.*

Tenancies

In Florida, estates in land may be owned in a variety of ways, depending on the number of people involved and their relationship. These various forms of ownership are called *tenancies.* *Tenancy in severalty* is ownership by one person. *Tenancy in common* is a form of ownership by two or more persons. Each one owns an *undivided interest,* which means that he owns a fraction of each part of the realty. In this arrangement, each is entitled to his share of the profits and is responsible to the other owners for his share of the costs and expenses. No part of the land may be disposed of without the consent of all, unless they have a specific arrangement whereby less than unanimity can force a decision. Tenants in common need not own equal shares. They may dispose of their shares in any way they choose, unless they have specifically agreed upon some limitation; this means that A and B may buy real estate as tenants in common and later on B may sell his share to C, making A and C tenants in common. Further, a tenant in common may will his share to someone else or give it away.

Joint tenancy is similar to tenancy in common except for one important difference: joint tenants have the *right of survivorship.* This means that if a joint tenant dies her share is divided proportionally among the surviving joint tenants. Consequently, a joint tenant cannot will her share to someone else. However, she can sell or give her interest away; the new owners will then have the status of tenants in common.

Tenancy by the entireties is a special form of joint ownership allowed only to married couples. In states where it is used, it protects the rights of the family to jointly owned property by providing the same basic rights and responsibilities as joint tenancy while also protecting the property against any foreclosure due to judgment or debt against one of the parties.

All of the forms of tenancy just discussed have to do with freehold estates. There are two major types of tenancies that refer to nonfreehold estates:

Tenancy at will occurs when there is a lease arrangement, but no specific time period is agreed upon. Essentially, then, either party can terminate the arrangement whenever he wants (i.e., at will), so its duration is uncertain.

Tenancy at sufferance occurs when a tenant remains on the property after the expiration of a lease. This differs from tenancy at will in that often some aspects of the original lease contract may be considered to be in force (such as those requiring notice before termination or prohibitions against certain kinds of uses or activities by the tenant). Many states have enacted laws requiring that, even in cases of tenancy at sufferance or tenancy at will, the parties give one another certain minimum notice before termination of the arrangement.

Limitations on Estates and Interests

Very few estates or interests are completely free of restrictions or encumbrances; one or more of the following will affect most of them: easements, restrictive covenants, or liens. The following are common in Florida.

EASEMENTS

An *easement* is the right of one landowner to use land belonging to another for a specific purpose. The most common kinds of easements are access easements, utility easements, and drainage easements. All of these allow someone who is *not* an owner of the affected property to make use of that property for some reason. An *access easement* allows someone to cross a property to reach (i.e., obtain access to) another property. These rights exist where one parcel of land is completely blocked by others from access to a public right-of-way. A *utility easement* is a right held by a utility company to put its utility lines on private property, usually for the purpose of providing service to that property. A *drainage easement* requires that a property owner not disturb a natural or man-made drainage pattern that crosses his land.

Easements are created in all the ways that estates are; most commonly, however, they are created by voluntary alienation or adverse possession. In some states, a person who sells a part of his land that does not have direct access to a public right-of-way is legally bound to provide the purchaser with an access easement.

DEED RESTRICTIONS

Deed restrictions, or *restrictive covenants,* are agreements whereby a group of neighboring landowners agree to do (or *not* to do) a certain thing or things so as to mutually benefit all. Covenants most commonly occur in residential subdivisions and are created by the developer as a means of assuring prospective buyers that the neighborhood will be required to meet certain standards. Examples of covenants are prohibitions against using a lot for more than one single-family dwelling, limitations on the minimum size of structures to be built, and specification of architectural style. Deed restrictions can last indefinitely or may contain time limitations.

Deed restrictions must be enforced by someone who is a party to them, since they are private contracts. If a violation occurs, the remedy is the same as for a violation of any other contract: an offended party must bring suit in civil court. In this case, the aggrieved party (one of the neighbors who is a party to the broken restriction) would seek an injunction from the court ordering that the offending activity be stopped, any damage repaired, and that it not be started up again in the future.

LIENS

Liens are claims against the owner of a property, with that property being usable as security for the claim. Claims for unpaid property taxes are liens, as are mortgages. In Florida, those who have done work to improve real estate, or have supplied materials for such work, may secure a *mechanic's lien* against the property if they are not paid as contracted for their work and/or materials. The work must have been done under contract from the owner of the real estate. Owners, however, are protected from claims by subcontractors, so long as they can prove that the general contractor was paid in full as agreed. If liens are not paid in the legal manner, the holder of the lien can foreclose against the property. *Foreclosure* is a legal process whereby a person holding a legal claim against a property may have the court order the property to be sold so as to provide funds to pay the claim.

Liens, restrictive covenants, and easements are, legally speaking, *a part of the property* and cannot be separated from it without the consent of all parties involved. A person who is considering buying property must be aware that all encumbrances on the property will remain with it after she acquires title, unless something is done to remove them.

Condominium

All states have passed laws that permit the establishment of *condominium* interests in land. *Condominium* is a legal term, describing a certain kind of ownership of land; it does *not* refer to any particular architectural style. In theory, any kind of property, serving any use, can be owned in condominium. In this form of ownership, one has title to a part of a larger piece of property, with the right to use his part exclusively and the right to share some of the rest with the other owners. Typically, in a residential condominium one would have the right to use his own dwelling unit, and no right to enter the units owned by others. However, one would share the right, with the others, to use the "common property," which might include private drives within the project, recreational facilities, common hallways, and elevators. Most important, the law allows an owner of a condominium unit to mortgage and otherwise encumber his unit; if he defaults, a lienholder may force the sale of his unit, but the other owners in the condominium project cannot be held responsible for anything.

A residential condominium development usually has a "homeowner's association" or some similar group that is elected by the owners of the units in the project. The function of the association is to ensure that the common property in the development is taken care of and also to make and enforce whatever rules the owners as a group want to enforce within their private community. Many people who have bought condominium units have found later that the rules and regulations of the association do not permit them to do everything they want to. For example, the association may have a rule limiting overnight guests to no more than two per unit, or requiring that only certain kinds of flowers be planted in the front yards. An owner who may wish to have more guests, or to plant different flowers, can find herself in conflict with the association and will be required to conform to the rules.

Many condominium projects have quite a lot of common property; swimming pools, park areas, parking lots, bicycle paths, tennis courts, clubhouses, and gatehouses are examples. The owners of units in the project own these common elements together, as a group. Their association looks after the common property and assesses each unit owner a fee (called a *condominium fee*), usually monthly, to get the funds necessary to maintain it. An owner who does not pay this fee will usually find that the association has the legal power to file a lien on his unit in order to collect the money.

Cooperative Ownership

Cooperative ownership has existed much longer than condominium, but in Florida, it is not very common outside the Miami area. In a cooperative, the entire real estate is owned by a *cooperative corporation*. Instead of owning his/her unit outright, the cooperative owner owns a proportion of the *shares of stock* of the cooperative corporation, along with the right to exclusive use of his/her unit. The owners elect a board of directors which is responsible for the operation of the corporation and, therefore, of the property. Each owner pays monthly assessments to the corporation which, in turn, pays its property taxes, mortgage payments, maintenance bills, and so forth. A big disadvantage of cooperative ownership is that if one or more of the owners does not pay, the others will have to make up the difference or face the risk of having the entire property foreclosed.

Title and Recordation

A person who owns real estate is said to hold *title* to the land. There is no such thing as "title papers" to real estate, as there are with automobiles and certain other chattels. The term *title* refers to the validity of the available evidence that backs up one's claim to land. Normally, all deeds, liens, restrictions, and easements affecting land are recorded, usually in the courthouse of the county in which the land is located. Some leases, contracts of sale, and other documents may be recorded as well. The object of *recordation* is to provide a means whereby anyone may check the validity of any claim to land. In a legal sense, therefore, the ownership of all land and all rights to land should be a matter of record. These records are public, which means that anyone may examine them. It also means that anything that is recorded gives everyone *constructive notice* of the information recorded; therefore, in a court of law one is assumed to be aware of all information in the public records.

The total of the evidence in the records will be the validity of the *title* an owner holds. *Good title* is title that cannot be impeached by the records. Title that appears to be good but is not is said to be *color of title*.

Eminent Domain and Escheat

There are two special ways in which the government may acquire title to real estate. The most important is *eminent domain*; this is the right of the government to acquire privately owned property to be put to a public use, even if the private owner is unwilling to dispose of it. Government needs this power in order to operate efficiently for the benefit of everyone. Imagine the problems if, when the government decided to build a road, it had to look all over to find willing sellers for land needed for the project—the road might wander all around, and quite possibly it couldn't be built at all.

In an eminent domain situation the government can't just seize the land; it must pay the owner the "fair market value" of the land. However, once the government has established that it needs the land for a legitimate public use, there is no way to stop it. All a landowner can do is to dispute the price being offered; if he thinks it is unfair, he may sue for a higher award and have the court make the final decision. Usually the government will approach the landowner to work out an amicable arrangement, and quite often the landowner agrees to the offered price and there is no dispute. If, however, the landowner is reluctant or refuses to negotiate, the government will *condemn* the affected land. Condemnation is a legal process whereby the owner is dispossessed of the property and must leave. He retains the right to dispute the price being offered; but once condemnation has begun, a time will come when he must leave the land, which will be transferred to the government whether or not the payment question has been settled. All levels of government have power of eminent domain; also, many states have granted limited eminent domain power to private enterprises such as railroads, and utility companies.

Escheat is a process whereby land for which no legal owner exists reverts to government, which then can dispose of it or use it as it sees fit. Escheat most commonly occurs when someone dies intestate and no legal heirs can be found.

Questions on Chapter 3

1. Which of the following is most accurately described as personal property?
   (A) A fixture
   (B) A chattel
   (C) An improvement
   (D) Realty

2. Which of the following is *not* corporeal property?
   (A) A fee simple estate
   (B) A leasehold
   (C) An easement
   (D) A fixture

Questions 3–5 concern the following situation:

Mr. Jones died; his will left to Mrs. Jones the right to use, occupy, and enjoy Mr. Jones's real estate until her death. At that time the real estate was to become the property of their son Willis.

3. Mrs. Jones is a
   (A) remainderman
   (B) life tenant
   (C) joint tenant
   (D) tenant in common

4. Willis is a
   (A) remainderman
   (B) life tenant
   (C) joint tenant
   (D) tenant in common

5. Mrs. Jones has a
   (A) fee simple estate in joint tenancy with Willis
   (B) fee simple estate as tenant in common with Willis
   (C) life estate
   (D) life estate in joint tenancy with Willis

6. Which of the following is *not* realty?
   (A) A fee simple estate
   (B) A leasehold for indefinite duration
   (C) Lumber
   (D) A life estate

7. Real estate is defined as
   (A) land and buildings
   (B) land and all permanent attachments
   (C) land and everything growing on it
   (D) land only

8. An item of personalty that is affixed to realty so as to be used as a part of it is
   (A) a fixture
   (B) a chattel
   (C) personal property
   (D) an encumbrance

9. A freehold estate is
   (A) one acquired without paying anything
   (B) any leasehold
   (C) any estate wherein one may use the property as he wishes
   (D) an estate of uncertain duration

10. Which is *not* considered a permanent attachment to land?
    (A) Anything growing on it
    (B) Fixtures
    (C) Chattels
    (D) Anything built upon the land

11. A person who has some rights to use land, but not all possessory rights, is said to have
    (A) an interest in land
    (B) an estate in land
    (C) a life estate in land
    (D) a tenancy in common

12. A person who has permission to use land, but has no other rights, has
    (A) tenancy at sufferance
    (B) tenancy in common
    (C) license to use
    (D) a fee simple estate

13. A person who receives title to land by virtue of having used and occupied it for a certain period of time, without actually paying the previous owner for it, receives title by
   (A) will
   (B) descent
   (C) alienation
   (D) adverse possession

14. A person who dies leaving no will is said to have died
   (A) intestate
   (B) without heirs
   (C) unbequeathed
   (D) unwillingly

15. A person who owns an undivided interest in land with at least one other, and has the right of survivorship, is said to be a
   (A) tenant in common
   (B) tenant at will
   (C) joint tenant
   (D) tenant at sufferance

16. Tenancy in severalty refers to
   (A) ownership by one person only
   (B) ownership by two persons only
   (C) ownership by at least three persons
   (D) a special form of joint ownership available only to married couples

17. Dower rights are rights that assure that
   (A) a husband receives a certain portion of his deceased wife's estate
   (B) wives (and in some states children) receive a certain portion of a deceased husband's (or father's) estate
   (C) a homeowner cannot lose his entire investment in his home
   (D) husbands and wives share equally in property acquired during marriage

18. An easement is
   (A) the right to use the property of another for any purpose
   (B) the right to use the property of another for a specific purpose
   (C) a private contract and does not permanently affect the realty
   (D) the right to keep another from using one's land illegally

19. The process whereby a person holding a claim against property can have the property sold to pay the claim is
   (A) a lien
   (B) a covenant
   (C) a mechanic's lien
   (D) foreclosure

20. A person who appears to own property, but does not, is said to have
   (A) good title
   (B) recorded evidence of title
   (C) constructive notice
   (D) color of title

21. Two people who own undivided interests in the same realty, with right of survivorship, have
   (A) tenancy in severalty
   (B) tenancy in common
   (C) tenancy at sufferance
   (D) joint tenancy

22. A fee simple estate is
   (A) a freehold estate
   (B) a life estate
   (C) an estate for years
   (D) an estate in abeyance

23. Which of the following is considered a permanent attachment to land?
   (A) Improvements to land
   (B) A fixture
   (C) Trees growing on the land
   (D) All of the above

24. A person who has some rights to land, but not all the possessory rights, has
(A) a life estate
(B) an interest in land
(C) an estate at will
(D) a fixture

25. A person who has color of title to land has
(A) the appearance of title
(B) forgeries of state title papers
(C) a right to one-half the income from the land
(D) foreign ownership

ANSWERS

1. **B**	8. **A**	15. **C**	22. **A**
2. **C**	9. **D**	16. **A**	23. **D**
3. **B**	10. **C**	17. **B**	24. **B**
4. **A**	11. **A**	18. **B**	25. **A**
5. **C**	12. **C**	19. **D**	
6. **C**	13. **D**	20. **D**	
7. **B**	14. **A**	21. **D**	

PART II: REAL ESTATE BROKERAGE IN FLORIDA

Chapter 4/*Florida Agency Law*

A licensed real estate broker or salesperson in Florida is an *agent*; therefore his practice comes under the *laws of agency*. He is also affected by Florida real estate license law, a topic that will be discussed in Chapter 5.

An agency relationship involves two parties: the *principal* and the *agent*. The agency relationship is contractual, but it also is covered by the general precepts of agency law. In the real estate business, a broker acts as an agent for his *employer*, or principal, who is the owner of the property for which the broker is seeking a buyer or tenant. A licensed salesperson usually is treated as the agent of the *broker*, because license law does not permit salespersons to act without the supervision of a broker.

A real estate broker is a *special agent*. He is called this because his powers are limited, usually to finding someone with whom his principal can deal. A *general agent* is a person whose powers are broader and may extend so far as to commit her employer to action. It should be noted that a real estate broker usually has little or no power actually to commit his principal to anything; the principal may refuse to deal with anyone the broker brings to her, although she still may be liable to pay the broker a commission.

Duties of Parties

An agent is employed to deal with third parties on behalf of his principal. The agent is an employee of the principal and must follow his principal's instructions implicitly. Furthermore, he has a duty to act in his employer's best interests, even when doing so means that he cannot act in his own favor. More specifically, agency law requires that the agent abide by the following obligations to his principal:

- He must *obey* his principal's instructions (except, of course, when he is instructed to do something illegal).
- He must be *loyal* to his principal's interests.
- He must act in *good faith*.
- He is expected to use *professional judgment, skill,* and *ability* in his actions. This is particularly true in the case of licensed agents such as real estate brokers, who are assumed to have met certain standards by virtue of having to be licensed.
- He must be able to *account* for all money belonging to others that comes into his possession. Real estate brokers often collect rents, earnest money payments, and other money on behalf of their principals.
- He must perform his duties *in person*. Normally, this would mean that he could not delegate his duties to anyone else unless the principal approved of the arrangement. Because of the nature of the real estate brokerage business and the establishment of the broker-salesperson relationship by all state licensing laws, however, a real estate broker has the implied right to delegate his function to duly licensed salespersons and brokers in his employ.
- He must keep his principal *fully informed* of developments affecting their relationship. A real estate broker should report all offers made on the principal's property, as well as all other information he acquires that may affect the principal's property, price, or other relevant factors.

The principal has obligations to the agent as well. Most of these have to do with money: the principal is obliged to *compensate* the agent for his services, to *reimburse* the agent for expenses paid on behalf of the principal, and to *secure* the agent against any loss due to proper performance of his duties. The principal also has the implied duty to make the agent fully aware of his duties and to inform him fully about anything that will affect his performance.

Real Estate Agency Contracts

Agency contracts are *employment* contracts. In real estate, an agency contract is called a *listing*. The details of drawing up these contracts are discussed in Chapter 11. The Statute of Frauds requires most listings to be written. Here, however, we can briefly distinguish among the various kinds of listings. Florida license law requires real estate listings to be written. Among listings of property for *sale* are the following:

In an *open* listing the principal agrees to compensate the agent only if the agent actually finds the buyer with whom the principal finally deals. A single owner may have open listings with many brokers, since she is obliging herself to pay only upon performance, and the broker makes his effort at his own risk.

In an *exclusive agency* listing the principal agrees to employ no other broker, and if the property is sold by any licensed agent a commission will be paid to the listing broker. State license law usually requires that any other agent must work *through* a broker having an exclusive listing; the participating brokers must then agree on a means by which they will share in the commission. However, the commission always will be paid to the listing broker, who then may pay a share to the other broker(s) who cooperated in the deal.

An *exclusive-right-to-sell* listing guarantees that the principal will pay the broker a commission regardless of who actually sells the property. This applies even if the principal herself finds the buyer, with no aid at all from the broker. (Note that under an exclusive agency listing the principal does not have to pay a commission if she herself finds the buyer.)

Usage of the term *exclusive listing* varies from one place to another. In some localities the term refers to an exclusive agency; in others it refers to the exclusive right to sell; in still others it refers to both types interchangeably.

A *net* listing is one in which the principal agrees to receive a given net amount. The excess by which the sale price exceeds the net amount goes to the broker as his commission. Net listings are "discouraged" by Florida authorities, because agents are strongly tempted to act in their own interest rather than that of their employer. To illustrate, suppose a net listing contract with a proposed net to the seller of $30,000 is agreed upon. By law, any time the broker solicits an offer he must report it to the principal. However, let us assume that an offer of exactly $30,000 is made; if the broker transmits it, the seller probably will accept and the broker will receive no compensation. Clearly there is the temptation to illegally "hide" the offer, and any subsequent offers, until one yielding a satisfactory excess over the listed price is received; obviously such action is contrary to the agent's legal responsibilities to his employer. A further source of trouble with net listings arises when a knowledgeable agent deals with a naive seller; there may exist an opportunity for the agent to convince the seller to sign a net listing at a low price, thereby guaranteeing the agent a large commission when he finds a buyer who will pay true market value.

The Agency Relationship in Real Estate Brokerage

In a *listing contract* (see Chapter 11), the agency relationship is between the owner of the listed real estate and the broker whom the owner hires to sell or lease the real estate. This makes sense; however, in the real estate brokerage business it is very common for other brokers to be involved in the transaction. Brokers very often *cooperate* with one another: they agree to allow one another to seek buyers (or tenants) for each others' listings. If another broker finds a buyer (tenant), then the listing broker agrees to share with that other broker the commission paid by the property owner.

Traditionally, *all* brokers involved in a transaction are *agents of the seller* (the owner of the listed property); since the selling broker is a "subagent" of the listing broker, the agency relationship between listing broker and owner passes down to them. This means that the broker who works with the buyer actually is supposed to represent the *seller's* best interests, and not to work on behalf of the buyer, thereby creating an awkward situation. Most buyers (especially homebuyers) don't realize that the salesperson showing them around isn't supposed to look out for their interests. Sales technique itself also leads to a natural inclination to work on behalf of the person(s) with whom one is working, particularly since common practice normally prevents an agent working with a prospective buyer from having much direct contact with the seller (offers and other communications normally are passed to the seller through the listing broker, and not directly). For decades the real estate brokerage business has been uncomfortable with this situation; in recent years several developments have evolved to deal with it.

Buyer Agency and Dual Agency

Some recent trends in the real estate brokerage business have aimed at overcoming this agency problem. One has been the growth of *buyer agency*; another has been the increasing use of *dual agency*.

Buyer agency. Here the broker and the buyer have their own contract in which the broker agrees to represent the buyer's interests, and not the seller's. Since this arrangement, although not illegal, is not the traditional one of exclusive seller agency by all brokers, the seller and the seller's broker must be notified that the buyer's broker is not representing the seller in the transaction. The key point is that everyone involved in the transaction must be aware of what the agency relationships are before the negotiations for a transaction begin. Florida requires that agency relationships be disclosed at first contact with the buyer, seller, and/or the seller's broker.

In many transactions there is little problem identifying the agents and their principals. However, there can arise the problem of *dual agency*. A salesperson lists a home for sale, and in the contract and disclosure agreement is named as the seller's agent. So far so good; when other agents arrive with buying prospects, no problem arises. But suppose the listing agent also has agreed to represent a buying prospect who subsequently becomes interested in this newly listed home? Suppose she decides she likes the property so much that she wants to buy it herself? Whose agent is she? Can she represent *both* buyer and seller? Usually yes, so long as both buyer and seller are aware of the dual agency, and both realize that the agent represents *neither* of them exclusively. This can be a very dicey situation, though, and agents are well advised to avoid it unless they are absolutely certain that no problems will arise. When in doubt, it is best to have another salesperson in the same brokerage firm represent the buyer for this particular property. One thing must always be remembered: in Florida, it is illegal for an agent in a transaction to represent more than one party to a transaction (dual agency) without the express knowledge of *all* parties involved in the transaction.

Florida law now requires that an agency disclosure form be signed by prospective brokerage customers before any meaningful broker-customer activity occurs.

Agency Disclosure

Figure 4-1 shows an *agency disclosure form* that must be presented by real estate salespeople to anyone they deal with (prospective buyers or sellers) upon first contact with them. An agent taking a listing normally would be the seller's agent. One showing property to a prospective buyer could be either a buyer's or a seller's agent. In times past, *all* salespeople were thought of as agents of the seller because they all shared in the commission paid by the seller and were therefore considered sub-agents of the seller's broker. A big problem with this has been that most buyers believed that the broker or salesperson they dealt with represented *them*. Nowadays, however, it is becoming common in Florida for licensees showing property to prospective buyers to agree to be the buyer's agent. It is customary that a buyer's agent still will be compensated out of the commission paid by the seller to the listing agent; this is arranged by including wording in offers submitted to sellers which state that the buyer's agent represents the buyer, but that the seller agrees for the buyer's agent to be paid out of the commission that the seller pays to his/her broker. Normally sellers will not object to such an arrangement, if they feel that the deal offered is a good one. So long as everyone is aware of the compensation arrangement, there is no problem.

AGENCY DISCLOSURE

Florida real estate licensees are required by law to disclose which party they represent in a transaction and to allow a party the right to choose or refuse among the various agency relationships.

The purpose of the AGENCY DISCLOSURE is to acknowledge that the disclosure occurred and that the consumer has been informed of the various agency relationships which are available in a real estate transaction. The following descriptions of terms, agency relationships and the respective duties and obligations are based upon Florida Law (Chapter 475, Florida Statutes).

Seller's Agent

A licensee who is engaged by and acts as the agent of the Seller only is known as a Seller's agent. A Seller's agent has the following duties and obligations:

To the Seller:

(a)   The fiduciary duties of loyalty, confidentiality, obedience, full disclosure, accounting and the duty to use skill, care and diligence.

To the Buyer and Seller:

(a)   A duty of honesty and fair dealing.

(b)   A duty to disclose all facts known to the Seller's agent materially affecting the value of the property which are not known to, or readily observable by, the parties in a residential transaction.

Buyer's Agent

A licensee who is engaged by and acts as the agent of the Buyer only is known as the Buyer's agent. A Buyer's agent has the following duties and obligations:

To the Buyer:

(a)   The fiduciary duties of loyalty, confidentiality, obedience, full disclosure, accounting and the duty to use skill, care and diligence.

To the Seller and Buyer:

(a)   A duty of honesty and fair dealing.

Disclosed Dual Agent

A disclosed dual agent is a licensee who, with the informed written consent of Seller and Buyer, is engaged as an agent for both Seller and Buyer.

As a disclosed dual agent, the licensee shall not represent the interests of one party to the exclusion or detriment of the interests of the other party. A disclosed dual agent has all the fiduciary duties to the Seller and Buyer that a Seller's or Buyer's agent has except the duties of full disclosure and undivided loyalty.

A disclosed dual agent may not disclose:

(a)   To the Buyer that the Seller will accept less than the asking or listed price, unless otherwise instructed in writing by the Seller;

(b)   To the Seller that the Buyer will pay a price greater than the price submitted in a written offer to the Seller, unless otherwise instructed in writing by the Buyer;

(c)   The motivation of any party for selling, buying, or leasing a property, unless otherwise instructed in writing by the respective party; or

(d)   That a Seller or Buyer will agree to financing terms other than those offered, unless otherwise instructed in writing by the respective party.

AGENCY DISCLOSURE

_____ is a _____ buyer _____ seller and is hereby informed that

Name

_____ and _____

Name of Brokerage   Name(s) of Licensee(s)

are acting as   _____ Seller's Agent   _____ Buyer's Agent

You have the explicit right to choose or refuse among these relationships. Other brokerage firms may offer you other brokerage relationships. You are free to seek any brokerage firm offering the type of relationship you desire.

CONSENT TO DUAL AGENCY

Sign only if you are giving your informed written consent to the brokerage firm and its licensees acting as a dual agent representing both seller and buyer. Your signature also acknowledges that you have received a copy of this disclosure.

_____   _____

Date   Seller

                                                                       _____

                                                                       Seller (print name)

_____   _____

Date   Buyer

                                                                       _____

                                                                       Buyer (print name)

THE AGENCY DISCLOSURE form has been adopted by the Florida Real Estate Commission and is required to be used by real estate licensees pursuant to Rule 6IJ2-10.036 of the rules of the Commission.

BPR70-01-003.025

Figure 4-1.   Florida Agency Disclosure Form

DUAL AGENCY CONFIRMATION

Seller: _____

Buyer: _____

Property: _____

    (Check if this paragraph is applicable.) This Dual Agency consent is an addendum to and made part of the contract dated _____, 19___, between Seller and Buyer for the purchase and sale of the Property.
The undersigned acknowledges that they have received the following information regarding disclosed dual agency:

    1.   A disclosed dual agent is a licensee who, with the informed written consent of Seller and Buyer, is engaged as an agent for both Seller and Buyer.

    2.   As a disclosed dual agent, the licensee shall not represent the interests of one party to the exclusion or detriment of the interests of the other party. A disclosed dual agent has all the fiduciary duties to the Seller and Buyer that a Seller's or Buyer's agent has except the duties of full disclosure and undivided loyalty.

    3.   A disclosed dual agent may not disclose:

    (a)   To the Buyer that the Seller will accept less than the asking or listed price, unless otherwise instructed in writing by the Seller;

    (b)   To the Seller that the Buyer will pay a price greater than the price submitted in a written offer to the Seller, unless otherwise instructed in writing by the Buyer;

    (c)   The motivation of the Seller or Buyer for selling, buying, or leasing a property, unless otherwise instructed in writing by the respective party; or

    (d)   That a Seller or Buyer will agree to financing terms other than those offered, unless instructed in writing by the respective party.

    Seller and Buyer hereby confirm that they give their informed consent to the disclosed dual agency of

_____ and _____ who
Name of Brokerage Firm   Name(s) of Licensee(s)

represent both Seller and Buyer in this transaction.

_____   _____
Date   Seller

                            _____
                            Seller (print name)

_____   _____
Date   Buyer

                            _____
                            Buyer (print name)

THE AGENCY DISCLOSURE form has been adopted by the Florida Real Estate Commission and is required to be used by real estate licensees pursuant to Rule 61J2-10.036 of the rules of the Commission.

BPR 70-01-002.025

Figure 4-2.   Dual Agency Confirmation

The agency disclosure form (Figure 4-1) must be used as follows:

Single agency (the traditional kind, where the broker represents only one side of the transaction). The form must be signed by the broker's employer before a representation contract (listing or buyer agency) is signed. After that, the form must be signed by other parties (the ones the broker does not represent) upon "first substantive contact."

An agent representing a seller makes first substantive contact with a prospective buyer whenever any of the following occur:

1. Showing the property.
2. Eliciting confidential information from a buyer concerning the buyer's real estate needs, motivations or financial qualifications.
3. Executing a contractual offer or lease agreement by the buyer/tenant.

The Real Estate Commission has excluded the following from the definition of first substantive contact unless any of the events described above also take place:

1. A bona fide open house or model home showing.
2. Preliminary conversation or "small talk" about about price ranges, location, property styles.
3. Responding to a factual question from a buyer about property advertised for sale or lease (such as "how many bedrooms/baths?" "what is the asking price," etc.).

An agent representing a buyer makes first substantive contact with a seller by showing, or requesting to show, the seller's property for sale or lease.

Dual Agency. When a licensee is to act as agent for both sides, both buyer and seller must give their consent at the bottom of the agency disclosure form. *In addition*, buyer and seller must *confirm* their consent by signing the Dual Agency Confirmation form (Figure 4-2).

Transaction Brokerage

A licensee who facilitates a brokerage transaction between buyer and seller without representing either party takes on, in Florida, the role of *transaction broker*. A transaction broker has no agency duty to either party except the duties of accounting and the obligation to use skill, care, and diligence. In such a transaction, the licensee must give written notification to all parties that he/she is acting as a transaction broker. Transaction brokerage is not common in residential sales; however, it is sometimes encountered in sales of expensive investment properties. Here, the parties are likely to have experience and knowledge, as well as their own legal and accounting advisors, and so are able to adequately "represent" their own interests.

Property Disclosure

Long ago the rule of *caveat emptor* (let the buyer beware) prevailed in most transactions. Not any more—consumer protection laws and other laws mandating certain disclosures are very common. Since brokers and salespeople are sellers' agents, they too can be held responsible for not disclosing relevant problems concerning property sold. It's hard to say just what must be disclosed and what needn't be. Obvious dangers such as construction faults, instability of land or foundations, leaks of hazardous materials, and a host of environmental hazards, should be disclosed. More subtle problems can be difficult to judge (although in one case a court decided that, since the sellers didn't notify the buyers that the house was haunted, the buyers could void the sale!). Florida law requires that anyone offering improved property for sale must disclose any termite infestation and/or damage, and, if one exists, must disclose an existing termite bond or contract.

In recent years environmental hazards have become matters of great public concern. The environment, of course, is real estate, so it is possible that real estate offered for sale by a broker may be subject to environmental problems such as contamination, pollution, or other natural hazards. Asbestos, lead-based paint, aluminum wiring, urea-formaldehyde insulation, are problems associated with construction materials used in building. Most can be cured only by removal. Other types of problems can include radon gas, and various kinds of pollution.

Earning the Commission

Under common law, a broker earns his commission when he produces a buyer (or tenant) with whom the principal is willing to deal. From then on, the risk that the deal actually will go through rests with the principal. However, many listing contracts today put the risk back on the broker by specifying that the commission is not payable until the sale closes.

As mentioned previously, the principal is not obliged to deal with anyone whom the broker brings; that is, the principal, by hiring the broker, incurs no legal responsibility to the *third party*. Consequently, a buyer who is willing to pay the asking price and meet all the conditions set down by the principal in the listing agreement normally will have no legal recourse if the principal refuses to deal with him, unless the buyer's civil rights have been violated.

Nevertheless, the principal's obligations to the broker remain. In the listing agreement an acceptable price and terms of sale are specified. If the broker produces a bona fide offer that meets all these conditions, then the principal is liable to pay the broker a commission even if she chooses not to accept the offer. This is required, because the broker has satisfied the terms of his employment contract, and there *is* a contract between him and the principal. There is *no* contract however, between the principal and third parties, so she is not liable to them.

If the broker's principal refuses to pay him a commission that the broker feels he has earned, he may sue in court to receive it. To be successful, he must prove three things:

1. That he was *licensed* throughout the time, beginning with the solicitation of the listing until the closing of the deal and the passing of title (or the notification by the principal that she will not accept an offer that meets the terms of the listing agreement).
2. That he had a contract of employment with the principal. The best evidence here is a written contract, and indeed some state licensing laws require that listings be written to be enforceable.
3. That he was the "efficient and procuring cause" of the sale; that is, that he actually brought about the sale within the terms of the listing contract. In an open listing this would mean that he actually found the eventual buyer. In an exclusive agency listing, he must have found the buyer or the buyer must have been found by a licensed agent. An exclusive-right-to-sell listing effectively defines the broker as having earned a commission when and if the property is sold.

Termination of an Agency Contract

Agency contracts can be terminated by a variety of events, though some of them are relatively uncommon. In a broad sense, contracts can be terminated in two ways: by the *actions of the parties* to them, or *by law* when certain events occur.

Termination by the actions of the parties includes the following:

The contract is terminated by *performance* when both parties perform their duties as prescribed and the event for which the agency is created ends. In the real estate business, a listing agency contract is terminated by performance when there is a "meeting of the minds" between the principal and the third party found by the agent. Sometimes, however, the contract will specify some other event (usually title closing, in the event of a listing for sale) as the actual termination of the contractual relationship.

The parties may *mutually agree* to terminate the relationship before it has been terminated by performance.

The agent may *resign*. In this case, the agent may be liable to the principal for damages due to his breach of the contract, but he cannot be held to perform under the contract.

The principal may *discharge* the agent. Once again, the principal, too, can be liable for damages due to her breach of the contract, but she cannot be forced to continue the employment of the agent.

The agent may resign, or the principal may discharge the agent, without penalty if it can be proved that the other party was not properly discharging his or her duties under the contract. An agent would be justified in resigning if, for example, his principal did not provide him with enough information to do his job well or required that he perform some illegal act in the execution of his duties. An agent could be discharged justifiably if it could be shown that he was not faithful to his duties or was acting contrary to the interests of the principal.

Termination of the contractual relationship also occurs automatically, *by law*, with the occurrence of certain events, such as the following:

The *death of either party* terminates an agency relationship.

If either party becomes *legally incompetent*, the agency relationship ceases.

Bankruptcy of either party, so as to make continuation of the relationship impossible; terminates the relationship.

Destruction of the subject matter terminates any agency relationship. In real estate this would include such events as the burning down of a house or the discovery of another claim on the title that would make it impossible for the owner of the property to pass good and marketable title.

Questions on Chapter 4

1. A real estate broker is a
   (A) general agent
   (B) special agent
   (C) secret agent
   (D) travel agent

2. Which of the following is *not* required of an agent with respect to his principal?
   (A) To be loyal
   (B) To act in person
   (C) To account for his own personal finances
   (D) To act in the principal's best interests

3. A listing contract that says that the broker will receive a commission no matter who sells the property is called
   (A) an open listing
   (B) a net listing
   (C) an exclusive agency listing
   (D) an exclusive-right-to-sell listing

4. Which of the following does *not* terminate an agency relationship?
   (A) Making an offer
   (B) The death of either party
   (C) The resignation of the agent
   (D) The destruction of the subject matter

5. To prove her right to a commission a broker must show
   (A) that she was licensed throughout the transaction
   (B) that she had a contract of employment
   (C) that she was the "efficient and procuring cause" of the sale
   (D) all of the above

6. A net listing
   (A) requires the broker to seek a net price for the property
   (B) is legal in all states
   (C) is one that most ethical brokers would prefer to use
   (D) is discouraged in Florida

7. Among other things, the principal is obligated to
   (A) compensate the agent for his services
   (B) give the agent full authority to accept or turn down offers
   (C) give the agency the principal's financial statement
   (D) none of the above

8. A real estate agent
   (A) must always represent the seller
   (B) may represent the buyer if the buyer-broker agency is disclosed to all parties
   (C) may not take listings if she represents buyers
   (D) need not disclose a buyer-broker agency relationship

9. A special agent is one
   (A) whose powers are limited to certain specific functions
   (B) who must report to a licensing agency
   (C) who has less then a certain amount of experience as an agent
   (D) who is not a licensed agent

10. Among other things, an agent is obligated to
    (A) act in the principal's best interests unless these conflict with the agent's own interests
    (B) keep an accurate account of all money he receives on behalf of the principal
    (C) never disclose the agency relationship to anyone
    (D) represent only one principal at a time

11. In Florida, which of the following is illegal?
    (A) Selling agent represents only the buyer
    (B) Selling agent represents both buyer and seller
    (C) Buyer's agent represents both buyer and seller
    (D) All of the above are illegal

12. The agency disclosure form must be executed
    (A) when the sale closes escrow
    (B) only if there is a dual agency
    (C) when a salesperson agrees to work for a broker
    (D) upon first substantive contact with a potential seller or buyer

ANSWERS

1. B	5. D	9. A
2. C	6. D	10. B
3. D	7. A	11. A
4. A	8. B	12. D

Chapter 5/*Florida Real Estate License Law*

Since 1923, Florida has required licensure of real estate brokers and salespeople. Real estate licensing is an exercise of the state's *police power*, granted to the government by the United States Constitution. When you get your application materials from the Division of Real Estate, you also should order (for $10.00) a copy of the *Florida Real Estate Commission Handbook*. It contains the Florida Real Estate License Law (Chapter 475 of the Florida Statutes, as amended), the rules and regulations of the Florida Real Estate Commission, and reprints of several other bodies of regulation governing the real estate business. It is required that this book be used in required prelicensing courses in Florida, so you may already have it; however, if it has been some time since you took the course (or if you haven't taken it yet), you should get an updated copy. Be sure to read the *Handbook* carefully. We can't possibly cover everything that is in this book's 200+ pages, but we will hit the important parts that are most likely to appear on the exam. About 20 percent of the salesperson's exam and the broker's exam concerns license law and agency (described in Chapter 4).

Brokerage, Broker and Salesperson

A *real estate brokerage* business is one which, in an agency relationship and for compensation, sells, leases, solicits buyers, sellers, tenants or lessors for real estate owned by others. A real estate brokerage business may be a sole proprietorship (owned and operated by an individual), a corporation, or a partnership. With a few exceptions (see below), anyone who performs any of these brokerage-related activities must be licensed either as a broker or a salesperson.

A *real estate broker* is one who is licensed to independently operate a real estate brokerage business. A *real estate salesperson* performs brokerage functions, but must be employed by a licensed broker, and may not operate independently. A real estate broker is not required to operate independently; an *associate broker* is a broker licensee who is employed by another broker just as a salesperson licensee would be. Licensed salespersons and associate brokers may not operate or manage a brokerage business, may not hold or control a majority of the stock in a corporate brokerage, and may not be a director or officer in a corporate brokerage. A corporate brokerage must be operated by a licensed broker. In a brokerage partnership, all partners must be licensed brokers.

A salesperson may not receive *any* form of compensation for brokerage-related activity except *directly from* his/her employing broker. The salesperson's employment agreement with the broker must be in writing. However, the manner in which the salesperson is paid (salary, commission, and how much) is subject to negotiation between the salesperson and broker. These rules also apply to associate brokers employed by another broker.

In any brokerage business, the licenses of all licensees (brokers, associate brokers, and salespersons) associated with the business must be available to the public for inspection. The managing broker's license must be posted in public view; the rest only have to be readily available upon request.

Real estate brokers also may deal in businesses, as well as real estate. For example, a building that houses a shoe store is real estate (the building and land) and the business that occupies the real estate can be a shoe retailing business.

Exemption from Licensing

Some people who perform what seems to be real estate brokerage activity do not have to be licensed:

1. Most people buying or selling their own real estate.
2. An attorney-at-law, in the course of his/her duties to clients.
3. Anyone who has a properly executed power of attorney allowing them to act for a party to a transaction.
4. A trustee selling under a deed of trust.
5. Anyone acting under an order of any court.
6. A trustee, or receiver, in bankruptcy.
7. An officer of a corporation performing such functions for the corporation without receiving special compensation (i.e., a commission) for doing so.

Although there are some other less frequently encountered exceptions mentioned in the law, these are the main ones, and the ones which are likely to appear on licensing examinations.

Obtaining the License

Review Chapter 1 for education and experience necessary to qualify to take the licensing examination. An application for the examination is available by calling or writing the Division of Real Estate offices in Orlando at (407) 245-0810. The packet includes the application for the examination. Applicants must prove that they have had the required education by having the proper forms submitted by the educational institution(s) they attended for the required instruction. Salesperson applicants must complete a 63-hour course in Real Estate Fundamentals, called Course I, before taking the examination. Broker applicants must complete an additional 72-hour course (Course II), and must have been active real estate salespersons for at least twelve months during the five years preceding the application. Also, one cannot take Course II until one has accumulated at least six months of experience as an active salesperson.

In addition to the specified real estate-related instruction that is required, applicants for real estate licenses must be at least 18 years of age and have the equivalent of a high school education. They also must submit a set of their fingerprints with the application, as well as two 2×2-inch photographs suitable for identification purposes. The application fee is $185 for the salesperson's examination and $195 for the broker's examination.

Real estate licenses are good for two years. They may be renewed for additional two-year periods by paying a renewal fee ($70 brokers, $60 salespersons), provided that the licensee has completed the required continuing education (described in the next paragraph) during the two-year license period. If a license is not renewed, it expires, and the holder is no longer allowed to engage in any activity for which the license is required. However, for the first two years after a license expires it still can be renewed by paying a (higher) late renewal fee. Anyone whose license still has not been renewed, once this two-year period has passed, must go thorough the entire licensing process again, including the examination, to become licensed anew.

Even after the license is received, and the education requirements for initial licensure have been met, the law requires licensees to receive *continuing education*. This education is not required during the first two-year licensing period for new licensees. After that, in order to renew the license, the licensee must submit, with each renewal application, proof of having attended and passed a qualifying course of at least 14 hours.

Administration of License Law

The *Florida Department of Business and Professional Regulation* (also called DBPR) administers and enforces the Florida real estate licensing laws through its *Division of Real Estate* (DRE). The *Florida Real Estate Commission* is an appointed body of seven members; however, it has no staff, which is why DRE administers licensing examinations and administers and enforces license law and the rules and regulations of the Real Estate Commission.

The Real Estate Commission has the power to restrict, suspend, or revoke licenses of those who violate the law. Through DRE it investigates complaints against licensees, provided that complainants submit them in writing. The Commission can take statements from anyone involved, including the licensee, and can examine records such as bank, escrow, title records, etc., that are relevant to the complaint. The licensee may have an attorney, if desired. If the charges are proven, the Commission can restrict, suspend, or revoke the license. The penalty depends upon the severity of the licensee's offense.

Escrow Funds

Most brokerage firms have occasion to be entrusted with other people's money. Common examples are deposits made by buyers when a purchase contract is executed, or rents received by brokers who are managing and leasing property. Any escrow monies received by a broker (or other broker or salesperson employed by the broker) must, *by the next business day*, (a) be given to the principal on whose behalf they were received, or (b) deposited in the broker's escrow money bank account that the broker must keep at a Florida financial institution. This escrow money does not belong to the broker although, for convenience, he/she often "keeps" it; the escrow money account allows the broker to keep the escrow money safely. Since the broker is merely the trustee of the account, the law recognizes that the funds in the account do not belong to the broker and can never be taken by anyone who may have a claim against the broker. Interest-bearing accounts are permitted, with some restrictions, but the accounting involved is such a nightmare that most brokers do not use them.

Under certain circumstances, the broker does not have to put the money in safekeeping immediately. With the knowledge of the broker's principal, the broker can hold a postdated check, or a promissory note, or some such device until an agreed upon time. Also, during the negotiation of a purchase contract, the prospective buyer may instruct the broker, in writing, not to deposit the check unless and until a purchase contract has been agreed upon.

There are two grievous sins that brokers can commit with respect to escrow accounts. First, they can fail to keep meticulous escrow account records. The law requires the records to be accurate and up to date; inspectors from DRE have the right to enter a broker's place of business, unannounced, anytime during reasonable business hours to inspect the records. The second deadly sin is *commingling*. This refers to mixing the broker's own business and/or personal funds with escrow account funds. Since the whole idea of the escrow account is to keep escrow monies safely segregated from the broker's own funds, it is obvious why commingling is such a serious offense.

Notification to the DRE

DRE must be kept up-to-date with the business addresses of all licensed brokers and with the broker affiliation of all licensed salespeople. A broker must notify the DRE of any change of business address. When a salesperson is first licensed, the salesperson and broker apply to have the salesperson's new license issued to the broker. (Note that salespeople are not issued their own licenses; the licenses are held by their brokers.) If the broker discharges a salesperson, DRE must be notified immediately. If a salesperson leaves one broker and affiliates with another, the first broker gives the salesperson his/her license; the salesperson notes the change on it and gives it to the new broker. The salesperson and new broker must notify the DRE of the change within five days of the new employment.

If a broker or salesperson surrenders his license, or his license is suspended or revoked, he must immediately cease all real estate brokerage activity. Any salespeople employed by a broker whose license is surrendered, suspended, or revoked also must cease all real estate brokerage activity until they can affiliate with a different broker, and DRE is notified of the new association. The same applies to any salesperson discharged by a broker.

Record Keeping

Brokers must keep records of all business for at least three years after the business is concluded. For all real estate transactions, this means keeping records for three years after escrow settlement. For escrow accounts, it means records of each transaction must be kept for three years after the transaction is concluded. Salesperson's contracts, copies of the DRE forms, notifications, and similar documents must be kept for three years, as well as the business's bank statements, other employee records, etc.

Nonresident Licenses

Persons who are not residents of Florida must obtain Florida nonresident licenses if they wish to engage in the real estate business in Florida. For residents of most states, this means that they must take the appropriate Florida licensing examination (and, therefore, meet the education and experience requirements as well). However, Florida has reciprocity with some other states with respect to nonresident broker's and salesperson's licenses. With respect to those states, this means that, without taking any examinations, Florida licensees may obtain nonresident licenses in the other states, and their licensees may obtain Florida licenses without taking the Florida licensing examination. Anyone taking advantage of this reciprocity must pay the normally required license fees.

Violations of License Law

Following, in outline form, are the most common violations of license law. Or, to put it in a more realistic fashion, here are the many ways in which you can *lose your license!*

A. MISHANDLING MONEY BELONGING TO OTHERS

1. Commingling trust (or escrow) money with one's own funds.
2. Not remitting funds quickly, once they are received.
3. Salesperson's not remitting funds quickly to broker.
4. Accepting noncash payments on behalf of principal without principal's agreement. (Checks are considered to be cash.)

B. MISREPRESENTATION AND FRAUD
All of these practices are *misrepresentation or fraud.*

1. False advertising.
2. Intentionally misleading someone.
3. Acting for more than one party to a transaction without the knowledge of all parties.
4. Using a trademark or other identifying insignia of a firm or organization (such as the National Association of Realtors®) of which one is not a member.
5. Salesperson's pretending to be a broker or to be employed by a broker not his own.
6. Not identifying oneself as a licensee in any transaction in which one is also a party.
7. Taking kickbacks, referral fees, commissions, placement fees, and so on in association with one's duties from persons who are not one's principal, and without the principal's knowledge.
8. Guaranteeing future profits.

9. Offering property on terms other than those authorized by the principal.

10. Pretending to represent a principal by whom one is not actually employed.

11. Failing to identify the broker in all advertising.

C. IMPROPER BUSINESS PRACTICE

1. Failing to submit all offers to the principal.

2. Attempting to thwart another broker's exclusive listing.

3. Inducing someone to break a contract.

4. Accepting a net listing.

5. Failing to put an expiration date in a listing.

6. Putting one's sign on a property without the owner's permission.

7. Failing to post a required bond; failing to keep the bond up to date.

8. Blockbusting.

9. Discriminating.

D. FAILURE TO IMPART REQUIRED INFORMATION

1. Failure to leave copies of contracts with all parties involved.

2. Failure to deliver a closing statement to all parties entitled to one (brokers only).

3. Failure to inform some or all parties of closing costs (brokers only).

E. IMPROPER HANDLING OR PAYMENT OF COMMISSIONS

1. Paying a commission to an unlicensed person.

2. Paying a commission to a licensee not in one's employ.

3. Salesperson's receiving a commission from anyone other than her employing broker.

F. AGENCY DISCLOSURE

1. Failing to disclose to prospective buyers that broker is agent of the seller.

2. Failing to disclose buyer-broker agency to seller or seller's broker (including when to do so).

3. Required form to use for agency disclosure.

G. OTHER

1. Being convicted of certain crimes.

2. Violating any part of the license law.

3. Making false statements on the license application.

4. Showing any evidence of "incompetence," "unworthiness," "poor character," and so on. This is a "catch-all" provision usually found at the end of the list of specific offenses to drive home the point that *any* improper action can cost a licensee his license.

Questions on Chapter 5 _____

Note that some of these questions may not be answered by the material in Chapter 5. Remember, we encouraged you to read the *Florida Real Estate Commission Handbook*. You will find that some of the following questions are answered in that publication.

1. A licensee's license must be
   (A) carried in his wallet at all times
   (B) kept on the wall in his home
   (C) available for examination in the broker's office
   (D) kept on the wall at the DRE

2. A person must be licensed if she is to sell
   (A) her own home
   (B) property belonging to an estate for which she is executor
   (C) property belonging to clients who pay her a commission
   (D) property she has inherited

3. A broker must place funds belonging to others in
   (A) his office safe, to which only he knows the combination
   (B) a safety deposit box
   (C) an account maintained by the DRE
   (D) a trust, or escrow, account

4. License laws forbid
   (A) collecting a commission from more than one party to a transaction
   (B) soliciting for listings before one is licensed
   (C) both A and B
   (D) none of the above

5. A licensee's license can be revoked for
   (A) closing a deal
   (B) intentionally misleading someone into signing a contract that she ordinarily would not sign
   (C) submitting a ridiculous offer to a seller
   (D) all of the above

6. Real estate licenses, once received,
   (A) remain in effect indefinitely
   (B) are good for a limited period of time
   (C) must be filed in the county records
   (D) may be inherited by the licensee's spouse

7. A broker's unlicensed secretary may
   (A) sell property provided that he does it under the broker's direct supervision
   (B) sell or negotiate deals so long as he does not leave the office
   (C) refer interested clients to the broker or her employed licensees
   (D) all of the above

8. A broker may use escrow moneys held on behalf of others
   (A) for collateral for business loans
   (B) for collateral for personal loans
   (C) to make salary advances to licensees in his employ
   (D) none of the above

9. In order to do business, a licensee must
   (A) make proper application for a license
   (B) pass a licensing examination
   (C) have a license issued by the appropriate state agency
   (D) all of the above

10. A licensee can lose his license for which of the following?
    (A) Paying a commission to a nonlicensed person
    (B) Using moneys received as commissions to pay office help
    (C) Both A and B
    (D) Neither A nor B

11. A licensee can lose her license for
    (A) selling properties quickly, at low prices
    (B) buying property for her own use from her principal
    (C) both A and B
    (D) neither A nor B

12. Which of the following is not required to have a real estate license?
    (A) A resident manager of an apartment project
    (B) A resident manager of an apartment project who, for a fee, sells a house across the street
    (C) A student who sells houses as part of a research project
    (D) All of the above

13. A licensed salesperson
    (A) must be under the supervision of a broker
    (B) can collect commission payments only from his broker
    (C) must have his license held by his employing broker
    (D) all of the above

14. In order to sell property belonging to a trust for which he is trustee, the trustee must have a
    (A) broker's license
    (B) salesperson's license
    (C) trustee's license
    (D) none of the above

15. A person who is employed to lease property, but not to sell it,
    (A) must be licensed   (C) may be paid a salary or commission
    (B) is an agent   (D) all of the above

16. The Florida real estate licensing laws are part of the
    (A) Business and Professions Code
    (B) Code of Licenses
    (C) Florida Statutes
    (D) Health and Public Safety Code

17. Licensed salesperson Fleming is independently wealthy. She feels that real estate brokerage is potentially a very lucrative business. However, she has tried and failed to pass the broker's examination numerous times. She forms a corporation, XYZ Realty, Inc., of which she owns 75 percent of the shares. The other 25 percent are owned by Broker Hansen, who has agreed to be the broker of the company.
    (A) They must have at least two more stockholders to satisfy the Corporations Code.
    (B) This arrangement violates the law.
    (C) Broker Hansen can't be the broker and own shares at the same time.
    (D) All of the above are correct.

18. Broker Johnson receives a cash deposit from Jones, who has signed a purchase contract to buy real estate from Smith. Which of the following may Broker Johnson *not* do?
    (A) Give the money to Smith.
    (B) Deposit the money in the brokerage's trust money bank account.
    (C) Put the money in the brokerage office safe for safekeeping.
    (D) None of the above.

19. Morgan is treasurer of ABC, Inc. ABC wished to buy land for a new plant, and Morgan negotiated the entire deal at a price and terms very favorable to ABC. As a result, ABC paid Morgan a commission of 10 percent of the purchase price of the land. Morgan does not have a real estate license.
    (A) The law limits Morgan's payment to no more than 5 percent, since he has no license.
    (B) This practice is within the law.
    (C) This practice violates the License Law.
    (D) By making this deal, Morgan automatically becomes licensed under the "grandfather clause" of the license law.

20. A Florida Real Estate license is good for negotiating
    (A) anywhere in the state of Florida
    (B) the sale of any kind of real property
    (C) the sale of property outside Florida, if negotiation occurs inside Florida
    (D) all of the above

21. A licensed salesperson may act independently (i.e., not in the employ of a broker)
    (A) in any transaction valued at less than $10,000
    (B) to sell her own house, provided all parties know she holds a license
    (C) if he owns at least 51 percent of the stock in the brokerage firm that employs him
    (D) if all other parties involved in the transaction are also licensed

22. The Real Estate Commission is composed of ____ members.
    (A) 5
    (B) 7
    (C) 9
    (D) 12

23. For how long after a transaction is concluded must a broker keep his/her records of the transaction?
    (A) two years
    (B) three years
    (C) four years
    (D) five years

24. The license renewal fee for a real estate salesperson is
    (A) $60
    (B) $70
    (C) $185
    (D) $195

25. Real estate broker's and salesperson's licenses are good for
    (A) two years
    (B) three years
    (C) four years
    (D) five years

26. The license fee for a real estate broker is
    (A) $50
    (B) $100
    (C) $150
    (D) $200

27. Licensees must complete ____ hours of qualifying continuing education every two years.
    (A) 15
    (B) 22½
    (C) 30
    (D) 37½

28. Violation of license law
    (A) is a misdemeanor
    (B) is impossible if you have a license
    (C) is punishable only by the DRE
    (D) will always result in permanent revocation of the license

29. Licensees must pay fees for which of the following?
    (A) Transferring employment to another broker
    (B) Replacing a lost pocket card
    (C) Reactivating an inactive license
    (D) All of the above

30. If a licensee's license has become inactive, the licensee can activate it within ____ without having to retake the examination.
    (A) two years
    (B) one year
    (C) four years
    (D) three years

ANSWERS

1. C	11. D	21. A
2. C	12. A	22. B
3. D	13. D	23. B
4. B	14. D	24. A
5. B	15. D	25. A
6. B	16. C	26. C
7. C	17. B	27. B
8. D	18. B	28. A
9. D	19. C	29. D
10. A	20. B	30. A

PART III: REAL ESTATE CONTRACTS

Chapter 6/*Introduction to Contracts*

Most people have a little familiarity with contracts, though these documents may appear more awesome than any others. A popular misconception is that a contract must be filled with obscure, legalistic language and printed in nearly invisible type. Many contracts do appear this way, but often these features are unnecessary.

While it is true, as we shall see, that contracts must conform to certain standards, usually the only requirement of the *language* is that it *say clearly what it is supposed to say*. These days there is an admirable trend to simplify and clarify the language of most contracts, eliminating elaborate language that serves no useful purpose.

We can approach the study of contracts with confidence; a little familiarity with them will reveal the basic logic behind the laws and customs that surround them and will eliminate the mystery that usually clouds the layperson's view of these documents.

Contracts and Real Estate

The real estate business is dominated by contracts. Buying, selling, mortgaging, leasing, and listing real estate all involve particular kinds of contracts. To become familiar with the real estate business, we must devote a considerable part of our study to contracts *in general*, as well as to the *specific kinds* that concern real estate.

For convenience we divide real estate contracts into two rather loosely defined groups. Our *major* contracts are associated with the kinds of real estate dealings that most frequently occur: these are *listings, purchase contracts, deeds, mortgages,* and *leases*. Other contractual arrangements, which involve particular kinds of circumstances and so are less frequently encountered, constitute our *minor* contracts. Note that this division into major and minor is a grouping we are making for our own convenience. The law and the courts do not make this distinction: to them a contract is a contract, and the parties to all contracts have the same rights of access to the courts and to legal enforcement of their contractual promises.

REAL ESTATE CONTRACTS

Figure 6-1 arranges the major contracts in the order in which they might be encountered in a typical series of transactions. First an owner (a seller) enters into a *listing contract* with a broker; in this contract the seller agrees to pay a commission when the broker has found an acceptable buyer for the listed property. In many states, when a buyer is contacted, the law requires that an *agency disclosure* be made to the buyer by the seller's broker at that time (see Chapter 4 for discussion of agency disclosure). When a buyer becomes interested in the listed property, negotiations begin; if there is a buyer-broker agency relationship (see Chapter 4), disclosure of it must be made to the seller and/or his broker during the negotiations. If the buyer and the seller agree to transact, they will sign a *contract for sale*, in which they agree that at some time in the future the seller will convey the property to the buyer; this conveyance will occur when the *deed* is executed by the seller and delivered to the buyer. The buyer may then seek to borrow part of the cost of the property, so he offers a lender a *mortgage* as collateral for the *note*, which serves as evidence of the debt he owes. Also, he decides to rent part of the premises to someone else, with whom he enters into a *lease* contract.

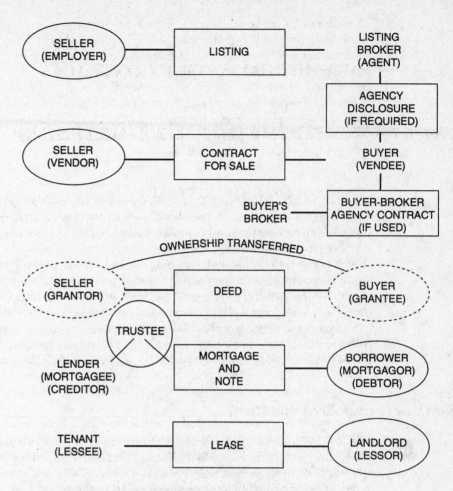

Figure 6-1.   Major Real Estate Contracts.

PARTIES TO CONTRACTS

In each of these contracts, the parties have specific names. In a listing contract, the seller is the *employer* and the broker is the *agent*. In the contract for sale, the seller becomes the *vendor* and the buyer is the *vendee*. The parties to the deed are the *grantor* and the *grantee*; the mortgage contract is between the *mortgagor* (owner) and *mortgagee* (lender). The *lessor's* real estate is made available to the *lessee* in a lease contract. Generally, the suffix -*or* refers to the person who conveys rights, privileges, or something else of value to the person whose title has the suffix -*ee*. In subsequent chapters each of the real estate contracts will be discussed in detail, but first we examine the basic principles that apply to all contracts.

WHAT IS A CONTRACT?

A contract is an agreement between two or more *parties*, in which each of the parties pledges to do, or is shown to have done, *something* that will benefit the others. This "something" can take a multitude of forms. A common one is a payment of money, though contracts involving no money payment can be perfectly valid. Each of the parties must be shown to benefit, so contracts must involve *exchanges* of benefits. A gives something to B, in return for which B gives something to A. A common example is a purchase: I give money to you, and you give the thing I am buying from you. However, a valid contract need not involve money: I can swap my automobile for your lawn mower, or we can agree that neither of us will build on our land an ugly structure that will be in the line of sight of the other.

Although there are other requirements that must be met, the critical test of the validity of a contract is the issue of whether or not the parties can be shown to benefit from it. The amount of benefit doesn't really matter; but if benefit to one or both parties is totally lacking, then usually there is no contract, for it is an ancient precept of law that no one should give something for nothing. If *any* measurable or identifiable benefit is mentioned in the contract, that will suffice. If you and I sign an agreement that says simply I will give you my automobile next Tuesday, no court will require me to live up to this promise, because no benefit *to me* is mentioned. However, if our agreement says that I will give you my car next Tuesday in return for one dollar paid by you to me, the courts *will* enforce the agreement against me: it will be a contract because I am receiving some benefit. The fact that my car may be worth much more than one dollar is immaterial here; all that matters is that *both* parties receive *some* benefit: you get my car and I get your dollar.

ENFORCEMENT OF CONTRACTS

A valid contract has the "force of law" among the parties to it. It is as if they had agreed to "pass" a law among themselves and promised to abide by it. However, when a person violates the provisions of a contract, the police, or a flock of judges and bailiffs, do not descend upon him and demand that he keep his bargain. In fact, the law will do nothing about private contractual disputes unless one of the injured parties petitions the court to intervene. At that point, the law requires the affected parties to appear and to present their arguments. Then the court (i.e., a judge or a jury) makes a decision as to what is to be done, and by whom. (This description, of course, is somewhat oversimplified; resolving a contractual dispute—or any other—in court often consumes considerable time and expense.) It is likely that many violated contracts never reach court because the offended parties do not want the bother of a court case. Even so, there is always that possibility; all parties to a contract have the inherent right to request the court to render judgment if they feel that other parties to the agreement are not living up to it.

Generally, a person who brings a contract to court has two remedies available. First, she can ask that the court require *specific performance* of the offending party, that is, that the court order the other party to live up to the agreement. Often, however, by the time a contract dispute reaches court it is too late for mere performance to do any (or enough) good. In such a case, the injured party may seek *damages*. Here she would claim that she had suffered some loss because of the other party's violation of the contract and would ask that the court order the violator to make the loss good. Note the use of the words *court order* here. Once the court has reached a decision, the parties to the dispute are *required by law* to abide by it.° If they do not, they are in contempt of court and can be jailed or fined if need be. In this manner, behind every contractual arrangement there lies the threat of court action, which can be backed up by potentially severe penalties.

Most contract cases that come to court are not cut and dried. Rarely does a person enter into a contract with the intention to violate it; furthermore, one who *knows* that he is in violation of a contract rarely has the stubbornness (or foolishness) to go ahead with a court showdown he knows he will lose. What usually happens is that *all* parties to a dispute think they are right and the other(s) wrong. The parties *interpret* their agreement differently and are unable to resolve their differences. By taking the matter to court, they ask the court to render a judgment as to who is right and what is to be done.

Requirements of Valid Contracts

A contract cannot be considered by a court unless it is valid. While certain kinds of contracts may have additional requirements for validity, *all* contracts must have the following attributes:
1. Mutual agreement
2. Consideration
3. Legally competent parties

°This assumes that the decision is not appealed. But an appeal only delays an eventual unappealed, or unappealable, decision, which must be respected.

4. Lawful purpose
5. Legal form

1. MUTUAL AGREEMENT

Mutual agreement (often referred to as *offer and acceptance, reality of consent, mutual assent, meeting of the minds*, and similar phrases) means that all parties recognize that an offer has been made and has been accepted by the other parties. All are agreed as to what each party has done, with respect to the contract, as well as to what each party is still required to do in the future. Generally, the parties will agree to do, or not to do, some thing or things, in return for some kind of obligation from the others.

Provided that the other essentials of a contract are present, once an offer has been accepted, a contract exists. The one making the offer is the *offeror*, and the one to whom it is made is the *offeree*. The actions of both of them in creating the contract must be shown to be intentional and deliberate: generally their signatures to a written contract are evidence of this, provided that no fraud, misrepresentation, duress, or mistake is present. However, many binding contracts need not be written; in such cases it is the testimony of the affected parties that provides the evidence that an agreement exists. (Duress, misrepresentation, and fraud are discussed later in this chapter.)

2. CONSIDERATION

Legal consideration refers to the "benefit" received by the parties. Each party must be shown to be obligated to do (or not to do) something, in return for some action or nonaction by the other parties to the contract. The benefit can take many forms; all that must be shown is that the party receiving the benefit agreed that it was of use to him and that he was willing to obligate himself in some way in order to get it. Payment of money is always consideration, as is the transfer of ownership of anything that can be shown to have a market value. In addition, the transfer of many *rights* is consideration; for example, a lease transfers rights to use property, but not ownership of the property.

Examples. Here are some examples of consideration in a contractual relationship:
1. A pays $50,000 to B. B transfers ownership of the house to A.
2. A pays B $200 per month. B gives A the right to use an apartment for each month for which A pays.
3. A pays B $2.50. B lets A watch a movie in B's theater.
4. A agrees not to hang her laundry outside where B and C can see it. B agrees not to hang his laundry where A and C can see it. C agrees not to hang her laundry where A and B can see it.
5. A agrees to use his best efforts to try to find a buyer for B's house. B agrees to pay A a commission of 6 percent of the sale price if A finds a suitable buyer.
6. A agrees to pay B $92,000 in 60 days, at which time B will transfer to A ownership of a particular house.
7. A pays B $1000. B gives A the right to purchase B's land for $25,000 at any time of A's choosing during the next 6 months.
8. A transfers ownership of her house to B. B transfers to A the ownership of his parking lot, four albums of rare stamps, two sets of dishes, and a mongrel dog.
9. A pays B $10,000. B transfers to A the ownership of a producing diamond mine in South Africa.
10. A transfers to his son, A, Jr., the ownership of the family estate in return for the "love and affection" that A, Jr. has given to A in the past.
11. A pays B $10,000. B agrees to pay A $126.70 per month for the next 10 years.
12. A pays B $10,000. B gives A the right to have B's house sold if B defaults on her debt to A.

In all of these instances there exists legal consideration; these examples show but a few of the many forms it can take. In many cases it includes the payment of money; in (4), (8), and (10), however, no money changes hands. In most, the consideration involves the parties doing something or performing some act; in (4), however, the parties agree *not* to do something. Examples (2), (3), (4), (7), and (12) include the exchange of rights; (5) includes the exchange of services; and the others involve the exchange of ownership of things.

These are examples of real estate contracts we will examine in more detail later. Example (2) is a *lease*; (4) is a *restrictive covenant*; (5) is a *listing*; (6) is a *contract of sale*; (7) is an *option*; (12) is a *mortgage*; and (1), (8), (9), and (10) are *deeds*. Many of these contracts are purchases of one kind or another; examine (11) closely and you will discover that it is a *loan* or a *note*: A lends B $10,000, which B agrees to repay (at a 9 percent interest rate) in equal monthly installments of $126.70 for the next 10 years. Example (5) is a *listing*; it is also an *employment contract*, wherein the services of one of the parties are purchased by the other party.

Good and Valuable Consideration

In all except (10) we have *"valuable" consideration*. Valuable consideration is anything that is of value to practically everyone and thus can be sold for money. Money, of course is "valuable," as is ownership of things, the receipt of someone's services, receipt of various kinds of rights, and the like. However, things such as friendship, love, and affection are not valuable consideration, because their value is entirely subjective. You may set a very high value upon the attention and friendship you receive from your best friend, but to most of the rest of us the attention is valueless, since we don't even know him. Furthermore, a person's affection is not a transferable benefit. Rights, ownership, money, services, and such things can be passed on (or sold) to practically anyone, but you can't sell your best friend's affection to someone else. Consequently, such things as friendship and love are called *"good" consideration*. They are of value to the one who receives them, and if she agrees to transfer benefit in return for them she can be held to her bargain.

The law does *not* require that *equal* consideration accrue to all parties. So long as consideration is there, the law is satisfied, provided of course that there no fraud or duress is involved. There is only one exception: the courts will not enforce a contract requiring the simultaneous exchange of different sums of money.

3. LEGALLY COMPETENT PARTIES

Competent parties are persons who have the legal right to enter into contractual arrangements. Not all legal persons are human beings: corporations, partnerships, trusts, and some other organizations can also be parties to a contract. You can contract to purchase an automobile from ABZ Auto Sales, Inc., even though this company is not a living, breathing being. Furthermore, not all humans are competent to contract; many are legally unable to do so, and many more may contract only under carefully defined circumstances.

Nonhuman Parties

Usually each party to a contract must assure himself of the other's legal competence. Although the law places few restrictions upon the possible contracting ability of nonhuman parties, often these organizations will operate under self-imposed restrictions. A corporation's charter, for example, can permit or prevent certain kinds of contractual agreements on the part of the organization; in addition, it can provide that some or all of the permitted functions be carried out in certain ways. For this reason a person who contracts with an organization must assure himself, first, that the outfit is permitted to engage in such a contract, and, second, that the contract is executed and carried out in consistency with the organization's permitted limitations and prescribed methods.

People

Among people, there are two major categories of incompetent parties: infants and insane persons, along with several minor ones: drunkards, convicts, and others.

a. Infants (or *minors*).   These are people who have not yet attained the age of majority, which is 18 in Florida. While you may not think that a hulking 17-year-old football star could be incompetent at *anything*, the law says he is. Furthermore, a person who may be immature, ignorant, or naive in business judgment still may be considered by the law to be perfectly competent to take responsibility for her actions if she has attained the age of majority. Minors are not prohibited from contracting, so no law is broken if a minor signs a contract. However, the contract is viewed in a special way by the law: the minor can *void* the contract later on, if he wishes, but adult parties to the contract do *not* have that privilege. The minor may not, however, void (or *disaffirm*) only *part* of the contract; he must abandon it entirely. If he contracts to buy property from an adult, he will have the right to declare the contract void, if he wishes, any time before it is carried out. The adult, however, must honor the contract unless and until the minor actually disaffirms it. If the adult does not keep his bargain, the minor can sue. The adult will receive no help from the courts if the minor disaffirms. However, the minor cannot, say, disaffirm the part of the contract that specifies he must pay for the property, while at the same time requiring the adult to transfer it to him anyway; he must abandon the *entire* contract. Furthermore, if he disaffirms it after the adult has provided him some benefit under it, he may have to pay for that which he had already received by the time he decided to void the contract.

The whole idea behind the legal specification of some people as incompetent is a matter of protection. An *infant* is considered too young to bind herself to agreements; the law gives her protection by allowing her to void most agreements that she gets herself into. Once an infant attains the age of majority she becomes an adult and loses this protection, but she *is* given a "reasonable" time beyond the attainment of majority to decide whether she will disaffirm any contracts that she entered into as a minor.

b. Insane Persons.   The law also extends this "protection" to other categories of people, the largest being *insane persons*. Unlike infancy, however, insanity is a state that can come and go. One who is sane can become insane, and one who is insane can become cured and so become sane again. Also, it is possible for a person who is under severe stress or suffering from some other transitory disturbance to become so disoriented that the law may extend the protection of incompetence to him during that episode.

Legal protection of an insane person takes two forms. First, if he has had a guardian appointed by the court, then all contracts he enters into are *void*, and he has no capacity to contract at all. Notice that an infant's contracts are *voidable*, whereas the contracts of an insane person under guardianship are *void*. If the insane person has no guardian, his contracts, too, are voidable rather than void. He has the choice to require that his bargains with others be carried out or to disaffirm the contracts.

Neither the infant nor the insane person may disaffirm *all* kinds of contracts; generally, courts will enforce against them contracts for *necessaries*. Examples of necessaries are food, clothing, and shelter; sometimes other things are included as well. For example, in some cases contracts for employment or for education may be considered necessaries. Once again, the law is extending another form of protection: an adult usually will not care to contract with an infant or someone else she knows may later plead incompetence and void the contract. Consequently, a truthful incompetent may be at a serious disadvantage if his personal circumstances *require* him to contract. Therefore, the law allows some incompetents what amounts to a limited competency. For things that are "necessary" to them they are allowed to create binding contracts, which they cannot disaffirm and which a court can enforce against them. As a result, competent parties receive the protection *they* seek in a contractual arrangement and any reluctance they may have to deal with an incompetent is eliminated.

c. Other Incompetency.   Certain other forms of incapacity "earn" one the legal protection of incompetency. A contract made by a person who is severely intoxicated with alcohol or is under the dominating influence of drugs known to affect judgment may later be considered voidable. Many states consider felon prisoners to be without the right to contract; this situation is described by the rather grim term of *civilly dead*. Usually when the sentence has been served, and sometimes at the time parole is secured, most rights will be restored.

4. LAWFUL PURPOSE

A contract that requires any of its parties to violate the law usually is void. However, if it is possible to do so without impairing the contract's basic purpose, a court will uphold the contract but strike out that part requiring an illegal act. A very good example concerns the Federal Fair Housing Act of 1968. Among other things, this law declared illegal certain restrictive deed covenants that required buyers of some real estate to agree they would resell only to people of certain racial or cultural backgrounds. At the time the law was enacted, vast numbers of deeds to homes contained such clauses, but that fact did not void those deeds in their entirety. The outlawing of these clauses had no great effect upon the main purpose of the deeds, which was to transfer title to realty in return for consideration. However, if someone had created a special agreement for the sole purpose of restricting the racial or cultural background of purchasers of certain real estate, then that entire contract would have been voided by the enactment of the law. If this kind of agreement came into being after the law was passed, it would be void from the beginning and would *never* be a contract.

The essential rule of lawful purpose, then, is that a contract that exists substantially for the purpose of requiring an illegal act is void. So also is a contract in which an illegal act is required, the elimination of which would materially alter the purpose or effect of the contract. When, however, an illegal act is included in a contract but is not essential to the basic intent or purpose of the agreement, a court often will void only the illegal part while letting the rest stand.

5. LEGAL FORM

Some contracts are required to follow a certain form or to be drawn in a certain manner. For example, deeds and contracts of sale require that "legal" descriptions of the property be included; if they are missing or are defective, the entire contract may be invalid. It should be pointed out, though, that much of the wordy, archaic language that frequently appears in contracts is *not* required by any law and appears only as a result of tradition.

Statute of Frauds: Real Estate Contracts Must Be Written

For most real estate contracts, however, there is one critical requirement with respect to form: generally, all real estate contracts, except (1) listings and (2) leases for 1 year or less, *must be written*. This requirement is an outgrowth of the fact that Florida has a law called the Statute of Frauds, which requires that all contracts of certain types be *written* if legal means are to be used to enforce them. Included in these categories are all contracts in which land or an interest in land is sold and contracts that cannot be performed within 1 year. This latter category, then, includes lease contracts extending for more than 1 year.

As noted in Chapter 4, a listing contract, however, does not require the sale of land or an interest in land among its parties (although it often is tied into such a sale to a third party). It is a contract of *employment,* which is a category not covered by the Statute of Frauds. However, License Law requires that listings also be in writing.

The definition of "land or an interest in land" is very specific and also quite broad. It includes future interests, so, in addition to deeds, contracts of sale must be written. It includes partial interests, so mortgages must be written. It includes improvements to land and attachments to it, so contracts involving purchase of buildings or growing plants must be written, even if the actual land beneath them is not part of the transaction. However, once an attachment to land is severed from it (e.g., trees are cut down or crops are reaped), the attachment becomes personal property and is no longer subject to the part of the Statute of Frauds that covers realty. This law covers much more than just realty contracts, though, so it is quite possible that many other nonrealty contracts can be required to be written.

Duress, Misrepresentation, and Fraud

All parties to a valid contract must have entered into it willingly and without having been misled as to pertinent facts concerning the arrangement. Consequently, you cannot expect a court to enforce a contract against someone if you pointed a gun at his head to force him to sign, or if you deliberately or unintentionally misled him so that he agreed to its terms, on the basis of this false information. The former kind of situation is described as one of *duress*; the latter is either *misrepresentation* or *fraud*.

DURESS

Duress can take any number of forms. When circumstances force a person to do something against her will, one could say that duress exists, but the law does not always see the situation in that way. If the duress is caused by a party who benefits under the contract, then a court usually will recognize it as such; this covers situations such as forcing someone's assent by threatening her illegally. But other circumstance can also create duress: Jones discovers that he has a rare, expensive disease and must sell his home in order to raise money to pay for the cure. A person who buys from him at this time might make an advantageous deal legally, if Jones is in a hurry to sell. If the duress is caused by one's own action, the court is reluctant to recognize it. If you buy a new house and therefore are desperate to sell your old home, that situation is pretty much your own fault. If you create your own duress, you usually have to suffer with it.

MISREPRESENTATION AND FRAUD

Misrepresentation and fraud go a few steps further: here someone is led into a bad bargain on the basis of false information. Misrepresentation is loosely defined as the *unintentional* giving of false information, whereas fraud is *deliberate*. There is another difference, too: fraud is a *crime* as well as a civil wrong. This means that, whereas a victim of either fraud or misrepresentation is entitled to compensation for what he was misled into losing, a victim of fraud may sue also for punitive damages, which are a form of extra payment required of the culprit as a kind of punishment. Finally, the perpetrator of a fraud may also be prosecuted in criminal court and may end up being convicted and imprisoned.

Proving Misrepresentation or Fraud

A victim must prove three things to show that misrepresentation or fraud exists: (1) that the incorrect information was relevant to the contract she is disputing—that is, it was *material*; (2) that it was reasonable for her to rely on this false information; and (3) that this reliance led her to suffer some loss as a result.

Let's consider an example. Brown considers buying Green's house. Brown asks Green whether the house is free of termites, and Green says that it is. Actually the house is infested. If Brown later buys the house based, in part, upon Green's information and subsequently discovers termite infestation, he may have a case. The point at issue is material: it is reasonable for Brown to base his decision to buy at least partly upon the assurance that no termites inhabit the premises. When he finds them, it is obvious that he has suffered a loss; therefore the first and third conditions are met. Now he must show that it was reasonable to rely upon Green (the owner at the time) to give him accurate information on this matter. If the court agrees with Brown, he has proved his case. If Green knew about the termites and deliberately lied, then he committed fraud. If he truly thought there were no termites, then he misrepresented.

If one or more of the three conditions are missing, fraud or misrepresentation cannot be claimed successfully. If Brown had not bought Green's house, he could not claim relief, since he suffered no loss due to the falsehood. Also, if he had asked a neighbor a few houses away about the termite problem in Green's house and had depended on the neighbor's incorrect information, it is unlikely that he could get help from the court, because he would have great difficulty showing that it was reasonable to rely on a neighbor for this kind of information.

Some Information Must Be Divulged

For some kinds of contracts, the law requires that certain information be divulged by at least some of the parties. If it is not, then misrepresentation or fraud may exist. For example, most licensing laws require that brokers inform other parties if the brokers are acting as principals in the contract, as well as agents. Also, California requires a broker to disclose which party she is acting for, especially if more than one party to a transaction is paying her a commission.

Discharge and Breach of Contracts

Contractual arrangements can be terminated in two general ways. *Discharge* of a contract occurs when no one is required to perform under it anymore. *Breach of contract* occurs when one party makes performance impossible, even though other parties are willing, by refusing to do his part or by otherwise preventing discharge of the contract.

DISCHARGE

Discharge can be considered the "amicable" situation in which the parties to a contract agree that the arrangement is terminated. Most often, discharge occurs by *performance*; that is, everyone has done what he has promised to do and nothing more is required of anyone. Other forms of discharge include agreement to terminate a contract, for one reason or another, before it would have been discharged by performance. Such a reason might be the substitution of a new party for one of the original parties; this original party, then, would have had her duties discharged. Sometimes the parties may decide to terminate one agreement by substituting another one for it. Discharge can also occur when the parties simply agree to abandon the contract without substituting a new party or another agreement for it.

Statute of Limitations

The law limits the time during which contracting parties can take a dispute concerning a contract to court; this is the Statute of Limitations, and it sets different kinds of limits on different kinds of contracts. Once the limit has passed, a dispute will not be heard in court, so, in that sense, the contract may be said to be discharged, because it can no longer be enforced. It is greatly advisable that any agreement discharging a contract for reasons other than performance or limitation be in writing. Under some situations (particularly when some, but not all, parties have performed or begun to perform under the contract) an agreement discharging an existing contract *must* be in writing.

BREACH

Breach occurs when a party violates the provisions of a contract; often this action can be serious enough to terminate the contract by making it impossible to continue the arrangement. The injured parties must seek remedy from the court; usually it takes the form of a judgment for *damages* against the party causing the breach. Sometimes, however, it may be feasible to secure a judgment for *specific performance*, which requires the breaching party to perform as he had agreed. To be successful in court, the injured parties must be able to show that a breach has indeed occurred. Failure by a party to perform entirely as specified in the contract constitutes a breach, as does a declaration that he does not intend to perform. Finally, there is a breach if a party creates a situation wherein it is impossible for every party to the contract to perform as specified. Once any of these events has occurred, there is a breach, and one attribute of a breaching of a contract is that it terminates the obligations of the other parties as well. The person who has breached a contract cannot have that agreement held good against any of the other parties.

INJUSTICE

The court will not enforce a contract if doing so will result in an obvious injustice. While the law is precise, its enforcement is allowed to be compassionate. Consider a case where Smith and Jones come to an *oral* agreement, wherein Smith pays money to Jones, and Jones transfers title to a piece of land to Smith. Smith then builds a house upon the land, whereupon Jones claims title to the land (and to the attachments, including the house) on the grounds that the contract transferring title was oral and therefore invalid. In a case as cut and dried as this, the court would award title to Smith, despite the absence of a written contract, for two reasons. First, there is a principle of law that recognizes an oral contract of this nature provided that the purchaser has "substantially" improved the property; otherwise he clearly would suffer unjustly. Second, if Jones had engineered the entire scheme specifically in order to take advantage of Smith, then Jones's case would be dismissed; a person can't use the law to obtain an unfair advantage over someone else who is acting in good faith.

OUTSIDE CIRCUMSTANCES

Finally, a contract can be terminated because of some outside circumstance. For example, new legislation may invalidate some kinds of contracts. The death of one of the parties usually will void a contract; also, if a party becomes ill or injured to the point where she cannot perform, she often can void a contract without penalty. If it turns out that the parties have made a mistake as to what their agreement constitutes, then the contract can be nullified. For example, if Emmett thinks a contract of sale involves his purchase of Ted's property on *First* Street and Ted thinks he has agreed to sell Emmett the property he owns on *Twenty-first* Street, there is no contract, because there hasn't been a meeting of the minds. Finally, if the subject matter of the contract is destroyed, the contract ceases to exist.

Questions on Chapter 6

1. A contract in which an owner of real estate employs a broker for the purpose of finding a buyer for the real estate is a
   - (A) deed
   - (B) contract of sale
   - (C) listing
   - (D) lease

2. A contract in which property is transferred from one person to another is a
   - (A) deed
   - (B) contract of sale
   - (C) listing
   - (D) lease

3. The two parties to a lease contract are the
   - (A) landlord and the serf
   - (B) rentor and the rentee
   - (C) lessor and the lessee
   - (D) grantor and the grantee

4. The requirement that all parties to the contract have an understanding of the conditions and stipulations of the agreement is
   - (A) reality of consent
   - (B) meeting of the minds
   - (C) offer and acceptance
   - (D) all of the above

5. Consideration that has value only to the person receiving it is
   - (A) illegal in any transaction
   - (B) good consideration
   - (C) valuable consideration
   - (D) contingent consideration

6. A person who is too young to be held to a contractual arrangement is called
   - (A) youthful
   - (B) incompetent
   - (C) an emancipated minor
   - (D) civilly dead

7. One who is otherwise incompetent to make a contract may be bound to contracts for
   - (A) anything but real estate
   - (B) real estate only
   - (C) necessaries
   - (D) food, clothing, and shelter not to exceed $100 per week

8. Which of the following contractual arrangements would be unenforceable?
   (A) A agrees to buy B's house.
   (B) A agrees with B that B shall steal money from C.
   (C) A agrees to find a buyer for B's car.
   (D) A agrees with B that B shall make restitution to C for money stolen by B.

9. In Florida, the law that requires that most real estate contracts be written to be enforceable is the
   (A) Statute of Limitations
   (B) **Statute of Frauds**
   (C) Statute of Written Real Estate Agreements
   (D) Statute of Liberty

10. A contract in which A agrees to allow B to use A's real estate in return for periodic payments of money by B is a
    (A) deed
    (B) contract of sale
    (C) lease
    (D) mortgage

11. When a person deliberately lies in order to mislead a fellow party to a contract, this action is
    (A) fraud
    (B) misrepresentation
    (C) legal if no third parties are hurt
    (D) all right if it is not written into the contract

12. Holding a gun to someone's head to force him to sign a contract is
    (A) attempted murder
    (B) permissible only in exceptional circumstances
    (C) duress
    (D) rude and inconsiderate but not illegal so long as the gun doesn't go off

13. When a party to a contract makes performance under it impossible, the result is
    (A) breach of contract
    (B) discharge of contract
    (C) performance of contract
    (D) abandonment of contract

14. A contract in which A agrees to purchase B's real estate at a later date is
    (A) a deed
    (B) an option
    (C) a contract of sale
    (D) a lease

15. In Florida, contracts made by a minor are
    (A) enforceable at all times
    (B) void
    (C) voidable by either party
    (D) voidable only by the minor

16. In Florida, incompetent parties include
    (A) minors
    (B) insane persons
    (C) people with court-appointed guardians
    (D) all of the above

17. The parties to a deed are the
    (A) vendor and vendee
    (B) grantor and grantee
    (C) offeror and offeree
    (D) acceptor and acceptee

18. If A and B have a contractual arrangement and B violates the contract, A may
    (A) do nothing but suffer the consequences
    (B) sue in court for damages and/or specific performance
    (C) call the police and have B arrested unless B agrees to cooperate
    (D) damage B to the extent that she has damaged A

19. A agrees to sell his brand new limousine to B in return for one dollar. Later A wishes to back out of the deal.
    (A) He may not do so.
    (B) He may do so because he is not getting the true value of the limousine.
    (C) He may only require that B pay a fair price for the limousine.
    (D) Both actions are clear evidence of insanity, so the contract is void.

20. A agrees to trade her car to B in exchange for a vacant lot that B owns.
    (A) This is a valid contractual arrangement.
    (B) This is not a contract, because no money changes hands.
    (C) This is not a contract, because unlike items can't be traded.
    (D) This is not a valid contract, because the car is titled in A's name.

ANSWERS

1. **C**	9. **B**	17. **B**
2. **A**	10. **C**	18. **B**
3. **C**	11. **A**	19. **A**
4. **D**	12. **C**	20. **A**
5. **B**	13. **A**	
6. **B**	14. **C**	
7. **C**	15. **D**	
8. **B**	16. **D**	

Chapter 7/*Description of Land*

Recognized, uniform methods of land description are essential to proper contractual transactions involving land. If the land in a transaction cannot be identified, our legal system will not recognize the transaction as binding. Therefore, proper description of the land involved is an essential part of contracts of sale, deeds, leases, options, mortgages, listings, and virtually all other kinds of real estate contracts.

There are four generally accepted methods of land description in the United States:
1. Rectangular survey
2. Metes and bounds descriptions
3. Lot and block number descriptions
4. Monument or occupancy descriptions

The purpose of all of these is to *identify* real estate. Often, in the terminology of the real estate business, descriptions are called "legal descriptions," giving the impression that there is some particular formula that must be followed. Actually, the only legal point of any importance is that the description be *sufficient to identify the property*. If the property can be identified from the description given, then the description is good. Otherwise, no matter how elaborate it may appear, it is faulty.

Most description methods are designed to demonstrate to a surveyor a means of marking the outline of the land on the ground. Most descriptions do not include buildings; remember that real estate is land *and all attachments to it*, so a description of the land automatically includes all improvements, unless they are *specifically excluded*.

Rectangular Survey Descriptions

The U.S. government rectangular survey is used in Florida, and in the states indicated in Figure 7-1. The government rectangular survey divides the land into squares 6 miles on a side; these are called *townships*. Each township is identified with respect to its distance from the *base line* and the *principal meridian*. There are several sets of principal meridians and base lines throughout the country, so each principal meridian carries a name or number to distinguish it from all the others; each one has a single base line paired with it.

Principal meridians are imaginary lines that run north-south. Base lines are imaginary lines that run east-west. Parallel to the principal meridians and 6 miles apart from each other are other *meridians*. Parallel to the base line are other lines called *parallels*; these are also 6 miles apart. Altogether, this system of north-south meridians and east-west parallels cuts the map up into a grid of 6-mile squares, as in Figure 7-2.

The vertical (north-south) rows of townships are called *ranges*, and the horizontal (east-west) rows of townships are *tiers*. Each township can be identified by labeling the range and tier in which it is found. The ranges and tiers are numbered according to their distances and directions from the principal meridian, or the base line. For example, the principal meridian will have a row of townships on each side of it. The one to the east is called *Range 1 East*, while the one to the west is *Range 1 West*. Similarly, the tier immediately north of the base line is called *Tier 1 North*, while the one below it is *Tier 1 South*.

To specify a particular township, a description must state both the tier and the range in which the township appears. These specifications usually are given in the form of abbreviations, such as T3N (Tier 3 North) or R4W (Range 4 West). Figure 7-2 identifies a number of

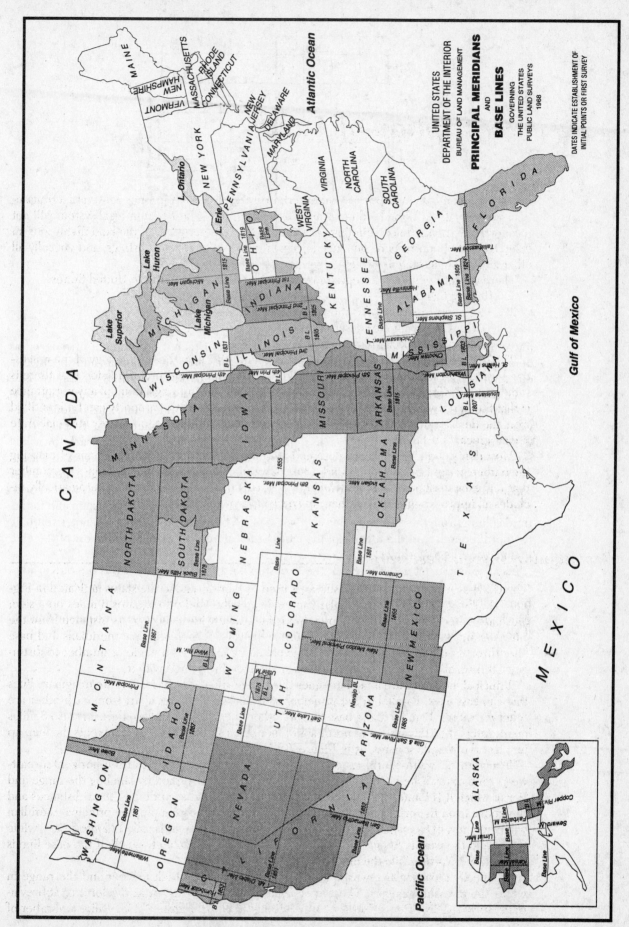

Figure 7-1.   Government Rectangular Survey

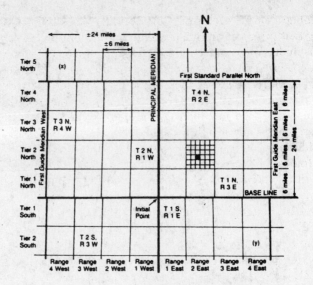

Figure 7-2.   Six-Mile Square Grid

townships by this kind of description; note that you simply count the number of ranges (or tiers) from the principal meridian (or the base line) to the particular township, and specify the direction taken. For practice, try to identify all the unmarked townships in Figure 7-2.

Of course, most tracts of land are less than 6 square miles, so it becomes necessary to identify which *part* of the township is the specific piece of land under consideration. This is done by dividing the township into smaller and smaller parcels until the one of interest is all that is left.

All townships are divided into 1-mile squares, as shown in Figure 7-3. Since each township is 6 miles square, it will contain 36 square miles. Each of these is always numbered, as shown in Figure 7-3. Each square-mile tract is called a *section*. Section 1 in any township, then, is the square mile at the very northeast corner of the township; Section 2 is immediately west of Section 1, and so on. Section 21 will be in the fourth row from the top of the township and in the third column from the west. In other words, the north border of Section 21 is 3 miles south of the north boundary of the township; the east border of Section 21 is 3 miles west of the east boundary of the township.

As an example, let us assume that the township illustrated in Figure 7-3 is the one in Figure 7-2 with the sections drawn in; that is, it is T2N, R2E. If, then, we wanted to describe Section 21 of this township, we would write, "Sec. 21, T2N, R2E." We would also have to specify which principal meridian we were using, although in states with only one principal meridian it is not strictly necessary to identify the meridian in a valid description.

6	5	4	3	2	1
7	8	9	10	11	12
18	17	16	15	14	13
19	20	21	22	23	24
30	29	28	27	26	25
31	32	33	34	35	36

N
↑

T2N, R2E

Figure 7-3.   Numbering for Sections

Notice that for each principal meridian there is only *one* T2N, R2E. All other townships using that principal meridian will be in different ranges or tiers, or both. Furthermore, each township has only *one* Section 21. Therefore, a description such as "Sec. 21, T2N, R2E, Tallahassee Meridian" describes a single square-mile tract of land in the Florida panhandle. "Sec. 21, T2N, R2E, Boise Meridian" describes a square-mile tract in southwestern Idaho.

If the tract of land under consideration is smaller than 1 square mile, we must further subdivide the section in which it appears. We do this by dividing the section into quarters or halves; if necessary, we further subdivide the resulting parts until we arrive at the tract we are considering. Figure 7-4 shows examples of how this is done. The entire section can be divided into four quarters: the northeast, northwest, southeast, and southwest quarters. These would be written as NE¼, NW¼, SE¼, and SW¼, respectively. In Figure 7-4 the SE¼ quarter is shown; the others have been further subdivided. The NW¼ quarter has been divided into two halves, E½ and W½. The proper descriptions of these subdivisions would be E½, NW¼, Sec. 21, T2N, R2E and W½, NW¼, Sec. 21, T2N, R2E.

The SW¼ quarter of this section has been divided into a number of smaller parcels; the proper description of each is given. The smallest is the shaded tract NW¼, SW¼, NW¼, SW¼, Sec. 21, T2N, R2E. The NE¼ quarter of the section has been divided slightly differently: the N½ is divided by the distance from the boundaries of N½, NE¼.

Each square mile contains 640 acres. The quarters, then, contain 160 acres each. Further subdivision yields smaller tracts that can be easily measured in terms of acreage; all the tracts subdivided in Figure 7-4 have the acreage indicated. In any case, it is a simple matter to determine acreage from most rectangular survey descriptions: multiply the series of fractions given in the description; then multiply the result by the 640 acres contained in the section. For example, the NW¼ quarter contains 160 acres: ¼ × 640 = 160. The very small tract cited in the preceding paragraph is NW¼, SW¼, NW¼, SW¼, so its acreage is ¼ × ¼ × ¼ × ¼ × 640 = 2½ acres.

Tracts such as those described in the N½, NE¼ subdivision aren't quite as easy to determine, since they aren't described entirely in fractions of the full section. For these, however, it is a relatively simple matter to determine the lengths of the sides in feet; then the total number of square feet can be determined. An acre contains 43,560 square feet; therefore by dividing the square footage of the entire tract by 43,560, we can obtain the acreage of the tract in question.

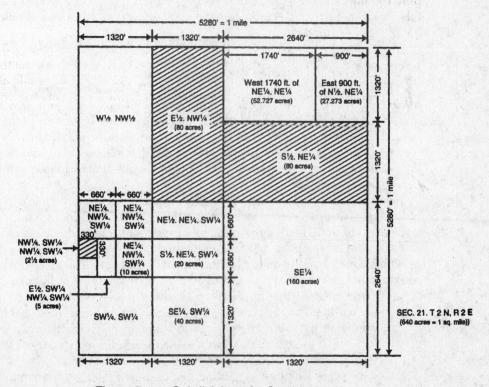

Figure 7-4. Subdivision of a Section

Sometimes a specific tract cannot be described using a single rectangular survey description; in such cases it is perfectly all right to use several descriptions, each for part of the tract, making sure that all the descriptions together will describe the entire tract. For example, the large L-shaped shaded tract in Figure 7-4 would be described as "E½, NW¼ and S½, NE¼; Sec. 21, T2N, R2E." Note, however, that it is almost always necessary that rectangular survey descriptions be of fairly regular tracts with straight sides. The boundaries almost always must run north-south or east-west. Usually the survey is not a good system for describing irregular tracts, tracts with curved or wandering boundaries, and very small tracts; these are better described using other methods.

One final feature of the rectangular survey description system must be noted: north-south lines on our planet are not parallel because they all meet at the poles. Therefore, the meridians must be adjusted every so often to keep them from getting too close together. This is done by shifting every *fourth* meridian, each 24 miles away from the base line. These meridians, called *guide meridians*, are shown in Figure 7-2. The parallels at which the adjustments take place, that is, every fourth parallel, are called *standard parallels*. Standard parallels and guide meridians are named to indicate their numbers and distance from the respective base line or principal meridian.

As you can see in Figure 7-1, all rectangualr survey descriptions in Florida use the Tallahassee Meridian.

Metes and Bounds Descriptions

Metes and bounds descriptions indicate to the surveyor how to locate the corners of a tract. By locating the corners, one also locates the sides, since they run from corner to corner. Following is a metes and bounds description of Lot 15 in Figure 7-5. This lot is shown enlarged in Figure 7-6.

> "BEGINNING at a point being the southeast corner of the intersection of Vicious Circle and Alongthe Avenue, thence one hundred and six and forty-hundredths feet (106.40') north 90°0'0" east, thence one hundred and twenty feet (120.00') south 0°0'0" east, thence seventy-three and fourteen-hundredths feet (73.14') south 90°0'0" west, thence one hundred and twenty-four and fifty-three hundredths feet (124.53') north 15°29'26" west to the point of beginning; said tract lying and being in Ooga Chooga County, Florida."

Note that a metes and bounds description must have the following components:
1. A properly identified *point of beginning*.
2. *Distance* and *direction* given for each side.

The preceding description contains all these. The point of beginning is identified as the intersection of two public streets; this is permissible, since a person may always consult the public records to find out exactly where these streets are. From that point, the surveyor is directed to proceed a certain distance, and in a certain direction. By following this description, he can arrive *only* at the specific points described, and these points are the corners of the lot. He will have outlined the particular plot of land in question by following this description; thus it is a good description.

The accuracy of the description is the only point of any consequence in a court of law. The description can progress clockwise or counterclockwise. Directions (north, south, etc.) may be capitalized or not. The description should include, of course, the name of the city (or county) and the state in which the real estate is located.

Often a metes and bounds description may include more language than in the fairly minimal example provided here. Common additional elements are as follows:
1. To define the street rights-of-way, lot lines of adjacent lots, and so on, along which directed lines travel. Example: ". . . thence one hundred feet (100.00') north 63°30'0" west along the southern right-of-way boundary of Thirtieth Street, thence one hundred feet (100.00') north 88°0'0" west along the southern boundary of Lot 44, . . .".
2. To end each direction with the words ". . . to an iron pin . . ." or ". . . to a point . . ." or some other language suggesting that there is a mark on the ground to refer to. More often than not, there is no marker now in existence, though at the time the lot originally

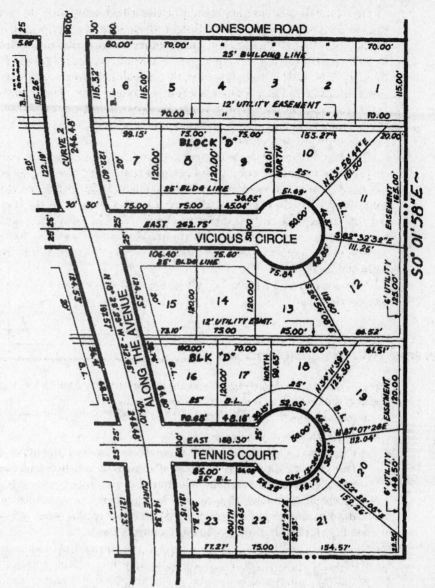

Figure 7-5.   Block D, Stripmine Estates, Gotham City, Ooga Chooga County, Florida

was laid out, many years ago, there indeed was. However, over the years these things disappear, erode, and otherwise become invisible.

3. To refer to actual things on the ground that can be found. If these things are relatively permanent and obvious, they are referred to as *monuments*. Examples: large, identifiable trees, visible streambeds, milestones, stone walls or other constructions, and occasionally genuine monuments placed at a location by the original surveyors for the very purpose of serving as references for descriptions. One serious point to keep in mind is that, if monuments are mentioned in a metes and bounds description, and the directed lines and monuments conflict, then the monuments rule. This means that, if the distance and measurement given say to go 200 feet due north to a certain milestone and the milestone actually is 193 feet, 6 degrees west of north, the latter measurement will rule in the description. For this reason, the inclusion of too many monuments in a description can sometimes cause confusion or error.

4. To add the statement ". . . containing x number of acres (square feet, etc.), more or less." This is convenient, but unnecessary; given the measurements and directions supplied by the description, it is always possible to calculate the area of the parcel if need be. The major reason for including the acreage is to protect the grantor against an error in the description that might indicate the transfer of much more (or much less) land.

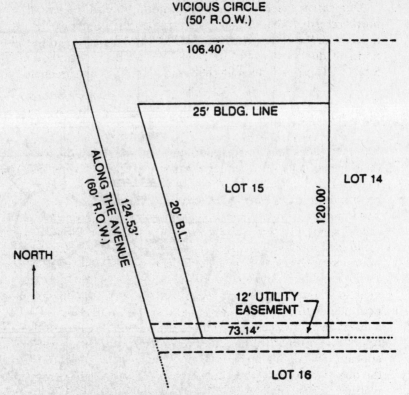

VICIOUS CIRCLE
(50' R.O.W.)

106.40'

25' BLDG. LINE

ALONG THE AVENUE
(60' R.O.W.)

124.53'

20' B.L.

LOT 15

120.00'

LOT 14

NORTH

12' UTILITY
EASEMENT

73.14'

LOT 16

Figure 7-6.   Lot 15, Block D, Stripmine Estates

For example, if the description mentions a tract of 100 acres, and the tract actually is only 10 acres, the inclusion of a statement of area would be an immediate indication that the description contained a mistake.

The point of beginning of a metes and bounds description must use a point of reference outside the description of the property itself. In urbanized areas, it is very common to use the nearest intersection of public roads or streets, as in the sample description given. [If that description had been of Lot 14, which is not at the corner, it would have begun as follows: "BE-GINNING at a point on the south boundary line of the right-of-way of Vicious Circle, one-hundred-and-six and forty-hundredths feet (106.40') east of the southeast corner of the intersection of the rights-of-way of Vicious Circle and Alongthe Avenue. . . ."] In some localities, official surveys, milestones, and so forth may exist, and reference points from these may be used. Indeed, one may refer to any point on earth that can be located using instructions from any publicly recorded document. Once the reference point has been defined, the actual beginning point of the parcel in question is identified by distance and direction from the reference point.

Distance may be expressed in any known unit of measurement, although the most common by far is feet. Directions are given according to the compass. However, there are two "sets" of compass directions: magnetic bearings and true bearings. Magnetic bearings refer to the magnetic poles; true bearings, to the geographic poles. If magnetic bearings are used, then, in order to achieve true bearings, they must be corrected for the location at which the survey was made and the date. The reason is that the magnetic pole is not at the same location as the true pole; furthermore, the magnetic pole "drifts" and so is located slightly differently at different times. From Florida, the compass needle (pointing at the magnetic North Pole) aims slightly *west* of true North.

By convention, compass bearings are described as numbers of degrees east or west (or south). There are 360 degrees in a full circle, 90 degrees in a right (square) angle. The symbol for *degree* is °, so 90° means 90 degrees. Each degree is divided into 60 *minutes* (symbol:') and each minute is composed of 60 *seconds* (symbol:"). The statement N 44°31'56" E is read as "north 44 degrees, 31 minutes, 56 seconds east."

Due east is exactly 90° away from north, toward the east; it is written as N 90° E. "Due" northeast is half that distance from true north, written as N 45° E. If directions are south of due east or west, they are measured by their deviations from true south. A direction slightly north of due west would be N 89° W; if it were slightly *south* of due west, it would be S 89° W. These and several other examples of various directions are shown in Figure 7-7.

Lot and Block Number

Lot and block number descriptions are common in urban areas where *plats* of subdivisions must be recorded. A plat is a map of the manner in which land is divided into lots; Figure 7-5 is an example of a plat. If the plat is a matter of public record (i.e., has been recorded), it is quite sufficient to refer to it for the legal description of property it illustrates. For example, it would be enough to describe Lot 15 on that plat as "Lot 15, Block D, Stripmine Estates, Gotham City, Ooga Chooga County, Florida." Given this description, a surveyor could look up this subdivision in the records, find the plat of Block D, and from it get all the information he needed to do an accurate survey of the lot.

Lot and block number descriptions are very simple to do and take little space. Therefore, in areas where the records are such that they can be used, they are very popular. It should be pointed out also that reference can be made to *any* recorded document in the preparation of a description. Thus, if lot and block descriptions are impossible, it may be possible simply to refer to a previous deed or other recorded instrument in which a description of the property appears. This should be done, however, only if the previous description is exactly the same as the one to be used at present; even so, it is potentially inconvenient in that, whereas copies of plats are easily obtained, and often can be received directly from developers and dealers, old deeds and other documents have to be dug out of the records.

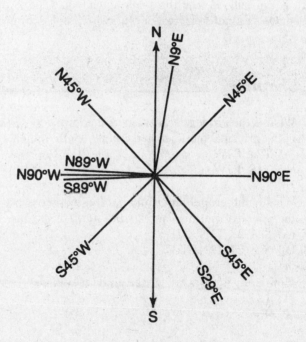

Figure 7-7. Compass Bearings

Monument and Occupancy Descriptions

Monument descriptions are similar superficially to metes and bounds descriptions. The difference is that monument descriptions rely entirely upon monuments and specify no distance or direction, except from the monuments themselves to important points of the survey. A monument description might read: "Beginning at the intersection of Highway 9 and County Road 445, thence along the right-of-way of County Road 445 to the end of a stone wall; thence from the end of the stone wall through the center of a large, freestanding oak tree to the center of a streambed; thence along the streambed to the point where the streambed intersects Highway 9; thence along Highway 9 to the point of beginning." Since this description can be followed in order to outline the property, it is a valid description, but there is always the risk that the monuments may move or disappear. These descriptions are used mainly for large rural tracts of relatively inexpensive land, where a full survey may entail much greater expense than is warranted by the usefulness of the land.

Occupancy descriptions are very vague: "All that land known as the Miller Farm"; "All that land bordered by the Grant Farm, Happy Acres Home for the Elderly, the Ellis Farm, and State Highway 42." With this kind of description one must rely on the community's general impression of what constitutes the Miller Farm, the Grant Farm, and so on. Occupancy descriptions are very weak because they indicate no specific boundaries at all. A similar situation arises when street addresses are used as descriptions. Although houses and other buildings usually have address numbers visibly displayed on them, these give no indication at all of the actual extent of the property.

Limits of Descriptions

It is important to understand that descriptions, while they may accurately describe land, do not provide any guarantee of *title* to that land. A deed that contains a perfectly usable description of a tract of land may be worthless if the grantor has little or no right to convey title to that particular tract. The mere fact that a deed or contract of sale contains a particular description does not guarantee to the buyer that his claim to the described land will hold up in court. It can only do so if the seller actually had the legal right to transfer the land she described. One cannot sell, give, or otherwise bargain away what one does not own.

Questions on Chapter 7

1. What is the proper description of the township whose *northeast* corner is 36 miles west of the principal meridian and 6 miles south of the base line?
   (A) T2S, R7W
   (B) T1S, R7W
   (C) T1S, R6W
   (D) T2S, R6W

2. What is the proper description of the section whose *northwest* corner is 5 miles east of the principal meridian and 2 miles north of the base line?
   (A) Sec. 23, T1N, R1E
   (B) Sec. 24, T1N, R1E
   (C) Sec. 29, T1N, R1E
   (D) Sec. 25, T1N, R1E

3. How many miles apart are the guide meridians?
   (A) 12
   (B) 4
   (C) 24
   (D) 18

4. The east-west lines at which guide meridians are adjusted are
   (A) adjustment lines
   (B) base line extensions
   (C) parallels of adjustment
   (D) standard parallels

5. The number of acres in 1 square mile is
   (A) 640
   (B) 5280
   (C) 1000
   (D) 160

Questions 6–13 concern Figure A, shown at right.

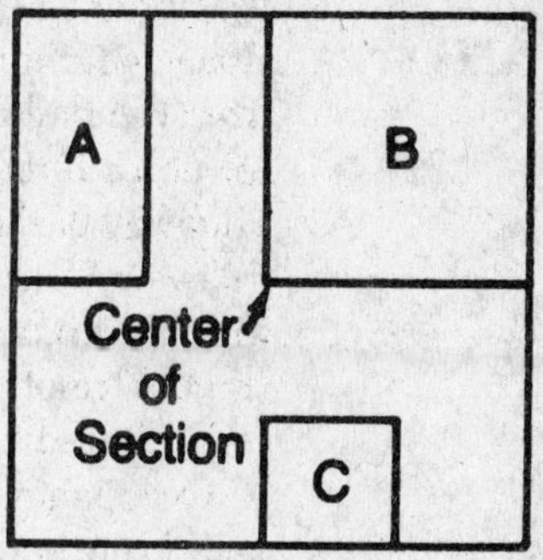

Figure *A.*
Diagram of a Section

6. How many acres does the tract marked A contain?
   (A) 640
   (B) 160
   (C) 80
   (D) 40

7. How many acres does the tract marked B contain?
   (A) 640
   (B) 160
   (C) 80
   (D) 40

8. How many acres does the tract marked C contain?
   (A) 640
   (B) 160
   (C) 80
   (D) 40

9. The description of Tract A is
   (A) NW¼, NW¼
   (B) N½, NE¼
   (C) W½, NW¼
   (D) W½, N½

10. The description of Tract B is
    (A) NE¼
    (B) NE½
    (C) NE¼, NE¼
    (D) NE¼, NE¼, N½

11. The description of Tract C is
    (A) SE¼, SE¼
    (B) SW¼, SW¼
    (C) SE¼, SW¼
    (D) SW¼, SE¼

12. Assume that the illustrated section is Section 8 of a particular township. What section would you be in if you traveled exactly 2¾ miles due *south* from the *center* of Section 8?
    (A) Sec. 11
    (B) Sec. 12
    (C) Sec. 20
    (D) Sec. 29

13. Assume that the southeast corner of the section is exactly 28 miles south of the base line and 11 miles west of the principal meridian. In what township is it located?
    (A) T2W, R5S
    (B) T5S, R2W
    (C) T6S, R2W
    (D) T6S, R3W

14. The line behind which all buildings on a lot must be placed is called the
    (A) set line
    (B) setback, or building line
    (C) construction limit
    (D) backup, or setdown line

15. Which of the following is most nearly due west?
    (A) N 88° W
    (B) N 79°66′43″ W
    (C) S 89°58′3″ W
    (D) W 0°4′ N

16. Which of the following would *not* be a proper way to begin a metes and bounds description of Lot 10?
    (A) "Beginning at the southwest corner of Lot 10 . . ."
    (B) "Beginning at the street intersection nearest Lot 10 . . ."
    (C) "Beginning at a point 110 feet northwest of Lot 10 . . ."
    (D) All of the above

17. "All that land known as the Jones Farm" is which kind of description?
    (A) Invalid
    (B) Occupancy
    (C) Metes only
    (D) Rural

Questions 18–23 refer to the plat shown in Figure B.

18. Which lot has the most footage on Circuit Court?
    (A) Lot 10   (C) Lot 20
    (B) Lot 18   (D) Lot 21

19. Which lot has the most street footage?
    (A) Lot 7   (C) Lot 20
    (B) Lot 18   (D) Lot 21

20. How many lots border on Circuit Court?
    (A) 9   (C) 16
    (B) 15   (D) 21

21. How many lots have sides that are *not* straight?
    (A) 8   (C) 10
    (B) 9   (D) 11

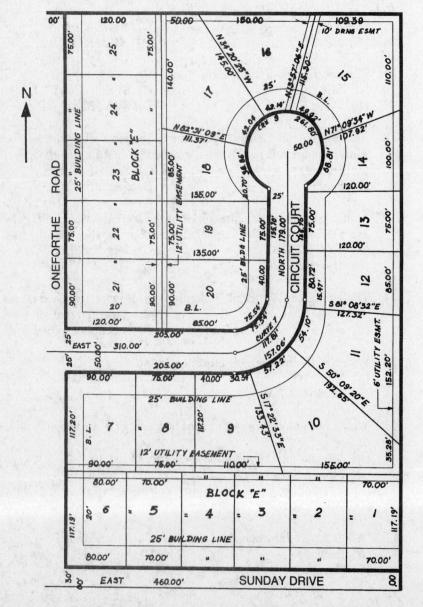

Figure B.   Block E Quagmire Village, Metropolis, Snakebite County, Florida

22. How many lots front on more than one street?
    (A) 1
    (B) 2
    (C) 3
    (D) 4

23. Which lots have the *fewest* straight sides?
    (A) Lots 10, 11, 14, 15, 16, 17, 20
    (B) Lots 10, 11, 14, 16
    (C) Lots 11, 14, 16
    (D) Lots 11, 16

ANSWERS

1. A	7. B	13. B	19. D
2. D	8. D	14. B	20. B
3. C	9. C	15. C	21. C
4. D	10. A	16. D	22. C
5. A	11. D	17. B	23. D
6. C	12. D	18. C	

Chapter 8/*Sales Contracts*

A contract for the sale of real estate is a document that sets forth the rights and obligations of the purchaser(s) and seller(s). Days, weeks, or months later, at a ceremony called a *closing*, the seller(s) will deliver a deed that transfers legal title to the property; the purchaser(s) will surrender payment for the property as set forth in the contract for sale.

A contract for sale of real estate is "*the deal.*" This means that all the provisions that the parties want, all the "ifs, ands, or buts," must be set forth in this contract; all the negotiation, "wheeling and dealing," "give and take," and the like have to occur and be settled *before* the contract for sale exists. Once there is a contract for sale, it is too late for any more negotiation; all the parties to the agreement must abide by it, and none of them can change anything in it unless all other parties agree to the change. Therefore, it is vitally important that the parties to this contract make sure that all the conditions and requirements that they want with regard to the sale and purchase of the real estate are contained in the sale contract.

It is possible to sell property merely by delivery of a deed in exchange for payment and thus bypass the contract for sale. However, the parties, especially the buyer, face a lot of risk. A title search must be performed to satisfy the buyer that the seller can give ownership, and time is required for such a search. The buyer may also need time to arrange financing. Most lenders will consider real estate loans only after they have studied the contract for sale. In short, it is indeed rare for a transfer of real estate to be completed without such a contract. Furthermore, it is of paramount importance that all parties involved in a transaction understand their contractual obligations and privileges.

Upon completion of the contract for sale, the purchaser (*vendee*) receives an "equitable" title. Equity, in law, attempts to treat things as they should be to be fair and considers the purchaser to have "equitable title," although legal title remains with the seller (*vendor*) until closing. Therefore, if there is a casualty loss—a fire, for example—before closing, the risk may be upon the purchaser. However, considering that equity is intended to be fair, the risk of loss before closing should not pass automatically to the purchaser in all instances. There are situations in which the seller should be responsible and courts will hold him to be so. *To avoid potential problems concerning risk of loss, the contract for sale should specify who has the burden of loss prior to closing and which party is obligated to complete the transaction and to receive the proceeds from insurance.*

The Statute of Frauds requires that contracts for the sale of real estate be in writing to be enforceable. The *parol evidence* rule prevents oral testimony from being introduced when it conflicts with better (written) evidence. Consequently, care should be exercised in the preparation of a contract for sale.

A contract for sale should contain any *contingency clauses*, or *contingencies*, that the parties want. These "what if?" provisions often allow a buyer or seller to cancel the deal without penalty if something does or doesn't happen (the *if* part). For example, the seller may have her home on the market because her employer is transferring her, but wants to be able to cancel the deal *if* the transfer falls through. A buyer may need to sell his own home in order to be able to buy the seller's property, so he wants to be able to cancel the deal *if* he can't make the sale of his own property within a reasonable time. A great many homebuying purchase contracts are *contingent upon financing*; this means that the buyer can cancel the deal *if* he is unable to get a suitable mortgage loan. Many preprinted contracts for sale have common contingencies already written into them: The buyer can cancel the deal *if* the seller can't provide clear title, *if* the property is severely damaged before closing, *if* termite infestation is found. The seller can cancel the deal *if* the buyer doesn't get financing approval within a certain time. (Note that Florida law will "provide" some of these contingencies automatically.)

Florida requires that the seller provide the buyer with a *disclosure* of certain conditions, defects, and so on, of the property; if there aren't any, then the seller must provide the buyer with a statement that no such conditions exist. If possible, the disclosure must be made available to a prospective buyer before an offer is made, usually when the first contact between prospect and seller and/or listing broker occurs. In a brokered transaction, such disclosure normally will be provided to the broker when the property is listed. The broker then will provide a copy of it to all potential buyers who examine the property. If the transaction is not brokered, it is the seller's responsibility to provide the disclosure to all potential buyers.

Figure 8-1 shows a Florida *Contract for Sale and Purchase* that is commonly used. Note that adequate provision is made for all parts discussed in the next two sections. *Read this contract carefully!* Note the provisions for various kinds of notices, disclosures, and so on. They all won't be used in every transaction, but many of these items could show up in examination questions.

A deposit, or *earnest money*, is not necessarily a legal requirement of a contract for sale (the parties' promises to perform in the future usually are sufficient as the required consideration), but is very common that the buyer put down a cash deposit at the time the contract for sale is agreed upon. It serves as evidence of his good-faith intentions to perform under the contract. Earnest money usually is held by the seller's broker, if there is one.

Requirements of a Valid Contract for Sale

There are six essentials of a valid contract for the sale of real estate:
1. Competent parties
2. Offer and acceptance
3. Adequate description of the property
4. Consideration
5. Lawful purpose
6. Written and signed

1. COMPETENT PARTIES

Parties must be considered legally competent. Insane persons, drunkards and drug users, sick persons, persons under great duress, and mentally handicapped persons may be considered incompetent. Those who have been declared incompetent by courts may sell property through their legal guardians. Corporation officers may contract for their corporation when they have such authority. A cautious party should request to see such authority in the corporation's by-laws and the minutes of directors' meetings.

Minors may buy and sell property, and they also have the right to disaffirm (repudiate) their transactions. Shortly after reaching adult age, minors can disaffirm sales and purchases, including unprofitable ones, whereas adults, even those who deal with minors, do not have this powerful right.

2. OFFER AND ACCEPTANCE

For a contract to be valid, the parties involved must be identified. Furthermore, one party must offer something and the other accept. When they reach an agreement, there is said to be a "meeting of the minds." A mutual mistake, misrepresentation, fraud, undue influence, and duress are possible reasons for a contract to be declared void.

One party who offers a contract to another may be presented with a counteroffer. At that point the person who made the original offer is no longer bound by it and may accept or reject the counteroffer as he pleases. There is no meeting of the minds until both parties agree to a contract.

Residential Sale and Purchase Contract
FLORIDA ASSOCIATION OF REALTORS®

1* Effective Date: _____ (To be completed by the last party to sign or initial acceptance of the final offer.)

PARTIES AND DESCRIPTION OF PROPERTY

3* **1. SALE AND PURCHASE:** _____ ("Seller")

4* and _____ ("Buyer")

5 agree to sell and buy on the terms and conditions specified below the property described as:

6* Address: _____

7* _____ County: _____

8* Legal Description: _____

9* _____

10* _____ Tax Folio No: _____

11 together with all improvements and attached items, including fixtures, built-in furnishings and appliances, ceiling fans, light
12 fixtures, attached wall-to-wall carpeting, rods, draperies and other window coverings. The only other items included in the
13* purchase are: _____

14* _____

15* The following attached items are excluded from the purchase: _____

16* _____

17 The real and personal property described above as included in the purchase is referred to as the "Property." Personal property
18 listed in this Contract is included in the sales price, has no contributory value and is being left for **Seller's** convenience.

PRICE AND FINANCING

20* **2. PURCHASE PRICE:** $_____ payable by **Buyer** in U.S. currency as follows:

22* (a) $_____ Deposit received (checks are subject to clearance) _____, 19_____ by
23* _____ for _____ ("Escrow Agent")
24 *Signature* *Name of Company*

25* (b) $_____ Additional deposit to be made by _____, 19_____
26* (c) _____ Total mortgages (see Paragraph **3** below) (express as a dollar amount or percentage)
27* (d) $_____ Other: _____
28* (e) $_____ Balance to close (not including **Buyer's** closing costs, prepaid items and prorations). All
29 funds paid at closing must be paid by locally drawn cashier's check or wired funds.

31* **3. FINANCING:** (Check as applicable) ❑ **(a) Buyer** will pay cash for the Property with no financing contingency.
32* ❑ (b) This Contract is contingent on **Buyer** qualifying and obtaining (1) and/or (2) below by _____, 19_____
33 (if left blank then Closing Date or within 45 days from Effective Date, whichever occurs first):
34* ❑ (1) A commitment for new ❑ conventional ❑ FHA ❑ VA financing for $_____ (including PMI, MIP, VA funding
35* fee) or _____% of the purchase price at the prevailing interest rate and loan costs (if FHA or VA , see attached addendum).
36* ❑ (2) Approval for **Seller** financing or assumption of mortgage (see attached addendum).
37* **Buyer** will apply for financing within _____ days from Effective Date (5 days if left blank) and will timely provide any and all
38 credit, employment, financial and other information required by the lender. Either party may cancel this Contract if **(i) Buyer**,
39 after using diligence and good faith, cannot obtain the financing, or **(ii)** the financing is denied because the Property
40 appraises below the purchase price and either **Buyer** elects not to proceed or the parties are unable to renegotiate the
41 purchase price. Upon cancellation, **Buyer** will return all **Seller**-provided title evidence, surveys and association documents
42 and **Buyer's** deposit(s) will be returned after Escrow Agent receives proper authorization from all interested parties.

CLOSING

44 **4. CLOSING DATE; OCCUPANCY:** This Contract will be closed, the deed and possession delivered, the Property swept clean
45* and **Seller's** personal property removed on or before _____, 19_____, unless extended by other provisions of this Contract.

47* **5. CLOSING PROCEDURE; COSTS:** ❑ **Buyer** ❑ **Seller** will select a closing agent acceptable to **Buyer** and **Buyer's** lender.
48 If title insurance insures **Buyer** for title defects arising between the title binder effective date and recording of **Buyer's** deed,
49 closing agent will disburse at closing the net sale proceeds to **Seller** and brokerage fees to Broker as per Paragraph **18**. In
50 addition to other expenses provided in this Contract, **Seller** and **Buyer** will pay the costs indicated below.
51 **(a) Seller Costs: Seller** will pay taxes on the deed and recording fees for documents needed to cure title; certified,
52 confirmed and ratified special assessment liens and, if an improvement is substantially completed as of Effective Date, an
53 amount equal to the last estimate of the assessment; up to 1.5% of the purchase price for repairs to warranted items
54 **("Repair Limit")**; and up to 1.5% of the purchase price for wood-destroying organism treatment and repairs **("Termite
55* Repair Limit")**; Title Evidence (see Paragraph **10**): (check one) ❑ (1) abstract ❑ (2) prior policy ❑ (3) owner's title
56* insurance commitment and policy; Other: _____
57 **(b) Buyer Costs: Buyer** will pay taxes and recording fees on notes and mortgages; recording fees on the deed and
58 financing statements; loan expenses; pending special assessment liens; lender's title policy; inspections; survey; flood
59 insurance; and owner's title insurance policy, if **Seller** provides an abstract or prior policy as title evidence.
60* **(c) Other Costs:** ❑ **Buyer** ❑ **Seller** ❑ **Both parties equally** will pay for the abstract/title search, examination, related charges.
61* ❑ **Buyer** ❑ **Seller** ❑ **N/A** will pay for a home warranty plan issued by _____ at a cost
62* not to exceed $_____. A home warranty plan provides for repair or replacement of a home's mechanical systems
63 and major built-in appliances in the event of breakdown due to normal wear and tear during the agreement period.
64 **(d) Prorations:** The following items will be made current (if applicable) and prorated as of the day before Closing Date: real estate
65 taxes, interest, bonds, assessments, association fees, insurance, rents and other current expenses and revenues of the Property.
66 If taxes and assessments for the current year cannot be determined, the previous year's rates will be used with adjustment for
67 homestead and other exemptions, improvements and increase due to change in ownership.
68 **(e) Tax Withholding: Buyer** and **Seller** will comply with the Foreign Investment in Real Property Tax Act, which may
69 require **Seller** to provide additional cash at closing if **Seller** is a "foreign person" as defined by federal law.

PROPERTY CONDITION

71 **6. INSPECTION PERIODS: Buyer** will complete the inspections referenced in Paragraphs **7** and **8(a)(2)** by
72* _____, 19_____ (within 10 days from Effective Date if left blank) ("Inspection Period"); the wood-
73* destroying organism inspection by _____, 19_____ (prior to closing if left blank); and the walk-through
74 inspection on the day before Closing Date or any other time agreeable to the parties.

75* **Buyer** (____)(____) and **Seller** (____)(____) acknowledge receipt of a copy of this page, which is Page 1 of 4 Pages.

FAR-3 Rev. 10/95 ©1995 Florida Association of REALTORS® All Rights Reserved

Figure 8-1. Contract for Sale

76 **7. REAL PROPERTY DISCLOSURE: Seller** represents that **Seller** does not know of any facts that materially affect the value
77 of the Property, including violations of governmental laws, rules and regulations, other than those that **Buyer** can readily
78 observe or that are known by or have been disclosed to **Buyer.**
79   **(a) Energy Efficiency: Buyer** may, within the Inspection Period, have the Property's energy efficiency rating determined,
80   but no contingency or repair obligation is connected with the outcome. **Buyer** acknowledges receipt of the Florida Building
81   Energy-Efficiency Rating System brochure. If this is a new home, the builder's FL-EPL card is attached as an addendum.
82   **(b) Radon Gas:** Radon is a naturally occurring radioactive gas that, when it has accumulated in a building in sufficient
83   quantities may present health risks to persons who are exposed to it over time. Levels of radon that exceed federal and
84   state guidelines have been found in buildings in Florida. Additional information regarding radon and radon testing may
85   be obtained from your county public health unit. **Buyer** may, within the Inspection Period, have an appropriately
86   licensed person test the Property for radon. If the radon level exceeds acceptable EPA standards, **Seller** may choose
87   to reduce the radon level to an acceptable EPA level, failing which either party may cancel this Contract.
88   **(c) Flood Zone: Buyer** is advised to verify by survey, with the lender and with appropriate government agencies which
89   flood zone the Property is in, whether flood insurance is required and what restrictions apply to improving the Property
90   and rebuilding in the event of casualty. If the Property is in a Special Flood Hazard Area or Coastal High Hazard Area and
91   the buildings are built below the minimum flood elevation, **Buyer** may cancel this Contract by delivering written notice to
92   **Seller** within 10 days from Effective Date, failing which **Buyer** accepts the existing location of the Property and buildings.
93   **(d) Lead Hazards:** If the Property was built before 1978, **Buyer** acknowledges receipt of an EPA lead-based paint
94   hazards brochure and lead-based paint warning statement (see attached addendum) before signing this Contract.

95 **8. MAINTENANCE, INSPECTIONS AND REPAIR: Seller** will keep the Property in the same condition from Effective Date
96 until closing, except for normal wear and tear ("maintenance requirement") and repairs required by this Contract. **Seller**
97 will provide access and utilities for **Buyer's** inspections. **Buyer** will repair all damages to the Property resulting from the
98 inspections and return the Property to its pre-inspection condition. If **Seller** is unable to complete required repairs or
99 treatments prior to closing, **Seller** will give **Buyer** a credit at closing for the cost of the repairs **Seller** was obligated to
100 make. **Seller** will assign all assignable repair and treatment contracts to **Buyer** at closing.
101   **(a) Warranty, Inspections and Repair:**
102   **(1) Warranty: Seller** warrants that non-leased major appliances and heating, cooling, mechanical, electrical, security,
103   sprinkler, septic and plumbing systems, seawall, dock and pool equipment, if any, are and will be maintained in working
104   condition until closing; that the structures (including roofs) and pool, if any, are structurally sound and watertight; and that
105   the Property has proper permits. **Seller** does not warrant and is not required to repair cosmetic conditions, unless the
106   cosmetic condition resulted from a defect in a warranted item. **Seller** is not obligated to bring any item into compliance
107   with existing building code regulations unless necessary to repair a warranted item. "Working condition" means
108   operating in the manner in which the item was designed to operate and "cosmetic conditions" means aesthetic
109   imperfections that do not affect the working condition of the item, including tears, worn spots and discoloration of floor
110   coverings/ wallpapers/window treatments; nail holes, scratches, dents, scrapes, chips and caulking in bathroom ceiling/
111   walls/ flooring/tile/fixtures/mirrors; and minor cracks in windows/driveways/sidewalks/pool decks/garage and patio floors.
112   **(2) Professional Inspection: Buyer** may have warranted items inspected by a person who specializes in and holds an
113   occupational license (if required by law) to conduct home inspections or who holds a Florida license to repair and
114   maintain the items inspected ("professional inspector"). **Buyer** must, within 5 days from the end of the Inspection
115   Period, deliver written notice of any items that are not in the condition warranted and a copy of the inspector's written
116   report, if any, to **Seller**. If **Buyer** fails to deliver timely written notice, **Buyer** waives **Seller's** warranty and accepts the
117   items listed in subparagraph (a) in their "as is" conditions, except that **Seller** must meet the maintenance requirement.
118   **(3) Repair: Seller** is obligated only to make repairs necessary to bring warranted items into the condition warranted,
119   up to the Repair Limit. **Seller** may, within 5 days from receipt of **Buyer's** notice of items that are not in the condition
120   warranted, have a second inspection made by a professional inspector and will report repair estimates to **Buyer**. If
121   the first and second inspection reports differ and the parties cannot resolve the differences, **Buyer** and **Seller** together
122   will choose, and equally split the cost of, a third inspector, whose written report will be binding on the parties. If the
123   cost to repair warranted items equals or is less than the Repair Limit, **Seller** will have the repairs made in a workmanlike
124   manner by an appropriately licensed person. If the cost to repair warranted items exceeds the Repair Limit, either
125   party may cancel this Contract unless either party pays the excess or **Buyer** designates which repairs to make at a
126   total cost to **Seller** not exceeding the Repair Limit and accepts the balance of the Property in its "as is" condition.
127   **(b) Wood-Destroying Organisms:** "Wood-destroying organism" means arthropod or plant life, including termites, powder-
128   post beetles, oldhouse borers and wood-decaying fungi, that damages or infests seasoned wood in a structure, excluding
129   fences. **Buyer** may, at **Buyer's** expense and prior to closing, have the Property inspected by a Florida-licensed pest
130   control business to determine the existence of past or present wood-destroying organism infestation and damage caused
131   by infestation. If the inspector finds evidence of infestation or damage, **Buyer** will deliver a copy of the inspector's written
132   report to **Seller** within 5 days from the date of the inspection. **Seller** will have 5 days from receipt of the inspector's report to
133   have reported damage estimated by a licensed building or general contractor and corrective treatment estimated by a
134   licensed pest control business. **Seller** will have treatments and repairs made by an appropriately licensed person at
135   **Seller's** expense up to the Termite Repair Limit. If the cost to treat and repair the Property exceeds the Termite Repair
136   Limit, either party may pay the excess, failing which either party may cancel this Contract. **Seller** is not obligated to treat
137   the Property if there is no visible live infestation, the Property has previously been treated and **Seller** transfers a current full
138   treatment warranty to **Buyer** at closing. If **Buyer** fails to timely deliver the inspector's written report, **Buyer** accepts the
139   Property as is with regard to wood-destroying organism infestation and damage, subject to the maintenance requirement.
140   **(c) Walk-through Inspection: Buyer** may walk through the Property solely to verify that **Seller** has made repairs required by
141   this Contract and has met the maintenance requirement. No other issues may be raised as a result of the walk-through
142   inspection. If **Buyer** fails to conduct this inspection, **Seller's** repair and maintenance obligations will be deemed fulfilled.

143 **9. RISK OF LOSS:** If any portion of the Property is damaged by fire or other casualty before closing and can be restored within 45 days
144 from the Closing Date to substantially the same condition as it was on Effective Date, **Seller** will, at **Seller's** expense, restore the Property
145 and the Closing Date will be extended accordingly. If the restoration cannot be completed in time, **Buyer** may accept the Property "as is"
146 with **Seller** assigning the insurance proceeds for the Property to **Buyer** at closing, failing which either party may cancel this Contract.

147   **TITLE**
148 **10. TITLE: Seller** will convey marketable title to the Property by statutory warranty deed or trustee, personal
149 representative or guardian deed as appropriate to **Seller's** status.
150   **(a) Title Evidence:** Title evidence will show legal access to the Property and marketable title of record in **Seller** in accordance
151   with current title standards adopted by the Florida Bar, subject only to the following title exceptions, none of which prevent
152   residential use of the Property: covenants, easements and restrictions of record; matters of plat; existing zoning and
153   government regulations; oil, gas and mineral rights of record if there is no right of entry; current taxes; mortgages that **Buyer**
154   will assume; and encumbrances that **Seller** will discharge at or before closing. **Seller** will, prior to closing, deliver to **Buyer**
155   **Seller's** choice of one of the following types of title evidence, which must be generally accepted in the county where the
156   Property is located (specify in Paragraph 5(a) the selected type). **Seller** will use option (3) in Palm Beach County. If **Seller**
157   uses option (1) or (2), delivery will be by the earlier of 20 days after Effective Date or 15 days before Closing Date.

158 Buyer (____) (____) and Seller (____) (____) acknowledge receipt of a copy of this page, which is Page 2 of 4 Pages.

FAR-3 Rev. 10/95   ©1995 Florida Association of Realtors®   All Rights Reserved

Figure 8-1.   Contract for Sale (*continued*)

159 (1) An existing abstract of title from a company satisfactory to **Buyer** and certified to Effective Date.
160 (2) **Seller's prior owner's title policy** acceptable to the proposed insurer as a base for reissuance of coverage along with
161 copies of all policy exceptions and an abstract continuation or computer printout from the policy effective date and certified
162 to **Buyer** or **Buyer's** closing agent, who may order the printouts at **Seller's** expense if necessary for certification purposes.
163 (3) A title insurance commitment issued by a qualified title insurer acceptable to **Buyer** and **Buyer's** lender in the
164 amount of the purchase price and subject only to title exceptions set forth in this Contract.
165 (b) Title Examination: **Buyer** will examine the title evidence and deliver written notice to **Seller**, within 5 days from receipt
166 of title evidence but no later than closing, of any defects that make the title unmarketable. **Seller** will have 30 days from
167 receipt of **Buyer's** notice of defects ("Curative Period") to cure the defects at **Seller's** expense. If **Seller** cures the
168 defects within the Curative Period, **Seller** will deliver written notice to **Buyer** and the parties will close the transaction on
169 Closing Date or within 10 days from **Buyer's** receipt of **Seller's** notice if Closing Date has passed. If **Seller** is unable to
170 cure the defects within the Curative Period, **Seller** will deliver written notice to **Buyer** and **Buyer** will, within 10 days from
171 receipt of **Seller's** notice, either cancel this Contract or accept title with existing defects and close the transaction.
172 (c) Survey: **Buyer** may, prior to Closing Date and at **Buyer's** expense, have the Property surveyed and deliver written notice
173 to **Seller**, within 5 days from receipt of survey but no later than closing, of any encroachments on the Property, encroachments
174 by the Property's improvements on other lands or deed restriction or zoning violations. Any such encroachment or violation
175 will be treated as a title defect and **Buyer's** and **Seller's** obligations will be determined in accordance with subparagraph **(b)**
176 above. If any part of the Property lies seaward of the coastal construction control line, **Seller** will provide **Buyer** with an
177 affidavit or survey delineating the line's location on the property, unless **Buyer** waives this requirement in writing.

MISCELLANEOUS

179 **11. EFFECTIVE DATE; TIME:** The "Effective Date" of this Contract is the date on which the last of the parties initials or signs
180 the latest offer. The last party to initial or sign the Contract should enter the date on the "Effective Date" line on page 1.
181 **Time is of the essence for all provisions of this Contract.** All time periods will be computed in business days (a "business
182 day" is every calendar day except Saturday, Sunday and national legal holidays) and will end at 5:00 p.m. local time of the
183 appropriate day. For purposes of this Contract, the term "local" means in the county where the Property is located.

184 **12. NOTICES:** All notices will be made to the parties and Broker by mail, personal delivery or electronic media. **Buyer's**
185 failure to deliver timely written notice to Seller, when such notice is required by this Contract, regarding any contingencies
186 will render that contingency null and void and the Contract will be construed as if the contingency did not exist.

187 **13. COMPLETE AGREEMENT:** This Contract is the entire agreement between **Buyer** and **Seller**, and all representations by
188 Broker or found in printed material about the Property, including the listing information sheet, on which the parties relied
189 are expressed in this Contract. **Except for brokerage agreements, no prior or present agreements or representations will**
190 **bind Buyer, Seller or Broker unless incorporated into this Contract.** Modifications of this Contract will not be binding
191 unless in writing, signed and delivered by the party to be bound. Signatures, initials and written modifications
192 communicated by electronic media will be binding. Handwritten or typewritten terms inserted in or attached to this
193 Contract prevail over preprinted terms. If any provision of this Contract is or becomes invalid or unenforceable, all
194 remaining provisions will continue to be fully effective. This Contract will not be recorded in any public records.

195 **14. ASSIGNABILITY; PERSONS BOUND: Buyer** may not assign this Contract without **Seller's** written consent. The terms
196 "**Buyer**," "**Seller**," and "**Broker**" may be singular or plural. This Contract is binding on the heirs, administrators, executors,
197 personal representatives and assigns (if permitted) of **Buyer**, **Seller** and Broker.

DEFAULT AND DISPUTE RESOLUTION

199 **15. DEFAULT: (a) Seller Default:** If for any reason other than failure of **Seller** to make **Seller's** title marketable after diligent effort,
200 **Seller** fails, refuses or neglects to perform this Contract, **Buyer** may choose to receive a return of **Buyer's** deposit without
201 waiving the right to seek damages or to seek specific performance as per Paragraph 16. **Seller** will also be liable to Broker for
202 the full amount of the brokerage fee. **(b) Buyer Default:** If **Buyer** fails to perform this Contract within the time specified, including
203 timely payment of all deposits, **Seller** may choose to retain and collect all deposits paid and agreed to be paid as liquidated
204 damages or to seek specific performance as per Paragraph 16; and Broker will, upon demand, receive 50% of all deposits
205 paid and agreed to be paid (to be split equally among cooperating brokers) up to the full amount of the brokerage fee.

206 **16. DISPUTE RESOLUTION:** This Contract will be construed under Florida law. All controversies, claims, and other matters in
207 question between the parties arising out of or relating to this Contract or its breach will be settled as follows:
208 (a) Disputes concerning entitlement to deposits made and agreed to be made: **Buyer** and **Seller** will have 15 days from
209 the date conflicting demands are made to attempt to resolve the dispute through **mediation**. If that fails, Escrow Agent
210 will submit the dispute, if so required by Florida law, to Escrow Agent's choice of mediation, arbitration, a Florida court
212 or the Florida Real Estate Commission. **Buyer** and **Seller** will be bound by any resulting settlement or order.
213 (b) All other disputes: **Buyer** and **Seller** will have 15 days from the date a dispute arises between them to attempt to
214 resolve the matter through mediation, failing which the parties will resolve the dispute through neutral binding
215 **arbitration** in the county in which the Property is located. The arbitrator may not alter the Contract terms or award
216 any remedy not provided for in this Contract. The award will be based on the greater weight of the evidence and will
217 state findings of fact and the contractual authority on which it is based. If the parties agree to use discovery, it will
218 be in accordance with the Florida Rules of Civil Procedure and the arbitrator will resolve all discovery-related
219 disputes. Any disputes with a real estate licensee named in Paragraph 18 will be submitted to arbitration only if the
220 licensee's broker consents in writing to become a party to the proceeding. This clause will survive closing.
221 (c) Mediation and Arbitration; Expenses: "Mediation" is a process in which parties attempt to resolve a dispute by
222 submitting it to an impartial mediator who facilitates the resolution of the dispute but who is not empowered to impose
223 a settlement on the parties. Mediation will be in accordance with the rules of the American Mediation Association or
224 other mediator agreed on by the parties. The parties will equally divide the mediation fee, if any. "Arbitration" is a
225 process in which the parties resolve a dispute by a hearing before a neutral person who decides the matter and
226 whose decision is binding on the parties. Arbitration will be in accordance with the rules of the American Arbitration
227 Association or other arbitrator agreed on by the parties. Each party to any arbitration will pay its own fees, costs and
228 expenses, including attorney's fees, and will equally split the arbitrators' fees and administrative fees of arbitration.

ESCROW AGENT AND BROKER

230 **17. ESCROW AGENT: Buyer** and **Seller** authorize Escrow Agent to receive, deposit and hold funds and other items in escrow
231 and, subject to clearance, disburse them upon proper authorization and in accordance with the terms of this Contract,
232 including disbursing brokerage fees. Escrow Agent will deposit funds in a federally insured escrow account. The parties
233 agree that Escrow Agent will not be liable to any person for misdelivery of escrowed items to **Buyer** or **Seller**, unless the
234 misdelivery is due to Escrow Agent's willful breach of this Contract or gross negligence. If Escrow Agent interpleads the
235 subject matter of the escrow, Escrow Agent will pay the filing fees and costs from the deposit and will recover reasonable
236 attorney's fees and costs to be paid from the escrowed funds or equivalent and charged and awarded as court costs in
237 favor of the prevailing party. All claims against Escrow Agent will be arbitrated, so long as Escrow Agent consents to arbitrate.

238 Buyer (____) (____) and Seller (____) (____) acknowledge receipt of a copy of this page, which is Page 3 of 4 Pages.

FAR-3   Rev. 10/95   ©1995 Florida Association of REALTORS®   All Rights Reserved

Figure 8-1.   Contract for Sale (*continued*)

239 **18. BROKERS:** The licensee(s) and brokerage(s) named below are collectively referred to as "Broker." **Seller** and **Buyer**
240 confirm the following agency or transaction brokerage relationship(s) and acknowledge that the brokerage(s) named
241 below are the procuring cause of this transaction. **Instruction to Closing Agent: Seller** and **Buyer** direct closing agent to
242 disburse at closing the full amount of the brokerage fees specified in separate brokerage agreements with the parties
243 and cooperative agreements between the brokers, or in the absence of such, as indicated below.

244 _____   _____
245 *Selling Real Estate Licensee*   *Listing Real Estate Licensee*
246 _____   _____
247 *Selling Brokerage / Brokerage Fee.* _____   *Listing Brokerage / Brokerage Fee:* _____
248 ❑ **Buyer's** agent ❑ disclosed dual agent ❑ transaction broker   ❑ **Seller's** agent ❑ disclosed dual agent ❑ transaction broker
249 ❑ **Seller's** agent
250

251 **19. PROFESSIONAL ADVICE; BROKER LIABILITY:** Broker advises **Buyer** and **Seller** to verify all facts and representations
252 that are important to them and to consult an appropriate professional for legal advice (for example, interpreting contracts,
253 determining the effect of laws on the Property and transaction, status of title, foreign investor reporting requirements, etc.)
254 and for tax, property condition, environmental and other specialized advice. **Buyer** and **Seller** hold Broker harmless and
255 release Broker and Broker's officers, directors, agents and employees from all liability for loss or damage, whether caused
256 by Broker's negligence or otherwise, in connection with **(1) Seller's** failure to disclose material facts in accordance with this
257 Contract; **(2)** Broker's representations regarding the Property's condition or square footage; **(3)** Broker's performance, at
258 **Buyer's** and/or **Seller's** request, of any task beyond the scope of services regulated by Chapter 475, F.S., as amended,
259 including Broker's referral, recommendation or retention of any vendor, **(4)** services or products provided by any vendor, and
260 **(5)** expenses incurred by any vendor. **Buyer** and **Seller** each assume full responsibility for selecting and compensating
261 vendors. For purposes of this paragraph, Broker will be treated as a party to this Contract. This paragraph will survive closing.
262

ADDENDA AND ADDITIONAL TERMS

264 **20. ADDENDA:** The following additional terms are included in addenda and incorporated into this Contract (check if applicable):
265 ❑ A. Condo. Assn.   ❑ G. New Mort. Rates   ❑ M. Housing Older Persons.   ❑ S. Sale of Buyer's Property
266 ❑ B. Homeowners' Assn.   ❑ H. As Is w/Right to Inspect ❑ N. Pre-1978 Housing Stmt.   ❑ T. Rezoning
267 ❑ C. Seller Financing   ❑ I. Self-Inspections   ❑ O. Interest-Bearing Account   ❑ U. Assignment
268 ❑ D. Mort. Assumption   ❑ J. Insulation Disclosure   ❑ P. Back-up Contract.   ❑ V. Additional Clauses
269 ❑ E. FHA Financing   ❑ K. Property Disclosure Stmt. ❑ Q. Broker - Pers. Int. in Prop. ❑ Other _____
270 ❑ F. VA Financing   ❑ L. Flood Insurance Reqd.   ❑ R. Rentals   ❑ Other _____
271

272 **21. ADDITIONAL TERMS:** _____
273 _____
274 _____
275 _____
276 _____
277 _____
278 _____
279 _____
280 _____
281 _____
282 _____
283 _____
284 _____

285 This is intended to be a legally binding contract. If not fully understood, seek the advice of an attorney prior to signing.

286   **OFFER**
287 **Buyer** offers to purchase the Property on the above terms and conditions. Unless this Contract is signed by **Seller** and a
288 copy delivered to **Buyer** no later than _____ ❑ a.m. ❑ p.m. on _____, 19____, this offer will be
289 revoked and **Buyer's** deposit refunded subject to clearance of funds.
290
291 Date: _____   **Buyer:** _____   Tax ID No: _____
292   Print name: _____
293 Date: _____   **Buyer:** _____   Tax ID No: _____
294   Print name: _____
295 Phone: _____   Address: _____
296 Fax: _____

297
298   **ACCEPTANCE / COUNTER OFFER / REJECTION**
299 ❑ **Seller** accepts **Buyer's** offer and agrees to sell the Property on the above terms and conditions.
300 ❑ **Seller** counters **Buyer's** offer (to accept the counter offer, **Buyer** must sign or initial the counter offered terms and deliver a
301 copy of the acceptance to **Seller** by _____ ❑ a.m. ❑ p.m. on _____, 19____): _____
302 _____
303 _____
304 ❑ **Seller** rejects **Buyer's** offer.
305
306 Date: _____   **Seller:** _____   Tax ID No: _____
307   Print name: _____
308 Date: _____   **Seller:** _____   Tax ID No: _____
309   Print name: _____
310 Phone: _____   Address: _____
311 Fax: _____

312 **Buyer** (____) (____) and **Seller** (____) (____) acknowledge receipt of a copy of this page, which is Page 4 of 4 Pages.

The Florida Association of REALTORS and local Board/Association of REALTORS make no representation as to the legal validity or adequacy of any provision of this form in any specific transaction. This standardized form should not be used in complex transactions or with extensive riders or additions. This form is available for use by the entire real estate industry and is not intended to identify the user as a REALTOR. REALTOR is a registered collective membership mark that may be used only by real estate licensees who are members of the National Association of REALTORS and who subscribe to its Code of Ethics.

The copyright laws of the United States (17 U.S. Code) forbid the unauthorized reproduction of blank forms by any means including facsimile or computerized forms.
FAR-3 Rev. 10/95   ©1995 Florida Association of REALTORS®   All Rights Reserved

Figure 8-1. Contract for Sale (*continued*)

3. ADEQUATE DESCRIPTION OF THE PROPERTY

To be adequate, a description need not be a fully accurate legal description but it must point out a specific piece of real estate in such a way that only one tract is identified. A house identified only by street number is generally adequate provided that the city, county, and state are noted. Property described as "my frame house" may be adequate provided that the seller owns only one such house.

4. CONSIDERATION

For a valid contract to exist, each party must promise to surrender something. The amount of money, other property, or services to be surrendered in exchange for the deed at closing should be clearly stated in the contract for sale.

5. LAWFUL PURPOSE

To be enforceable, an agreement must have a purpose that is not forbidden by law or is not contrary to public policy. If A writes, "I will deed my house to you provided that you promise to use it only as a place to sell drugs," there is not a legal object. The contract will be void.

6. WRITTEN AND SIGNED

To prevent fraudulent proof of a fictitious oral contract, the Statute of Frauds requires that contracts of sale for real estate be written. To be enforced by a principal, the contract must be signed by the other principal or by someone acting for him under a power of attorney. A person with a power of attorney, called an *attorney-in-fact*, need not be an attorney-at-law.

Parts of a Real Estate Contract for Sale

A contract for sale for real estate will normally contain certain parts. These parts and their purposes are as follows:

Part	Purpose
Parties	States the names of the seller (vendor) and buyer (vendee).
Property description	Provides a legal or an adequate description of the subject property and the fixtures included.
Sales price	States the amount to be paid at closing in cash and from the proceeds of financing.
Financing conditions	Purchaser stipulates acceptable conditions of financing, including the type of loan, loan-to-value ratio, interest rate, monthly payments.
Earnest money	Notes the amount of the good-faith deposit presented to the seller or his agent. Also called *hand money* or *escrow money*.
Type of deed	Describes the type of deed to be given at closing.
Title evidence	Describes the type of evidence to be considered satisfactory assurance that the seller can give title.
Title approval	Describes the rights of purchaser and seller in the event that the purchaser objects to a flaw in the title.
Property condition	States whatever changes (if any) are required to be made to the property.
Prorations	Calls for the proration of prepaid or unpaid taxes, insurance, rents, etc., between buyer and seller.
Loss	Affixes responsibility for casualty losses until closing.
Possession	Establishes a date for possession.

Closing	Establishes a date for closing.
Broker	Acknowledges the existence of a real estate broker, specifies the commission rate, and identifies the principal who will pay the commission.
Default	Describes the obligations of parties in the event one fails to perform.
Contingencies	Describes any "what if" provisions of the contract, and the conditions under which the parties may cancel the contract without penalty.
Miscellaneous provisions	States whatever other provisions buyer and seller agree upon.
Signatures	Principals, brokers, escrow agents.

Offer and Counteroffer

A common use for the contract for sale form is by the buyer in making an initial offer. The form is filled out the way the buyer wants it to be, signed by buyer and buyer's agent (if any) and submitted to the seller (through the seller's agent, if there is one). Real estate practice over the years has developed this method as the most efficient way to make and describe an offer. A very important thing to keep in mind is that if the seller signs the form without making any changes in it, *it becomes a binding contract.* Therefore, the prospective buyer, when making an offer, must be absolutely certain that the offer says everything that he/she wants it to say, no more and no less! Never forget that it must be something that the offeror will be willing to be bound by.

Usually, however, the seller will find fault with at least part of the buyer's offer, and will want to turn it down and make a *counteroffer.* Often this is accomplished by striking out the "offensive" parts of the offer, writing in any changes or other provisions desired, signing the document and initialing the changes—and then passing the revised document back to the original offeror for consideration. If this procedure goes back and forth a few times, you end up with a very messy and, possibly, very unclear instrument. Although this process is legal in Florida, it usually is avoided by writing a new contract for sale form if the first one becomes hard to read. Once a final contract is agreed upon (one party's offer accepted without change by the other), it is wise to write up the final agreement on a fresh form, if the existing one has a lot of cross-outs and changes on it.

When an offer is made, one of three things must happen:
(a) the offeree accepts it, and it becomes a contract
(b) the offeree rejects it
(c) the offeror withdraws it

To make a contract out of an offer, the offeree (person to whom the offer was made) must accept the offer in full, with no changes or amendments. Changing anything constitutes making a counteroffer, i.e., making an offer back to the original offeror. Making a counteroffer automatically means that the initial offer has been rejected; only one offer can be "on the table" at a time. However, the offeree doesn't have to make a counteroffer in order to reject an offer; an offer can be rejected without any other activity. Anytime before the offeree responds to an offer, the offeror may withdraw it. Once an offer has been rejected or withdrawn, it ceases to exist and can't be "revived" later, except as a new offer.

A very important thing to remember about the offer-counteroffer process is that *offers are not binding on anyone!* Until an offer is accepted in full (and therefore becomes a contract), there is no binding agreement of any kind. Furthermore, the language in a sale contract (toward the end) which states that the offer will expire at a certain time does *not* guarantee that the offer will remain open that long! It simply says that if there has been no response from the offeree, the offer will be automatically withdrawn at that time; however, the offeror is quite free to withdraw the offer sooner, so long as the offeree has not accepted it.

Questions on Chapter 8

1. Whenever all principals agree to the terms of a real estate contract, there has been
   (A) legality of object
   (B) meeting of the minds
   (C) reality of consent
   (D) bilateral consideration

2. The law that requires contracts for the sale of real estate to be in writing to be enforceable is the
   (A) Statute of Frauds
   (B) Statute of Limitations
   (C) Statute of Liberty
   (D) parol evidence rule

3. A person who has the power to sign the name of his principal to a contract for sale is a(n)
   (A) special agent
   (B) optionee
   (C) tenant in common
   (D) attorney-in-fact

4. A valid contract for purchase or sale of real property must be signed by the
   (A) broker
   (B) agent and seller
   (C) seller only
   (D) buyer and seller

5. Hand money paid upon the signing of a contract for sale is called
   (A) an option
   (B) a recognizance
   (C) a deposit
   (D) a freehold estate

6. What is *not* an essential element of a valid contract?
   (A) Offer and acceptance
   (B) Capacity of participants
   (C) Lack of ambiguity
   (D) Lawful purpose

7. A seller of real estate is also known as the
   (A) vendee
   (B) grantor
   (C) vendor
   (D) grantee

8. In any real estate contract for sale there must be
   (A) an offer and acceptance
   (B) a leasing arrangement
   (C) a mortgage loan
   (D) prepayment of taxes

9. If, upon receipt of an offer to purchase under certain terms, the seller makes a counteroffer, the prospective purchaser is
   (A) bound by his original offer
   (B) bound to accept the counteroffer
   (C) bound by the agent's decision
   (D) relieved of his original offer

10. A contract that has no force or effect is said to be
    (A) voidable
    (B) void
    (C) inconsequential
    (D) a contract of uncertain sale

11. A contract for sale, to be enforceable, must have
    (A) the signature of the wife of a married seller
    (B) an earnest money deposit
    (C) competent parties
    (D) witnesses

12. A party to a contract for sale normally has the right to
    (A) change the provisions in the contract if it is convenient to her
    (B) change the provisions in the contract if it will save her money
    (C) back out of the contract if she finds a better deal
    (D) none of the above

13. Which of the following would *not* be a contingency clause in a sale contract?
    (A) The settlement will be within 90 days.
    (B) The seller can cancel the deal if the buyer cannot get suitable financing.
    (C) The buyer can cancel the deal if Aunt Minnie won't lend him $10,000.
    (D) The deal is off if the property is infested with termites.

14. Which of the following is *not* true?
    (A) A contract for sale must contain a legal description of the land being sold.
    (B) An unwritten contract for sale is not enforceable in court.
    (C) Once a contract for sale is signed, there is no way to avoid going through with the deal.
    (D) A contract for sale should specify a time limit by which the sale will be closed.

15. Sam presents Joe with a real estate contract for sale, signed by Sam, offering Joe $100,000 for Joe's house. Joe agrees with all of Sam's offer, except that Joe wants the price to be $110,000. Joe should
    (A) wait for someone to make a better offer
    (B) wait for Sam to make a better offer
    (C) present Sam with a counteroffer form changing the price to $110,000
    (D) present Sam with a new real estate contract for sale with the higher price and everything else the same

16. To be valid, a real estate contract for sale must be signed by
    (A) a licensed real estate broker
    (B) the seller's attorney
    (C) the buyer's lender
    (D) none of the above

17. When a real estate contract for sale is agreed to, the buyer receives
    (A) equitable title
    (B) a new mortgage loan
    (C) the right to occupy the premises
    (D) the right to lease the property until escrow closes

18. A real estate contract for sale should include
    (A) a proper description of the real estate
    (B) the names of the buyer(s) and seller(s)
    (C) the signatures of all parties involved
    (D) all of the above

ANSWERS

1. **B**	7. **C**	13. **A**
2. **A**	8. **A**	14. **C**
3. **D**	9. **D**	15. **C**
4. **D**	10. **B**	16. **D**
5. **C**	11. **C**	17. **A**
6. **C**	12. **D**	18. **D**

Chapter 9/Deeds

To transfer (or *alienate*) an interest in real estate during the owner's lifetime, the owner (*grantor*) surrenders a *deed of conveyance* to another (the *grantee*). The deed of conveyance, also simply called a *deed*, is covered by the Statute of Frauds; consequently, it must be in writing to be enforceable. A deed should be recorded in the county courthouse to give constructive notice of its existence. Personal property is transferred by a *bill of sale*.

Types of Deeds

The parties to a deed are the *grantor* and the *grantee*. The grantor conveys title in the real estate to the grantee. There are three types of deeds: *warranty* (also known as *general warranty*), *special warranty*, and *quit claim*. In a deed, the warranty guarantees that the *title* (the ownership rights) is good; it does *not* make any guarantees as to the physical condition or usefulness of the real estate itself.

Warranty deed. In Florida, the warranty deed often is called the *statutory deed* (Figure 9-1). The warranty deed is the best one for a grantee to receive, because in this type of deed, the grantor warrants that the title is good, and that the grantor will guarantee the title *forever* against any defects that it may have had at the time the grantee received it. It contains the following assurances, or *covenants*, to the grantee:

1. the covenant of *seizin*, that the grantor has title to the property and the power to convey it.
2. the covenant of *quiet enjoyment*, that the title is good against the claims of others.
3. the covenant *against encumbrances*, that the property is free of encumbrances, except for those indicated in the public records, and/or mentioned in the deed itself.
4. the covenant of *further assurances*, that the grantor will perform whatever is necessary to make the title good.
5. The covenant of *warranty forever*, that the grantor will forever defend the rights of the grantee.

In many states deeds will enumerate each of these covenants separately. Florida law specifies that the language in the statutory deed shown in Figure 9-1 implicitly includes all these covenants. As you can see, the statutory deed is a very simple document; the meat of the document takes up fewer than eight full lines of text. The rest is for the names and signatures of the parties and for the use of the records office; the big blank space in the middle is for the description of the real estate.

Quitclaim. The quitclaim, in contrast, contains no warranties at all. In effect, in the quitclaim the grantor says to the grantee: "whatever claim that I may have to the indicated real estate is now yours," but does *not* say that the grantor has any claim at all. Basically, the grantor gives up all rights to the property without even implying that the grantor has or has ever had any claim against the specified title. It is up to the grantee to find out if, indeed, there is any claim that the grantor can convey. Obviously a quitclaim is not much use in transferring a fee simple title, because the grantor doesn't warrant anything and can't be held responsible for any title defects.

So, what use is the quitclaim? Mainly, it is used to clear up potential imperfections in the title. If a title search shows that the records are incomplete, or that it is uncertain whether someone may or may not have a claim to a particular title, a quitclaim from such a person can eliminate the problem. The language of the quitclaim is even simpler than the warranty deed:

"Grantor does remise, release and quitclaim to grantee, his heirs and assigns forever . . ." The use of the term *quitclaim* implies by law the characteristics described above.

Special warranty deed. A deed that contains some, but not all, of the covenants of a warranty deed is called a special warranty deed. Most commonly, the special warranty deed warrants only against title problems that arose during the grantor's tenure, or due to the actions or relationships of the grantor; it does not warrant against any title problems that originated previous to the grantor's involvement in the property. In contrast, the warranty deed guarantees against a defective title no matter when or how the defect(s) originated, even if from a time before the grantor owned the property.

Special warranty deeds are most often used by third-party grantors, such as executors, trustees, and the like. For example, when someone dies, his or her estate is administered and settled by an *executor*. If it involves real estate, the executor has to sell it or transfer it to the designated heirs. The executor doesn't own the property, so the executor wouldn't want to execute a warranty deed and thereby become responsible for the condition of the title. The use of a special warranty deed, in effect, tells the grantee, "I did my job properly, and I can be held responsible for it, but not for anything else." Common special warranty deeds are the *executor's deed*, the *trustee's deed* (used to transfer property from a trust), and a *referee's deed* or *sheriff's deed* (to transfer foreclosed property). In all of these, the deed is executed by someone acting on behalf of the owner; the grantor doesn't want to personally warrant the title, so the deed contains a warranty limited only to the actions and relationships of the grantor.

Deed Requirements

The following elements must be present in a deed for it to be considered valid:
1. A legally competent grantor
2. A designated grantee
3. Consideration—even though only a token amount is shown
4. Words of conveyance
5. The interest being conveyed
6. A description of the property
7. Grantor's proper signature
8. Delivery of the deed and acceptance

Parts of a Deed

The traditional deed has the following five parts:

Part of Deed	Purpose
1. Premises	Gives names of parties, exploratory facts, words of conveyance, consideration, legal description of the property
2. Habendum	Is the "to have and to hold" clause, which may describe a limit to the quantity of the estate being granted, such as "to have and to hold forever" or "to have and to hold for life"
3. Testimonium	Contains warranties (if any)
4. Execution	Contains date, signatures, and seal if applicable
5. Acknowledgment	Contains attestation by a public officer, usually a notary public, as to the genuineness of the grantor's signature. (Although acknowledgment is not required to transfer title, it is usually a requirement for the deed to be recorded.)

Execution of the Deed

To be considered complete, a deed must be signed by the grantor and delivered to the grantee or delivered in escrow (see below). Occasionally, problems arise when an undelivered deed is

This instrument was prepared by:
Name _____
Address _____
_____

Return to:
Name _____
Address _____
_____

Grantee #1 S.S. No. _____

Grantee #2 S.S. No. _____

Property Appraiser's
Parcel Identification No.
_____

WARRANTY DEED
(STATUTORY FORM — SECTION 689.02, F.S.)

This Indenture, made this _____ day of _____ 19 ___ , **Between**

_____
whose post office address is
of the County of _____ , State of _____ , grantor*, and

_____
whose post office address is
of the County of _____ , State of _____ , grantee*,

Witnesseth that said grantor, for and in consideration of the sum of
_____ Dollars,
and other good and valuable considerations to said grantor in hand paid by said grantee, the receipt whereof is hereby acknowledged, has granted, bargained and sold to the said grantee, and grantee's heirs and assigns forever, the following described land, situate, lying and being in _____ County, Florida, to-wit:

SAMPLE

and said grantor does hereby fully warrant the title to said land, and will defend the same against lawful claims of all persons whomsoever.

*"Grantor" and "grantee" are used for singular or plural, as context requires.

In Witness Whereof, grantor has hereunto set grantor's hand and seal the day and year first above written.
Signed, sealed, and delivered in our presence:

_____   _____ (Seal)
(First Witness)   Grantor
Printed or typed name: _____   Printed or typed name: _____

_____   _____ (Seal)
(Second Witness)   Grantor
Printed or typed name: _____   Printed or typed name: _____

STATE OF
COUNTY OF
THE FOREGOING INSTRUMENT was acknowledged before me this _____ day of _____ ,
19 ___ , by _____ , who is (or are) personally known to me or who has
produced _____ as identification and who did (did not) take an oath.

My commission expires: _____
                                                     Notary Public
                                     Printed, typed, or stamped name:

                                     _____

                                     _____
                                     (Serial Number, if any)   F-761 (rev. 12/91)

Figure 9-1.   Warranty Deed

found in the grantor's home after his death. The grantee named may claim ownership; but since the grantor never delivered the deed, courts will not agree that transfer was intended.

The requirement for delivery of the deed generally is considered very literally; that is, the grantee actually must have come into physical possession of the document in order for title to be considered transferred to her. The grantee may arrange for her agent to accept delivery for her. A common form of such delivery is *delivery in escrow*. In this situation, the grantor delivers the deed to a trustee or escrow agent, who holds it pending completion of some required action by the grantee (such as payment in full of a note given in payment for all or part of the price). In this case delivery is considered to have occurred as soon as the escrow agent or trustee received the deed, so title is transferred. However, since the grantee has no deed in her possession, she will have difficulty disposing of the title until she fulfills the necessary requirements to get the deed released to her by the agent.

Public Records and Title Search

Records concerning real estate are maintained in the courthouse of each county in Florida. Whenever someone receives a deed, a mortgage, a long-term lease (over three years in duration), or other key document in real estate, he or she may *record* it in the county courthouse. One need not record a deed to own property. By recording a deed, a person gives *constructive notice* to the world of his or her ownership interest. Constructive notice means that anyone in the world who would have an interest in a property is assumed to know what is in the recorded documents affecting that property. Anyone thereafter who searches courthouse records concerning this property would see the documents transferring ownership to the grantee and could avert a proposed transaction if good title were not available. A grantee who fails to record a deed runs the risk that an unscrupulous grantor may sell the property again, and that the other buyer, who doesn't know of the first buyer's rights, records the second deed. A dispute will arise and it is likely the second buyer's ownership interest will be upheld. The first buyer is unable to establish an earlier date of ownership because his or her deed was not recorded first (and perhaps is still not recorded), and the second buyer was innocent of wrongdoing and acted in good faith.

One who buys real estate in Florida will sign a real estate contract for sale (see Chapter 8) which will specify the deed to be given. Because of the potential risk of loss in every transaction, it is prudent for an attorney to be engaged to *search the title*. (If title insurance is acquired, the title insurance company will do this.) In any transaction where a new mortgage loan is also to be arranged, the potential lender will insist on a title search. Often, the attorney is associated with a title company (see below) as an agent or employee. The attorney may provide an *abstract of title*, which is a condensed history of the title, a summary of the chain of title, and a list of all liens, charges, and encumbrances affecting the title. Sometimes the attorney's work is simpler. If the property sold recently and the same title company searched the title previously, then an update from the previous title report may be adequate.

Title Insurance

The purpose of title insurance is to protect a purchaser's or a lender's interest in property. As a real estate transaction is closed (see Chapter 19 on settlement) the seller receives money and the buyer receives a piece of paper, the deed. How can the buyer be certain that the deed is good? Or suppose the seller was thought to be an heir to an estate, but the will naming him was successfully challenged? That is, suppose the seller was a fraud who forged the signature of the real heir? In these cases, the seller could not have given legal title, but there was nothing in the public records to show that fact. Since a buyer cannot get a larger interest than the seller has, a buyer in these circumstances would end up with nothing. Therefore, a buyer is critically interested in getting good title. Because a lender's collateral is the property, the lender also is most interested in assuring the buyer gets good title.

Based on the attorney's research, the title insurer will issue a *preliminary title report*, which is a promise to insure the title. This document may have a list of exceptions against which the title company will not insure. The buyer's and lender's attorneys should determine whether any of the exceptions are likely to have validity, and if one poses a threat to ownership, advise their client to not complete the transaction until this *cloud on the title* is cleared.

In most transactions there is no title problem and a title policy will be issued at closing. Payment for title insurance is made only once for property purchased, and is valid for as long as that party owns the property. Lenders will demand enough title insurance to cover the full amount they lend. Buyers would be well advised to insure the full amount that they paid, so as to cover their equity investment in the property. The additional cost will be very small, and the peace of mind well worth it.

Questions on Chapter 9

1. X hands Y a deed with the intent to pass title and orally requests Y not to record the deed until X dies. When is the deed valid?
   (A) Immediately
   (B) When Y records the deed
   (C) When X dies
   (D) Never

2. A quitclaim deed conveys only the interest of the
   (A) guarantee
   (B) property
   (C) claimant
   (D) grantor

3. Which of the following forms of deeds has one or more guarantees of title?
   (A) Quitclaim deed
   (B) Executor's deed
   (C) Warranty deed
   (D) Special-form deed

4. The part of conveyance that defines or limits the quantity of the estate granted is
   (A) habendum
   (B) premises
   (C) equity
   (D) consideration

5. The Statute of Frauds
   (A) requires certain contracts to be in writing to be enforceable
   (B) requires a license to operate as a broker or a salesperson
   (C) regulates escrow accounts
   (D) regulates fraud conveyance

6. For a deed to be recorded, it must be in writing and must
   (A) be signed by the grantee
   (B) state the actual purchase price
   (C) be acknowledged
   (D) be free of all liens

7. The most comprehensive ownership of land at law is known as
   (A) an estate for years
   (B) a life estate
   (C) a fee simple
   (D) a defeasible title

8. From the standpoint of the grantor, which of the following types of deeds creates the least liability?
   (A) Special warranty
   (B) General warranty
   (C) Bargain and sale
   (D) Quitclaim

9. The recording of a deed
   (A) passes the title
   (B) insures the title
   (C) guarantees the title
   (D) gives constructive notice of ownership

10. Title to real property may pass by
    (A) deed
    (B) bill of sale
    (C) both A and B
    (D) neither A nor B

11. Real property title may be conveyed by
    (A) adverse possession
    (B) inheritance
    (C) deed
    (D) all of the above

12. A warranty deed protects the grantee against a loss by
    (A) casualty
    (B) defective title
    (C) both A and B
    (D) neither A nor B

13. Deeds should be recorded
    (A) as soon as possible after delivery
    (B) within 30 days of delivery
    (C) within one year
    (D) none of the above

14. A deed of conveyance must be signed by
    (A) the grantee and the grantor
    (B) only the grantor
    (C) only the grantee
    (D) none of the above

15. A deed to be valid need not necessarily be
    (A) signed
    (B) written
    (C) sealed
    (D) delivered

16. The party to whom a deed conveys real estate is the
    (A) grantee
    (B) grantor
    (C) beneficiary
    (D) recipient

17. Deeds are recorded in the
    (A) county courthouse
    (B) city hall
    (C) Federal Land Book
    (D) state capital

18. A deed must
    (A) contain the street address of the property
    (B) state the nature of the improvement on the land (dwelling)
    (C) contain an adequate description to identify the property sold
    (D) state the total area in the tract

19. What is the maximum number of grantees that can be named in a deed?
    (A) Two
    (B) Four
    (C) Ten
    (D) There is no limit

20. Property is identified in a deed by the
    (A) habendum
    (B) consideration
    (C) description
    (D) acknowledgment

21. Attestation, by a notary public or other qualified official, of the signature on a deed or mortgage is called an
    (A) authorization
    (B) acknowledgment
    (C) execution
    (D) authentication

22. For which reason is a deed recorded?
    (A) To insure certain title
    (B) To give notice of a transaction to the world
    (C) To satisfy a requirement of state law
    (D) To save title insurance cost

23. Ownership of property is transferred when
    (A) the grantor signs the deed
    (B) the grantor's signature has been notarized
    (C) delivery of the deed is made
    (D) the correct documentary stamps are put on the deed and canceled

24. From the point of view of the grantee, the safest kind of deed that can be received is a
    (A) general warranty deed   (C) quitclaim or release deed
    (B) special warranty deed   (D) trustee's deed

25. Which of the following statement(s) is (are) true?
    (A) A quitclaim deed transfers whatever interest a grantee has in property.
    (B) A quitclaim deed carries a warranty of good title.
    (C) Both A and B
    (D) Neither A nor B

TRUE/FALSE
Write T for true, F for false.

_____26. The warranty in a deed guarantees that the real estate will be in good condition for a certain length of time.

_____27. A warranty deed is the best kind of deed for a grantee to receive.

_____28. A quitclaim normally does not include a description of the specific rights granted to the grantee.

_____29. A deed must be in writing, and if it is to be recorded it must be acknowledged as well.

_____30. An executor's deed contains a full and general warranty.

_____31. A deed must show consideration, though it is usually permissible to state a "nominal" amount (i.e., less than the true amount).

ANSWERS

1. A	8. D	15. C	22. B	29. T
2. D	9. D	16. A	23. C	30. F
3. C	10. A	17. A	24. A	31. T
4. A	11. D	18. C	25. D	
5. A	12. B	19. D	26. F	
6. C	13. A	20. C	27. T	
7. C	14. B	21. B	28. T	

Chapter 10/Leases and Property Management

A lease is a contract that transfers possession of property in exchange for rent.

The real estate owner is known as the *landlord* or *lessor*; the user is the *tenant* or *lessee*. The landlord retains a *reversionary right*; that is, he retains the right to use the property upon expiration of the lease. The tenant holds a *leasehold estate*, that is, a personal property interest that gives the tenant the right to use the property for the lease term and under the conditions stipulated in the lease.

Types of Leasehold Estates

1. Estate for years
2. Periodic estate
3. Tenancy at will
4. Tenancy at sufferance

An *estate for years* has a stated expiration date. The period included may be only 1 day or more than 50 years. When the lease term ends, the tenant is to vacate the property.

A *periodic estate* (*estate from period to period*) does not have a fixed expiration date. It is automatically renewed for another period (week, month, year) unless adequate notice for termination is given. One period of notice is generally adequate; less than 1 year is acceptable in the case of a year-to-year lease.

A *tenancy at will* allows the tenant to remain with the consent of the landlord. At any time, either the tenant or the landlord may terminate the agreement. "Emblements" arise by operation of law to give tenants-at-will the right to harvest growing crops.

A tenant who holds property beyond the lease term and without the landlord's consent is a "holdover tenant." The form of estate is called *tenancy at sufferance*. A holdover tenancy has the fewest rights of any leasehold estate.

Requirements of a Valid Real Estate Contract

Since a lease is a contract for the use of real estate, it must meet all the requirements for a valid real estate contract. These requirements include:

1. Offer and acceptance
2. Competent parties
3. Consideration
4. Adequate description of the property
5. Written form

In Florida, an oral lease for 1 year or less is binding. Any provision that is legal can be included in a lease. Some common lease provisions are discussed below.

SOME COMMON LEASE PROVISIONS

Rent

Rent may be payable in any form that the parties agree upon. Typically, rent is payable in money, but it may also be payable in crops, labor, and so on—whatever the landlord and tenant agree upon. *Straight* or *flat* leases call for level amounts of rent. *Step-up* or *step-down*, *graduated*, or *reappraisal* leases provide for fluctuating amounts of rent.

A *percentage lease* requires the tenant to pay, as rent, a percentage of sales. Usually a basic rent is stipulated to guarantee a minimum amount. For example, a lease may require that a retailer-tenant pay $10,000 rent annually, plus 2 percent of gross sales in excess of $500,000. Should sales be under $500,000, the rent is $10,000; for sales of $600,000, the rent is $12,000, that is, $10,000 basic plus 2 percent of the $100,000 excess sales.

Operating Expenses

A lease that requires the landlord to pay operating expenses, such as utilities, repairs, insurance, and property taxes, is called a *gross lease*. The lessor considers the rent to be gross income and receives net operating income after he pays operating expenses out of his own pocket. A *net lease* requires the tenant to pay operating expenses. The landlord receives the rent as a net return.

The terms *net* and *gross*, though often used, may be inadequate to describe a lease. *Hybrid, seminet,* and *net-net* are used to describe the degree to which a party may be responsible for operating expenses. Careful reading of a lease by interested parties is necessary to avoid misunderstandings.

Escalation

Escalation or *step* provisions are found in long-term gross leases. Should certain operating expenses exceed a designated amount, the increase is passed on to the tenant.

Assignment and Subletting

Unless specifically prohibited in a lease, a tenant has the right to assign or sublet. In either case, the original lessee remains liable to fulfill the lease contract.

An *assignment* occurs when the tenant transfers all the rights and obligations stipulated in the lease to a third party (the assignee).

Should the original tenant wish to keep a portion of the property for his own use or to rent the premises to a third party for a term shorter than his lease, he may sublet. *Subletting* involves a second lease; the original tenant becomes a lessor for part of the property or for the entire property for part of the lease term.

Sale of the Property

When leased property is sold, the lease survives the sale. The tenant is allowed to continue use under the lease terms.

Termination of a Lease

The normal termination of a lease is the result of *performance*. When both landlord and tenant have fulfilled their lease obligations, there is said to be performance.

Another method of terminating a lease is by *agreement*. Landlord and tenant may agree to terminate the lease before its stated expiration date. Compensation may be included in such an agreement.

A *breach* may also cause termination. When either party fails to perform under a lease, there is said to be a breach. Although a breach can terminate a lease, it does not cancel all provisions. The violating party may be held liable for damages. When a tenant has breached a lease, the landlord's remedy is in court. Using a court order, a landlord may eject or *evict* a tenant.

A tenant who vacates property before the fixed expiration date of a lease is responsible for the remaining rent. If the property is eventually leased, the tenant owes only the difference in rent, plus expenses incurred in obtaining a substitute tenant. However, vacating property fails to terminate a lease except by *constructive eviction*. In this form of breach the landlord makes it very difficult or impossible for the tenant to "enjoy" the leased premises as contracted. In effect, the landlord's actions force the tenant to leave. Examples are very noisy repair work that goes on night after night in an apartment building; turning off utilities for long periods of time; closing the parking lot in a retail shopping center.

A *ground lease* is a long-term lease of land or air space. The tenant usually builds whatever improvements are desired. The landlord receives what is called *triple-net* rent; this means that the tenant pays not only operating expenses, but also property taxes and mortgage payments. Ground leases are for very long periods of time, usually 25 to as many as 99 years.

Lease provisions frequently encountered are described below. (Not all of the provisions will be found in every lease.)

Provision	*Purpose*
Premises	Describes the property being leased
Term	States the term of the lease
Rent	Describes rental amount, date, and place payable
Construction of building and improvements	Describes improvements for proposed property or property to be renovated to suit tenant
Common area	Describes maintenance of common-use areas, such as those in shopping centers
Taxes	States who will pay ad valorem taxes and escalation amounts
Repairs	States which party is responsible for repairs and maintenance
Alterations	States responsibilities and rights of tenant to alter improvements
Liability insurance	Designates party who is responsible to carry liability insurance and the extent
Other insurance	Designates party who is responsible to carry hazard insurance and the extent
Damage by fire and casualty	Describes operation of lease in the event of a fire or other casualty
Payment for utilities	States which party must pay charges for water, heat, gas, electricity, sewage disposal, and other utilities
Subordination	Describes rights between landlord and tenant in the event of mortgage foreclosure
Certificate of lease status	Obligates tenant to inform mortgage lender of occupancy and rent status
Condemnation and eminent domain	Describes operation of lease in the event of a taking or partial taking of the property
Compliance of law	Requires landlord and tenant to comply with laws and ordinances
Access by landlord	Allows landlord to inspect property
Mechanic's liens	Describes the discharge of mechanic's liens
Assignment and subletting	Limits the tenant's rights to assign or sublet
Nonliability of landlord	Frees landlord from liability due to injury or damage within premises
Right to cure defaults	Allows landlord to cure tenant defaults and require reimbursement
Use	Permits tenant the use of property for specific purposes
Notices	Describes method to serve notice to a party
Definitions	Defines terms used in the lease
Partial invalidity	Describes operation of lease when parts of lease are held to be invalid
Waiver of redemption	Permits tenant to waive all rights upon lease expiration
Bankruptcy or insolvency	Describes required notice and operation of lease in the event of bankruptcy
Default	Defines lease default
Surrender	Describes how tenant is to leave property upon expiration of the lease

Provision	Purpose
Arbitration	Provides a method to settle disputes
Brokers	Notes whether a broker was involved in lease negotiation
Encumbrances	Describes rights and obligations of parties to deliver and return property (with respect to liens, easements, etc.)
Quiet enjoyment	Agreement by landlord that tenant, while he performs, may have, hold, and enjoy property without interferences
Other restrictions	May limit the leasing of space in a shopping center to a competitor
Entire agreement	States that the written lease is the entire agreement
Percentage clause	Stipulates conditions affecting a percentage lease
Recapture clause	Stipulates that in a percentage lease a lessor may terminate lease if lessee's revenues do not attain a specified level within a certain length of time

Florida Residential Landlord and Tenant Act

The Florida Residential Landlord and Tenant Act attempts to place tenants on an equal footing with landlords in an effort to stop potentially abusive practices. It applies to residential units and does not apply to commercial property leases, cooperative apartments, condominiums, or transient facilities including hotels and mobile home parks, but does apply to nontransient mobile homes. This act prohibits unconscionable rental agreements or practices, even when the fine print in a lease seems to bind a landlord or a tenant to an unreasonable or unjust condition.

Security Deposit

The purpose of a security deposit or advance rent is to guarantee that a property will be left in good condition. The landlord must do one of the three following procedures with a security deposit:

1. Place it in a separate noninterest-bearing Florida bank, not commingle it, not pledge it as security, nor use the money until it is due; or
2. Place it in a separate interest-bearing Florida bank, pay the tenant at least 75 percent of the amount it earns or 5 percent; not commingle it, not pledge it as security, nor use the money until it is due; or
3. Pay the tenant 5 percent per year, and post a surety bond equal to the lesser of $50,000 or the total amount of security deposits and advance rents. The surety bond is to be posted with the clerk of the circuit court in which the property is located.

The landlord is to inform the tenant, within 30 days from the receipt of the security deposit or advance rent, which method is being used. The landlord must also tell the tenant the bank name and address, amount of deposit, rate of interest, and date that interest will be paid to the tenant (at least once a year).

Maintenance Obligation. A landlord of a dwelling unit must meet all building, housing and health codes in the jurisdiction. If there are no codes in the area, the rented premises must be maintained in "good repair and capable of resisting normal forces and loads."

The landlord must provide an extermination service to get rid of bugs and vermin, provide garbage receptacles and periodic pickup, hot running water, and heat. The landlord may charge the tenant for these services. An exception is provided for a single-family dwelling unit or a duplex, where the landlord need not provide these services. A landlord and tenant may agree that the landlord is not responsible for these services (extermination, garbage, etc.), but the landlord is always responsible for meeting building, housing, and health codes.

A landlord is not responsible for conditions created by a tenant's wrongful acts or a tenant's negligence. A landlord is not responsible for a mobile home that the landlord doesn't own, even though the tenant is paying the landlord to rent the lot.

Tenant's Obligation

The tenant must comply with existing building, housing, and health codes. The tenant is to maintain the dwelling unit, including the plumbing, in a sanitary condition. The tenant is to be reasonable in his or her use of all plumbing, heat, and air-conditioning equipment. The tenant, his or her family and guests, is responsible for conducting themselves so as not to disturb the peace of other tenants.

Landlord's Access

The landlord is allowed to enter rented property for emergencies, but cannot abuse this right to harass a tenant. The landlord may also enter the property from time to time to:
1. Inspect the premises.
2. Make agreed or necessary repairs, improvements, decorations.
3. Provide promised services.
4. Show the apartment.

The landlord does not have the right to enter the apartment in other situations, even during an extended absence of the tenant.

Vacating Premises

If, after a lease expires, a landlord intends to keep part or all of a tenant's security deposit, the landlord must notify the tenant within 15 days of the vacancy. Should the landlord fail to give notice within 15 days, the landlord forfeits the right to keep any part of the deposit, and must return it with interest.

If the tenant is properly notified of the landlord's intent to keep part of the deposit, the tenant must submit an objection within 15 days of the time he or she receives the landlord's notice. If the dispute is settled in court, the loser must pay court costs plus reasonable attorney fees to the victor.

If the tenant should vacate before expiration of the lease, the tenant must give the landlord at least seven days written notice by certified mail or personal delivery. When a tenant fails to give such notice, the landlord is automatically released of the 15-day notice obligation. Of course, the seven-day-notice does not relieve the tenant of obligations under the lease. It simply maintains the landlord's requirement to account for the security deposit.

Lease Termination

This can be by either the tenant or landlord.

Tenant Termination. When a tenant has cause to terminate a lease, such as because the landlord failed to comply with the lease, the tenant may terminate the agreement provided the following procedure is followed:
1. Write to the landlord stating the reason for noncompliance and intent to cancel the lease if this is not corrected.
2. Wait seven days to give the landlord an opportunity to correct the problem.
3. If the problem is not corrected, the tenant may terminate the lease.

If the tenant wants the landlord to correct the landlord's noncompliance, but the tenant does not want to terminate the lease, the tenant has these options:
1. If the dwelling is still inhabitable, the rent may be reduced in proportion to the loss in rental value caused by the landlord's noncompliance.
2. If the dwelling is unhabitable, the tenant is not liable for the rent.

By the Landlord. If the tenant fails to comply with the lease, other than a failure to pay rent when due, the landlord may:
1. Write to the tenant stating the reason for noncompliance and intent to cancel the lease if this is not corrected.
2. Wait seven days to give the tenant an opportunity to correct the problem.
3. If the problem is not corrected, the landlord may terminate the lease.

If the tenant's noncompliance is a failure to pay rent when it is due, the landlord must observe the following procedure to terminate the agreement:

1. Give written notice (mailed, delivered by hand, or posted to the tenant's door) demanding the rent payment within 3 days or possession of the apartment.
2. The tenant has three days to surrender the apartment or pay rent. If the tenant doesn't do either, the landlord must go through the eviction process.

If the tenant vacates, the landlord must give the tenant written notice of any claim on the security deposit.

Eviction

The eviction process for apartments in Florida is as follows:

1. The landlord must notify the tenant (in writing, by mail or posted on the door) that he or she is demanding possession. The landlord should keep a copy of the notice and indicate the date and time it was served.
2. Assuming the tenant has not surrendered the premises within three days for nonpayment of rent (seven days for other breaches of the lease), the landlord files a *complaint eviction* in the county court where the apartment is located. The complaint, which is usually delivered by the sheriff, cites the reasons for the eviction.
3. The tenant is given five days to reply. If the tenant wishes to continue possession, the case will be decided in court.
4. If the tenant does not answer the complaint eviction, the landlord may go to court to obtain a final judgment.
5. After receiving a final judgment, the landlord must obtain a *writ of possession* from the court.
6. The sheriff will enforce the writ of possession. The sheriff will give 24 hours notice to the tenant, after which time the sheriff's department will physically remove the tenant and his or her belongings from the apartment.

The eviction process may take up to two months when the tenant is uncooperative. Any unpaid rent creates a lien on all of the tenant's property except for clothing and beds.

Property Management

Property management is the business of seeking and negotiating with tenants for the use of other people's real estate. It is a real estate brokerage function, and property managers in all states are required to hold real estate sales or brokerage licenses. (*Resident managers* of apartment buildings or projects are allowed to function without a license, provided that they do not manage any other properties and are employed either by the property owner or a properly licensed property manager.)

Some brokers who claim to be "property managers" may do little more than find tenants for vacant properties, and collect payment for doing so. Actually, a *professional* property manager does a lot more. In fact, he is able to do everything associated with the proper management of a property, so that the owner need do nothing at all. Property management functions include leasing, negotiating with potential tenants, advertising, developing leasing plans, arranging maintenance and repairs, and paying all bills (out of rent receipts). Of course, property managers are paid for their services. Normally, their payment is a commission on rent payments collected; however, they may instead (or also) receive a flat fee.

Certain special kinds of lease arrangements often are found in managed properties. Retail property (shopping centers, etc.) often features *percentage leases*. In this type of lease, all or part of the tenant's rent is a percentage of her gross business revenues. The theory here is that a well-managed and popular shopping center will generate good business for tenants, and so they will be willing to pay part of their intake as rent. Also, the property manager is encouraged to promote and advertise the shopping center because by doing so he gets more people to come to it, spend more money, and thus generate more rent.

Many percentage leases contain *recapture clauses*. These allow the property manager to void the lease if the tenant does not do at least a certain volume of business within a certain time. In this way the management avoids getting stuck with a poor tenant or one who does not do much business.

Questions on Chapter 10

1. Which of the following statements is correct?
   (A) The tenant is known as the lessor.
   (B) The owner leasing property is the lessee.
   (C) The tenant is the lessee.
   (D) None of the above

2. Under a net lease, who is liable for payment of insurance and repairs?
   (A) Lessor
   (B) Lessee
   (C) Sublessee
   (D) Both A and B

3. A gross lease requires the tenant to pay rent based on
   (A) gross sales
   (B) net sales
   (C) gross profit
   (D) none of the above

4. A percentage lease requires the tenant to pay a
   (A) percentage of taxes and insurance
   (B) percentage of net income as rent
   (C) percentage of sales as rent
   (D) none of the above

5. A tenant is delinquent in paying rent. The landlord should give written notice, then
   (A) call the sheriff to evict him
   (B) bring a court action
   (C) give him 30 days' notice
   (D) turn off water, lights, etc.

6. A lease that requires the landlord to pay the operating expenses of the property is called
   (A) a gross lease
   (B) an assigned lease
   (C) a percentage lease
   (D) a net lease

7. A lease for 1 year or less in Florida
   (A) may be oral
   (B) must be in writing
   (C) may be oral but must be reduced to writing within 1 year
   (D) is always invalid

8. Transfer, by a tenant, of the rights and obligations of an existing lease to another tenant is called
   (A) assignment of lease
   (B) a release
   (C) subletting
   (D) an eviction

9. A contract that transfers possession but not ownership of property is
   (A) a special warranty deed
   (B) an option
   (C) an easement
   (D) a lease

10. When an individual holds property past the expiration of a lease without the landlord's consent, the leasehold estate he has is a
    (A) tenancy at sufferance
    (B) freehold estate
    (C) common of pasturage
    (D) holdover tenant

11. A sublease is a
    (A) lease made by a lessor
    (B) lease made by a lessee and a third party
    (C) lease for basement space
    (D) condition of property

12. A landlord rents a store to a furniture retailer on a percentage lease. On which of the following is the percentage usually based?
    (A) Market value   (C) Tenant's gross sales
    (B) Sales price   (D) Tenant's net income

13. Which of the following will *not* terminate a lease?
    (A) Performance   (C) Surrender
    (B) Breach   (D) Vacancy

14. When a leased property is sold, what effect does the sale have upon the tenant?
    (A) The tenant must record the lease in the recorder's office.
    (B) The tenant must obtain an assignment from the purchaser.
    (C) The tenant must move out after reasonable notice.
    (D) There is no effect.

15. A lease for more than 1 year *must* be in writing to be enforceable because the
    (A) landlord or tenant might forget the terms
    (B) tenant must sign the agreement to pay rent
    (C) Statute of Frauds requires it
    (D) lease can then be assigned to another person

16. A lease can state that the rent is to be paid in
    (A) labor   (C) cash
    (B) crops   (D) any of the above

17. An estate at will is
    (A) a limited partnership   (C) an inheritance by will
    (B) a tenancy of uncertain duration (D) a life tenancy

18. A reversionary interest
    (A) expires when a lease is signed
    (B) allows land to escheat at the termination of a lease
    (C) is a landlord's right to use of property upon expiration of a lease
    (D) constitutes a breach of a lease

19. A leasehold estate is a
    (A) large home built on leased land
    (B) personal property interest in real estate
    (C) landlord's interest in realty
    (D) none of the above

20. Escalation clauses in a lease provide for
    (A) term extensions
    (B) elevator and escalator maintenance
    (C) increased rentals because of higher operating expenses
    (D) purchase options

21. Which of the following statements is true?
    (A) Property managers are required to be licensed in all states.
    (B) Percentage leases are illegal in many states.
    (C) An unlicensed person may solicit tenants for several properties provided that she works for a licensed property manager.
    (D) Property managers do not negotiate leases.

22. Which of the following is true?
    (A) Property management is a real estate brokerage function.
    (B) Resident managers of apartment complexes don't always have to be licensed.
    (C) Property managers usually are paid a percentage of rents collected as their fee.
    (D) All of the above

23. A person who remains on leased property, without the landlord's consent, after the expiration of a lease is
    (A) a tenant at will
    (B) a tenant *par duration*
    (C) a tenant in common
    (D) a tenant at suffrance

24. A lease that requires that all or part of the tenant's rent be based on the tenant's revenues is
    (A) a lease at will
    (B) a flat lease
    (C) a percentage lease
    (D) a gross lease

TRUE/FALSE

Write *T* for true, *F* for false.

_____25. The parties to a lease are the lessor and the lessee.

_____26. A tenancy at will may be terminated at any time by either tenant or landlord.

_____27. A lease that calls for a level amount of rent throughout the lease period is called a "straight" or "flat" lease.

_____28. A "net lease" requires the tenant to pay operating expenses.

_____29. A lease for more than 1 year must be in writing to be enforceable.

_____30. Property managers normally do not handle repairs and maintenance of the properties that they manage.

_____31. Property management is a brokerage function, so property managers are required to hold real estate licenses.

ANSWERS

1. C	8. A	15. C	22. D	29. T
2. B	9. D	16. D	23. D	30. F
3. D	10. A	17. B	24. C	31. T
4. C	11. B	18. C	25. T	
5. B	12. C	19. B	26. T	
6. A	13. D	20. C	27. T	
7. A	14. D	21. A	28. T	

Chapter 11/*Listings*

A *listing* is a contract of employment between a principal (property owner) and an agent (broker) to sell or lease real estate. Under the terms of the listing contract, the principal agrees to pay the broker a commission when the broker locates a party who is ready, willing, and able to buy or lease the listed property at its list price. Should an offer be tendered for less than the list price, the broker is entitled to a commission only if the transaction is consummated.

Normally, the seller pays the commission at closing. It is possible for a buyer to agree to pay a commission in lieu of the seller or in addition to the seller, so long as all parties are aware of the circumstances.

Types of Listings

Listings can be categorized into five broad types as follows:
1. Open listings
2. Exclusive agency listings
3. Exclusive right to sell listings
4. Multiple listings

(*Net listings*, described in Chapter 4, are discouraged in Florida.) Each type is described below.

1. OPEN LISTINGS

Using an open listing, the principal offers the broker a commission provided that the broker secures a purchaser. The owner reserves the right to list the property with other brokers or to sell the property himself. Thus, the open listing is open to other real estate brokers. All open listings are automatically canceled upon a sale of the property, so that the seller pays no more than one commission.

2. EXCLUSIVE AGENCY LISTINGS

In an exclusive agency listing one broker is employed to the exclusion of all other brokers. The owner retains the right to sell the property herself without paying a commission. However, if the property is sold by a broker other than the listing broker, the listing broker is still entitled to a commission.

3. EXCLUSIVE RIGHT TO SELL LISTINGS

The exclusive right to sell listing allows the employed broker to collect a commission upon the sale, no matter who sells the property. Whether the employed broker, another broker, or the owner procures a purchaser, a broker with an exclusive right to sell gains his fee upon the sale.

At first glance, such a contract may seem to be to a seller's disadvantage. Even if the seller procures a buyer on her own, or another broker finds one, the listing broker earns a commission. However, this rigid arrangement gives the listing broker the assurance that the property is available for sale by him only. Brokers employed by other types of listings may be dismayed to learn that property has been sold by the owner or another broker. Since this does not occur under an exclusive right to sell, the employed broker has more incentive to devote his efforts and to spend money to promote the sale of the listed property. In recognition of this fact, most real estate boards emphasize the exclusive right to sell listing, particularly for single-family dwellings.

4. MULTIPLE LISTINGS

Some brokers in a given geographical area may agree to pool all of their listings. They form a *multiple listing association* to coordinate activities. Through that association, brokers agree to share their exclusive right to sell listings; any cooperating broker may sell property that another has listed. Upon the sale of multiple-listed property, the commission is split between the listing and the selling broker in accordance with the agreement established by the multiple listing association. A small fraction of the commission is paid to the association to cover its expenses of operation, which include the periodic publication, in writing and/or by computer, of the features of all listed property of the brokers belonging to that multiple listing association.

Selecting a Form

No special form is required for a listing. However, it is important to read the form used, to gain an understanding of the type of listing. An example of a listing contract form is shown in Figure 11-1.

Agency Law

A broker is an agent for his principal. The broker's duties, obligations, and responsibilities to his principal are covered by the Law of Agency. Chapter 4 of this book describes this body of law as it pertains to real estate brokerage. Many states require that, upon first contact with a prospective buyer, a broker or salesperson must disclose to the prospect the agency relationship with the seller. Ordinarily this is accomplished by having the buyer sign and return to the agent a form (usually designed and prescribed by law) that describes the agency relationship, so that the prospect realizes that the agent's loyalty is to the seller. Sometimes brokers do represent buyers in negotiations and transactions. In such cases they are agents of the buyer, not the seller, and there has to be an agency contract between broker and buyer. Disclosure is required here, too; when negotiations begin with a seller (or seller's broker) of a property the buyer is interested in, the seller and/or listing broker must be notified of the buyer-broker agency relationship.

Rate of Commission

As a matter of law, commission rates for the sale of real estate are negotiable between the principal and his broker. The rate or amount should be specified in the listing contract to avoid misunderstandings. Antitrust suits have been brought against brokers who have agreed with one another about commission rates. Never discuss commissions with another broker or another broker's salesperson!

Listing Period

Contracts for the listing of real estate should have a fixed expiration date. Most contracts provide 60 to 120 days for the sale of single-family homes and up to 6 months for commercial property and apartment complexes. The law does not establish limits, so the actual period agreed upon is a matter of negotiation.

Exclusive Right of Sale Listing Agreement
FLORIDA ASSOCIATION OF REALTORS®

This Exclusive Right of Sale Listing Contract ("Contract") is between

_____ ("Seller") and

_____ ("Broker").

1. AUTHORITY TO SELL PROPERTY: **Seller** gives **Broker** the EXCLUSIVE RIGHT TO SELL the real and personal property (collectively "Property") described below, at the price and terms described below, beginning the _____ day of _____, 19____, and terminating at 11:59 p.m. the _____ day of _____, 19____ ("Termination Date"). Upon full execution of a contract for sale and purchase of the Property, all rights and obligations of this Contract will automatically extend through the date of the actual closing of the sales contract. **Seller** and **Broker** acknowledge that this Contract does not guarantee a sale. This Property will be offered to any person without regard to race, color, religion, sex, handicap, familial status, national origin or any other factor protected by federal, state or local law. **Seller** certifies and represents that he/she/it is legally entitled to convey the Property and all improvements.

2. DESCRIPTION OF PROPERTY:
  (a) Real Property Street Address: _____

    Legal Description: _____
    _____ ❑ See Attachment _____
  (b) Personal Property, including appliances: _____
    _____ ❑ See Attachment _____
  (c) Occupancy: Property ❑ is ❑ is not currently occupied by a tenant. If occupied, the lease term expires _____.

3. PRICE AND TERMS: The property is offered for sale on the following terms, or on other terms acceptable to **Seller**:
  (a) Price: _____
  (b) Financing Terms: ❑ Cash ❑ Conventional ❑ VA ❑ FHA ❑ Other _____
    ❑ **Seller** Financing: **Seller** will hold a purchase money mortgage in the amount of $_____ with the following terms: _____
    ❑ Assumption of Existing Mortgage: Buyer may assume existing mortgage for $_____ plus an assumption fee of $_____. The mortgage is for a term of _____ years beginning in 19____, at an interest rate of _____% ❑ fixed ❑ variable (describe) _____
    Lender approval of assumption ❑ is required ❑ is not required ❑ unknown. **Notice to Seller:** You may remain liable for an assumed mortgage for a number of years after the Property is sold. Check with your lender to determine the extent of your liability. **Seller** will ensure that all mortgage payments and required escrow deposits are current at the time of closing and will convey the escrow deposit to the buyer at closing.
  (c) **Seller** Expenses: **Seller** will pay mortgage discount or other closing costs not to exceed _____% of the purchase price; and any other expenses **Seller** agrees to pay in connection with a transaction.

4. BROKER OBLIGATIONS AND AUTHORITY: **Broker** agrees to make diligent and continued efforts to sell the Property until a sales contract is pending on the Property. **Seller** authorizes **Broker** to:
  (a) Advertise the Property as **Broker** deems advisable in newspapers, publications, computer networks and other media; place appropriate transaction signs on the Property, including For Sale signs and "Sold" signs (once **Seller** signs a sale contract procured through **Broker's** efforts); and use **Seller's** name in connection with marketing or advertising the Property;
  (b) Obtain information relating to the present mortgage(s) on the Property.
  (c) Place the Property in a multiple listing service ("MLS"). **Seller** authorizes **Broker** to report to the MLS this listing information and price, terms and financing information on any resulting sale for use by authorized Board / Association members, MLS participants and subscribers;
  (d) Provide objective comparative market analysis information to potential buyers;
  (e) Act as a ❑ disclosed dual agent ❑ transaction broker in accordance with **Broker's** office policy as explained in paragraph 8 and revert to **Seller's** agent status if the parties do not complete a transaction; and
  (f) (Check if applicable) ❑ Use a lock box system to show and access the Property. A lock box does not ensure the Property's security; **Seller** is advised to secure or remove valuables. **Seller** agrees that the lock box is for **Seller's** benefit and releases **Broker**, persons working through **Broker** and **Broker's** local Realtor Board / Association from all liability and responsibility in connection with any loss that occurs.
  ❑ Withhold verbal offers. ❑ Withhold all offers once **Seller** accepts a contract for sale and purchase of the Property.

5. SELLER OBLIGATIONS: In consideration of **Broker's** obligations, **Seller** agrees to:
  (a) Cooperate with **Broker** in carrying out the purpose of this Contract, including referring immediately to **Broker** all inquiries regarding the Property's transfer, whether by purchase or any other means of transfer.
  (b) Provide **Broker** with keys to the Property and make the Property available for **Broker** to show during reasonable times.
  (c) Inform **Broker** prior to leasing, mortgaging or otherwise encumbering the Property.
  (d) To indemnify **Broker** and hold **Broker** harmless from losses, damages, costs and expenses of any nature, including attorney's fees, and from liability to any person, that **Broker** incurs because of (1) **Seller's** negligence, representations, misrepresentations, actions or inactions, (2) the use of a lock box, (3) the existence of undisclosed material facts about the Property, or (4) a court or arbitration decision that a broker who was not compensated in connection with a transaction is entitled to compensation from **Broker**. This clause will survive **Broker's** performance and the transfer of title.
  (e) To perform any act reasonably necessary to comply with FIRPTA (Internal Revenue Code Section 1445).
  (f) Make all legally required disclosures, including all facts that materially affect the Property's value and are not readily observable or known by the buyer. **Seller** certifies and represents that **Seller** knows of no such material facts (local government building code violations, unobservable defects, etc.) other than the following: _____
_____

  Seller will immediately inform **Broker** of any material facts that arise after signing this Contract.

ERS-5   Rev. 10/95   © 1995 Florida Association of REALTORS®   All Rights Reserved

Figure 11-1. Listing Contract

6. **COMPENSATION: Seller** will compensate **Broker** as specified below for procuring a buyer who is ready, willing and able to purchase the Property or any interest in the Property on the terms of this Contract or on any other terms acceptable to **Seller. Seller** will pay **Broker** as follows (plus applicable sales tax):

   (a) _____% of the total purchase price OR $_____, no later than the date of closing specified in the purchase contract. However, closing is not a prerequisite for **Broker's** fee being earned.

   (b) _____ ($ or %) of the consideration paid for an option, at the time an option is created. If the option is exercised, Seller will pay **Broker** the paragraph 6(a) fee, less the amount **Broker** received under this subparagraph.

   (c) _____ ($ or %) of gross lease value as a leasing fee, on the date **Seller** enters into a lease or agreement to lease, whichever is soonest. This fee is not due if the Property is or becomes the subject of a contract granting an exclusive right to lease the Property.

   (d) **Broker's** fee is due in the following circumstances: (1) If any interest in the Property is transferred, whether by sale, lease, exchange, governmental action, bankruptcy or any other means of transfer, regardless of whether the buyer is secured by **Broker, Seller** or any other person. (2) If **Seller** refuses or fails to sign an offer at the price and terms stated in this Contract, defaults on an executed sales contract or agrees with a buyer to cancel an executed sales contract. (3) If, within _____ days after Termination Date ("Protection Period"), **Seller** transfers or contracts to transfer the Property or any interest in the Property to any prospects with whom **Seller, Broker** or any real estate licensee communicated regarding the Property prior to Termination Date. However, no fee will be due **Broker** if the Property is relisted after Termination Date and sold through another broker.

   (e) **Retained Deposits:** As consideration for **Broker's** services, **Broker** is entitled to receive _____% of all deposits that **Seller** retains as liquidated damages for a buyer's default in a transaction, not to exceed the paragraph 6(a) fee.

7. **COOPERATION WITH OTHER BROKERS: Broker's** office policy is to cooperate with all other brokers except when not in **Seller's** best interest, and to offer compensation to: ❏ Buyer's agents, who represent the interest of the buyer and not the interest of **Seller** in a transaction, even if compensated by **Seller** or **Broker.** ❏ Subagents.
❏ Transaction brokers, who represent neither **Seller** nor the buyer, but who facilitate the sales transaction.
❏ None of the above (if this box is checked, the Property cannot be placed in the MLS).

8. **SELLER'S AGENT; POTENTIAL FOR DUAL AGENCY:** By signing this Contract, **Broker** agrees to represent and act as **Seller's** agent within the scope of this Contract. A seller's agent owes the seller the fiduciary duties of loyalty, confidentiality, obedience, full disclosure, accounting and the use of skill, care and diligence in carrying out **Broker's** duties under this Contract. However, if (i) **Broker** represents a buyer who expresses interest in **Seller's** Property; or (ii) **Broker** or an agent in the listing office wishes to buy the Property, **Broker's** office policy is to act as a:
   ❏ **(a) Disclosed Dual Agent:** A disclosed dual agent has all the fiduciary duties except full disclosure between the buyer and **Seller.** This means that **Broker** will not reveal confidential information about the parties, such as **Seller's** motivation for selling or willingness to accept less than the listed price or the buyer's willingness to pay more than the offer price. When the situation arises, **Broker** will disclose to **Seller** all facts pertaining to the potential dual agency and will not undertake disclosed dual agency without the buyer's and **Seller's** written consent.
   ❏ **(b) Transaction Broker:** A transaction broker does not represent **Seller** or the buyer as an agent. Instead, **Broker** will treat both **Seller** and the buyer with honesty and fairness; will disclose all known facts materially affecting the value of residential property to both parties; will account to both parties for money or property that comes into **Broker's** possession; and will use skill, care and diligence in facilitating the transaction.

9. **CONDITIONAL TERMINATION:** At **Seller's** request, **Broker** may agree to conditionally terminate this Contract. If **Broker** agrees to conditional termination, **Seller** must sign a withdrawal agreement, reimburse **Broker** for all direct expenses incurred in marketing the Property and pay a cancellation fee of $_____ plus applicable sales tax. **Broker** may void the conditional termination and **Seller** will pay the fee stated in paragraph 6(a) less the cancellation fee if **Seller** transfers or contracts to transfer the Property or any interest in the Property during the time period from the date of conditional termination to Termination Date and Protection Period, if applicable.

10. **DISPUTE RESOLUTION:** This Contract will be construed under Florida law. All controversies, claims and other matters in question between the parties arising out of or relating to this Contract or the breach thereof will be settled by first attempting mediation under the rules of the American Mediation Association or other mediator agreed upon by the parties. If litigation arises out of this Contract, the prevailing party will be entitled to recover reasonable attorney's fees and costs, unless the parties agree that disputes will be settled by arbitration as follows:
   Arbitration: By initialing in the space provided, **Seller** (_____) (_____), Listing Agent (_____) and Listing Broker (_____) agree that disputes not resolved by mediation will be settled by neutral binding arbitration in the county in which the Property is located in accordance with the rules of the American Arbitration Association or other arbitrator agreed upon by the parties. Each party to any arbitration or litigation (including appeals and interpleaders) will pay its own fees, costs and expenses, including attorney's fees, and will equally split the arbitrators' fees and administrative fees of arbitration.

11. **MISCELLANEOUS:** This Contract is binding on **Broker's** and **Seller's** heirs, personal representatives, administrators, successors and assigns. **Broker** may assign this contract to another listing office. Signatures, initials and modifications communicated by facsimile will be considered as originals. The term "buyer" as used in this Contract includes buyers, tenants, exchangors, optionees and other categories of potential or actual transferees.

Broker advises Seller to consult an appropriate professional for related legal, tax, property condition, environmental, foreign reporting requirements and other specialized advice.

Date: _____ Seller: _____ Tax ID No: _____
Home Telephone: _____ Work Telephone: _____ Facsimile: _____
Address: _____

Date: _____ Seller: _____ Tax ID No: _____
Home Telephone: _____ Work Telephone: _____ Facsimile: _____
Address: _____

Date: _____ Authorized Listing Agent or Broker: _____
Brokerage Firm Name: _____ Telephone: _____
Address: _____

Copy returned to **Seller** on the _____ day of _____, 19_____ by: ❏ personal delivery ❏ mail ❏ facsimile.

This form is available for use by the entire real estate industry and is not intended to identify the user as a REALTOR. REALTOR is a registered collective membership mark which may be used only by real estate licensees who are members of the National Association of REALTORS and who subscribe to its Code of Ethics.
The copyright laws of the United States (17 U.S. Code) forbid the unauthorized reproduction of blank forms by any means including facsimile or computerized forms.
ERS-5   Rev. 10/95   ©1995 Florida Association of REALTORS®   All Rights Reserved

Figure 11-1. Listing Contract *(continued)*

Occasionally, after having been shown a particular piece of property through a broker, a prospect and the property owner may arrange a sale "behind the broker's back." Together they wait for the listing to expire, then contract for the sale without advising the broker, in an attempt to elude the payment of a commission. Despite the fact that the listing has expired, courts are likely to require payment to a licensed broker whose listing expired, if she can show that she was the procuring cause of the sale.

Termination of Listings

Listing agreements may be terminated either by the parties or by operation of law.
Termination by the parties can occur through:
1. *Performance.* The broker procures a purchaser; the listing contract is terminated when the sale is completed.
2. *Mutual consent.* Both parties agree to terminate the listing.
3. *Expiration of agreed time.* A listing generally has a definite expiration date. If it doesn't, the listing ends after a reasonable period. In many states a listing must have a fixed expiration date.
4. *Revocation by the principal.* At any time, the principal may revoke authority given to the broker. However, the principal may be liable for damages resulting from the breach of contract, but not if he can show the agent to have been negligent in her duties, as by disloyalty, dishonesty, or incompetence.
5. *Revocation by the broker.* An agent may terminate the listing contract or abandon it. However, he may be held liable for damages to the principal because of failure to complete the object of the listing contract.

Termination by law can occur through:
1. *Death of either party.* The death of either the principal or the broker generally causes termination of a listing contract.
2. *Bankruptcy of either party.* Bankruptcy of a principal or an agent normally terminates an agency.
3. *Insanity of either party.* If either party is judged to be insane, he is considered incapable of completing the contract; therefore, the listing contract will terminate.
4. *Destruction of the property.* If the property upon which the agency had been created is destroyed, the agency is terminated.

Questions on Chapter 11

1. When more than one broker is employed by an owner to sell real estate, there exists
    (A) an exclusive agency listing   (C) an exclusive right to sell
    (B) an open listing   (D) a unilateral listing

2. To collect a commission in court, a broker must show that
    (A) he is licensed
    (B) he had a contract of employment
    (C) he is the cause of the sale
    (D) all of the above

3. The broker's responsibility to the owner of realty is regulated by
    (A) the law of agency   (C) rendition superior
    (B) the law of equity   (D) investiture

4. What is a real estate listing?
    (A) A list of brokers and salespersons
    (B) A list of property held by an owner
    (C) The employment of a broker by an owner to sell or lease
    (D) A written list of improvements on land

5. Under an open listing
   (A) the seller is not legally required to notify other agents in the case of sale by one of the listing brokers
   (B) the owner may sell the property without paying a commission
   (C) both A and B
   (D) neither A nor B

6. If the listing owner sells her property while the listing agreement is valid, she is liable for a commission under a(n) _____ listing agreement.
   (A) net
   (B) exclusive right to sell
   (C) exclusive agency
   (D) open

7. Under an exclusive agency listing,
   (A) the seller may sell by his own effort without obligation to pay a commission
   (B) the broker receives a commission regardless of whether the property is sold
   (C) both A and B
   (D) neither A nor B

8. The listing agreement may not be terminated
   (A) without compensation if the broker has found a prospect ready, able, and willing to buy on the seller's terms
   (B) because of incompetence of the prospect
   (C) if the seller files for bankruptcy
   (D) if the listing agreement is for a definite time

9. A multiple listing
   (A) is illegal in certain states
   (B) is a service organized by a group of brokers
   (C) requires that members turn over eligible listings within 12 days
   (D) causes lost commission

10. Under which type of listing are brokers reluctant to actively pursue a sale, because of the risk of losing a sale to competing brokers?
    (A) An exclusive right to sell listing
    (B) A net listing
    (C) An open listing
    (D) A multiple listing

11. A principal may sell her property without paying a commission under
    (A) an open listing
    (B) an exclusive agency listing
    (C) both A and B
    (D) neither A nor B

12. The rate of commission is normally fixed under
    (A) a net listing
    (B) an open listing
    (C) both A and B
    (D) neither A nor B

13. Buyer and seller both may pay a commission so long as
    (A) all parties are aware of the situation
    (B) payments are made to the same broker
    (C) both A and B
    (D) neither A nor B

14. It is possible to terminate a listing by
    (A) revocation by the principal
    (B) revocation by the agent
    (C) both A and B
    (D) neither A nor B

15. An exclusive right to sell listing enables
    (A) the seller to sell the property himself without paying a commission
    (B) cooperating brokers to sell and earn a commission
    (C) both A and B
    (D) neither A nor B

TRUE/FALSE

Write *T* for true, *F* for false.

_____16. Real estate associations strongly suggest that members secure net listings.

_____17. A listing agreement may be terminated by agreement of the parties.

_____18. A listing agreement is terminated when the subject property is destroyed by fire.

_____19. The rate of commission is set by the National Association of REALTORS®.

_____20. If no expiration date is written in a listing contract, the contract is forever binding.

Questions 21 to 33 refer to the following narrative:

You are a salesperson for Able Realty. On May 10, 1996, you list a 10-year-old house owned by Mr. and Mrs. Nebulous under an exclusive right to sell listing for 3 months. The property is a one-story brick house with four bedrooms and two baths. It has a full basement, which measures 35 ft. × 40 ft. The lot measures 120 ft. × 70 ft.; it is fenced. It is described as Lot 9, Block F, of the Lake Alpine Subdivision, Banks County, Florida. It is also known as 1314 Geneva Drive, Hometown, Florida.

The house has central air conditioning and an entrance foyer. The living room measures 15 ft. × 12 ft. Bedrooms are about average size for this type of house, in your opinion. The house has an eat-in kitchen with a built-in oven and range. The owners state that the dishwasher and refrigerator will remain, but they plan to take the clothes washer and dryer.

The house is heated by natural gas. Water is heated the same way. Water is supplied by the county. The house is on a sewer line.

Bunn is the elementary school; Gunter, the junior high; Washington, the high school.

The tax rate is 24 mills; the latest tax appraisal is $85,000; the assessment ratio is 100 percent. There are no exemptions.

You list the house for $99,500. The commission rate is 6 percent. There is an existing, assumable 8.5 percent mortgage on the property. The current balance is $68,229.12, with equal monthly payments of $549.93. The owners will accept a second mortgage for up to $10,000 at a 9 percent interest rate for 7 years.

21. Which of the following is correct?
    (A) The washer and dryer remain
    (B) The refrigerator remain
    (C) Both A and B
    (D) Neither A nor B

22. The listing expires on
    (A) May 10, 1996
    (B) July 10, 1996
    (C) July 9, 1996
    (D) none of the above

23. Which of the following is correct?
    (A) Natural gas heats the house
    (B) The house is on a sewer line
    (C) Both A and B
    (D) neither A nor B

24. Taxes for the year are
    (A) $510
    (B) $2040
    (C) $5100
    (D) none of the above

25. If the house is sold at the listed price, the commission will be
    (A) $4489
    (B) $5441
    (C) $5970
    (D) none of the above

26. The balance on the existing mortgage is
    (A) $68,229.12
    (B) $71,156.15
    (C) $10,000
    (D) $99,500

27. Which of the following is correct concerning schools?
    (A) Gunter—junior high
    (B) Bunn—high
    (C) Washington—elementary
    (D) None of the above

28. Which features does the house have?
    (A) Central air conditioning
    (B) A fireplace
    (C) Both A and B
    (D) Neither A nor B

29. The basement measurements are
    (A) 30 ft. × 40 ft.
    (B) 40 ft. × 40 ft.
    (C) 35 ft. × 40 ft.
    (D) none of the above

30. The lot is in Block _____ of the Lake Alpine Subdivision.
    (A) A
    (B) B
    (C) C
    (D) None of the above

31. Which of the following is correct?
    (A) There is an eat-in kitchen.
    (B) The dining room is 15 ft. × 12 ft.
    (C) Both A and B
    (D) Neither A nor B

32. The listing is for a period of
    (A) 90 days
    (B) 3 months
    (C) both A and B
    (D) neither A nor B

33. The house has
    (A) four bedrooms
    (B) a wood exterior
    (C) both A and B
    (D) neither A nor B

ANSWERS

1. B	8. A	15. D	22. D	29. C
2. D	9. B	16. F	23. C	30. D
3. A	10. C	17. T	24. B	31. A
4. C	11. C	18. T	25. C	32. B
5. C	12. B	19. F	26. A	33. A
6. B	13. A	20. F	27. A	
7. A	14. C	21. B	28. A	

Chapter 12/*Other Real Estate Contracts*

People dealing in real estate may want to accomplish transactions that do not involve the categories of contracts discussed in Chapters 8 through 11. Contracts not included in those categories are:

1. Contracts for the exchange of real estate
2. Contracts for deed
3. Options
4. Assignments
5. Novations

Each of these contracts is discussed below.

Contracts for Exchange

A *contract for exchange* is used when principals want to exchange property. If both properties are of equal value and both are unencumbered, they may be swapped without additional consideration. This transaction may be beneficial to the principals. For example, one person may own land and want income-producing property, whereas the other party may have reverse holdings and needs. A swap accomplishes the objectives of both parties. Further, if it is an even swap of real estate used in trade or business or held as an investment, and no additional consideration is given, the transaction may possibly be tax-free for both parties, even though the properties exchanged are worth much more now than they cost originally.

More often than not, the properties exchanged are of different values. Then the party who gives up the lower valued property must also give other consideration so that the trade becomes a fair one, acceptable to both parties. Personal property (cash, cars, diamonds, etc.) put into an exchange to equalize the total value of all property exchanged is called *boot*. The party who receives boot may be taxed to the extent of the unlike property received or, if less, to the gain realized.

Mortgaged property can be exchanged. Suppose Mr. Jones owns a $10,000 vacant lot free and clear; Mr. Smith owns a $50,000 building with a $40,000 mortgage against it. Since the equity of both is $10,000, the exchange is a fair trade. Smith's boot received is relief from a $40,000 debt.

Two-way exchanges may be more or less difficult to accomplish than three-way trades, or trades involving four parties. There is no limit to the number of parties involved in an exchange.

Contract for Deed

In a *contract for deed* (sometimes called *land contract*), the property seller finances the sale but does not surrender the deed until all payments have been made. This type of contract typically allows the purchaser to gain possession, but not ownership, of the land while paying for it. Since the seller retains the deed until the final payment, he is well protected in the event of default. In many states, because the land is still legally his, he doesn't have to go through foreclosure; he can have the defaulting buyer evicted quickly and regain full possession and ownership of the land.

Options

An *option* gives its holder the right, but *not* the obligation, to buy specific property within a certain time at a specified price. The option need not be exercised. An *optionee* can elect not to purchase the property, in which case amounts paid to acquire the option belong to the property owner, who is the *optionor*.

Consideration must be paid with an option. Upon exercise of the option, the amount paid for the option may or may not apply to the sales price, depending upon the agreement.

An option may be used by a speculator who is uncertain whether a significant increase in the value of the property is forthcoming. Through purchasing an option, she can be assured of a fixed price for the property in a set time span. If the value increase materializes, she exercises the option. Otherwise, she lets it lapse and loses only the cost of the option. The holder of an option may sell the option itself (at a gain or a loss) if she wishes to do so.

Assignments

Assignments refer to the transfer of contracts. Through an assignment, a person may convey to someone else his rights under a contract. A lease may be assigned, as may a contract of sale, a deed, an option, and so on. The person who gives or assigns the contract is the assignor; the receiver, the assignee. It should be noted that the assignor is not automatically relieved of his duties to other parties under the earlier contract. If a lease contract exists and is assigned, for example, the original lessee is still bound to pay rent if the assignee fails to do so.

Novations

A *novation* is a contract used to substitute a new contract for an existing contract between the same parties. It may also be used to substitute or replace one party to a contract with a different party. Thus, a novation is used to amend an agreement or substitute the parties involved.

A novation must be bilateral: both parties must agree to it. Suppose a home is to be sold, with the buyer assuming the seller's mortgage. Since the seller made a contract to repay the debt, she cannot automatically substitute the new buyer for herself on the debt. Acceptance of the substitution must come from the lender. The process used for this substitution is called a *novation*. In such a case, the original contract has been assigned, while at the same time the assignor has been relieved of her obligations to other parties to the contract.

Questions on Chapter 12

1. Property, unlike real estate, that is used to equalize the value of all property exchanged is called
   (A) listing
   (B) gain
   (C) boot
   (D) equalizers

2. Mr. Hill has a 6-month option on 10 acres at $10,000 per acre. Mr. Hill may
   (A) buy the property for $100,000
   (B) sell the option to another
   (C) not buy the land
   (D) all of the above

3. A contract that gives someone the right but not the obligation to buy at a specified price within a specified time is
   (A) a contract for sale
   (B) an option
   (C) an agreement of sale
   (D) none of the above

4. A contract for deed also is known as
   (A) an installment land sales contract
   (B) a mortgage
   (C) a land contract
   (D) both A and C

5. Which of the following best describes an installment or land contract?
   (A) A contract to buy land only
   (B) A mortgage on land
   (C) A means of conveying title immediately, while the purchaser pays for the property
   (D) A method of selling real estate whereby the purchaser pays for the property in regular installments, while the seller retains title to the property

6. Mr. Beans owns land worth $50,000; Mr. Pork owns a house worth $300,000, subject to a $200,000 mortgage that Beans will assume. For a fair trade,
   (A) Pork should pay $50,000 cash in addition
   (B) Beans should pay $50,000 cash in addition
   (C) Beans and Pork may trade properties evenly
   (D) none of the above

7. A speculator can tie up land to await value enhancement, without obligating himself, through the use of
   (A) an installment land contract   (C) a contract for deed
   (B) an option   (D) A and C only

8. Ms. Smith wants to buy Jones's house and assume the 6 percent mortgage. Jones should
   (A) assign the debt
   (B) grant an option on the debt
   (C) ask the lender for a novation to substitute Smith
   (D) none of the above

9. Larry assigned his rights to use leased property to Allen. Allen stopped paying rent. Larry may
   (A) sue Allen for the rent
   (B) not pay the property owner since he hasn't received payment from Allen
   (C) both A and B
   (D) neither A nor B

10. Treasure Homes sold a lot to Mr. Kay under a real property land sales contract. Upon making the down payment, Kay is entitled to
    (A) a warranty deed   (C) a fee simple estate
    (B) use of the property   (D) all of the above

ANSWERS

1. **C**	5. **D**	9. **A**
2. **D**	6. **B**	10. **B**
3. **B**	7. **B**	
4. **D**	8. **C**	

PART IV: REAL ESTATE ANALYSIS

Chapter 13/*Mortgages and Finance*

Most real estate professionals learn very early in their careers that borrowed money is the lifeblood of the real estate business, because nearly all real estate purchases are made with borrowed funds. In addition, most real estate development and construction uses borrowed money. Without access to such funds, these aspects of the real estate business dry up quickly; such cessation of activity has occurred several times during periods of "tight" money, when interest rates are high and loanable funds scarce.

There are several reasons for this dependence on borrowed money in the real estate business. Perhaps the most significant reason is that real estate is *expensive*. Even a modest home costs more than $100,000; apartment projects, office buildings, shopping complexes, and the like often cost in the millions. Very few of the more than 60 percent of Florida families that own their own homes could do so if they had not been able to borrow a significant portion of the price at the time of purchase. Quite simply, very few families have the kind of ready cash necessary to buy a home without borrowing. Similarly, very few real estate developers or builders have enough cash on hand to finance completely the ventures they engage in.

Another fact that contributes to the importance of borrowed money in the real estate business is that real estate is *very good collateral* for loans. It lasts a long time and so can be used to back up loans that have very long repayment terms, such as the 20 to 30 years typical of most home mortgage loans. This enables real estate owners to spread the cost of an asset over a long payment term, so that they can afford more expensive units, as well as to spread the payment over the time they expect to use the asset.

Real estate is *stable in value*. Of course, some real estate values are more stable than others, but generally a lender can expect that real estate collateral will not depreciate quickly and may indeed rise in value.

Real estate investors like to borrow money to buy real estate because it gives them *leverage*. As a simple example, suppose someone buys an apartment complex costing $5 million by putting up $1 million of his own money and getting a mortgage loan for the other $4 million. In effect, he has gained "control" of a $5 million property but has used only $1 million to do it. By borrowing he is able to buy considerably more than if he used only his own money; if he is wise in his choices of the real estate to buy, he may improve his investment profits considerably by borrowing.

Mortgages and Notes

In the financing of real estate in Florida, two important documents are employed: the *loan*, the evidence for which is a *note* or *bond* and the *mortgage*, which is a pledge of property as security for a debt. A simplified sample of a note and of a mortgage is shown below.

NOTE OR BOND	MORTGAGE
Date I owe you $100,000, payable at the rate of $900 per month for 20 years, beginning next month. Signed, T. Borrower	Date If I don't pay on the attached note, you can take 34 Spring Street, Hometown. Signed, T. Borrower

Since the borrower gives the note and mortgage to the lender, the borrower is the *mortgagor*. The lender is the *mortgagee*. (The suffix *-or* always signifies the giver, whereas *-ee* describes the receiver.)

A mortgage and a note are both contracts. Any provisions that are agreed upon may be written into either contract, so long as such provisions are legal. The essential elements of a note are (a) a promise to pay at (b) a fixed or determinable time (c) a certain sum of money (d) to a payee or to bearer, (e) signed by the borrower.

Title and Lien Theory

Mortgages (also called *trust deeds* in several states) are viewed either as transfers of property (title theory) or as the creation of a lien (lien theory). Title theory holds that the property is transferred to the lender subject to an automatic return of the property to the borrower upon payment of the loan. Lien theory holds that a mortgage gives the lender a lien on the property, but not title to it.

Florida embraces the lien theory; that is, the mortgage lender has a lien against the property. In the event of default, the lender may foreclose and sell the property to satisfy the debt. Upon delinquency (being late on a payment or two), a *grace period* may be provided before a default is declared. In the absence of default, the property owner has the usual rights that accompany ownership, including use, enjoyment, and disposition. The mortgagor (borrower) is expected to keep the property in good repair (not commit *waste,* insure the property, pay all taxes and assessments, and pay interest and principal).

In a *deed of trust* (not commonly used in Florida), title is vested in a third party (trustee) for the benefit of the lender (beneficiary). This takes the foreclosure a step away from possible illegal acts of a too-aggressive borrower who is overly concerned with gaining the property.

Mortgage Loan Classification

Mortgages are often classified or described according to particular provisions. Several types of mortgages and their provisions are described below.

VA MORTGAGES (ALSO KNOWN AS GI MORTGAGES)

The Veterans Administration (VA) guarantees to private lenders that, in the event of default, the VA will make restitution. The VA guarantee is good for up to 60 percent of the original loan or the veteran's "entitlement," whichever is less. Eligible veterans have an entitlement of $36,000 (as of 1996, but the entitlement amounts are raised every few years). For a loan amount above $100,000, the VA may increase the entitlement to $50,750. A VA loan need not require a down payment. The maximum no-down-payment loan is four times the veteran's entitlement ($144,000 as of 1996). If the veteran does make any down payment, the maximum loan is four times the sum of entitlement plus down payment. Only an eligible veteran can originate a VA loan, but anyone, including a nonveteran, can assume the loan from the veteran. Once a veteran originates a loan, that loan will be "charged" against his entitlement until the loan either is paid off or is assumed by another eligible veteran who is willing to substitute her entitlement. However, it still may be possible for a veteran with an existing VA loan on his entitlement to get another VA loan. Entitlement is "used" only to the extent of 25 percent of the VA loan. For example, if a veteran had a VA loan for $70,000 that was assumed by someone else, then 25 percent of $70,000, or $17,500 of the veteran's $36,000 entitlement, would be "used." This would leave $18,500 (as of 1996) unused, so the veteran theoretically could buy another house for up to $74,000 with no money down.

The main advantage of the VA loan is its no-down-payment feature. Lenders have greater security because they may look to the borrower, the VA, and/or the property in the event of default. For example, suppose that a veteran borrows $60,000 on a VA mortgage, reduces it to $58,000, and then defaults. The property is foreclosed and sold for $40,000. The VA will repay the lender $18,000 (the outstanding balance less the amount realized at foreclosure) plus expenses of foreclosure.

FHA MORTGAGES

The Federal Housing Administration (FHA), which is now part of the Department of Housing and Urban Development (HUD), has many programs that help to provide housing. They insure single-family and multifamily housing loans, nursing home mortgage loans, and loans on mobile homes and other properties. Some FHA loans provide subsidies to eligible borrowers. An FHA-insured loan requires only a small down payment, which is the principal advantage to borrowers. Borrowers need their own cash only for the down payment and closing costs. The required down payment is 3 percent of the first $50,000 of price plus closing costs, and 5 percent of the amount over $50,000. There also are maximum limits on the amount of an FHA insured loan, from (as of 1994) as little as $67,500 in some low-cost areas to over $150,000 in designated high-cost areas.

The fee for FHA mortgage loan insurance is paid partly at origination (around 2 percent of the loan amount) and partly by a monthly fee. The insurance is supposed to be paid for by the borrower, although it is possible to bargain with the seller of the property to have him pay some or all of the fee due at origination. Even with the insurance premium, however, the cash requirement for an FHA loan is relatively small. This feature and the fact that borrower qualification standards are somewhat less stringent then for conventional loans are the main attractions of FHA loans to borrowers. The main attraction to lenders is the insurance of the loan balance. Note that property, lender, and borrower all must meet FHA qualifications.

CONVENTIONAL MORTGAGES

Conventional mortgages are loans that are neither guaranteed by the VA nor insured by the FHA. These mortgages may be insured privately, with *private mortgage insurance* (called "PMI" in the mortgage business). Normally, on conventional loans with 80% loan-to-value ratio or less, no PMI is required. However, if the loan is for more than 80 percent of the lower of (a) the appraised value of the mortgaged property or (b) its sale price, lenders will require PMI, which is paid for by the borrower. Conventional loans may be for as much as 100 percent of the purchase price, provided that PMI covering the loan amount in excess of 80% loan-to-value can be purchased. However, as a practical matter, the cost of PMI makes loans of much more than 90% loan-to-value so expensive as not to be worthwhile for a borrower.

PURCHASE MONEY MORTGAGES

Sometimes a *seller* provides financing for a purchaser by accepting a mortgage loan in lieu of cash for all or part of the purchase price. A mortgage of this type, where the seller accepts a mortgage loan, is called a *purchase money mortgage*. The seller effectively gives purchase money to the buyer.

CONSTRUCTION LOANS AND PERMANENT MORTGAGES

Construction loans are used by builders or developers to improve land. Construction loan advances are permitted as construction progresses. When commercial property is completed, a *permanent loan* is used to pay off completely the construction loan. Construction loans on single-family homes usually continue until a residence is sold and the occupant arranges permanent financing.

The word *permanent* as it is used in real estate financing is a misnomer. Permanent mortgage loans seldom have terms beyond 30 years, and most will be repaid before their full terms. Recent experience has shown that the typical mortgage loan is outstanding for about 12 years.

TERM LOANS, AMORTIZING LOANS, AND BALLOON PAYMENT LOANS

A *term loan*, or *straight term loan,* requires only interest payments until maturity. At the end of the maturity term, the *entire* principal balance is due.

Amortizing loans require regular, periodic payments. Each payment is greater than the interest charged for that period, so that the principal amount of the loan is reduced at least slightly with each payment. The amount of the monthly payment for an amortizing loan is calculated to be adequate to retire the *entire* debt over the amortization period.

A *balloon payment loan* requires interest and some principal to be repaid during its term, but the debt is not fully liquidated. Upon its maturity, there is still a balance to be repaid.

HOME EQUITY LINES OF CREDIT

The *home equity line of credit* is like a second mortgage loan, but the borrower does not have to take possession of all of the money at one time. This type of loan is well suited for borrowers who anticipate that they will need more money in the near future, but do not need it immediately.

Setting up a home equity line can be like applying for a credit card. However, because a second mortgage is involved, there is processing, including an appraisal of the property. The application fee may be up to 2 percent of the line of credit, though some lenders may reduce or even waive this fee. Some plans also charge an annual fee to encourage the borrower to use the line once it has been granted. In addition, many plans require the borrower to take out a minimum amount when the loan is granted.

Home equity lines of credit offer a flexible way to access home equity, thereby financing periodic needs with tax-deductible interest. (Up to $100,000 of home equity loans generate tax-deductible housing interest, whereas personal interest is no longer deductible.) Borrowers may tailor the plan to the way they want to handle the payments and can draw upon the line with checks (good for infrequent, large withdrawals) or credit cards (for frequent, smaller withdrawals).

BUDGET MORTGAGES

Budget mortgages require a homeowner to pay, in addition to monthly interest and principal payments, one-twelfth of the estimated taxes and insurance into an escrow account. These mortgages reduce a lender's risk, for the lender is thus assured that adequate cash will be available when an annual tax or insurance bill comes due.

PACKAGE MORTGAGE

Package mortgages include appliances, drapes, and other items of personal property in the amount loaned. The lender tends to exercise more control over a borrower's monthly obligations, and the borrower is able to spread the payment for such items over a lengthy period.

CHATTEL MORTGAGE

A *chattel mortgage* is a mortgage on personal property. The property may be a car, boat, furniture, or the like.

BLANKET MORTGAGE

A *blanket mortgage* covers more than one parcel of real estate. *Release provisions* are usually included to allow individual parcels to be released from the mortgage upon payment of part of the mortgage principal.

Mortgage Repayment

For decades only one mortgage repayment method was available for home loans: *fixed-interest, fixed-payment amortization*. On these loans, the interest rate was always the same, the monthly payment was always the same, and when all the scheduled payments had been made, the loan balance was paid in full. Beginning in the 1970s, however, a variety of other methods entered the mortgage market. Today, the most popular loans are fixed-rate mortgages (FRMs) and adjustable rate mortgages (ARMs), each of which has several variations.

FIXED-RATE MORTGAGES

The *fixed-rate mortgage (FRM)* is the most popular modern mortgage instrument. It features an interest rate that does not change; it is "fixed" over the life of the loan. Fixed-rate loans can have any term up to 30 years (even longer in certain restricted government-subsidized programs). The most popular term, however, is 30 years, followed by 15 years and 20 years. In a typical FRM the monthly payment remains the same throughout the loan term; by the end of the term the loan has been completely repaid to the lender. However, there are some plans in which the monthly payment is not always the same; the most common of these are graduated payment mortgages and balloon mortgages.

Graduated Payment Mortgage (GPM)

The GPM is designed to allow a relatively low monthly payment in the first years of the loan; the payment is increased by some amount (or percentage) every year until it becomes high enough to fully amortize (pay off) the loan over the remaining term. Typically, this final payment level will be reached after 5 to as many as 10 years. One unpleasant feature of most GPMs is *negative amortization* in the early years. The loan amount actually goes up instead of down at first, because the payments during the first 3 to 5 years aren't even enough to pay the accumulating interest on the loan; the unpaid interest is added to the loan amount, which keeps growing until the payments become high enough to cover the interest.

Balloon Mortgage

The balloon mortgage features reasonable monthly payments, but a term too short to allow for the loan to be fully paid. Therefore, at the end of the term a large final payment (the "balloon" payment) is due. A typical arrangement is for the borrower to make payments as though the loan had a 30-year term; however, after 10 or 15 years the loan comes due and the entire unpaid balance must be paid.

ADJUSTABLE-RATE MORTGAGES

Adjustable rate mortgages (ARMs) feature interest rates that change every so often. A change in the interest rate, of course, usually means a change in the amount of the monthly payment as well. ARMs were first introduced in the 1970s, but did not become really popular with borrowers until the 1980s, by which time several modifications had been introduced that helped overcome consumer reluctance. When ARMs were first offered, a wide variety of terms and conditions were available. Nowadays the ARM has been fairly well standardized into a few popular versions that have many features in common. All have *periodic adjustment,* an interest rate based upon some *index* of interest rates, and both periodic and lifetime *caps* on interest rates.

The *period* of the loan is the frequency at which adjustments occur; common periods are 6 months and 1 year, but longer periods (3 to 5 years) are gaining in popularity. Today most ARMs have the interest rate adjusted every year. Interest rates aren't adjusted arbitrarily; they are based upon an *index* of interest rates. The ARM contract specifies the index used and the *margin*. Each time the rate is adjusted, this margin will be added to the index rate to get the new rate for the ARM loan for the following period.

The *caps* are limits on changes in the interest rate. The *periodic cap* limits the amount of change for any one period; the *lifetime cap* provides upper and lower interest rate limits that apply for the entire life of the loan. The most popular cap arrangements are "1 and 5" (limited largely to FHA and VA loans) and "2 and 6." The first number is the periodic cap; the second, the lifetime cap. An "annual ARM with 2 and 6 caps" will be adjusted every year (annually), by no more than 2 percentage points (the periodic cap) above or below the previous year's rate, and over the life of the loan the interest rate can't rise by more than 6 percentage points (the lifetime cap) above the original rate. ARMs are popular with lenders, who don't want to get stuck with low-interest loans in a period of rising rates, but have been difficult to "sell" to borrowers, most of whom are unwilling risk a rise in interest rates, which would increase their loan payments. The mortgage industry is addressing this concern with a variety of features and concessions tied to ARM loans. The most popular and effective of these are *convertibility* and *teaser rates*.

The convertibility feature, which is not an automatic part of all ARM loans, allows the borrower to convert the ARM loan to an FRM loan at some time in the future, usually 3, 4, or 5 years after the loan is originated. Typically a fee, usually 0.5 to 1 percent of the loan amount, is charged for conversion. The appeal of convertibility is that the loan doesn't have to be an ARM forever, and the borrower feels "safer" with the ARM because of the conversion privilege.

Teaser rates are unusually low *initial* interest rates. They are very common in ARMs with annual (or shorter) adjustment periods. An interest rate that is attractively low for the first year or two of the ARM translates into low initial payments and thus into genuine money savings for the borrower. Teaser rates can have another useful effect: if the lifetime cap applies to the initial loan rate, then the maximum interest rate on the loan will be relatively low as well. Teaser rates are typically 3 or more percentage points below current FRM interest rates. For example, if FRM loans are available at 8.5 percent interest for 30-year mortgages, the teaser rate for a 30-year annual ARM with 2 and 6 caps probably will be around 5.5 percent, or maybe even lower. This would result in a lifetime cap of 5.5 percent + 6 percent, or 11.5 percent. Even if a year after origination the interest rate were to rise by the full 2 percent annual cap, the second year's rate would be 7.5 percent, still a full point less than the original FRM rate.

To illustrate, for a 30-year FRM for $100,000, at 8.5 percent interest, the monthly payment would be $769. An ARM of $100,000, with a 5.5 percent teaser rate, would require a monthly payment of $568 for the first year, and a maximum possible payment (at 7.5 percent interest) of $696 the second year. The ARM borrower would be more than $2,400 ahead the first year and another $876 ahead the second year, for total cash savings of almost $3,300 over the first 2 years. This "money in the pocket" provides many borrowers with a strong incentive to choose the ARM, particularly if it also has the convertibility feature.

ARMs with longer adjustment periods (3, 5, and even 7 years) are becoming more popular. If they have teaser rates, these rates are much closer to the FRM rate (1 percent to 1.5 percent less, at the most); periodic caps on these loans are higher, although a lifetime cap of about 6 percent is common.

OTHERS

Reverse Annuity Mortgage (RAM)

Here the lender makes the payments to the borrower, gradually advancing money to a (typically elderly) homeowner. The amounts advanced, plus interest, become the principal of the loan. Payments to the lender are deferred until a sale of the property, the death of the homeowner, or a time when the balance owed approaches the market value of the home. RAMs also can be arranged whereby money, borrowed against the home, is used to purchase an annuity contract that will pay the homeowner for life. The homeowner then pays the mortgage interest with income from the annuity.

Biweekly Mortgages

Here the lender figures the monthly payment on a 30-year amortizing loan, then requires half to be paid every 2 weeks. Because there are twenty-six 2-week periods in a year, this is the equivalent of paying for 13 months per year. As a result the loan is retired in 18 to 22 years. For borrowers who are paid every 2 weeks, such a mortgage may fit the budget well. However it may not appeal to those who are paid monthly.

Open-End Mortgage

Using this type of mortgage, the balance can be increased; that is, the funding remains open for an increase in the mortgage amount. A homeowner may buy a house needing extensive repair work. Initially paying $125,000, and getting a $100,000 loan, the balance may be increased to, say, $200,000, as repair work progresses.

Flexible Payment Mortgage

In an ARM (adjustable rate mortgage), the adjusted payment directly follows the change in interest rates, whereas in a flexible payment loan, changes in the interest rate may not be directly felt in the payment. Instead, there may be payment caps that limit the change in payments. Rather than the payment rising to pay for the higher interest requirement, the principal balance increases.

Wraparound Loan

This is really a second mortgage that includes an existing first mortgage in its balance. Suppose property is worth $1 million and has a $600,000 first mortgage at a low interest rate, say 6 percent. A lender might be willing to advance $150,000 at 10 percent in the form of a second mortgage, but there are negative legal or image characteristics associated with the second mortgage. So the potential second mortgage advances $150,000 in cash, and calls the loan a $750,000 wraparound ($600,000 plus $150,000 = $750,000). The interest rate on the wraparound is 8 percent. The borrower pays the wraparound lender the payment on $750,000, and the wraparound lender pays the first mortgage payment.

Swing Loan

This is a loan that allows a borrower to "swing a deal." Suppose a homeowner is buying a new house, but hasn't sold the old one. A swing loan is provided by a bank to a home buyer for a short term to use as equity in the new house; the loan must be repaid when the old house is sold.

Construction Loan

This type of loan funds construction by advancing money in steps as the project is developed. Generally it is considered high risk and is accompanied by a high interest rate, discount points, and fees. Underwriting is more difficult for a proposed project than for one that exists on the market. The construction lender does not want to advance more than is put into the project, so the loan is made in increments—when the land is purchased, streets and utilities installed, foundations, framing, and roofing built, and so on. Before providing a construction loan, a lender generally wants there to be a commitment for permanent financing when an income property is built.

For a *subdivision loan,* release provisions allow parcels to be removed as collateral so the lots may be sold. Releasing a lot requires a payment against the loan.

Bridge Loan

This is a short-term loan to cover the period between the construction loan and the permanent loan. There may be a time lag during which a short-term loan is needed.

Gap Loan

A gap loan is used to fill in for a shortfall until certain conditions have been met, such as an occupancy percentage rate for an office building. The permanent financing may have a floor amount, payable when construction is complete, and a higher amount, payable when occupancy reaches a certain level. A gap loan funds the difference until occupancy reaches the specified level.

Home Equity Loan

For a household that is "house rich" and "cash poor," a home equity loan may be a tempting way to finance a child's college education, or pay for medical bills or some other need. A home equity loan is likely to simply be a second mortgage, but it carries a lower rate than other types of consumer finance.

Land Contract

This is also called a *contract for deed* or an *installment sales contract*. Title does not pass until the final payment is made. This is often used to finance recreational or resort property, or for buyers with poor credit ratings. These are common in Florida because of the popularity of resort and recreational property.

Sale Leasebacks

A lease and a loan share many of the same characteristics, so a lease can be structured to be like a loan. Instead of borrowing to raise money, and then repay the loan, one can sell property and lease it back for a long term (25 or 30 years). The sale generates cash (like borrowing a mortgage), and the rental payments are similar to mortgage payments. At the end of the lease term, there may be a purchase option at a small amount for the property user. This is sometimes a method to arrange 100 percent financing, and to control property without a legal purchase.

Lenders

SAVINGS AND LOAN ASSOCIATIONS

Savings and loan associations hold about 45 percent of all residential mortgages in the United States. They keep most (about 75 percent) of their funds invested in residential mortgages; almost 90 percent of their mortgages are conventional ones. Such percentages have declined with recent laws concerning deregulation of these institutions.

COMMERCIAL BANKS

Commercial banks hold some residential mortgages; they are more active, however, in the construction loan field and in other types of lending. They have a great deal of latitude in the types of activity in which they engage, but strict limitations are imposed for each type. Only about 10 percent of their assets is invested in residential mortgages; of those, about 85 percent are conventional loans.

MUTUAL SAVINGS BANKS

Mutual savings banks have no stockholders; they operate for the benefit of depositors. More than half of their assets are invested in residential mortgages; of these mortgages, slightly over half are conventional loans.

LIFE INSURANCE COMPANIES

Life insurance companies invest about 15 percent of their total assets in residential mortgage loans and hold about 7.5 percent of all residential mortgages. About two thirds of their mortgages are conventional loans; the balance are FHA or VA loans. Life insurance companies are quite active in permanent mortgage loans on income-producing property, including apartments, shopping centers, and office buildings.

FEDERAL NATIONAL MORTGAGE ASSOCIATION

The *Federal National Mortgage Association* (also known as *FNMA* or *"Fanny Mae"*) is a federally chartered, privately owned and managed corporation. It does not make direct loans to homeowners; rather, it purchases first mortgage loans, originated by others, in the secondary mortgage market. FNMA thereby aids in the liquidity of mortgage investments, making mortgages more attractive investments. FNMA presently owns more than 6 percent of all residential mortgages.

MORTGAGE COMPANIES

Mortgage companies, also known as *mortgage bankers,* are the most common sources of home mortgages. However, these businesses do not lend their own money; they are not financial institutions. Rather, they originate and service home mortgage loans on behalf of large investors (insurance companies, banks, pension funds, etc.) in mortgage loans. Mortgage bankers receive a fee for originating loans and fees for servicing them: collecting payments, holding escrows, dunning late payers, and the like.

FEDERAL HOME LOAN MORTGAGE CORPORATION

The FHLMC, or Freddie Mac, is a privately owned corporation that, like FNMA (Federal National Mortgage Association—Fanny Mae), buys mortgages on the secondary market. It buys most of its inventory from savings and loan associations and commercial banks. It also sells participations in pools of mortgages.

GOVERNMENT NATIONAL MORTGAGE ASSOCIATION

This entity, GNMA, or Ginnie Mae, is a U.S. government entity that encourages low income housing. It will subsidize low income mortgages by paying the difference between the 1 percent interest charged to the qualified borrower/homeowner and the market rate paid to the lender.

GNMA also guarantees securities sold to investors by mortgage bankers. The securities are backed by VA and FHA loans.

FARMERS HOME ADMINISTRATION

This agency, FmHA, which has regional branches, provides financing for the purchase and operations of farms and rural homes, and guarantees loans on such properties made by others.

Lender Criteria

Institutional lenders perform a process called *underwriting.* The purpose of this is to assess the risks of making the loan. They look at the property, as well as the borrower. Regarding the property, the lender typically arranges for an appraisal (the cost is paid by the borrower), which will provide information about the property's value, its location and market conditions, including comparable sales.

The lender will get a credit report on the borrower, financial statements, and letters from employers concerning salary, term of employment, and prospects for the continuation of employment. Lenders will verify bank accounts and other assets of the borrower, as well as his or her liabilities.

For a conventional loan on a single-family home, the lender will normally require a 20 percent down payment; if a borrower seeks a greater loan, they will be forced to get private mortgage insurance (PMI). Up to 90 and 95 percent loan-to-value ratios may be obtained. For a duplex or four-unit property, a larger down payment (25 percent) is normally required.

Lenders have certain guidelines to follow if they want to be able to have a truly marketable loan, that is a loan which can be sold to FNMA or FHLMC. This is called a *conforming* loan. The lender will provide a *qualifying ratio* of housing-payments-to-gross-income of 33 percent, and total fixed-payments-to-gross-income of 38 percent. For example, suppose the Andersons earn $10,000 per month. The maximum housing payments they would be allowed are $3,300 per month, including interest, principal, taxes, and insurance. When payments on other long-term debt, such as car loans, are considered, the maximum allowed would be 38 percent ($3,800).

Many lenders will offer *nonconforming* loans to those who don't otherwise qualify. These loans do not conform to FNMA/FHLMC guidelines, and a higher rate of interest is charged. But a nonconforming loan may allow a marginal borrower to purchase the home desired.

With income-producing property, a lender will also look to the debt coverage ratio, and insist that the net operating income from the property exceed debt service by a comfortable margin, that is, by 25 percent or more. So a debt service coverage ratio of 1.25 times net operating income may be required.

When considering a loan on the stock in a cooperative apartment, lenders will consider the risk. If it were an existing, sold-out development, it is less risky than one that is to be built or converted from rental apartments. For those, the developer or sponsor's filings of stock with the Attorney General may offer clues as to the likelihood of success.

Features of Mortgage Loans

POINTS

One *point* is 1 percent of the amount of the loan. Some mortgage loan charges are expressed in terms of points. These charges are either *fees* or *discounts*. Typical fees expressed in points are origination fees, conversion fees (ARM to FRM; see page 129), prepayment penalties, and so on. The actual dollar amount of such a fee depends upon the dollar amount of the loan involved. For example, some new mortgage loans have origination fees. Usually the fee is about one point, or 1 percent of the loan amount. For a loan of $100,000, then, the fee will be $1,000 (1 percent of $100,000); for a loan of $75,000 the fee will be $750, and so on.

Discount points are something else, although they too are expressed as percentages of the loan amount. Discounts are paid at origination in order to reduce the interest rate on the loan. (You can think of discounts as somewhat like interest paid in advance.) Depending upon the amount of the discount required, a lender will offer a variety of interest rates on new mortgage loans. For example, a "menu" of interest rates might be: 8.5 + 0, 8.25 + 1.25, 8.0 + 2.5. These mean that the lender will offer an interest rate of 8.5 percent with no discount (usually called "par"); 8.25 percent in return for a payment of 1.25 percent of the loan amount (a 1.25-point discount); and 8 percent in return for a 2.5-point discount. For a $100,000 loan from this menu, the borrower's interest rate will be 8.5 percent if no discount is paid, 8.25 percent if $1,250 is paid in advance, and 8 percent for an advance payment of $2,500. Why would anyone pay discounts? Actually, most borrowers don't. However, *sellers* often do for a variety of reasons, usually concerned with making a sale more attractive to a buyer.

Because some non-VA loans may have discounts, lenders usually will provide potential borrowers with a selection of interest rates—and associated discounts. For example, the lender may offer 10 percent interest with a 5-point discount, 10.5 percent with a 3-point discount, and 11 percent with no discount at all.

Discounts also are used as *buydowns,* often in association with teaser interest rates. Buydowns substitute an initial charge for interest later in the loan. Most often they are used to provide an unusually low interest rate during the early period of a loan. For example, if the "normal" rate of interest is 11 percent, a lender may offer a buydown (for a fee of about 5.5 percent of the loan amount) that will give the loan an interest rate of 8 percent the first year, 9 percent the second, and 10 percent the third. After the third year, the interest rate will be 11 percent for the rest of the loan period.

PREPAYMENT PENALTIES AND PRIVILEGES

Some mortgage loans allow the borrower to pay off the principal balance at any time. Others require a penalty, such as 3 percent of the outstanding balance, for early debt retirement.

ACCELERATION CLAUSES

An *acceleration clause* states that the full principal balance becomes due upon certain default. If one or more payments are past due (depending on the agreement), the entire loan becomes due.

SALE OF PROPERTY

When mortgaged real estate is sold, the seller often retires the debt from the proceeds of the sale. A prepayment penalty may be imposed. To purchase the property, the buyer, at closing, may pay cash or may have obtained a new loan. In many cases the buyer assumes the existing loan (assumption), or takes on the debt without being personally liable (subject to), as described below.

LOAN ASSUMPTION

Property offered for sale may be encumbered by a loan bearing a low interest rate, which makes it attractive to the real estate purchaser. The buyer may pay the seller for his equity (the difference between the property value if free and clear and the amount of debt) and then *assume* the loan. The purchaser then becomes liable for the loan and its required payments. The original borrower, however, is not automatically freed from his obligation. He may ask the lender for a *novation* (see page 123), which serves to release him from responsibility, and then substitute the new property owner as the sole debtor. In the absence of a novation, the lender may look to the property and to both the original borrower and the subsequent purchaser for repayment.

Rather than assume a loan, a purchaser may agree to take the property *subject* to a mortgage loan. In doing so, the buyer acknowledges the debt, but it does not become her personal liability. In the event of default, she stands to lose no more than her investment.

USURY

Florida has laws prescribing maximum permitted interest rates. Charging a higher interest rate than that permitted by law is considered *usury*. Penalties for usury differ widely depending on the type of loan.

ESTOPPEL CERTIFICATE

An *estoppel certificate* is a statement that prevents its issuer from asserting different facts at a later date. For example, a mortgage originator may wish to sell the mortgage loan (the right to collect payments) to another. The loan purchaser may ask for an estoppel certificate, whereby the borrower states the amount he owes. Later, the borrower is stopped from asserting that he owed less at the time he signed the estoppel certificate.

RELEASING FROM PROPERTY MORTGAGES

Four methods by which property may be released from mortgages are:
1. *Satisfaction piece.* This document from the lender states that the loan is paid off and that the lender releases property from the lien.
2. *Parcel or land release.* This releases part of mortgaged property from the mortgage, usually upon payment of part of the debt.
3. *Postponement of lien.* The lien is not satisfied but is subordinated, meaning that it assumes a lower priority.
4. *Foreclosure.* This is described in detail below.

FORECLOSURE, DEFICIENCY JUDGMENTS, AND EQUITY OF REDEMPTION

Upon certain default, a lender may be allowed to go through an authorized procedure, known as *foreclosure*, to have the property applied to the payment of the debt. Should the property sell at foreclosure for more than the unpaid first mortgage loan plus the expenses of the foreclosure action, the excess belongs to the junior lenders, if any. After all lenders have received full payment, any excess funds go to the borrower.

It is more likely that the proceeds from a foreclosure will be inadequate to pay mortgage indebtedness. In this case, the lender may attempt to get a *deficiency judgment* for the amount of the loan that remains unpaid. This requires the borrower to pay the deficiency personally. Deficiency judgments are difficult to establish in many jurisdictions. Commercial property mortgagors are frequently able to negotiate *exculpatory* clauses in their loans. Exculpatory clauses cause loans to be *nonrecourse;* when such a clause exists, a defaulting borrower may lose the real estate that he has pledged, but he is not personally liable for the debt. The lender may look only to the property as collateral.

Should property be foreclosed, the borrower has the right to redeem the property by repaying in full the principal owed. This is known as *equity of redemption*.

THE FINANCIAL INSTITUTIONS REFORM, RECOVERY AND ENFORCEMENT ACT (1989)

Until the late 1970s, the savings and loan (S&L) industry operated very conservatively. S&Ls took in their depositors' savings (in savings accounts and certificates of deposit) and made home mortgage loans with that money. However, competitive pressures from the banking industry and other forms of investment (notably high interest rates on U.S. government securities) ate into the deposits of the S&Ls and led to "deregulation." This process gradually allowed the S&L industry to diversify its investments into riskier areas and thus make enough income to pay depositors higher rates.

During the 1980s, however, some of the areas into which some S&Ls had channeled their funds turned out to be poor ventures. The rapid drop in oil prices created severe economic times in the "oil patch" states; hardest hit were Texas, Colorado, and Louisiana. These states had previously been experiencing a real estate boom, which lured mortgage loan money from investors, including S&Ls, throughout the country. In addition, the deregulated situation also allowed S&Ls to venture into areas of lending in which they had no expertise.

The result was that a large number of S&Ls became insolvent in the final years of the 1980s. Although deposits in S&Ls were insured by the Federal Savings and Loan Insurance Corporation (FSLIC), the spate of failures rapidly exhausted the FSLIC's reserves. Nevertheless, the federal government technically still remained responsible for up to $150 billion (by some estimates) of shortfall in insured deposits.

The result was the passage, in August 1989, of the Financial Institutions Reform, Recovery and Enforcement Act (FIRREA), a 1000-page law referred to in the news media as the "S&L bailout." FIRREA replaced the FSLIC and FHLBB (Federal Home Loan Bank Board, the agency that formerly regulated the S&L industry) with a new agency, the Resolution Trust Corporation (RTC). RTC is supervising the orderly liquidation of insolvent S&Ls, and may issue bonds to obtain the money needed to pay off depositors. Insurance of deposits in institutions not threatened with insolvency has been taken over by the FDIC (the agency that insures deposits in the banking system).

Questions on Chapter 13 _____

1. The major source of single-family home mortgage loan funds is
   (A) mortgage bankers
   (B) commercial banks
   (C) savings and loan associations
   (D) the Federal National Mortgage Association (FNMA)

2. A conventional mortgage is
   (A) amortizing
   (B) guaranteed by the FHA
   (C) not guaranteed by any government agency
   (D) approved by the VA

3. A chattel mortgage is usually given in connection with
   (A) realty
   (B) farms
   (C) personal property
   (D) commercial property

4. The lending of money at a rate of interest above the legal rate is
   (A) speculation
   (B) usury
   (C) both A and B
   (D) neither A nor B

5. One discount point is equal to
   (A) 1 percent of the sales price
   (B) 1 percent of the interest rate
   (C) 1 percent of the loan amount
   (D) none of the above

6. Discount points in FHA and VA loans are generally paid by the
   (A) lender
   (B) purchaser
   (C) seller
   (D) broker

7. The main appeal of VA mortgages to borrowers lies in
   (A) low interest rates
   (B) minimum down payments
   (C) an unlimited mortgage ceiling
   (D) easy availability

8. When a loan is assumed on property that is sold,
   (A) the original borrower is relieved of further responsibility
   (B) the purchaser becomes liable for the debt
   (C) the purchaser must obtain a certificate of eligibility
   (D) all of the above

9. An estoppel certificate is required when the
   (A) mortgage is sold to an investor
   (B) property is sold
   (C) property is being foreclosed
   (D) mortgage is assumed

10. An owner who seeks a mortgage loan and offers three properties as security will give
    (A) a blanket mortgage
    (B) an FHA mortgage
    (C) a conventional mortgage
    (D) a chattel mortgage

11. A clause in a mortgage or accompanying note that permits the creditor to declare the entire principal balance due upon certain default of the debtor is
    (A) an acceleration clause
    (B) an escalation clause
    (C) a forfeiture clause
    (D) an excelerator clause

12. Which of the following statements is (are) false?
    (A) VA loans are insured loans
    (B) FHA loans are guaranteed loans
    (C) Both A and B
    (D) Neither A nor B

13. A second mortgage is
    (A) a lien on real estate that has a prior mortgage on it
    (B) the first mortgage recorded
    (C) always made by the seller
    (D) smaller in amount than a first mortgage

14. A large final payment on a mortgage loan is
    (A) an escalator
    (B) a balloon
    (C) an amortization
    (D) a package

15. A requirement for a borrower under an FHA-insured loan is that he
    (A) not be eligible for a VA or conventional loan
    (B) have cash for the down payment and closing costs
    (C) have his wife sign as coborrower
    (D) certify that he is receiving welfare payments

16. A mortgaged property can
    (A) be sold without the consent of the mortgagee
    (B) be conveyed by the grantor's making a deed to the grantee
    (C) both A and B
    (D) neither A nor B

17. In the absence of an agreement to the contrary, the mortgage normally having priority will be the one
    (A) for the greatest amount
    (B) that is a permanent mortgage
    (C) that was recorded first
    (D) that is a construction loan mortgage

18. The mortgagor's right to reestablish ownership after delinquency is known as
    (A) reestablishment
    (B) satisfaction
    (C) equity of redemption
    (D) acceleration

19. The Federal National Mortgage Association is active in the
    (A) principal mortgage market
    (B) secondary mortgage market
    (C) term mortgage market
    (D) second mortgage market

20. The money for making FHA loans is provided by
    (A) qualified lending institutions
    (B) the Department of Housing and Urban Development
    (C) the Federal Housing Administration
    (D) the Federal Savings and Loan Insurance Corporation

21. Amortization is best defined as
    (A) liquidation of a debt
    (B) depreciation of a tangible asset
    (C) winding up a business
    (D) payment of interest

22. A mortgage is usually released of record by a
    (A) general warranty deed
    (B) quitclaim deed
    (C) satisfaction piece
    (D) court decree

23. Loans from savings and loan associations may be secured by mortgages on
    (A) real estate
    (B) mobile homes
    (C) both A and B
    (D) neither A nor B

24. The borrower is the
    (A) mortgagee
    (B) creditor
    (C) mortgagor
    (D) both A and B

25. In an amortizing mortgage, the
    (A) principal is reduced periodically along with the payment of interest for that period
    (B) principal is paid at the end of the term
    (C) lenders have greater security than in an unamortizing mortgage
    (D) loan-to-value ratio does not exceed 30 percent

26. A term mortgage is characterized by
    (A) level payments toward principal
    (B) interest-only payments until maturity
    (C) variable payments
    (D) fixed payments including both principal and interest

27. Mortgage bankers
    (A) are subject to regulations of the Federal Reserve System
    (B) are regulated by federal, not state, corporation laws
    (C) act as secondary lenders
    (D) earn fees paid by new borrowers and lenders

28. The seller of realty takes, as partial payment, a mortgage called
    (A) sales financing
    (B) note toting
    (C) primary mortgage
    (D) purchase money mortgage

29. In Florida, a borrower retains title to the real property pledged as security for a debt, which is a
    (A) lien theory state
    (B) title theory state
    (C) creditor state
    (D) community property state

30. A state in which a mortgage conveys title to the lender is known as a
    (A) lien theory state
    (B) title theory state
    (C) conveyance state
    (D) community property state

31. A biweekly mortgage requires
    (A) monthly payments to increase by predetermined steps each year
    (B) payments every 2 weeks
    (C) that the lender share profits from resale
    (D) none of the above

32. The use of reverse annuity mortgages
    (A) is widespread because of inflation
    (B) helps elderly people who are house rich but cash poor
    (C) is losing importance with inflation
    (D) none of the above

33. As to whether a lender is the owner or lien holder, Florida embraces the
    (A) title theory
    (B) lien theory
    (C) trustee theory
    (D) torrens theory

34. A gap mortgage is one used to
    (A) include in its balance an underlying first mortgage
    (B) lend on the equity of one's unsold house to help buy another house
    (C) fund the difference when the amount of a permanent loan will be increased due to tenant occupancy increases
    (D) finance educational or medical costs by someone with substantial equity in a house

35. A swing loan is one used to
    (A) include in its balance an underlying first mortgage
    (B) lend on the equity of one's unsold house to help buy another house
    (C) fund the difference when the amount of a permanent loan will be increased due to tenant occupancy increases
    (D) finance educational or medical costs by someone with substantial equity in a house

36. A wraparound mortgage is one used to
    (A) include in its balance an underlying first mortgage
    (B) lend on the equity of one's unsold house to help buy another house
    (C) fund the difference when the amount of a permanent loan will be increased due to tenant occupancy increases
    (D) finance educational or medical costs by someone with substantial equity in a house

37. A home equity loan is one used to
    (A) include in its balance an underlying first mortgage
    (B) lend on the equity of one's unsold house to help buy another house
    (C) fund the difference when the amount of a permanent loan will be increased due to tenant occupancy increases
    (D) finance educational or medical costs by someone with substantial equity in a house

38. The Federal National Mortgage Association
   (A) is where a home buyer applies for a loan
   (B) buys home loans that already exist
   (C) owns the FHA
   (D) is also known as FHLMC

ANSWERS

1. C	9. A	17. C	25. A	33. B
2. C	10. A	18. C	26. B	34. C
3. C	11. A	19. B	27. D	35. B
4. B	12. C	20. A	28. D	36. A
5. C	13. A	21. A	29. A	37. D
6. C	14. B	22. C	30. B	38. B
7. B	15. B	23. C	31. B	
8. B	16. C	24. C	32. B	

Chapter 14/Appraisals

Examination Content Outline

Salesperson and broker applicants, in addition to those who are seeking specific appraisal designations, should study the material in this chapter.

Florida offers four designations of appraisers:

- **Registered appraiser.** This is an "apprentice" or "trainee" designation that does not require an examination.
  Education. Requires 75 classroom hours of precertification education including coverage of the Uniform Standards of Professional Appraisal Practice.
  Experience. None.
- **Licensed appraiser.** This designation allows its holder to appraise residential properties of one to four units valued up to $1 million.
  Education. Requires 75 classroom hours of precertification education including coverage of the Uniform Standards of Professional Appraisal Practice.
  Experience. 120 appraisal reports, at least two years.
- **Certified residential appraiser.** This designation allows its holder to appraise residential properties of one to four units, having no limit on the value.
  Education. Requires 120 classroom hours of precertification education including coverage of the Uniform Standards of Professional Appraisal Practice.
  Experience. 120 appraisal reports, at least two years.
- **Certified general appraiser.** This designation allows its holder to appraise any property of any value.
  Education. Requires 165 classroom hours of precertification education including coverage of the Uniform Standards of Professional Appraisal Practice.
  Experience. Minimum of 15 narrative appraisal reports or 8 narrative and 90 nonnarrative. At least two years, of which at least 50 percent must be in nonresidential work.

Appraisal Examinations

All three of the examinations (no examination is required to be a registered appraiser) consist of 100 questions, and candidates are given 4 hours for completion. A score of 75 percent is passing for all exams.

To apply for an appraisal license, an applicant must show that he or she:

1. Is 18 years or older.
2. Has a high school diploma or equivalent.
3. Shows successful completion of educational requirements.
4. Makes it possible for the Appraisal Board to begin an inquiry as to competence and qualifications by disclosing records of crimes or proceedings, mental disabilities, and disclosures of suspensions or revocations of other professional licenses.

The application is submitted to:

Division of Real Estate
400 West Robinson Street
Orlando, FL 32801
(407) 317-7251

The text of Chapters 14 and 15 and the questions at the end of each chapter follow the same sequence as the Examination Content Outline given below. Some of the items are covered elsewhere in this book; these items generally concern real estate law or real estate financing. The text is not repeated; instead the appropriate chapter of this book is cited. Multiple-choice questions at the end of each chapter mix pure appraisal questions with more general ones.

Examination Content Outline
Certified General, Certified Residential, and Licensure
Real Property Appraisal Classifications

Percentages represent the estimated proportionate numbers of questions on the examination.

I. **INFLUENCES ON REAL ESTATE VALUE** (page 152)
   Certified general examination 2–3%
   Certified residential examination 3–4%
   Licensure examination 3–4%
   A. Physical and environmental
   B. Economic
   C. Governmental and legal
   D. Social

II. **LEGAL CONSIDERATIONS IN APPRAISAL** (page 152)
   Certified general examination 7–8%
   Certified residential examination 6–8%
   Licensure examination 6–8%
   A. Real estate vs. real property
   B. Real property vs. personal property
      1. Fixtures
      2. Trade fixtures[†]
      3. Machinery and equipment[†]
   C. Limitations on real estate ownership
      1. Private
         a. Deed restrictions
         b. Leases
         c. Mortgages
         d. Easements
         e. Liens
         f. Encroachments
      2. Public
         a. Police power
            (1) Zoning
            (2) Building and fire codes
            (3) Environmental regulations
         b. Taxation
            (1) Property tax
            (2) Special assessments
         c. Eminent domain
         d. Escheat
   D. Legal rights and interests
      1. Fee simple estate
      2. Life estate
      3. Leasehold interest
      4. Leased fee interest
      5. Other legal interests
         a. Easement
         b. Encroachment

[†]Certified general exam only

E. Forms of property ownership
  1. Individual
  2. Tenancies and undivided interest
  3. Special ownership forms
    a. Condominiums
    b. Cooperative
    c. Timesharing*
F. Legal descriptions
  1. Metes and bounds
  2. Government survey
  3. Lot and block
G. Transfer of title
  1. Basic types of deeds
  2. Recordation

III. **TYPES OF VALUE** (page 153)
Certified general examination 2–3%
Certified residential examination 3–5%
Licensure examination 3–5%
A. Market value or value in exchange
B. Price
C. Cost
D. Investment value
E. Value in use
F. Assessed value
G. Insurable value
H. Going-concern value†

IV. **ECONOMIC PRINCIPLES** (page 155)
Certified general examination 3–5%
Certified residential examination 7–9%
Licensure examination 7–9%
A. Anticipation
B. Balance
C. Change
D. Competition
E. Conformity
F. Contribution
G. Increasing and decreasing returns
H. Opportunity cost†
I. Substitution
J. Supply and demand
K. Surplus productivity

V. **REAL ESTATE MARKETS AND ANALYSIS** (page 157)
Certified general examination 5–7%
Certified residential examination 5–7%
Licensure examination 5–7%
A. Characteristics of real estate market
  1. Availability of information
  2. Changes in supply vs. demand
  3. Immobility of real estate
  4. Segmented markets
  5. Regulations
B. Absorption analysis
  1. Demographic data
  2. Competition

---

†Certified general exam only
*Licensure and certified residential exam only

        3. Absorption
        4. Forecasts
        5. Existing space inventory[†]
        6. Current and projected space surplus[†]
        7. New space[†]
  C. Role of money and capital markets
        1. Competing investments
        2. Sources of capital
  D. Real estate financing
        1. Mortgage terms and concepts
            a. Mortgagor
            b. Mortgagee
            c. Principal and interest
        2. Mortgage payment plan
            a. Fixed rate, level payment
            b. Adjustable rate
            c. Buy down
            d. Other
        3. Types of mortgages
            a. Conventional
            b. Insured

VI. VALUATION PROCESS (page 160)
Certified general examination 2–4%
Certified residential examination 4–6%
Licensure examination 4–6%
  A. Definition of problem
        1. Purpose and use of appraisal
        2. Interests to be appraised
        3. Type of value to be estimated
        4. Date of value estimate
        5. Limiting conditions
  B. Collection and analysis of data
        1. National and regional trends
        2. Economic base
        3. Local area and neighborhood
            a. Employment
            b. Income
            c. Trends
            d. Access
            e. Locational convenience
        4. Site and improvements
  C. Analysis of highest and best use
  D. Application and limitations of each approach to value
        1. Sales comparison
        2. Cost
        3. Income capitalization
  E. Reconciliation and final value estimate
  F. Appraisal report

VII. PROPERTY DESCRIPTION (page 163)
Certified general examination 2–4%
Certified residential examination 2–4%
Licensure examination 2–4%
  A. Site description
        1. Utilities
        2. Access

[†]Certified general exam only

3. Topography
4. Size
B. Improvement description
1. Size
2. Condition
3. Utility
C. Basic construction and design
1. Techniques and materials
a. Foundations
b. Framing
c. Finish (exterior and interior)
d. Mechanical
2. Functional utility
VIII. **HIGHEST AND BEST USE ANALYSIS** (page 163)
Certified general examination 5–7%
Certified residential examination 5–7%
Licensure examination 5–7%
A. Four tests
1. Physically possible
2. Legally permitted
3. Economically feasible
4. Maximally productive
B. Vacant site or as if vacant
C. As improved
D. Interim use
IX. **APPRAISAL MATHEMATICS AND STATISTICS** (page 165)
Certified general examination 3–5%
Certified residential examination 1–3%
Licensure examination 1–3%
A. Compound interest concepts†
1. Future value of $1†
2. Present value of $1†
3. Future value of an annuity of $1 per period†
4. Present value of an annuity of $1 per period†
5. Sinking fund factor†
6. Installment to amortize $1 (loan constant)†
B. Statistical concepts used in appraisal
1. Mean
2. Median
3. Mode
4. Range
5. Standard deviation
X. **SALES COMPARISON APPROACH** (page 165)
Certified general examination 10–12%
Certified residential examination 21–24%
Licensure examination 21–24%
A. Research and selection of comparables
1. Data sources
2. Verification
3. Units of comparison
a. Income†
(1) Potential gross income multiplier†
(2) Effective gross income multiplier†
(3) Overall rate†

†Certified general exam only

        b. Size
- (1) Square feet
- (2) Acres
- (3) Other

        c. Utility (examples only)
- (1) Motel and apartment units[†]
- (2) Theater seats[†]
- (3) Rooms[*]
- (4) Beds[*]
- (5) Other

        d. Data sources[*]

B. Elements of comparison
1. Property rights conveyed
   - a. Easements
   - b. Leased fee/leasehold
   - c. Mineral rights[†]
   - d. Others
2. Financing terms and cash equivalency
   - a. Loan payment
   - b. Loan balance
3. Conditions of sale
   - a. Arm's length sale
   - b. Personalty
4. Market conditions at time of contract and closing
5. Location
6. Physical characteristics
7. Tenant improvements[†]

C. Adjustment process
1. Sequence of adjustments
2. Dollar adjustments
3. Percentage adjustments
4. Paired-sales analysis

D. Application of sales comparison approach

XI. SITE VALUE (page 169)
Certified general examination 3–5%
Certified residential examination 4–6%
Licensure examination 4–6%

A. Sales comparison
B. Land residual
C. Allocation
D. Extraction
E. Ground rent capitalization[†]
F. Subdivision analysis[†]
1. Development cost: direct and indirect[†]
2. Contractor's overhead and profit[†]
3. Forecast absorption and gross sales[†]
4. Entrepreneurial profit[†]
5. Discounted value conclusion[†]

G. Plottage and assemblage

XII. COST APPROACH (page 170)
Certified general examination 9–12%
Certified residential examination 8–10%
Licensure examination 8–10%

A. Steps in cost approach

[†]Certified general exam only
[*]Licensure and certified residential exam only

      1. Reproduction vs. replacement cost
        a. Comparative unit method
        b. Unit-in-place method
        c. Quantity survey method
        d. Cost service index
      2. Accrued depreciation
        a. Types of depreciation
          (1) Physical deterioration
            (a) Curable
            (b) Incurable
            (c) Short-lived
            (d) Long-lived
          (2) Functional obsolescence
            (a) Curable
            (b) Incurable
          (3) External obsolescence
            (a) Locational
            (b) Economic
        b. Methods of estimating depreciation
          (1) Age-life method
          (2) Breakdown method and sequence of deductions
    B. Application of the cost approach

XIII. INCOME APPROACH (page 173)
Certified general examination 20–24%
Certified residential examination 7–9%
Licensure examination 7–9%
    A. Estimation of income and expenses
      1. Gross market income
      2. Effective gross income
        a. Vacancy
        b. Collection loss
      3. Operating expenses
        a. Fixed expenses
        b. Variable expenses
        c. Reserve for replacements
      4. Net operating income
    B. Operating statement ratios[†]
      1. Operating expense ratio
      2. Net income ratio[†]
      3. Break-even ratio[†]
    C. Direct capitalization
      1. Relevance and limitations[†]
      2. Overall capitalization rate[†]
      3. Gross income multiplier and net income ratio
      4. Band of investment (mortgage equity) techniques[†]
      5. Residual techniques[†]
        a. Land (building value given)
        b. Building (land value given)
        c. Equity (mortgage value given)
    D. Cash flow estimates (before tax only)[†]
      1. Operating years[†]
        a. Estimating NOI with a change in NOI[†]
        b. Estimating NOI using lease information[†]
        c. Cash flow (NOI less mortgage payment)[†]

[†]Certified general exam only

    2. Reversion[†]
        a. Estimating resale with a change in value[†]
        b. Estimating resale with a terminal capitalization rate[†]
        c. Cash flow (sale price less mortgage balance)[†]
        d. Deductions for cost of sales and legal fees to arrive at a net reversion[†]
  E. Measures of cash flow[†]
    1. Equity dividend rate (cash on cash rate)[†]
    2. Debt coverage ratio[†]
  F. Discounted cash flow capitalization (DCF)[†]
    1. Relevance and limitations[†]
    2. Potential gross income and expense estimate[†]
        a. Market vs. contract rents[†]
        b. Vacancy and lease commissions[†]
        c. Tenant improvements and concessions[†]
    3. Discount rates and yield rates (definition and concept but no calculations of yield rate)[†]
    4. Discounting cash flows (from operations and reversion where all cash flows are projected in dollar amounts and tables or calculators can be used)[†]

XIV. PARTIAL INTERESTS (page 174)
Certified general examination 4–6%
Certified residential examination 1–3%
Licensure examination 1–3%
  A. Interests created in a lease
    1. Leased fee
    2. Leasehold
    3. Subleasehold[†]
    4. Renewal options[†]
    5. Tenant improvements[†]
    6. Concessions[†]
  B. Lease provisions[†]
    1. Overage rent[†]
    2. Expense stops[†]
    3. Net leases[†]
    4. Minimum rent[†]
    5. Percentage rent[†]
    6. CPI adjustments[†]
    7. Excess rent[†]
  C. Valuation considerations[†]
    1. Identifying cash flows to different interests, including turnover ratio[†]
    2. Discount rate selection for different interests[†]
    3. Relationship between values of interests[†]
  D. Other partial interest
    1. Life estates
    2. Undivided interest in commonly held property
    3. Easements
    4. Timeshares
    5. Cooperatives

XV. APPRAISAL STANDARDS AND ETHICS (page 175)
Certified general examination 7–11%
Certified residential examination 7–11%
Licensure examination 7–11%

[†]Certified general exam only

Appraisal

An *appraisal* is an expert's opinion of value. Appraisals are used in real estate when a professional's opinion of value is needed. Because each property is unique and is not traded in a centralized, organized market, value estimates require the collection and analysis of market data.

To understand what appraisals are, please examine the preceding definition more closely. By *an expert*, we mean a person with the competence and experience to do the type of analysis required. You can get opinions of value from the sales agent, the owner, the tenant, or anyone else familiar with the property. However, these opinions may not be very useful and probably won't be convincing as evidence of value. Usually, an appraisal expert has attained some type of designation through formal study and examination by a recognized body such as the state or a professional organization.

An *opinion* is a judgment supported by facts and logical analysis. The appraiser considers all available information that reflects on the value of the property and then follows a logical process to arrive at an opinion. The result is not merely a guess but is a careful reading of the facts in the case.

The appraisal process is a sequence of steps that an appraiser uses in a systematic fashion to derive an estimate of value.

THE APPRAISAL OR VALUATION PROCESS

The preparation of an appraisal report is an eight-step problem-solving exercise that begins with *defining the problem*, for example, "to estimate market value." The second step is to *plan the appraisal*. The third is *data collection and verification*. Fourth, the *highest and best use* of the site is considered, and fifth, the *land value* is estimated. Three *approaches to appraisal: cost, market data* (or direct sales comparison), and *income* (or capitalization) are applied as a sixth step. Each approach provides an independent value estimate. The seventh step is *reconciliation*, in which the value estimates from the three approaches are considered and a *final value conclusion* is reached. The last step is to provide a written *report*. See Figure 14-1, The Appraisal Process.

GOVERNMENT REGULATION

At one time, anyone could claim to be an appraiser, since there was no mandatory test of the skills required to estimate property value. The higher qualifications of some individuals were (and still are) recognized by professional designations conferred by appraisal associations, but such designation was not a requirement for practice as an appraiser. Since 1992, however, a real estate appraiser must be licensed or certified in Florida in order to appraise property in a federally related transaction. Since federally related transactions include any in which an FDIC-insured bank, or FSLIC, FNMA, FHLMC, or GNMA, is involved, probably 90 percent or more of real estate appraisals are now prepared by a state-licensed or -certified appraiser. A licensed real estate broker or salesperson may appraise real estate in situations where there is not a federally related transaction.

Government regulation was imposed as a result of the savings and loan association débacle of the 1980s, when numerous savings institutions collapsed, largely as a result of defective or nonexistent real estate appraisals. An appraisal serves as evidence that a loan is properly supported by collateral and thus serves to protect our nation's financial institutions.

NEED FOR APPRAISAL

An appraisal may be sought for any of a number of purposes, including the following:
1. To help buyers and/or sellers determine how much to offer or accept.
2. To assist lenders in determining the maximum prudent amount to lend on real estate.
3. To arrive at fair compensation when private property is taken for public use.
4. To determine the amount to insure, or the value loss caused by a natural disaster.
5. To determine the viability of a proposed building, renovation, or rehabilitation program.

```
┌─────────────────────────────────────────────────────┐
│          STEP ONE: DEFINITION OF THE PROBLEM          │
│        a. Purpose of assignment                       │
│        b. Type of value sought                        │
│        c. Identification of property and legal interests │
│        d. Date of appraisal                           │
└─────────────────────────────────────────────────────┘
                          ↓
┌─────────────────────────────────────────────────────┐
│             STEP TWO: PLAN OF APPRAISAL               │
│        a. Determine data requirements                 │
│        b. Identify appropriate methodology            │
│        c. Estimate time and personnel needs           │
│        d. Provide fee and assignment proposal         │
└─────────────────────────────────────────────────────┘
                          ↓
┌─────────────────────────────────────────────────────┐
│    STEP THREE: COLLECTION AND VERIFICATION OF DATA    │
│        a. Area and neighborhood                       │
│        b. Site and off-site                           │
│        c. Improvement analysis                        │
│        d. Law and government                          │
│        e. Economic activity data—income, costs, sales │
└─────────────────────────────────────────────────────┘
                          ↓
┌─────────────────────────────────────────────────────┐
│   STEP FOUR: ANALYSIS OF HIGHEST AND BEST USE OF LAND │
│        a. As if vacant                                │
│        b. As improved                                 │
└─────────────────────────────────────────────────────┘
                          ↓
┌─────────────────────────────────────────────────────┐
│            STEP FIVE: ESTIMATE LAND VALUE             │
└─────────────────────────────────────────────────────┘
                          ↓
┌─────────────────────────────────────────────────────┐
│     STEP SIX: APPLICATION OF RELEVANT VALUATION       │
│                     APPROACHES                        │
│        a. Income approach                             │
│        b. Market approach                            │
│        c. Cost approach                              │
│        d. Analysis                                    │
└─────────────────────────────────────────────────────┘
                          ↓
┌─────────────────────────────────────────────────────┐
│             STEP SEVEN: RECONCILIATION                │
│        a. Review of facts as related to valuation principles │
│        b. Statistical and probability indications    │
│        c. Logic and judgment                          │
│        d. Final indicated value conclusions           │
└─────────────────────────────────────────────────────┘
                          ↓
┌─────────────────────────────────────────────────────┐
│    STEP EIGHT: REPORT OF FINAL VALUE ESTIMATE         │
│  Letter of opinion ←──────────────→ Full narrative    │
└─────────────────────────────────────────────────────┘
```

Figure 14-1. The Appraisal Process

Source: INCOME APPRAISAL ANALYSIS, Jack P. Friedman and Nicholas Ordnay, © 1988. Adapted by permission of Prentice Hall, Inc., Upper Saddle River, New Jersey.

6. To assist in corporate mergers, reorganizations, and liquidations.
7. To determine taxes due, including income, gift, estate, and ad valorem taxes.

Comparative Market Analysis

Very often property owners want to get an idea of what their real estate is worth, without paying for a full appraisal. For example, a homeowner may contact a broker or salesperson to list her house, and will accept the broker's or salesperson's judgment regarding its value or the amount for which the house should be listed on the market. A broker may not wish to spend the time to prepare a complete appraisal just to solicit a listing, even if the broker is perfectly qualified to do so. Further, unless the broker is licensed or certified by Florida, the appraisal could not be used to support a loan by a federally chartered bank or savings association.

A Comparative Market Analysis (CMA) will be prepared by the broker or salesperson for this purpose. Unlike the standard pre-printed forms required for Fannie Mae/Freddie Mac residential appraisals, there is no standard form for a CMA. Brokers are free to include whatever information they wish to use, and present it in any manner.

A CMA is likely to show recent sales of other houses in the neighborhood, and salient characteristics. It may also show properties currently on the market for sale. Consider the following data:

Property	Price	Date	Sq. Ft.	# Bedrooms	# Baths	Stories	Per SF
Subject	?	Now	2,000	4	2	1	?
Comp 1	$210,000	Last yr.	2,100	4	2	2	$100.00
Comp 2	$190,000	Last yr.	1,950	3	1.5	1	$97.44
Comp 3	$235,000	6 months	2,250	4	2.5	1	$101.44
Asking 1	$215,000	Now	2,050	3	2	2	$104.87
Asking 2	$225,000	Now	2,100	3	2	1	$107.14

Figure 14-2. Comparative Market Analysis

This particular CMA might be used to judge a market range (highest and lowest prices per square foot). However, it offers no information on special features, the age or condition of the houses, nor how long it took to sell them, or how long the existing listings have been on the market. So a CMA is not as detailed or thorough as an appraisal, though it may provide a reasonable indication of property value.

Residential Market Analysis

A residential market analysis (RMA) provides information on the current housing market situation. It tries to answer the question, "How is the market?" A response may be, "There are currently 102 homes for sale in northeast Tallahassee. Twenty homes were newly listed last month, and twenty-seven sold last month. The average time on the market was 62 days for those that sold. Of those sold, 67 percent were in the $200,000 to $250,000 price range, with ten percent in the $250,000 to $300,000 range, and five percent above $300,000. Eight percent sold below $150,000, and ten percent between $150,000 and $200,000. Houses with fewer than two full bathrooms are not selling well. About half of the buyers are local "move-ups," the other half are transferees. Prices seem to be rising slightly."

As is apparent, the purpose of an RMA is to describe the current condition of the real estate market. This may help answer the question of whether this is a good time to buy or sell, and whether prices are rising or falling.

Evaluations

An *evaluation* of real estate is a study which does *not* lead to an estimate of market value. An evaluation may be performed to consider the feasibility of a proposed use (feasibility study), the highest and best use of property, or a market study which considers the supply and demand in the current market for a certain type of land use.

I. Influences on Real Estate Value

Forces affecting real estate values operate on the international and national, regional, and local community levels. These forces can be categorized as follows:
1. Physical and environmental
2. Economic-financial
3. Political-governmental-legal
4. Sociological

PHYSICAL AND ENVIRONMENTAL

Physical and environmental forces include such factors as dimensions, shape, area, topography, drainage, and soil conditions, as well as utilities, streets, curbs, gutters, sidewalks, landscaping, and the effect of legal restraints (zoning, deed restrictions) on physical development.

Nuisances and hazards are also to be considered, including contaminated air and water and environmentally hazardous building materials such as asbestos, PCBs, and urea formaldehyde.

ECONOMIC-FINANCIAL

The fixed location of land and its immobility distinguish land from other assets. Land is dependent on where it is and what surrounds it. Urban land derives its value from its location. The most significant determinants of value are the type of industry in the area, employment and unemployment rates and types, interest rates, per capita and household income, and stability. These matters also affect the individual property, including real estate prices and mortgage payments.

POLITICAL-GOVERNMENTAL-LEGAL

Political-governmental-legal factors focus on the services provided, such as utilities, spending and taxation policies, police and fire protection, recreation, schools, garbage collection, and on planning, zoning, and subdivision regulations. Building codes and the level of taxes and assessments are also important considerations.

SOCIOLOGICAL

Sociological factors are concerned with the characteristics of people living in the area, the population density and homogeneity, and compatibility of the land uses with the needs of residents.

II. Legal Considerations in Appraisal

Appraisers are expected to know and consider legal matters affecting real estate in making their appraisals. These matters are covered elsewhere in this book. Specific topics and coverage follow:
  A. Real estate vs. real property (Chapters 2 and 3)
  B. Real property vs. personal property (Chapters 2 and 3)
    1. Fixtures

      2. Trade fixtures
      3. Machinery and equipment
  C. Limitations on real estate ownership (Chapters 2 and 3)
      1. Private
         a. Deed restrictions
         b. Leases
         c. Mortgages
         d. Easements
         e. Liens
         f. Encroachments
      2. Public
         a. Police power
            (1) Zoning
            (2) Building and fire codes
            (3) Environmental regulations
         b. Taxation
            (1) Property tax
            (2) Special assessments
         c. Eminent domain
         d. Escheat
  D. Legal rights and interests (Chapters 3 and 10)
      1. Fee simple estate
      2. Life estate
      3. Leasehold interest
      4. Leased fee interest
      5. Other legal interests
         a. Easement
         b. Encroachment
  E. Forms of property ownership (Chapter 3)
      1. Individual
      2. Tenancies and undivided interest
      3. Special ownership forms
         a. Condominiums
         b. Cooperative
         c. Timesharing
  F. Legal descriptions (Chapter 8)
      1. Metes and bounds
      2. Government survey
      3. Lot and block
  G. Transfer of title (Chapter 10)
      1. Basic types of deeds
      2. Recordation

III. Types of Value

There are numerous types of value that the appraiser may be asked to estimate.

MARKET VALUE

The most common type is *market value*, which is defined below.

> *The most probable price which a property should bring in a competitive and open market under all conditions requisite to a fair sale, the buyer and seller each acting prudently and knowledgeably, and assuming the price is not affected by undue stimulus. Implicit in this definition is the consummation of a*

sale as of a specified date and the passing of title from seller to buyer under conditions whereby:

1. *buyer and seller are typically motivated;*
2. *both parties are well informed or well advised, and acting in what they consider their best interests;*
3. *a reasonable time is allowed for exposure in the open market;*
4. *payment is made in terms of cash in United States dollars or in terms of financial arrangements comparable thereto; and*
5. *the price represents the normal consideration for the property sold unaffected by special or creative financing or sales concessions granted by anyone associated with the sale.*[1]

Persons performing appraisal services on property that may be subject to condemnation are cautioned to seek the exact definition of market value applicable in the jurisdiction where the services are being performed.

CONTRASTED VALUE WITH COST AND PRICE

Value, cost, and price are not the same. *Value* is a measure of how much a purchaser would likely be willing to pay for the property being appraised. *Cost* is a measure of the expenditures necessary to produce a similar property. Depending on several factors, this cost could be higher or lower than the current value. *Price* is the historic fact of how much was spent on similar properties in past transactions. Neither past prices nor cost will necessarily represent a fair measure of current value.

OTHER KINDS OF VALUE

Different kinds of value are necessary because of different needs and functions. Included are such values as *loan value, insurable value, market value, book value, rental value, fair value, salvage value, investment value*, and many others. Certain of the more common types are described below.

LOAN VALUE OR MORTGAGE VALUE

Loan or *mortgage value* is the same as market value. Property serving as collateral for a loan or mortgage is normally valued at market value.

INVESTMENT VALUE

Investment value is the estimated value of a certain real estate investment to a particular individual or institutional investor. It may be greater or less than market value, depending on the investor's particular situation. For example, the investment value of vacant land in the path of growth would be greater for a young, aggressive investor who has time to wait for fruition than for an elderly widow who needs available cash for living expenses. Similarly, the investment value of a tax shelter is greater for a high-tax-bracket investor than for a tax-exempt pension plan.

VALUE IN USE AND VALUE IN EXCHANGE

Value in use, which tends to be subjective because it is not set in the market, is the worth of a property to a specific user or set of users. It considers the value of the property when put to a specific use as part of a going concern. For example, the use of a factory where automobiles are assembled may have a high value to the manufacturer, even though the market value of the property is difficult to measure and may be low because there are few interested buyers. Value in use is distinguished from *value in exchange*, which is the value of a commodity, in terms of

---

[1]Uniform Standards of Professional Appraisal Practice, Appraisal Standards Board of the Appraisal Foundation, 1996, pp. 9–10.

money, to people in general rather than to a specific person. Value in exchange is a more objective measure and is commonly identified with market value.

ASSESSED VALUE

The *assessed value* (or *assessed valuation*) is the value of property established for tax purposes. Although tax assessors try to value most property at market value (or some specified fraction of market value), the fact that they must assess a great number of properties periodically on a limited budget often means that assessed values are quite different from market values.

INSURABLE VALUE

The *insurable value* of a property is the cost of total replacement of its destructible improvements. For example, suppose a home that sold for $100,000 ten years ago would cost $200,000 to rebuild today, not including land cost. Its insurable value would be $200,000 even if its current market value, including the land, was only $175,000.

GOING-CONCERN VALUE

Going-concern value is the worth of a business, such as a hotel, based on its operations. The replacement cost of the property may be much more or much less than the business is worth.

IV. Economic Principles

Economics involves combining the *factors of production* to result in a product that is worth more than the cost of the individual factors. The factors of production are land, labor, capital, and entrepreneurship. For example, to produce a bushel of wheat may require $1 for land rent, $1 for labor, $1 for equipment, and $1 for the business management and risk-taking entrepreneur. This is a total of $4, so the farming operation would not occur unless the expected selling price was $4.01 or more per bushel. Many economists recognize only three factors of production, regarding profit as the owners' compensation for their risk taking and inputs of management and entrepreneurship. Certain economic principles are associated with real estate valuation. The major principles are explained below.

ANTICIPATION

Anticipation is determination of the present worth of income or other benefits one expects to receive in the future from the ownership of property. For income-producing properties, value is based on the anticipated net receipts from the operation of the assets plus any amounts to be received upon resale.

BALANCE (PROPORTIONALITY)

For any type of land use, there are optimal amounts of different factors of production that can be combined to create maximum land values. Land, labor, capital, and entrepreneurship can be combined in different proportions, as is demonstrated by the number of houses that may be erected on a parcel of land. Values are maximized when factors are in proportion, or *balance* is achieved.

CHANGE

Real estate values tend not to remain constant, but to vary over time. New technology and social patterns create new demands for real estate. Demographic *changes* create needs for different kinds of housing. People's desires and tastes undergo transitions. Neighborhoods go through a life cycle of growth, maturity, decline, and renewal. Any of these factors and many others can change the utility of real estate at a given location.

Objects wear out. New businesses are started, and others end. The land use pattern is modified by private and public actions. Money supply and interest rates fluctuate. Economic conditions create opportunities or stifle growth.

COMPETITION

When profits exceed the income necessary to pay for the factor of production, *competition* will tend to enter the market, causing average net incomes to fall. This principle is important to an analyst attempting to estimate the value of property that is selling above the cost of its replacement. Its high cost attracts builders and developers, who can earn a large profit from new construction.

CONFORMITY

Conformity is a measure of how well the architectural style and levels of amenities and services offered by a real estate development meet market needs and expectations. A project that fails to conform to market standards is likely to suffer a financial penalty. This does not mean, for example, that all buildings in a particular location must be of the same architectural style. However, the architectural styles and the land use must be compatible. Consider the consequences of building a brightly painted Victorian house replete with architectural gingerbread in a neighborhood of split-level houses. Consider also what would happen if a municipal incinerator were constructed next to a nursing home. The nursing home might have to close because of the health hazard posed by the smoke and other pollution.

CONTRIBUTION

Contribution is the amount by which the value or net income of an economic good is increased or decreased by the presence or absence of some additional factor of production. Contribution is the value increment or detriment to an economic good by the addition of some new factor, rather than the actual cost of the new factor itself. In real estate, some things add more than their cost of production, whereas others may actually detract from value. For example, a new exterior paint job may improve the appearance of a house and make it more salable. On the other hand, a potential buyer may regard a swimming pool as a liability rather than an asset.

An example of the principle of contribution would be a builder's deliberation over whether to add a tennis court to an apartment complex. The cost of this feature is $25,000. With the added tennis court, the complex is worth $1,100,000. Without it, it is worth only $1,000,000. Thus, the tennis court would add $75,000 to the overall value. Since the cost of adding this amenity is less than its contribution, a prudent builder would construct the tennis court.

INCREASING AND DECREASING RETURNS

As resources are added to fixed agents in production, net returns will tend to increase at an increasing rate up to a certain point. Thereafter, total returns will increase at a decreasing rate until the increment to value is less than the cost of resource unit input. A common problem faced by the owners of land is the determination of how intensively their land should be developed. Development should become more intensive as long as profit increases. For example, the profit on a downtown office building, to be sold above cost, may increase with the height of the building, up to a point. Above that height, the profit may decline.

OPPORTUNITY COST

Opportunity cost is the return forfeited by not choosing an alternative. A person with $25,000 to invest may choose to buy equity in a rental residence rather than to purchase a certificate of deposit. The opportunity cost is the interest not received on the CD.

SUBSTITUTION

The maximum value of a property is set by the lowest price or cost at which another property of equivalent utility may be acquired. This *substitution* principle underlies each of the three traditional approaches to value used in the appraisal process: (1) direct sales comparison, (2) income, and (3) cost. A rational purchaser will pay no more for a property than the lowest price being charged for another property of equivalent utility. Likewise, it is not prudent to pay more for an existing project if another one of equivalent utility can be produced, without unreasonable delay, for a lower cost. If an investor is analyzing an income stream, the maximum price is set by examining the prices at which other income streams of similar risk and quality can be purchased.

SUPPLY AND DEMAND

Supply is the quantity of goods, such as real estate, available at a given price schedule; *demand* is the quantity of goods desired at this price schedule. Demand is based on the desire of potential purchasers to acquire real estate, provided that they also have sufficient sources of financing to act on their desires. Together, supply and demand interact to establish prices.

In the long run, supply and demand are relatively effective forces in determining the direction of price changes. An excessive supply or lack of demand will tend to depress price levels. A contrary pressure, which serves to raise prices, occurs when there is either an inadequate supply or a high demand.

SURPLUS PRODUCTIVITY

Surplus productivity is the net income attributed to land after the costs of labor, capital, and entrepreneurship have been paid. Because land is physically immobile, the factors of labor, capital, and entrepreneurship must be attracted to it; therefore, these factors are compensated first. If any money is left over, this residual amount is paid as rent to the owner. In economic theory, land is said to have "residual value" and has worth only if a surplus remains after paying for the other factors of production.

V. Real Estate Markets and Analysis

This topic is concerned with the characteristics of the real estate market, the analysis of use of additional space (absorption), the role of money and capital markets, and the financing terms available for a property. Market analysis and absorption are discussed below. Mortgages and finance were considered in Chapter 13.

REAL ESTATE MARKETS

Real estate is not a single market but consists rather of a series of submarkets with different desires and needs that can change independently of one another. Consequently, real estate markets are said to be *segmented*. The market for retail space in north Atlanta may be quite different from that in east, west, or south Atlanta. Even within the directional quadrants there are significant differences, depending on the distance from downtown and from the nearest major artery or intersection. Within a narrow geographic area there may be a saturation of one type of retail space but not enough of another. For example, neighborhood shopping centers, which typically have a supermarket and a drugstore as anchor tenants, may be abundant, whereas there is no convenient regional mall.

AVAILABILITY OF INFORMATION

One key to successful appraisal is the ability to locate reliable, consistent data. Sources of market data for rental income and expense are described below.

Nationally Disseminated Rental and Operating Expense Data

Certain national organizations collect information from owners and managers in major cities regarding local rents and operating expenses. Such information can be used judiciously to determine whether the data for a particular property appears consistent with experience reported nationally. Because the real estate market is fragmented, a data source appropriate for the specific property must be used.

Office Buildings.   The Building Owners and Managers Association (BOMA) International provides information on office building rental rates and operating expenses experienced by their members in major U.S. cities. BOMA's address is:

Building Owners and Managers International
1250 Eye Street NW, Suite 200
Washington, DC 20005

Shopping Centers.   The Urban Land Institute (ULI) releases a new edition of *Dollars and Cents of Shopping Centers* every 2 years. Another source of shopping center information is the *Department Store Lease Study*, published by the National Retail Merchants Association. Addresses are:

Urban Land Institute
625 Indiana Ave., Suite 400
Washington, DC 20004

National Retail Merchants Association
100 W. 31st Street
Florida, NY 10001

Apartments, Condominiums, and Cooperatives.   The Institute of Real Estate Management (IREM) of the National Association of Realtors periodically provides the *Income/Expense Analysis* for various types of buildings (elevator, walk-up, others) in different cities. IREM's address is:

Institute of Real Estate Management
430 N. Michigan Avenue
Chicago, IL 60611

Hotels and Motels.   Sources of information on national and local trends include Smith's Travel Research and Pannell Kerr Forster's *Trends in the Hotel Industry*. Addresses are:

Smith's Travel Research
P.O. Box 659
Gallatin, TN 37066

Pannell Kerr Forster
262 North Belt E
Houston, TX 77060

Local Sources of Real Estate Data

Local organizations often collect real estate data, usually for membership use or sale to interested parties. These include the following:

Local Boards of REALTORS.   Most metropolitan areas have a Board of REALTORS, or other broker group, that sponsors a multiple listing service (MLS). Upon the sale of property listed through the MLS, the broker must supply information about the completed transaction. Each property sold and its terms of sale are therefore available on computer or in a published book. Some REALTOR boards provide information to members only; some share with other real estate organizations.

Local Tax Assessing Offices.   Assessing offices usually keep a file card on every property in the jurisdiction, noting property characteristics, value estimate, and data from which the estimate was derived. Many jurisdictions are notified of every sale or building permit, for immediate update of affected properties.

Local Credit Bureaus and Tax Map Companies. These may have data on certain parcels; since their main business is not evaluation, however, they are not regular sources.

University Research Centers. University research centers, many of which are supported by state broker and salesperson license fees, may have aggregated data on real estate transactions collected from other sources throughout the state. These data are often helpful in identifying trends established over time and by city for various types of property. Additional research and educational information may also be available from such centers.

Private Data Sources. Many real estate investors retain files on their property. They will often share information, usually for reciprocity rather than payment.

Property Owners. Property owners' records include permanent records such as deeds, leases, and copies of mortgages (lenders have the original mortgage documents), as well as periodic accounting and tax return information about a property's recent past. An owner's report may be of limited immediate use, however, because it may be disorganized, contain extraneous information, or be arranged poorly for appraisal purposes. Also, data from a single property cannot offer a broad perspective on the market.

DEMAND FOR PROPERTY

An appraiser must always be concerned about the demand for a property. People must want to use the property enough to pay the rent asked. If the demand to use the property is high, the demand to buy the property will also be high. High demand means top rents, low vacancies, and good resale prospects. Poor demand means rent reductions, high vacancies, and a property that is hard to sell.

The following are the key items that produce demand for real estate:

Economic growth in the local area increases demand for all properties. New jobs and more residents increase the need for developed real estate. Rising incomes mean higher rents and prices, as well as more retail sales.

Good-quality property raises demand. A property should have all the standard features expected in the market, plus something extra that the competition doesn't have. Appearance, features, size, and services are valued in the market.

A *good location* improves demand. Location can make a poor-quality property profitable, while a good property in the wrong place can suffer.

A *competitive price* can increase demand. If a property is less than ideal, it may be able to compete on the basis of price. It is important to know what segment of the market the property is intended to serve and to price accordingly.

The *cost of alternatives* also determines demand. Apartments are more popular when house prices are high. Houses sell better when interest rates are low.

The demand for a type of property can be estimated by a market analysis. This will indicate whether there is room for more of that type of property in the market. The demand for a specific property can be determined by comparing its features, location, and price to those of similar properties.

Market Analysis

Market analysis is the identification and study of current supply and demand conditions in a particular area for a specific type of property. Such a study is used to indicate how well a particular piece of real estate will be supported by the market. It identifies the most likely users of the project and determines how well they are being served by the existing supply of properties. In essence, the study shows whether there is a need for a new project, or whether an existing project has a good future.

For example, suppose a developer is considering construction of new luxury apartments in a certain town. A market study will first examine the sources of demand for the units. It will identify a *target market*: the type of tenants most likely to be attracted to the property. Description of the target market may include family income, typical family structure, and the features that potential buyers will desire in a residence. The analysis will then survey the market area and use all relevant available data sources to see how many people of this type exist and where they live. A good study will project growth trends in the target market, since a likely source of tenants will be new arrivals.

Next, the study will examine supply conditions. The number and the location of similar properties are identified. A survey of vacancies indicates how well supply matches demand. Features and characteristics of competing properties should be described, and some indication of market rents found. In addition, any new projects that will come along should be identified.

An appraiser should determine whether the market is unbalanced. When the supply of a certain type of real estate is short, rents and prices may be high, but only temporarily. New competition will add to the supply and drive prices down. By contrast, when a market is oversupplied, the price must be low enough to offer an attractive investment.

Market analysis is used to estimate the pace of rent-up or sales for a new project. This *absorption rate* may be expressed as an overall rate ("The market needs 1000 new apartment units per year") or as a specific rate for the project ("Given current competition, the project should capture 200 new rentals per year"). An absorption rate estimate is important in projecting the revenue production of a property.

A market analysis may indicate that there is little demand for the type of project envisioned. Then a change in plans is needed; the project can be redirected to a different target market. The study may also be used to help in the design of the project. It may identify some feature lacking in the existing supply that, if included in the proposed project, will offer a competitive advantage. At the same time, it will probably be necessary to offer the standard features of the competition. The market study will also help in pricing the product for the indicated target market.

Feasibility Analysis

A *feasibility study* tests not only market conditions but also the financial viability of a proposed project. It is not enough to describe the market for rental units; one must also explore whether the cost of production can be maintained at a price that allows a profit or meets some investment objective.

VI. The Valuation Process

As noted earlier in this chapter, the steps in the appraisal or valuation process are as follows:
1. Define the problem to be solved.
2. Plan the appraisal.
3. Collect and verify data.
4. Analyze the highest and best use of the land.
5. Estimate the land value.
6. Apply relevant valuation approaches.
7. Reconcile the value indications and make a final value estimate.
8. Report the final value estimate.

DEFINE THE PROBLEM

In defining the problem to be solved, the appraiser must ascertain a number of items. A definition of value should be formulated at the outset of the valuation process. The property to be valued and the property rights to be appraised must be identified. Also, the date of the estimate of value must be determined. The use of the appraisal should be addressed, in order to determine the needs and requirements of the client. Finally, the appraiser must consider and set forth any special limiting conditions that will be part of the appraisal.

PLAN THE APPRAISAL

The second step is planning the appraisal. This includes determining the data needed and identifying potential data sources, identifying the methodology to be applied, estimating the time and personnel needed, estimating the fee, and scheduling the work to be performed.

COLLECT AND VERIFY DATA

Part three of the valuation process involves gathering data related to the subject property and its environs (region and immediate neighborhood), and comparable market data. A narrative report often starts with national trends, then proceeds to the region and local area. General data gathering relates to the region in which the property is located and the interaction of social, economic, governmental, and environmental forces. A neighborhood description is included. A *neighborhood* is an area of complementary land uses that may be delineated by natural barriers, political boundaries, income levels of inhabitants, or streets.

The appraiser, in gathering specific data and completing research into general data, should seek to identify any factors that directly or indirectly influence the subject property, so that these factors can be considered in the appraisal. Specific data are those related directly to the subject property. These include site data, improvement data, zoning data, ad valorem tax data, and market data. *Market data* is a broad term referring to all real estate sales, listings, leases, and offers that are used in developing the three approaches to value (see below). Thus, data requirements are set by the appraisal problem to be addressed. Not only must data be collected, but also the accuracy of the collected information must be verified.

ANALYZE THE HIGHEST AND BEST USE

After describing and analyzing the subject environs, site, and improvements, the appraiser analyzes the *highest and best use* of the property. The highest and best use analysis for improved properties has a twofold purpose: (1) to determine the highest and best use of the site as if vacant, and (2) to analyze the highest and best use of the property as improved. The highest and best use of the site as if vacant is required so that land with similar highest and best uses can be used for comparison purposes in the land value estimate section of the appraisal. Also, the existing improvements are evaluated in regard to the highest and best use of the site as if vacant. If the existing improvements do not conform to this use of the site, changes or modifications should be considered. The highest and best use of a property is a very crucial conclusion, as the three approaches to value are developed on the basis of this determination.

ESTIMATE THE LAND VALUE

The next step in the valuation process involves estimating the value of the site as if vacant. In determining this value, consideration must be given to the highest and best use of the site. One or more of the following methods can be used to arrive at an indication of the value of the site as if vacant:

1. Sales comparison
2. Allocation
3. Extraction
4. Subdivision development
5. Land residual technique
6. Ground rent capitalization

APPLY VALUATION APPROACHES

After the site value estimate, the three approaches to value: the cost approach, the direct sales comparison (market data) approach, and the income approach are developed. Sometimes, one or more of the three approaches is not applicable to a given property and is not developed in the appraisal. In this case, the appraiser should state why the approach is not applicable. This can be determined, however, only by careful analysis of the property being appraised in relation to the analytical tools available to the appraiser. A short explanation of each approach follows; the three approaches are considered in detail later in this chapter.

COST APPROACH

The cost approach is based on the principle of substitution. It recognizes that buyers often judge the value of an existing structure by comparing it with the cost to construct a new structure of the same type. In developing the cost approach, the appraiser estimates the cost to replace or reproduce the improvements, deducts depreciation (if any), and then adds to this figure the estimated value of the site or land as if vacant. The major limitation of this approach is the difficulty in estimating accrued depreciation, particularly when depreciation is present in more than one form.

DIRECT SALES COMPARISON APPROACH

The direct sales comparison approach recognizes that no informed and prudent person will pay more for a property than it would cost to purchase an equally desirable substitute property (the principle of substitution). In developing this approach, the appraiser locates sales of properties similar to the property being appraised (called *comparable sales*) and provides details describing them in the appraisal report. These sale properties are then compared to the property being appraised, and adjustments are made for differences between each such property and the property under appraisal. The reliability of this approach is directly related to the quality and quantity of the sales data.

INCOME CAPITALIZATION APPROACH

The income capitalization approach is based on the principle of anticipation, which states that value is created by the anticipation of future benefits to be derived from ownership of a given property. The appraiser is primarily concerned with the future benefits to be derived from operation of the subject property—the net operating income (NOI), or cash flow. The steps in this approach include estimating potential gross income by comparison with competing properties, deducting a market derived vacancy and collection loss allowance, and estimating expenses (derived from historical and/or market experience) to determine a projected stream of net operating income. The income stream is then capitalized into an indication of value by using capitalization rates extracted from competitive properties in the market, or by using other techniques when applicable.

RECONCILIATION

It should be noted that all three approaches are closely interrelated, and that all three use market data: the cost approach utilizes data from the market on labor and materials costs, the direct sales comparison approach analyzes sales of similar properties, and the income capitalization approach determines the market investment return rates. Also, data and conclusions from one approach are often used in one or more of the other approaches. If good data are available for application of all three approaches, the resulting indications should fall within a narrow range.

Among the factors considered in the final estimate of value are the accuracy, reliability, and pertinence of the information available for each approach. Major considerations in the *reconciliation* of value indications are which approach has the best data, which is the most likely to be free of error, and which is the most reliable for the type of property being appraised. A final value estimate should be rounded so as not to give a false impression of the precision associated with an opinion.

REPORT

The final step in the appraisal process is the report of defined value. Although such a report can take many forms, the preferred and most common form for income property is the written *narrative appraisal report*. A properly written narrative report should lead the reader through the appraisal process in such a way that he or she reaches the same conclusion or conclusions that were arrived at by the appraiser. A *letter report* is frequently too brief to explain all the data and reasoning. A *form* report is used predominantly for one- to four-family residential property. A *narrative demonstration report*, the most detailed and complete, is typically used only to gain a professional designation. Since July 1994, a *summary* report is allowed whereby the presentation of certain data is not provided, and a *restricted report* is allowed, which is solely for one user.

VII. Property Description

The site, improvements, and construction design must be described in an appraisal to allow the reader to understand the physical qualities of the property.

SITE DESCRIPTION

The size and shape of the site are described, and any impediment to development or any superior qualities are noted. If a parcel is narrow or awkwardly shaped, this fact is mentioned. Road frontage (or lack of access) and topography are noted. Zoning is described, detailing allowable uses and the current use. The appraiser should note, with reference to maps, whether the property is in a flood-prone area. The availability of utilities at the site, including water supply and sewers, gas and electricity, and, if appropriate, cable television, is noted.

IMPROVEMENTS DESCRIPTION

The size, condition, and utility of the improvements must be described in the appraisal report, accompanied by photographs of the property, both inside and out. Photographs give the reader a visual impression in addition to the written description of the information to be conveyed. Anything relevant about the usefulness (or lack thereof) and condition of the property is described.

BASIC CONSTRUCTION AND DESIGN

When plans and specifications are available, the appraiser can refer to them in describing the design and construction. Otherwise, he must rely on visual impressions and answers to questions provided by owners, lessees, or neighbors. At the least, the report should describe the foundation (concrete slab, pier and beam), framing, finish (inside and out), and electrical and mechanical systems.

The usefulness of the building is important. Functionality is affected by such factors as ceiling height for warehouse space, pedestrian traffic flow for retail locations, and layout of office space for office buildings.

VIII. Highest and Best Use Analysis

Highest and best use is defined as follows:

> *The reasonably probable and legal use of vacant land or an improved property, which is physically possible, appropriately supported, financially feasible, and that results in the highest value. The four criteria the highest and best use must meet are legal permissibility, physical possibility, financial feasibility, and maximum profitability.*[2]

---

[2]*The Dictionary of Real Estate Appraisal*, 3rd ed. (Chicago: Appraisal Institute 1993), p. 171.

The four criteria are applied in sequential order. Potential uses are narrowed through the consideration of each criterion so that, by the time the last criterion is applied, only a single use is indicated. A property often will have numerous uses that are physically possible; a lesser number that are both physically possible and legally permissible; fewer still that are physically possible, legally permissible, and financially feasible; and only a single use that meets all four criteria.

As the definition implies, there are two types of highest and best use: the highest and best use of land or a site as if vacant, and the highest and best use of property as improved. The highest and best use of land or a site as if vacant can be specifically defined as follows:

> *Among all reasonable, alternative uses, the use that yields the highest present land value, after payments are made for labor, capital, and coordination. The use of a property based on the assumption that the parcel of land is vacant or can be made vacant by demolishing any improvements.*[3]

In valuing an improved parcel, consideration should be given to the additional value, if any, of the improvements. The highest and best use of property as improved is defined as follows:

> *The use that should be made of a property as it exists. An existing property should be renovated or retained as is so long as it continues to contribute to the total market value of the property, or until the return from a new improvement would more than offset the cost of demolishing the existing building and constructing a new one.*[4]

HIGHEST AND BEST USE OF THE LAND AS IF VACANT

This type of use forms the basis of land value in the cost approach. Four tests are employed in the effort to determine the highest and best use of land. The first three are physical, legal, and financial. Uses that meet the first three tests are then considered to determine which is the maximally productive. Highest and best use analysis assumes that any existing building can be demolished.

PHYSICALLY POSSIBLE

The appraiser describes the uses surrounding the site and in the neighborhood, along with the traffic flow on the subject's street and nearby thoroughfares. Visibility and access are described as they affect potential uses. The size and shape are considered, and the question of whether these attributes lend themselves to certain uses or are impediments is discussed. Nearby transportation systems (bus, subway, rail) are also considered. Availability of utilities is a physical factor that can limit or impede development.

LEGALLY PERMISSIBLE

Legal restrictions include private restrictions and existing public land use regulations—in most cities, zoning. Often, only a title search by a competent attorney will uncover deed restrictions. It is therefore recommended that a title search be made if any question regarding deed restrictions arises. If common restrictions (e.g., utility and drainage easements) exist, the appraiser can state whether they appear to adversely affect the site's development potential. The appraiser should specify what is allowed within the zoning classification.

FINANCIALLY FEASIBLE

The financial feasibility of the physically possible and legally permissible uses of the site is considered. In this analysis, consideration is given to the supply and demand levels for residential, retail, and industrial properties within the area.

---

[3]Ibid.

[4]Ibid.

MAXIMALLY PRODUCTIVE

On the basis of surrounding existing uses, most probable type of use and, within this range, possible alternatives (e.g., office/warehouse or office/laboratory for industrial property) are stated. Although a great deal of judgment is involved, the appraiser provides a conclusion as to the highest and best use. This use need not be one that can be implemented immediately, but may be something to consider for the future.

HIGHEST AND BEST USE OF THE PROPERTY AS IMPROVED

When the property is already improved with a substantial building, there are only two practical alternatives for the subject: razing the improvements or continued operation as improved. When the improvements have lost much of their utility because of their effective age, obsolescence, and condition, demolition could be considered. However, it is often not economically feasible to demolish when there is sufficient income and utility to justify continued operation of the building for an interim period.

IX. Appraisal Mathematics and Statistics

Math concepts in appraisal fall into two categories:
1. The arithmetic of real estate finance, which is covered in Chapter 18.
2. Statistical concepts of mean, median, mode, range, and standard deviation, which follow.
   - *Mean*—the average of a set of numbers. It is found by adding the amounts and dividing by the number of items.
   - *Median*—the middle item in a ranking.
   - *Mode*—the most popular amount, that is, the one that occurs most frequently in a list.
   - *Range*—the difference between the largest and the smallest numbers in a list.

     For example, consider seven homes that sold for the following amounts:

Number	Price
1	$150,000
2	170,000
3	200,000
4	210,000
5	240,000
6	240,000
7	270,000
Total	$1,480,000

     The *mean*, or average, is found by totaling all the prices and then dividing by the number of sales (seven). In this example, the mean is $211,429. The *median* is $210,000, as three houses sold for more and three for less. The *mode* is the most popular price—in this case, $240,000, as two houses sold for that price and only one for every other price. The *range* is from $150,000 to $270,000, or $120,000.
   - *Standard deviation*—a term used to describe the variance of the observations from the mean. It is important to remember that 66 percent of observations fall within one standard deviation from the mean, and 95 percent fall within two standard deviations.

X. Sales Comparison Approach

The sales comparison approach is based primarily on the principle of substitution, which holds that a prudent individual will pay no more for a property than it would cost to purchase a comparable substitute property. The approach recognizes that a typical buyer will compare asking prices and seek to purchase the property that meets his or her wants and needs for the lowest cost. In developing the sales comparison approach, the appraiser attempts to interpret and measure the actions of parties involved in the marketplace, including buyers, sellers, and investors.

COLLECTION OF DATA

Data are collected on recent sales of properties similar to the subject, called *comparables* (*comps*). Sources of comparable data include Realtor publications, public records, buyers and sellers, brokers and salespersons, and other appraisers. Salient details for each comp are described in the appraisal report. Because comps will not be identical to the subject, some price adjustment is necessary. The idea is to simulate the price that would have been paid if the comp were actually identical to the subject. Differences that do not affect value are not adjusted for. If the comp is *superior* to the subject, an amount is *subtracted* from the known sales price of the comp. *Inferior* features of the comp require that an amount be *added* to the comp's known sales price. From the group of adjusted sales prices, the appraiser selects an indicator of value that is representative of the subject.

SELECTION OF COMPARABLES

No set number of comparables is required, but the greater the number, the more reliable the result. How are comps selected? To minimize the amount of adjustment required, comps should be closely similar to the subject. How current and how similar the comps are depends on the availability of data. Comps should be verified by calling a party to the transaction. The appraiser must ascertain that comps were sold in an *arm's length* market transaction; that is, that the sales price or terms were not distorted by, for example, the fact that buyer and seller were relatives.

The following are common shortcomings in the selection process:
- The sale occurred too long ago. (The market may have changed since the sale took place.)
- The location is too different. (Location and surroundings have important effects on value.)
- Special financing was used in a comparable sale. (The price may have been based in part on favorable financing terms.)
- Too few comparables can be found. (One or two sales may not represent the market.)
- The comparable was not an open market transaction. (A sale to a relative or an intracompany sale, foreclosure, or the like is not considered an open market or arm's length transaction.)

When the subject is unusual or when market activity is slow, one or more of these problems may be unavoidable. However, if this is the case, the problem(s) should be acknowledged and taken into consideration when the final value opinion is rendered.

STEPS IN APPROACH

The steps involved in developing the sales comparison approach are as follows:
1. Research the market to obtain information pertaining to sales, listings, and sometimes offerings of properties similar to the property being appraised.
2. Investigate the market data to determine whether they are factually accurate and whether each sale represents an arm's length transaction.
3. Determine relevant units of comparison (e.g., sales price per square foot), and develop a comparative analysis for each.
4. Compare the subject and comparable sales according to the elements of comparison, and then adjust each sale as appropriate.
5. Reconcile the multiple value indications that result from the adjustment of the comparables into a single value indication.

UNITS OF COMPARISON

Units of comparison (see step 3 above) are defined as "the components into which a property may be divided for purposes of comparison."[5] For example, apartment complexes are typically

---

[5]*The Dictionary of Real Estate Appraisal*, 3rd ed. (Chicago: Appraisal Institute 1993), p. 380.

analyzed on the basis of one or more of the following three units of comparison: sales price per square foot of rentable area, sales price per apartment unit, and gross income multiplier. Land is sold by the acre, front foot (along a road or street), square foot, and developable unit. All appropriate units of comparison should be analyzed for the property type being appraised, and the resulting value indications reconciled to a single indicated value or value range. The best unit of comparison for any property is the unit that is considered important in the market for that property type.

Adjustments are usually required to compare the comparable properties selected to the subject property. The adjustments may be applied either to the total sales price or to the unit or units of comparison. Income multipliers are not normally adjusted, however. The comparable sales are adjusted for differences in *elements of comparison*, which are defined as "the characteristics or attributes of properties and transactions that cause the prices paid for real estate to vary."[6] The adjustment process is an effort to isolate the amount paid for different features or sizes; thus it rests on the principle of contribution.

USE OF UNITS OF COMPARISON IN APPRAISALS

Real estate is more easily appraised using units of comparison. Just as meat is sold by the pound, fabric by the yard, precious metals by the troy ounce, and liquids by the fluid ounce, quart, or gallon, real properties are compared by a unit of comparison after adjustments are made to comparables to obtain a uniform quality level. The unit of comparison used may vary depending on the property type or use. Units of comparison may be used in all approaches to value.

LAND

Farm land and large vacant tracts are normally sold by the *acre* (1 acre equals 43,560 square feet). Valuable tracts are sold by the *square foot*, although land along a highway suitable for commercial development or waterfront property may be sold by the number of *front feet* (length along the highway or shoreline). A certain minimum or typical depth is associated with the frontage. Another way that land may be sold is per unit of allowable development. For example, when zoning permits 12 apartment units per acre, the price may be $120,000 per acre (or stated as $10,000 per developable unit).

IMPROVED PROPERTY

Improved properties may be sold by varying units of measurement, depending on their use. For example, office or retail space may be sold on a per-square-foot, motels on a per-room, and theaters on a per-seat basis. However, quality, condition, and other elements are also considered, and an adjusted price is estimated before the units are compared so that the units of comparison are truly comparable.

ELEMENTS OF COMPARISON

The following *elements of comparison* should be considered in the sales comparison approach:
1. Real property rights conveyed
2. Financing terms
3. Conditions of sale
4. Market conditions on date of sale
5. Location
6. Physical characteristics

Adjustments for these are made to the actual selling price of the comparable property.

---

[6]Ibid., p. 114.

REAL PROPERTY RIGHTS CONVEYED

In most situations, fee simple title will be conveyed. However, when the comparables differ from the subject in the extent of rights conveyed, adjustment is required. The appraiser must also be aware of the effects of easements and leaseholds on the price and must apply adjustments accordingly.

FINANCING TERMS

Generally the seller will receive cash from the sale, even when the buyer arranges a loan from a third party. When the property is sold with special financing, however, the price will be affected. Therefore, when the seller provides financing or pays points or excessive fees for the buyer's loan, the price received should be adjusted to a cash equivalent to result in the market value. Terms of financing, whether good or poor, affect the price but not the value.

CONDITIONS OF SALE

In some transactions, sellers or buyers may be unusually motivated, so that the price agreed upon does not necessarily reflect market value. This is true in cases of foreclosure and bankruptcy, as well as transactions in which a buyer requires a certain adjacent parcel for business expansion. A parent may sell property to a child at a bargain price, or a stockholder may sell to his wholly owned corporation at a high price, both in relation to the market. An appraiser must adjust these non-arm's-length transactions to the market, or not use them as comparables.

MARKET CONDITIONS ON DATE OF SALE

Especially during periods of inflation or local economy changes, it is possible to determine shifts in price levels over time. In a rising market, a comparable property sold just a few months ago would fetch a higher price if sold now. For this reason it is important to identify the date of sale of each comparable. Unless a comparable sale is very recent, an adjustment may be needed for market conditions.

LOCATION

Since real estate prices are greatly affected by location, an adjustment is warranted for this characteristic when a comparable's location differs significantly from the subject's. Because each location is unique, the adjustment is often subjective. For retail properties, traffic count is often a key variable.

PHYSICAL CHARACTERISTICS

Physical characteristics of the property warrant adjustment. These characteristics include age, condition, construction, quality, maintenance, access, visibility, and utility.

THE ADJUSTMENT PROCESS

Adjustments may be made in terms of percentages or in dollar amounts. Either the total sales price may be adjusted, or the adjustments can be applied to one or more units of comparison. The adjustments should be made in sequential order, with the adjustment for real property rights always made first, the adjustment for financing terms then made to the sales price adjusted for real property rights conveyed, and so on. Adjustments for location and physical characteristics can be grouped together as a single cumulative amount or percentage. If characteristics are interrelated or interdependent, then cumulative percentage adjustments may be used. If they are independent, however, each should be applied to the actual price of the comparable property.

The *paired sale* technique is useful in adjusting for just one feature. If other sales are found for properties that are similar except for just one feature, the value of that feature can be captured. It is then applied to the comparable properties.

After adjustment, the sales will indicate a range in total value or unit value for the property being appraised. If the sales data are highly comparable, and the sales occurred in a reasonably efficient market, the range in indicated values should be tight. When market conditions are imperfect and comparable sales data are limited, however, the range in indicated values may be wider.

In reconciling the value indications provided by the comparable sales, the appraiser should consider the amount of adjustment required for each sale. Sales requiring lesser degrees of adjustment are typically more comparable and are given greater weight than sales requiring greater adjustment. Other factors must be considered, however, including the reliability of the sales data and the degree of support of the required adjustments. After consideration of these factors, a final point value or value range is set forth.

XI. Site Value

A *site* is land that has been cleared, graded, and improved with utility connections so that it is ready to be built upon. In a real estate appraisal, the site value is typically estimated even though the purpose of the appraisal is to estimate the value of the entire property, the improved real estate. The site value is estimated as part of the cost approach.

Site value may also give information about the entire property. For example, suppose that the site value is almost equal to the improved property value; this fact may provide a clue about the highest and best use of the property. It may help also in analyzing the possibility of replacing the existing building, or give information on the useful life of the present improvements.

There are several ways to estimate site value; sales comparison, land residual, allocation, extraction, and plottage and assemblage are discussed below.

SALES COMPARISON

The sales comparison technique for land is similar to that described above for improved properties, but it is easier to apply to land because there are fewer factors to consider. It is the most commonly used technique for land valuation.

LAND RESIDUAL

Improved properties may generate annual income. If the building value is known, the income attributable to the building may be subtracted from the total income; the difference is the income to the land. That amount may be converted to a land value by dividing by a capitalization rate (rate of return).

ALLOCATION

Allocation is a method of estimating land value as a fraction of total value. Suppose that, for the type of property in question, data from numerous comparables indicate that land is typically 25 percent of total value. The land value for the subject property is then estimated at 25 percent of total value unless there is some reason not to apply this technique (such as the presence of excess land on the subject).

EXTRACTION

The *extraction* method of estimating land value involves subtracting the depreciated cost of improvements from the total value of the property. It is used to best advantage when the improvements have little value.

PLOTTAGE AND ASSEMBLAGE

These terms relate to combining two or more parcels of land. The combination is called *assemblage*. When the combined parcel is worth more, because of increased utility, than the parcels would be if sold separately, the increment of value added is called *plottage*.

XII. Cost Approach

The cost approach to appraising is predicated on the assumption that the value of a structure does not exceed the current cost of producing a replica of it. This tends to hold true when a site is improved with a new structure that represents the highest and best use of the site.

Typically, an appraiser estimates the reproduction cost of the subject property, then subtracts for depreciation. The market value of the site (land prepared for use) is then added to the depreciated reproduction cost to arrive at a final estimate of value.

Steps in the cost approach, also called the *summation approach*, follow:

1. Estimate the value of the site as if vacant and available to be put to its highest and best use as of the date of the appraisal.
2. Estimate the reproduction or replacement cost new of the improvements.
3. Estimate all elements of accrued depreciation, including physical, functional, and economic obsolescence.
4. Subtract the total accrued depreciation from the replacement cost new of the improvements to determine the present worth of the improvements.
5. Add the estimated depreciated worth of all site improvements.
6. Add the total present worth of all improvements to the estimated site value to arrive at the value of the property as indicated by the cost approach.

The procedure for estimating land value was described in the Sales Comparison Approach.

REPRODUCTION COST VERSUS REPLACEMENT COST

Reproduction cost is the cost of building a replica; *replacement cost* is the cost of replacing the subject with one that has equivalent utility but is built with modern materials and to current standards of design and function. Replacement cost new tends to set the upper limit on current value.

MEASURING REPRODUCTION COST OR REPLACEMENT COST

Four methods of measuring reproduction or replacement cost are as follows:

1. *Quantity survey*, whereby each type of material in a structure is itemized and costed out (the price of each nail, brick, etc., is reflected). Overhead, insurance, and profit are added as a lump sum.
2. *Unit-in-place*, whereby the installed unit cost of each component is measured (e.g., exterior walls, including gypsum board, plaster, paint, wallpaper, and labor). Equipment and fixtures are added as a lump sum.
3. *Segregated cost* or *trade breakdown*, which is similar to the unit-in-place method except that the units considered are major functional parts of the structure, such as foundation, floor, ceiling, roof, and heating system. Fixtures and equipment are added as a lump sum.
4. *Comparative unit*, whereby all components of a structure are lumped together on a unit basis to obtain the total cost per square foot or cubic foot. Costs include materials, installation, and builder's overhead and profit.

COST SERVICES

Companies that provide cost data, either through on-line computer services or as hard copy, include Marshall & Swift (Marshall Valuation Service), R.S. Means, Dow/Dodge (McGraw-Hill), and Boeckh.

COST INDEXES

Cost indexes are prepared, using a construction inflation index, to update costs from the latest price schedules to the present time. Another index, a local multiplier, is printed for selected cities to show the variation from the benchmark region or city.

DEPRECIATION

Depreciation is a reduction in value, due to all sources, from cost new. *Accrued depreciation* is the total loss of value from all causes, measured from reproduction cost new. Depreciation is broken down into three elements—physical, functional, and external or economic—and each is further classified as curable or incurable.

PHYSICAL DETERIORATION

Physical deterioration is a reduction in the utility of improvements resulting from an impairment of physical condition and is commonly divided into curable and incurable components. *Curable physical deterioration* considers items (referred to as "deferred maintenance") that a prudent purchaser would anticipate correcting immediately upon acquisition of the property. It is assumed that the cost of effecting the correction will not be greater than the anticipated gain in value accrued by virtue of correcting the problem. This estimate is usually computed as a cost to cure. *Incurable physical deterioration* refers to items that cannot be physically or economically corrected.

FUNCTIONAL OBSOLESCENCE

Functional obsolescence is a loss of value due to characteristics inherent in the structures themselves. It results in a decreased capacity of the improvements to perform the functions for which they were intended, in accordance with current market tastes and standards of acceptability. Something becomes outmoded. As mentioned above, functional obsolescence consists of curable and incurable items.

Curable Functional Obsolescence

Curable functional obsolescence may be the result of either a deficiency or an excess. The measure of a deficiency is the excess cost to cure, whereas the measure of an excess is the reproduction cost of the superadequacy, less physical deterioration already charged, plus the cost to cure. As noted, in order for an item to be considered curable, the necessary cost to cure must not exceed the anticipated increase in value due to the cure.

Incurable Functional Obsolescence

Incurable functional obsolescence is caused by either a deficiency or an excess that, if cured, would not warrant the expenditure. In other words, the owner/purchaser would not be justified in replacing items whose cost would exceed the anticipated increase in value. If caused by a deficiency, obsolescence is estimated as the capitalized value of the rent loss due to the condition. An excess is measured by the reproduction cost of the item, less physical deterioration already charged, plus the present worth of the added cost of ownership due to the subject property and other factors relating to this property.

EXTERNAL OR ECONOMIC OBSOLESCENCE

External or economic obsolescence is a diminished utility of the structure due to negative influences from outside the site. It is almost always *incurable* on the part of the owner, landlord, or tenant. External obsolescence can be caused by a variety of factors, such as neighborhood decline; the property's location in a community, state, or region; market conditions; or government regulations.

DEPRECIATION CALCULATIONS

There are a number of ways to calculate the value loss from depreciation. These include the economic age-life method, the breakdown method, and market extraction. Definitions of two important terms are offered below as an aid to understanding depreciation calculations.

Economic life is the period over which improvements to real estate contribute to the value of the property. Economic life establishes the capital recovery period for improvements in the traditional residual techniques of income capitalization. It is also used in the estimation of accrued depreciation (diminished utility) in the cost approach to value estimation.

Effective age, as applied to a structure, is the age of a similar structure of equivalent utility, condition, and remaining life expectancy, as distinct from *chronological age*; that is, effective age is the age indicated by the condition and utility of the structure. If a building has had better than average maintenance, its effective age may be less than the actual age; if there has been inadequate maintenance, it may be greater. A 40-year-old building, for example, may have an effective age of 20 years because of rehabilitation and modernization.

ECONOMIC AGE-LIFE METHOD

The ratio between the effective age of a building and its total economic life is its *economic age-life*. To estimate the building's incurable physical depreciation, this ratio is applied to the cost of the building or components after deferred maintenance has been subtracted.

BREAKDOWN METHOD

With this method, the loss in value is separated into physical, functional, and external causes.

Cost Approach Example
Replacement Cost New

Office/warehouse building:		
(24,208 SF @ $20.78/SF)		$503,042
Site improvements and equipment:		
Parking lot	$75,000	
Signage, landscaping, misc.	5,000	
Subtotal, site improvements		80,000
Subtotal, hard costs		583,042
Developer/contractor profit:		
Building cost new @ 15%		87,456
Ad valorem taxes at 2.6% × $70,000		1,800
Marketing, misc.		1,000
Replacement cost new		673,298
Less: Accrued depreciation:		
Physical depreciation (based on direct cost)		
Curable	$60,000	
Incurable	401,343	
Subtotal	$461,343	
Obsolescence		
Functional	50,000	
External	110,000	
Subtotal	$160,000	
Total accrued depreciation		(621,343)
Estimated present value of improvements		51,955
Add: Estimated land value		70,000
Indicated value via cost approach		$121,955
Rounded to:		$120,000

Cost Approach Estimate of Value $120,000

XIII. Income Approach

Most of the income approach methodology will be found in the general certification section of Chapter 15. All appraisal candidates, however, are expected to understand gross rent multipliers (or gross income multipliers) and to be able to estimate income and expense.

GROSS INCOME MULTIPLIER

The *gross income multiplier* is simply the sales price divided by the rental income, generally on an annual basis. For example, if a building sold for $1,200,000 and earns $200,000 a year in rent, the multiplier is 6 ($1,200,000/$200,000 = 6). This multiplier is often used on a monthly rent basis, especially for houses. If a home sold for $120,000 and rents for $1,000 per month, the monthly multiplier is 120. The multiplier is applied to the subject's rent to estimate its value.

Generally, the gross rent multiplier is used as a sales comparison measure for income property. It may be used as the income approach for single-family housing.

ESTIMATE OF INCOME AND EXPENSES

The income most commonly used is called *net operating income (NOI)*, which is found for rental properties as follows:

1. Estimate *potential gross income* (the rental collected if all units are rented for an entire year).
2. Subtract a vacancy and collection allowance.
3. Subtract *operating expenses*. These include insurance, maintenance and repairs, real estate taxes, utilities, and other expenses essential to the operation of the property.

    Operating expenses are categorized as fixed or variable. *Fixed expenses* remain constant regardless of occupancy, whereas *variable expenses* go up and down depending on occupancy.

    Another category of operating expenses consists of reserves for the replacement of appliances, carpets, and other short-lived assets. Since these may last only 5–10 years, an amount is set aside annually as a provision to prevent distorting the income in the year these assets are replaced.

    Interest and principal payments and depreciation are *not* operating expenses.

The result—(1) minus (2) and (3)—is net operating income. NOI is then divided by a capitalization rate, which is the rate used to convert an income stream into a lump sum capital value. The capitalization rate must be adequate to provide for a return on the entire investment, as well as a recovery of the portion of the property that is subject to depreciation.

The rate of return on the entire investment can be estimated as in the following example:

> ***Basic Rate:***
>
> | | |
> |---|---:|
> | *Safe, liquid rate of return on investment* | |
> | *(U.S. government bonds, insured savings)* | 5% |
> | *Provision for illiquidity* | 1% |
> | *Provision for investment management* | 1% |
> | *Provision for risk* | 2% |
> | Rate of return on investment | 9% |
> | *Plus capital recovery: 80% of cost represented by improvements,* | |
> | *which are subject to a 40-year life = 80% × 2½% (straight-line* | |
> | *annual depreciation)* | 2% |
> | Capitalization rate | 11% |

If net operating income is estimated at $100,000, the resulting value is $100,000 ÷ 0.11 = $909,091, rounded to $910,000. The formula employed is as follows:

$$\text{Value} = \frac{\text{Income}}{\text{Capitalization Rate}}$$

XIV. Partial Interests

The residential appraiser is expected to know the effects of certain partial interests, namely:
- Leaseholds and leased fees
- Life estates
- Easements
- Timeshares
- Cooperatives
- Undivided interests in common areas

LEASEHOLDS AND LEASED FEES

When property is leased, the tenant has a *leasehold*. This may be a valuable interest, particularly when the lease rent (called the *contract rent*) is below market rent and the lease is for a long term. The landlord's position is called *leased fee*. An appraiser should determine the effect of a lease on the market value of the fee simple and ascertain the definition of value being sought. Is it a leased fee value, or fee simple unencumbered?

LIFE ESTATES

A *life estate* allows a person to use property for his or her own lifetime or for the life of another person (*pur autre vie*). Upon death, the remainderman becomes the sole owner. Thus, the market value of the property is divided between two persons: one with the right of use for life and another whose use commences upon the life tenant's death.

EASEMENTS

An *easement* is the right to use property owned by another for a specific purpose. For example, billboards may be erected on easements, and power company transmission line paths and other land needed for utilities are often provided by the use of easements. Easements may enhance the value of real estate when they generate adequate revenue (billboard rent), attract desired services (utilities to the property), or provide access to other properties. They may detract from value when they represent nuisances (unsightly utility wires), indicate flood plains, or prevent alternative profitable property uses. Unless easements are specifically excluded by the appraisal report, an appraiser should ascertain the effect of easements on property being considered as well as easements on others' properties that the subject property owner can enjoy.

TIMESHARES

A *timeshare* is the right to use property for a given period of time each year. Often used for resort property, a timeshare may be ownership of a specific apartment unit for a specific period, such as the first week in April of each year, or it may represent the right to use any of a number of identical units in a condominium development for any week during a certain period (with prices varying for peak and off-season periods). The price of a weekly timeshare, when multiplied by 52 weeks, may exceed two to three times the value of the unit if sold in its entirety, but timeshare ownership often includes amenities (such as utilities, laundry service, and periodic redecoration) that would not be included in ownership of the unit itself.

COOPERATIVES

Some apartment buildings, especially in Florida, are owned as cooperatives (co-ops). A corporation owns the building and can mortgage it. Stockholders own certain shares, which give each stockholder the right to occupy a certain unit. Stockholders are generally tenants and must pay their pro rata shares of maintenance expenses. Special tax laws allow the tenants to deduct interest on the mortgage and real estate taxes. An appraiser must recognize the valuation process for this type of property and understand how the stock is valued.

UNDIVIDED INTERESTS IN COMMON AREAS

Condominiums provide for separate ownership of individual units with the right to mortgage each unit. Common areas such as walkways, recreational facilities, and exterior walls are owned jointly. Each condo owner owns a share of the common area and may use it, as may all other condo owners.

XV. *Appraisal Standards and Ethics*

The Uniform Standards of Professional Appraisal Practice (USPAP) have been developed by the Appraisal Foundation. Appraisers belonging to an organization that is a member of the Appraisal Foundation adhere to these standards. The following are highlights of certain parts of the USPAP.

PREAMBLE

- The appraisal must be meaningful to the client and not misleading in the marketplace.
- The appraiser is to observe all the ethical standards set forth below.
- Certain competency provisions are to be observed.
- If departure provisions are utilized, the rules concerning their use must be observed. A departure provision is a "loophole," or provision for the appraiser to depart from the standards. For example, a departure provision allows an approach to be waived provided that the appraiser explains why that approach was not used.
- Users of an appraiser's services are encouraged to demand work in conformance with the standards.

ETHICS

The appraiser is to observe the highest standards of professional ethics. These include standards of conduct, management, confidentiality, and record keeping.
- *Conduct*. The appraiser must not engage in conduct that is unethical, illegal, or improper, and should remain impartial, objective, and independent.
- *Management*. The appraiser may not accept an assignment or compensation that would be biased in any way, or accept undisclosed compensation. Advertising may not be false or misleading.
- *Confidentiality*. The appraiser must protect the confidential nature of the appraiser-client relationship.
- *Record keeping*. The appraiser must keep records for at least 5 years after preparation, or 2 years after judicial settlement, whichever period expires last.

COMPETENCY

The appraiser must properly identify the problem to be addressed and have the knowledge and experience to complete the assignment competently. If the appraiser does not have the required knowledge or experience, she must:
1. Disclose this fact to the client before accepting the engagement.
2. If engaged, take all steps necessary to complete the assignment competently.
3. Describe the deficiency and the steps taken to complete the assignment competently.

STANDARDS

The following are some standards to be followed in appraising real estate.
- *Standard 1*. In developing a real property appraisal, an appraiser must be aware of, understand, and correctly employ the recognized methods and techniques necessary to produce a credible appraisal.
- *Standard 2*. In reporting the results of a real property appraisal, an appraiser must communicate each analysis, opinion, and conclusion in a manner that is not misleading.

- *Standard 3.* In reviewing an appraisal and reporting the results of that review, an appraiser must form an opinion as to the adequacy and appropriateness of the report being reviewed and must clearly disclose the nature of the review process undertaken.
- *Standard 4.* In performing real estate or real property consulting services, an appraiser must be aware of, understand, and correctly employ the recognized methods and techniques necessary to produce a credible result.
- *Standard 5.* In reporting the results of a real estate or real property consulting service, an appraiser must communicate each analysis, opinion, and conclusion in a manner that is not misleading.

Questions on Chapter 14

1. All of the following types of broad forces affect value *except*
   (A) physical
   (B) intellectual
   (C) political
   (D) social
   (E) economic

2. Social, economic, governmental, and environmental influences that affect property value are called
   (A) laws
   (B) forces
   (C) factors
   (D) consequences
   (E) impacts

3. Compared with other assets, real estate is
   (A) immobile
   (B) expensive
   (C) long-lived
   (D) mortgageable
   (E) all of the above

4. The truly distinguishing characteristic of real estate as compared with other assets is
   (A) large size
   (B) long life
   (C) high price
   (D) uniqueness
   (E) fixed location

5. The primary economic distinguishing characteristic of land is
   (A) homogeneity
   (B) high cost
   (C) immobility
   (D) slow depreciation
   (E) no depreciation

6. Urban land derives its value primarily from its
   (A) size
   (B) natural beauty
   (C) concentration of population
   (D) location
   (E) buildings

7. Which of the following is a basic component of value?
   (A) Utility
   (B) Scarcity
   (C) Demand coupled with purchasing power
   (D) Transferability
   (E) All of the above

8. The value of real estate is determined in the market mainly by its
   (A) price
   (B) productivity
   (C) mortgage
   (D) size
   (E) height

9. Which of the following is an important governmental influence on neighborhood values?
   (A) Zoning code
   (B) Income level
   (C) Owner occupancy
   (D) Flood plain mapping
   (E) Ethnic concentration

10. *Realty* is best defined as rights in
    (A) land
    (B) improvements on and to land
    (C) buildings
    (D) fixtures
    (E) real estate

11. Built-in appliances are legally classified as
    (A) real estate
    (B) trade fixtures
    (C) chattels
    (D) personal property
    (E) amenities

12. The term *improvements to real estate* refers to
    (A) buildings only
    (B) buildings, fences, walkways, etc.
    (C) trees and buildings
    (D) all of the above
    (E) none of the above

13. Rights of condemnation are held by a
    (A) state government agency
    (B) local agency or authority representing a federal government agency
    (C) utility company
    (D) small municipality
    (E) all of the above

14. Eminent domain requires
    (A) appraisal processes for the estimation of real property value
    (B) just compensation for specific types of financial loss
    (C) due process for the taking of property through condemnation
    (D) both A and B
    (E) both B and C

15. Zoning and environmental protection regulations represent the exercise of
    (A) land use politics
    (B) public use
    (C) escheat
    (D) eminent domain
    (E) police power

16. All of the following are considered legal encumbrances *except*
    (A) leases
    (B) utilities
    (C) zoning
    (D) mortgages
    (E) liens

17. *Real property* is defined as
    (A) leased and unleased space
    (B) rights in realty
    (C) land and all improvements
    (D) the right to use or occupy real estate
    (E) realty

18. Which of the following expires upon the owner's death?
    (A) Fee tail
    (B) Remainder interest
    (C) Simple interest
    (D) Life estate
    (E) Estate for years

19. The most complete interest in real property is
    (A) fee tail
    (B) joint tenancy
    (C) tenancy in common
    (D) fee simple
    (E) life estate *pur autre vie*

20. A deed should be recorded in order to
    (A) give constructive notice of the transaction
    (B) comply with federal and state law
    (C) pass title
    (D) make the deed a legal document
    (E) establish the priority of claim of the purchaser

21. Property description is necessary to
    (A) identify and locate the subject property
    (B) identify the property rights being appraised
    (C) find the appropriate section in the report
    (D) find the official map coding of the subject property
    (E) tell where the property deed is recorded

22. One way in which land may be legally described is by
    (A) highest and best use
    (B) acreage
    (C) mailing address
    (D) metes and bounds
    (E) front footage

23. "Block 17, lot 5 of the Woodcreek Subdivision" is an example of a land description using which of the following systems?
    (A) Lot and block
    (B) Rectangular method
    (C) Metes and bounds
    (D) Government survey
    (E) Monuments survey

24. A value estimate is a(n)
    (A) estimate of a selling price
    (B) prediction that property will sell for exactly the amount named
    (C) projection or extrapolation of historic price to future price
    (D) sophisticated guess by expert
    (E) promise or option to buy

25. *Loan value* is the same as
    (A) investment value
    (B) market price
    (C) replacement value
    (D) book value
    (E) market value

26. *Mortgage value* is synonymous with
    (A) market price
    (B) liquidation value
    (C) market value
    (D) assessed value
    (E) insurable value

27. An objective kind of value that can be estimated for property bought and sold in the market is called
    (A) value in use
    (B) value in exchange
    (C) economic value
    (D) potential value
    (E) insurable value

28. In appraisal, "market value" is most commonly identified with
    (A) value in use
    (B) value in exchange
    (C) assessed value
    (D) listing value
    (E) none of the above

29. Price and value are
    (A) not necessarily the same
    (B) synonymous
    (C) different, depending on financing terms
    (D) close together in an inactive market
    (E) used interchangeably in a report

30. Market price is the amount for which a property
    (A) should sell
    (B) was sold
    (C) will sell
    (D) could sell
    (E) would be appraised

31. All of the following statements are true *except:*
    (A) *Real property* refers to items that are not permanently fixed to a part of the real estate.
    (B) Appraising is the art and science of estimating the value of an asset.
    (C) Assets typically requiring appraisal include real and personal property.
    (D) Asset values change with time.
    (E) Markets change with supply and demand.

32. *Investment value* is best described as
    (A) market price
    (B) market value
    (C) the cost of acquiring a competitive substitute property with the same utility
    (D) the present worth of anticipated future benefits to a certain individual or institutional investor
    (E) value in exchange

33. Assessed value is usually based on
    (A) cost value
    (B) book value
    (C) market value
    (D) insurable value
    (E) replacement cost

34. The principle of anticipation
    (A) is future oriented
    (B) is past oriented
    (C) involves the "as of" date for an appraisal
    (D) predicts the loan-to-value ratio for the subject property
    (E) is substitution oriented

35. Which principle of value best affirms that value is the present worth of expected future benefits?
    (A) Supply and demand
    (B) Balance
    (C) Substitution
    (D) Anticipation
    (E) Conformity

36. What principle states that value levels are sustained when the various elements in an economic or environmental mix are in equilibrium?
    (A) Anticipation
    (B) Equivalence
    (C) Substitution
    (D) Balance
    (E) Highest and best use

37. The fundamental valuation principle underlying the sales comparison process is
    (A) contribution
    (B) substitution
    (C) conformity
    (D) change
    (E) anticipation

38. Which principle of value best affirms that the maximum value of a property generally cannot exceed the cost of its replacement?
    (A) Increasing and decreasing returns
    (B) Supply and demand
    (C) Substitution
    (D) Balance
    (E) Anticipation

39. The fact that the value of a property tends to equal the cost of an equally desirable substitute is an example of the principal of
    (A) balance
    (B) substitution
    (C) contribution
    (D) diminishing returns
    (E) supply and demand

40. The principle of substitution holds that a purchaser will pay no more for a property than
    (A) the maximum he can afford
    (B) the cost of acquiring an equally desirable substitute
    (C) the price of a previously owned property
    (D) the price of a property with greater utility
    (E) none of the above

41. The function(s) of a real estate market is (are) to
    (A) facilitate exchanges
    (B) set prices
    (C) allocate resources
    (D) adjust supply to demand
    (E) all of the above

42. In estimating current market value, an appraiser assumes all of the following *except that*:
    (A) The buyer is typically motivated.
    (B) The parties are knowledgeable.
    (C) A reasonable time will be allowed for market exposure.
    (D) The property will be marketed by a professional expert.
    (E) The property will be sold for cash or equivalent terms.

43. In which market are there many potential buyers but few properties available?
    (A) Demand
    (B) Buyer's
    (C) Seller's
    (D) Low-priced
    (E) Normal

44. A perfect market occurs when
    (A) there are numerous buyers and sellers who are knowledgeable and free to trade
    (B) all products are interchangeable and can be transported to better markets
    (C) the government allocates supply and demand perfectly
    (D) all of the above are true
    (E) A and B only are true

45. The identification and study of a pertinent market is called
    (A) market analysis
    (B) neighborhood review
    (C) property research
    (D) market segmentation
    (E) market interaction

46. If the typical occupancy rate in an area is 95 percent, what conclusion would you most likely draw about a subject property that has 100 percent occupancy?
    (A) Advertising is average.
    (B) The rents are high.
    (C) The rents are low.
    (D) Management is incompetent.
    (E) New construction will occur soon.

47. Which type of studies test the ability of various proposed improvements to meet investment objectives?
    (A) Market
    (B) Feasibility
    (C) Marketability
    (D) Cost-benefit
    (E) Prospectus

48. A decrease in land value is the result of
    (A) functional obsolescence
    (B) physical deterioration
    (C) market forces
    (D) wear and tear
    (E) obsolescence

49. To estimate market value, an appraiser follows the
    (A) appraisal report
    (B) valuation process
    (C) evaluation methodology
    (D) appraisal guidelines
    (E) report evolution technique

50. In appraising, the most important judgment is probably called for in
    (A) projecting selling rates
    (B) reconciling value indications
    (C) selecting good comparable data
    (D) performing neighborhood analysis
    (E) making rental market estimates

51. An "as of" date is specified in appraisals to
    (A) show when the appraiser inspected the property
    (B) indicate the prevailing price level
    (C) indicate the market conditions on which the value is estimated
    (D) indicate when the buyer agreed to purchase the property
    (E) indicate the value as of the closing date

52. An appraisal of real estate
    (A) guarantees its value
    (B) assures its value
    (C) determines its value
    (D) estimates its value
    (E) segments its value

53. Residential appraisers generally provide an estimate of
    (A) market price
    (B) mortgage loan value
    (C) cash value
    (D) assessed value
    (E) market value

54. Commercial real estate appraisers are most frequently asked to estimate
    (A) assessed value
    (B) liquidation value
    (C) insurable value
    (D) market value
    (E) intrinsic value

55. Legal transactions that frequently require appraisals are
    (A) income-tax-deductible charitable contribution of property, estate tax, and property settlement upon divorce
    (B) damage lawsuits, loan foreclosures, and security for bail bonds
    (C) company merger, tax basis, and loan assumptions
    (D) all of the above
    (E) none of the above

56. Knowledge of land value is required for all of the following *except*
    (A) condemnation actions
    (B) fire insurance
    (C) property taxation
    (D) a ground lease
    (E) a grazing lease

57. A market value estimate provided in an appraisal
    (A) changes with the use to which it is put
    (B) changes with the function of the appraisal
    (C) remains the same regardless of whom the appraisal is prepared for
    (D) depends upon the use or function of the appraisal
    (E) always reflects market value

58. In preparing an appraisal, definition of the problem identifies all of the following *except*
    (A) the real estate being appraised
    (B) the highest and best use for the property
    (C) the real property rights
    (D) the date of the value estimate
    (E) the use to which the appraisal will be put

59. In appraising, the data requirements are set by the
    (A) client
    (B) lender
    (C) seller
    (D) appraisal problem
    (E) appraiser

60. The requirement to verify data in an appraisal report varies according to
    (A) the appraiser's "gut feelings" about the reliability of the data
    (B) the purpose and intended use of the appraisal report
    (C) legal restrictions on the property
    (D) the type of value being sought
    (E) the use to which the property has been put

61. A property's immediate environment is
   (A) its pivotal point
   (B) a "comp" grid
   (C) a neighborhood
   (D) the adjacent uses
   (E) a natural boundary

62. The life cycle of a neighborhood illustrates the principle of
   (A) substitution
   (B) highest and best use
   (C) change
   (D) conformity
   (E) anticipation

63. The data required for an appraisal assignment are established by the
   (A) lending association
   (B) appraiser
   (C) buyer
   (D) Office of Thrift Supervision
   (E) nature of the appraisal problem

64. Which of the following exhibits is *least* frequently used in an appraisal?
   (A) A photograph of the subject property
   (B) An aerial photograph of the surrounding area
   (C) A plot plan
   (D) A floor plan
   (E) A photograph of a comparable property

65. In which market is the direct sales comparison approach most applicable?
   (A) Seller's
   (B) Buyer's
   (C) Reasonable
   (D) Active
   (E) Calm

66. The criteria for determining highest and best use include all of the following *except*
   (A) physical possibility
   (B) financial feasibility
   (C) legal permissibility
   (D) maximal productivity
   (E) effect on community welfare

67. The three approaches to estimating value are
   (A) cost, income, and replacement
   (B) replacement, income, and reproduction
   (C) cost, direct sales comparison, and income capitalization
   (D) reproduction, cost, and income
   (E) market, building residual, and multiplier

68. In appraising a dwelling built 50 years ago, the appraiser usually relies on the
   (A) current reproduction cost
   (B) original construction cost
   (C) current replacement cost
   (D) direct sales comparison approach
   (E) superior construction technique

69. Which approach would be best when appraising a 15- to 20-year-old house?
    (A) Cost
    (B) Feasibility study
    (C) Sales comparison
    (D) Income capitalization
    (E) Replacement cost new less accrued depreciation

70. The appraiser's final value estimate should be based on
    (A) an average of the three value indications given by the three approaches to value
    (B) a weighing of the reliability of the information analyzed in each of the three approaches to value
    (C) an average of the values in the three closest comparable sales
    (D) the correlation technique
    (E) adjustments for the most recent indicators in the local market

71. Before reconciliation the appraiser should
    (A) reinspect the subject property
    (B) evaluate the reliability of each approach to value
    (C) review the overall appraisal process and check for technical accuracy
    (D) seek the property owner's opinion
    (E) average the results from the approaches used

72. Since each value approach has its own strengths and weaknesses, an appraiser should
    (A) choose the approach that is the most popular with lenders
    (B) choose the approach that is the most popular with buyers
    (C) weigh the strengths and weaknesses of each approach and decide which is the most reliable for the subject property
    (D) weight each approach equally
    (E) use the approach that the client feels is most appropriate

73. The cost approach is often given more weight in the appraisal of
    (A) old or obsolete buildings
    (B) single-family houses more than 10 years old
    (C) new buildings or special-use buildings
    (D) commercial and industrial properties
    (E) vacant land

74. In reconciliation and conclusion of value, the appraiser should
    (A) describe the relevance of each value approach explored
    (B) discuss the reliability of the data used
    (C) provide arguments to justify his or her final conclusion of value
    (D) explain his or her judgments and reasoning
    (E) do all of the above

75. Value indications are reconciled into a final value estimate
    (A) throughout the appraisal
    (B) after the report of defined value
    (C) after each approach is completed
    (D) at the preliminary stage to let the client know what result to expect
    (E) after all three approaches have been completed

76. During the reconciliation process, an appraiser should ask:
    (A) How appropriate is each approach?
    (B) How adequate are the data?
    (C) What range of values do the approaches suggest?
    (D) All of the above
    (E) A and C only

77. Which of the following is the longest and most detailed type of appraisal report?
(A) Letter report
(B) Form report
(C) Narrative demonstration report
(D) Subdivision report
(E) Detailing report

78. All of the following are main sections in the typical narrative appraisal report *except*
(A) introduction
(B) engagement letter
(C) description, analyses, and conclusion
(D) addenda
(E) valuation

79. An oral appraisal report
(A) is not worth the paper it is written on
(B) should not be provided
(C) is unethical
(D) is impossible
(E) is a legitimate substitute for a written report

80. Standardized residential form reports
(A) are adequate for all appraisals
(B) may not be as detailed or complete as written reports
(C) are seldom adequate for appraisals
(D) allow little space for neighborhood analysis
(E) are difficult to computerize

81. The highest and best use of a site is its
(A) existing use
(B) most probable use
(C) immediate next use
(D) ordinary and necessary use
(E) least expensive use

82. The important reason(s) for inspecting and analyzing the subject site is (are) to
(A) ascertain its highest and best use
(B) note any unusual characteristics
(C) find comparable sales
(D) be certain the property exists
(E) all of the above

83. The length of a tract of land along a street is called the land's
(A) depth
(B) width
(C) frontage
(D) abutment
(E) lineage

84. The number of square feet in 1 acre is
(A) 64,000
(B) 460
(C) 440
(D) 43,560
(E) 34,560

85. The livable square footage of a single-family residence is usually measured from the
    (A) total interior (including interior walls)
    (B) inside room dimensions
    (C) interior plus basement
    (D) exterior
    (E) exterior, with adjustment for wall width

86. The most important item an appraiser needs for recording data during a building inspection is a
    (A) plat map
    (B) tape measure
    (C) checklist
    (D) clipboard
    (E) ruler

87. A large home built in an area of small cottages is an example of:
    (A) overimprovement
    (B) underimprovement
    (C) land regression
    (D) functional obsolescence
    (E) environmental aesthetics

88. The period over which a building may be profitably used is its
    (A) actual life
    (B) physical life
    (C) useful life
    (D) normal life
    (E) effective age

89. An improvement's remaining economic life is
    (A) its chronological age
    (B) its effective age
    (C) the future time span over which the improvement is expected to generate benefits
    (D) its effective age minus its chronological age
    (E) its effective age plus its chronological age

90. To be considered as a possible alternative for highest and best use, a use must be
    (A) physically and legally possible and financially feasible
    (B) physically and legally possible
    (C) already in existence and legal
    (D) physically possible and appropriate
    (E) legal and profitable

91. When applying the concept of highest and best use of land as if vacant, the assumption is made that
    (A) any existing building can be demolished
    (B) zoning cannot be changed
    (C) the basic characteristics of a site can be changed
    (D) vacant land produces maximum income
    (E) land is not subject to erosion

92. The highest and best use of land as if vacant forms part of the basis for
    (A) mortgage equity analysis
    (B) a property rights adjustment
    (C) an operating expense estimate
    (D) the cost approach
    (E) the square footage approach

93. The best assurance of appraisal accuracy results from the use of
    (A) the greatest number of adjustments
    (B) a gross dollar amount of adjustments
    (C) a large number of truly comparable properties
    (D) a net dollar amount of adjustments
    (E) market segmentation

94. The direct sales comparison approach to appraising derives an estimate of value from
    (A) sales of comparable properties
    (B) comparison of the architecture of properties
    (C) comparison of loans made on properties
    (D) original costs of comparable properties
    (E) checking prices in the *Wall Street Journal* stock market report

95. A gross rent multiplier is often used in the
    (A) direct sales comparison approach for single-family housing
    (B) income approach for income property
    (C) income approach for single-family property
    (D) cost approach
    (E) back-door approach to valuation

96. Gross rent multiplier analysis is
    (A) required in almost every residential appraisal
    (B) applicable to every residential appraisal
    (C) applicable to residential property valuation only
    (D) part of the direct sales comparison approach to valuation of commercial properties
    (E) seldom used for houses

97. In estimating site value, the direct sales comparison approach
    (A) does not apply to older residences
    (B) is the most reliable method available
    (C) is considered inferior to other methods
    (D) is used only when the subject property is unimproved
    (E) is used for real estate but not for personal property appraisals

98. In an open market transaction, the subject property sold would not be
    (A) listed for at least 30 days
    (B) listed on a multiple listing service
    (C) advertised in local newspapers
    (D) sold to a relative
    (E) closed by a title company

99. The minimum number of comparable sales needed to apply direct sales comparison is
    (A) 3
    (B) 4
    (C) 10
    (D) 30
    (E) no set number

100. Physical units of comparison include
    (A) seats in a theater
    (B) rooms in a hotel
    (C) square feet of a house
    (D) cubic feet of a warehouse
    (E) all of the above

101. In GRM analysis an estimate of market value is derived by
    (A) dividing market rental by GRM
    (B) multiplying market rental by GRM
    (C) dividing GRM by market rental
    (D) multiplying net income by GRM
    (E) multiplying comparable sales by GRM

102. To apply the direct sales comparison approach, there need not be
    (A) an active market
    (B) many comparable properties
    (C) property representing the highest and best use
    (D) a long trend of historical data
    (E) informed buyers and sellers

103. Comparable sales that require little or no adjustment to the subject are usually sales
    (A) made within 2 years
    (B) of properties equal in square footage to the subject
    (C) of houses in the same neighborhood as the subject
    (D) of contiguous properties
    (E) in new developments with homes nearly identical to the subject

104. The date of sale of a comparable identifies
    (A) the motivation for the sale
    (B) the point in time when adjustments take place
    (C) the terms of sale
    (D) the market conditions when the sale was made
    (E) the functional utility of the property

105. A sale between relatives is suspected to be
    (A) a bona fide sale
    (B) a sale made at a distorted price
    (C) an arm's length sale
    (D) a seller-financed sale
    (E) a cash equivalence sale

106. Any recent previous sale of the subject property
    (A) should be considered confidential
    (B) may not under any circumstances be considered in estimating the current market value of the property
    (C) should be discussed in the appraisal report
    (D) is not an arm's length sale
    (E) should be used as a comparable sale, but adjusted for time and terms of sale

Questions 107–112 are based on the following information:

Factor	Subject	Comparable #1	Comparable #2	Comparable #3
Price		$270,000	$265,500	$261,000
Living area (square feet)	1,500	1,600	1,450	1,400
Condition	Good	Fair	Excellent	Good
Garage	One-car	Two-car	One-car	Two-car
Time of sale	Now	Last year	Last year	This year

Adjusted Sales Price: Prices have been rising by 5 percent per year in the area for this type of property.

Other Adjustments: Each square foot of livable area is judged to be worth $30; condition grades are fair, good, and excellent, with each difference in condition grade worth 5 percent; a two-car garage is judged to be worth $4,500 more than a one-car garage.

107. What is the size adjustment for Comparable #1?
    (A) +$4,500
    (B) −$4,500
    (C) 0
    (D) +$9,000
    (E) −$9,000

108. What is the size adjustment for Comparable #2?
    (A) +$4,500
    (B) −$4,500
    (C) 0
    (D) +$9,000
    (E) −$9,000

109. What is the condition adjustment for Comparable #1?
    (A) 0
    (B) +$13,500
    (C) −$13,500
    (D) +$27,000
    (E) −$27,000

110. What is the condition adjustment for Comparable #2?
    (A) 0
    (B) +$13,275
    (C) −$13,275
    (D) +$26,550
    (E) −$26,550

111. What is the garage adjustment for Comparable #2?
    (A) 0
    (B) +$4,500
    (C) −$4,500
    (D) +$9,000
    (E) −$9,000

112. What is the garage adjustment for Comparable #3?
    (A) 0
    (B) +$4,500
    (C) −$4,500
    (D) +$9,000
    (E) −$9,000

113. What would be the indicated value of a property that rented for $2,250 per month, using a monthly gross rent multiplier of 110, if the expenses attributable to the property were $375 per month?
    (A) $227,010
    (B) $247,500
    (C) $206,250
    (D) $183,375
    (E) $41,250

114. A 7-year-old residence is currently valued at $216,000. What was its original value if it has appreciated by 60 percent since it was built?
    (A) $81,000
    (B) $113,400
    (C) $135,000
    (D) $345,600
    (E) none of the above

115. An adjustment for market conditions would be made to reflect
    (A) a loan assumption
    (B) a sale between relatives
    (C) financing differences
    (D) a decrease in demand
    (E) differences in government regulation

116. For residential property, market value appraisals assume that
    (A) the purchaser pays all cash; no money is borrowed
    (B) an FHA or VA mortgage is used
    (C) a purchase money mortgage is considered
    (D) the value estimate is based on no special financing
    (E) the seller pays no more than 5 points

117. In considering comparable sales in a direct sales comparison appraisal,
    (A) the seller's motivation is significant
    (B) the date of sale is significant
    (C) the proximity of the comps to the subject property is most important
    (D) both A and B
    (E) none of the above

118. In estimating the market value of a comparable sale, an appraiser must consider all of the following *except*
    (A) whether the transaction was made in cash, terms equivalent to cash, or other precisely revealed terms
    (B) whether the property had reasonable exposure in a competitive market
    (C) whether a fair sale was transacted, with neither the seller nor the buyer acting under duress
    (D) whether the replacement cost of the property corresponds to its market value
    (E) whether the seller was related to the buyer

119. The terms of financing, whether good or bad,
    (A) have no effect on the market price
    (B) have no effect on the market value
    (C) have no effect on affordability
    (D) depend on the fiscal and monetary policy of the government
    (E) should be ignored when adjusting comparables

120. A tract home builder offers new houses for sale with different financing plans offered. The price is $300,000 if the builder pays no discount points, and $2,800 more for each point paid on the buyer's loan. Numerous recent sales have been made on these terms. You are appraising a house that sold with 2½ points. If you found no adjustments to make compared to other sales, the market value of the house would be
   (A) $300,000
   (B) $305,600
   (C) $307,000
   (D) $308,400
   (E) $308,000

121. In a 100-unit apartment building, rentals vary as follows:

Number of Units	Monthly Rental
15	$980
25	$1,020
30	$1,060
20	$1,100
10	$1,140

   What is the modal rent for this building?
   (A) $1,054
   (B) $1,060
   (C) $1,038
   (D) $1,100
   (E) $1,076

Questions 122–126 are based on the following information:
   In a subdivision with 160 homes, the houses have varying numbers of bedrooms, as shown below:

Number of Bedrooms	Number of Homes
2	18
3	77
4	53
5	12

122. What is the mean number of bedrooms?
   (A) 3.37
   (B) 3.00
   (C) 4.00
   (D) 3.50
   (E) Not shown

123. What is the median number of bedrooms?
   (A) 3.37
   (B) 3.00
   (C) 4.00
   (D) 3.50
   (E) Not shown

124. What is the modal number of bedrooms?
   (A) 3.37
   (B) 3.00
   (C) 4.00
   (D) 3.50
   (E) Not shown

125. What is the average number of bedrooms?
    (A) 3.37
    (B) 3.00
    (C) 4.00
    (D) 3.50
    (E) Not shown

126. What is the range for the number of bedrooms?
    (A) 3.37
    (B) 3.00
    (C) 4.00
    (D) 3.50
    (E) Not shown

127. The adjustment process in the direct sales comparison approach relies on the principle of
    (A) contribution
    (B) substitution
    (C) complexity
    (D) supply and demand
    (E) conformity

128. In selecting properties for a paired-sale comparison,
    (A) one of the pair should be next door or on the same street as the subject
    (B) the pair should offer different financing
    (C) the pair should be nearly identical to each other except for one important feature being considered
    (D) the pair should be virtually identical to each other, as is a pair of shoes or earrings
    (E) the pair should be selected to be quite different and to embody as many different features as possible

129. In the direct sales comparison approach, dollar adjustments for elements of comparison are made to the
    (A) sales prices of subject properties
    (B) listing prices of subject properties
    (C) sales prices of comparable properties
    (D) listing prices of comparable properties
    (E) appraised values of comparables

130. In the cost approach, land valuation is based on the principle of
    (A) variable proportions
    (B) highest and best use
    (C) diminishing returns
    (D) contribution
    (E) conformity

131. To be used as comparables, land sales must be
    (A) competitive with the subject
    (B) relatively recent
    (C) open-market transactions
    (D) adjusted to cash equivalent prices
    (E) all of the above

132. Price per front foot is
    (A) a physical unit of comparison
    (B) not as accurate as price per square foot
    (C) rarely used in commercial site analysis
    (D) an accurate guide to site marketability
    (E) useful when there are major physical differences between sites

133. What is plottage?
    (A) The value of land between the subject property and another property
    (B) The bonus that is sometimes obtained by combining parcels
    (C) The price of land per plot
    (D) The value estimated while slowly walking on the land
    (E) The age of a piece of land since it was mapped

134. When two or more sites are assembled or created to produce greater utility, the value increase is called
    (A) capital gain
    (B) plottage
    (C) enclosure
    (D) physical adaptation
    (E) assembly

135. The act of combining two or more sites in an effort to develop one site with a greater value than the two sites have separately is called
    (A) assemblage
    (B) plottage
    (C) surplus land
    (D) excess land
    (E) a land contract

136. All of the following are cost estimation methods *except*
    (A) unit-in-place
    (B) unit-breakdown
    (C) quantity survey
    (D) comparative-unit
    (E) segregated cost

137. Which of the following tends to set the upper limits of value?
    (A) Replacement cost new
    (B) Market data approach
    (C) Income approach
    (D) Gross rent multiplier
    (E) Double declining balance method

138. A building that is too large for the neighborhood is an example of functional obsolescence in the form of overimprovement. Another example of functional obsolescence is
    (A) a sound building with a worn-out heating system
    (B) an awkwardly shaped floor plan in an office building
    (C) a residence abutting a new freeway
    (D) a building that will probably cost more to repair than the value added to the structure
    (E) an older building with modernized elevators

139. An inefficient floor plan would generally be classified as
     (A) physical depreciation
     (B) economic obsolescence
     (C) functional obsolescence
     (D) environmental obsolescence
     (E) none of the above

140. *Effective age* refers to
     (A) chronological age
     (B) average age
     (C) apparent age, considering the physical condition and marketability of a structure
     (D) warranty expiration
     (E) the ageless depreciation method

141. The effective age of a building will probably exceed its actual age when
     (A) a normal maintenance program has been carried out and the property experiences typical economic obsolescence
     (B) an inadequate maintenance program has been used
     (C) an above-average maintenance program has been used
     (D) the property is in a moderate climate
     (E) there is a full-time maintenance crew

142. Functional obsolescence in a house can be caused by
     (A) deterioration of the foundation
     (B) factors inherent in the house
     (C) factors external to the property
     (D) failure to paint when needed
     (E) worn-out carpeting

143. All other things being equal, when the building being appraised is much larger than the benchmark building described in the cost manual, the subject building's unit cost is probably
     (A) higher
     (B) lower
     (C) the same
     (D) adjustable by a local multiplier
     (E) none of the above

144. Reproduction cost is
     (A) original cost adjusted for inflation
     (B) the cost new of an exact replica of the subject
     (C) the cost of acquiring an equally desirable substitute
     (D) the current cost of constructing a functionally equivalent structure
     (E) available from brokerage offices

145. Determinants of building cost include
     (A) design
     (B) construction type
     (C) quality rating
     (D) local costs
     (E) all of the above

146. Subtracting an improvement's current market value from its reproduction cost new indicates
    (A) its sale price
    (B) the owner's profit
    (C) its replacement cost
    (D) accrued depreciation
    (E) replacement cost new

147. *Replacement cost new* refers to the cost of
    (A) constructing an exact replica of the subject building
    (B) constructing a building that would have similar or equivalent utility
    (C) reproducing the subject building on a different site
    (D) buying another property
    (E) an investment yielding similar returns

148. Examples of functional obsolescence do *not* include
    (A) poor room layout
    (B) peeling paint on exterior trim
    (C) a relatively short or narrow garage
    (D) inconveniently placed building support columns
    (E) uneconomical high ceilings

149. Which of the following best illustrates curable functional obsolescence?
    (A) Poor room layout with immovable load-bearing walls
    (B) Poorly located building support columns on an office floor
    (C) Inadequate electrical wiring in an older single-family house
    (D) A narrow, short carport that can be enlarged at low cost
    (E) Stains on the ceiling due to water penetration

150. What appraisal approach can be used for a public building?
    (A) Direct sales comparison
    (B) Income
    (C) Cost
    (D) Insurance
    (E) None of the above

151. Functional obsolescence that cannot be economically remedied is known as
    (A) physical depreciation
    (B) incurable depreciation
    (C) physical deterioration
    (D) locational deterioration
    (E) a curable loss

Questions 152–155 are based on the following information:
A residence is 12 years old but has been so well cared for that it is in as good condition as a typical 8-year-old property. Residences in this area typically last 60 years, and even that life span may be extended with extensive renovation.

152. The effective age of the residence is
    (A) 100 years
    (B) 60 years
    (C) 12 years
    (D) 8 years
    (E) none of the above

153. The chronological age of the residence is
     (A) 100 years
     (B) 60 years
     (C) 12 years
     (D) 8 years
     (E) none of the above

154. The remaining economic life of the residence is
     (A) 100 years
     (B) 60 years
     (C) 52 years
     (D) 48 years
     (E) none of the above

155. Normal life expectancy of the residence is
     (A) 100 years
     (B) 60 years
     (C) 12 years
     (D) 8 years
     (E) none of the above

156. The construction of a luxury home in a neighborhood almost completely developed with
     one- and two-bedroom apartments would
     (A) produce functional inadequacies
     (B) be called an underimprovement
     (C) result in plottage value
     (D) result in neighborhood amenities
     (E) be reasonable and appropriate

157. In the cost approach, a site is valued
     (A) as raw land
     (B) as if vacant
     (C) via the leased fee method
     (D) less accrued depreciation
     (E) as if unzoned

158. Functional obsolescence attributed to a property may result from
     (A) factors outside the property
     (B) physical deterioration
     (C) economic factors
     (D) changes in popular taste
     (E) functional area analysis

Questions 159–167 are based on the following information:
You are appraising a 20-year-old, single-family residence. It is typical of other houses in the neighborhood, and its estimated effective age is the same as its chronological age. Items needing immediate work at the time of the appraisal include exterior painting, with an estimated cost of $3,600, interior paint and decorating at $2,700, and storm door replacement at $450.

You have noted the following short-lived items and have estimated for each the cost new, effective age, and normal life expectancy.

Component	Cost	Effective Age (years)	Normal Life (years)
Roof	$4,500	5	20
Heating equipment	4,800	20	25
Light fixtures	2,400	20	25
Plumbing fixtures	6,000	20	40

The total estimated reproduction cost new of the house is $240,000. After completion of the work above, you estimate the house will have an effective age of only 15 years. Similar houses in the neighborhood are estimated to have an economic life new of 50 years. The subject has only one bathroom in a neighborhood of two-bathroom houses. It is rented for $1,800 per month, and this is its maximum rent. Several similar houses in the area with two bathrooms are rented for $1,950 per month. A number of sales of rented houses were analyzed, and a gross rent multiplier of 125 was indicated. A contractor has given you an estimate of $25,500 for adding another bathroom to the house.

159. Estimate curable physical deterioration.
  (A) $6,300
  (B) $3,600
  (C) $6,750
  (D) $450
  (E) None of the above

160. Estimate the dollar amount of *deferred* curable physical deterioration of the roof.
  (A) $4,500
  (B) 0
  (C) $2,250
  (D) $1,125
  (E) None of the above

161. Estimate the dollar amount of *deferred* curable physical deterioration of the heating equipment.
  (A) $3,840
  (B) $2,400
  (C) $3,600
  (D) 0
  (E) None of the above

162. Estimate the dollar amount of *deferred* curable physical deterioration of the light fixtures.
  (A) $1,800
  (B) $2,400
  (C) $1,536
  (D) $1,920
  (E) None of the above

163. What is your estimate of the dollar amount of *deferred* curable physical deterioration of the plumbing fixtures?
    (A) $4,800
    (B) $1,200
    (C) $2,400
    (D) $6,000
    (E) $3,000

164. For determination of incurable physical deterioration, what dollar amount is assigned to the remaining portion of the main structure?
    (A) $222,300
    (B) $240,000
    (C) $233,250
    (D) $215,550
    (E) None of the above

165. The functional obsolescence experienced by this property is
    (A) curable
    (B) deferred curable
    (C) incurable
    (D) deferred incurable
    (E) partially curable

166. What is your estimate of the dollar amount of functional obsolescence?
    (A) $15,000
    (B) $18,750
    (C) $22,500
    (D) $45,000
    (E) $48,000

167. What is your estimate (rounded) of the depreciated reproduction cost of the improvement?
    (A) $132,000
    (B) $168,000
    (C) $192,000
    (D) $204,000
    (E) $240,000

168. In appraisal, accrued depreciation is normally subtracted from
    (A) historic cost
    (B) actual cost new as of the date of the appraisal
    (C) reproduction cost new as of the date of the value estimate
    (D) depreciated cost as of the date of the value estimate
    (E) balance sheet assets

169. The cost of plumbing, heating, elevators, and similar building components may represent a smaller proportion of total costs when these components are installed in a large building than in a smaller one. This may be reflected in the
    (A) unit-in-place method
    (B) land-to-building ratio
    (C) quantity survey method
    (D) comparative-unit method
    (E) segregated cost method

170. The anticipated income that remains after deducting all operating expenses from effective gross income but before subtracting mortgage debt service is
    (A) cash flow
    (B) net operating income
    (C) potential gross income
    (D) after-tax cash flow
    (E) net income before debt service

171. The cost of painting and redecorating an apartment is
    (A) an operating expense
    (B) a fixed expense
    (C) an unnecessary expense if you have 100% occupancy
    (D) set aside in an owner's bank account as a reserve for redecoration
    (E) always justified for aesthetic reasons

172. Which of the following might be classified as a tangible rather than an intangible amenity?
    (A) Pride of ownership
    (B) A sense of security
    (C) Free utilities
    (D) Work satisfaction
    (E) Clean air

173. The lessor's interest in leased property is referred to as the
    (A) leasehold estate
    (B) leased fee estate
    (C) fee simple estate
    (D) remainder estate
    (E) residual estate

174. An ownership right retained by a landlord is
    (A) apparent authority
    (B) leased fee estate
    (C) leasehold estate
    (D) ingress and egress
    (E) fee tail

175. The monthly rental being paid under a lease for a comparable rental property is called the
    (A) market rental
    (B) net rental
    (C) effective rental
    (D) economic rent
    (E) contract rent

176. Timeshare units are most often used by
    (A) commuters
    (B) gardeners
    (C) attorneys
    (D) salespersons
    (E) vacationers

177. Which of the following is (are) important for good appraisal communication?
    (A) Word choice
    (B) Reading level
    (C) Sentence structure
    (D) Clarity
    (E) All of the above

178. Valuation estimates for which of the following purposes are normally outside the scope of a real estate appraiser's function?
    (A) Divorce (home valuation)
    (B) Mortgage financing
    (C) Condemnation
    (D) Personal injury
    (E) Insurance

179. An appraiser's workload should determine
    (A) the length and context of the appraisal report
    (B) the approaches included
    (C) the inspection detail
    (D) clerical responsibilities
    (E) none of the above

180. The purpose of which of the following is to analyze a property's potential for success?
    (A) Feasibility study
    (B) Marketability study
    (C) Market segmentation study
    (D) Appraisal report
    (E) Need study

181. The objective of the appraisal should be stated in the report because
    (A) it identifies the function of the report
    (B) it defines the problem and identifies the value sought
    (C) it absolves the appraiser of liability
    (D) the market needs this information
    (E) there are too many definitions of market price

182. It is___for an appraiser to receive or pay finder's or referral fees.
    (A) reasonable
    (B) unethical
    (C) necessary
    (D) customary
    (E) honest

183. Professional appraisal services are rendered
    (A) for professional attorneys
    (B) in a courtroom setting
    (C) on a fee basis only
    (D) generally on a retainer
    (E) contingent on the value estimate

184. For an appraiser to use the assistance of another appraiser is
    (A) inconsiderate
    (B) unethical
    (C) illegal
    (D) ethical
    (E) questionable

185. To provide a value range to a client who requests it and understands its meaning and use is
    (A) foolish
    (B) appropriate
    (C) unethical
    (D) impossible
    (E) improper but not unethical

ANSWERS

1. B	32. D	63. E	94. A	125. A	156. A
2. B	33. C	64. B	95. C	126. B	157. B
3. E	34. A	65. D	96. D	127. A	158. D
4. E	35. D	66. E	97. B	128 C	159. C
5. C	36. D	67. C	98. D	129. C	160. D
6. D	37. B	68. D	99. E	130. B	161. A
7. E	38. C	69. C	100. E	131. E	162. D
8. B	39. B	70. B	101. B	132. A	163. E
9. A	40. B	71. C	102. D	133. B	164. D
10. E	41. E	72. C	103. E	134. B	165. C
11. A	42. D	73. C	104. D	135. A	166. B
12. B	43. C	74. E	105. B	136. B	167. A
13. E	44. E	75. E	106. C	137. A	168. C
14. E	45. A	76. D	107. E	138. B	169. D
15. E	46. C	77. C	108. A	139. C	170. B
16. B	47. B	78. B	109. B	140. C	171. A
17. B	48. C	79. B	110. C	141. B	172. C
18. D	49. B	80. B	111. A	142. B	173. B
19. D	50. B	81. B	112. C	143. B	174. B
20. A	51. C	82. E	113. B	144. B	175. E
21. A	52. D	83. C	114. C	145. E	176. E
22. D	53. E	84. D	115. D	146. D	177. E
23. A	54. D	85. D	116. D	147. B	178. D
24. A	55. A	86. C	117. D	148. B	179. E
25. E	56. B	87. A	118. D	149. D	180. A
26. C	57. C	88. C	119. B	150. C	181. B
27. B	58. B	89. C	120. A	151. B	182. B
28. B	59. D	90. A	121. B	152. D	183. C
29. A	60. B	91. A	122. A	153. C	184. D
30. B	61. C	92. D	123. B	154. C	185. B
31. A	62. C	93. C	124. B	155. B	

Chapter 15 / *Certified General Appraiser*

This chapter is of primary interest to a person who wishes to be licensed as a certified general appraiser. Much of the material will be of interest also to brokers, salespersons, and other appraisers but is not presently required by licensing examinations for those groups.

Items indicated by a dagger (†) in the Examination Content Outline in Chapter 14 are specifically covered here.

Legal Considerations in Appraisal

Property is generally classified as either real or personal. Whatever is more or less permanently affixed to land or buildings is *real property*; all other property is *personal property*. Questions frequently arise as to whether or not fixtures are part of the real estate in question; if they *are* part, they are included in the appraised value.

TRADE FIXTURES

A *trade fixture* is attached to a rented facility by a tenant who uses that fixture in conducting a business. No matter how trade fixtures are attached to real estate, they are personal property. Some examples are booths, counters, and bar stools in a restaurant, tanks and pumps in a service station, and shelves in a retail store. The tenant may remove these at the expiration of the lease.

In determining whether an item is a trade fixture, courts will consider:

1. *The manner of attachment.* Personal property can generally be removed without damage.
2. *The adaptation of the article to the real estate.* Items that are built specifically to be installed in a particular building and are unlikely to be used in another are probably real estate.
3. *The intent of the parties when the property was attached.*

MACHINERY AND EQUIPMENT

An appraiser needs to know whether or not to include these items in the real estate value estimate. For example, in a hotel there may be equipment in laundry facilities, guest exercise rooms, or restaurants that could be considered either real or personal property. In the office section of a warehouse, there could be heating, ventilation, and air conditioning equipment, lighting, and plumbing facilities for office workers. Depending on the same criteria described for fixtures, the appraiser has to classify the machinery and equipment as real or personal property.

Types of Value

All types of value were covered in Chapter 14 except *going-concern value*. This is the difference between the market value of a business and the market value of its assets. For example, a restaurant may be worth $1 million as a business even though its building, land, furniture, fixtures, and equipment have an aggregate market value of only $600,000. The $400,000 excess is the going-concern value.

When appraising business real estate, such as a hotel or motel, retail store, or storage service facility, an appraiser needs to recognize the difference between the business value and the real estate value. The value conclusion will, of course, depend on what is being appraised.

Economic Principles

All of these principles were discussed in Chapter 14 except *opportunity cost*, that is, the cost of an opportunity forgone by not choosing it. For example, suppose an investor buys mortgages on real estate that yield 10 percent rather than corporate bonds yielding 9 percent. The opportunity cost is the 9 percent yield on the bonds that were not bought.

Similarly, if an appraiser accepts an assignment for $8,000 that requires his full-time effort for a month, requiring him to turn down another assignment at $6,000 because of a time conflict, the $6,000 is the opportunity cost.

Real Estate Market Analysis

The three items of the Examination Content Outline that were not covered in Chapter 14 are *existing space inventory*, *current and projected space surplus*, and *new space*.

EXISTING SPACE INVENTORY

Existing space may be inventoried and categorized for a market or market segment. For example, for each office building in a city, a database may be used that includes, at a minimum, the following information:

Building name	*Year built*
Building location	*Class (A, B, C)*
Square feet retail	*Occupancy rate*
Square feet office	
Rent rate asked	*Typical lease terms*

The database can then be sorted in various ways: by amount of space in each section of the city or by class, rent range, vacancy rate, and so on.

CURRENT AND PROJECTED SPACE SURPLUS

Using the database model described above, one can estimate an occupancy ratio for each part of the city and class of building, for example, and can then compare historical absorption rates with existing surplus space to estimate future occupancy. This comparison must be tempered by knowledge of specific important changes to come, such as the impending relocation of a corporate headquarters to another city. The analysis will provide insights as to the likelihood of a tightening of supply or a surplus of space.

NEW SPACE

The planning or engineering department of the city can provide information on the issuance of permits authorizing new construction. Since these permits will be for specific buildings, they will provide locations and sizes that may be added to the database. Construction and leasing activity will be recognized for new space; together these can offer a picture of the supply of space for the next 2 to 3 years in an office market, for example.

Appraisal Math and Statistics

All compound interest functions are reserved for the appraiser general certification examination. There are six of these functions; each is described below. All six functions are variations on the compound interest formula, which holds that interest in each period is based on the initial principal plus accrued but unpaid interest earned in prior periods. The six functions (and their column locations in standard six-function tables) are as follows:

- Future value of $1 (Column 1)
- Future value of an annuity of $1 per period (Column 2)
- Sinking fund factor (Column 3)
- Present value of $1 (Column 4)
- Present value of an annuity of $1 per period (Column 5)
- Installment to amortize $1 (Column 6)

FUTURE VALUE OF $1

This function is compound interest. Interest that has been earned and left on deposit becomes principal. In the next period, that principal will earn interest along with the initial principal. The formula for compound interest is as follows:

$$S^n = (1 + i)^n$$

where S^n = sum after n periods; i = periodic rate of interest; n = number of periods.

Table 15-1 indicates the growth of a $1.00 deposit that earns 10 percent compound interest for 5 years. Figure 15-1 illustrates the growth of $1.00 at compound interest.

Although Table 15-1 illustrates a compounding interval of 1 year, compounding may occur daily, monthly, quarterly, or semiannually. Interest rates are usually stated at a nominal annual

Table 15-1
FUTURE VALUE OF $1
$1.00 Deposit at 10% Interest Rate for 5 Years

Year		Compound Interest and Balance
0	Deposit	$1.00
1	Interest earned	0.10
1	Balance, end of year	1.10
2	Interest earned	0.11
2	Balance, end of year	1.21
3	Interest earned	0.121
3	Balance, end of year	1.331
4	Interest earned	0.1331
4	Balance, end of year	1.4641
5	Interest earned	0.1464
5	Balance, end of year	$1.6105

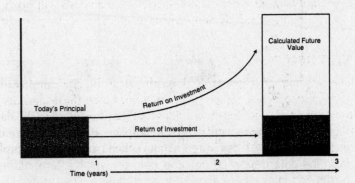

Figure 15-1. Growth of Principal at Compound Interest

figure, such as 10 percent, but more frequent compounding increases the effective rate. The general formula is the same: $S^n = (1 + i)^n$.

FUTURE VALUE OF AN ANNUITY OF $1 PER PERIOD

This function offers the future value of a series of equal amounts deposited at the ends of periodic intervals. It is the sum of all these individual amounts, each deposited at the end of an interval, (period), plus appropriate interest. Note that this differs from the future value of $1 factor in two ways. First, the future annuity factor is based on a series of deposits, whereas the future value of $1 involves a single deposit. Second, the accumulation is based on a deposit at the end of each interval, whereas compound interest is based on a deposit made at the beginning of the total period.

The formula for the future value of $1 per period is as follows:

$$S_n = \frac{s^n - 1}{i} \quad \text{or} \quad \frac{(1 + i)^n - 1}{i}$$

where Sn = future value of annuity of $1 per period; i = periodic interest rate; n = number of periods considered.

Table 15-2 shows the annual interest earned and end-of-period balances of the future value

Table 15-2
FUTURE VALUE OF AN ANNUITY OF $1 PER PERIOD
Illustrated at 10% Interest Rate for Four Periods

End of period 1, initial deposit	$1.00
Interest, period 1	0.00
Balance, end of period 1	1.00
Interest, end of period 2	0.10
Deposit, end of period 2	1.00
Balance, end of period 2	2.10
Interest, end of period 3	0.21
Deposit, end of period 3	1.00
Balance, end of period 3	3.31
Interest, end of period 4	0.331
Deposit, end of period 4	1.00
Balance, end of period 4	$4.641

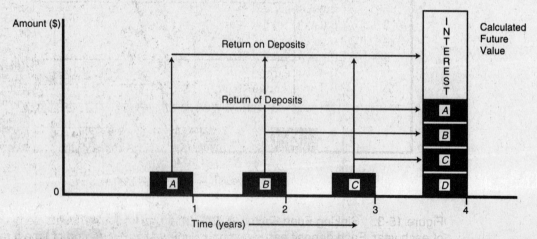

Figure 15-2.   Accumulation of $1 per Period (Future Value of an Annuity). *A, B, C,* and *D* each represent $1 deposited at the end of a year. Each deposit earns compound interest from the date deposited until the date on which a terminal amount is sought. Thus, all deposits and interest are allowed to accumulate. The terminal value is the sum of all deposits plus compound interest.

of an annuity of $1 per period at 10 percent interest. Figure 15-2 is an illustration of the function for four periods.

SINKING FUND FACTOR

This factor shows the deposit that is required at the end of each period to reach $1.00 after a certain number of periods, considering interest to be earned on the deposits. It is the reciprocal of the future value of an annuity of $1 per period.

For example, at a 0 percent rate of interest, $0.25 must be deposited at the end of each year for 4 years to accumulate $1.00 at the end of 4 years. If, however, the deposits earn compound interest at 10 percent, only $0.215471 need be deposited at the end of each of the 4 years.

Table 15-3 indicates how four periodic deposits grow to $1.00 with interest. Figure 15-3 offers a graphic presentation of the same data.

Table 15-3
SINKING FUND FACTOR
Illustrated to Reach $1.00 in Four Periods at 10% Interest Rate

Deposit, end of period 1	$0.215471
Interest for period 1	0.000000
Balance, end of period 1	0.215471
Interest for period 2	0.021547
Deposit, end of period 2	0.215471
Balance, end of period 2	0.452489
Interest for period 3	0.045249
Deposit, end of period 3	0.215471
Balance, end of period 3	0.713209
Interest for period 4	0.071321
Deposit, end of period 4	0.215471
Balance, end of period 4	$1.000000

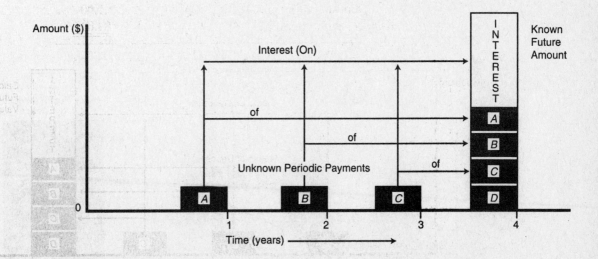

Figure 15-3.   Sinking Fund Factor. A, B, C, and D are equal amounts deposited at the end of each year. Each deposit earns compound interest for the period of time it remains on deposit. At the end of the time period considered, the depositor can withdraw the terminal value. The sinking fund factor is computed in such a way that the terminal value will always equal $1.

PRESENT VALUE OF $1

This factor offers the value now of $1 to be received in the future. Money has a time value; a dollar to be received in the future is worth less than a dollar now. The amount of discount depends on the time between the cash outflow and inflow and the necessary rate of interest or discount rate.

Since the purpose of investing is to receive returns in the future, applying the present value of $1 factor to anticipated future income is a crucial step in valuing an investment. When applying a present value factor, the terms *discounting* and *discount rate* are used, as contrasted with *compounding* and *interest rate*, which are used in computing future values. Mathematically, the present value of a reversion is the reciprocal of the future value of $1.

For example, at a 10 percent discount rate, $100.00 that is expected 1 year from now has a present value of $90.91. As an arithmetic check, consider that, if an investor has $90.91 now and earns 10 percent during the year, the interest will amount to $9.09, making the principal in 1 year $100.00 ($90.91 original principal + $9.09 interest).

An investor who will get $100.00 in 2 years and pays $82.64 now receives a 10 percent annual rate of interest. As a check, consider that, after 1 year, $82.64 will grow to $90.91 with 10 percent interest, then to $100.00 in 2 years.

The formula for the present value of $1 is as follows:

$$V^n = \frac{1}{(1 + i)^n} \quad \text{or} \quad \frac{1}{S^n}$$

where V = present value of $1; i = periodic discount rate; n = number of periods.

Table 15-4 shows the present value of a reversion at 10 percent interest for 4 years. Figure 15-4 illustrates the present value of $1.

Table 15-4
PRESENT VALUE OF $1
Illustrated at 10% Interest Rate for 4 Years

Year	Compound Amount	Reciprocal		Present Value of $1.00 Reversion
1	1.1	1/1.1	=	$0.909091
2	1.21	1/1.21	=	0.826446
3	1.331	1/1.331	=	0.751315
4	1.4641	1/1.4641	=	0.683013

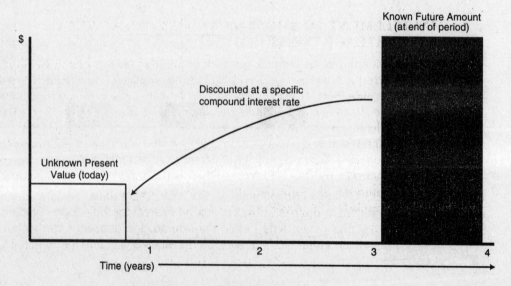

Figure 15-4. Present Value of a Reversion

PRESENT VALUE OF AN ANNUITY OF $1 PER PERIOD

An ordinary annuity is a series of equal payments beginning one period from the present. It is also defined as a series of receipts. For example, the right to receive $1.00 at the end of each year for the next 4 years creates an ordinary annuity.

Table 15-5 shows the present value of an annuity of $1 each year for 4 years at a 10 percent interest rate. Figure 15-5 provides an illustration.

Table 15-5
PRESENT VALUE OF AN ANNUITY OF $1 PER PERIOD
Illustrated for 4 Years at 10% Interest Rate

Year	Present Value of Reversion	Present Value of Annuity
1	$0.9091	$0.9091
2	0.8264	1.7355
3	0.7513	2.4868
4	0.6830	3.1698

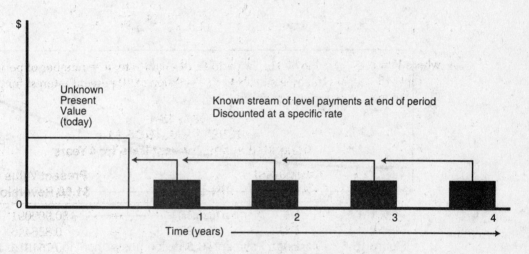

Figure 15-5. Present Value of an Ordinary Annuity

INSTALLMENT TO AMORTIZE $1 (LOAN CONSTANT OR MORTGAGE CONSTANT)

This function shows the periodic payment required to retire a loan, with interest. It is the sum of the interest (or discount) rate and the sinking fund factor. It is the reciprocal of the present value of an annuity of $1 per period. This factor, which shows the constant payment necessary to amortize a loan in equal periodic installments, considers the term, interest rate, and principal of the loan.

As the interest rate increases or the amortization term shortens, the required periodic payment is increased. Conversely, lower interest rates and longer repayment periods reduce the required periodic payment. Each level payment in the installment to amortize $1 factor is a blend of interest and a reduction of the original principal.

The formula for the installment to amortize $1 is as follows:

$$\frac{1}{a_n} = \frac{i}{1 - V^n} \text{ or } \frac{1}{a_n} = \frac{i}{1 - \dfrac{1}{(1 + i)^n}}$$

where a_n = present value of annuity of \$1 per period; i = interest rate; n = number of periods; V^n = present value of \$1.

Table 15-6 shows that the installment to amortize \$1 is the reciprocal of the present value of an annuity of \$1 factor. Figure 15-6 illustrates the distribution of periodic payments to interest and principal retirement.

Table 15-6
INSTALLMENTS TO AMORTIZE $1 AS RECIPROCAL
OF PRESENT VALUE OF ANNUITY
Illustrated for 4 Years at 10% Interest Rate

Year	Present Value of Annuity	Installment to Amortize $1
1	$0.9091	$1.10
2	1.7355	0.5762
3	2.4868	0.4021
4	3.1698	0.3155

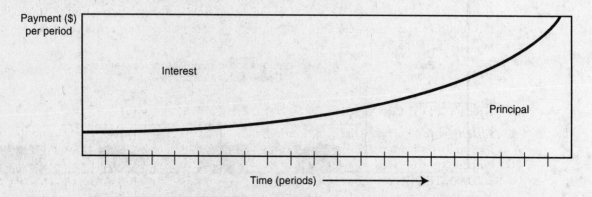

Figure 15-6.   Mortgage Payment Application (Installment to Amortize $1)

As an example of use, suppose that a \$100 loan requires four equal annual payments at 10 percent interest. The required payment will be \$31.55. As a check, one can construct an amortization schedule as shown in Table 15-7.

Table 15-7
AMORTIZATION SCHEDULE FOR A $100 LOAN
Level Payments at 10% for 4 Years

Year	Loan Balance at Beginning of Year	Add Interest at 10%	Less Interest and Principal Payment	Balance at End of Year
1	$100.00	$10.00	$31.55	$78.45
2	78.45	7.85	31.55	54.75
3	54.75	5.48	31.55	28.68
4	28.68	2.87	31.55	-0-

Sales Comparison Approach

Chapter 14 covers most of the details associated with sales comparisons. Here, gross income multipliers and overall rates are discussed, along with certain units of comparison, mineral rights and other vertical interests, and tenant improvements.

GROSS INCOME MULTIPLIERS

Gross income multipliers can be used to compare comparable properties to the subject property. The *gross income multiplier (GIM)* indicates the relationship between the annual revenues from a property and its selling price or value. In nearly all situations, the sales price is several times greater than the revenues and therefore is the numerator, with the revenues the denominator. The resulting factor is expected to be greater than 1, most frequently between 4 and 20.

POTENTIAL GROSS INCOME MULTIPLIER

Potential gross income (PGI) is the amount that would be received from rental properties if all units were fully occupied all year. For example, if a building contained 100 apartments, each renting for $1,000 per month, the PGI would be 100 × $1,000 × 12 months, or $1,200,000. If this building were to sell for $10 million, the *potential gross income multiplier (PGIM)* would be 8.333 ($10,000,000 ÷ $1,200,000).

EFFECTIVE GROSS INCOME MULTIPLIER

Effective gross income (EGI) is determined by subtracting an allowance for vacancy and collection losses from potential gross income. In the example above, if the appropriate allowance percentage rate is 5 percent of the $1,200,000 potential gross income, the allowance is $60,000. The EGI is therefore $1,200,000 minus $60,000, or $1,140,000. The *effective gross income multiplier (EGIM)* is the selling price divided by the EGIM, that is, $10,000,000 ÷ $1,140,000, or 8.772.

OVERALL RATE OF RETURN

The *overall rate of return* is the percentage relationship between the *net operating income (NOI)* and the sales price. Since NOI is a revenue amount, this ratio is almost always less than 1, typically 0.05 to 0.30.

NOI is EGI minus operating expenses (OE). Operating expenses are payments that must be made to run the property, but not financing expenses, such as interest, nor depreciation. Operating expenses include maintenance and repairs, payroll and payroll taxes, real estate property taxes, advertising, utilities, management fees, grounds maintenance, and replacement reserve.

Suppose, in the preceding example, that annual operating expenses are $440,000. Then NOI is $1,140,000 (EGI) minus $440,000 (OE), or $700,000. The overall rate of return is

$$\frac{\text{NOI}}{\text{Sales Price}} = \frac{\$700,000}{\$10,000,000} = 7 \text{ percent}$$

UNITS OF COMPARISON

The certified general appraiser is expected to be knowledgeable about some less obvious units of comparison, including those for specialized properties, such as motels and theaters. Units of comparison for these include the price per room for a motel and the price per seat for a theater. The computation is straightforward: after appraisal adjustments are made for the elements of comparison described below, the adjusted price is divided by the number of units.

An appraisal should emulate market conditions; for example, in the case of multiscreen theaters, the number of screens may become a unit of comparison.

MINERAL RIGHTS AND OTHER VERTICAL INTERESTS

A real estate appraiser is not expected to be a geologist or to be able to value subsurface rights (*mineral rights*), but she must recognize that in certain regions the minerals may have value. When some comparables sell with mineral rights and some without, the appraiser must take care to make the appropriate adjustments from the comparables to the subject property. The paired-sale technique (see Chapter 14) may be useful for this purpose.

An appraiser may need also to value other *vertical interests*, such as *air rights* (the right to build above property, starting from a certain height) and tunneling.

TENANT IMPROVEMENTS

Tenant improvements, known in the trade as TIs, are allowances given to a tenant to adapt the property for his use. For example, a retail tenant agrees to a 5-year lease at a rent of $25 per square foot per year. The landlord offers bare walls and will advance $15 per square foot, before occupancy, for the tenant to adapt the property to his use. If costs exceed the allowance, the tenant will be responsible.

When comparing rents, an appraiser must also consider TIs. One building may offer a low rent but contribute no TIs, whereas another has higher rents and a generous TI allowance. The appraiser must understand the market so as to properly estimate the market rent for the subject property.

Site Value

Two methods of estimating site value, in addition to those given in Chapter 14, are *ground rent capitalization* and *subdivision analysis*. These methods apply only in certain situations.

GROUND RENT CAPITALIZATION

In a few places, notably Hawaii, Baltimore, and Manhattan, there is a high concentration of ground lease ownership; that is, the building owner does not own the land but, as a tenant, leases it from the landowner. An appraiser can estimate land value by *capitalization*, that is, by dividing the annual rent by an appropriate capitalization rate. As a simple example, suppose that the rent on a lot in Baltimore is $120 per year, renewable forever. The appropriate rate of return on investment is 6 percent. Then the land value is $120 ÷ 0.06 = $2,000.

SUBDIVISION ANALYSIS

Subdivision analysis is a method of estimating the maximum that a subdivider can pay for a tract of land. This method involves a sales estimate (usually monthly or quarterly) and a cost estimate over time. Cash flows are then discounted to a present value.

The example shown in Table 15-8 was prepared on an annual basis. As can be seen from the table, $137,285 is the maximum that can be paid for land, and still allow the subdivision to be developed, under the assumptions shown.

Table 15-8
SUBDIVISION DEVELOPMENT ANALYSIS

	Year 1	Year 2	Year 3	Year 4
Lost sales units	-0-	10	15	20
Price per lot		$ 20,000	$ 22,000	$ 25,000
Total sales	-0-	200,000	330,000	500,000
Costs:				
Engineering	$ 40,000			
Utility installation	70,000	100,000		
Clearing and grading	50,000			
Advertising	25,000	25,000	25,000	25,000
Streets and sidewalks	50,000	50,000	60,000	-0-
Permits	10,000			
Contractor's overhead and profit	10,000	10,000	10,000	10,000
Legal and accounting	15,000			
Interest	20,000	15,000	15,000	15,000
Entrepreneurial profit			50,000	50,000
Total costs	$290,000	$200,000	$160,000	$100,000
Cash flow (total sales less Total costs)	(290,000)	-0-	170,000	$400,000
Discount rate @ 10%	× .90909	× .8264	× .7513	× .683
Present value	(263,636)	-0-	$127,721	$273,200
Sum of present value		$137,285		

Income Approach

A certified general appraiser is expected to know how to appraise income-producing property on the basis of the revenue it is expected to generate. A number of techniques used for this purpose are described below.

ESTIMATION OF INCOME AND EXPENSES

Income property valuation begins with an estimate of income and expenses, which was described, to a limited extent, under the sales comparison approach. The levels of income generated by a given property range from a top level, potential gross income, to a bottom level, owner's cash flow. Table 15-9 on the next page is a chart of income levels.

In addition to income, operating expenses must be considered, and an operating statement derived.

POTENTIAL GROSS INCOME

Potential gross income is the rent collectible if all units are fully occupied.

Types of Rent

In estimating potential gross income, the appraiser distinguishes between *market rent* (economic rent) and *contract rent*. Market rent is the rate prevailing in the market for comparable properties and is used in calculating market value by the income approach. Contract rent is the actual amount agreed to by landlord and tenant. If the leases are long-term, contract rent is important in calculating investment value.

Table 15-9
LEVELS OF REAL ESTATE INCOME

	Potential gross income
Less:	Vacancy and collection allowance
Plus:	Miscellaneous income
Equals:	**Effective gross income**
Less:	Allowable expenses
	Maintenance and operating
	Administrative
	Utilities
	Real estate taxes
	Replacement reserves
	Etc.
Equals:	**Net operating income**
Less:	Debt service
	Mortgage principal
	Mortgage interest
Equals:	**Before-tax cash flow**
	(Cash throw-off or equity dividend)

Market rents represent what a given property should be renting for, based on analysis of recently negotiated contract rents for comparable space—but only those that are considered bona fide "market" rents. The market rent should be the amount that would result from a lease negotiated between a willing lessor and a willing lessee, both free from influence from outside sources.

Rental Units of Comparison

Rents must be compared in terms of a common denominator. Typical units of comparison are square foot, room, apartment, space, and percentage of gross business income of the tenant, as shown in Table 15-10.

Table 15-10
RENTAL UNITS OF COMPARISON
FOR TYPES OF INCOME-PRODUCING PROPERTY

Rental Unit of Comparison	Type of Income-Producing Property
Square foot	Shopping centers, retail stores, office buildings, warehouses, apartments, leased land
Room	Motels, hotels, apartment buildings
Apartment	Apartment buildings
Space	Mobile home parks, travel trailer parks, parking garages
Percentages of gross business income	Retail stores, shopping centers, restaurants, gas stations

When the square foot unit is used for an office building or shopping center, the appraiser should note that some leases are based on *net leasable area (NLA)* and others on *gross leasable area (GLA)*. NLA is the floor area occupied by the tenant. GLA includes NLA plus common areas such as halls, restrooms, and vestibules. An office building with 100,000 square feet of GLA may have only 80,000 square feet of NLA, a difference of 20 percent. When leases are compared, it must be known whether rent is based on GLA or NLA.

EFFECTIVE GROSS INCOME

Effective gross income is the amount remaining after the vacancy rate and collection (bad debt) allowances are subtracted from potential gross income and miscellaneous income is added. Calculating effective gross income is an intermediate step in deriving the cash flow.

Vacancy and Collection Allowance

The losses expected from vacancies and bad debts must be subtracted from potential gross income. These losses are calculated at the rate expected of local ownership and management.

Miscellaneous Income

Miscellaneous income is received from concessions, laundry rooms, parking space or storage bin rentals, and other associated services integral to operating the project.

OPERATING EXPENSES

The potential list of operating expenses for gross leased real estate includes:
- Property taxes: city, county, school district, special assessments
- Insurance: hazard, liability
- Utilities: telephone, water, sewer or sewage disposal, electricity, gas
- Administrative costs: management fees, clerical staff, maintenance staff, payroll taxes, legal and accounting expenses
- Repairs and maintenance: paint, decoration, carpet replacement, appliance repairs and replacement, supplies, gardening/landscaping, paving, roofing
- Advertising and promotion: media, business organizations

Fixed Versus Variable Expenses

Operating expenses may be divided into two categories. *Fixed expenses* do not change as the rate of occupancy changes. *Variable expenses,* on the other hand, are directly related to the occupancy rate: as more people occupy and use a building, variable expenses increase.

Fixed expenses include property taxes, license and permit fees, and property insurance. Variable expenses generally include utilities (such as heat, water, sewer), management fees, payroll and payroll taxes, security, landscaping, advertising, and supplies and fees for various services provided by local government or private contractors. There may be a fixed component in expenses normally classified as variable—for example, a basic fixed payroll cost regardless of the occupancy rate.

Replacement Reserve

Provision must be made for the replacement of short-lived items (e.g., carpeting, appliances, and some mechanical equipment) that wear out. Such expenditures usually occur in large lump sums; a portion of the expected cost can be set aside every year to stabilize the expenses. A replacement reserve is necessary because the wearing out of short-lived assets causes a hidden loss of income. If this economic fact is not reflected in financial statements, the net operating income will be overstated. An appraiser should provide for a replacement reserve even though most owners do not set aside money for this purpose.

NET OPERATING INCOME

Net operating income (NOI) is estimated by subtracting operating expenses and the replacement reserve from effective gross income. Any interest or principal payments are not considered in computing NOI.

NOI for each comparable sale should be estimated in the same way that the subject property's NOI is considered. All relevant income and operating expenses are included in consistent amounts or rates to uniformly apply a capitalization rate. Each dollar of error in stating NOI will be multiplied, perhaps by 10 or more, in the resulting value estimate.

OPERATING STATEMENT RATIOS

Operating statement ratios are informative comparisons of expenses to income. The *operating expense ratio* is the percentage relationship of operating expenses to potential or effective gross income. There are typical ratios for each type of property in a market area, and much higher or lower ratios may be a clue to the effectiveness of management policies, efficient or inefficient.

The *net income ratio* is the reciprocal of the operating expense ratio. It tells what the fraction of property net operating income is compared to potential gross income. The *break-even ratio* is the occupancy rate needed to have zero cash flow. It is the sum of operating expenses plus debt service, divided by potential gross income.

INCOME CAPITALIZATION

Income capitalization is a process whereby a stream of future income receipts is translated into a single present-value sum. It considers:
1. Amount of future income (cash flow).
2. Time when the income (cash flow) is to be received.
3. Duration of the income (cash flow) stream.

A *capitalization rate* is used to convert an income stream into a lump-sum value. The formula used is as follows:

$$V = \frac{I}{R}$$

where V = present value; I = periodic income; R = capitalization rate.

Direct Capitalization

Direct capitalization involves simple arithmetic division of two components to result in a capitalized value, as shown below:

$$Property\ Value = \frac{Net\ Operating\ Income}{Overall\ Rate\ of\ Return}$$

The appraiser considers other properties that have been sold and the net operating income generated by each to derive an *overall rate of return (OAR)*. A market-derived OAR is then divided into the subject's NOI to estimate the latter's value.

Overall Capitalization Rate

To derive an overall capitalization rate from market data, the appraiser must select similar properties that have sold recently and are characterized by income streams of risk and duration similar to those of the subject property. If sufficient comparables are available, an OAR can be derived directly from the market and the appraiser can use direct capitalization to convert forecast NOI into a market value estimate.

To illustrate, suppose an appraiser has found the following data:

Comparable	NOI	Sales Price	Indicated OAR
#1	$240,000	$2,000,000	0.120
#2	176,000	1,600,000	0.110
#3	210,000	2,000,000	0.105

If adequate data of this nature were consistently available, appropriate overall rates could be developed for all types of properties, and other methods of capitalization would be of little importance. Unfortunately, reliable, verified sales data are not plentiful, and caution should be exercised in using this capitalization method. The comparability of the sale properties to the subject property must be analyzed carefully. Appropriate application requires that the comparables considered be consistent in these respects:

- Income and expense ratios
- NOI calculations
- Improvement ratio
- Remaining economic life
- Date and terms of sale

The simplicity of direct capitalization makes it attractive, even though complex relationships of income, expenses, and rates of return may underlie the computation. Various ways to derive rates are described in this chapter.

The *overall capitalization rate* must include a return on and a return of investment. Return *on* investment is the compensation necessary to pay an investor for the time value of the money, risk, and other factors associated with a particular investment. It is the interest paid for the use of money, also referred to as *yield*. Return *of* investment deals with repayment of the original principal, referred to as *capital recovery*. The capitalization rate taken from the market presumably incorporates other factors, such as expected inflation, income tax effect on the property, and interest rates and loan terms. However, this is a presumption, without actual numbers being tested to validate the expectation.

The yield rate is a rate of return on investment. Since real estate tends to wear out over time, though its economic useful life may be 50 years or longer, an investor must receive a recovery *of* the investment in addition to a return on it. There are three ways to provide a return of investment:

1. Straight line
2. Annuity
3. Sinking fund at safe rate

Straight Line. The straight-line technique is useful when building income is forecast to decline. Under a straight-line method, an annual depreciation rate is computed as an equal percentage for each year of the asset's life. When the life is 50 years, the rate is 2 percent per year, totaling 100 percent over 50 years. Thus, 2 percent would be added to the 10 percent return on investment to provide a 12 percent capitalization rate. That rate is divided into the estimated building income to derive an estimate of building value.

Annuity. An annuity method is useful when the income is projected to be level annually for a finite life. The appraiser determines the capital recovery rate at the sinking fund factor at the investment's rate of return. At 10 percent return on investment for 50 years, this factor is 0.000859, offering a total capitalization rate of 0.100859 (0.10 + 0.000859).

Sinking Fund at Safe Rate. The sinking fund factor at a safe rate is used when reinvestment assumptions are conservative. The 5 percent sinking fund factor for 50 years is 0.004777. This provides a capitalization rate of 0.104777 (0.10 + 0.004777) when given a 10 percent rate of return on investment.

BAND OF INVESTMENT

Net operating income from real estate is typically divided between mortgage lenders and equity investors. Rates of return can be weighted by the portions of purchase capital contributed, to result in a rate of return applicable to the entire property. This method is called the *band of investment*. The yield or interest or discount rate is then used to capitalize all of the NOI into one lump-sum property value. This value would assume that a capital recovery provision is unnecessary since neither amortization nor recovery of equity invested is considered.

For example, suppose that lenders typically contribute 75 percent of the required purchase capital and seek a 10 percent rate of return on investment. Equity investors want a 12 percent rate of return on investment. The rate for the entire property would be 10.5 percent, as shown in Table 15-11 on the next page. This rate consists purely of interest and assumes no principal

Table 15-11
RATES OF RETURN FOR A MORTGAGED PROPERTY

Source of Funds	Portion of Purchase Capital		Rate of Return on Investment		Weighted Rate
Mortgage	0.75	×	0.10	=	0.075
Equity	0.25	×	0.12	=	0.030
Yield or discount rate for entire property					0.105

retirement of the loan and no capital appreciation or depreciation of the equity investment. Further, all of the NOI is paid each year to each investor, mortgage and equity. Repayment of all purchase capital will be made upon a resale of the property at an indefinite time in the future.

GROSS INCOME MULTIPLIERS

In the case of multipliers, gross rent (income) estimates are frequently used by investors. The estimated annual gross income is multiplied by a factor that has been derived as an accurate representation of market behavior for that type of property. A monthly gross income multiplier is typically used for residential housing, whereas annual multipliers are used for other types of property.

Ease of computation makes a rent multiplier a deceptively attractive technique. For appropriate application, however, everything about the subject being appraised and the comparables used must be alike, including the lease terms, tenant strength, operating expenses, and physical setting. The rent multiplier is, at best, a crude measuring device.

RESIDUAL TECHNIQUES

Residual techniques can be applied to income-producing property. The term *residual* implies that, after income requirements are satisfied for the known parts of the property, the residual, or remaining, income is processed into an indication of value for the unknown part. The three most commonly used types are (1) land, (2) building, and (3) equity residual techniques.

Land Residual Technique

The land residual technique is useful when improvements are relatively new or have not yet been built. Their values (or proposed costs) can be closely approximated, as can their estimated useful lives. For example, suppose recently constructed real estate improvements cost $1 million and have a 50-year economic useful life. The appropriate rate of return on investment is 10 percent because that rate is competitive with other investment opportunities perceived to have equal risk. Straight-line capital recovery is considered appropriate for the improvements. The annual recovery rate is 2 percent (100 percent ÷ 50 years = 2 percent per year), so the total required rate of return for the improvements is 12 percent. Annual net operating income for the first year is estimated to be $150,000. The improvements require a 12 percent return on $1 million of cost, which equals $120,000 of income. Subtracting this amount from the $150,000 net operating income leaves a $30,000 residual for the land. This amount, capitalized in perpetuity at 10 percent, offers a land value of $300,000. Capitalization of land income in perpetuity is appropriate because land is thought to last forever. This technique is summarized in Table 15-12.

The land residual technique is used also in estimating the highest and best use of land. Costs of different proposed improvements can be estimated, as can the net operating income for each type of improvement. A capitalization rate is multiplied by the estimated improvement cost, and the result subtracted from forecast net operating income. The result is forecast land income. Whichever type or level of improvement offers the highest residual

Table 15-12
LAND RESIDUAL TECHNIQUE—STRAIGHT-LINE
CAPITAL RECOVERY FOR BUILDINGS

Net operating income (first year)	$150,000
Less: Income attributable to improvements:	
10% (on) + 2% (of) = 12%; 0.12 × $1,000,000	120,000
Residual income to land	$30,000
Capitalized at 10% return on investment in perpetuity	$300,000

The total property value is then estimated at $1.3 million
($1 million for improvements plus $300,000 for land).

income to land is the highest and best use of the land, subject to legal and physical constraints.

Building Residual Technique

The building residual technique works in reverse of the land residual technique. When the land value can be estimated with a high degree of confidence (as when there are many recent sales of comparables), income attributable to the land is subtracted from net operating income. The residual income is attributable to the improvements and can be capitalized to estimate their value. Then the capitalized value of the improvements is added to the land value to obtain a total property value estimate.

As an example of the building residual technique, suppose that the land value is estimated at $200,000 through a careful analysis of several recent sales of comparable vacant tracts of land. A 10% discount rate is considered appropriate. Of the estimated $150,000 of annual NOI, $20,000 is attributable to the land. Capital recovery for land income is unnecessary since the land will last forever. The $130,000 balance of NOI is attributable to the improvements, which would be worth $1,083,333 using a straight-line capital recovery rate and 50-year life. The building residual technique is summarized in Table 15-13.

Table 15-13
BUILDING RESIDUAL TECHNIQUE

Net operating income	$150,000
Less: Income to land: 10% of $200,000	20,000
Income to improvements	$130,000
Improvement value at straight-line capital recovery: (over 50 years) $130,000 ÷ 0.12	$1,083,333

Equity Residual Technique

The equity residual technique is an effort to estimate the value of the property when the mortgage amount and terms are known. Net operating income is calculated as in other techniques, and debt service is subtracted to result in cash flow. The cash flow is capitalized at an appropriate equity dividend rate to obtain equity value, which is added to the mortgage principal to provide a value estimate.

OWNER'S CASH FLOW FROM OPERATIONS

In this technique, net operating income is forecast for a number of years to some period in the future when a property sale is expected to occur. The cash flows from operations and resale are discounted by an appropriate discount rate, then totaled to offer a property value estimate.

ADJUSTMENTS TO CAPITALIZATION RATES

Depending on lease and market information, net operating income may be forecast to be level, to grow, or to decline. An appraiser must use known information and provide market evidence for the projections.

Financial results from real estate depend on lease terms and economic conditions. If the tenant's credit is triple A and the lease is long term at a fixed net rental rate, income should be assured. If the tenant's credit rating is not high, or the lease is not net or its term is short, value will depend on such factors as inflation, competition, interest rates, and economic conditions.

Current values may be strongly affected by expectations of future resale prices. An appraiser must therefore consider resale expectations when selecting a capitalization rate. This "cap rate" is raised when value decline is expected in the future, lowered when appreciation is anticipated.

ESTIMATING RESALE PRICE

Reversion

It is sometimes helpful to estimate a resale price based on expectations for the future. The resale price, less selling costs and outstanding debts, has a present value that, added to the present value of net operating income for each year, may be used to estimate today's value. The estimated resale price is diminished by selling expenses, including commissions and legal expenses, to result in proceeds from sale. Table 15-14 shows how a $1,000,000 resale price is diminished by transaction costs.

Table 15-14
RESALE PRICE DIMINISHED BY TRANSACTION COSTS

Resale price		**$1,000,000**
Less seller's estimated expenses of sale:		
Title insurance policy	$ 3,000	
Attorney's fees	4,500	
Release of lien	200	
Survey of property	600	
Escrow fees	500	
Recording fees	200	
Broker's professional service fee (commission)	40,000	
Subtotal		49,000
Estimated receipts to seller		**$ 951,000**

Other Methods of Resale Price Estimation

The resale price can be estimated in several other ways. First, today's market value with a percentage annual growth or depreciation rate is applied. This method assumes that future values are related to today's value, often adjusted by expected inflation. Second, income forecast for the year after the sale is capitalized to obtain a resale price. Third, the sales price of encumbered property may be the cash flow after debt service, capitalized at an equity dividend rate, and added to the mortgage balance.

MEASURING RATE OF CASH FLOW

Cash flow is usually defined as the amount left after debt service. The rate of cash flow can be derived in two ways: dividend and yield.

EQUITY DIVIDEND RATE

The *equity dividend rate* (also called *cash-on-cash return*) is cash flow divided by the equity paid for the property. The result is a measure of cash return on investment. When cash flow can be measured accurately, it may be divided by a market-derived equity dividend rate to obtain the equity value. Equity value, plus mortgage balance, offers a property value estimate.

DEBT COVERAGE RATIO

The *debt coverage ratio* indicates a lender's margin of safety. It is computed by dividing net operating income by debt service. Lenders typically want a ratio ranging from at least 1.1 for the safest property, secured by a net lease from a tenant with triple A credit, up to 1.2 to 1.5 for apartments or office buildings and a minimum of 2.0 for recreational property.

DISCOUNTED CASH FLOW (YIELD) CAPITALIZATION

By contrast to first-year capitalization techniques, yield capitalization rates employ compound interest/present value factors. These rates are typically found in six-function compound interest tables, described on page 206, which offer a precise value for periodic cash flow and reversion based on a specific rate of return on investment.

DISCOUNTED CASH FLOW APPLICATION

Discounted cash flow capitalization is best applied when income from the property and a resale price can be forecast with reasonable certainty. This requires income forecasts of rents, operating expenses, and tenant improvements, as previously discussed.

The key to discounted cash flow is the *discounting process*, which is based on the fact that money to be received at some time in the future is worth *less* than money received today. The value that we assign to such *future incomes* is called *present value*, or *present discounted value*. Exactly what the present value of a future income is will depend on the answers to two questions: (1) when will the income accrue and (2) what is the *discount rate*? The discount rate is a rate of return, similar to an interest rate, that measures the risk and time value of the income to be received. How a discount rate is arrived at is discussed below, but there are a couple of basic rules that are useful: (1) the longer we have to wait for a future income, the less it is worth to us *today* (i.e., the lower is its present value), and (2) the higher the discount rate applied to a future income, the lower its present value (and vice-versa).

Appraisers value an income property by examining the net income that the property can be expected to provide in the future, and then finding a present value for that income. This can be done fairly easily using six-function tables or a financial calculator. However, most states don't allow applicants for licenses to use financial calculators (not yet, anyway), so we will take a brief look at the math involved.

Essentially, we derive a present value for each part of the future income stream, and then add all the values. For example, suppose we are appraising a property that will produce a net income of $10,000 per year for 5 years; at the end of 5 years it can be sold for $50,000. (This one-time income at the end of the holding period, either sale price or salvage value, is called a *reversion* by real estate appraisers.) Let's assume that we're using a discount rate of 12 percent. This means that we need a return of 12 percent a year (compounded) for this investment. To simplify, let's assume also that the incomes accrue at the *end* of each year. Then our income stream will be $10,000 a year for 4 years, with a fifth-year income of $10,000 *plus* the sale proceeds of $50,000, for a total fifth-year income of $60,000. Our income stream looks like the column below headed "Income."

Time	Income	Factor		Present Value
Year 1	$10,000	$1/1.12$	$= 0.892857$	$ 8,928.57
Year 2	$10,000	$1/(1.12)^2$	$= 0.797194$	7,971.94
Year 3	$10,000	$1/(1.12)^3$	$= 0.711780$	7,117.80
Year 4	$10,000	$1/(1.12)^4$	$= 0.635518$	6,355.18
Year 5	$60,000	$1/(1.12)^5$	$= 0.567427$	34,045.61
	Present value total			**$64,419.10**

We arrived at a present value of about $64,400. What we're saying, with this number, is that a future income of $10,000 a year for 5 years, plus a reversion of $50,000 at the end of 5 years, when discounted at 12 percent a year, is worth about $64,400 *today*. In other words, $64,400 invested today, at 12 percent annual return, will yield the income we project for the property.

How exactly did we do this? Let's look at the first year's income of $10,000. We don't get it for a year, but we have to pay for it *now*. Basically, we ask, "How much money, invested today, will grow to $10,000 in 1 year, given a 12 percent annual return?" This first year's income, then, will have a present value of $10,000/1.12 because we are looking for an amount that, once it has earned a 12 percent return, will *become* $10,000. What we did in the table was to figure out the *factor* for 12 percent for 1 year, which is the decimal equivalent of 1/1.12, and then multiply it by $10,000. The advantage of this method is that, once we figure out what 1/1.12 is, we can use that number to get the present value of *any* amount to be received 1 year from now at a rate of 12 percent.

For the 12 percent *factors* for periods beyond 1 year, we just divide by 1.12 *again* for *each* year longer that we have to wait for the income. For the present value of the second year's income, we multiply $10,000 by 1/1.12 *twice* (once for each year): $10,000 \times 1/1.12 \times 1/1.12$, which is the same as $10,000 \times 1/(1.12)^2$. For the third year we use $1/(1.12)^3$, and so on. Once we've figured out the present value of each of the five annual incomes, we just add them. You can check these numbers out yourself. For each year's income, start with the present value. Multiply it by 1.12; do this for each year that you have to wait, and you should end up with $10,000 for each of the first 4 years, and $60,000 for the fifth year.

Yield Rate Selection

An appraiser can attempt to construct a yield rate using the *buildup method,* by identifying the components of a required rate of return. Although there is general agreement in identifying the components (see below), the proportion of each component in the overall rate is arbitrary. Furthermore, the buildup is unnecessary because an investor acquires the entire property, which provides one rate. Although the buildup method is theoretical, it helps us to understand capitalization rates and to compare them with non-real estate investments.

To construct a built-up rate, begin with a liquid, risk-free rate, such as the rate on passbook accounts offered by financial institutions whose depositors' accounts are insured by a U.S. government agency. The rate is the minimum that must be paid as compensation for the time value of money.

Add to this risk-free rate a provision for the risk associated with the specific type of real estate being appraised. For example, risk is low where there is a strong tenant with captive customers, but high for property leased to weak tenants who have fickle customers.

Provisions must be made for illiquidity. *Liquidity* is a measure of how quickly an asset can be converted into cash. Compared to stocks and bonds, real estate is illiquid, particularly in a weak market or tight-money economy.

The burden of investment management must also be included. This is the decision making required of the investor and is distinguished from the everyday process of property management.

The components of the build-up method and their proportions in the overall built-up rate are summarized as follows:

Risk-free rate	5%
Risk of subject property	3%
Illiquidity of subject property	2%
Investment management	1%
Rate of return on investment	11%

Selecting the appropriate yield rate depends on numerous factors, especially the availability of accurate market data. An appraiser must consider the duration, quality, and amount of income from the property forecast for each future year. Other relevant factors include the earnings or yield rate required by the market and the portion of investment that is subject to capital recovery.

Ratio capitalization requires a realistic estimate of net operating income, which is divided by a supportable capitalization rate. The mathematical composition of the cap rate is derived from the market, tempered by property performance expectations.

Valuation of Partial Interests

The certified general appraiser is expected to have an extensive knowledge of partial interests in real estate. These include interests in a lease, lease provisions, and the identification of the various ownership positions within a property having different risk features.

LEASE INTERESTS

A *subleasehold* may be carved out of a lease interest. A subleasehold is the interest of the tenant's tenant; that is, a tenant may sublease his property, becoming a landlord to another tenant. The subtenant's interest may be valuable.

Renewal options in a lease give the tenant the right, but not the obligation, to extend the lease at whatever rent and terms are described in the option. This encumbrance can affect the value of the property either positively or negatively.

Tenant improvements must be analyzed to determine how they affect the property value. Are they to remain after the lease expires? Would a substitute tenant find them useful and pay a premium for them, or would they be expensive to demolish on demand?

Concessions granted in the market or by the property to attract tenants must be assessed. For example, suppose an office building rents for $25 per square foot on a 5-year lease, with the first year free. The property is appraised in the second year of the lease. Is the correct rent $25/per square foot or much less? How much rent can be capitalized? The appraiser needs to understand the market.

LEASE PROVISIONS

Net Versus Gross Leases

A lease is typically referred to as *net* or *gross*, although most leases are neither absolutely net nor absolutely gross. In an absolute net lease the tenant (lessee) pays taxes, insurance, and operating expenses: maintenance, including repairs, alterations, replacements, and improvements, ordinary or extraordinary repairs whether interior or exterior, and so on. A net lease is the most straightforward approach for a single-tenant structure. The terms *triple-net* and *net-net-net* lease are often used to indicate a greater degree of net-ness than that for other leases. As to specific taxes, tenants pay taxes, special assessments, and the like; however, tenants do not pay obligations of the landlord (lessor), such as gift, income, inheritance, franchise, or corporate taxes, or a tax on the rental receipts of the landlord.

The real estate owner is a passive investor when a net lease is used, relying on net rent to provide a return on investment. The property is the owner's investment, not a business.

With a gross lease the landlord pays all operating expenses. The owner must become a businessperson, keeping firm control over operating expenses and assuring that money spent to comply with the lease is spent prudently.

With a *stop* (or *escalation*) clause in a gross lease, the landlord pays a base-year amount for the expense and the tenant pays the increase in expense each year. A net lease or stop clauses reduce the need for frequent rent adjustments, cost of living indexes, or short-term leases.

Operating Expenses

A properly written lease should specify whether landlord or tenant pays for each operating expense. It should also specify that the responsible party must present proof of payment, such as a paid property tax bill or insurance policy in conformity with requirements of the lease, to provide assurance of protection from risks covered by the lease. If the lessee in a net lease does not supply the information, the lessor should request it.

PERCENTAGE LEASES

A *percentage lease,* commonly used for a retail tenant, provides incentive to the landlord to make the property attractive and thus encourage retail sales. The landlord must be prepared to audit the tenant's retail sales records and to enforce provisions of the lease that protect the lessor's rights to a percentage of sales.

Most percentage leases require a fixed *minimum base rent* plus a percentage rent based on gross sales in excess of a certain amount. The base rent is often set as an anticipated average amount of sales per square foot for the particular type of business. For example, suppose industry norms for a ladies' fashion shop indicate that sales of $200 per square foot (SF) are typical. Rent for a 10,000-SF shop could be $100,000 per year plus 5 percent of sales above $2 million (10,000 SF × $200 typical sales = $2,000,000). Percentage rents would be imposed only when sales exceed the norm of $200/SF of floor area.

Different types of businesses have different typical percentage rents. For example, a jewelry store or other retailer selling luxury items tends to be relatively small, and has a high markup and low inventory turnover in comparison to a grocery or discount store. The percentage rental rate thus tends to be higher for the luxury or specialty store.

Certain lease provisions are necessary to assure fairness to both parties in administering a percentage lease. Monthly or annual sales reports may be required; and the landlord may have the right to hire an auditor, whose fee will be paid by the tenant if sales are understated or by the landlord if no discrepancies are found.

COST OF LIVING INDEX

Leases for multiple years without rent adjustments result in hardships to landlord or tenant during highly inflationary or deflationary periods. A long-term lease may have a *cost of living adjustment* that calls for changes in rent based on the change in some published index.

The index used and the frequency and amount of adjustment are negotiable. The Consumer Price Index (CPI), published by the Bureau of Labor Statistics of the U. S. Department of Labor, is usually chosen because of its frequency of computation and publication. A lesser known local index tied to rental rates, operating expenses, or real estate values may be satisfactory but can introduce elements of instability or potential manipulation, possibly resulting in litigation.

The adjustment period may be a single year or a multiple of years. This period should be short for a gross lease but may be longer for a net lease. With a net lease the landlord has less financial exposure to the risk of inflation because the tenant pays operating expenses.

The degree of adjustment may be only part of the full change in the index selected. For example, if 50 percent of the index was selected as the multiplier and the index rose by 20 percent, rent would increase by 10 percent. This provides some protection to the landlord (who perhaps bought the property with preinflation dollars) but does not inflict the full effect of inflation on the tenant.

EXCESS RENT

Excess rent is the difference between contract and market rents; the term implies that the tenant is paying more than would be paid for comparable property. If a property has several leases, the appraiser should prepare a schedule with the expiration date of each lease to assist in estimating the quality and duration of the income stream.

VALUATION CONSIDERATIONS

A property may have been fractionated, that is, split into different interests. For example, there may be two mortgages and/or a land lease. The appraiser needs to determine the volatility of income, the priorities of cash distributions, and the risks and rewards for each interest. In doing so, the value to each party having a fractional interest can be estimated by the appraiser.

Summary

The certified general appraiser is expected to have knowledge of income property valuation techniques and an understanding of their applications to specialized properties and interests that are beyond the expectations for a residential appraiser, broker, or salesperson.

Questions on Chapter 15

1. The fact that rents tend to be set by the market for equally desirable space reflects the principle of
   (A) balance
   (B) substitution
   (C) externalities
   (D) supply and demand
   (E) conformity

2. The net income that remains after the proper costs of labor, capital, and entrepreneurship have been paid is
   (A) surplus rent
   (B) opportunity cost
   (C) effective income
   (D) land rent
   (E) contract rent

3. All of the following are essential to the viability of an industrial district *except*
   (A) labor
   (B) materials
   (C) transportation
   (D) high technology
   (E) entrepreneurship

4. The present and future demand for a property and its absorption rate are considered in a
   (A) valuation report
   (B) market feasibility study
   (C) market segmentation study
   (D) highest and best use analysis
   (E) narrative appraisal

5. Real estate markets
   (A) are national in scope
   (B) do not meet the criteria for a perfect market
   (C) are centralized in nature
   (D) consist of used property only
   (E) are prevalent in former Communist countries

6. The federal discount rate, which is the interest rate that banks pay on the funds they borrow from the Federal Reserve, is most closely linked to
   (A) the inflation rate
   (B) the prime rate
   (C) long-term yield rates
   (D) interest rates on 30-year bonds
   (E) municipal bond rates

7. Credit-regulating devices used by the Federal Reserve include
   (A) moral suasion
   (B) reserve requirements
   (C) the federal discount rate
   (D) the Federal Open Market Committee
   (E) all of the above

8. Monetary policy helps control inflation by
   (A) regulating the money supply
   (B) encouraging rent control
   (C) reducing taxes
   (D) refusing to balance the budget
   (E) using a noncalendar year

9. The secondary mortgage market is where
   (A) mortgage bankers originate mortgage loans
   (B) second mortgages are originated
   (C) existing mortgages are bought and sold
   (D) the FNMA and GNMA make mortgage loans
   (E) the RTC searches for buyers of savings and loan associations

10. When inflation is expected to be high, investors tend to avoid
    (A) equity investments
    (B) long-term fixed-income investments
    (C) short-term investments
    (D) money market instruments
    (E) tangibles

11. Mortgage financing affects
    (A) equity dividends from real estate
    (B) equity yields from real estate
    (C) monetary policy
    (D) fiscal policy
    (E) both A and B

Questions 12–14 are based on the following information:
   A $1,500,000 loan is issued with 5 discount points. The loan bears a 12% interest rate and has a 12.5% mortgage constant, with annual payments.

12. The original annual payment was
    (A) less than $180,000
    (B) $180,000
    (C) $187,500
    (D) more than $190,000
    (E) none of the above

13. The annual mortgage constant is
    (A) 12%
    (B) 12.25%
    (C) 12.5%
    (D) 12.75%
    (E) above 12.75%

14. What is the amount of the loan discount?
    (A) less than $75,000
    (B) $75,000
    (C) $100,000
    (D) $150,000
    (E) More than $150,000

15. Which of the following is a valuation study?
    (A) Market value appraisal
    (B) Market and marketability study
    (C) Absorption analysis
    (D) Feasibility study
    (E) Technical impact study

16. Generally, the *least* reliable sources of sales data are
    (A) bankers
    (B) appraisers
    (C) newspaper articles
    (D) brokers
    (E) sellers

17. Operating income data do *not* include
    (A) vacancy rate
    (B) reproduction cost
    (C) operating expenses
    (D) utilities provided by the owner
    (E) lease terms

18. Industrial buildings are typically measured in terms of
    (A) gross living area
    (B) gross building area
    (C) net leasable area
    (D) gross rentable area
    (E) interior area

19. The appropriate time adjustment for a property is concluded to be an increase of 7% per year compounded. The time adjustment for a comparable sales property that sold for $40,000 two years ago is
    (A) −$5,796
    (B) −$5,600
    (C) −$2,800
    (D) +$5,600
    (E) +$5,796

20. How much must be deposited today, in a bank that pays 10% rate of interest with annual compounding, in order to realize $10,000 in 4 years?
    (A) $40,000
    (B) $9,077
    (C) $6,830
    (D) $4,000
    (E) $2,500

21. Ms. Brown has just paid $5 for a purchase option on some land. The option gives her the right to buy the property for $10,000 at the end of 2 years. The $5 paid for the option will not be applied to the purchase price. How much must Ms. Brown put aside today, in a bank that pays a 10% rate of interest with monthly compounding, to achieve a balance of $10,000 in 2 years?
    (A) $12,100
    (B) $10,000
    (C) $8,194
    (D) $6,720
    (E) $5,000

22. A sample of 100 residences had an average square footage of 1500 with a standard deviation of 120 and normal distribution. This means that
    (A) about 2 out of 3 have between 1380 and 1620 sq. ft.
    (B) about 9 out of 10 have between 1380 and 1620 sq. ft.
    (C) almost every home has between 1140 and 1560 sq. ft.
    (D) almost every home has between 1380 and 1620 sq. ft.
    (E) none of the 100 homes has any standard construction defect

23. In problem 22, two standard deviations would be
    (A) 50 homes
    (B) 1500 sq. ft.
    (C) 240 sq. ft.
    (D) 67% of all homes
    (E) none of the above

Questions 24–28 are based on the following information:
   Eleven recent sales of rental income property provided the following data:

Sale Number	Sales Price	Gross Monthly Rent
1	$162,000	$1,500
2	184,000	1,600
3	152,000	1,440
4	160,000	1,470
5	183,000	1,580
6	134,000	1,400
7	144,000	1,350
8	176,000	1,560
9	132,000	1,350
10	183,800	1,650
11	153,000	1,380

24. The range of gross rent multipliers is
    (A) $1,350 to $1,650
    (B) $132,000 to $184,000
    (C) $95.7 to $115.8
    (D) $150
    (E) none of the above

25. The mean monthly rental is
    (A) $1,350
    (B) $1,400
    (C) $1,470
    (D) $1,480
    (E) none of the above

26. The median monthly rental is
    (A) $1,350
    (B) $1,400
    (C) $1,470
    (D) $1,480
    (E) none of the above

27. The mode of the monthly rentals is
    (A) $1,350
    (B) $1,400
    (C) $1,470
    (D) $1,480
    (E) none of the above

28. The best estimate of the gross rent multiplier is
    (A) 92
    (B) 100
    (C) 108
    (D) 116
    (E) none of the above

29. In the sequence of adjustments in the sales adjustment process, the item adjusted for first should usually be
    (A) location
    (B) terms of financing
    (C) size
    (D) time
    (E) It makes no difference which is first.

30. The land development method in appraisal is used to estimate the value of vacant acreage that is ready to be subdivided. This method requires
    (A) study of current sales of subdivided lots
    (B) projection of land development costs
    (C) RTC approval
    (D) both A and B
    (E) none of the above

Questions 31–36 are based on the following information:
You are appraising a 20-acre tract of unimproved land. The site is zoned for single-family residential use. All utilities are available along the street on which the land fronts. From the engineers who will plat the proposed subdivision, your learn that 20% of the land area will be used for streets and sidewalks. You find that zoning will permit four lots per acre of net developable land after deducting streets. Research indicates that lots similar to those that will be available on the subject land sell for $18,000 and that the entire tract can be developed and sold in 1 year. You find that 40% of the sale price of each lot must be allocated to selling costs, overhead, contingencies, carrying cost, and developer's profit. Finally, your research discloses that 2000 feet of streets (including water, storm sewer, and sanitary sewer lines) must be installed at a cost of $80 per foot.

31. How many lots can be developed?
    (A) 20
    (B) 64
    (C) 80
    (D) 88
    (E) 16

32. What is the gross sales price from the sale of all lots?
    (A) $288,000
    (B) $360,000
    (C) $1,152,000
    (D) $1,440,000
    (E) $1,584,000

33. What is the cost of installing streets and water and sewer lines?
    (A) $16,000
    (B) $32,000
    (C) $64,000
    (D) $160,000
    (E) None of the above

34. What is the total of selling cost, overhead, contingencies, carrying costs, and developer's profit?
    (A) $144,000
    (B) $460,800
    (C) $576,000
    (D) $633,600
    (E) None of the above

35. What is the total cost of development and overhead, including developer's profit?
    (A) $304,000
    (B) $320,000
    (C) $620,800
    (D) $733,600
    (E) None of the above

36. What is the developer's potential profit on the 20-acre tract?
    (A) less than $160,000
    (B) $160,000
    (C) $531,200
    (D) $1,152,000
    (E) $1,440,000

37. When there is a dearth of recent land sales data, which technique may the appraiser use to estimate land value?
    (A) Land residual
    (B) Property residual
    (C) Building residual
    (D) Mortgage residual
    (E) Property reversion

38. The annual net operating income from an apartment house is $22,000. With a capitalization rate of 11%, the indicated market value is
    (A) $2,420
    (B) $126,000
    (C) $176,000
    (D) $200,000
    (E) $242,000

39. A small office building sold for $1,200,000. The monthly net operating income is $13,000 per month. What was the overall capitalization rate?
    (A) 1.08%
    (B) 9.2%
    (C) 10.8%
    (D) 12%
    (E) 13%

40. For which of the following would the lowest ratio of operating expenses to gross income be incurred by the landlord?
    (A) Resort hotel
    (B) Net-leased retail store
    (C) Office building
    (D) Apartment building
    (E) Nursing home for the elderly

41. The band-of-investment technique is most useful when equity investors are primarily concerned with
    (A) land appreciation rates
    (B) building tax shelters
    (C) gross rent multipliers
    (D) equity capitalization rates
    (E) noise abatement

42. Which of the following is the preferred method of deriving a capitalization rate?
    (A) Summation
    (B) Band of investment
    (C) Direct comparison
    (D) Bank of investment
    (E) Monetary policy

43. Capitalization is employed in the
    (A) cost approach
    (B) direct sales comparison approach
    (C) income approach for income properties
    (D) income approach for residential properties
    (E) none of the above

44. Capitalization is the process whereby
    (A) income is converted to an indication of value
    (B) syndicates are formed
    (C) an asset is removed from accounting records
    (D) both A and B
    (E) none of the above

45. The operating expense ratio for income property is typically
    (A) between 4 and 10
    (B) under 100%
    (C) under 10%
    (D) under 2%
    (E) more than 10

46. In determining income and expenses, the first step is
    (A) a lease and rent analysis
    (B) an effective gross income estimate
    (C) an operating expense estimate
    (D) a reconstructed operating statement
    (E) a market analysis

47. A forecast using discounted cash flow analysis would include
    (A) income, vacancy, and operating expenses
    (B) an economic analysis
    (C) reversion at the end of the holding period
    (D) discounting expected future cash flows to a present value
    (E) all of the above

48. If the overall capitalization rate for income property were to increase while estimated net operating income remained the same, the resulting value estimate would
    (A) increase
    (B) decrease
    (C) remain the same
    (D) any of the above could occur
    (E) none of the above would occur

49. Estimated income property values will decline as a result of
    (A) increased net cash flows
    (B) lower capitalization rates
    (C) lower vacancy rates
    (D) increased discount rates
    (E) higher standard of living

50. *Income capitalization* is the term used to describe the process of estimating the value of income property by studying expected future income. This process
    (A) converts the net operating income of a property into its equivalent capital value
    (B) reflects the time value of money by reducing or discounting future income to its present worth
    (C) focuses on the present worth of future benefits
    (D) uses market interest rates
    (E) all of the above

51. When estimating the value of an income-producing property, the appraiser will *not* consider
    (A) income taxes attributable to the property
    (B) the remaining economic life of the property
    (C) potential future income
    (D) net operating income
    (E) expected future income patterns

52. In income capitalization, value is measured as the present worth of the
    (A) forecast reversion with a growth factor
    (B) forecast cash flow capitalized in perpetuity
    (C) forecast effective gross income (EGI) plus the reversion
    (D) forecast net operating income plus the reversion
    (E) cost of production

53. Income capitalization techniques are typically *not* used in valuing
    (A) retail properties
    (B) apartment buildings
    (C) office buildings
    (D) motels
    (E) single-family residences

54. The lump sum that an investor receives upon resale of an investment is called
    (A) net income
    (B) gross income
    (C) equity dividend
    (D) reversion
    (E) residual

55. The most commonly used capitalization rate is the
    (A) income rate
    (B) composite capitalization rate
    (C) interest rate
    (D) overall rate
    (E) underall rate

56. An ordinary annuity is
    (A) level in amount and timing
    (B) different from a variable annuity
    (C) received at the end of each period
    (D) a stream of income
    (E) all of the above

57. The procedure used to convert expected future benefits into present value is
    (A) residual analysis
    (B) capitalization
    (C) market capitalization
    (D) equity capitalization
    (E) compounding

58. A reconstructed operating statement for an owner-operated property should include
    (A) income tax
    (B) book depreciation
    (C) management charges
    (D) wages earned outside the property
    (E) imputed interest

59. *Yield* is defined as
    (A) overall capitalization
    (B) stopping to review work
    (C) letting another speak first
    (D) rate of return on investment
    (E) rate of return of investment

60. Which of the following is a specific expense item rather than a category?
    (A) Replacement reserve
    (B) Property taxes
    (C) Operating expenses
    (D) Fixed charges or expenses
    (E) Variable expenses

61. In yield capitalization, investor assumptions are
    (A) accrued
    (B) critiqued
    (C) regulated
    (D) questioned
    (E) simulated

62. The basic formula for property valuation via income capitalization is
    (A) $V = IR$
    (B) $V = I/R$
    (C) $V = R/I$
    (D) $V = SP/GR$
    (E) $V = I/F$

63. All of the following consider the time value of money *except*
   (A) net present value
   (B) discounted cash flow
   (C) internal rate of return
   (D) payback period
   (E) compound interest

64. A rent survey of apartment buildings reveals that one-bedroom units have a considerably higher occupancy factor than two-bedroom units. If the subject property contains only two-bedroom units, the appraisal should probably project
   (A) an average of the vacancy factors for all units surveyed
   (B) a higher vacancy factor than was found for one-bedroom units
   (C) a lower vacancy factor than was found for one-bedroom units
   (D) the same vacancy factor as was found for one-bedroom units
   (E) Projection from the information provided is impossible.

65. The quality of a forecast future income stream is indicated by its
   (A) amount
   (B) length
   (C) timing
   (D) mortgage
   (E) risk

66. The total anticipated revenue from income property operations after vacancy and collection losses are deducted is
   (A) net operating income
   (B) before-tax cash flow
   (C) effective gross income
   (D) potential gross income
   (E) property residual income

67. Which of the following is used in direct capitalization?
   (A) Internal rate of return
   (B) Overall capitalization rate
   (C) Building capitalization rate
   (D) Mortgage capitalization rate
   (E) Equity yield rate

68. Which of the following statements is true?
   (A) If the overall yield on the property is less than the mortgage rate, favorable leverage occurs.
   (B) When negative leverage occurs, the owner receives a cash yield on the property that is greater than if the property were not financed.
   (C) If the overall property yield equals the mortgage rate, the owner receives an additional yield on his investment by trading on the equity.
   (D) Financing the property at higher rates of interest than the overall rate may not be beneficial to the owner in terms of yield on the equity investment.
   (E) When a property generates cash flow, its owner pays tax on the money received.

69. Which of the following statements is true?
   (A) An investor usually considers the return from a property in the light of the risk being assumed.
   (B) An investor who assumes higher risk usually expects lower investment yield.
   (C) Higher-risk investments are generally associated with lower investment returns.
   (D) To maximize the overall risk position, the investor may wish to diversify real and/or personal property investments.
   (E) The lowest-risk investment is real estate.

70. *Capitalization rate* is
    (A) the annual rent divided by the purchase price
    (B) annual income and all gains or losses prorated to an effective annual amount—an internal rate of return.
    (C) the percentage or decimal rate that, when divided into a periodic income amount, offers a lump-sum capital value for the income
    (D) unchanging with time
    (E) none of the above

Questions 71–75 are based on the following information:

A $12 million office building is purchased with an 80% loan-to-value ratio mortgage, payable over 30 years at 11% interest with monthly payments of $91,423. At 100% occupancy, rents would be $2 million. The vacancy trend in the area is 2.5%. Operating expenses amount to $650,000, including $50,000 placed in a replacement reserve. The land is considered to be worth $2 million.

71. What ratio, expressed as a percentage, is between 80 and 85?
    (A) Improvement
    (B) Overall rate
    (C) Mortgage constant
    (D) Vacancy
    (E) Operating expense

72. What ratio, expressed as a percentage, is between 10 and 11?
    (A) Improvement
    (B) Overall rate
    (C) Mortgage constant
    (D) Vacancy
    (E) Operating expense

73. What ratio, expressed as a percentage, is between 11 and 12?
    (A) Improvement
    (B) Overall rate
    (C) Mortgage constant
    (D) Vacancy
    (E) Operating expense

74. What ratio, expressed as a percentage, is between 30 and 40?
    (A) Improvement
    (B) Overall rate
    (C) Mortgage constant
    (D) Vacancy
    (E) Operating expense

75. What ratio, expressed as a percentage, is between 0 and 5?
    (A) Improvement
    (B) Overall rate
    (C) Mortgage constant
    (D) Vacancy
    (E) Operating expense

76. Investors for apartments are seeking a 10% cash-on-cash return in the current market. The current interest rate on a 30-year mortgage for this type of property is 12% with monthly payments. Lenders will fund up to a 75% loan-to-value ratio. What is the overall rate of return using the band of investment technique?
    (A) 10–10.5%
    (B) 10.51–11%
    (C) 11.01–11.25%
    (D) 11.26–12%
    (E) None of the above

Questions 77–81 are based on the following information:
    A certain older office building in the heart of a downtown metropolitan area currently generates $40,000 net operating income. Income is expected to decline systematically over the estimated 10 remaining years of the building's useful life. Therefore, straight-line capital recovery (declining income to the building) is considered appropriate. The land is currently valued at $250,000, based on numerous recent sales of comparable properties. For this type of property, investors want a 10% interest (yield to maturity) rate.

77. How much of the first year's $40,000 net operating income is attributable to the land?
    (A) $15,000
    (B) $20,000
    (C) $25,000
    (D) $30,000
    (E) $40,000

78. How much of the net operating income is attributable to the building?
    (A) $15,000
    (B) $20,000
    (C) $25,000
    (D) $30,000
    (E) $40,000

79. What is the building capitalization rate, assuming straight-line capital recovery?
    (A) 5%
    (B) 10%
    (C) 15%
    (D) 20%
    (E) 25%

80. What is the value of the building, using the building residual technique?
    (A) $75,000
    (B) $100,000
    (C) $125,000
    (D) $130,000
    (E) $140,000

81. What is the combined value of the building and land?
    (A) $275,000
    (B) $300,000
    (C) $325,000
    (D) $330,000
    (E) $340,000

Questions 82–86 are based on the following information:
A freestanding retail store is under a triple net lease for the next 25 years, with $20,000 rent payable at the end of each year. The tenant has a purchase option to buy the property at the end of the lease term for $150,000. The property is free and clear of debt. For this situation, investors seek a 12% rate of return on investment.

82. What is the present value of the rental income?
    (A) less than $100,000
    (B) $100,000 to $150,000
    (C) $150,000 to $175,000
    (D) $175,000 to $200,000
    (E) $200,000 to $250,000

83. On the assumption that the tenant will exercise her purchase option, what is the present value of the reversion?
    (A) less than $10,000
    (B) $10,000 to $20,000
    (C) $20,000 to $100,000
    (D) $100,000 to $150,000
    (E) More than $150,000

84. What is the present value of the property?
    (A) less than $100,000
    (B) $100,000 to $150,000
    (C) $150,000 to $175,000
    (D) $175,000 to $200,000
    (E) $200,000 to $250,000

85. What is the overall rate of return?
    (A) 10–10.5%
    (B) 10.5–11%
    (C) 11–11.25%
    (D) 11.25–11.5%
    (E) More than 11.5%

86. What is the equity dividend rate?
    (A) 10–10.5%
    (B) 10.5–11%
    (C) 11–11.25%
    (D) 11.25 12%
    (E) None of the above

87. The most common type of partial-interest appraisal involves
    (A) a leased property
    (B) a timeshare residence
    (C) a condominium
    (D) rezoning
    (E) condemnation

88. When contract rent exceeds market rent, the leasehold interest
    (A) is subleased
    (B) must be appraised
    (C) has no positive value
    (D) should be mortgaged
    (E) is the same as the leased fee

89. Lease provisions may describe all of the following *except*
    (A) rental payments and the term of use and occupancy
    (B) whether landlord or tenant pays operating expenses
    (C) rent escalations and renewal or purchase options
    (D) the credit rating of the tenant
    (E) assignment or subletting rights

90. *Overage rent* is the
    (A) actual rent over the entire lease term
    (B) percentage rent above guaranteed minimum rent
    (C) amount by which contract rent exceeds market rent
    (D) rent that is past due
    (E) rent the property could command in the open market if not subject to its lease

91. A lease normally states all of the following *except*
    (A) agreed terms of occupancy
    (B) rental payments
    (C) tenant's responsibilities and obligations
    (D) financing of the property
    (E) actions causing default

92. All of the following lease provisions are advantageous to the lessee *except*
    (A) an escape clause
    (B) a renewal option
    (C) a purchase option
    (D) an escalation clause
    (E) All of the above are advantageous.

93. Homeowners' associations are usually found in
    (A) planned unit developments (PUD)
    (B) condominiums
    (C) timeshares
    (D) both A and B
    (E) none of the above

ANSWERS

1. B	20. C	39. E	58. C	77. C
2. D	21. C	40. B	59. D	78. A
3. D	22. A	41. D	60. B	79. D
4. B	23. C	42. C	61. E	80. A
5. B	24. C	43. C	62. B	81. C
6. B	25. D	44. A	63. D	82. C
7. E	26. C	45. B	64. B	83. A
8. A	27. A	46. A	65. E	84. C
9. C	28. C	47. E	66. C	85. A
10. B	29. B	48. B	67. B	86. E
11. E	30. D	49. D	68. D	87. A
12. C	31. B	50. E	69. A	88. C
13. C	32. C	51. A	70. C	89. D
14. B	33. D	52. D	71. A	90. B
15. A	34. B	53. E	72. B	91. D
16. C	35. C	54. D	73. C	92. D
17. B	36. C	55. D	74. E	93. D
18. B	37. A	56. E	75. D	
19. E	38. D	57. B	76. D	

Chapter 16/*Taxation and Assessment*

Real estate, because it is valuable and also hard to hide, has been subject to tax for nearly all of human history. Consequently, it is easy for officials to assess taxes on real estate. The property tax is an *ad valorem* tax; that is, it is based on the *value* of the thing being taxed. In effect, then, the tax bill on a large, valuable property should be more than the bill on a small, relatively low-valued one.

The property tax usually is the major source of income for city, village, town and county governments. In a sense, this may be just, because the real estate that provides the bulk of the taxes collected also benefits greatly from many of the services local government pays for with the property taxes it collects. Most important of these is fire protection, which accrues almost exclusively to real estate. Police protection and the provision and maintenance of local streets and roads also provide obvious benefits. Nearby, locally provided public amenities such as schools and parks make many kinds of real estate more valuable. The control of real estate development through zoning and building codes also tends to preserve the values of existing real estate improvements, as does the provision of planning services. In addition, local courthouses store the records that are necessary for the documentation of title to real estate.

Property is also subject to a special assessment for improvements installed by the municipality that serve to benefit only certain property owners. These are typically to pay for sidewalks, streetlights, or curbs in a particular area. Their cost is apportioned to the various properties served in accordance with the perceived benefit received by each property.

Tax Assessment

Real estate taxation is relatively straightforward, but some elements can be fairly confusing unless the process is studied carefully.

Because the tax is based upon the value of the real estate, some method must be available for determining the values of all parcels of real estate in the taxing jurisdiction. For this purpose, there is a county tax assessor.

More often than not, a single property will be in *more* than one taxing jurisdiction. Most commonly, a property may be in a particular county, as well as in a specific city, town, or school district; each may levy taxes. The county tax assessor sets the value for all jurisdictions located within the county.

All property in Florida is to be assessed at *just value*, which means the same as market value. To estimate just value, county assessors must consider these items:
- Present cash value of the property.
- Size or quantity.
- Present and immediate future highest and best use.
- Condition.
- Net income.
- Expected net proceeds from sale.
- Location.
- Replacement cost of improvements.
These items are included in the three standard appraisal approaches (market, cost, income).

Exemption from Property Taxes

Not all real estate is subject to the real property tax; some of it is *exempt*. Exactly what is exempt and what is not is a matter decided by both state and local law. Some kinds of property, however, are exempt almost everywhere.

GOVERNMENT PROPERTY

Primary among these is any property owned by government. This exemption seems to make sense: it would be peculiar for the government to pay taxes to itself. Of course, there are several governments; although it is conceivable that they could pay taxes to one another, they usually don't. Therefore, *all* government-owned property, no matter which government owns it, is exempt from property taxes. In some areas, where a very large proportion of the property is government-owned, this situation can work a hardship on local taxpayer-owners of property, especially when the government-owned property receives many of the services paid for by local taxes. Examples of such "problem" areas are state capitals, including Tallahassee, FL, and many small cities and towns that provide school and other services for large government (usually military) establishments. In such cases the benefiting branch of government often will provide some direct grant of money to the affected local government to make up for the unpaid property tax.

PRIVATE PROPERTY

Some privately owned property may also be exempt from tax. Most areas will exempt certain kinds of land uses that seem to provide other benefits to the community, making them desirable even when exempt from property tax. These uses usually include churches, nonprofit private schools, hospitals, and some other charitable organizations. In some localities, *all* property owned by such organizations is exempt from tax; however, the current trend is toward granting the exemption only to property that actually is used by the organization for its basic purposes. In such an area, then, a church building used for religious purposes would be exempt, but an apartment project owned by the congregation would not be—even if all its profits went to the church.

Homestead tax exemption ($25,000). Any permanent legal resident of Florida who owns and resides on that property is allowed a $25,000 exemption from the assessed value. The exemption applies to city, county, and school board assessed values. First-time home buyers generally file for the exemption by visiting the county tax office in person by March 1 of the year following purchase. Renewals of homestead vary by county with some counties requiring the homeowner to renew by sending out a notice and having the owner return the notice by mail. Other counties seek return of the notices only when a change has occurred. The $25,000 is significant; few, if any, other states are as generous to its permanent residents. For someone who owns a $100,000 home, only $75,000 is subject to the *ad valorem* tax.

This $25,000 homestead exemption may be claimed together with any of the $500 exemptions noted below. For example, a surviving spouse may claim a $25,500 exemption.

Surviving spouse ($500). An unremarried widow or widower who was a Florida resident on January 1 of the year the spouse died may claim a $500 exemption. This does not apply if divorce preceded the death. Eligibility expires upon remarriage.

Disability ($500). Any permanent resident of Florida who is totally disabled may claim a $500 exemption. Any 10 percent disabled veteran may claim it.

Blind persons ($500). Any Florida resident who is certified as blind may claim this exemption.

Military service-connected total and permanent disability tax exemption. A qualified resident who is an honorably discharged veteran with service-related disabilities that are total may claim a total property tax exemption, which could continue to a spouse after death.

Totally and permanently disabled. A total exemption is allowed for a quadriplegic, or a hemiplegic or other totally and permanently disabled person, or one who is legally blind, provided they meet the following tests:

1. Have been a Florida resident for five consecutive years before the application.
2. Fall within a certain household gross income limit.

ANNUAL APPLICATION

Each of the exemptions requires an in-person application for the first time. Annual reapplication is required between January 1 and March 1 of each year in a manner prescribed by each county.

Payment of Taxes

Past-due property taxes automatically become a lien on the property so affected. If the taxes remain unpaid, the taxing government eventually can foreclose and have the property sold in order to pay the taxes. A tax lien takes priority over all other liens, including mortgages, even ones that have been entered on the records before the tax lien.

Normally, a property owner has a considerable period of time between the time the taxes actually are levied and the date payment is due. The specific schedule follows:

January 1	Tax year begins. Property is assessed, a lien attached.
	Tax exemption filing period begins.
March 1	Tax exemption filing period ends.
April 1	Taxes for previous year become delinquent.
November 1	Property taxes for current year are due.
December 31	Tax year ends.

A homeowner often is spared the chore of remembering when taxes are due, because his mortgage lender requires him to make a supplemental payment into an escrow account with each monthly payment. This money mounts up to create a fund from which the lender pays taxes (and usually insurance) when they are due. Generally the lender is contractually responsible to the borrower for paying the taxes out of these funds; if a mistake is made, or a penalty is required for late payment, the lender can be held liable to the borrower.

Calculation of Property Taxes

To calculate property taxes, two figures are necessary: the *assessed value* of the property and the *tax rate*. Just value, minus the homestead and any other tax exemptions, is the assessed value. The tax rate is applied to the assessed value in order to find the tax due. In effect, the tax rate will be a certain proportion, such as 0.766 percent of the assessed valuation, or $.766 per $100 of valuation, or 7.66 mills per dollar of valuation. All three of these represent the same tax rate, expressed in three different ways.

To determine the tax rate, it usually is easiest to turn the rate into a percentage figure, because that can be easily applied to the assessed valuation through simple arithmetic procedures. Rarely, however, is the tax rate expressed as a percentage; instead, it usually is given as a *millage rate*. A millage rate specifies how many *mills* must be paid for each *dollar* of assessed valuation. A *mill* is $^1/_{10}$ of a cent; therefore, there are 1000 mills in 1 dollar. The millage rate, then, shows how many *thousandths* of the assessed valuation must be paid in tax.

Millage rates are easy to convert to percents: percents measure hundredths, so to change a millage rate to a percentage rate, *the decimal point is moved one place to the left*. This is the same as dividing by 10, since there are 10 thousandths in each hundredth. Consequently, a millage rate of 7.76 is the same as .776 percent. Sometimes the millage rate is expressed as so many dollars per thousand dollars of assessed valuation. In either case, the figure is in thousandths, so the numerical value is the same: 7.76 mills per dollar is the same as $7.76 per thousand dollars.

Once the tax rate is expressed as a percent, the next step is to determine the assessed valuation to which it must be applied. In Florida, the appraised valuation is the same as the just value of the property as estimated by the tax assessor. Florida has a *homestead exemption*, which exempts $25,000 of the appraised valuation from taxation. Once exemptions are determined, they are subtracted from the appraised valuation to arrive at the assessed figure upon which the tax is based.

When the assessed valuation subject to tax has been determined, the tax rate is applied to it to determine the tax to be paid. For example, assume that a property has a taxable assessed valuation of $20,000, and the millage rate is 7.76, or .776 percent; then .776 percent of $20,000 will be the tax to be paid. This is found by changing the percentage into a decimal and multiplying: .00776 × $20,000 = $155.20. The tax, then, is $155.20.

Enforcement

On January 1, taxes become a lien on the property.

In Florida, a property tax lien is superior to all other liens. Special assessments are next in priority. In order to collect a delinquent tax, the city or county issues a *property tax certificate* for each delinquent property. The city or county publishes the list of properties having delinquent taxes in a local newspaper with general circulation. The published list specifies a date, time, and place for the public auction of tax certificates on each property. This serves as notice to the property owner(s) that their tax certificates will be sold if the tax lien is not removed before the date of sale.

The public auction is then held. Any qualified person can bid on a tax certificate for any property. The tax certificate allows the bidder to collect interest up to 18 percent on a property. The bids are by the rate of interest, starting at 18 percent and going down with competitive bids. To remove the lien, the property owner pays the taxing authority the amount of tax plus all accrued interest.

A party who has held a tax certificate for more than two years after the taxes were first declared delinquent can request a tax deed. This begins a process whereby the property can be offered for sale at a public auction. If the tax certificate holder is the successful bidder, he or she claims the property. If someone else is the successful bidder, the holder of the tax certificate will be paid the amount he or she has invested in the tax certificate plus interest.

Rate Setting

The process of setting a tax rate begins with a budget that is adopted by the city council or other board. Then there is an appropriation that authorizes spending the money. The assessor estimates the property value within the jurisdiction, and a tax rate is set. For example, if there is $1,000,000,000 of taxable property in the city, and the city's budget is $10,000,000, then the tax rate must be one percent, applied to all taxable property.

The tax rate may be expressed as a percentage or a millage rate. As described above, a one percent rate is the same as 10 mills. Each owner will then get a tax bill for one percent of his property value.

TAX RATE CEILING

Florida placed a ceiling (cap) of 10 mills on the basic rate that a city, county, or school district may assess; however, a school board's tax rate is comprised of two components:
1. Construction.
2. Operations.
Up to 2 mills may be assessed for construction, in addition to 10 mills for operations.

Any tax district may have a voter-approved bond issue. Debt service on voter-approved bonds may be assessed in addition to the basic tax rate.

SPECIAL ASSESSMENTS

A special assessment is made against property that is to benefit from certain improvements, including street paving, sidewalks, and sewer lines. These types of special assessments are generally charged against each property that benefits, usually depending on the length of frontage (front feet) of the tract. Special assessments are often funded by a bond issue, and property owners are assessed over the life of the bonds.

Appeals or Protests

If a property owner believes that his property is assessed at too high a value, he can appeal. The first step is to visit the assessor within 25 days after the assessment notice was mailed. One should be prepared to do more than talk; documentation is needed. If the property was not measured or described accurately, the assessor will almost surely issue a correction and, on request, will perhaps allow an adjustment retroactively. If the owner or representative can show the property is not being taxed uniformly, in comparison to neighboring properties, it is helpful to supply proof. Even though the assessment may be less than the property's market value, there may be room for a reduction when neighboring properties are assessed at a lower proportion of market value. If that process does not provide satisfaction, the owner may continue.

The next step is to file an appeal petition with the Value Adjustment Board. This is a five-person board that has authority to change the tax assessor's valuation amount.

The third step is to go to court. The owner must file this suit against the county appraiser and collector within 60 days after the tax role is certified, so the owner's deadline is approximately October 15.

Green Belt and Blue Belt Law

Florida's Green Belt law is intended to protect farmers from being assessed at prohibitive amounts based on the land's value at its highest and best use. Instead, the land is taxed on its agricultural land value. Classification must be applied for on March 1 of each year. This annual classification application requirement is needed to ensure that farmers, not speculators, get the benefit.

The Blue Belt law allows appraisers to assess land that provides high rates of recharge to Florida's aquifers, and recreational use land by a favorable method. Such land is taxed at its value in current use, rather than highest and best use.

A Sample Property Tax Problem

Following is an example of the calculation of property tax. This problem is for illustrative purposes, so it may be somewhat more complicated than what you are likely to encounter, either on licensing examinations or in actual practice.

> *Jones wishes to determine what the tax will be on the home he just bought for $122,500. Current practice in his area is for the assessor to estimate the value of newly sold property as 95 percent of the sale price. Taxes are levied on 30 percent of estimated value. There is a homestead exemption of $5000 of taxable value. The city tax rate is 21.1 mills. County taxes that Jones's property is subject to have a millage rate of 14.5. In addition, the city school system levies a 34.4 mill tax, and there is a state tax of 0.5 mill. The homestead exemption does not apply to county taxes. The city allows an additional $2000 exemption on its taxes for the elderly; Jones is 72 years old, so he qualifies for this exemption.*

(1) The first step is to determine the assessed valuation. First we find 95 percent of $122,500 to get the estimated value:

$$0.95 \times \$122,500 = \$116,375 \text{ estimated value}$$

The assessed valuation is 30 percent of this figure:

$$0.30 \times \$116,375 = \$34,912.50 \text{ assessed valuation}$$

(2) Actually, there are four separate taxes: city, county, school, and state. They can be computed separately; however, the school and state taxes are computed on the same base, so they can be combined for efficiency. We will show both ways.

First, the school tax of 34.4 mills (which is 3.44 percent or 0.0344) is applied to the tax base of $29,912.50 (which is the assessed valuation of $34,912.50 minus the $5000 homestead exemption):

$$0.0344 \times \$29,912.50 = \$1028.99 \text{ school tax}$$

Next, the state tax rate of 0.5 mill (which is 0.5 percent or 0.0005) is applied to the same base:

$$0.0005 \times \$29,912.50 = \$14.96 \text{ state tax}$$

These two taxes add up to $1043.95. This total could have been arrived at by adding the two tax rates, and then applying the total to the assessed valuation of $29,912.50:

$$34.4 \text{ mills} + 0.5 \text{ mill} = 34.9 \text{ mills combined tax rate} = 3.49\% = 0.0349$$
$$0.0349 \times \$29,912.50 = \$1043.95 \text{ combined state and school taxes}$$

(3) Now the city tax must be calculated. Since the city has an extra $2000 exemption for the elderly, for which Jones qualifies, this tax is applied to a base calculated by adjusting the assessed valuation to reflect both the homestead exemption and the city's exemption for the elderly:

$$\$34,912.50 - (\$5000 + \$2000) = \$27,912.50 \text{ city tax base}$$

The city tax rate is 21.1 mills, which is 2.11 percent or 0.0211. The tax is calculated as follows:

$$0.0211 \times \$27,912.50 = \$588.95 \text{ city tax}$$

(4) The county tax allows no homestead exemption at all, so it is figured on a base that is the full appraised valuation of $34,912.50. The county tax rate is 14.5 mills, which is 1.45 percent or 0.0145. The county tax is calculated as follows:

$$0.0145 \times \$34,912.50 = \$506.23 \text{ county tax}$$

(5) Now that the four separate taxes have been calculated, they are added together to arrive at the total property tax on Jones's house:

School tax	$1,028.99
State tax	14.96
City tax	588.95
County tax	506.23
Total property tax	$2,139.13

State Taxes on Real Estate Transfers

STATE DOCUMENTARY STAMP TAX ON DEEDS

Florida requires the payment of a documentary stamp tax on conveyances, including deeds. The rate is $.70 per $100, based on the full price. This is a one-time tax paid when recording the purchase.

STATE DOCUMENTARY STAMP TAX ON NOTES

Florida requires the payment of a documentary stamp tax on notes and written monetary obligations. The rate is $.35 per $100, based on the full amount of the note. An exemption is allowed for the renewal of a note by the same borrower as the original borrower, provided the balance had not increased. This is a one-time tax paid at inception of recording the note.

STATE INTANGIBLES TAX ON MORTGAGES

Florida requires the payment of a state intangibles tax on mortgages prior to their being recorded. The rate is $.20 per $100 of debt. This is a one-time charge.

Checklist for Your Locality's Property Taxation Practices _____

Obtain the answers to the following questions from the literature supplied by the local tax assessor's office in your area.

What proportion of the estimated market value is subject to tax? _____ %

Are any of the following exemptions applicable to the tax base?
- ☐ Veteran's exemption
- ☐ Old-age exemption
- ☐ Exemption for the poor
- ☐ Other(s): _____

Is it possible for a property to be subject to taxes by more than one governmental body?
- ☐ No; taxes are levied only by _____
- ☐ Yes; these include:
  - ☐ State government
  - ☐ County government
  - ☐ City (township) government
  - ☐ School district
  - ☐ Special assessment district
  - ☐ Improvement district
  - ☐ Other(s): _____

Questions on Chapter 16 _____

1. An ad valorem tax is based on
   (A) income earned
   (B) the value of the thing being taxed
   (C) the size of the thing being taxed
   (D) something other than A, B, or C

2. The property tax is a form of
   (A) sales tax   (C) income tax
   (B) ad valorem tax   (D) excise tax

3. The major source of income for local government usually is
   (A) income taxes   (C) property taxes
   (B) licenses and fees   (D) parking meters

4. Which of the following is (are) always exempt from real property taxes?
   (A) Income-producing property owned by a church.
   (B) Government-owned property.
   (C) Most restaurants.
   (D) A private, for-profit school.

5. A millage rate of 8.45 mills is the same as
   (A) $8.45 per $1000
   (B) 0.845 percent
   (C) both A and B
   (D) none of the above

6. If a property is assessed at $60,000 and the millage rate is 32.5, the tax is
   (A) $19.50   (C) $1,950
   (B) $195.00   (D) $19,500

7. The appraised valuation of a property is $85,000. The city tax is 10 mills; the county tax is 8 mills. Which of the following is true?
   (A) The city tax is $680.
   (B) The county tax is $850.
   (C) The city and county taxes combined add up to $1,530.00.
   (D) The city and county taxes combined add up to $7,650.00.

8. A lien for unpaid property taxes
   (A) can be sold at auction
   (B) takes priority over all other liens except a first mortgage
   (C) cannot exist unless taxes are at least 36 months overdue
   (D) is a form of adverse possession

9. Which of the following is *not* a good reason why real property taxes are so popular?
   (A) Real estate ownership is easy to hide.
   (B) Real estate is valuable.
   (C) Real estate is easy to find.
   (D) Real estate can be foreclosed to provide payment of unpaid tax levies.

10. Real property taxes are justifiable because
    (A) real property benefits from many services provided by property taxes
    (B) real property owners are wealthy and can afford to pay taxes
    (C) real property taxes are legal everywhere, whereas many other kinds of taxes are not
    (D) none of the above

TRUE/FALSE

Write *T* for true, *F* for false.

_____11. There is no way that a property owner can appeal an assessment he considers incorrect.

_____12. A tax lien takes priority over all other liens.

_____13. The property tax rate is always applied to the market value of the property.

_____14. Real estate owners benefit from many of the services provided by local government with the money collected from real property taxes.

_____15. Some properties may be subject to real property taxes levied by more than one jurisdiction.

FILL-INS

Fill in the blanks with the appropriate words or phrases.

16. Unpaid and overdue property taxes become a _____ on the property.

17. If the assessed valuation is $40,000 and the tax rate is 7.7 mills, the tax is _____ .

18. A *mill* is an amount of money equal to _____ .

19. A millage rate can also be expressed as so many dollars per _____ .

20. The property tax is based on the value of the thing taxed, so it is a form of _____ _____ tax.

21. The amount of the homestead exemption in Florida is $ _____.

22. In Florida, the tax assessor measures the market value of property, which is called _____.

23. *Just value*, minus the homestead exemption and any other exemptions, is called _____.

24. If a property owner wishes to appeal the assessed value, the owner should come prepared with _____.

25. The disability tax exemption is $ _____.

ANSWERS

1. **B**	6. **C**	11. **F**	16. **Lien**	21. **$25,000**
2. **B**	7. **C**	12. **T**	17. **$30.80**	22. **just value**
3. **C**	8. **A**	13. **F**	18. **⅒ of 1 cent**	23. **assessed value**
4. **B**	9. **A**	14. **T**	19. **$1000**	24. **documentation (or data)**
5. **C**	10. **A**	15. **T**	20. **ad valorem**	25. **$500**

Chapter 17/*Real Estate Investment*

Real estate has been the path to riches for many investors. In addition, it has provided security and income to those who had the foresight to build an estate. Success in real estate investing requires knowledge, capital, and the willingness to take risks. An investor must know how to select properties, when to buy and sell, how to finance and operate a rental property.

Fundamentals of Real Estate Investment

Real estate has proven itself to be a lucrative investment through the years. There are many ways to invest in real estate and each offers distinct benefits. About two thirds of Americans own their own homes, and this basic level of real estate investment frees them from dependence on a landlord, and hopefully provides financial rewards in the form of value appreciation. In addition to their homes, many people have acquired small holdings of income property. Often self-managed, these properties provide periodic income, some of which is tax sheltered, and opportunity for appreciation gains.

Investors may put their money into a limited partnership or a Real Estate Investment Trust (REIT). This is like a mutual fund for real estate. Through such entities, investors can own a part of large properties or diversified holdings. This form also provides the advantages of professional property and investment management.

INVESTMENT ADVANTAGES

Regardless of the form of investment, investors look for several advantages from real estate. Real estate often offers higher cash returns than alternative investments. In part, this can be attributed to greater risk and difficulty of resale (illiquidity) associated with the property. Returns may be increased by using borrowed money, called leverage. Real property tends to be a good hedge against inflation since rents may be increased as costs rise. Well-located properties may even beat inflation and offer resale profits from appreciation in value. Finally, tax shelter has traditionally been an attraction of real estate investment. Opportunities for tax shelter have been diminished by recent tax law changes. However, in some cases, tax benefits still exist. Each of these attractions are described in greater detail in this chapter. Real estate investments cover a wide range from the relatively secure to the highly speculative. In general, the most secure investments emphasize current income production from highly creditworthy tenants. Speculative investments emphasize appreciation potential from future developments.

INVESTMENT DRAWBACKS

There are serious drawbacks to real estate investing. One factor that limits the field of real estate investors is the size of the required investment. A down payment on even a modest rental home requires several thousand dollars. Purchasing a sizable commercial property or assembling a diversified portfolio of properties means a much larger investment, certainly beyond the means of the typical investor. Syndicators overcome this problem by gathering a group of investors each of whom purchases shares of a large property or inventory of properties. Partnership interests may be acquired for as little as $1000. Furthermore, the investor may buy into several partnerships to gain further diversification.

Real estate is an *illiquid* investment. This means that, once the investment is made, it is difficult to get money out quickly. It takes at least several weeks, and sometimes months, to sell a property. Market conditions may prevent a sale at a reasonable price. If liquidity is desired, you may purchase shares in a publicly traded syndication, or a REIT. Many of these are traded on the major stock exchanges and offer immediate conversion to cash.

Since real estate is a physical asset, it requires ongoing management. Purchase of a property is like buying a small business. The owner is responsible for maintaining the property and keeping it productive. Professional property managers or resident managers can be hired to take on many of these responsibilities. The owner still must decide on tenant selection, rental rates, marketing, alterations, and when to sell.

Real estate markets are local in nature. There is a shortage of available information about current prices, rental, and vacancy rates. The typical purchaser is in the market infrequently and cannot stay attuned to current conditions. Therefore, it is difficult to decide on the best offering price for a property or rental rate to charge.

Aside from the size of the investment, the costs of purchasing a property are increased by transaction expenses. These include sales commissions, attorney fees, title insurance, appraisal and surveying costs, loan fees, and transfer taxes. A seller may pay as much as ten percent of the price of the property in transaction costs. In addition, the buyer may pay five or more percent. These costs tend to make real estate a long-term investment. Short-term profits would have to be substantial to offset transaction costs.

Real estate is *immobile*. For the investor, this means the performance of the property is determined by local market conditions. The demand for the property may be depressed by an economic downturn or an abundant supply of similar properties. The property cannot be moved to another location where conditions are better. In addition to local market conditions, a property is affected by the quality of the neighborhood and what happens to surrounding properties. Therefore, location is a major factor in a property's performance. Furthermore, these conditions may change over time. A big part of investment analysis involves evaluating trends in the local market and surrounding area.

What you can do with your property is subject to government policies. On a broad scale, government influence on interest rates and economic trends will affect demand for the property. On a local scale, government can limit your use of the property through zoning ordinances, building codes, health codes, and environmental laws. In some places a residential project may come under rent controls. Decisions to extend streets and utilities can change the attractiveness of your property. For these reasons, real estate investors often take an active interest in the affairs of their local government.

Investment Analysis

Investment analysis is deciding if a particular investment opportunity is a good choice. A projection of expected investment returns is helpful in making the decision. Since the return from real estate investments depends on future rent, operating expenses, financing, and tax considerations, an estimation of what these will be will help you estimate how the property will perform. Projections may be the main determinant of the decision or may supplement other sources of information. The important thing to remember is that projections are only as good as the assumptions used to make them.

PRO FORMA STATEMENTS

Pro forma statements show expected returns from operating a property. One of the most important results is cash flow, the money produced by an investment that you get to keep. Basically, this amounts to the cash, if any, left over after all expenses have been paid. Expenses include those to operate the property and to meet all loan requirements.

Cash flow represents the money produced by operating the investment. It does not reflect any appreciation gains that may eventually be received at resale nor equity buildup due to mortgage amortization. Since these types of return are realized only in the future, cash flow is a measure of the current performance of the investment. For that reason, some investors base their decision to acquire a property on a simple *cash-on-cash* return. This measure is cash flow divided by the required equity investment. For example, a property which is expected to produce a cash flow of $10,000 per year and requires a cash investment of $100,000, has a cash-on-cash return of ten percent.

The following is an example of how to calculate the cash flow from a real estate investment.

STATEMENT OF OPERATIONS

PRO FORMA

Total rental income if building full (Potential Gross Income)		$200,000
Less allowance for vacancies and bad debts		10,000
Effective Gross income		$190,000
Operating expenses:		
Management	$ 10,000	
Maintenance	25,000	
Utilities	7,000	
Property taxes	15,000	
Insurance	3,000	
Repairs	10,000	
Total operating expenses		70,000
Net operating income		$120,000
Debt service (mortgage payments):		
Principal	$ 5,000	
Interest	80,000	
Total debt service		85,000
Before-tax cash flow		$ 35,000

A property seller or broker may offer a *pro forma statement of operations*, such as the one above, as part of a sales presentation. The rental income may be attractive estimates rather than actual amounts earned by the property. Or, operating expenses may be based on last year's rates while property taxes, insurance, or utilities have jumped in the current year. You may have to recast the amounts to determine what you are likely to incur in costs or receive in cash flow. Get the owner's rent roll, which is a list of the tenants, space occupied (i.e., apartment number), and rent, and compare the figures to the pro forma statement. Or look at actual operating statements, not forecasts.

Expected cash flow can be an indication of how speculative an investment is. When appreciation rates are high, it is not uncommon for properties to be purchased with negative cash flow. The investor expects to have to "feed" the property (pay the cash flow deficit out of other income or capital reserves) until the property is sold. An expected large profit at resale offsets the period of negative cash flow. In other cases, investors may purchase properties with turnaround potential—those that are currently losing money but which may become productive given renovation or marketing effort. These properties are expected to have negative cash flow for a time, but eventually produce positive income and resale profits. In any case, where the cash-on-cash return is low or negative, the investment is speculative in nature. Eventual returns are based on anticipated improvements in market conditions or the appeal of the property, and this introduces risk that the improvement will not materialize.

Short-term analysis can be used to screen properties. The following indicators may be calculated quickly with a few bits of information that are based on current performance:

Gross Rent Multiplier

This is the total gross rent divided by the price of the property. The lower the number, the less you are paying for the gross income.

Overall Rate of Return or Capitalization Rate

This is the net operating income (rent less operating expenses) divided by the value of the property. This measure is preferred to the gross rent multiplier because it accounts for operating expenses. Also, it offers a percentage rate, which is a customary way to express rate of return.

Cash-on-cash Return or Equity Dividend Rate

This is the cash flow divided by the required equity investment, and is especially useful when you know how the property will be financed. You may use before-tax or after-tax cash flow. If after-tax cash flow is used, you should adjust the returns on alternative types of investment for taxes to make a meaningful comparison.

Long-term analysis requires more information and assumptions since you are projecting several years into the future. If you are considering a property whose value is likely to increase or decrease in the near future, or if inflation is significant, long-term analysis is probably worthwhile. The analysis requires that you project growth rates for rents, operating expenses, and property value. Changes in debt service and taxes are also considered. The result of the analysis can be a measure of yield to maturity called the *internal rate of return*. This is the projected annual rate of return over the entire holding period. It can be used to compare other investments with the same holding period. Alternatively, you may calculate the *net present value* of the investment based on your required rate of return. This is often useful when comparing investments that require different levels of cash investment or when putting together a portfolio of several investments. Fortunately, there are computer programs available to do long-term investment analysis.

Investment Strategy

INVESTMENT LIFE CYCLE

Like most things, a real estate investment has a beginning and an end. You purchase a property (or share in a partnership) and later sell it, hopefully for a profit. In between, the property may provide income if well managed. This middle period of operation may be long or short, depending on market conditions and the reasons for buying the property. Because of high transaction costs, most investors end up holding real estate for several years.

There are important considerations at each stage of the life cycle of the investment.

PURCHASE

The investor will be concerned with getting the right property at a good price and with favorable financing terms. The property should fit the investment objectives. If cash flow is desired, pick a property with proven ability to produce cash flow. If you want appreciation, pick a property with potential for increased value. The price you pay will have a lot to do with appreciation. If you pay above market value, the property will have to improve for you to break even. Financing may determine whether the property makes money or even whether you can keep the property. You must decide how much leverage to use, knowing that high leverage increases possible returns but may reduce income.

OPERATION

During this phase, the property should produce some cash flow. This is the income to you as an investor. Some properties have negative cash flow, which means you must pay some expenses out of your pocket. A part of cash flow may be due to tax benefits. Depending on your tax situation, these benefits allow you to shelter some property income from taxes. Remember that cash flow may vary from year to year and it depends on your ability to keep a sufficient amount of paying tenants and minimize operating expenses.

SALE

The main benefit from sale is capital gain, the profit on the sale. To make a profitable sale, you will want to maximize the sales price and minimize taxes on the sale. The highest price depends on the timing of the sale. You want to sell when the market is strong. Sometimes, a better price can be had if you are willing to help finance the purchase. To limit your exposure to taxes, you may wish to structure the sale as an *installment sale*. This allows you to spread the income from the sale over several years and may reduce the tax rate on the gain. Also, you may want to arrange an exchange. If properly done, an exchange can avoid payment of taxes altogether.

The key to a successful investment is to consider all of the income expected through the cycle, and its timing, to determine whether it is worth the cost.

When to Sell

How long should investment real estate be held? Its optimal holding period varies with the property type, market conditions, and each individual investor. Perhaps the most important factor is what you'll do with the money.

Do you plan to spend the money on a new boat, or reinvest it wisely? If you really just want to buy the boat, then investment strategy doesn't matter. However, as an investor considering the sale, think about the net amount you'll realize and how you'll reinvest it. If you can't equal or exceed the return that you'll get from continuing to hold the property, keep what you have. You might consider refinancing, which allows you to get some money out of the property without selling it.

Here's an example: Suppose you bought a rental house a few years ago for $50,000 and now it's worth $100,000. It generates annual income of $10,000, net of operating expenses. If you sell, you'll pay a brokerage commission ($6000), expenses of sale ($3000), and income taxes ($11,000). You'll be left with $80,000 to reinvest. Suppose the best investment opportunity is one that yields eight percent; that will provide only $6400 annually, much less than the $10,000 you're now getting. If you can't exceed $10,000 of income on a new investment opportunity, keep the house. But if the $80,000 is needed to go into a business that promises to pay a 50 percent annual return, sell the house. The rate of return is like a speedometer—if your vehicle is too slow, get a faster one, if you can.

Considering a sale requires more thought than just estimating a rate of return, because it must include risk factors. The problem becomes more complex when debt is involved. As to risk, a bond may provide more safety, whereas the business venture may be much riskier than the rental house. So your personal judgment must temper a higher rate with increased risk of loss or volatility. As to financing, one must subtract the debt on property owned to determine exactly how much money will be realized from a sale. This adds more mathematics to the problem. The effect of depreciation and capital gains can add complications to the income tax estimate.

Highly leveraged real estate that appreciates in value will provide a very high yield on the equity investment. To sustain such a high yield, there is a temptation to sell and buy another larger, highly leveraged property in a year or two. However, this sort of pyramiding is financially dangerous—like playing "double-or-nothing"—one loss and you're completely wiped out. A longer holding period tends to be safer, and you eliminate the risk associated with a new purchase.

Sometimes cash can be extracted from real estate by refinancing, thus extending the optimal holding period. Refinancing costs money but eliminates most of the expenses of a sale, including income taxes. Refinancing may provide the cash for a new boat or additional investment. But be sure you can handle the increased payments of a new loan with increased principal.

Available Financing

Arranging the best financing can be as important as negotiating the best price for a property. Before you talk to a lender, however, you should understand how the various terms of a loan can affect your investment.

INTEREST RATE

Interest is a charge for the use of money. The lower the rate, the more attractive the loan. The degree of leverage is also important. Many investors will pay a significantly higher interest rate in order to enjoy a lower cash down payment and therefore be able to exercise more leverage. Some equity investors will pay higher prices for property to achieve more leverage. Sellers sometimes accommodate by providing financing to buyers or by paying *discount points* on a buyer's loan, but they will try to raise their price to compensate. Consequently, prices are generally increased by favorable financing.

DEGREE OF LEVERAGE

When interest rates are low, the loan amount is usually limited by the *loan-to-value* (L/V) ratio. When rates are high, the *debt coverage ratio* (DCR) usually sets the maximum loan amount. For conservative lenders, the L/V ratio is usually in the range of 65 to 70 percent. Other lenders may use L/V ratio criteria of 75 to 80 percent. A conservative DCR is around 1.25.

AMORTIZATION TERM

The longer the amortization term of a mortgage loan, the lower the annual debt service, and therefore the greater the annual cash flow. However, once loan terms are stretched beyond 30 years, the annual mortgage payment requirement declines, but the change is quite small. Annual debt service can never become less than the interest due on the principal balance. Many loans on income property become due years before being fully amortized. These are called *balloon payment* loans.

PREPAYMENT PRIVILEGES

In this circumstance, the borrower has the right to pay off the remaining debt before it is due. Some loans include penalties for prepayment, although usually the penalty declines with time. For example, the penalty may be three percent if the loan is prepaid during the first five years, two percent for the next five years, then declining by 0.5 percent for each of the following years until there is no penalty. Some mortgage loans are locked in for the first five to ten years; prepayment without the lender's consent is prohibited.

EXCULPATION

Exculpation is freedom from liability. When a mortgage loan includes an exculpatory clause, the property is the sole collateral for the loan. Should the property be foreclosed, the lender can look only to the property for full satisfaction of the debt, not to other property you own. In the absence of exculpation, you are usually personally liable for the debt. *Nonrecourse* is another term used to describe mortgages with exculpatory clauses; the lender's only recourse in the event of borrower default is to the property itself, not to your personal assets.

ASSUMABILITY

This right allows the borrower to transfer the mortgage loan with the property to another party. Since the new owner may not be as good a credit risk as the original owner, lenders often reserve the right to approve a loan assumption. In recent years, some lenders have been willing to approve changes routinely, provided that they can *escalate* (increase) the interest rate on the debt. Such provisions in mortgage loans make assumption privileges less attractive. Despite lender approval of changes in assumption, original borrowers remain liable for the mortgage debt. So if there is a default on an assumed loan, sellers are liable, but they can try to collect from their buyer. By contrast, if the buyer took the property "subject to" the loan, but did not assume it, the sellers remain solely liable for default.

CALL OR ACCELERATION PROVISIONS

These provisions effectively permit balloon payments. Although the loan has a 25 or 30 year term, lenders, at their option, can accelerate payment of the principal after ten or fifteen years, regardless of whether the loan is in default. This obviously puts the lender in a strong position. Upon reaching the "call" date, the lender can force repayment or escalate the interest rate.

SUBORDINATION

Moving a mortgage loan to a lower priority. The priority of a lender's claim is where the lender stands in line for collection after a foreclosure. Land financed by a seller with a first mortgage and now ready for development is not acceptable collateral for a construction lender. Construction lenders want a first lien. If the holder of an existing mortgage is willing to subordinate, the existing mortgage will be reduced to a second lien position to allow a first lien for the new mortgage. If a subordination clause will be needed, you should attempt to insert it initially; lenders are reluctant to reduce collateral later. Subordinated loans are more favorable to borrowers because they increase the flexibility of first-mortgage financing.

Property Types and Investment Characteristics

Real estate comes in many different forms and can be leased or financed in so many different ways that the lease or mortgage will alter its investment characteristics. These characteristics vary from very passive investments to management-intensive ones, and from the lowest to the highest levels of risk.

APARTMENTS

Ownership

Traditionally dominated by independent individuals or partnerships. Relatively little in institutional, corporate or large developer portfolios.

Characteristics

Individual investors have been attracted to rental housing for several reasons.
1. Familiarity with housing
2. Liberal borrowing opportunities
3. Management need and ability
4. Tax incentives offered by government to encourage housing

Attractive Features

1. Leverage opportunities
2. Ability to respond quickly to market conditions (short leases)
3. Greater liquidity than other real estate investments
4. Tax shelter for high bracket investors
5. Inflation hedge
6. Greater immunity to recession than other property types

Risks

1. Rent control
2. Competition
3. Local economy dependence

OFFICE BUILDINGS

Ownership

Dominated by institutional, corporate, or large developer portfolios.

Characteristics

The institutional investor and large developer is attracted to office buildings because of:
1. Perceived quality and quantity of income stream
2. Large capital requirement prevents others from bidding
3. Ability to acquire competent property and investment management services

Attractive Features

1. Cash flow
2. Ability to respond to market conditions
3. Long-term nature of investment and physical asset: attractive for long-term investors such as pension funds and insurance companies
4. Inflation hedge
5. Perceived long-term stability
6. Expected diversification benefits vs. securities

Risks

1. Effect of recession on space needs
2. Competition
3. Local economy dependence
4. Functional obsolescence

SHOPPING CENTERS

Ownership

Shopping center investors may be categorized into the following groups:
1. Major national and regional shopping center developers
2. Local shopping center developers
3. Commercial property investors
4. Institutional investors and Pension Funds
5. Investment Banking and Security firms
6. Syndications and Real Estate Investment Trusts
7. Foreign investors

Physical Characteristics

1. Unified architectural treatment for the building or buildings, providing space for tenants that are selected, and managed as a unit for the benefit of all tenants
2. Unified site, suited to the type of center called for by the marketplace
3. An easily accessible location within the trade area with adequate entrances and exits
4. Sufficient on-site parking to meet the demands generated by the retail commercial users
5. Service facilities

6. Site improvements, such as landscaping, lighting, and signage, to create a desirable, attractive, and safe shopping environment
7. Tenant grouping that provides merchandising interplay among stores and the widest possible range and depth of merchandise
8. Surroundings that are agreeable and comfortable for shopping and that create a sense of identity and place

Attractive Features

1. Long-term viability from long-term leases with selected creditworthy tenants.
2. Financial stability and security when there are financially strong national chain stores as tenants.
3. Value enhancement and appreciation through the sales performance of tenants.
4. Limitations on expense exposure with "net" leases and periodic recycling opportunities.

Risks

1. Locational obsolescence
2. Leasing, when terms of tenants become undesirable
3. Financing, when interest rates or payment requirements are burdensome
4. Tenant use requirement in lease
5. Expense pass-through
6. Governmental activities: ordinances, rules, statutes or governmental laws, or regulations

Categories of Shopping Centers

Shopping centers are divided into four distinct categories: the neighborhood shopping center, the community shopping center, the regional shopping center, and the super-regional shopping center.

TABLE 17-1

CHARACTERISTICS OF SHOPPING CENTERS

Center Type	Leading tenant (Basis for Classification)	Typical GLA* (Square Feet)	General Range in GLA (Square Feet)	Usual Minimum Site area (Acres)	Minimum Population Support Required
Neighborhood Centers	Supermarket	50,000	30,000–100,000	3–10	3000 40,000
Community Centers	Junior Department Store, Large Variety, Discount, or Department Store	150,000	100,000–300,000	10–30	40,000 150,000
Regional Centers					
Regional Center	One or More Full-line Department Store(s)	400,000	300,000–900,000	10–60	150,000 or more
Super Regional Center	Three or More Full-line Department Store(s)	800,000 800,000	500,000–1.5 million or	15–100 or more	300,000 or more

*GLA=Gross Leasable Area

Source: International Council of Shopping Centers

INDUSTRIAL PROPERTIES

Ownership

1. Corporate users
2. Developer/investors
3. Joint ventures with developers and users
4. Pension funds
5. Life insurance companies
6. Long-term individual investors

Investment Characteristics

1. Cash flow
2. Stable values
3. Long life

Risks

1. Tenant default
2. Environmental obsolescence
3. Local economic conditions
4. Illiquidity
5. Functional obsolescence
6. Environmental problems

Types of Uses

1. Service center
2. Office warehouse
3. Distribution
4. Manufacturing
5. Research and development

LOCATION

An expression in real estate is that the three key aspects of success are "location, location, location." Very similar buildings can have very different values depending on where they are located. In fact, the value of undeveloped land is almost totally determined by where it is located.

The reason location is so important is that real estate is more than just space in an economic sense. Its surroundings have a lot to do with how useful the property is. One big reason to buy or rent a piece of property is to be near other activities.

The type of location desired varies with the type of property:

For *residential properties,* people will want to be relatively close to their job and shopping, but not so close that there is a lot of traffic in their neighborhood. Being in a good school district is important to many home buyers. The neighborhood should be pleasant and well-cared for. A prestigious address can add a great deal of value. If the property has apartments, being on a bus route might be important.

Stores and shopping centers need visibility and traffic flow. The property should be near areas where shoppers live or work, depending on the type of stores. Big stores should not be too close to their competitors, but small stores often like to be near big stores, hoping to attract shoppers coming and going to the larger store.

Office buildings should be close to business activities. Lawyers want to be near courthouses or government offices; consultants want to be near corporate headquarters or banks; doctors need to be near hospitals or nursing homes, and other businesses need to be near customers.

Because of the necessity to be close together, downtown areas used to be the best place for offices. Today, suburban locations may be just as valuable because of improvements in communications.

Industrial properties should be close to the source of their materials and labor. They have great need for good transportation, with heavy industry often locating on rail lines or near seaports. A good highway is almost a necessity.

In real estate, the best locations get the top dollar. As an investor, you have to look at more than the property alone. Remember, however, that the quality of a location can change over time. Sometimes, a lesser location can become the best place to be.

Sources of Market Data for Income and Expenses

Apartments, Condos and Co-ops

The Institute of Real Estate Management (IREM) of the National Association of Realtors periodically provides the *Income/Expense Analysis* for various types of buildings (elevator, walk-up, others) in different cities. Write to:

> *Institute of Real Estate Management*
> *430 North Michigan Ave.*
> *Chicago, Illinois 60611*

Office Buildings

The Building Owners and Managers Association (BOMA) International provides information on office building rental rates and operating expenses experienced by their members in major U.S. cities.

> *Building Owners and Managers International*
> *1250 Eye Street, Suite 200*
> *Washington, D.C. 20005*

Shopping Centers

The Urban Land Institute (ULI) releases a new edition of *Dollars and Cents of Shopping Centers* every three years.

> *Urban Land Institute*
> *625 Indiana Ave., NW Suite 400*
> *Washington, D.C. 20004*

The Department Store Lease Study

Published by the National Retail Merchants Association.

> *National Retail Merchants Association*
> *100 West 31st Street*
> *New York, NY 10001*

Hotels and Motels

Sources of information on national and local trends include Pannell Kerr Forster's *Trends in the Hotel Industry*.

> *Pannell Kerr Forster*
> *262 North Belt East*
> *Houston, TX 77060*

REIS (Real Estate Information Systems)

REIS maintains current and historical data on more than 30,000 buildings, and is able to offer trend data on nominal and effective rental rates for 60 urban markets.

> *REIS*
> *11 East 36th Street*
> *New York, NY 10016*

Other sources of national real estate data include the SREA Market Data Center (Chicago), National Association of Realtors (Chicago), and International Association of Assessing Officers (Chicago).

Local Sources of Real Estate Data

Local organizations often collect real estate data, usually for membership use or sale to interested parties. These include the following:
- Local Board of Realtors/Multiple Listing Service
- Local tax assessor's office
- Local credit bureaus, and tax map reproduction firms
- University research centers
- Private brokerage or appraisal firms

Local Boards of Realtors

Most metropolitan areas have a Board of Realtors, or other broker group, that sponsors a multiple listing service (MLS). Upon the sale of property listed through MLS, the broker must supply information about the completed transaction. Each property sold and its terms of sale are therefore available on computer or in a published book. Some realtor boards provide information to members only; some share with other real estate organizations.

Local Tax Assessor's Offices

Assessor's offices usually keep a file on every property in the jurisdiction, with property characteristics, value estimate, and how the estimate was derived. Many jurisdictions are notified of every sale or building permit, for immediate update of affected properties.

Local Credit Bureaus and Tax Map Companies

These may have data on certain parcels; since their main business is not evaluation, they are not a regular source.

University Research Centers

University research centers, many of which are sponsored by broker and salesperson state license fees, may have aggregated data on real estate transactions collected from other sources throughout the state. This data is often helpful in identifying trends established over time, and by city, for various types of property. Additional research and educational information may be available from such centers.

Private Data Sources

Many real estate appraisers and brokers retain file data for property owned by their clients and others. They will often share information, usually for reciprocity rather than payment.

Property Owner

Property owner's records include permanent records such as deeds, leases, and copies of mortgages (lenders have the original mortgage document), as well as periodic accounting and tax return information about the property's recent past. An owner's report may be of limited immediate use, however, because it may be disorganized, have extraneous information, or be arranged poorly for appraisals. Also, data from a single property cannot offer a broad perspective on the market.

Return on Investment

Return on investment is the actual earnings from the investment; this is apart from any returns which represent repayment (called amortization) of the principal invested. The difference is like distinguishing the fruit from the tree on which it grows. Both can be sold for money, but selling the tree provides a different type of income than would picking the fruit each year.

In real estate, it is sometimes difficult to determine how much of income is return *on* investment and how much is a return *of* investment. For example, if you rent a property that depreciates in value, some of the rental income must go toward significant repairs, or the eventual possibility of replacing the building when it becomes useless from age or obsolescence.

Why is this important? It makes a difference in evaluating the performance of the investment. The return on investment determines how well your money is invested. Return of investment affects risk of capital. The sooner your investment is recovered, the less risk there is of losing it.

Measures of return on investment include the *equity dividend rate*, based on a one-year analysis, and the *internal rate of return*, based on a multiyear projection (see DISCOUNTED CASH FLOW ANALYSIS). Consider that the rate of return you get includes these:

A Safe Rate

This is the rate you could get if you put your money into a perfectly safe, liquid investment, such as a federally insured passbook savings account.

A Liquidity Premium

This compensates you for the difficulty of, and time required, to sell your property. Stocks and bonds may be sold at market value within a moment's notice, whereas selling real estate may take months or years.

A Management Premium

This is for the burden of monitoring and making decisions about the investment.

A Risk Premium

This accounts for the chance that you may not get all your money back or that the return will be lower than expected.

You may use a buildup approach to evaluating the return on a particular investment. Consider a real estate investment that promises an annual return of 14 percent before taxes. You would hold the property for at least ten years. The safe liquid rate, as measured by the current yield on passbook savings accounts, is five percent. The real estate looks like a superior investment. But you must remember to account for the premiums included in the rate. The following increased rates are estimates that will vary with the type of property, economic situation, and tenant or user.

The real estate is difficult to sell, so add another 3 percent for illiquidity. The real estate requires more investment decisions, add two percent. Finally, there is much more risk that the real estate will deviate from the promised return. Add four percent more. The built-up rate is now 14 percent. Using these estimates, the real estate should offer at least a 14 percent rate of return on investment. If it doesn't, you might be better off with the savings account.

RETURN OF INVESTMENT

Hopefully, any investment will provide a stream of future income. A portion of this income represents the *return of* the investor's original invested cash. Any excess is a *return on investment*. The return of investment may appear in a lump sum at the end of the investment term. For example, if you deposit money in a savings account or buy a certificate of deposit, your money is refunded when you close the account. In other cases, the return may a part of the periodic income stream. If you were to borrow a self-amortizing mortgage loan, the principal is paid down with each payment. At maturity there is no lump sum payment.

The return from a real estate investment is less clear-cut. Whether periodic income includes return of investment depends on how much is realized at resale. Consider an investment of $100,000 that provides an annual cash flow of $15,000. If the property is sold later for $100,000, the resale proceeds provide all of the return *of* investment and all of the annual cash flow is return *on* investment. If the sale is made for less than $100,000, a portion of the annual cash flow is actually return *of* investment.

Guard against investments that offer illusory returns. Suppose someone offers you an investment that provides a 20 percent return each year for five years. If there is no resale amount, you will have just received your money back with absolutely no return on investment.

Likewise, if a property produces negative cash flow, all return of and on investment is pushed to resale. During times of rapid inflation, investors may purchase properties strictly for appreciation. The price paid is often so high that net operating income fails to cover debt service. In effect, the investor must invest new capital in the property each year. The hope is that resale proceeds will be sufficient to return the original investment, all annual cash flow deficits, and provide a return on investment. Be sure that the expected value enhancement is sufficient to cover the long wait to receive returns, with compound interest.

By contrast, if you receive periodic income, and then sell for a profit, the resale proceeds not only provide the return of capital but some return on investment as well.

The use of depreciation tax deductions affects the pattern of return. Depreciation allows you to receive some return on investment before resale through tax savings. If your property depreciates in value at the same rate as it is depreciated for tax purposes (resale price equals adjusted tax basis), all tax savings due to depreciation deductions is return of investment, not a return on investment.

In summary, consider the entire cycle of an investment, from purchase to resale, all of the investment returns and contributions, and their timing.

RISK

Risk is the chance that things will not turn out as planned. Since no one knows what will occur in the future, risk is an unavoidable fact of life. However, it is possible to anticipate or forecast the future and project a reasonable range of possible outcomes. This is what is meant by the term calculated risk. It does not imply that risk can be precisely measured, but that sources of risk can be identified. In this way, it is possible to rank investment opportunities according to their riskiness.

Why would an investor choose to take more risk? Greater risk ought to mean the chance of higher returns. Risk not only introduces the chance that the return will be lower than expected, but also that it will be higher. (For example, the potential reward from playing the lottery is much higher than the maximum yield from a savings account, but you typically lose your entire "investment" in the lottery, which you won't do in the savings account.) Since most people are averse to risk, high risk ventures must offer a high potential return to attract investors. Put another way, society often rewards those who are willing and able to take risks. Therefore, to get a high return, you must accept higher risk.

Most people are said to be risk-averse. This normally means that people prefer less risk to more risk. However, some investors are more sensitive to risk than others. Some are prone to worry about things going wrong and are probably better off with relatively risk-free investments. It should be recognized that no investment is truly risk-free. Real estate rises and falls in value. It is illiquid. Even investing in government-insured passbook accounts exposes the investor to the *purchasing power risk* that inflation will wipe out any real return.

Some investors have a greater *capacity* to undertake risk. This capacity depends on the consequences of the investment not working out as planned. If you need cash flow from the investment for the basic necessities of life, you have a low capacity for risk. Any reduction in income would be serious. Likewise, if the invested income is your entire wealth, risk capacity is low. You could weather a reduction in cash flow but would be harmed by loss of capital. An investor with *venture capital,* which is money that he or she is willing to place at risk, can take on more risk. Some investors have what they call "play money" that is not crucial to their financial support and which they can use for speculative ventures. It is important to determine how much risk you are prepared to take and choose investments accordingly.

There are different types of risk. Possibly the most familiar type is *business risk.* This is the chance that the investment will not perform as expected. It may turn out that more capital investment is needed to keep the property going. For example, a major component of the building may fail unexpectedly and need replacing. Or a storm may damage the building. Revenues may drop due to a rise in vacancies or the need to lower rental rates. Operating expenses may increase. Expected appreciation may not be realized when the property is sold. It is even possible that changes in tax laws may affect the return over time. Some of these risks can be reduced by using *hazard insurance.* Others may be minimized by diversifying investment among different locations and types of property.

A second type of risk is *financial risk.* This is the chance that you will be unable to make the debt service payments on the property and thus become insolvent. Financial risk is increased by the use of *leverage.* The more money borrowed to purchase the property, the higher the chance that a declining net operating income will fail to cover debt service. This is especially a problem if you are poorly capitalized or have most of your capital tied up in illiquid assets. This is why any investment is made more risky by using financial leverage. (Likewise, leverage increases the potential return). The use of short-term financing also exposes you to *interest rate risk.* This is the chance that interest rates will increase and adversely affect return. Such financing as balloon loans or adjustable rate mortgages present the possibility that debt service costs will increase if interest rates rise.

Tax Considerations

One of the traditional attractions of real estate investment is its ability to generate tax losses. These losses arise from certain deductions and credits that reduce taxable income but do not require cash outlays. In other words, a property may show a loss for tax purposes, yet produce positive *cash flow.* When this occurs, the loss is said to shelter income from taxation. Reduced taxes are a form of investment income.

Most of the expenses associated with rental property are deductible from taxable income. These include operating expenses and interest payments on the mortgage loan. Mortgage principal repayment is never deductible. (If the property is your personal residence, you may deduct property taxes and interest payments.)

While business expenses are deductible for rental property, they represent real cash outlays. Therefore, they do not provide tax shelter. Deductions for tax depreciation reduce taxable income but do not require cash outlays. Rather, they are a way of accounting for the gradual decline in value of man-made structures. You are allowed to deduct a portion of the property's original value each year to compensate for this decline in value. These deductions can shelter part or all of the income produced by the property. Except for high income investors, you may also shelter income up to $25,000 that is earned from sources outside the property by showing tax losses of the property.

While tax shelter has long been an advantage of real estate investment, it is very limited in today's tax environment. For properties placed in service after 1986, depreciation deductions are based on a life of 27.5 years for residential properties and 39 years for nonresidential properties. The amount of annual deduction is approximately 1/27.5, or 1/39, of the purchase price of buildings. Land is not depreciable. In most cases, depreciation deductions under this schedule are too small to provide shelter. Any tax losses produced may be applied only against *passive income.* Basically, passive income is produced by rental properties. This prevents many real estate losses from offsetting income from wages, salaries, or other types of investments, such as dividends or interest earnings. If you *actively participate* in the management of the property, up to $25,000 of nonpassive income may be offset by passive losses. This begins to be phased out as adjusted gross income (AGI) rises above $100,000, and it is eliminated at $150,000 of AGI. "Active participation" refers to investors who own property directly and make most of the investment decisions.

Even under these restrictions, depreciation does reduce taxes on the income from the property. In addition, it may be possible to put together a tax strategy whereby investments with tax losses are matched with properties with passive income. The result could be a source of tax-free income.

An example serves to show how tax shelter is calculated:

ASSETS

Purchase cost of entire property	$1,150,000
Land purchase cost	150,000
(land cannot be depreciated)	
Building cost	$1,000,000

Divide building cost by depreciable life, in this case 27.5 years, to derive annual depreciation. (or multiply by the IRS factor which is .0364 per year)	$36,363

OPERATING STATEMENT

Rental collections	$ 150,000
Less operating expenses	$ 50,000
Less interest paid	85,000
Less depreciation	36,363
Taxable income from property	$ −21,363

Because the income is negative, the property provides over $21,000 of tax shelter to be applied against income from other passive investments. Any unused losses may be carried forward to future tax years.

As a special incentive, the tax code sometimes provides tax credits for certain types of investment expenses. In the past, credits have been given for purchasing capital equipment (such as elevators), rehabilitating historically significant structures, and for taking energy conservation measures. Credits are applied directly against taxes owed rather than as deductions against income. Credits may be available for investors who build, renovate or purchase housing for low-income tenants.

Depreciation Tax Deductions

A key to real estate investments is depreciation claimed for federal income tax purposes. The Internal Revenue Service allows an owner of business or investment property to claim depreciation as a business expense, even when the property increases in value. Land is not considered to wear out so depreciation cannot be claimed on it. Appliances, carpets, and furniture can be depreciated over a relatively short life, and buildings over a longer period. The exact life to be used has changed frequently. Almost every time the tax law has changed in recent years, the depreciable life has been changed. Usually tax changes affect new owners, whereas present owners continue the depreciable life they started with.

Depreciation allows a tax deduction without the owner paying for it in cash. This gives the owner the best possible benefit—a tax deduction that doesn't reduce cash flow. For example, suppose an investor buys a small building for $100,000 and is allowed a 27.5-year depreciable life using the straight-line method of depreciation. The owner may claim a tax deduction of $3640 annually (the first year can be less depending on the month the property was acquired). This deduction reduces the owner's taxable income which will in turn save income taxes. The deduction was created merely by a bookkeeping entry and can be claimed even though the property rises in value. Thus the owner gains by reducing taxes on property that provides cash flow from rents and would otherwise generate taxable income.

However, the taxpayer must be prepared to return the benefits received from depreciation when the property is sold. There is a concept called *basis*—the point from which gain or loss is measured. In general, basis begins as the price paid for the property. As you claim depreciation as a tax deduction, you reduce the basis. This increases the gain when property is sold. If the investment remains the same in value, or rises, all of the depreciation becomes taxable as a gain when sold. In this way, depreciation that was claimed while owning the property generates taxable gain on a sale, unless the property actually loses value more quickly than the investor depreciates it on his/her tax return.

Tax depreciation should not be confused with an actual reduction or loss in value. Tax depreciation does not measure the actual loss in value of property sustained in a year. It is an arbitrary deduction allowed by tax law.

To summarize, depreciation claimed for tax purposes allows the investor to save on taxes, perhaps having to pay them back later. It is not a measure of a property's loss in value.

Tax-Free Exchanges

In most real estate investment programs, there comes a time when you need to change properties. Your property may have grown in value and now it is time to move up to a larger property. You may want to get into a different type of property, such as moving from rental housing to an office building. If you move, you may want to keep your investments close at hand. You may have several small properties and want to consolidate into one large property.

Many have found that the best way to change properties is thorough exchanging. They merely trade properties with another investor. This may be simpler than selling the property and reinvesting in a new one. It means you need only one transaction instead of two (or more). Financing is often exchanged along with the property, so you don't necessarily need to get a new loan. There is no need to get out of the market and then get back in, taking the chance that the market changes during that time.

Another big advantage of exchanging is that you may save taxes. If your property has appreciated, you will owe taxes on capital gains when you sell. An exchange can let you defer paying those taxes until some time in the future when you sell the new property. To do this, you must trade for other investment real estate (the property traded or received can't be your home). If you end up with some cash from the exchange, you may have to pay some taxes. In most cases, you will need to trade up in the exchange. If you end up with a smaller debt, you may have to pay some taxes. However, in cases where you pay some taxes, they may be less than if you sold your property for cash.

The rules of a tax-free exchange are described in Section 1031 of the Internal Revenue Code. They now allow a sale to qualify as a tax-free exchange, provided that, within 45 days, replacement property is identified, and is purchased within 180 days. Be sure to enlist professional tax advice when considering a trade.

Questions on Chapter 17

1. Investment real estate may offer
    (A) cash flow
    (B) appreciation in value
    (C) income tax shelter
    (D) all of the above

2. REIT is a
    (A) Really Energized Income Tax
    (B) Real Estate Investment Trust
    (C) Real Estate Income Target
    (D) None of the above

3. A REIT is like
   (A) tenancy in common
   (B) a joint tenancy
   (C) community property
   (D) a mutual fund

4. Refinancing is
   (A) arranging a new loan to replace an existing loan
   (B) a wraparound mortgage
   (C) done to postpone income taxes
   (D) reduces operating expenses

5. Depreciation claimed for income tax purposes
   (A) reduces cash flow
   (B) reduces taxable income
   (C) increases potential gross income
   (D) increases operating expenses

6. A list of tenants, their space identified, and rent amounts, is called
   (A) an operating statement
   (B) a tenant list
   (C) a rent roll
   (D) an operating role

7. One of the important drawbacks to direct real estate investing is
   (A) illiquidity
   (B) location
   (C) small size
   (D) disclosure requirements

8. Instead of selling property and paying a tax on the gain, one may prefer
   (A) a capital gain
   (B) Section 1231
   (C) a tax-free exchange
   (D) ordinary income

9. A projection of what is expected to occur from operating a property is a _____ statement.
   (A) conforming
   (B) nonconforming
   (C) consistent
   (D) pro forma

10. Neighborhood, community, regional, are descriptive of
    (A) apartments
    (B) office buildings
    (C) warehouses
    (D) shopping centers

ANSWERS

1. **D**	6. **C**
2. **B**	7. **A**
3. **D**	8. **C**
4. **A**	9. **D**
5. **B**	10. **D**

Chapter 18/*Real Estate Arithmetic and Problem Solving*

Real Estate Arithmetic Is Familiar

Many applicants for real estate license examinations worry about the part of the examination that features "mathematics." Actually, the science of mathematics encompasses such things as algebra, calculus, and a variety of exotic fields of study, NONE of which appears on real estate license examinations. It would be better, and less frightening, to refer to the real estate "mathematics" as real estate *arithmetic*, because that is actually what it is.

You have been through all the necessary arithmetic before! Every state requires applicants for real estate licenses to have a high school education or the equivalent. The "mathematics" you will encounter on the licensing examination is the kind of arithmetic taught in the sixth and seventh grades, so you should have been exposed to it at least that one time if you are eligible to take the licensing examination in your state. Of course, the arithmetic problems in elementary and junior high school probably didn't deal with real estate situations, but the arithmetic used (the manipulation of numbers) is similar to that required on the licensing examination.

To pass the licensing examination, you should know:

> *Basic manipulations:*
> addition
> subtraction
> multiplication
> division
> *How to work with:*
> fractions
> decimals
> percentages
> *How to figure areas of simple figures:*
> quadrilaterals (four-sided figures, including squares and rectangles)
> triangles
> circles

Every day you may work with many of the necessary arithmetic concepts, even though you may not realize it:

- You work with *decimals* whenever you deal with money. Decimals show numbers in tenths, hundredths, thousandths, and so on. The sum $17.62 is seventeen dollars and sixty-two cents. It is also 17.62 dollars, or seventeen and sixty-two one-hundredths dollars. You add and subtract decimals whenever you check a restaurant bill, balance your checkbook, or count a pocket full of loose change. You multiply with decimals when you figure the cost of four paperback books, each costing $4.99. You divide with decimals when the store is selling mousetraps at three for $1.99 and you want to buy only one.
- You work with *percentages* when you try to figure out sales taxes on purchases you make, when you figure out your income tax, and when you try to determine what an item will cost if the store sign says that everything is 40 percent off the price marked. If you work on a commission basis, you almost certainly work with percentages, since commission payments (including those in the real estate business) are nearly always expressed as percentages of

sales. Finally, if you ever try to compute the interest on a loan, once again you will be manipulating percentages.

- You work with *fractions* when you follow a recipe that calls for 1⅓ cups of this and 2½ teaspoons of that, and you want to make three times as much because you're having a lot of people over for a party. Often when you're dealing with percentages and decimals, you are also dealing with fractions, because fractions, decimals, and percents are just three different ways of saying basically the same thing. Don't forget that in your pocket you may have a *half*-dollar or a *quarter*.
- You may even work with *areas* more than you think. Wrapping paper, paper towels, tissue paper, and the like all are measured in square feet or square inches. Wallpaper, carpeting, and the size of your house are all measured in terms of area, as is any land you may own.

A review of basic arithmetic isn't a function of this book; we assume that you can handle the arithmetic concepts described above. If you feel, however, that your arithmetic skills are *really* rusty, go to your local bookstore and buy Barron's *Arithmetic Made Easy*. It will give you all the help you'll need. You should find it in or near that same section where this book is sold (usually called "Study Aids," or something similar).

Calculators

What really helps with the arithmetic on the examination is that you *will be allowed to take a calculator in with you*. There may be some restrictions on the kind of calculator: usually, they don't allow "programmable" ones (so you can't "set up" problems in advance) or the kind that beep or make other disturbing noises.

You certainly don't need a fancy one. All you'll be doing is adding, subtracting, multiplying, and dividing. The cheapest calculators (in the blister packs at the checkout stand) perform these functions, of course, and most of them have some sort of memory, figure percents, and maybe even handle square roots. So big bucks are not going to be a problem. However, there are two things you should avoid.

Don't get a solar calculator. These don't have batteries; they use energy from a nearby light source such as a lamp. What happens if you take the exam in a big room and the nearest light is a fluorescent fixture 20 feet above your head? Get a calculator that runs on batteries, and make sure the batteries are *fresh*.

Also, don't buy one of those credit-card-sized things. You don't want to waste your time trying to find and hit tiny keys, and squinting to make out a small, dim display. Get a standard sized calculator, with a large, clear, easy-to-read display.

Once you have your calculator, work with it and get used to it. Read the instruction book. Learn how the memory works and how the percent (%) key is used.

Measurements

Make sure that you know certain measurements, because you can be certain that the exam questions will assume a familiarity with them.

Linear measures:
12 inches	=	1 foot
3 feet	=	1 yard
5280 feet	=	1 mile

Area measures:
144 square inches	=	1 square foot
9 square feet	=	1 square yard
640 acres	=	1 square mile

and here is one that *you absolutely must remember:*

1 acre = 43,560 square feet

Burn this into your memory! You can bet the farm (and all of its acreage) that you'll be asked questions that *require* you to know the number of square feet in an acre.

Word Problems

The mathematics problems you will encounter on the licensing examination are most likely to be in the form of *word problems*; that is, problems that describe a situation for which you have to find a mathematical answer. Here is an example of a simple word problem:

> *I have three apples. John has four apples. How many apples do John and I have together?*

Here is an example of a very complicated word problem[*]:

> *Ms. Jones owns a building that is rectangular in shape: 40 ft. × 66 ft. 3 in. She wishes to construct a sidewalk around the perimeter of the building. The sidewalk will be made of concrete and crushed stone. It will be 4 ft. wide and will be poured to a depth of 3½ in. The composition will be 85 percent concrete and 15 percent crushed stone. Concrete costs $313.00 per cubic yard. Crushed stone is $27.83 per ton; 1 cu. yd. of crushed stone weighs 3282 lb. 15 oz. Labor required to construct the sidewalk is $19 per hour; in 1 hour a laborer can finish 188 sq. ft. of sidewalk. The laborer must be paid for at least 4 hours every time he works, even if it takes him less time to finish the job. How much will the sidewalk cost?*

In spite of the complicated appearance of the second problem, the process for solving it is basically the same as the process for solving the first:

1. *Read* the question.
2. Determine *what* is being asked for.
3. Determine *how* to arrive at the answer.
4. *Calculate* the answer.
5. *Check* the answer.

The last step is particularly important, especially when the problem is a complicated one; you have to make sure that you did all the calculations correctly, or your answer will be wrong. On most examinations, knowing *how* to do a problem will get you no credit; you must provide the *correct answer* as evidence that you know how to do that particular problem. You should be aware of one more fact: on mathematics questions offered in a multiple-choice format you have both an advantage and a possible disadvantage.

The advantage, which is always present, is that *you are given the correct answer to the problem*! Obviously, it *must* be among the ones you are to choose from; all you have to do is to figure out *which* one it is.

A possible disadvantage is that some of the *incorrect* answers may be answers you would arrive at by making common mistakes. You may be lulled into choosing the incorrect answer by assuming that, since your calculations gave you an answer that appears among the ones you must choose from, it *must* be correct. You should especially be on your guard if one of the choices given is something like "none of the above" or "none of the other answers is correct." This kind of choice *may* mean that none of the answers is correct, but it may also be included as a red herring.

Mistakes on mathematics problems may result from:

1. Incorrect reading of the problem. *Solution*: Read carefully!
2. Misunderstanding what is being asked for. *Solution*: Read carefully and slowly; you have plenty of time, so don't rush!
3. Not knowing how to do the problem correctly. *Solution*: Study this chapter carefully, so that you know how to approach all kinds of problems.

---

[*]This question is answered on pages 270–271 and 294–295.

4. Incorrect calculation of the answer. *Solution*: Study the methods of calculation for all kinds of real estate problems, as outlined in this chapter.

5. Mistakes in arithmetic. *Solution*: Check your work to make sure that you did your arithmetic correctly.

Note that these five common sources of errors can be controlled by applying the five steps in problem solving offered at the beginning of this chapter.

In discussing the various kinds of real estate mathematics problems, we are going to assume in this chapter that you have an adequate knowledge of basic arithmetic. Have your calculator ready before you tackle the sample problems; use this opportunity to become familiar with the calculator, if you aren't already. You must get used to doing these kinds of problems with a calculator because you'll be using one for the exam.

Special Terms You Should Know

You must know the following special *terms* used in real estate measurement; these are illustrated in Figure 18-1.

Depth refers to the straight-line distance from the front-lot line to the rear-lot line. If these lot lines aren't parallel, the term *depth* will refer to the *longest* straight-line distance between them. The lot shown in Figure 18-1 has a depth of 272 feet.

Frontage is the *lineal distance* (see *lineal foot* below) of the lot line that is also a part of a public street or other right-of-way. Frontage of corner lots usually is expressed as separate figures for the distance fronting on each of the streets the lot bounds. This would also apply to very deep lots that border streets at both ends, and so on. The frontage of the lot in Figure 18-1 is 133 feet.

Front foot refers to the distance that a lot borders on a street. For the lot illustrated in Figure 18-1, we can say that it has *133 feet of frontage* or that it has *133 front feet*. (To say that the lot has 133 front feet of frontage is redundant.)

Lineal foot refers to the distance between two particular spots. Note that lineal feet need not be a *straight* measure; rather, the term refers to the number of feet traveled while following a *particular path connecting the particular points involved*. In real estate, this term is used normally to describe irregular lot sides (such as the east side of the lot in Figure 18-1, which is 363 lineal feet on a lot that has only 272 feet of depth), irregular paths along roads, and so on.

Right-of-way (R.O.W.) refers to the area owned by the government within which a road is

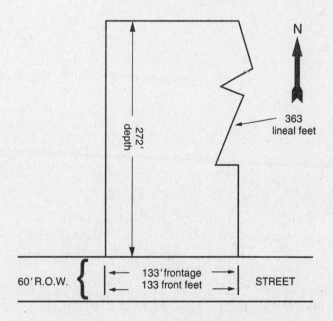

Figure 18-1. Real Estate Measurement

located. On maps, plats, and so on, the term R.O.W. usually refers to the width of the right-of-way area (which usually exceeds *pavement* width).

You are also assumed to be familiar with the basic methods of calculating distance, area, and volume; here we will confine ourselves to particular kinds of real estate problems that you will encounter. Most of them can be characterized as specific *forms* of problems that are easy to recognize.

Before showing how to deal with them, however, we should pass on one very crucial hint for solving these kinds of problems:

Draw a picture of the problem, if you possibly can. Then, with the picture as your guide, go through the problem step by step.

We cannot stress this process too much. By drawing a picture of the problem, you can *look* at it. A picture really is valuable, especially if it helps you to visualize a problem. (Sometimes, of course, the problem on the exam will include a picture or diagram. But if it doesn't, supply your own!) Then when you do the problem, work it very carefully, step by step. Even if you feel you can take some shortcuts, or do part of it in your head, DON'T! Solving problems this way may be boring or tedious, but it helps to eliminate mistakes.

SIDEWALK QUESTIONS

The complicated problem presented in Chapter 17 is a "sidewalk question." You are asked to compute the cost of constructing a strip of something that *surrounds* another area. Figure 18-2A also illustrates a sidewalk problem, using some of the information from the first question. Here the problem is (in part) to find the area of the surface of the sidewalk; this is the shaded area in Figure 18-2A.

Probably the most common mistake made in such problems is to treat the *corners* improperly in one of two ways:

(a) By forgetting the corners entirely: if you calculate the sidewalk as 66 ft. 3 in. + 40 ft. + 66 ft. 3 in. + 40 ft. = 212 ft. 6 in. in length, and 4 ft. wide, you get all *but* the shaded areas in Figure 18-2B.

(b) By counting the corners *twice*: here the calculation measures the sidewalk along the outside, getting an area of 74 ft. 3 in. + 48 ft. + 74 ft. 3 in. + 48 ft. = 244 ft. 6 in. Thus, each of the shaded areas in Figure 18-2B is counted *twice*.

The correct way is first to *draw* your picture. Start out with a diagram like Figure 18-2A, except that you don't have to shade anything in. Then divide the sidewalk area into easily measured sections, making sure you don't leave anything out. The best way is to divide the picture into a set of rectangles; one way of doing that is shown in Figure 18-2C. Here we have two rectangles that are 74 ft. 3 in. × 4 ft., and two that are 40 ft. × 4 ft. To solve the problem of finding the area of the sidewalk, we proceed as follows:

$$\text{Area} = [(74.25 \text{ ft.} \times 4 \text{ ft.}) + (40 \text{ ft.} \times 4 \text{ ft.})] \times 2$$
$$= (297 + 160) \times 2$$
$$= 914 \text{ sq. ft.}$$

Of course there are other ways of dividing the sidewalk into easily computed rectangular areas. Once you have finished such a problem, you should choose a different way of dividing up the sidewalk and then use that way as a *check* on your answer.

Note that sidewalk problems don't always involve sidewalks. You would use the same technique to find the area of a yard surrounding a house, the area of a field surrounding a lake, the area of a parking lot surrounding a building, and so on.

Sometimes it may be easier to use a second method of solving sidewalk problems, especially when there is a fairly small area inside a fairly large one. Here you simply figure the area of the small space and *subtract* it from the area of the large one. For the problem we just did, the large area is the area covered by the building *and* the sidewalk. The small area inside it is the area of the building alone. Obviously, if you subtract the area of the *building* from the area of the *building and the sidewalk*, what is left is the area of the *sidewalk* alone.

Again let's use the problem diagramed in Figure 18-2. The outside area is 74.25 ft. × 48 ft. = 3564 sq. ft.; the inside area is 66.25 ft. × 40 ft. = 2650 sq. ft. Subtracting the area of the

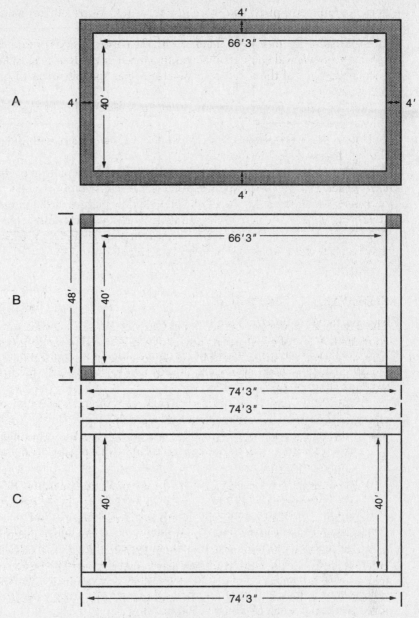

Figure 18-2. Sidewalks

building from the area of the building and the sidewalk, we get 3564 − 2650 = 914 sq. ft., the same answer we got previously.

If you wish, you can use both methods when you solve a sidewalk problem, using one as a check against the other. (The rest of the problem is answered on pages 294–295.)

ROAD PROBLEMS

Road problems are a lot like sidewalk problems in that the most common mistake is to forget the corners. All or part of a road problem involves finding the area of a road that usually has one or more corners or bends to it. The example shown in Figure 18-3A is a *two-step* problem in that some initial calculations are needed before we can get to the calculations that produce the final result.

> *The lot shown in Figure 18-3A is exactly square and is ¼ sq. mi. in area. The road passing through it has a right-of-way 150 ft. wide. All corners are right angles. What is the road's area?*

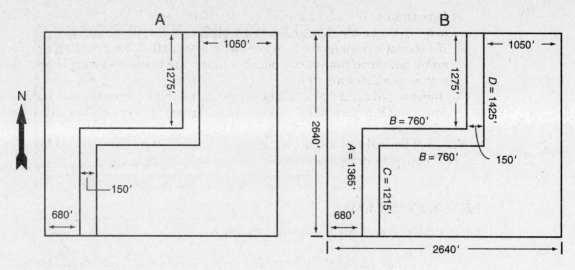

Figure 18-3. Roads

Step one is to find the remaining measurements of the road so that we can calculate its area. The way to do this is to find the measurements of the lot. We have a major clue: it is square, so all its sides are the same length. Since it contains ¼ sq. mi., it must be ½ mi. on a side: ½ × ½ = ¼. We know that ½ mi. = 2640 ft.; therefore the lot is 2640 ft. on a side. Now we can get the measurements we need, which are all shown in Figure 18-3B, as follows:

(A) 2640 ft. − 1275 ft. = 1365 ft.

(B) 2640 ft. − (680 ft. + 150 ft. + 1050 ft.) = 760 ft. Here we have to remember the width of the road when we make our calculations! It is 680 ft. from the west side of the lot to the right-of-way of the road; the road is 150 ft. wide. At the top of the lot, it is 1050 ft. from *the other side of the road* to the east side of the lot. Between its turns, therefore, the road actually traverses only 760 ft.

(C) is the side of the road opposite (A); it should be 150 ft. *shorter* than (A) because of the turn in the road: 1365 ft. − 150 ft. = 1215 ft.

(D) is the side of the road opposite the one side for which the measurement was given; because of the turn in the road, it should be 150 ft. longer: 1275 ft. + 150 ft. = 1425 ft.

Given all this information, we now can proceed to step two, using the same method as in the sidewalk questions: Divide the area of the road into easily calculated rectangles, making sure no part of the road is left out. Then calculate the area of each rectangle and add the areas.

The dotted lines in Figure 18-3B show one suggested way of dividing the road; there are three rectangles, each of which is 150 ft. wide. The three are 760 ft., 1215 ft., and 1425 ft. in length. The total area of the road, then, is as follows:

$$150 \text{ ft.} \times 760 \text{ ft.} = 114,000 \text{ sq. ft.}$$
$$150 \text{ ft.} \times 1215 \text{ ft.} = 182,250 \text{ sq. ft.}$$
$$150 \text{ ft.} \times 1425 \text{ ft.} = 213,750 \text{ sq. ft.}$$
$$114,000 \text{ sq. ft.} + 182,250 \text{ sq. ft.} + 213,750 \text{ sq. ft.} = 510,000 \text{ sq. ft.}$$
$$510,000 \text{ sq. ft.} \div 43,560 \text{ sq. ft.} = 11.708 \text{ acres, the area of the road.}$$

To check such a problem, divide the road into different rectangles and do the problem again.

You should be aware of a special way in which such a problem can be stated: the lot within which the road appears can be described, using a *legal description*. This is particularly tempting for examination officials in states that use the government rectangular survey description of land, since descriptions can be given very briefly and usually will involve fairly regular shaped lots. Other times, you may be given an entire plat of a subdivision, with lot dimensions and directions all spelled out. As part of the analysis of such a plat, you may get a road problem.

An outgrowth of road problems are *path* problems. Here you are asked the *straight-line* distance from one specified point to another. These problems usually appear in connection with plats or government rectangular survey descriptions. Some sample questions that need not be answered here are:

(1) How far would a rabbit have to hop from the center of NW¼, NW¼, Sec. 22, T3N, R4W to get to the eastern boundary of T3N, R5W?

(2) If I start at a point on the base line and travel exactly 155.6 miles in a straight line *due north*, how many townships (checks, sections) will I cross over completely? Identify the *section* in which I will stop.

(3) (Referring to a plat that would be supplied) How far is it from the northeast corner of A Street and B Avenue to Lake Mudhole, if you travel in a straight line to the *nearest* part of the lake?

For all of these the procedure is the same: *Draw a picture*. Once you do that, the answer can be found quite straightforwardly.

FENCE PROBLEMS

Fence problems are usually stated as follows:

> *Jones has a lot 50 ft. by 90 ft. He wants to build a fence 4-ft.-high all the way around the lot. Fence posts have to be put in every 10 ft. Special posts are used at the corners. There will be one gate assembly; the gate is 10 ft. wide, between two regular posts. Fence posts cost $10 each. Corner posts cost $22 each. The gate costs $125. Fence fabric costs 27¢ per square foot. The gate requires no fabric. How much will the materials for the fence cost?*

A similar type of problem requires you to find the area of (or the cost of the materials for) the sides of a house or other structure. A variation of the problem has a fence that does not go all the way around the property.

Once again, the way to proceed is to *draw a picture* first because you have to know how many fence posts and corner posts and how much material to buy. The question tells you that there will be only one gate.

Figure 18-4 shows you one way of drawing the picture. Of course, during the examination you don't have to be as neat so long as what you draw makes sense to you. Here is how to get the answer to the problem above:

(a) We need one gate, because that's what we're told.

(b) We need four corner posts, because the lot is rectangular.

(c) We need 24 fence posts. We can calculate this simply by counting the fence posts in our drawing. A shortcut method would be to count the posts on one side and the bottom and multiply by 2, since the other side and the top will require the same number. Notice something important: each side uses only 8 fence posts, even though the side is 90 ft. long and a post is used every 10 ft. This occurs because there is a corner post at each end of the side, so fence posts are only needed *between* them.

(d) We will need 1080 sq. ft. of fence fabric. This is found as follows: each side is 90 ft. long, the top is 50 ft., and the bottom is only 40 ft., because 10 ft. is taken up by the *gate*. These add up to 270 lineal ft. of fence. The fence is 4 ft. high, so the area of the fence is 4 ft. × 270 ft. = 1080 sq. ft.

A slightly different way is to figure the full perimeter of the lot as 280 ft., and then subtract 10 ft. for the gate, to get the 270 lineal ft. of fence.

Now we can calculate the cost of the fence:

1 gate @ $125	$125.00
4 corner posts @ $22	88.00
24 fence posts @ $10	240.00
1080 sq. ft. of fence fabric @ 27¢	291.60
TOTAL	$744. 60

Remember: the key to solving this kind of measurement problem is to draw a picture of the problem and to reason from there. Note that this example was fairly comprehensive, in that you had to calculate the total cost of the materials used to build the fence. Some problems may

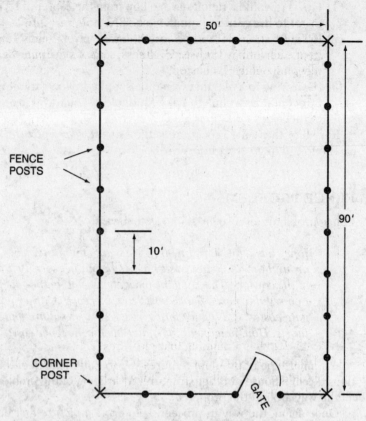

Figure 18-4. Fences

be fairly simple, asking only how much fence fabric is necessary or how much the fence fabric alone would cost.

A variation of the fence problem is a question asking how much paint would be needed to paint the outside of a house. Here you must be careful to note any mention of windows and glass in doors, since these spaces would *not* be painted. (The problem we just did had a similar situation with the gate.) This sort of question might ask how much paint would be needed, after telling how many square feet of surface a given amount of paint would cover. Instead, it might state the price of a given amount of paint and then ask the cost of the paint needed to do the job.

Problem Set A

The following problems deal with lengths, areas, and measures. The answers, along with the methods of solution, are given at the end of the chapter. Use the space below each question to work it out.

1. Brown's home measures 55 ft. long and 30 ft. wide. The outside walls are 8½ ft. high. Brown is going to paint these walls and wants to know how much the paint will cost him. There are two doors, each 3 ft. × 7½ ft., one picture window 12 ft. × 5 ft., and 6 windows 2½ ft. × 4 ft. The doors and windows will not be painted. Each gallon can of paint will cover 320 sq. ft. and will cost $9.98.

2. Ms. Orsini wishes to subdivide her 76-acre tract into building lots. She will have to use 665,000 sq. ft. of land for streets, roads, parks, and so on. If the zoning code requires that each lot have at least 7500 sq. ft., what is the *maximum* number of lots that she can develop out of this land?

3. Steinfeld has a building that measures 65 ft. long × 35 ft. deep. One of the 65-ft. sides fronts directly on the sidewalk; he wants to build a sidewalk 8 ft. wide to surround the building on the other three sides. If the sidewalk costs $1.15 per square foot to build, what will be the total cost?

4. Johnson's lot is rectangular and contains 313 sq. yds. If the frontage is 41 ft., how deep is the lot?

5. A triangular plot of land is 500 ft. wide at the base and 650 ft. deep to the point of the triangle. What is the value of this lot, at $600 per acre?

6. Huang purchased the NW¼ of the SE¼ of a section of land. A road 66 ft. wide goes due north-south through the parcel, splitting it into two pieces. Huang did *not* acquire title to the road. How much land did he get?

Percent Problems

A great many real estate problems involve percents; these include commissions, interest, mortgage payments, loan discounts (points), depreciation, profit and loss, and return on investment. We will discuss each of these, but it should be remembered that the mathematics involved is the same for all of them: you will be looking for one of three things—a base, a rate, or a result.

Every percent problem can be stated as one of three variations of the following statement:

$$A \text{ is } B \text{ percent of } C.$$

Numerical examples of such a statement are "14 is 50 percent of 28" and "63 is 90 percent of 70." Of course, if you know all three numbers, you don't have a problem.

All percent problems are like the statement above, except that one of the numbers is missing: the problem is to find that missing number.

Type 1: *A is B percent of ?*   (*C is missing.*)
Type 2: *A is ? percent of C*   (*B is missing.*)
Type 3: *? is B percent of C*   (*A is missing.*)

The solutions to these problems are as follows:

$$A = B \times C$$
$$B = A \div C$$
$$C = A \div B$$

An easy way to remember these is that *A* is *B* multiplied by *C*. To find either *B* or *C*, you divide *A* by the other. Here are some examples illustrating the three variations of the percent problem:

1. What is 88.5 percent of 326?   (*? is B percent of C.*)
2. 16 is what percent of 440?   (*A is ? percent of C.*)
3. 43 is 86 percent of what?   (*A is B percent of ?.*)

The solutions are as follows:

1. The missing item is *A*. $A = B \times C$. $A = 0.885 \times 326$. $A = 288.51$.
2. The missing item is *B*. $B = A \div C$. $B = 16 \div 440$. $B = 0.0363636 = 3.63\%$
3. The missing item is *C*. $C = A \div B$. $C = 43 \div 0.86$. $C = 50$.

COMMISSION PROBLEMS

Commission problems naturally are very popular on real estate examinations because most licensees are paid in commissions. A real estate commission is simply what the employer pays the agent for performing his function. Most often, the commission is a portion of the sale price received by a seller because of the efforts of the agent to secure a buyer. Typical commission rates vary from as low as 1 percent or less to over 10 percent, depending on the kind of property, the prevailing custom in the area, and the success of the agent, or the employer, in negotiating the listing contract.

The simplest commission problems are like this one:

> *Jones sells Smith's house for $327,000. Jones's commission is 6 percent of the sale price. What is her commission, in dollars?*

Here the solution is to find 6 percent of $327,000; $0.06 \times \$327,000 = \$19,620$.

This *same* problem, which is the type 1 described above, can also be stated as a type 2 or type 3 problem:

> Type 2:   *Jones sells Smith's house for $327,000 and receives a commission of $19,620. What is her commission rate?*
>
> Type 3:   *Jones sells Smith's house and receives a commission of $19,620, which is 6 percent of the sale price. What was the sale price?*

These problems are simple. To make them more "interesting," they are often expanded in one of two ways. The first way is to make them more complicated, and there are two methods of doing that. The second way is to develop the question *backwards*; this often traps many unwary examinees, but if you pay attention it won't fool you.

First, let's look at the more elaborate kinds of commission problems. The two methods used are (a) to have you calculate the salesperson's share of a total commission and (b) to make the means of determining the commission more complicated.

Here (a) is illustrated:

> *O'Reilly sells Marino's house for $197,000. The commission is 6½ percent of the sale price. O'Reilly's broker receives 45 percent of this amount from the listing broker as the selling broker's share. O'Reilly himself is entitled to 60 percent of all commissions that he is responsible for bringing in. How much does O'Reilly get?*

This may look complicated, but it is just three consecutive simple percent problems.

(1) How much was the total commission? *A* is 6½ percent of $197,000.00; $A = \$12,805$.

(2) O'Reilly's broker received 45 percent of this amount. *A* is 45 percent of $12,805 = $5,762.25.

(3) O'Reilly gets 60 percent of that amount. *A* is 60 percent of $5,762.25 = $3,457.35.

This is the second kind (b):

> *Albertson sold Harding's house for $115,000. The commission rate is 7 percent of the first $50,000 of the sale price, 4 percent of the next $50,000, and 1.5 percent of everything over that. What was Albertson's total commission?*

Once again, we have several simple percentages to calculate: 7 percent of the first $50,000 is $3500; 4 percent of the next $50,000 is $2000; adding $2000 to $3500 yields a commission of $5500 on the first $100,000 (or $50,000 + $50,000). This leaves a balance of $15,000, to which we apply the commission rate of 1½ percent to get another $225, for a total commission of $5725.

This question could have been complicated further by going an additional step and asking, "What was the effective commission rate on the sale?" Here the question is, "What percent of the sale price is the actual commission?" First we say, $5725 is ? percent of $115,000. Then we take the additional step: $B = 5725 \div 115,000 = 0.0498$, so the percentage = 4.98 percent.

Now let's turn to the other general category of complicated commission problems—those in which the question is developed *backwards*. Here the question is phrased like this:

> *Baker sold her house; after paying a 7 percent commission she had $371,535 left. What was the sale price of the house?*

Many people will find 7 percent of $371,535, add it on, and GET THE WRONG ANSWER!! Their mistake is that the commission should be figured on the *sale price*, and they are figuring it on what the seller had left *after* the commission was paid. The way to solve these problems is simple: If Baker paid a 7 percent commission, then *what she had left* was 93 percent (or 100 percent − 7 percent) of the sale price. Now the problem becomes a familiar variation: $371,535 is 93 percent of ? $C = 371,535 \div 0.93 = $399,500.

As you can see, this question is "backwards" in that you don't actually have to figure the dollar amount of the commission. On your examination be sure to look out for these kinds of problems; the best way to spot them is to follow the rule of *reading* the question and *then* trying to determine what you are asked to do.

You should be aware of the terminology used in commission figuring. The *commission* is the dollar amount arrived at by applying the *commission rate* to the *sale price*. If you are asked for the "commission," you are being asked to tell *how many dollars and cents* the commission payment was. If you are asked for the "commission rate" or the "rate," you are being asked to provide the *percent rate* of the commission.

INTEREST PROBLEMS

Interest is money paid to "rent" money from others. It is typically expressed as an annual percentage rate; that is, for each year that the money is borrowed, a certain percentage of the loan amount is charged as interest. Interest will most often be stated in annual percentage terms even for loans that have a duration of much less than 1 year. As an example, the "interest rate" on charge accounts, credit card accounts, and the like may be charged monthly, and the bill may be due within a month, but the interest rate still is expressed as an annual rate. This practice is becoming even more prevalent as a result of federal truth-in-lending laws, which *require* that the annual percentage rate (APR) be stated.

Usually, for short-term arrangements a monthly or quarterly rate will also be specified. If you are given only an annual rate and are required to calculate based on a monthly or quarterly rate, simply divide the annual rate by 12 to get the monthly rate, and by 4 to get the quarterly rate. If a problem gives a monthly or quarterly rate, multiply a monthly rate by 12 or a quarterly rate by 4 to get the annual rate. For example:

> *A rate of 12 percent annually is 1 percent monthly and 3 percent quarterly.*
> *A rate of 9½ percent annually is 2.375 percent quarterly or 0.791666 . . . percent monthly.*

A rate of 0.6 percent monthly is 1.8 percent quarterly or 7.2 percent annually.

Interest is calculated in two ways, *simple* and *compound*.

Simple interest is calculated quite straightforwardly. To determine the interest charge for any period of time, we calculate the proportional interest, based on the annual rate. If the annual rate is 12 percent, interest for 2 years is 24 percent, interest for 6 months is 6 percent, and so on.

When *compound interest* is used, interest is charged on unpaid interest, as well as on the unpaid debt. This adds a complicating element to the calculation, since some sort of adjustment may be necessary to allow for the fact that interest is not being paid periodically, but is being allowed to accumulate over all or part of the term of the debt. Since in real life most debts are paid in monthly installments, one does not frequently encounter interest compounding in the payment of debts. One *does* encounter it in savings accounts, where a well-advertised feature is that, if a depositor does not withdraw the interest his principal earns, it is added to his balance and begins to earn interest too.

Before compound interest can be calculated, the compounding frequency must be given. This is expressed in units of time. Compounding can be daily, quarterly, semiannually, annually—indeed it can be over any period of time, even "continuously." Given a compounding term, interest is figured by first deriving an interest rate for the term involved. Then interest is calculated for *each* term, taking into account the fact that some or all of the interest earned so far may not have been paid out. Here is an example:

> *Berger borrows $1000 at 8 percent annual interest. The interest is compounded quarterly. How much interest will Berger owe after 9 months?*

First we must change the annual rate to a quarterly rate: $8 \div 4 = 2$, so the quarterly interest rate is 2 percent. For the first quarter, interest is 2 percent of $1000, or $20.

To calculate interest for the second quarter, we add the first quarter's interest to the balance to get $1020, upon which interest for the second quarter is due. Therefore, the second quarter's interest is 2 percent of $1020.00, or $20.40. In effect, for the second quarter there is $20 interest, again, on the initial balance of $1000, plus another 40¢ interest on the unpaid $20 of interest earned in the first quarter.

Interest for the third quarter of the 9-month period will be based on a balance of $1040.40, which is the original balance plus the interest accumulated in the first two quarters. Therefore, interest for the third quarter is 2 percent of $1040.40, or $20.81. The total interest for the 9 months (three quarters) will be $20.00 + $20.40 + $20.81, or $61.21.

Notice that compound interest will amount to *more* than simple interest, if the interest period extends over more than one compounding term. We can show this with the same problem, this time assuming that simple interest is paid. In this case, the interest is $20 each quarter, for a total of only $60, compared to the $61.21 charged under compound interest. The reason is that, with simple interest, interest is calculated only on the original loan balance. Compound interest includes interest on earned but unpaid interest as well as on the original principal, so a larger amount becomes subject to interest once the first compounding term has passed.

In real estate problems, interest questions usually involve *mortgage loans* and *loan discounts*, or *points*.

Mortgage Loans

Mortgage loans are like any other loans in that interest is charged for the use of someone else's money. Usually these loans require monthly payments, with part of the payment used to pay the interest due since the last payment and the remainder used to reduce the amount of the loan (the *principal*). Eventually, in this manner the loan will be fully paid off.

A very common question on this type of loan concerns the interest payable in any given month. This requires you to calculate the loan balance for that month before you can find the interest payment due. Here is an example:

> *Smith borrows $300,000 on a 30-year mortgage loan, payable at 9 percent interest per year. Payments are $2413.87 per month. How much interest is to be charged in each of the first 3 months?*

The first step in the solution is to determine the *monthly* interest rate, since the mortgage interest payments are being made monthly. Therefore, we divide the annual rate of 9 percent by 12 and get an interest rate of ¾ percent, or 0.75 percent per month.

Now we can find the interest payable in the first month. Since no payments have yet been made, the balance for the first month is the full loan amount of $300,000. So, the first month's interest is 0.0075 × $300,000 = $2250.00. The monthly loan payment is $2413.87, so the loan is paid down in the first month by: $2413.87 − $2250 = $163.87. The balance for the second month, then, is $300,000 − $163.87 = $299,836.13.

With this number we can find the interest payment for the second month; it's done the same way: 0.0075 × $299,836.13 = $2248.77 of interest paid on the loan with the second payment. Therefore, the pay down in the second month is $2413.87 − $2248.77 = $165.10. The loan balance after the second payment will be $299,836.13 − $165.10 = $299,671.03.

Using the same methods, the third month's interest can be shown to be $2247.53, and the third month's pay down to be $166.34, leaving a new balance of $299,504.69. All of these results can be tabulated as follows:

Month	Loan Balance (Beginning of Month)	Loan Payment	Interest	Loan Payoff
1	$300,000.00	$2413.87	$2250.00	$163.87
2	299,836.13	2413.87	2248.77	165.10
3	299,671.03	2413.87	2247.53	166.34
4	299,504.69	. . . .	. . . .	. . . . . .

There is a whole family of questions that would be answered using this same method, *making these same calculations.* Here are some examples, using the same information in the question we just solved ($300,000 30-year loan, monthly payments, 9 percent interest per year). Note that all of them can be answered using the information in the table above—information we've *already* calculated.

1. *What is the total amount of interest to be paid in the first three months?*
2. *How much interest will be paid in the third month?*
3. *How much will the loan be paid down in the first three months?*
4. *What will the loan balance be after three months?*
5. *What will the loan balance be at the beginning of the fourth month?*
6. *What will the loan balance be after the third payment is made?*

Here are the answers:

1. Just add up the three interest amounts for months 1, 2, and 3:
    $2250.00 + $2248.77 + $2247.53 = **$6746.30.**
2. The interest amount for month 3: **$2247.53.**
3. Add up the three loan payoff amounts: $163.87 + $165.10 + $166.34 = $495.31. Another way: subtract the balance at the end of 3 months from the original balance: $300,000 − $299,504.69 = **$495.31.**
4, 5, and 6 are all different ways of asking *exactly the same question.* The answer is, of course, **$299,504.69.**

This kind of loan is called *self-amortizing, equal payment.* The monthly payments are equal. However, as the loan balance is reduced a little each month, the portion of the payment representing interest decreases monthly, while the portion going to reduce the loan increases.

In some loans, called *level principal payment loans*, the loan amount is reduced the *same* amount with each payment. This means that the payments themselves get smaller each time, as the interest due decreases because the loan balance is decreasing. Here is an example:

> *Smith borrows $24,000 for 10 years at an annual rate of interest of 12 percent. He pays it back in the level principal payment manner each month. What will be his payments for the first, fourth, and tenth months?*

The first thing we must do here is to calculate the amount of the monthly level principal payment. Since 10 years is 120 months, the monthly principal payment is $24,000 ÷ 120 = $200. The monthly interest rate is 12% + 12 = 1%.

In the first month, the entire $24,000 is on loan, so the payment is the level $200 payment plus 1 percent of $24,000, which is another $240. Therefore, the first month's total payment is $200 + $240 = $440.

For the fourth month, Smith will owe the original balance of $24,000 *less* the $200 payments that were made for each of the first 3 months. That amount totals $600, so for the fourth month he owes $24,000 − $600 = $23,400. Then, 1 percent of $23,400 is $234; this added to the level payment of $200 gives a payment of $434 for the fourth month.

The payment for the tenth month is calculated in the same way. At that time, nine payments will have been made, so the loan will have been reduced by 9 × $200 = $1800, leaving a loan amount of $22,200. Since 1 percent of that amount is $222, the full payment for the tenth month will be $422.

[If you are studying for the salesperson's license examination, skip to page 293. Broker and appraiser applicants: keep reading!]

Loan Discounts (Brokers and Appraisers only)

The purpose of loan discounts is briefly explained in Chapter 13 ("Mortgages and Finance"). A loan discount is very simple to calculate, since it is merely a given percentage of the loan amount. You should be aware of the terminology, though, since these discounts often are referred to as *points*. One discount point is the same as a charge of 1 percent of the loan amount. Therefore, a discount of three points (often just referred to as "three points") is 3 percent of the loan amount. Frequently, a problem involving discounts will require you first to determine the loan amount; this can trap the unwary examinee, who makes the mistake of calculating the discount based on the purchase price instead of the *loan amount*. Here is an example:

> *Murgatroyd bought a home costing $54,900. She got a 95 percent loan, on which there was a charge of 3¾ points. What was the discount in dollars and cents?*

First we calculate the loan amount, which is 95 percent of $54,900: 0.95 × $54,900 = $52,155.

Now we can calculate the discount, which is 3¾ points, or 3¾ percent of the loan amount: 0.0375 × $52,155 = $1955.81.

Depreciation (Brokers and Appraisers only)

Although the tax laws allow all sorts of complicated ways to calculate depreciation, the only one you have to worry about on licensing examinations is the simplest one, which is called *straight-line depreciation*. Straight-line depreciation assumes that the property depreciates an *equal* amount each year.

We will not argue here whether real estate does or does not, in fact, depreciate. Some does and some does not seem to. However, there are many reasons why one should be aware of the possibility of depreciation, not the least of which is that in the long run a real estate asset *will* wear out. The 50-year-old house that is being offered for ten times the original cost of construction also has a new roof, modernized heating and air-conditioning, new wiring, carpeting, kitchen installations, and plumbing. Nearly every visible surface has been repainted and remodeled.

When calculating depreciation, you must know the *useful life* of the property (sometimes referred to as *economic life*, or just plain *life*). Once you know this, you can easily calculate an annual *depreciation rate*: divide the useful life, in years, *into* 100 percent to get the percent rate of depreciation per year. For example:

> *10-year life: 100% ÷ 10 = 10% depreciation per year*
> *50-year life: 100% ÷ 50 = 2% depreciation per year*
> *35-year life: 100% ÷ 35 = 2.857% depreciation per year*

Once this has been done, most depreciation problems become only slightly elaborated versions of the standard three types of percentage *problems*. For example:

(a) *Madison owns a building for which he paid $550,000. If it has a total useful life of 30 years, what is its value after 5 years?*

(b) *Madison owns a building for which he paid $550,000. If it has a 40-year life, in how many years will it be worth $426,250?*

(c) *Madison owns a building worth $550,000. If it depreciates to $440,000 in 9 years, what is the total useful life?*

(d) *If a building depreciates at a 2½ percent per year, in how many years will it be worth 85 percent of its original value?*

Here is how the answer to each of these is found:

(a) Here you are asked to determine the value after 5 years, so you must determine how much the building depreciates each year. A 30-year life yields 3⅓ percent depreciation per year. Five years' depreciation, then, is 16⅔ percent. Therefore, in 5 years the building will be worth 83⅓% (100% − 16⅔%) of its original value: 0.8333 × $550,000 = $458,333.33, its value after 5 years.

(b) Here you want to know how long it takes for a certain depreciation to take place. A 40-year life is depreciation at 2½ percent per year. $426,250 is 77½ percent of $550,000 (426,250 ÷ 550,000). 100% − 77½% = 22½% total depreciation. At 2½ percent per year, that would take 9 years to accumulate (22.5 ÷ 2.5 = 9).

(c) Here you have to determine the useful life. $440,000 is 80 percent of $550,000 (440,000 ÷ 550,000 = 0.80). Therefore, the building depreciates 20 percent in 9 years, or 2.2222 . . . percent per year. Divide this figure into 100 percent to get the total number of years required for the building to depreciate fully: 100 ÷ 2.2222 = 45. Thus, the useful life is 45 years.

(d) In this problem you don't have to calculate the depreciation rate, since it is given to you (2½ percent per year). If the building depreciates to 85 percent of its original value, it will have depreciated 15 percent. 15% ÷ 2½% = 6 years' worth of depreciation.

Profit and Loss (Brokers and Appraisers only)

Calculation of profit and loss is another slightly different version of the three types of percentage problems. The important thing to remember is that profit and loss are always expressed as percentages of *cost*. Cost is the original price that the seller paid for the property when he acquired it. If *his* selling price is higher than cost, he has a profit. If it is lower, he has a loss.

The *dollar value* of profit or loss is the difference between purchase price and sale price.

The *rate* of profit or loss is the percentage relationship between the purchase price and the dollar value of profit or loss.

Here are some examples:

(a) *Martin bought her house for $89,900 and sold it later for $111,800. What was her rate of profit?*

(b) *Samson Wrecking Company mistakenly tore down part of Habib's home. Before the home was damaged, it was worth $150,000. Afterward, it had sustained 28 percent loss. What was its value after the wrecking?*

(c) *Harrison sold his home for $210,250 and made a 45 percent profit. What had he paid for the home?*

Here are the solutions:

(a) First, determine the dollar value of the profit: $111,800 − $89,900 = $21,900. Then determine what percentage proportion the dollar value is of the *purchase price* ($21,000 is ? percent of $89,900). 21,900 ÷ 89,900 = 24.36 percent.

(b) The loss was 28 percent of the original value of $150,000: 0.28 × $150,000 = $42,000. $150,000 − $42,000 = $108,000 value afterward.

(c) The original price of the house, plus 45 percent, is now equal to $210,250. Therefore,

$210,250 is 145 percent of the original price of the home (? is 145 percent of $210,250). $210,250 ÷ 1.45 = $145,000. As a check, Harrison's profit is $62,500 ($210,250 less $145,000), which is 45 percent of $145,000 ($65,250 ÷ $145,000 = 0.45).

Return on Investment (Brokers and Appraisers only)

The concept of return on investment is very similar to the concept of interest payments on loans. In the investment case, an investor spends money to buy an income-producing asset. She wants to make money from it; otherwise there is no point to the investment. She calculates her return and expresses it as a *percentage* of her investment being paid back to her each year. In a sense, she can be thought of as "lending" her money to the investment and having it "pay" her "interest" on her money.

It is possible to make deceptively simple-sounding investment questions so complicated that they can best be answered with the aid of a computer or a very sophisticated calculator. This fact needn't concern you, though. On licensing examinations the questions are kept simple enough that they can be calculated quickly by hand or, in states that allow their use, with simple, hand-held calculators that do no more than add, subtract, multiply, and divide.

If you think of return on investment problems as similar to interest problems, you should have no trouble with them. Here are some examples:

(a) *Bennett owns a building that cost him $650,000. How much income should the building produce annually to give Bennett a 15 percent return on his money?*
(b) *Maximilian paid $174,000 for a triplex apartment building. All units are identical. He lives in one unit and rents the other two. The total net income per month from rental is $1420. What annual rate of return is he getting on his investment in the rental units?*
(c) *What monthly income should a building costing $38,500 produce if the annual return is to be 15 percent?*

Here are the solutions:

(a) The building should produce an income each year of 15 percent of $650,000: 0.15 × $650,000 = $97,500.
(b) This problem involves a lot of steps, but they are simple ones. First we must determine how much of the purchase price should be allocated to the two rental units. Since all three are the same, one-third of the purchase price ought to be allocated to each. This means that two-thirds of the price should be allocated to the two rental units: ⅔ × $174,000 = $116,000. Next we must determine the annual dollar amount of income received. The monthly income is $1420, so the annual income is $1420 × 12 = $17,040. Now we must find out what percent $17,040 is of $116,000 ($17,040 is ? percent of $116,000). $17,040 ÷ $116,000 = 14.69 percent, the annual rate of return.
(c) Here we must calculate a monthly dollar income. The annual income must be 15 percent of $38,500.00, or $5775.00. The monthly income is one-twelfth of that amount, or $481.25.

Problem Set B

Here are some practice problems involving percents. The questions cover all of the kinds we have just discussed, including common variations. Answers are given at the end of the chapter.

1. Peters sold her home for $497,000 and made a 42 percent profit. How much did she pay for the home?

2. Rodriguez's home cost $249,500. He financed the purchase with a 90 percent loan. The discount was three points. How much was the dollar amount of discount?

3. Going back to question 2, assume that the interest rate on Rodriguez's loan was 8½ percent per year and that the loan was for a 25-year period. How much interest would be payable with the first payment?

4. Talbot sold her building for $242,218.75. She had owned it for 7 years and had originally paid $287,500.00 for it. What was the annual rate of depreciation?

5. Sam Zealous, the real estate agent, sold I. M. Sellar's home for him. After paying Zealous a commission of 7½ percent of the sale price, Sellar ended up with $184,907.50. What was the sale price?

6. Winken, Blinken, and Nod are partners in the ownership of a certain property worth $440,000. The property produces a 21 percent return per year, in income collected monthly. Winken owns a 37 percent share of the building. How much is Winken's monthly income from the property?

7. In problem 6, Blinken owns a 22 percent share and Nod owns the rest. If $198,000 originally was paid for the property, what would be the dollar value of Nod's share of the profit if the partners were to sell the property today for its current value? What rate of profit does this represent?

8. Bernie, a real estate salesman for Gettum Realty, Inc., gets 52½ percent of all real estate commissions he brings into the firm. Bernie just sold Fred's home for $223,750. Fred had listed the home with a different broker in the same Multilist group as Bernie's broker. According to the Multilist rules, the listing broker received 40 percent of the commission, and the selling broker received the rest after a fee of 3 percent of the commission was paid to the Multilist group to cover its expenses. How much (dollar amount) of the 6½ percent commission on this sale was paid to Bernie?

9. Mr. Selkirk borrowed $5000 to install a new kitchen island in his home. The loan was for one year, with no payments to principal to be made until the loan term was past. The interest rate was 10½ percent per year, with the interest payable quarterly. How much was the quarterly interest payment? If the interest had been allowed to compound quarterly, how much *extra* interest would Mr. Selkirk have had to pay in excess of simple quarterly interest?

10. Ms. Jessup just sold for $62,500 a building she bought 8 years earlier for $93,000. What was the percent rate of her loss? What was the annual rate of depreciation she sustained?

[Note: From this point on, the discussion applies only to the broker's license exam. If you're not studying for that exam, turn to page 293.]

Proration (Brokers only)

Proration, which is a necessary input into the calculation of closing statements, normally will come up only on examinations for broker's licenses. If you are seeking a brokerage license, you should cover the material in this section. Appraisal or salesperson candidates can skip it.

Two kinds of prorating methods are in common use. The most widely used one employs the *statutory year*; the other, the *actual year*.

The function of proration is to distribute equitably the costs of a particular charge that two or more people must share. In real estate, these costs usually are created by transactions associated with a title closing, in which allocations are made for charges that apply over the period in which both buyer and seller own the property. The most commonly prorated items are these:

- Real property taxes
- Property insurance
- Interest on assumed mortgage loans
- Prepaid or later-paid rentals

Property taxes are usually paid by the year; when a transaction occurs in the middle of a year, part of that year's property tax usually will be deemed, by the parties to the sale, to be payable by each one. Note that the government that collects the taxes does *not* prorate them; it collects the *full* amount of the taxes from whoever owns the property at the time the taxes are due. If, when the sale occurs, the year's property taxes have *already* been paid, the seller will have paid them and the buyer must recompense the seller for the portion of the taxes that apply to the part of the year when the buyer will own the property. On the other hand, if the taxes are due *after* the close of the sale, the buyer will have to pay them in full, for the entire year, when they come due. At the closing the seller pays the buyer for the share that applies during the period of the tax year when the seller owned the property.

Insurance usually is paid in advance. Often insurance policies are multiyear policies, although the premiums generally are payable annually. On licensing examinations, however, problems that involve closing often assume that the entire multiyear premium was paid at once when the policy was purchased; this is a device to see whether examinees read the questions completely. Since insurance usually is paid in advance, the buyer, if he assumes the existing insurance policy, recompenses the seller for the prepaid unused portion of the policy that the buyer gets from her.

When the buyer assumes the seller's mortgage loan, and the closing date is not the day after the loan payment is due and paid, the month's interest must be prorated between buyer and seller. Loan payments are due at the end of the monthly payment periods. When the next payment is due, the buyer will have to pay it in full, including the interest for an entire month during which he actually owned the property only part of the time. Therefore, the seller will have to pay the buyer for her share of the mortgage interest.

Rents work the other way, since they are payments *to* the owner rather than *by* the owner. Rent usually is paid in advance, but it is possible to have a situation where rent is paid at the *end* of the month or lease period. If rent is paid in advance, the seller will have been paid a full month's rent for the month in which the closing occurs; she must pay the buyer his prorated share of that month's rent already received. If the rent is paid at the end of the month, the buyer will get a full month's rent covering the month of sale, and he must recompense the seller for the period during which she owned the property. Because of these two types of situations examinees must read rent questions carefully.

COMPUTING PRORATIONS

To compute prorations an examinee must know three things:

1. How much—in money—is the item to be prorated?
2. To whom is payment to be made?
3. How much time is involved?

The discussion above covers the question of who pays whom what charges, but in summary we can state two easily remembered rules:

1. If the item was paid *before* closing, the buyer recompenses the seller.
2. If the item will be paid *after* closing, the seller recompenses the buyer.

These rules are fair because the seller had to pay all items due before closing, and the buyer will have to pay everything that comes due after closing.

Calculation of the amount of money due in the payment will vary, depending on the complexity of the problem. Sometimes the amount is specified exactly; other times it will have to be calculated. It is quite popular in licensing examinations to require the examinee to calculate the property tax bill before he can begin to prorate it (see Chapter 16). Usually the insurance premium and rentals will be given, since it is difficult to incorporate a sensible calculation method for them into a problem. Proration of the interest on assumed mortgages is another favorite candidate for calculation.

Calculation of the proration itself includes apportioning the time involved among the parties. Rent and interest usually are apportioned over 1 month, taxes over 1 year, and insurance over 1 or more years.

To prorate correctly, you must have two important pieces of information:
1. Who (buyer or seller) is supposed to "have" the day of closing?
2. Which calculation year (statutory or calendar) is being used?
You must be given this information somewhere in the examination. If you can't find it, ask one of the examination supervisors.

The Closing Day

The day of closing can be counted either as the buyer's first day or as the seller's last day. Which it is to be usually reflects local custom, so we can't state a general rule (although in the East and the South, the closing day most often is considered the seller's, while it tends to be the buyer's in the West).

The Statutory Year

Prorating items over a full year can involve very messy calculations, since everything has to be divided by 365 (or 366), the number of days in a year. Many banks and other financial institutions therefore have substituted the 360-day "statutory year" as a means of simplifying calculation. This system assumes the year to be made up of twelve 30-day months. Numbers such as 360 and 30, while large, can be divided easily by many other numbers, so that calculations involving them are less cumbersome.

For items paid monthly, such as interest and rent, the statutory year rarely is used, since its application can create visible distortion in 31-day months and, especially, in February. However, spread over a year or more, the error introduced with the statutory year becomes very small, so it is sometimes used for calculation of prorated taxes and insurance.

To prorate an item using the statutory year, first find the payment for the full period. Next, divide this payment by the number of months in the period to get the monthly cost, and divide the monthly cost by 30 to find the daily cost. After determining who pays whom, and for what length of time, you can calculate the prorated payment.

Using the statutory year was helpful when calculations were made by hand or with adding machines; now that calculators and computers are in common use, dividing by 365 (or 366) instead of 360 isn't such a big deal. As a result, the recent trend has been to use the actual year instead of the statutory year.

The Actual Year

If using the statutory year is forbidden, the actual year must be used. In this case, you need to calculate how many days of the period must be paid for. You then multiply this sum by the *daily* cost of the item to get the prorated payment. The difficulty comes in the fact that to get the daily rate you must divide the annual rate by 365, or 366 in leap years. Further, it often is confusing to try to count days elapsed in a significant part of a year, especially when dealing with odd beginning and ending dates. To try to figure how many days elapse between January 1 and July 26 of a given year is bad enough; to calculate the number of days that elapsed from, say, October 23 of one year to March 14 of the following year is even worse. If you must use the actual year, you have no alternative; you need to remember the number of days in each month and whether or not you're dealing with a leap year. Be sure to keep your calculator in good working order, and to be familiar with its use, to help you make actual-year computations.

Calculating Time with the Statutory Year

The statutory year lends itself well to calculation of elapsed time. In this type of calculation you want to find out how many days have elapsed between two dates, one of which is usually the closing date. To do this, write each date *numerically* as follows: YEAR—MONTH—DATE.

June 17, 1996, would be 96—6—17. July 4, 1998, would be 98—7—4. To find the elapsed time, "subtract" the earlier date from the later one. Remember that you can "borrow" from adjacent left-hand columns just as you do in normal arithmetic subtraction. Also remember that you're borrowing months and years, not digits. Each month has 30 days, and each year has 12 months.

In the following example, we want to find the elapsed time between December 28, 1996, and March 19, 1997:

$$
\begin{array}{r}
97 - 3 - 19 \\
- 96 - 12 - 28 \\
\hline
? \quad\; ? \quad\; ?
\end{array}
$$

First, we find the number of days; here we would have to subtract 28 from 19, and we can't do that. We must borrow a month (30 days) from the month column, to change the 19 to 49. $49 - 28 = 21$, so we have:

$$
\begin{array}{r}
{}^{2}\qquad {}^{49} \\
97 - 3 - 19 \\
- 96 - 12 - 28 \\
\hline
? \quad\; ? \quad\; 21
\end{array}
$$

Now we look to the months; we must subtract 12 from 2. We can't do that, so we borrow a year, or 12 months, from the year column, and subtract 12 from 14:

$$
\begin{array}{r}
{}^{14} \\
{}^{96}\quad {}^{\not{2}}\quad {}^{49} \\
97 - \not{3} - \not{1}9 \\
- 96 - 12 - 28 \\
\hline
? \quad\; ? \quad\; 21
\end{array}
$$

Since 96 subtracted from 96 leaves 0, the elapsed time between December 28, 1996 and March 19, 1997 is 2 months and 21 days.

Rounding in Proration

One very important warning must be given here. When you are calculating prorations, always carry your intermediate results (i.e., daily and monthly charges) to *at least two decimal places beyond the pennies*. Do *not* round to even cents until you have arrived at your *final* answer, because when you round you introduce a tiny error. This is acceptable with respect to your final answer, but intermediate answers will later be operated on, including multiplication by fairly large numbers. Each time a rounded number is multiplied, the rounding error is multiplied also! To prevent such errors from affecting your final result, always carry intermediate steps two extra decimal places beyond what your final answer will have.

PRORATION EXAMPLES

Here is an example of proration for each of the four commonly prorated items: rent, interest, taxes, insurance.

Rent

Rent usually is paid in advance.

> *The closing date is May 19, 1996, and rent is payable for the calendar month on the first of each month. Who pays whom what in the proration of rent of $265 per month?*

Since the seller received the May rent payment on May 1, he should pay the buyer the portion of rent covering the part of the month *after* the closing date. May has 31 days; the closing date is May 19. Therefore, the buyer will own the property for $31 - 19 = 12$ days during May.

The daily rent for May is ⅟₃₁ of the monthly rent, since there are 31 days: $265.00 ÷ 31 = $8.5484. (Remember to carry to two extra decimal places.) The buyer's share of the rent, then, is 12 × $8.5484 = $102.5808, which rounds to $102.58. (Note that, if we had rounded the daily rental to $8.55 and then multiplied by the 12 days, the result would have been $102.60, or 2¢ off.)

Interest

Interest is paid after it has accrued. Normally, the interest period ends the day *before* a payment is due—that is, a payment due on the first of the month covers the preceding month; one due on the 18th of the month covers the period from the 18th of the preceding month through the 17th of the current one.

> The closing date is September 22, 1996. Interest is payable, with the payment on the 16th of the month. The loan amount as of September 16, 1996, is $44,881.10. The interest rate is 9¼ percent per year. If the loan is assumed, who pays whom what for prorated interest?

We have to calculate the monthly interest due and determine how much of that amount is paid by whom. First, the dollar amount of interest—this is ⅟₁₂ of 9¼ percent of the loan balance of $44,881.10: ⅟₁₂ × 0.0925 × $44,881.10 = $345.96. Note that we rounded off the monthly interest, because the lender does that, too, each month.

The period involved here is 30 days, since September has that length. The seller will have to pay the buyer for all of the interest between September 16 and September 22, since on October 16 the buyer is going to have to pay the full month's interest. The seller will own the property for 7 days of that time. (At a glance, this appears incorrect since 22 − 16 = 6. However, the seller owns the property on both the 16th and the 22nd, so we must add a day. Another way is to count the days on our fingers, starting with the 16th and ending with the 22nd.)

Now we must determine the daily interest charge, which is $345.96 ÷ 30 = $11.5320. We multiply this by 7 to get the seller's share for 7 days: $11.5320 × 7 = $80.724 = $80.72 rounded off.

Taxes

Taxes are usually assessed for a full year, so we would use the statutory year for calculation, if permitted.

> The closing date is April 27, 1996. Taxes are $1188.54 per year. The tax year is March 1 to February 28 (or 29) of the following year. Who pays whom how much in prorated taxes? Use both the statutory and the actual year, assuming (a) that taxes are paid on June 1 and (b) that taxes are paid on March 15 of the tax year.

This sample problem is probably more complex than any you will encounter on a licensing examination, but it demonstrates all the possibilities.

In situation (a) the seller pays his share to the buyer, since the taxes are due after the closing date and so must be paid by the buyer. In situation (b) the buyer pays the seller her share, because the taxes for the full tax year were paid by the seller before the closing date.

Statutory Year Calculations. The closing date is April 27, 1996, and the tax year begins March 1, 1996. Therefore the seller owns the property for 1 month and 27 days:

$$\begin{array}{r} 96 \quad 4 \quad 28 \\ -\,96 \quad 3 \quad\ \ 1 \\ \hline 1 \quad 27 \end{array}$$

Note that we did not use April 27, the closing date, in this calculation, because we consider the closing date as belonging to the seller. April 28, then, is the first day that the seller does *not* own the property, and so we must count from that day.

The seller's share is for 1 month and 27 days. The total tax payment is $1188.54 per year. Dividing by 12 yields a monthly tax charge of $99.0450. Dividing this amount by 30 yields a daily tax charge of $3.3015.

$$
\begin{array}{rll}
\text{1 month @ } \$99.0450 & = & \$99.0450 \\
+ \text{ 27 days @ } \$3.3015 & = & + \quad 89.1405 \\
\hline
\text{Total seller's charge} & & \$188.1855 = \$188.19
\end{array}
$$

The seller's share is $188.19, so the buyer's share is the rest, or $1188.54 − $188.19 = $1000.35.

In situation (a), then, the seller pays the buyer $188.19.

In situation (b) the buyer pays the seller $1000.35.

Actual Year Calculations. When calculating using the actual year, we reduce everything to days. The year has 365 days,* so, using the same problem, the daily tax charge is $1188.54 ÷ 365 = $3.25627. The seller owns the property for a total of 58 days: 31 days of March and 27 days of April of the tax year. Therefore the seller's share is 58 × $3.25627 = $188.8654 = $188.87. The buyer's share would be $1188.54 − $188.87 = $999.67.

In situation (a), taxes are paid on June 1 and the seller pays the buyer $188.87.

In situation (b), taxes are paid on March 15 and the buyer pays the seller $999.67.

Note two things about this calculation. First, the results are 68¢ different from those obtained with the statutory year method; this discrepancy occurs because of the different calculation technique. Second, when the daily charge was calculated, it was carried to *three* extra decimal places. In the actual year calculation, we might have to multiply by a number as large as 365, and the rounding error would be multiplied by that much. Carrying to three extra decimal places reduces this error.

Insurance

> A 3-year insurance policy, dated October 22, 1993, is assumed on the closing date of August 11, 1995. The full 3-year premium of $559.75 was paid at the time the policy was bought. Who pays whom what if this policy is prorated?

First we calculate the monthly insurance charge, which is ¹⁄₃₆ (3 years, remember) of the premium of $559.75: $559.75 ÷ 36 = $15.5486. The daily charge is ¹⁄₃₀ of that amount: $15.5486 ÷ 30 = $0.5183.

Now we must calculate how long the buyer will use the policy. If the policy is dated October 22, 1993, then it expires on October 21 (at midnight) of 1996.

$$
\begin{array}{rrr}
96 & 10 & 21 \\
- 95 & 8 & 11 \\
\hline
1 & 2 & 10
\end{array}
$$

The buyer will own the policy for 1 year, 2 months, and 10 days. He will pay the seller the prorated share, since the seller paid for the full 3 years when she bought the policy. (Now we just go ahead and figure 1 year and 2 months to be 14 months, to save the problem of calculating the annual premium.)

$$
\begin{array}{rll}
\text{14 months @ } \$15.5486 & = & \$217.6804 \\
\text{10 days @ } \$0.5183 & = & + \quad 5.1830 \\
\hline
\text{Total payable to seller} & & \$222.8634 = \$222.86
\end{array}
$$

Calculating insurance according to the actual year can be cumbersome. To do this we ought to calculate first the annual premium, which is ⅓ of $559.75 = $186.58333. The daily premium charge is this amount divided by 365: $186.58333 ÷ 365 = $0.51119. Note that once again we are carrying actual year calculations to an extra *three* decimal places.

---

* 1996 is a leap year, but the 1996–97 tax year begins on March 1, 1996, which is *after* February 29; thus, the 1996–97 tax year has only 365 days.

In this example, figuring the time of ownership by the buyer is a lot more trouble. From October 22, 1995, to October 21, 1996, is 1 full year. From August 11, 1995, to October 21, 1995, is an additional 71 days—20 in August, plus 30 in September and 21 in October.

$$
\begin{array}{rcl}
1 \text{ year @ } \$186.58333 & = & \$186.58333 \\
71 \text{ days @ } \$0.51119 & = & +\ \ 36.29449 \\
\hline
\text{Total payable to seller} & & \$222.87782 = \$222.88
\end{array}
$$

Problem Set C

Here are some proration problems for you to practice with. Answers are given at the end of the chapter.

1. The closing date is June 26, 1995. Taxes are collected on a calendar year basis and are payable on June 1 of each year. Taxes for the year are $779.90. A 2-year insurance policy, dated May 2, 1995, is to be assumed. A full 2-year premium of $345.76 was paid when the policy was issued. A mortgage loan of $28,883.00 as of June 1, 1995, will be assumed. Its interest rate is 7¾ percent per year, with interest payable on the first of each month. Part of the property is rented, with rent of $125 per month payable in advance. Use the statutory year. Who pays whom what at closing?

2. The closing date is December 15, 1996. Taxes are $982, and cover the period from May 1, 1996, to April 30, 1997; they are not due and payable until the last day of the tax year. An insurance policy of 1 year, dated March 19, 1996, and costing $360, is to be assumed. The property is not rented, and the loan is not to be assumed. Use the *actual* year. Who pays whom what?

3. Use the statutory year for insurance and taxes. The closing date is April 20, 1995. Taxes are $1188 per year and are payable in four quarterly installments due March 31, June 30, September 30, and December 31 of each year. Quarterly tax payments are equal. An insurance policy costing $1046.55 for 5 years, dated July 16, 1992, is to be assumed. The property is not rented. Who pays whom what?

4. The closing date is September 25; use the statutory year. In this area, two property taxes are paid. A $555.10 *city* tax must be paid by August 15, while a $303.25 *county* tax must be paid by October 15. Taxes cover the calendar year in which they are paid. What is the *net* amount payable? Who pays it to whom?

Hints on Handling Mathematical Problems on Examinations

Now that the different kinds of mathematics problems that appear on licensing examinations have been discussed, a few remarks dealing with the proper ways to approach them are in order.

You should remember that your objective on the examination is to get a passing grade. It is *not* necessary that you get 100 percent—only enough to pass. Mathematical problems can be terrible time-consumers; therefore you should devote your time at the outset to the problems that do not take a lot of time. Save the complicated ones for later, when you have had the chance to answer all the "easy" questions. Many examinees determinedly tackle the mathematics first or spend tremendous amounts of time on a very few problems, only to find later that they have to rush just to have a chance of getting to every question on the examination.

Try to determine just how long a problem will take *before* you tackle it. If it's going to take a lot of time, postpone it. Then when you get back to the time-consuming questions, do first those that are worth the most points. This may mean that you will turn in your examination without finishing one or two of the really long arithmetic problems. That doesn't mean you're stupid—it means you're smart. Instead of slaving away over the few points these unfinished problems represented, you used your time to build up a good score on the other parts of the examination that could be answered quickly. However, before turning in your test paper, try to mark an answer for *every* question, even math problems not attempted. You might just guess the right answer!

Another point to remember concerning arithmetic questions is that you may not need all the information given. After you read the question and determine just what you are being asked to do, begin to search for the information you need to provide the answer. Do not assume that just because some information is included you must find some way of using it in your solution. Fairly often extra information has been included just to sidetrack or confuse examinees whose arithmetic skills make them unsure of themselves.

ANSWERS

Before looking at the answers for Problem Set A, let's finish doing the long problem that appears in Chapter 17. This very complicated "sidewalk question" was partially answered in association with Figures 18-1A, B, and C. On pages 270–271, we got as far as calculating the area of the sidewalk to be 914 sq. ft.

(1) Calculate the *volume* of the sidewalk, given that its area is 914 sq. ft. and the depth is 3½ in.
First, convert everything into inches: 1 sq. ft. = 144 sq. in.
914 × 144 sq. in. = 131,616 sq. in.
Now find the volume, in cubic inches, of the sidewalk.
Volume = 3½ × 131,616 sq. in. = 460,656 cu. in.

(2) Change the cubic inches into cubic yards: 1 cu. yd. = 36 × 36 × 36 cu. in., or 46,656 cu. in.
460,656 cu. in. ÷ 46,656 cu. in. = 9.87346 cu. yd.

(3) Figure out how much stone and concrete are necessary.
Concrete is 85 percent of the sidewalk. 0.85 × 9.87346 cu. yd. = 8.39244 cu. yd. of concrete.
Stone is 15 percent of the walk. 0.15 × 9.87346 cu. yd. = 1.48102 cu. yd. of stone.

(4) Figure out how many tons of stone: 1 cu. yd. of stone weighs 3282 lb. 15 oz. (Change the 15 oz. to $^{15}/_{16}$ lb., or 0.9375 lb., to get 3282.9375 lb.) Since we are using 1.48102 cu. yd. of stone, there will be
1.48102 cu. yd. × 3282.9375 lb. = 4862.0961 lb. of stone.
Since 1 ton is 2000 lb., we will use
4862.0961 ÷ 2000 = 2.43105 tons of stone.

(5) Figure out how much labor is necessary. A worker can do 188 sq. ft. of walk per hour; there are 914 sq. ft., so use
914 sq. ft. ÷ 188 sq. ft. = 4.862 hours of labor.

(6) Now (finally!), figure out the cost of the walk:

8.39244 cu. yd. of concrete @ $313 per cu. yd.	$2626.83
2.43105 tons of stone @ $27.83 per ton	67.66
4.862 hours of labor @ $19 per hour	92.38
Total cost of sidewalk	$2786.87

Problem Set A

1. **$39.92** total cost
The house is 55 ft. × 30 ft., or 170 ft. around. Since it is 8½ ft. high, the total wall area is
170 ft. × 8.5 ft. = 1445 sq. ft.
Now we must subtract for doors, the picture window, and other windows:
Doors: 3 ft. × 7.5 ft. = 22.5 sq. ft. each
Picture window: 12 ft. × 5 ft. = 60 sq. ft.
Windows: 2.5 ft. × 4 ft. = 10 sq. ft. each
Unpainted area includes:

2 doors @ 2.5 sq. ft.	45 sq. ft.
Picture window	60 sq. ft.
6 windows @ 10 sq. ft.	60 sq. ft.
Total unpainted area	165 sq. ft.

If 165 sq. ft. are unpainted, then 1280 sq. ft. (1445 − 165) must be painted. A gallon of paint covers 320 sq. ft. Therefore, we will need:
1280 sq. ft. ÷ 320 sq. ft. = 4 gal. of paint @ $9.98 = **$39.92** total cost

2. **352** lots
76 acres is 3,310,560 sq. ft. (76 × 43,560). Subtracting 665,000 sq. ft. for roads, parks, etc., leaves 2,645,560 sq. ft. to be devoted to lots. Each lot must be 7500 sq. ft.
2,645,560 sq. ft. ÷ 7500 sq. ft. = 352.74
Therefore, Orsini can get no more than **352** lots out of the land.

3. **$1389.20** total cost
The following diagram shows that the walk can be divided into two parts, each 43 ft. × 8 ft., and one part 65 ft. × 8 ft. These contain 344 + 344 + 520 = 1208 sq. ft. If 1 sq. ft. costs $1.15, then 1208 sq. ft. cost 1208 × $1.15 = **$1389.20**.

4. **68.707** ft.
There are 9 sq. ft. in 1 sq. yd., so the lot contains 313 × 9 = 2817 sq. ft. If the plot is rectangular, with frontage of 41 ft., the depth must be
2817 sq. ft. ÷ 41 ft. = **68.707** ft.

5. **$2238.29** total value
The formula for the area of a triangle is $A = ½ × B × H$. The base (B) is 500 ft.; the height, or depth (H), is 650 ft.

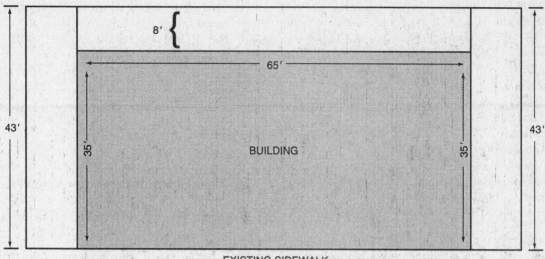

EXISTING SIDEWALK

500 ft. × 650 ft. = 325,000 sq. ft.
325,000 sq. ft. × ½ = 162,500 sq. ft.
162,500 sq. ft. ÷ 43,560 sq. ft. = 3.73049 acres
The land is valued at $600 per acre, so the total value is

$600 × 3.73049 acres = **$2238.29**

6. **38** acres
One section (1 square mile) contains 640 acres. (You have to know that fact.) The NW¼ of the SE¼ of a section, then, contains

¼ × ¼ × 640 = 40 acres

Now we must determine how much of that 40-acre tract is taken up by the road. The road is 66 ft. wide. The 40-acre tract is ¼ mi. on a side (draw a diagram, if necessary, as shown); ¼ mi. is 1320 ft. (or 5280 ft. ÷ 4). Therefore, the road is 66 ft. × 1320 ft., since it crosses the entire tract.

1320 ft. × 66 ft. = 87,120 sq. ft.

87,120 sq. ft. ÷ 43,560 sq. ft. = 2 acres
If the road contains 2 acres, then Huang ended up with the rest of the 40 acres, or **38** acres.

Problem Set B

1. **$350,000** purchase price.
If Peters sold her home for $497,000 and made a 42 percent profit, then $497,000 is 142 percent of her original purchase price: $497,000 ÷ 1.42 = **$350,000** purchase price.

2. **$6736.50** discount on loan.
First, the amount of the loan, which is 90 percent of the price of $249,500, or $224,550. The three-point discount is three percent of the loan amount: 0.03 × $224,550 = **$6736.50**.

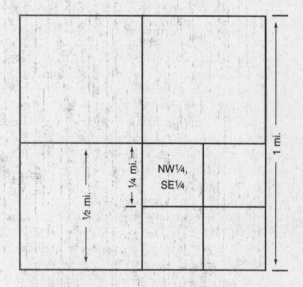

3. **$1590.56** interest for the first month.
The interest for the first month will be ½ of a year's interest on the full loan amount, since none of it will be paid back yet. 0.085 × $224,550 = $19,086.75 annual interest. Divide that by 12 to get **$1590.56**. (Note that the term of the loan—25 years—has nothing to do with this problem. The interest for the first month is the same no matter how long or short the loan term is.)

4. **2¼%** depreciation per year.
The building had depreciated a total of $45,281.25, which is $287,500 − $242,218.75. Next we determine what percent $45,281.25 is of $287,500: $45,281.25 ÷ $287,500 = 15¾%.

This occurred over 7 years, so we divide the total depreciation of 15¾ percent by 7 to get **2¼%**.

5. **$199,900** sale price.
   If Sellar paid a 7½ percent commission, his $184,907.50 represents 92½ percent of the sale price (100% − 92½% = 7½%). $184,907.50 is 92.5% of ?. $184,907.50 ÷ .925 = **$199,900** sale price.

6. **$2849** is Winken's share of the monthly income.
   The building's annual return is 21 percent of $440,000: $440,000 × .21 = $92,400 annual income. Divide by 12 to get the monthly building income of $7700. Winken gets 37% of that amount: $7700 × .37 = **$2849**.

7. **$99,220** Nod's share; **122.22%** rate of profit.
   Because Winken owns 37 percent and Blinken owns 22 percent, that leaves 41 percent for Nod (100 − 37 − 22 = 41). The total profit is $242,000 ($440,000 − $198,000). Nod's share is 41 percent of this: $242,000 × .41 = **$99,220**. Nod started with $81,180 (41% of $198,000) and his profit of $99,220 would be 122.22% of that amount ($99,220 ÷ $81,180 = 1.2222). Note that the rate of profit for the entire building is the same as it is for each of the three investors. This just means that all three of them experienced the same growth in wealth as did the entire investment. If you're skeptical about this, work it out for each of the other two investors and for the building as a whole.

8. **$4,352.22** paid to Bernie.
   This problem is cumbersome and time consuming, but not difficult. First we determine what percentage of the total commission goes to Bernie's broker: the other broker gets 40%; 3% goes to the Multilist group, so 57% is left for Bernie's broker (100 − 40 − 3 = 57). Now we figure the dollar amount of the 6½% commission: $223,750 × .065 = $14,543.75 total commission. Bernie's broker gets 57% of that: $14,543.75 × .57 = $8289.94 to Bernie's broker. Bernie gets 52½% of that: $8289.94 × .525 = **$4352.22**.

9. **$131.25** quarterly payment; **$21.04** more per year for compounding
   The simple interest due quarterly is ¼ of the annual interest, which is 10½ percent of $5000, or 0.105 × $5000 = $525. The quarterly simple interest is $525 ÷ 4 = $131.25.
   To find accumulated compound interest requires additional computation. We already know, from the calculations we just did, that the interest for the first quarter is $131.25. For the second quarter, then, we will have $5000.00 +

$131.25 = $5131.25 on which to calculate interest. Thus, ¼ × 0.105 × $5131.25 = $134.70, the interest due for the *second* quarter. At this point, a total of $265.95 of unpaid interest has accrued ($131.25 + $134.70), so for the third quarter interest must be calculated on $5265.95: ¼ × 0.105 × $5265.95 = $138.23. At the end of the third quarter a total of $404.18 in unpaid interest has accrued ($265.95 + $138.23); therefore, for the fourth quarter interest will be calculated on $5404.18. The interest for the fourth quarter is ¼ × 0.105 × $5404.18 = $141.86, giving a total interest for the year of $546.04 ($404.18 + $141.86).
   Simple interest would have been 4 × **$131.25** = $525.00, so with compound interest a total of **$21.04** more is paid ($546.04 − $525).

10. **32.8%** loss; **4.1%** annual depreciation rate
    The total amount of the loss is $93,000 − $62,500 = $30,500. This is 32.8 percent of $93,000 ($30,500 ÷ $93,000 = 0.328). Profit and loss are calculated based on the *purchase* price originally paid. Since this depreciation occurred over an 8-year period, the annual depreciation rate is **32.8%** ÷ 8 = **4.1%**.

Problem Set C

1. Taxes: **$398.62** payable to seller
   Insurance: **$319.35** payable to seller
   Interest: **$161.67** payable to buyer
   Rent: **$16.67** payable to buyer
   Taxes: June 26 represents 5 months and 26 days that the seller will own the property during the year; he has already paid the taxes, since they are due June 1. Therefore, the buyer must pay the seller for the 6 months and 4 days that she will own the property during the tax year. One month's tax charge is $779.90 ÷ 12 = $64.9917. One day's tax charge is $64.9917 ÷ 30 = $2.1664.

6 months @ $64.9917 =	$389.9502
4 days @ $2.1664 = +	8.6656
Total taxes payable to seller	$398.6158 =

   $398.62
   Insurance: The policy expires May 1, 1997, so the buyer will own it for 1 year, 10 months, and 5 days. The yearly charge is $345.76 ÷ 2 = $172.88. The monthly charge is $172.88 ÷ 12 = $14.4067. The daily charge is $14.4067 ÷ 30 = $0.4802.

One year @ $172.88 =	$172.88
10 months @ $14.4067 =	144.0670
5 days @ $0.4802 = +	2.4010
Total due seller for insurance	$319.3480 =

   $319.35

Interest: The payment date is July 1, covering all of June. The seller owns the property for 26 days of June, so he pays $^{26}/_{30}$ of the interest charge for that month to the buyer. The monthly interest charge is $^{1}/_{12} \times 0.0775 \times \$28,883.00 = \$186.5360$. One day's interest is $\$186.5360 \div 30 = \$6.2179$. The seller's portion of the interest is $\$6.2179 \times 26 = \$161.6654 = \textbf{\$161.67}$ payable to the buyer.

Rent: The seller has been paid for the entire month a total of $\$125.00$; 4 days of that is due to the buyer. One day's rent proration is $\$125.00 \div 30 = \$4.1667$; $4 \times \$4.1667 = \$16.6668 = \textbf{\$16.67}$ payable to the buyer.

2. Taxes: **\$616.10** payable to buyer
   Insurance: **\$91.73** payable to seller
   Taxes: The taxes due cover from May 1 to December 15 for the seller, who has to pay his share to the buyer at closing, since the buyer will be liable for the entire year's tax bill at the end of the tax year. One day's tax charge is $\$982.00 \div 365 = \$2.69041$. The seller owns the property for 229 days (31 days each in May, July, August, and October; 30 days each in June, September, and November; and 15 days in December): $229 \times \$2.69041 = \$616.10389 = \textbf{\$616.10}$ payable to the buyer.

   Insurance: One day's insurance is $\$360 \div 365 = \$0.98630$. The buyer must pay the seller, since the seller paid the full premium when the policy was bought. The buyer will own the property from December 16 (the day after closing, for prorating purposes!) through the expiration of the policy on March 18. She will own it for 93 days (16 in December, 31 in January, 28 in February, 18 in March): $93 \times \$0.98630 = \$91.7259 = \textbf{\$91.73}$ payable to the seller.

3. Taxes: **\$66** due to buyer
   Insurance: **\$468.04** due to seller
   Taxes: Taxes here are paid quarterly and not annually. The closing date is April 20, so the March 31 payment already has been made. The only payment that must be prorated is the June 30 payment, since it covers a period in which both buyer and seller will own the property. Quarterly taxes are $\$1188.00 \div 4 = \$297.00$.

Monthly taxes are $\$297.00 \div 3 = \$99.00$. Daily taxes are $\$99.00 \div 30 = \$3.30$. These numbers all come out even, and no rounding will be necessary, so no extra decimal places are required.

The seller will own the property for the 20 days of April during the second quarter. Therefore, he must pay the buyer $20 \times \$3.30 = \textbf{\$66}$ for his share of the second quarter's taxes.

Insurance: The 5-year policy cost $\$1046.55$; 1 year's insurance charge is $\$1046.55 \div 5 = \$209.31$. One month's charge is $\$209.31 \div 12 = \$17.4425$. One day's charge is $\$17.4425 \div 30 = \$0.5814$. The policy expires July 15, 1997.

$$\begin{array}{ccccc} & \overset{7}{9}7 & - & \overset{6}{\cancel{7}} & - & \overset{45}{1\cancel{5}} \\ - & 95 & - & 4 & - & 20 \\ \hline & 2 & & 2 & & 25 \end{array}$$

The buyer will own the policy for 2 years, 2 months, and 25 days.

2 years @ \$209.31	=	\$418.62
2 months @ \$17.4425	=	34.885
25 days @ \$0.5814	=	+ 14.535
Total due seller for insurance		**\$468.04**

4. Seller owes **\$76.75** to buyer.
   In this problem, part of the tax is payable before the closing (by the seller) and part is payable after the closing (by the buyer). The seller owns the property for 8 months and 25 days of the year; the buyer owns it for 3 months and 5 days.

   City tax: This is payable by the buyer to the seller, since it was paid August 15. One month's tax is $\$555.10 \div 12 = \$46.2583$; one day's tax is $\$46.2583 \div 30 = \$1.5419$. The seller receives payment for 3 months and 5 days, or $\$146.48$ from the buyer.

   County tax: This is payable by the seller to the buyer, since it is due *after* closing. The tax is $\$303.25 \div 12 = \$25.2708$ monthly; daily it is $\$25.2708 \div 30 = \$0.8424$. The seller owes a total of $\$223.23$ to the buyer. Therefore, the seller owes a net of $\$223.23 - \$146.48 = \textbf{\$76.75}$ to the buyer.

Chapter 19 / *Settlement*

Quite some time ago, it was common practice for real estate brokers (but not salespeople) to prepare the closing statements (also called settlement statements, escrow statements) for the transactions they and their salespeople effected. Therefore, it is traditional for several questions about closing statements to appear on broker's license examinations. Salesperson's examinations rarely have anything more than an occasional very simple question about closing statements. Nowadays, although licensing laws usually require brokers to make sure that a closing statement is provided to both buyer and seller, common practice is for someone other than the broker actually to prepare the statement. Often the lender providing a new mortgage loan for the buyer will do so; otherwise closings can be handled by title companies, abstract companies, or escrow agents.

Purpose of Closing Statements

Closing statements provide an accounting of all funds involved in a real estate transaction. These statements show the amount that the buyer must pay and that the seller will receive from the transaction. Buyer and seller each are given an accounting of all items they must pay for or are credited with in the transaction. Brokers should prepare a reconciliation for each sale as well, to "button up" the statements.

Debits and Credits

You need not be a bookkeeper to understand closing statements. Two columns are shown for the buyer and two for the seller. The two columns for each party are a debit column and credit column. Totals of debit and credit columns must agree with each other.

Listed in the debit column are amounts that the party being considered, buyer or seller, is charged for. Listed in the credit column are those that the party will receive credit for. Cash is needed to balance.

As a simple example, assume the sale of a $130,000 house on January 30, 1995. The seller already has paid taxes of $1714.81 for the entire 1995 calendar year. The seller should be credited with the payment of $130,000 for the house, and $1576.67 of prepaid taxes for the remainder of the 1995 year (January 31 to December 31, 1995, during which time the buyer will own the house). Cash will be the offsetting debit.

The buyer will be debited for the house and paid-up taxes; cash is the offsetting credit. The closing statements will appear as follows:

	Seller		Buyer	
	Debit	Credit	Debit	Credit
Real property		$130,000.00	$130,000.00	
Prepaid taxes		1,576.67	1,576.67	
Cash due from buyer				$131,576.67
Cash due to seller	$131,576.67			
Totals	$131,576.67	$131,576.67	$131,576.67	$131,576.67

(NOTE: If you cannot easily tell how the $1576.67 of prorated property tax was calculated, you should review the section entitled "Proration" in Chapter 18.)

Now let us consider the same transaction, except that we will add two more items: A broker was involved, who earned a commission of $7800 for making the sale; also, the buyer must pay $75 for a survey. The seller is to pay the commission, so the seller's statement will show a debit of the $7800 broker's commission. The buyer's statement will show a debit of $75 for the survey. The new closing statement will appear as follows:

	Seller Debit	Seller Credit	Buyer Debit	Buyer Credit
Real property		$130,000.00	$130,000.00	
Prepaid taxes		1,576.67	1,576.67	
Sales commission	$ 7,800.00			
Survey fee			75.00	
Cash due from buyer				$131,651.67
Cash due to seller	$123,776.67			
Totals	$131,576.67	$131,576.67	$131,651.67	$131,651.67

An item that affects only one party is shown as a debit or a credit *only on the statement of the party affected.* For example, if the sales commission is paid by the seller, the amount appears only on the seller's closing statement. If the buyer pays for a survey, it appears only as a debit to him.

Items of value that are sold, exchanged, or transferred between buyer and seller are shown in *opposite* columns of *both* parties. For example, the transferred property is shown as a credit to the seller *and* as a debit to the buyer. *Never should an item transferred, exchanged, or taken over be shown as a credit to both parties or as a debit to both.* If an item is transferred, sold, or exchanged, it is a debit to one party and a credit to the other.

Items usually *debited* (charged) to the buyer that are likely to be encountered include the following:
1. Purchase price of the real property
2. Purchase price of personal property
3. Deed-recording fees
4. Title examination
5. Title insurance
6. Hazard insurance
7. Survey
8. Appraisal fee (sometimes charged to seller)
9. Prepaid taxes
10. Loan assumption fees

Items that are likely to be *credited* to the buyer are:
1. Earnest money deposits
2. Proceeds of a loan he borrows
3. Assumption of a loan
4. Mortgage to the seller (purchase money)
5. Current taxes unpaid to closing
6. Tenant rents paid in advance (the seller collected these)
7. Balance due to close (paid by buyer to close)

Items likely to be *debited* to a seller are:
1. Sales commission
2. Current but unpaid taxes
3. Existing debt, whether assumed or to be paid off
4. Loan prepayment penalties
5. Discount points for buyer's VA or FHA loan. Discount points on *conventional* loans may be charged to buyer or to seller depending on contractual arrangements, custom in the area, local law, etc.
6. Rent received in advance
7. Deed preparation

Items usually *credited* to a seller are:
1. Sales price of real property

2. Sales price of personal property
3. Prepaid taxes
4. Prepaid insurance (only if policy is assumed by buyer)
5. Escrow balance held by lender

COMPREHENSIVE SAMPLE PROBLEM

Abe Seller and Will Buyer are to close on Seller's house on January 30, 1996. The purchase price is $130,000. In addition, Buyer will pay $650 for appliances. Seller is to pay a commission of 6 percent of the sale price to XYZ Realty, Inc. County property taxes for calendar 1996 were $1714.81, and were due on January 15, 1996. They were paid in full on that date by Mr. Seller. Since the house is in an unincorporated area, there is no city property tax.

The property was occupied by Ms. Happy Tenant, whose lease survives the sale. Her monthly rental is $775, paid on the first of each month. Rent is to be prorated to the date of closing.

Abe Seller owes $88,277.12 on a mortgage loan carrying an interest rate of 11¾ percent, which must be paid off at closing, plus interest for the entire month of January. He also will incur a 1 percent mortgage prepayment penalty. In addition, he has agreed to pay two discount points on Mr. Buyers $122,500 VA mortgage loan.

Mr. Buyer will take over Mr. Seller's hazard insurance policy. The policy anniversary date is January 26, 1996. Mr. Seller has not yet paid the $730 annual premium, so Mr. Buyer will have to pay it at a later date.

At closing, Mr. Seller will be charged $125 for a termite inspection. Mr. Buyer will pay $75 for a survey, $125 for a credit report, $66 for mortgage-recording fees, and $12 to record the deed. He also will be charged $670 for title insurance. Mr. Buyer will execute a mortgage in favor of Mr. Seller to secure a purchase money mortgage loan of $7500 from Mr. Seller to Mr. Buyer. A $2000 earnest money deposit from Mr. Buyer is being held in escrow by XYZ Realty, Inc., to be applied to the purchase price at closing.

Using Figure 19-1 and the information given above, complete the closing statement.

The properly completed closing statement is shown in Figure 19-2.

SETTLEMENT DATE:	BUYER'S STATEMENT		SELLER'S STATEMENT	
	DEBIT	CREDIT	DEBIT	CREDIT

Figure 19-1. Settlement Statement Worksheet

SETTLEMENT DATE: 1/30/96	BUYER'S STATEMENT		SELLER'S STATEMENT	
	DEBIT	CREDIT	DEBIT	CREDIT
PURCHASE PRICE	130,000.00			130,000.00
EARNEST MONEY		2,000.00		
TRUST DEED		122,500.00		
SECOND TRUST DEED		7,500.00	7,500.00	
PRORATED TAXES	1,576.67			1,576.67
PRORATED INSURANCE		8.00	8.00	
PRORATED RENT		25.00	25.00	
PERS. PROPERTY PURCH.	650.00			650.00
TRUST DEED PAYOFF			88,277.12	
ACCRUED MORTGAGE INT.			827.60	
PREPAYMENT PENALTY			882.77	
BROKERAGE COMMISSION			7,800.00	
DISCOUNT POINTS			2,450.00	
TERMITE INSPECTION			125.00	
DEED RECORDING	12.00			
TRUST DEED RECORDING	66.00			
SURVEY	75.00			
CREDIT REPORT	125.00			
TITLE INSURANCE	670.00			
DUE FROM BUYER/TO SELLER		1,141.67	24,331.18	
	133,174.67	133,174.67	132,226.67	132,226.67

Figure 19-2. Completed Settlement Statement Worksheet

Broker's Reconciliation

A broker's reconciliation worksheet is used to assure that all cash receipts and disbursements are accounted for properly. Like a closing statement, it has two columns, which can be described as "cash receipts" and "cash disbursements," respectively. The totals of the two columns must agree.

The reconciliation can be prepared using the following steps:
1. Go down the debit column of the purchaser's closing statement.
    A. List the items that the broker will pay from the purchaser's account in the "disbursements" column of the reconciliation.
    B. On a separate worksheet called "Loan Proceeds" (page 302), list the items that the new mortgage lender will receive directly from the buyer or will withhold from the loan amount.
2. Go down the credit column of the buyer's closing statement.
    A. List on the broker's reconciliation, as a receipt, all cash paid by the buyer. Be sure to include the earnest money and cash paid at closing.
    B. On the top of the loan proceeds worksheet, list the amounts of mortgage money supplied at closing. Do not include assumed mortgages or those taken by the seller in partial payment.
3. Go down the debit column of the seller's closing statement.
    A. List any amounts to be paid by the broker on behalf of the seller as a "disbursement" on the broker's reconciliation.
    B. List the sales commission as a disbursement on the broker's reconciliation.
    C. On the loan proceeds worksheet, list the balance of loans to be paid off, accrued interest, prepayment penalties, and discount points charged to the seller.

4. Go down the credit column of the seller's closing statement. If the seller has paid cash and not received something from the buyer in return, it must be reconciled.

Items not selected in steps 1–4 include the property being sold and prorated charges. These items will not appear on the broker's reconciliation.

5. On the loan proceeds worksheet, sum all items, excluding the principal of the new loan, which was written on top of the page. Subtract the sum from the new loan principal to get the loan proceeds, and insert that amount as a receipt on the broker's reconciliation.
6. Total the receipts and the disbursements columns of the reconciliation. They should agree to complete the reconciliation.

Amounts shown in each column should be received/disbursed by the broker who has earned a commission.

LOAN PROCEEDS WORKSHEET

Amount borrowed on new loan		$122,500.00
Less: Discount points	$ 2,450.00	
Existing mortgage loan payoff	88,277.12	
Prepayment penalty	882.77	
Accrued interest payable	827.60	
. . . .	$92,437.49	− 92,437.49
Loan proceeds		$30,062.51

Figure 19-3 shows a broker's cash reconciliation statement for the sample problem described in the preceding section.

Real Estate Settlement Procedures Act

The *Real Estate Settlement Procedures Act* (RESPA) covers most residential mortgage loans used to finance the purchase of one- to four-family properties. Included are a house, a condominium or cooperative apartment unit, a lot with a mobile home, and a lot on which a house will be built or a mobile home placed using the proceeds of a loan.

PURPOSE OF RESPA

The purpose of RESPA is to provide potential borrowers with information concerning the settlement (closing) process so that they can shop intelligently for settlement services and make informed decisions. RESPA does not set the prices for services; its purpose is merely to provide information about settlement (closing) and costs.

MATERIALS TO BE RECEIVED UNDER RESPA

Under RESPA, a person who files a loan application for property covered must receive from the lending agency a pamphlet titled *Settlement Costs and You* and a good-faith estimate of the costs of settlement services. The lender has 3 business days after receiving a loan application to mail these materials. From that time until settlement, the loan applicant has an opportunity to shop for loan settlement services. One business day before settlement, if the loan applicant requests, he has the right to inspect a Uniform Settlement Statement (page 301), which shows whatever figures are available at that time for settlement charges. At settlement the completed Uniform Settlement Statement is given to the borrower or his agent. When there is no actual settlement meeting, the Uniform Settlement Statement is mailed.

UNIFORM SETTLEMENT STATEMENT (HUD-1 FORM)

As discussed, the Uniform Settlement Statement (usually called the *HUD-1 Form*) is used in all RESPA-affected transactions (which include practically all residential transactions). The form is shown in Figure 19-4; it has been filled in using the same information as in the

Address: 1999 Somewhere Parkway   **Closing Date:** January 30, 1996

Mr. Abe Seller	Mr. Will Buyer
(Seller)	**(Buyer)**

	Receipts	Disbursements
From Buyer		
Earnest Money Deposited	2,000.00	
Check for Balance	1,141.67	
To Seller		
Check for Balance		24,331.18
Expenses		
Real Estate Commission		7,800.00
Preparation of Warranty Deed		
Preparation of Security Deed and Promissory Notes		
Title Fees		
Recording Mortgage Security Deed		66.00
Recording Warranty Deed		12.00
Survey		75.00
Special Assessments		
First Mortgage Proceeds	30,062.51*	
Survey and Credit Report		
Termite Inspection		125.00
Title Insurance		670.00
	33,204.18	33,204.18

*See worksheet attached

Figure 19-3.   Cash Reconciliation Statement

comprehensive sample problem described on page 300. Note that one item not mentioned in the sample problem is flood insurance, and no dollar figure is given on the form. Instead the notation "POC" ("paid outside closing") is used to show an item that may be important to the deal at hand, but was paid for or otherwise settled by the parties before closing.

SETTLEMENT COSTS AND YOU

The pamphlet *Settlement Costs and You* contains information concerning shopping for services, homebuyer's rights, and homebuyer's obligations. It also includes a sample Uniform Settlement Statement (HUD-1 Form) and describes specific settlement services. In addition, it provides information concerning a comparison of lender costs and describes reserve accounts and adjustments between buyer and seller.

A. **Settlement Statement**

U.S. Department of Housing
and Urban Development

OMB No. 2502-0265

B. Type of Loan				
1. ☐ FHA 2. ☐ FmHA 3.☐ Conv. Unins. 4. ☒ VA 5. ☐ Conv. Ins.	6. File Number	7. Loan Number	8. Mortgage Insurance Case Number	

C. **Note:** This form is furnished to give you a statement of actual settlement costs. Amounts paid to and by the settlement agent are shown. Items marked "(p.o.c.)" were paid outside the closing; they are shown here for informational purposes and are not included in the totals.

D. Name and Address of Borrower	E. Name and Address of Seller	F. Name and Address of Lender
WILL BUYER 404 W. MAIN SOMEWHERE	ABE SELLER 915 OAK ST. SOMEWHERE ELSE	W. E. GOTCHA 4821 BIGG BLDG. ANYPLACE

G. Property Location	H. Settlement Agent	
915 OAK ST.	DUE ITRIGHT & CO.	
	Place of Settlement	I. Settlement Date
	4372 BIGG BLDG. ANYPLACE	1-30-96

J. Summary of Borrower's Transaction		K. Summary of Seller's Transaction	
100. Gross Amount Due From Borrower		**400. Gross Amount Due To Seller**	
101. Contract sales price	130,000.00	401. Contract sales price	130,000.00
102. Personal property (APPLIANCES)	650.00	402. Personal property (APPLIANCES)	650.00
103. Settlement charges to borrower (line 1400)	948.00	403.	
104.		404.	
105.		405.	
Adjustments for items paid by seller in advance		*Adjustments for items paid by seller in advance*	
106. City/town taxes to		406. City/town taxes to	
107. County taxes to	1,576.67	407. County taxes to	1,576.67
108. Assessments to		408. Assessments to	
109.		409.	
110.		410.	
111.		411.	
112.		412.	
120. Gross Amount Due From Borrower	133,174.67	**420. Gross Amount Due To Seller**	132,226.67
200. Amounts Paid By Or In Behalf Of Borrower		**500. Reductions In Amount Due To Seller**	
201. Deposit or earnest money	2,000.00	501. Excess deposit (see instructions)	
202. Principal amount of new loan(s)	122,500.00	502. Settlement charges to seller (line 1400)	10,375.00
203. Existing loan(s) taken subject to		503. Existing loan(s) taken subject to	
204. PURCHASE MONEY MORTGAGE	7,500.00	504. Payoff of first mortgage loan	88,277.12
205.		505. Payoff of second mortgage loan	
206.		506. 1ST MORTGAGE INTEREST	827.60
207.		507. 1ST MORTGAGE PREPAY. PENALTY	882.77
208.		508. PURCHASE MONEY MORTGAGE	7,500.00
209.		509.	
Adjustments for items unpaid by seller		*Adjustments for items unpaid by seller*	
210. City/town taxes to		510. City/town taxes to	
211. County taxes to		511. County taxes to	
212. Assessments to		512. Assessments to	
213. PRORATED INSURANCE	8.00	513. PRORATED INSURANCE	8.00
214. PRORATED RENT	25.00	514. PRORATED RENT	25.00
215.		515.	
216.		516.	
217.		517.	
218.		518.	
219.		519.	
220. Total Paid By/For Borrower	132,033.00	**520. Total Reduction Amount Due Seller**	107,895.49
300. Cash At Settlement From/To Borrower		**600. Cash At Settlement To/From Seller**	
301. Gross Amount due from borrower (line 120)	133,174.67	601. Gross amount due to seller (line 420)	132,226.67
302. Less amounts paid by/for borrower (line 220)	(132,033.00)	602. Less reductions in amt. due seller (line 520)	(107,895.49)
303. Cash ☒ From ☐ To Borrower	1,141.67	603. Cash ☒ To ☐ From Seller	24,331.18

Previous Edition Is Obsolete

Forms and Worms Inc.,® 315 Whitney Ave., New Haven, CT 06511 1(800) 243-4545

HUD-1 (3-86)
RESPA, HB 4305.2
Item # 230700

Figure 19-4.   HUD-1 Form

L. Settlement Charges

700. Total Sales/Broker's Commission based on price $ 130,000.00 @ 6 % = 7,800.00	Paid From Borrower's Funds at Settlement	Paid From Seller's Funds at Settlement
Division of Commission (line 700) as follows:		
701. $ 7,800.— to XYZ REALTY		
702. $ to		
703. Commission paid at Settlement		7,800.00
704.		
800. Items Payable In Connection With Loan		
801. Loan Origination Fee %		
802. Loan Discount 2 %		2,450.00
803. Appraisal Fee to		
804. Credit Report 125 to MESSUP, INC.	125.00	
805. Lender's Inspection Fee		
806. Mortgage Insurance Application Fee to		
807. Assumption Fee		
808. HAZARD INSURANCE to MILFORD INS. AGENCY		P.O.C.
809. FLOOD INSURANCE to MILFORD INS. AGENCY		P.O.C.
810.		
811.		
900. Items Required By Lender To Be Paid In Advance		
901. Interest from to @ $ /day		
902. Mortgage Insurance Premium for months to		
903. Hazard Insurance Premium for years to		
904. years to		
905.		
1000. Reserves Deposited With Lender		
1001. Hazard Insurance months @ $ per month		
1002. Mortgage Insurance months @ $ per month		
1003. City property taxes months @ $ per month		
1004. County property taxes months @ $ per month		
1005. Annual assessments months @ $ per month		
1006. months @ $ per month		
1007. months @ $ per month		
1008. months @ $ per month		
1100. Title Charges		
1101. Settlement or closing fee to		
1102. Abstract or title search to		
1103. Title examination to		
1104. Title insurance binder to		
1105. Document preparation to		
1106. Notary fees to		
1107. Attorney's fees to		
(includes above items numbers:)		
1108. Title insurance 67000 to RJL TITLE CO.	670.00	
(includes above items numbers:)		
1109. Lender's coverage $		
1110. Owner's coverage $		
1111.		
1112.		
1113.		
1200. Government Recording and Transfer Charges		
1201. Recording fees: Deed $ 12.00 ; Mortgage $ 66.00 ; Releases $	78.00	
1202. City/county tax/stamps: Deed $; Mortgage $		
1203. State tax/stamps: Deed $; Mortgage $		
1204.		
1205.		
1300. Additional Settlement Charges		
1301. Survey $75 to JONES LAND SURVEY	75.00	
1302. Pest inspection to ABC TERMITE CO.		125.00
1303.		
1304.		
1305.		
1400. Total Settlement Charges (enter on lines 103, Section J and 502, Section K)	948.00	10,375.00

© 1984 Forms and Worms® Inc. 315 Whitney Ave. New Haven, Ct. 06511 All Rights Reserved 1 (800) 243-4545

Figure 19-4. HUD-1 Form *(continued)*

Requirement to Report to the Internal Revenue Service _____

The Federal Tax Reform Act of 1986 created a new requirement that brokers and/or settlement agents report the details of some real estate transactions to the U.S. Internal Revenue Service. The primary responsibility lies with the settlement agent, the person who actually handles the closing.

If there is no settlement agent, the responsibility rests with the buyer's broker and the seller's broker, in that order. Not all transactions need be reported.

Questions on Chapter 19 _____

1. The purchase price is shown on the purchaser's closing statement as
   (A) a debit   (C) both A and B
   (B) a credit   (D) neither A nor B

2. The purchaser's earnest money held by a broker until closing is shown as
   (A) a debit to the purchaser   (C) both A and B
   (B) a credit to the seller   (D) neither A nor B

3. If property taxes for the current year have not yet been paid, they should be shown as
   (A) a credit to the buyer   (C) both A and B
   (B) a debit to the seller   (D) neither A nor B

4. A tenant paid rent at the beginning of the month. The sale of the property takes place during the middle of the month. The rent is prorated by
   (A) crediting the seller   (C) both A and B
   (B) debiting the buyer   (D) neither A nor B

5. The buyer has arranged new financing for property. Closing statements, with respect to the mortgage principal, should show
   (A) a credit to the buyer   (C) both A and B
   (B) a debit to the seller   (D) neither A nor B

6. The seller will pay a broker's commission. The commission is shown as
   (A) a credit to the seller   (C) a debit to the buyer
   (B) a debit to the seller   (D) A and C only

7. The buyer will take over the seller's insurance policy. The premium has been paid by the seller. The unexpired premium should be shown as
   (A) a credit to the seller   (C) both A and B
   (B) a debit to the buyer   (D) neither A nor B

8. The seller will accept a second mortgage from the buyer. The amount owed is shown as
   (A) a credit to the buyer   (C) both A and B
   (B) a debit to the seller   (D) neither A nor B

9. The sale price of personal property to be paid for at closing is shown as
   (A) a credit to the buyer   (C) both A and B
   (B) a debit to the seller   (D) neither A nor B

10. An existing mortgage on the property is to be assumed by the buyer. The closing statements show the mortgage principal as
    (A) a credit to the buyer   (C) both A and B
    (B) a debit to the seller   (D) neither A nor B

11. The buyer must pay $100 for a survey and credit report at closing. The settlement statements show
    (A) a debit to the buyer
    (B) a credit to the seller
    (C) both A and B
    (D) neither A nor B

12. The buyer has arranged a 10½ percent VA mortgage loan with two discount points. The discount points are shown as
    (A) a debit to the seller
    (B) a debit to the buyer
    (C) both A and B
    (D) neither A nor B

13. The buyer is to assume the seller's mortgage loan and must also maintain the tax and insurance escrow account held by the mortgage lender. The escrow account balance is shown as a
    (A) debit to the buyer
    (B) credit to the seller
    (C) both A and B
    (D) neither A nor B

14. The tenant has a $250 security deposit in an account to be taken over by the buyer. At closing, the security deposit should be shown as a
    (A) credit to the buyer
    (B) credit to the seller
    (C) debit to the buyer
    (D) B and C only

15. The seller incurs a prepayment penalty to pay off his mortgage loan. The penalty is shown as
    (A) a credit to the seller
    (B) a debit to the seller
    (C) a credit to the buyer
    (D) B and C only

16. The buyer, in connection with her new financing, must establish, at closing, a $500 escrow account for taxes and insurance. The escrow deposit is shown as
    (A) a debit to the buyer
    (B) a credit to the buyer
    (C) a credit to the seller
    (D) A and C only

17. The buyer will pay for deed recording and title insurance at closing. These items are shown as
    (A) a credit to the buyer
    (B) a debit to the buyer
    (C) a credit to the seller
    (D) A and C only

18. RESPA is intended to
    (A) regulate charges for settlement services
    (B) provide information about settlement services to home loan applicants
    (C) both A and B
    (D) neither A nor B

19. After a home loan application is filed, how many business days does a lender have to provide a good faith estimate of settlement charges?
    (A) 1
    (B) 2
    (C) 3
    (D) 15

20. Upon the loan applicant's request, he has the right to inspect
    (A) the seller's credit report
    (B) a final Uniform Settlement Statement
    (C) the broker's financial statement
    (D) a Uniform Settlement Statement with whatever figures are available

ANSWERS

1. **A**	6. **B**	11. **A**	16. **A**
2. **D**	7. **C**	12. **A**	17. **B**
3. **C**	8. **C**	13. **C**	18. **B**
4. **D**	9. **D**	14. **A**	19. **C**
5. **A**	10. **C**	15. **B**	20. **D**

PART V: OTHER LAWS AFFECTING REAL ESTATE

Chapter 20/*Fair Housing Law*

The Federal Fair Housing Act, Public Law 90–284, was enacted into law on April 11, 1968, as Title VIII of the Civil Rights Act of 1968.

Purpose

The purpose of the Fair Housing Act is expressed by Section 801 of the law, which states:

> *It is the policy of the United States to provide, within constitutional limitations, for fair housing throughout the United States.*

The following explanation of the need for fair housing is quoted directly from *Understanding Fair Housing*, U.S. Commission on Civil Rights.[*]

> *Housing is a key to improvement in a family's economic condition. Homeownership is one of the important ways in which Americans have traditionally acquired financial capital. Tax advantages, the accumulation of equity, and the increased value of real estate property enable homeowners to build economic assets. These assets can be used to educate one's children, to take advantage of business opportunities, to meet financial emergencies, and to provide for retirement. Nearly two of every three majority group families are homeowners, but less than two of every five nonwhite families own their homes. Consequently, the majority of nonwhite families are deprived of this advantage.*
>
> *Housing is essential to securing civil rights in other areas. Segregated residential patterns in metropolitan areas undermine efforts to assure equal opportunity in employment and education. While centers of employment have moved from the central cities to suburbs and outlying parts of metropolitan areas, minority group families remain confined to the central cities, and because they are confined, they are separated from employment opportunities. Despite a variety of laws against job discrimination, lack of access to housing in close proximity to available jobs is an effective barrier to equal employment.*
>
> *In addition, lack of equal housing opportunity decreases prospects for equal educational opportunity. The controversy over school busing is closely tied to the residential patterns of our cities and metropolitan areas. If schools in large urban centers are to be desegregated, transportation must be provided to convey children from segregated neighborhoods to integrated schools.*
>
> *Finally, if racial divisions are to be bridged, equal housing is an essential element. Our cities and metropolitan areas consist of separate societies increasingly hostile and distrustful of one another. Because minority and majority group families live apart, they are strangers to each other. By living as neighbors they would have an opportunity to learn to understand each other and to redeem the promise of America: that of "one Nation indivisible."*

---

[*]From *Understanding Fair Housing*, U.S. commission on Civil Rights, Clearinghouse Publication 42, February 1973, p.1.

Property Covered

The federal Fair Housing Act of 1988 extended the property covered to all single or multifamily dwelling units, with the few exceptions noted below. A *dwelling* is defined as any building or structure designed as a residence to be occupied by one or more families; included are mobile-home parks, trailer courts, condominiums, cooperatives, and time-sharing units. Community associations and "adult-only" communities are clearly included unless they qualify under an exception.

Adult-only communities are reserved for older persons: specifically, 100 percent of the units must be rented to residents 62 years of age or older, or 80 percent of the units must be occupied by people of at least age 55, *and* significant facilities and services designed for use by elderly persons must be in place. Special facilities include an accessible physical environment, communal dining facilities, social and recreational programs, the availability of emergency and other health care facilities, and other amenities intended for the elderly. The apartments must publish and adhere to policies that demonstrate an intent to serve persons aged 55 and over.

Apartment complexes with four or fewer units are exempt from the federal Fair Housing Act when the owner occupies at least one unit, and single-family homes sold or rented by an owner are exempt. However, the exemption applies only to persons owning no more than three properties at one time and is subject to other restrictions. In selling, the owner may not use a real estate salesperson or broker and may not print, publish, or otherwise make any reference to preference, limitation, or discrimination on the basis of race, color, religion, sex, national origin, familial status, or handicap.

Discrimination in Sale or Rental

Section 804 of the Fair Housing Act makes it unlawful to do any of the following:

(a) *To refuse to sell or rent after the making of a bona fide offer, or to refuse to negotiate for the sale or rental of, or otherwise make unavailable or deny, a dwelling to any person because of race, color, religion, sex, national origin, familial status, or handicap.*

(b) *To discriminate against any person in the terms, conditions, or privileges of sale or rental of a dwelling, or in the provision of services or facilities in connection therewith, because of race, color, religion, sex, national origin, familial status, or handicap.*

(c) *To make, print, or publish, or cause to be made, printed, or published any notice, statement, or advertisement, with respect to the sale or rental of a dwelling that indicates any preference, limitation, or discrimination based on race, color, religion, sex, national origin, familial status, or handicap, or an intention to make any such preference, limitation, or discrimination.*

(d) *To represent to any person because of race, color, religion, sex, national origin, familial status, or handicap that any dwelling is not available for inspection, sale, or rental when such dwelling is in fact so available.*

(e) *For profit, to induce or attempt to induce any person to sell or rent any dwelling by representations regarding the entry or prospective entry into the neighborhood of a person or persons of a particular race, color, religion, sex, national origin, familial status, or handicap.*

Discrimination in New Construction

Under the 1988 amendments, newly constructed multifamily facilities (four or more units) must be accessible to the handicapped. In buildings with elevators, the handicapped must have access to 100 percent of the units, but only ground-floor units of garden-type apartments are required to be accessible.

Common areas in buildings must be accessible to all handicapped persons, and doors and hallways must be wide enough to allow passage of wheelchairs.

New living units must be constructed in a way that allows access for the handicapped, including the appropriate location of light switches, plugs, and environmental controls. Bathroom walls must be reinforced to allow future installation of grab rails, and the occupant must be allowed to install them. Requirements for removal, when the handicapped person vacates, are uncertain.

Discrimination in Financing

Section 805 of the Fair Housing Act applies to transactions after December 31, 1968. It states that it is unlawful for:

> *any bank, building and loan association, insurance company or other corporation, association, firm or enterprise whose business consists in whole or in part in the making of commercial real estate loans, to deny a loan or other financial assistance to a person applying therefore for the purpose of purchasing, constructing, improving, repairing, or maintaining a dwelling, or to discriminate against him in the fixing of the amount, interest rate, duration, or other terms or conditions of such loan or other financial assistance, because of the race, color, religion, sex, or national origin of such person or of any person associated with him in connection with such loan or other financial assistance or the purposes of such loan or other financial assistance, or of the present or prospective owners, lessees, tenants, or occupants of the dwelling or dwellings in relation to which such loan or other financial assistance is to be made or given: Provided, that nothing contained in this section shall impair the scope or effectiveness of the exception contained in Section 803(b).*

Section 803(b) exempts a single-family house sale or lease by owner, if certain provisions are met. This exemption was described on page 310.

Discrimination in Brokerage Services

Section 806 of the Fair Housing Act states:

> *After December 31, 1968, it shall be unlawful to deny any person access to or membership or participation in any multiple-listing service, real estate brokers' organization or other service, organization, or facility relating to the business of selling or renting dwellings, or to discriminate against him in the terms or conditions of such access, membership, or participation, on account of race, color, religion, sex, national origin, familial status, or handicap.*

Blockbusting

"Blockbusting," that is, the soliciting of homeowners by unscrupulous real estate agents, brokers, or speculators who feed upon fears of homeowners, is prohibited by the Fair Housing Act. Blockbusters attempt to buy properties at very low prices from whites in racially transitional neighborhoods and then broker or sell them to blacks at high prices. Some blockbusters deliberately incite panic and white flight to achieve their greedy, unlawful goal.

Two Specific Exemptions

There are two specific, limited exemptions to the Fair Housing Laws. One exemption allows a religious organization to discriminate with respect to its noncommercial property. It does not, however, allow this exemption if the religion discriminates on the basis of race, color, sex, national origin, familial status, or handicap with respect to its membership. The other exemption allows private clubs that provide lodging as an incident to their main purpose to give preferential treatment to club members.

Enforcement by the Federal Government

Any person who claims to have been injured by a discriminatory housing practice or who believes that he will be irrevocably injured by a discriminatory housing practice that is about to occur (hereafter "person aggrieved") may file a complaint with the Secretary of the Department of Housing and Urban Development (HUD). Complaints must be in writing, must state the facts, and must be filed within 1 year after the alleged discriminatory housing practice occurred. The Attorney General conducts all litigation in which the Secretary of HUD participates as a party pursuant to the Fair Housing Act.

Enforcement by Private Persons

The rights granted to private persons by the Fair Housing Act may be enforced by civil action in appropriate U.S. district courts without regard to the amount in controversy, and in appropriate state or local courts of general jurisdiction. A civil action must be commenced within 1 year after the alleged discriminatory housing practice occurred.

Upon application by the plaintiff and in such circumstances as the court may deem just, a court of the United States in which a civil action under this section has been brought may appoint an attorney for the plaintiff and may, upon proper showing, authorize the commencement of a civil action without the payment of fees, costs, or security. A court of a state or subdivision thereof may do likewise to an extent not inconsistent with the law or procedures of the state or subdivision.

The court may grant as relief, as it deems appropriate, any permanent or temporary injunction, temporary restraining order, or other order, and may award to the plaintiff actual damages, injunctive or other equitable relief, and civil penalties up to $50,000 ($100,000 for repeat violators), together with court costs and reasonable attorney fees in the case of a prevailing plaintiff, provided that said plaintiff, in the opinion of the court, is not financially able to assume said attorney's fees.

Penalty for Intimidation

Under Section 901 of the Civil Rights Act of 1968 (Title IX) whoever
   A.   injures or threatens to injure or interfere with any person because of his race, religion, color, sex, national origin, familial status, or handicap, and who is selling, leasing, occupying, financing, etc., property, or
   B.   intimidates persons who deal with others in housing on account of race, religion, color, sex, national origin, familial status, or handicap, or
   C.   discourages others from dealing with others in housing on account of race, religion, color, sex, national origin, familial status, or handicap
shall be fined up to $1000 or imprisoned for up to 1 year, or both. If bodily injury results, the penalty is a fine of $10,000 maximum or up to 10 years in prison, or both. If death results, the wrongdoer shall be imprisoned for any term of years or for life.

1988 Amendments

Amendments to the federal Fair Housing Act that became law in 1988 extended protection to familial status and handicap. Familial status refers to members of a family. The amendment prohibits discrimination against people with children, adults living with or in the process of acquiring legal custody, of anyone under age 18, and pregnant women.

The physically and mentally handicapped are also covered. *Handicap* is defined as a mental or physical impairment that substantially limits a person's major life activities; included are persons with records of impairment. Current drug addicts, persons convicted of drug-related felonies, and transvestites are not protected as handicapped under the law, but alcoholics are covered.

The law also appears to prohibit restrictions that would prevent the handicapped from using necessary aids. For example, a person who requires a seeing-eye dog should be allowed to have one even if pets are otherwise prohibited in an apartment building. Similarly, that person would be allowed to take the dog through the hallway, even if dogs are generally prohibited in public parts of the building.

Today, nearly all dwelling units are subject to the Fair Housing Law.

Other Fair Housing Laws

The Fair Housing Act was not the first law intended to prevent discriminatory practice in housing. The Supreme Court of the United States, in the 1917 *Buchanan* case, prohibited, on constitutional grounds, local governments from requiring residential segregation. This ruling is noteworthy because in 1896 the Supreme Court had established the doctrine that legally compelled segregation in such areas as public transportation and public education was constitutionally permissible. The Buchanan decision destroyed the doctrine as it applied to housing. In 1948, in *Shelley* v. *Kraemer*, the Supreme Court struck down as unconstitutional the legal enforcement of racially restrictive covenants.

The executive branch of the government took fair housing action for the first time in 1962, when President Kennedy issued an executive order on equal opportunity in housing. Although it represented a significant legal step forward, this executive order was limited. Its guarantee of nondiscrimination was restricted largely to housing provided through the insurance and guaranty programs administered by FHA and its sister agency, the Veterans Administration (VA), after the date of the order's issuance (November 20, 1962). Housing financed through conventional loans was not covered by the President's order, which also left hundreds of thousands of existing housing units receiving FHA and VA assistance immune from the nondiscrimination mandate. In fact, barely 1 percent of the nation's housing was covered by President Kennedy's executive order.

In 1964, Congress enacted Title VI of the Civil Rights Act of 1964, prohibiting discrimination in any program or activity receiving federal financial assistance. Among the principal programs affected by this law were low-rent public housing, a program directed to providing housing for the poor, and urban renewal. Like President Kennedy's executive order, Title VI excluded conventionally financed housing. It also excluded most FHA and VA housing that the executive order covered. Less than half of 1 percent of the nation's housing inventory was subject to the nondiscrimination requirement through Title VI.

In 1968, Congress enacted Title VIII of the Civil Rights Act of 1968, the federal Fair Housing Law. This law, which is the one described at the beginning of the chapter, prohibits discriminatory practices by all real estate brokers, builders, and mortgage lenders.

In June 1968, two months after enactment of Title VIII, the Supreme Court of the United States, in the landmark case of *Jones* v. *Mayer*, ruled that an 1866 civil rights law passed under the authority of the Eighteenth Amendment (which outlawed slavery) bars all racial discrimination in housing, private as well as public.

Today, over 90 percent of all U.S. housing is subject to the Fair Housing Law.

The Americans with Disabilities Act

The Americans with Disabilities Act (ADA), passed in 1992, considerably broadens the scope to which society in general must accommodate persons with disabilities. Many provisions of the act address discrimination in employment and access to public services. However, some of the most pervasive problems facing disabled persons have necessarily been involved with real estate: buildings are the most "barrier-prone" part of the physical environment. Narrow doors and hallways, variations in floor levels that require the negotiation of stairs, built-in facilities too high for the wheelchair-bound—the list of problems goes on and on.

Most new construction that may serve the public in general (almost anything except single-family housing) must meet barrier-free standards. Also, existing businesses with 15 or more employees must eliminate physical barriers that prevent disabled workers or customers from "functioning in the marketplace"; this *requirement* obviously requires considerable "retro-fitting" of existing real estate.

Questions on Chapter 20

1. The 1968 Fair Housing Act prohibits housing discrimination on the basis of
    (A) race and color
    (B) race, color, and religion
    (C) race, color, religion, and national origin
    (D) race, color, religion, national origin, sex, familial status, or handicap

2. The prohibitions of the 1968 Fair Housing Act apply to privately owned housing when
    (A) a broker or other person engaged in selling or renting dwellings is used
    (B) discriminatory advertising is used
    (C) both A and B
    (D) neither A nor B

3. The prohibitions of the 1968 Fair Housing Act apply to
    (A) multifamily dwellings of five or more units
    (B) multifamily dwellings of four or fewer units if the owner occupies one of the units
    (C) both A and B
    (D) neither A nor B

4. A single-family house privately owned by an individual owning fewer than three such houses may be sold or rented without being subject to the provisions of the Fair Housing Act unless
    (A) a broker is used   (C) both A and B
    (B) discriminatory advertising is used   (D) neither A nor B

5. The limiting of sale, rental, or occupancy of dwellings owned or operated by a religious organization for noncommercial purposes, provided that membership in said religion is not based on race, color, or national origin
    (A) is prohibited by the Fair Housing Act
    (B) is prohibited by the Civil Rights Act
    (C) both A and B
    (D) neither A nor B

6. A single-family house privately owned by an individual owning fewer than three such houses may be sold or rented without being subject to the provisions of the Fair Housing Act if
    (A) no more than one such house is sold in any 2-year period
    (B) a broker is employed to sell the house
    (C) both A and B
    (D) neither A nor B

7. What are the broker's responsibilities under the 1968 Fair Housing Act?
    (A) To show all houses to all prospects
    (B) To treat all prospects equally
    (C) Both A and B
    (D) Neither A nor B

8. Complaints about discrimination may be brought
   (A) to the Secretary of Housing and Urban Development
   (B) directly to court
   (C) both A and B
   (D) neither A nor B

9. If a minority prospect asks to be shown homes in white neighborhoods, the broker
   (A) obliges and shows homes in white neighborhoods
   (B) responds and shows homes as requested
   (C) both A and B
   (D) neither A nor B

10. The 1968 federal Fair Housing Law states that it is illegal to discriminate against any person because of race, color, religion, national origin, sex, familial status, or handicap
    (A) in the sale, rental, or financing of housing or residential lots
    (B) in advertising the sale or rental of housing
    (C) both A and B
    (D) neither A nor B

11. The broker's obligation in complying with the requirements for equal opportunity in housing is
    (A) to replace white residents with minority homeowners
    (B) to avoid any acts that would make housing unavailable to someone on account of color
    (C) both A and B
    (D) neither A nor B

12. The Civil Rights Act of 1968
    (A) makes it illegal to intimidate, threaten, or interfere with a person buying, renting, or selling housing
    (B) provides criminal penalties and criminal prosecution if violence is threatened or used
    (C) both A and B
    (D) neither A nor B

13. Court action may be taken by an individual under the Fair Housing Act
    (A) only if a complaint is filed with HUD
    (B) if action is taken within 1 year of the alleged discriminatory act
    (C) if the alleged discriminatory act occurred on public property
    (D) if the alleged discriminatory act caused damage of at least $500

TRUE/FALSE

Write *T* for true, *F* for false.

_____14. The Fair Housing Act does not apply to an owner selling her own house, if it is the only house she owns.

_____15. The Fair Housing Act does not apply to a building containing three dwelling units, one of which is occupied by the owner.

_____16. It is illegal for someone to intimidate another person into violating the Fair Housing Act.

_____17. Today over 90 percent of all housing in the United States is subject to the Fair Housing Act.

_____18. A part-time real estate salesperson is not required to abide by the Fair Housing Act.

_____19. Familial status and the handicapped became covered by 1988 amendments to the federal Fair Housing Act.

ANSWERS

1. **D**	6. **A**	11. **B**	16. **T**
2. **C**	7. **B**	12. **C**	17. **T**
3. **A**	8. **C**	13. **B**	18. **F**
4. **C**	9. **C**	14. **T**	19. **T**
5. **D**	10. **C**	15. **T**	

Chapter 21/*Truth in Lending Law*

Regulation Z of the Federal Reserve System, known as the Truth in Lending Act, became effective on July 1, 1969. Amendments established on April 1, 1981, became mandatory on April 1, 1982. The provisions affecting credit transactions in real estate are emphasized here, although the act covers other types of credit.

The purpose of Regulation Z is to let borrowers and consumers know the prevailing cost of credit so that they can compare costs among various credit sources and thus avoid the uninformed use of credit. Regulation Z also regulates the issuance of credit cards and sets maximum liability for their unauthorized use. In addition, it provides a procedure for resolving billing errors that occur in open end credit accounts. Regulation Z does not set maximum or minimum interest rates or require any charge for credit.

Coverage

Generally, Regulation Z applies to each individual or business that offers or extends credit when four conditions are met:
1. The credit is offered or extended to consumers.
2. The offering or extension of credit is done regularly (see definition of *creditor* below).
3. The credit is subject to a finance charge or is payable, pursuant to a written agreement, in more than four installments.
4. The credit is primarily for personal, family, or household purposes.

Definition of Creditors

Creditors are those who must comply with Regulation Z. A *creditor* is defined for this purpose as a person who arranges or extends credit more than 25 times a year (or more than 5 times in a year in the case of transactions secured by a dwelling).

As of February 19, 1982, the term *creditor* does not include a person (such as a real estate broker) who arranges seller financing of a dwelling or real property. However, a real estate broker or salesperson is not exempt from coverage in all transactions. For example, a real estate broker may be a creditor in the following situations:
1. The broker acts as a loan broker to arrange for someone other than the seller to extend credit, provided that the extender of credit (the person to whom the obligation is initially payable) does not meet the *creditor* definition.
2. The broker extends credit, provided that the broker otherwise meets the *creditor* definition.

Penalties for Violation of Regulation Z

A lender who fails to make disclosures as required under the Truth in Lending Act may be sued for actual damages plus twice the amount of the finance charge, as well as court costs and attorneys' fees. The finance charge portion of damages is subject to a minimum of $100 and a maximum of $1000. If lenders are convicted in a criminal action for willfully or knowingly disobeying the act or the regulation, they may be fined up to $5,000, imprisoned for up to 1 year, or both.

Exempt Transactions

The following transactions are exempt from the Truth in Lending Law:
1. Business, commercial, agricultural, or organizational credit.
2. Extension of credit to other than a natural person, including credit to government agencies.
3. Credit over $25,000 not secured by real property or a dwelling.
4. Extension of credit that involves public utility service.
5. Securities or commodities accounts.
6. Home-fuel budget plans.

Annual Percentage Rate

Regulation Z takes ten printed pages to define *annual percentage rate (APR)*. Briefly summarized, APR means the true interest rate charged for the use of money.

Finance Charge

DEFINITION

The *finance charge* is the cost of consumer credit as a dollar amount. It includes any charge payable directly or indirectly by the consumer, and imposed directly or indirectly by the creditor, as an incident to or a condition of the extension of credit. It does not include any charge of a type payable in a comparable cash transaction.

EXAMPLES

1. Interest, time-price differential, and any amount payable under an add-on or a discount system of additional charges.
2. Service, transaction, activity, and carrying charges, including any charge imposed on a checking or other transaction account to the extent that the charge exceeds the charge for a similar account without a credit feature.
3. Points, loan fees, assumption fees, finder's fees, and similar charges.
4. Appraisal, investigation, and credit report fees.
5. Premiums or other charges for any guarantee or insurance that protects the creditor against the consumer's default or other credit loss.
6. Charges imposed on a creditor by another person for purchasing or accepting a consumer's obligation, if the consumer is required to pay the charges in cash, as an addition to the obligation, or as a deduction from the proceeds of the obligation.
7. Premiums or other charges for credit life, accident, health, or loss-of-income insurance, written in connection with a credit transaction.
8. Premiums or other charges for insurance against loss of or damage to property, or against liability arising out of the ownership or use of property, written in connection with a credit transaction.
9. Discounts for the purpose of inducing payment by a means other than the use of credit.

The following charges are not finance charges:
1. Application fees charged to all applicants for credit, whether or not credit is actually extended.
2. Charges for actual unanticipated late payment, for exceeding a credit limit, or for delinquency, default, or a similar occurrence.

3. Charges imposed by a financial institution for paying items that overdraw an account, unless the payment of such items and the imposition of the charge were previously agreed upon in writing.
4. Fees charged for participation in a credit plan, whether assessed on an annual or other periodic basis.
5. Seller's points.
6. Interest forfeited as a result of an interest reduction required by law on a time deposit used as security for an extension of credit.
7. The following fees in a transaction secured by real property or in a residential mortgage transaction, if the fees are bona fide and reasonable in amount:
   a. Fees for title examination, abstract of title, title insurance, property survey, and similar purposes.
   b. Fees for preparing deeds, mortgages, and reconveyance, settlement, and similar documents.
   c. Notary, appraisal, and credit report fees.
   d. Amounts required to be paid into escrow or trustee accounts if the amounts would not otherwise be included in the finance charge.
8. Discounts offered to induce payment for a purchase by cash, check, or certain other means.

Premiums for certain types of insurance are also excludable if certain conditions are met, and certain taxes and fees prescribed by law are excludable.

Content of Disclosures

The following are disclosure requirements for closed-end loans. Most real estate mortgages are considered closed-end because there are no subsequent credit advances. For each transaction, the creditor shall disclose the following information as applicable:
1. Creditor. The identity of the creditor making the disclosures.
2. Amount financed. The "amount financed," using that term, and a brief description such as "the amount of credit provided to you or on your behalf." The amount financed is calculated by:
   a. determining the principal loan amount or the cash price (subtracting any down payment);
   b. adding any other amounts that are financed by the creditor and are not part of the finance charge; and
   c. subtracting any prepaid finance charge.
3. Itemization of amount financed.
   a. A separate written itemization of the amount financed. (Good faith estimates of settlement costs for transactions subject to the Real Estate Settlement Procedures Act [RESPA] are acceptable substitutes.) These items include:
      i. The amount of any proceeds distributed directly to the consumer.
      ii. The amount credited to the consumer's account with the creditor.
      iii. Any amounts paid to other persons by the creditor on the consumer's behalf. The creditor shall identify those persons. (Generic names or general terms are acceptable for certain persons such as public officials, credit reporting agencies, appraisers, and insurance companies.)
      iv. The prepaid finance charge.
   b. The creditor need not comply with paragraph 3-a above if the creditor provides a statement that the consumer has the right to receive a written itemization of the amount financed, together with a space for the consumer to indicate whether it is desired, and the consumer does not request it.
4. Finance charge. The "finance charge" using that term, and a brief description such as "the dollar amount the credit will cost you."
5. Annual percentage rate. The "annual percentage rate," using that term, and a brief description such as "the cost of your credit as a yearly rate."

6. Variable rate. If the annual percentage rate may increase after ⏤ation, the following disclosures must be included:
   a. The circumstances under which the rate may increase.
   b. Any limitations on the increase.
   c. The effect of an increase.
   d. An example of the payment terms that would result from an increase.
7. Payment schedule. The number, amounts, and timing of payments scheduled to repay the obligation.
   a. In a demand obligation with no alternative maturity date, the creditor may comply with this paragraph by disclosing the due dates or payment periods of any scheduled interest payments for the first year.
   b. In a transaction in which a series of payments varies because a finance charge is applied to the unpaid principal balance, the creditor may comply with this paragraph by disclosing the following information:
      i. The dollar amounts of the largest and smallest payments in the series.
      ii. A reference to the variations in the other payments in the series.
8. Total of payments. The "total of payments," using that term, and a descriptive explanation such as "the amount you will have paid when you have made all scheduled payments."
9. Demand feature. If the obligation has a demand feature, that fact shall be disclosed. When the disclosures are based on an assumed maturity of one year, that fact shall also be disclosed.
10. Total sale price. In a credit sale, the "total sale price," using that term, and a descriptive explanation (including the amount of any down payment) such as "the total price of your purchase on credit, including your down payment of $_____." The total sale price is the sum of the cash price, the items described in paragraph 2-b, and the finance charge disclosed under paragraph 4 above.
11. Prepayment.
    a. When an obligation includes a finance charge computed from time to time by application of a rate to the unpaid principal balance, a statement indicating whether or not a penalty may be imposed if the obligation is prepaid in full.
    b. When an obligation includes a finance charge other than the finance charge described in paragraph 11-a above, a statement indicating whether or not the consumer is entitled to a rebate of any finance charge if the obligation is prepaid in full.
12. Late payment. Any dollar or percentage charge that may be imposed before maturity due to a late payment, other than a deferral or extension charge.
13. Security interest. The fact that the creditor has or will acquire a security interest in the property purchased as part of the transaction, or in other property identified by item or type.
14. Insurance. The items required by law in order to exclude certain insurance premiums from the finance charge.
15. Certain security interest charges. The disclosures required by law in order to exclude from the finance charge certain fees prescribed by law or certain premiums for insurance in lieu of perfecting a security interest.
16. Contract reference. A statement that the consumer should refer to the appropriate contract document for information about nonpayment, default, the right to accelerate the maturity of the obligation, and prepayment rebates and penalties. At the creditor's option, the statement may also include a reference to the contract for further information about security interests and, in a residential mortgage transaction, about the creditor's policy regarding assumption of the obligation.
17. Assumption policy. In a residential mortgage transaction, a statement as to whether or not a subsequent purchaser of the dwelling from the consumer may be permitted to assume the remaining obligation on its original terms.
18. Required deposit. If the creditor requires the consumer to maintain a deposit as a condition of the specific transaction, a statement that the annual percentage rate does not reflect the effect of the required deposit.

DISCLOSURE FOR CERTAIN RESIDENTIAL MORTGAGE TRANSACTIONS

1. Time of disclosure. In a residential mortgage transaction subject to the Real Estate Settlement Procedures Act the creditor shall make good faith estimates of the disclosures described above before consummation, or shall deliver or place them in the mail not later than three business days after the creditor receives the consumer's written application, whichever is earlier. (See Figures 21-1, 21-2, and 21-3.)
2. Redisclosure required. If the annual percentage rate in the consummated transaction varies from the annual percentage rate disclosed by more than ⅛ of 1 percentage point in a regular transaction or more than ¼ of 1 percentage point in an irregular transaction, the creditor shall disclose the changed terms no later than consummation or settlement.

SUBSEQUENT DISCLOSURE REQUIREMENTS

1. Refinancings. A refinancing occurs when an existing obligation that was subject to this part of Regulation Z is satisfied and replaced by a new obligation undertaken by the same consumer. A refinancing is a new transaction requiring new disclosures to the consumer. The new finance charge shall include any unearned portion of the old finance charge that is not credited to the existing obligation. The following shall not be treated as a refinancing:
   a. A renewal of a single payment obligation with no change in the original terms.
   b. A reduction in the annual percentage rate with a corresponding change in the payment schedule.

Mortgage Savings and Loan Assoc.

Date:

ANNUAL PERCENTAGE RATE The cost of your credit as a yearly rate.	FINANCE CHARGE The dollar amount the credit will cost you.	Amount Financed The amount of credit provided to you or on your behalf.	Total of Payments The amount you will have paid after you have made all payments as scheduled.
10.85 %	$106,500.74	$44,605.66	$151,106.40

Your payment schedule will be:

Number of Payments	Amount of Payments	When Payments Are Due
360	$419.74	Monthly beginning 6/1/96

This obligation has a demand feature.

You may obtain property insurance from anyone you want that is acceptable to Mortgage Savings and Loan Assoc. If you get the insurance from Mortgage Savings and Loan Assoc. you will pay $ 150-/year

Security: You are giving a security interest in:
☒ the goods or property being purchased.
☐ _____

Late Charge: If a payment is late, you will be charged $ ___5___ % of the payment.

Prepayment: If you pay off early, you may have to pay a penalty.

Assumption: Someone buying your house may, subject to conditions, be allowed to assume the remainder of the mortgage on the original terms.

See your contract documents for any additional information about nonpayment, default, any required repayment in full before the scheduled date, and prepayment refunds and penalties.

_e_ means an estimate

Figure 21-1. Sample of Mortgage with Demand Feature

State Savings and Loan Assoc.   **Account number**

ANNUAL PERCENTAGE RATE The cost of your credit as a yearly rate.	FINANCE CHARGE The dollar amount the credit will cost you.	Amount Financed The amount of credit provided to you or on your behalf.	Total of Payments The amount you will have paid after you have made all payments as scheduled.
9.00 %	$83,452.22	$44,000.00	$127,452.22

Your payment schedule will be:

Number of Payments	Amount of Payments	When Payments Are Due
360	$354.03	Monthly beginning 6-1-96

Variable Rate

The annual percentage rate may increase during the term of this transaction if the prime rate of State Savings and Loan Assoc. increases. The rate may not increase more often than once a year, and may not increase by more than 1% annually.

The interest rate will not increase above _15.00_%. Any increase will take the form of higher payment amounts. If the interest rate increases by __1__% in __one year__, your regular payment would increase to $ _385.64_ .

Security: You are giving a security interest in the property being purchased.

Late Charge: If a payment is late, you will be charged 5% of the payment.

Prepayment: If you pay off early, you   □ may   □ will not   have to pay a penalty.

Assumption: Someone buying your house may, subject to conditions, be allowed to assume the remainder of the mortgage on the original terms.

See your contract documents for any additional information about nonpayment, default, any required repayment in full before the scheduled date, and prepayment refunds and penalties.

_____
e means an estimate

Figure 21-2.   Sample of Variable-Rate Mortgage

   c.   An agreement involving a court proceeding.

   d.   A change in the payment schedule or a change in collateral requirements as a result of the consumer's default or delinquency, unless the rate is increased, or the new amount financed exceeds the unpaid balance plus earned finance charge and premiums for continuation of insurance of certain types.

   e.   The renewal of optional insurance purchased by the consumer and added to an existing transaction, if disclosures relating to the initial purchase were provided as required by this subpart.

2.   Assumptions. An assumption occurs when a creditor expressly agrees in writing with a subsequent consumer to accept that consumer as a primary obligor on an existing residential mortgage transaction. Before the assumption occurs, the creditor shall make new disclosures to the subsequent consumer, based on the remaining obligation. If the finance charge originally imposed on the existing obligation was an add-on or a discount finance charge, the creditor need only disclose:

   a.   The unpaid balance of the obligation assumed.

   b.   The total charges imposed by the creditor in connection with the assumption.

   c.   The information required to be disclosed under section 226.18(k), (l), (m), and (n) of Regulation Z.

   d.   The annual percentage rate originally imposed on the obligation.

   e.   The payment schedule under section 226.18(g) and the total of payments under section 226.18(h), based on the remaining obligation.

Convenient Savings and Loan   Account number:

ANNUAL PERCENTAGE RATE The cost of your credit as a yearly rate.	FINANCE CHARGE The dollar amount the credit will cost you.	Amount Financed The amount of credit provided to you or on your behalf.	Total of Payments The amount you will have paid after you have made all payments as scheduled.
15.37 %	$177,970.44	$43,777	$221,546.44

Your payment schedule will be:

Number of Payments	Amount of Payments	When Payments Are Due	
12	$446.62	Monthly beginning	6/1/96
12	$479.67	" "	6/1/97
12	$515.11	" "	6/1/98
12	$553.13	" "	6/1/99
12	$593.91	" "	6/1/00
300	varying from $637.68 to $627.37	" "	6/1/01

Security: You are giving a security interest in the property being purchased.

Late Charge: If a payment is late, you will be charged 5% of the payment.

Prepayment: If you pay off early, you

- [X] may   [ ] will not   have to pay a penalty.
- [X] may   [ ] will not   be entitled to a refund of part of the finance charge.

Assumption: Someone buying your home cannot assume the remainder of the mortgage on the original terms.

See your contract documents for any additional information about nonpayment, default, any required repayment in full before the scheduled date, and prepayment refunds and penalties.

_____

e means an estimate

Figure 21-3.   Sample of Graduated-Payment Mortgage

Rescission

The right to rescind (cancel) a transaction is called *rescission*. Most lending contracts have a 3-day right of rescission period; in other words, anytime during the first 3 *business days* after the transaction is agreed to, the borrower can decide to cancel the transaction without penalty. The practice of many lenders is not to advance funds until this 3-day period has expired. One significant exception to the right of recission concerns real estate loans that are part of a contract of sale (i.e., they represent seller financing that is agreed to in the sale contract).

To rescind a credit transaction, the borrower may notify the creditor of the rescission by mail, telegram, or other written means of communication. Generally, the right to rescind expires on midnight of the third business day following the loan transaction, delivery by the creditor of the notice of the right to rescind, or delivery of all material disclosures, whichever occurs last.

EFFECT OF RESCISSION

A consumer who exercises his right to rescind is not liable for any finance or other charge, and any security interest becomes void upon rescission. Within 20 days after receipt of a notice of rescission, the creditor shall return to the consumer any money or property given as earnest money, down payment, or otherwise, and shall take any action necessary or appropriate to reflect the termination of any security interest created under the transaction. If the creditor has delivered any money or property to the consumer, the consumer may retain possession of it until the performance of the creditor's obligations under this section. Then the consumer shall tender the property to the creditor, except that, if return of the property in kind would be impracticable or inequitable, the consumer shall tender its reasonable value. Tender of property shall be made at the location of the property or at the residence of the consumer, at the option of the consumer. Tender of money shall be at the creditor's place of business. If the creditor does not take possession of the property within 20 days after tender by the consumer, ownership of the property vests in the consumer without obligation on his part to pay for it.

Residential Mortgage Transactions: Summary of Distinctions

There are five parts of Regulation Z that provide different treatment for residential mortgage loans as compared to other types of credit. These are as follows:

1. Certain fees in connection with a residential mortgage can be excluded from finance charges. These are fees for title examination, title insurance, title abstract, survey, preparing deeds and mortgage documents, notary, appraisal and credit report, and amounts paid into an escrow account if such amounts are not otherwise included in a finance charge.
2. In a residential mortgage transaction, the creditor must include a statement as to whether a subsequent purchaser of the dwelling may assume the remaining obligation on its original terms.
3. The timing of disclosure under Regulation Z for residential mortgage transactions, which are also covered by the Real Estate Settlement Procedures Act (RESPA), coincides with RESPA's requirements.
4. When a mortgage loan is assumed, the creditor must look at the intentions of the party assuming it to determine the required disclosures. If this party will use the property as a principal dwelling, disclosures applicable for such use are necessary, even if the original borrower did not use the property for that purpose.
5. A transaction to construct or acquire a principal dwelling is not eligible for the right of rescission. The lien status (first or junior mortgage) does not matter. However, a transaction that is separate from the purchase, such as one to improve a residence, is covered by this right of rescission.

Questions on Chapter 21

1. The purpose of Regulation Z is to
   (A) set the maximum interest rates that may be charged
   (B) let borrowers know the cost of credit
   (C) both A and B
   (D) neither A nor B

2. Regulation Z applies to
   (A) all real estate salespersons and brokers
   (B) all retail stores
   (C) wholesale establishments only
   (D) none of the above

3. Regulation Z covers
   (A) borrowing from relatives
   (B) borrowing by a business
   (C) real estate credit transactions
   (D) inheritances

4. Under Regulation Z, borrowers must be told in writing of
   (A) the annual percentage rate for credit
   (B) the total dollar amount of the finance charge
   (C) both A and B
   (D) neither A nor B

5. Which of the following must be included as a "finance charge" for real property credit transactions?
   (A) Fee for title insurance   (C) Monthly payment, in dollars
   (B) Fee for deed preparation   (D) None of the above

6. The annual percentage rate (APR) means the
   (A) true interest rate charged
   (B) total dollar amount of finance charges
   (C) monthly payment, in dollars
   (D) percentage of loan paid off each year

7. Under Regulation Z, a borrower may have the right to cancel, within 3 days, a
   (A) second mortgage used to improve his dwelling
   (B) first mortgage loan used to purchase his dwelling
   (C) home-improvement loan more than 1 year old
   (D) none of the above

8. To cancel a credit transaction, the borrower must inform the lender, within 3 days,
   (A) by phone   (C) both A and B
   (B) in writing   (D) neither A nor B

9. If a borrower cancels the contract within the 3-day period, she is responsible for
   (A) a 10 percent finance charge   (C) 3 days' interest
   (B) a 1 percent finance charge   (D) none of the above

10. The maximum penalty for conviction, in a criminal action, for willfully disobeying Regulation Z is up to
    (A) a $5000 fine   (C) both A and B
    (B) 1 year's imprisonment   (D) neither A nor B

TRUE/FALSE

Write *T* for true, *F* for false.

_____11. The purpose of the Truth in Lending Act is to make sure that borrowers know only how much their monthly payment is to be on a loan.

_____12. The only lender who is obliged to provide all the information required under Truth in Lending is the lender who charges the highest rate of interest.

_____13. All real estate credit transactions, except agricultural credit, are covered under the Truth in Lending Act.

_____14. Appraisal fees are not considered finance charges in real estate credit transactions.

_____15. Loan discounts are considered finance charges in real estate credit transactions.

_____16. Charges or premiums for credit life insurance required by the lender are considered finance charges.

_____17. If lenders fail to make required disclosures, they may be sued for actual damages, plus twice the amount of the finance charge as well as court costs and attorneys' fees.

ANSWERS

1. **B**	6. **A**	11. **F**	15. **T**
2. **D**	7. **A**	12. **F**	16. **T**
3. **C**	8. **B**	13. **T**	17. **T**
4. **C**	9. **D**	14. **T**	
5. **D**	10. **C**		

Chapter 22 / *Subdividing, Building and Development, Environmental Concerns*

Subdividing

Subdividing is the process of acquiring raw land and improving it to the point where it is prepared to be built on. At that point it is called a site and it can be sold to a builder or a prospective homeowner who will build on it. *Building* is putting a structure on the site. *Development* is both activities combined, usually including financing.

Subdividing is more than just preparing a map showing the boundaries of each lot. First, a subdivider gains control of the land through an option or contract. He may buy the land, though most subdividers don't want to use their own money at that point. A subdivider wants to be assured of financing before paying for the land.

Land

The value of land depends on what is around it. Land is a prisoner of its environment, so its location is crucial. Attributes of land may be described in four categories: physical, financial-economic, legal-political, and social. Physical characteristics include size, shape, topography, eye appeal, access to utilities, climate, and soil quality. Financial-economic issues include employment and unemployment in the area, wage rates, industry type and growth, interest rates, and inflation rates. Legal-political matters include zoning, building codes, and taxation. Social forces include school quality, hospitals, houses of worship, and availability of services. A key determinant of land value is the rate of inflation and expectations. This is because tangibles such as land are considered a hedge against inflation.

The value of land is most often appraised using a direct sales comparison (market) approach. Another method is by land development, whereby the final aggregate selling price of the lots are estimated and, working backwards, one subtracts the cost of development and adjusts for time and risk.

The cost of the finished lots for a homesite is typically four to five times the cost of the raw land. For example, if the raw land is purchased for $40,000 per acre, a finished lot of one-quarter acre can be expected to sell for $40,000 to $50,000.

The subdivider must have appropriate zoning for end use. For example, the land may be zoned R-1, which in that jurisdiction allows four houses per acre; or R-2, which may allow six houses. The subdivider must engage an architect and engineer to examine the subdivision and file a plat to be approved (map of the subdivision) by the planning and zoning and the engineering departments of the city.

A building permit must be obtained from the city before ground can be broken. The municipality's engineer checks the suitability of the land for the planned building. Later, assuming construction progresses, the city's inspector will inspect the foundation, heat and ventilation system, wiring, and plumbing and roofing, for compliance with the building code. Upon completion of construction, a certificate of occupancy will be issued.

Acquisition and Development Loans

Often a commercial bank is the likely source of an acquisition and development loan. Such loans generally carry interest at the prime rate plus three to five discount points. The loan is funded in stages, as the development proceeds. A subdivision or any other construction loan is considered high risk. Until sales occur in sufficient quantity, money is poured in without any coming out. It is the financial equivalent of swimming underwater. Economics in the area could change, as could the national economy. Home building is sensitive to interest rates and local growth, especially employment. Buyers are fickle—building a home is easily put off.

The first funds loaned are to purchase the land. Then, as the land is graded and potential drainage problems are cured, another installment is due. Connecting utilities to each lot—electricity, natural gas, water, sewer, and perhaps cable television, are costly. Another construction draw is due. Paving streets and putting in sidewalks deserve another draw. Advertising and selling expenses must be funded. So the construction loan balance is increased in steps, with the lender assuring that work has been done before advancing the money.

When lots are to be sold, they must be released from the subdivision loan to allow for construction financing of the house. Generally, these release provisions require more money for a given lot than the proportionate amount of subdivision loan. For example, if there is a $3 million loan on a 100 unit development, or $30,000 per lot, the loan may require that $40,000 be paid to release a lot from the subdivision loan. That way the lender forces the subdivider to stay with the project and earn a profit only after the development has proven its success through a near sell-out.

To keep loans and costs under control, the subdivider will build in phases, having enough inventory of lots to satisfy demand, but not too much, because of cost considerations.

City inspectors will examine the work at various stages to give approvals. Approvals are generally to determine compliance with city codes for safety reasons, but they are also to protect the public. Installation of pipes must be done properly to insure they won't leak natural gas, will carry sewage without leaking, and that water pipes won't get contaminated. Inspectors also assure that electrical connections are safe.

Generally, lots are considered a sale of real estate and may be sold by licensed real estate brokers and salespeople. If lots are offered for sale out of state, the subdividers must file a statement with the Office of Interstate Land Sales Registration. This is to make buyers aware of risks, especially buyers who might not visit the property. This is often the case for resort property.

Development

Development is not only getting the land prepared for use, it is also building on it and often financing a permanent loan. Matters to be considered when developing real estate are the site, market, financial feasibility, lease, financing and construction.

SITE—ZONING AND ADJACENT LAND USES

A site must have proper zoning before development can begin. Frequently, sites suitable for residential development are not zoned that way, or those intended for retail use are not zoned for commercial. Then, there must be an exploration of the attitudes of the local residents, municipal zoning staff, and the various governmental bodies that approve a proposed project, such as the Zoning Board of Appeals and City Council.

PROXIMITY OF COMPETITION AND TRAFFIC-GENERATING BUSINESSES

Conditions outside the site affect the success of the proposed development. Adjacent uses may generate desirable or undesirable traffic depending upon the type of business. For example, fast food restaurants typically find that shopping centers, high schools, and theaters are desired traffic generators. A residential development wants quiet neighbors. Both would tend to feel that salvage yards, factories, and auto dealerships generate undesired traffic.

SIZE AND SHAPE

Most developments need some street frontage. Rectangular sites are preferred for some uses because they make the most efficient layout for building, parking, and access.

TRAFFIC ACCESS, COUNT, AND CURB CUTS

A user must be able to enter and exit a site safely without causing traffic congestion. Although many developers prefer at least two curb cuts, some cities will not allow more than one curb cut for small development of under, say, 150 feet of frontage.

VISIBILITY

Some uses, such as retail properties, require good visibility. Poor visibility of a site is related to accessibility: a site that is difficult to see is also difficult to enter. A person traveling at 35 miles per hour should be able to see the property (or its sign) in time to enter the parking area safely. Corner lots generally provide better visibility and access than interior lots. Sign requirements vary by city; one should check with the planning or zoning department.

TOPOGRAPHY, DRAINAGE, AND UTILITIES

A flat site is preferred for commercial development, whereas many homebuyers prefer land with scenic qualities—a lake, stream, or hillside. The contour of the land affects the site development and building design. A level or gently sloping (less than three percent) grade is easier to build on; slopes of more than five percent require special consideration. Low-lying areas with poor drainage may require storm sewers, water retention ponds, or structural building considerations. The unavailability of gas, water, sewer, or electric service at or near the site is a major problem.

PARKING AND LANDSCAPING REQUIREMENTS

For a commercial development, the parking area must support the property's image of attractiveness and convenience. Therefore, the layout, dimensions and arrangements, grading, paving, landscaping, and lighting must all be considered in the site planning process.

Financial Feasibility

There are two methods of trying to assure the financial feasibility of a proposed development. One is to determine the cost (or operating expenses and debt service) that a completed building will incur. The price (or rental rate) is established to exceed that sum by a reasonable amount, depending on the equity capital required. This method is appropriate when attempting to build a unique structure with special market acceptance. However, when building into a competitive market, determine the going price (or rental rate) in the market. Then construction and related building costs must be kept within a strict budget so that market rents will be ample to pay for debt service and operating expenses, and to provide an adequate return on equity. Costs to be included are:
- Land
- Land acquisition fees
- Interest during construction
- Construction loan fees
- Permanent loan fees
- Permits
- Building and paving
- Site work
- Utility hookups
- Legal and accounting
- Builder's and developer's profit

Leasing

The lease is the key to developing real estate for a nonspeculative rental project. It allows property development and reduces risk for all parties who may be concerned—the landlord, tenant, lender, developer, builder, and investor.

The strength of a lease provides the basis for issuing credit. An institutional lender will provide a commitment for permanent financing based on the terms of a lease and credit standing of a tenant. The lease should specify, in sufficient detail, all aspects of the development. The permanent lender is obligated to fund the project upon completion of all terms described in the lease. The commitment need not be funded if the lease terms are not met, for example, if the completed building differs from the lease specifications or doesn't meet building codes, or there are other unfulfilled lease provisions. A permanent financing commitment paves the way to construction financing. When financing is arranged, the money is available to begin the project.

Financing

The two types of real estate financing are equity and debt. Equity funds are the owner's money in the property. Debt funds are obtained from third parties, predominantly from financial institutions.

EQUITY FINANCING

When the prospective owner's cash resources are insufficient to provide needed equity, other sources may be available. A partnership is one option. Joint ventures are similar to partnership agreements, but are for owning and operating one specific business; they terminate upon disposition of that business.

DEBT FINANCING

Under normal circumstances, financing for a newly built real estate development is obtained from two different lenders: a long-term (permanent) lender, and an interim (construction) lender. The permanent lender issues a takeout commitment that promises to repay the construction loan upon project completion. Only with a takeout commitment (or acceptable substitute), can a construction loan be arranged. The borrower prefers a permanent loan commitment from a long-term lender rather than a short-term lender.

Financing alternatives include a permanent loan (with or without participation) or a miniperm or balloon loan. Each may be structured to pay interest only for a specified period followed by amortization at a specified rate, with level payments, or an adjustable-rate mortgage (ARM). The ARM rates on commercial properties are usually indexed to short-term rates such as the prime or U.S. treasury bill rate. Rate adjustments may have annual caps and a ceiling on the rate over the life of the ARM.

Participation mortgages provide an inflation hedge to the lender as compensation for increasing market interest rates. The borrower gives up a portion of annual earnings and pays annual debt service plus a percentage of gross income or net operating income above a specified level. Lenders prefer to use gross income because values are easier to validate.

LENDERS

Savings and loan associations, commercial banks, and mortgage bankers are the primary sources of loans for housing.

Mortgage REITs finance every step of a real estate development. REITs may originate loans or purchase them from other originators. *Pension fund* investment managers typically place a portion of their assets in bank trust departments, trust companies, and life insurance companies. These assets are placed in commingled funds for investment in real estate equities and mortgages.

Insurance companies are interested in investing in commercial real estate mortgages, often through mortgage bankers who have correspondents. *Finance companies* are construction and gap financing lenders for commercial real estate. Underwriting criteria are competitive with commercial banks. Loan structures are also similar. Finance companies will accept more risk in higher L/V ratios than commercial banks with corresponding higher commitment fees, points, and interest rates.

The Loan Process

The loan process includes four steps. In *loan submission,* a comprehensive package of the borrower's financial condition and the project's characteristics and feasibility is presented to the lender. *Loan processing* includes analysis of the loan submission to verify borrower and project information submitted. *Loan underwriting* includes analysis of the borrower's creditworthiness and project feasibility to reach a lending decision. Negotiations between borrower and lender are needed to reach an agreement regarding loan terms. *Loan closing* activates the borrower and lender decisions and establishes contractual arrangements.

Construction Financing

The construction loan is secured by the land and subsequent improvements. The lender expects the loan to be repaid in a lump sum when construction is completed. For commercial property, with key tenants committed, and a permanent loan package arranged, the developer-borrower can shop for an interim (construction) loan. Institutional loans, other third party loans, and joint ventures, are three options usually available for construction financing.

The lender usually contracts with an independent architect or engineer and legal counsel to conduct the inspections. On each disbursement, county records are examined to be sure that no new liens have been filed. Typically, funds are disbursed to cover costs up to five to ten percent less than work in place plus stored materials.

Ten percent of the total construction loan amount is typically retained after construction completion, disbursed when the lender has verified that all subcontractors, materialmen, and the general contractor have been paid and no mechanics' liens have been filed on the property. With the final disbursement, the construction lender expects the property to be occupied and the permanent loan to be funded, paying off the interim loan.

These steps do not eliminate construction and economic risks. Construction risks include stoppages due to labor problems, unfavorable weather, unanticipated increase in construction costs, errors in plans and specifications, poor construction management, misappropriation of construction funds, and developer insolvency. Economic risks include market change that reduces demand, neighborhood decline, poor space design and construction defects, and poor marketing analysis leading to incorrect pricing and marketing strategy.

Physical Development

To physically develop the property, the landowner must act as a builder or hire a construction firm. If the landowner is the general contractor and developer, construction knowledge is essential. Since many landowners do not have the required time or expertise, most projects are built by firms in the construction business.

Construction Arrangements

A contractor will agree to do the specified work by a certain date for a fixed price or a certain markup above cost. Generally, contracts are complex and consist of several documents including:
  1. Invitation to bid

2. Instructions to bidders
3. General legal conditions of the contract
4. Supplementary operating conditions of the contract
5. Technical specifications
6. Drawings and blueprints
7. Bid bond
8. Contract agreement(s)
   a. Owner-architect
   b. Owner-contractor
   c. Contractor-subcontractor
9. Performance bond

The construction requirements and specifications of the project are exposed for bids; generally, the contract is awarded to the low bidder unless there are extenuating circumstances.

There are several cost estimation services available to help estimate the cost of alternative construction features; three are the *Boeckh Building-Cost Manual*, the *F. W. Dodge Construction Cost Manuals*, and the *Marshall Valuation Service*.

To reduce the chances for conflict between owners, architects, engineers, and contractors, standardized contract documents are commonly used. The American Institute of Architects offers a variety of forms that are frequently used. The National Society of Professional Engineers, the American Public Works Association, and the Associated General Contractors of America also provide standardized contract forms.

Types of Contracts

Although there are many variations, most contracts fall into one of the following categories and are awarded through competitive bidding, negotiation, or a joint venture.

A *fixed-price contract* requires the contractor to complete the project for a specific dollar amount. With a *guaranteed-maximum-price contract*, the owner pays for only the actual cost incurred (including a contractor's fee) within the maximum price guarantee. A *cost-plus contract* reimburses the contractor for actual costs incurred plus an additional percentage or fixed amount.

Selecting a Contractor

There are several questions to be raised in selecting a contractor. Does the contractor have prior experience building similar projects? Can a list of these projects be provided, along with original cost estimates and the actual cost of each? Does the contractor have experience building in the local area?

Building regulations, labor supplies, and the source of materials vary with each city; a contractor not familiar with local conditions may have conflicts, time delays, or greater expenses. Also, it is easier to check the references of a local contractor with lenders, government agencies, trade unions, and building supply houses.

Will the contractor provide a financial statement to indicate that (a) the firm has sufficient funds to be responsible for specific performance, (b) the firm is able to handle the cash flow requirements, and (c) there are no excessive short-term debts that might create problems after the project is started? Who are the subcontractors to be used for each major activity area? What is their reputation for quality and reliability, and their relationship with the general contractor? The general contractor is only as good as the subcontractors used.

Condominiums and Cooperatives

Developers or converters of a proposed condominium or cooperative, or any other shared housing arrangement, must file a statement indicating their plan. The developer must provide disclosure of the plans. This includes an architect's or engineer's report, past or expected expenses, management arrangements, and other legal and financial arrangements. It should include the conditions, covenants, and restrictions of use.

Condominium and co-op converters must follow specific rules in their community, depending on the converter's plans to allow for eviction of existing nonbuyers or a noneviction plan.

Housing offerings are printed in red on at least part of the first page (red herrings) upon preliminary review, then final plans are printed in black ink.

Environmental Considerations

Increased environmental sensitivity has raised the liability of those involved in real estate. Every gas station could have a leaking tank, pump, or pipe that contaminates ground water. Dry cleaners and car washes may use chemicals that, if released, are harmful. Even seemingly innocent property uses such as golf courses and agricultural land are suspect because of fertilizer and pesticide applications.

Recently, the Federal Home Mortgage Corporation proposed guidelines of due diligence for environmental standards of single-family homes which, until now, were defined as noncontaminating. A house may host radon (suspected of causing lung cancer), have had pesticides liberally applied to the lawn, have urea formaldehyde or asbestos insulation. It may be near a landfill, or have been built on contaminated land. Due diligence for the investigation of homes is being proposed. It would require an inspection of records of prior ownership and land use, and an inspection of the property.

LIABILITY

Superfund is the common name for the 1980 law that affects many issues of real estate contamination. Superfund, reauthorized in 1986 as SARA, includes stronger clean-up standards, disclosure requirements, and funding. *Superfund* requires the clean-up, but pays only in extreme situations, and it can render property worthless. It imposes liability on those involved with hazardous materials, liability that is *strict, joint and several, and retroactive.* Liability is created by Superfund in any connection with the property: as an owner, operator, generator, or transporter. Strict means that it doesn't matter whether such a person acted knowingly or reasonably—that person bears liability. The absence of negligence or other wrongdoing is not a defense. There are some legal defenses, but they are limited.

Joint and several liability means that every responsible party is liable for the full cost. The government or Superfund claimant may find anyone with a "deep pocket" to pay costs, and it doesn't have to sort out who was responsible for how much damage. Huge clean-up costs could conceivably be assessed against someone who took title for an instant during a closing to facilitate a transaction, but otherwise had no involvement with the property. The unlucky party would be responsible for the full amount, but could seek reimbursement from other responsible parties.

Retroactive liability means that it reaches back to prior owners and operators. This overrides "as is" clauses in sales contracts. It also precedes any mortgage lien.

ACTIVITIES

Activities that may cause contamination include manufacturing, assembly, repair, laboratory, storage, machine shop services, and cleaning. A partial list of types of businesses that may be perpetrators includes any that use, manufacture, or supply products to these uses: electronics, leathers, paints, pesticides, petroleum, pharmaceutical, plastics, refining, smelting, or textiles. In addition to those activities, events that may cause serious problems include fires, explosions, spills, and tank, pump, and pipe leaks.

CONTAMINATED ITEMS

Contamination can be found in buildings, soil, and groundwater. Within a building, asbestos may have been used for insulation and pipe-wrapping. There is no problem unless the asbestos is friable, which means it crumbles. Interior components of a building may have thick residues of chemicals that were used—these may have migrated through concrete floors into the soil.

Contamination that spreads through groundwater can cause problems to adjacent property. An extensive site assessment might be needed to determine the extent of damage.

DETECTION

A proper site assessment by a qualified professional is the best approach when considering a purchase. More and more lenders are requiring one as a requisite for a mortgage loan on commercial or industrial property, as contaminants can render a property worthless, and a foreclosure makes the lender an owner who is liable. Site assessment costs range from a few thousand to hundreds of thousands, and include drilling tests, electrical conducting, ground penetration, and laboratory analysis. An aerial photograph may help identify suspect points including ditches, landfills, lagoons, pits, ponds, tanks, and waste piles.

Other methods of due diligence to determine detection include reviewing public records and newspapers and checking with the local fire department and state or federal environmental or pollution agencies.

A Phase I assessment should be performed by a buyer as part of the due diligence acquisition process; it will help avoid clean-up liability under Superfund. Phase II is to estimate the cost of clean-up, and Phase III is to perform the work.

Acquisition Due Diligence

Due diligence relates to the process of inquiring about the property before buying. Because buyers and brokers are not engineers or geologists, it is in their best interest to hire qualified personnel to inspect the property.

Every house should be inspected for wood-destroying insects by a qualified, licensed pest control operator. Termites, carpenter ants, old house borers, and other pests should be discovered and the damage assessed. A qualified inspector will check the plumbing, electrical, and mechanical systems. Finally, a structural engineer may be helpful to determine soundness.

Commercial properties may need those types of inspectors, and a high level engineer. Environmental inspections may include searching for contaminants such as lead-based paints, the presence of underground storage tanks, groundwater contaminants from adjacent properties, asbestos, and pollution from the subject property into the air and water.

Due diligence for income property also includes a review of market conditions including proposed competition, tenant leases, and often financing availability.

Florida Uniform Land Sales Practices Act

The purpose of this law is to provide prospective buyers full and fair disclosure of information concerning the property being considered. The law created the Division of Land Sales, Condominiums and Mobile Homes, whose purpose it is to investigate the sale of subdivision land. This applies when 50 or more lots, parcels, or units of interest are created. The law specifies the content of public offering statements, which is similar to the federal Interstate Land Sales Full Disclosure Act.

Questions on Chapter 22

1. Subdividing is a process of
   A. passive investment in land
   B. clearing land of unwanted debris
   C. preparing land to be built on
   D. building on land

2. A developer is
   A. the same as a subdivider
   B. one who subdivides, builds, and generally finances
   C. a builder and tenant
   D. a broker who builds

3. Land appraisal is most frequently done by which approach?
   A. Income
   B. Replacement Cost
   C. Direct sales comparison
   D. All of the above

4. Construction loan funds are
   A. provided in steps as construction progresses
   B. loaned at the start of a project
   C. loaned at the completion of a project
   D. always the same dollar amount as permanent loan funds

5. Land for commercial uses ideally is on a (an)
   A. slope or grade
   B. heavily travelled street or road
   C. in a residential neighborhood
   D. interstate freeway

6. Banned health hazard products include all except
   A. radon
   B. asbestos
   C. radioactive materials
   D. Drano

7. Construction cost sources include all except
   A. Wiley
   B. Dodge
   C. Boechk
   D. Marshall

8. A condominium converter must
   A. not renew leases of tenants
   B. file a plan and provide disclosure
   C. make a special deal with each tenant over age 65
   D. not evict anyone under any circumstances

9. Before breaking ground, a _____ must be obtained from the city.
   A. construction loan
   B. red herring
   C. occupancy plan
   D. building permit

10. The final stage of building inspection is the granting of a
    A. prospectus
    B. certificate of occupancy
    C. inspection certificate
    D. conforming use certificate

Answers

1. **C**	5. **B**	8. **B**
2. **B**	6. **D**	9. **D**
3. **C**	7. **A**	10. **B**
4. **A**		

PART VI: REAL ESTATE LICENSING EXAMINATIONS

Chapter 23/*Exam Preparation and Strategy*

Studying for the Exam

You can't expect to walk into the examination room cold and pass with flying colors. You have to be ready for the exam. This means more than just doing a lot of reading and trying to cram your head full of facts. You have to be psychologically ready and properly prepared to take the examination so that you can *do your best* on it. To do this you have to acquire the following things:

1. Knowledge
2. A positive attitude
3. Information about exam taking
4. Confidence
5. Rest

Let's take these things one by one:

1. Knowledge. Of course you have to have the knowledge to get through the examination; this means knowing the subject matter well. Begin by studying this book and your state's license laws. Also, Florida provides special examination preparation materials, study those, too. You can't expect to acquire all the requisite knowledge if you start just a short while before the examination. You should follow a *reasonable* study schedule so that you will be at maximum readiness the day of the examination (see Chapter 1).

2. A positive attitude. Your attitude should be one of confidence; after all, if you have worked hard to learn all the real estate concepts, then you DO know the required material. The exam simply is the place where you get your chance to demonstrate that you are qualified for a real estate license.

3. Information about exam taking. Some people panic at the prospect of taking an exam and end up doing badly as a result. This sort of thing does happen; but if you look at the examination in the proper perspective, it won't happen to you. If you are concerned about taking an examination after having been out of school for such a long time, the thing to do is to practice: take the model examinations in Chapter 24. Set up actual "examination conditions." Give yourself a time limit, and go right through each practice exam just as if it were the real thing. Use all the examination-taking techniques you'll read about in this chapter. Each model exam has a key at the end of the book so that you can grade your own performance. To guide your future study, note the areas where you did well and those where you did badly. Do this for *each* practice examination: first take the exam and grade it, then do more studying in your weaker areas before you take the next one.

In this way you'll accomplish three important objectives. First, you'll get used to the examination situation. Second, you'll gain practice in answering the kinds of questions featured on most real estate license examinations. Third, you'll be able to keep track of the subject areas where you need more study and practice.

4. Confidence. Here are the areas of subject matter that examinees worry most about: (a) arithmetic, (b) contracts, and (c) for broker examinees, closing statements. We have included detailed sections on all of these, as well as on all other real estate subjects. The arithmetic you need to know is exactly the same sort you had to do for homework in the sixth and seventh grades. Contracts inspire awe because they're supposed to be the province of lawyers. By now you know that a contract is just a piece of paper on which people put down facts concerning an agreement they've made. In regard to a contract, all you have to be sure of is to write what you are supposed to and to be clear in what you say. Even property description doesn't have to look like mumbo-jumbo. Metes and bounds descriptions just need to tell where the boundaries of a property lie; lot and block number descriptions are great because they're simple and explicit.

Closing statements worry broker examinees because they look so mysterious. Actually, they're nothing but a record of where people's money goes in a real estate transaction. Once again, the important thing is accuracy. Also, if you think a bit about most of the items involved, it is easy to see if they should be paid by (or to) the seller or the buyer. All that's left is to line up all the numbers neatly so that they can be added easily. The tricky part about closing statements usually is the prorating of various items. As Chapter 18 explains, there is nothing mysterious about prorating; however, the calculations are long and clumsy, so there's room for error to sneak in if you're not careful.

Throughout this book an important aim has been to explain everything thoroughly. If you understand the subjects discussed, you should have no confidence problem: you *know* the basic principles of real estate.

5. Rest. Don't stay up studying the night before the exam! People are not at their best when tired or short of sleep. The day before the exam should be one of rest and relaxation.

You can, however, design a little last-minute study session that actually will help you, without disturbing your relaxation. Prepare a brief outline of the *important* points on which you know you need special effort. If contracts bug you, make a list of all the contracts and a brief description of each. Study this material for one-half hour in the morning, one-half hour in the afternoon, and one-half hour in the evening, but finish your studying *at least* two hours before bedtime. In that way you'll be strengthening your weaknesses, but you won't be spending so much time on studying that it interferes with the really important task at hand: getting yourself relaxed. The morning of the examination, if you have time, you can spend another half hour going over those notes one last time.

Two Important Rules

Your objective when you take any examination is to get as high a score as possible. The way to do that is to provide as many right answers as you can. This leads us directly to the most important rule of all in taking examinations.

ALWAYS ANSWER EVERY QUESTION. Even if you have to guess, write down an answer. If you leave the question blank, you can be certain that it will be counted as wrong because a blank answer is a wrong answer. If you guess, there is always the chance that the guess will be correct. Boiled down, the situation is as simple as this: you know you will get the question wrong if you leave it blank, but if you guess at an answer you may guess the right one.

The second rule is SKIP THE HARD QUESTIONS AT FIRST AND SAVE THEM FOR LAST. Many people start at the beginning of an examination and work their way through, one question at a time, until they run out of time. If they encounter a hard question, they battle with it for a long time and won't go on until they've licked it (or it has licked them). These people are lucky to get to the end of the exam before they run out of time; if they don't get to the end, they never even see some of the questions—and they might have been able to answer enough of those questions to earn a passing grade on the exam. On all of the Florida Real Estate Licensing and Appraisal Certification examinations, all questions are worth the same. So what sense is there in spending 15 minutes, half an hour, or more on a single question, when you can use that same time to read and answer a couple of *dozen* questions correctly?

When you take the exam, start at the beginning. Read the instructions, then read the first question. Answer it if you can, and then go on to number 2. Answer that one if you can, and then go on to the next and the next and the next. When you come across a hard question that you have to think about, or that will take a lot of time to answer even if you know exactly how to get the answer (some arithmetic problems can be like that), skip it for the time being. Come back to it later, after you have gone all the way through the exam and answered all the questions that you can do fairly quickly.

Strategies for Handling Questions

The Florida real estate exams are composed entirely of multiple-choice questions, in the following style:

The title of this chapter is
(A) How to Hammer a Nail
(B) Examination Strategy
(C) I Was an Elephant for the FBI
(D) None of the above

Always remember that with a multiple-choice question you are looking at the right answer! You just have to pick it out. Your strategy for answering such questions is as follows:

1. Read the question *completely* and *carefully*. Many people miss little key words such as *if*, *not*, *but*, and *except* that can completely change or limit the meaning of a sentence.

2. If the answer is obvious to you, mark it properly and go on to the next question. Then forget about the question you have just answered. Almost always the answer you pick first is the right one, and you will very rarely improve an answer by coming back and stewing over it later.

3. If the answer is not obvious, begin the guesswork strategy. First look for all the choices that you know are wrong. You may not be sure of the right answer, but that doesn't mean you can't find some answers you know are wrong. Then guess an answer from the ones that are left.

   Remember to make your guesses educated. Usually you will be able to guide your guesswork by using some of your knowledge. You may be able to decide that a certain answer is much more likely to be right than the others. Always be sure to eliminate answers you *know* are wrong in order to limit your choices and thus improve your chances of guessing the right one. However, if it looks as though a long time will be needed to reach even a guesswork answer, skip the question and come back to it later if you have the time.

Using Computer Answer Forms

Figure 23-1 is an example of a computer examination form. Do not expect the form you will use for your examination to be *identical* to Figure 23-1. The big advantage to these forms is that they are graded by a machine that can evaluate and grade thousands of examinations a day, thereby saving an enormous amount of time and labor.

If you have to use one of these answer forms, you will be given the form and a *test booklet*. The examination questions and instructions will be written in the test booklet; you will "code" your answers onto the answer sheet. Usually you will be asked to make no marks at all on the test booklet; you should put your name and any other identification asked for in the appropriate spaces on the answer sheet. Remember one critical rule: *Do not make any marks at all on either the test or the answer sheet unless and until you are instructed to*. Normally the test booklet will contain very detailed and specific instructions on how to enter the necessary information on the answer sheet; in addition, the people administering the examination will give an oral and visual presentation on the same subject.

Using these answer sheets is really quite simple. Below is an example of a set of answer spaces for three different questions:

```
1  ::A::   ::B::   ::C::   ::D::
2  ::A::   ::B::   ::C::   ::D::
3  ::A::   ::B::   ::C::   ::D::
```

For each question you have four answers to choose from: A, B, C, and D. When you have picked your answer, enter it on the examination form by *shading* the appropriate space with your pencil. Suppose, for example, you choose C:

NAME_____ SESSION_____ AM ☐ PM ☐

LAST   FIRST   MIDDLE

SOC. SEC. # _____/_____/_____   Enter your IDENT. NUMBER   EXAM CODE # _____

DATE_____ BOOK # ¥ _____

PLACE OF EXAM_____ SALESMAN ☐ BROKER ☐

TITLE OF EXAM_____

IMPORTANT: IN MARKING YOUR ANSWERS FILL IN ANSWER BOX COMPLETELY

	4 :A: :B: :C: :D:	8 :A: :B: :C: :D:	12 :A: :B: :C: :D:
1 :A: :B: :C: :D:	5 :A: :B: :C: :D:	9 :A: :B: :C: :D:	13 :A: :B: :C: :D:
2 :A: :B: :C: :D:	6 :A: :B: :C: :D:	10 :A: :B: :C: :D:	14 :A: :B: :C: :D:
3 :A: :B: :C: :D:	7 :A: :B: :C: :D:	11 :A: :B: :C: :D:	15 :A: :B: :C: :D:

	19 :A: :B: :C: :D:	23 :A: :B: :C: :D:	27 :A: :B: :C: :D:
16 :A: :B: :C: :D:	20 :A: :B: :C: :D:	24 :A: :B: :C: :D:	28 :A: :B: :C: :D:
17 :A: :B: :C: :D:	21 :A: :B: :C: :D:	25 :A: :B: :C: :D:	29 :A: :B: :C: :D:
18 :A: :B: :C: :D:	22 :A: :B: :C: :D:	26 :A: :B: :C: :D:	30 :A: :B: :C: :D:

	34 :A: :B: :C: :D:	38 :A: :B: :C: :D:	42 :A: :B: :C: :D:
31 :A: :B: :C: :D:	35 :A: :B: :C: :D:	39 :A: :B: :C: :D:	43 :A: :B: :C: :D:
32 :A: :B: :C: :D:	36 :A: :B: :C: :D:	40 :A: :B: :C: :D:	44 :A: :B: :C: :D:
33 :A: :B: :C: :D:	37 :A: :B: :C: :D:	41 :A: :B: :C: :D:	45 :A: :B: :C: :D:

	49 :A: :B: :C: :D:	53 :A: :B: :C: :D:	57 :A: :B: :C: :D:
46 :A: :B: :C: :D:	50 :A: :B: :C: :D:	54 :A: :B: :C: :D:	58 :A: :B: :C: :D:
47 :A: :B: :C: :D:	51 :A: :B: :C: :D:	55 :A: :B: :C: :D:	59 :A: :B: :C: :D:
48 :A: :B: :C: :D:	52 :A: :B: :C: :D:	56 :A: :B: :C: :D:	60 :A: :B: :C: :D:

	64 :A: :B: :C: :D:	68 :A: :B: :C: :D:	72 :A: :B: :C: :D:
61 :A: :B: :C: :D:	65 :A: :B: :C: :D:	69 :A: :B: :C: :D:	73 :A: :B: :C: :D:
62 :A: :B: :C: :D:	66 :A: :B: :C: :D:	70 :A: :B: :C: :D:	74 :A: :B: :C: :D:
63 :A: :B: :C: :D:	67 :A: :B: :C: :D:	71 :A: :B: :C: :D:	75 :A: :B: :C: :D:

	79 :A: :B: :C: :D:	83 :A: :B: :C: :D:	87 :A: :B: :C: :D:
76 :A: :B: :C: :D:	80 :A: :B: :C: :D:	84 :A: :B: :C: :D:	88 :A: :B: :C: :D:
77 :A: :B: :C: :D:	81 :A: :B: :C: :D:	85 :A: :B: :C: :D:	89 :A: :B: :C: :D:
78 :A: :B: :C: :D:	82 :A: :B: :C: :D:	86 :A: :B: :C: :D:	90 :A: :B: :C: :D:

	94 :A: :B: :C: :D:	98 :A: :B: :C: :D:	
91 :A: :B: :C: :D:	95 :A: :B: :C: :D:	99 :A: :B: :C: :D:	
92 :A: :B: :C: :D:	96 :A: :B: :C: :D:	100 :A: :B: :C: :D:	
93 :A: :B: :C: :D:	97 :A: :B: :C: :D:		

	104 :A: :B: :C: :D:	108 :A: :B: :C: :D:	112 :A: :B: :C: :D:
101 :A: :B: :C: :D:	105 :A: :B: :C: :D:	109 :A: :B: :C: :D:	113 :A: :B: :C: :D:
102 :A: :B: :C: :D:	106 :A: :B: :C: :D:	110 :A: :B: :C: :D:	114 :A: :B: :C: :D:
103 :A: :B: :C: :D:	107 :A: :B: :C: :D:	111 :A: :B: :C: :D:	115 :A: :B: :C: :D:

	119 :A: :B: :C: :D:	123 :A: :B: :C: :D:	127 :A: :B: :C: :D:
116 :A: :B: :C: :D:	120 :A: :B: :C: :D:	124 :A: :B: :C: :D:	128 :A: :B: :C: :D:
117 :A: :B: :C: :D:	121 :A: :B: :C: :D:	125 :A: :B: :C: :D:	129 :A: :B: :C: :D:
118 :A: :B: :C: :D:	122 :A: :B: :C: :D:	126 :A: :B: :C: :D:	130 :A: :B: :C: :D:

	134 :A: :B: :C: :D:	138 :A: :B: :C: :D:	142 :A: :B: :C: :D:
131 :A: :B: :C: :D:	135 :A: :B: :C: :D:	139 :A: :B: :C: :D:	143 :A: :B: :C: :D:
132 :A: :B: :C: :D:	136 :A: :B: :C: :D:	140 :A: :B: :C: :D:	144 :A: :B: :C: :D:
133 :A: :B: :C: :D:	137 :A: :B: :C: :D:	141 :A: :B: :C: :D:	145 :A: :B: :C: :D:

	149 :A: :B: :C: :D:		
146 :A: :B: :C: :D:	150 :A: :B: :C: :D:		
147 :A: :B: :C: :D:			
148 :A: :B: :C: :D:			

Figure 23-1.   Computer Examination Form

Here are three easy sample questions. Answer them by shading the appropriate space in the answer set that follows.

1. If John has two apples and I have three, together we have
   (A) 4   (C) 6
   (B) 5   (D) 7

2. The capital of France is
   (A) London   (C) Paris
   (B) Washington   (D) Des Moines, Iowa

3. Those things in the middle of your face that you see with are
   (A) eyes
   (C) nose
   (B) ears
   (D) fingernails

```
1 ::A: ::B: ::C: ::D:
2 ::A: ::B: ::C: ::D:
3 ::A: ::B: ::C: ::D:
```

The answers are obvious: 1 is B, 2 is C, 3 is A. The properly marked answer form is as follows:

```
1 ::A: ■■ ::C: ::D:
2 ::A: ::B: ■■ ::D:
3 ■■ ::B: ::C: ::D:
```

There are two things you must be careful of with respect to using computer answer forms. First, make sure you have enough pencils. Be certain that you are or are not required to bring your own pencils; if you are, get ordinary #2 pencils—the kind you can buy at any stationery store. And bring a little hand pencil sharpener along, too. After you sharpen a pencil, be sure to blunt the point by scribbling on some scratch paper before marking the answer form. You don't want to poke holes in it.

Second, our strategy of skipping the hard questions and saving them to the last means that you have to *make absolutely certain that you are putting the answer in the right space for that question!* Be especially careful here. The computer is very stupid! If you put answer marks in the wrong spaces, it will count them wrong.

By the way, the computer form used on the exam you take may be slightly different from the sample form shown here. However, it will be used in just the same way we use ours.

On-Site Scoring Systems (Keypad Answering and Scoring)

Florida still uses pencil-and-paper examinations but eventually they will be replaced by various kinds of computerized exams. One form uses a "keyboard" attached to a small terminal (screen) that displays the questions and the answer choices. You enter your choice of answer on the keypad, which also has keys allowing you to "erase" an answer, "scroll" back and forth in the exam, skip a question, and so on. Other forms use what appears to be a typical desktop personal computer, complete with a normal keyboard. If such a system is used, you usually can get some literature ahead of time that explains how to use the system. Naturally, it is important to know as much about it as you can in advance. Also, before you take the exam, the administrators will provide a detailed explanation and demonstration of how to use the equipment. Whatever the system, usually the instructions for using it (entering answers, erasing, scrolling, etc.) either appear on the screen (usually at the bottom or top) or can be accessed easily.

These devices have advantages and disadvantages. There are two major advantages. First, the machines make it easier to skip around within the exam without losing track of where you are and without any risk that you will put your answers in the wrong spaces. Second, most of the machines allow for instant scoring of your exam. When you are done, you "lock" the machine by pressing a special key. After that time, you no longer can enter or change answers. At that point, the administrators of the exam can instantly provide your score, since your answers are entered into the computer already. Usually you will be given a sheet that will tell you which questions you answered correctly and which you missed. In some examining centers, if the exam isn't over yet, you may be allowed to check your answers against the exam you just took and so tell exactly where you went wrong on the questions you missed.

The disadvantage of the examination machine is that it is unfamiliar to most people. However, it is no more complicated to use than an ordinary calculator. Rest assured that, if your examining center uses such a machine, it will be thoroughly explained before the exam starts, and there will be a brief practice session so that you can get familiar with it.

In Florida, real estate examinations are given *once a month* at test sites in Miami and Orlando, and *once every two months* in Panama City.

Chapter 24/*Model Examinations*

Following are nine practice examinations for you to take under conditions similar to those you will experience when you take the actual exam. There are two sample salesperson's licensing exams, and two sample broker's licensing exams. Both sales and broker examinations in Florida have 100 questions, and a 2½ hour time limit. The last three examinations are sample appraiser certification exams; each has 100 questions. Residential certification applicants need answer only the first 75 questions in each exam; general certification applicants should answer all 100 questions.

We suggest that applicants for broker's licenses or appraiser certification take the salesperson's exams as well as the ones they are practicing for. Because all the material covered on the typical salesperson's licensing examination is also covered on the broker's license exam and on both types of appraiser certification exams, valuable additional practice will be gained by taking the salesperson's exams.

Note that the practice exams contain no questions on license law. For this subject matter, go over your notes, materials you obtained from the examination authorities, and the text and questions in Chapter 5.

Chapter 25 provides special supplemental examinations on listing contracts, contracts of sale, closing statements. These are for broker applicants, to provide extra testing in areas particularly emphasized in the broker exam. Chapter 26 has keys to the model examinations and the special exams in Chapter 25, as well as explanations of the arithmetic questions in the exams.

Salesperson Examination 1

Answer the following questions. Use one of the answer forms at the back of the book. You have 2 hours and 30 minutes to complete this examination. Answer key is on page 430. Answers to arithmetic problems are on page 433. Mark your answers clearly on the answer sheet.

1. If, upon receipt of an offer to purchase under certain terms, the seller makes a counter-offer, the prospective purchaser is
   (A) bound by his original offer
   (B) bound to accept the counteroffer
   (C) bound by the agent's decision
   (D) relieved of his original offer

2. A broker who makes profitable investments with earnest money deposits
   (A) must share 50 percent of the profits with the owners of the money he used
   (B) has done something illegal
   (C) may keep all the profits
   (D) must turn over the profits to the state's licensing authorities

3. A real estate broker must comply with
   (A) agency law
   (B) her state's real estate licensing law
   (C) both A and B
   (D) neither A nor B

4. Smith makes an offer on Jones's property and states that the offer will remain open for 3 days. The day after Smith has made the offer, he decides to withdraw it since Jones has neither rejected nor accepted it.
   (A) Smith cannot do this.
   (B) Smith can do this only if Jones was planning to reject the offer anyway.
   (C) Smith must give Jones at least half the remaining time to make a decision.
   (D) Smith may withdraw the offer.

5. In order to sell property belonging to a trust for which she is trustee, the trustee must have
   (A) a broker's license
   (B) a salesperson's license
   (C) a trustor's license
   (D) none of the above

6. Appraised valuation is $250,000. Tax is based on 100 percent of appraised valuation. City tax is 10 mills; county tax is 8 mills. Which of the following is true?
   (A) Tax is $2,500.
   (B) Tax is $20,000.
   (C) City and county tax add up to $6,000.
   (D) None of the above

7. In the absence of an agreement to the contrary, the mortgage normally having priority will be the one that
   (A) is for the greatest amount
   (B) is a permanent mortgage
   (C) was recorded first
   (D) is a construction loan mortgage

8. A development in which a person owns her dwelling unit and, in common with other owners in the same project, also owns common property is
   (A) a leased fee
   (B) a condominium
   (C) a homestead
   (D) none of the above

9. Which of the following is true?
   (A) A condominium owner need not pay condominium fees that he feels are too high.
   (B) Condominium units are attached housing units.
   (C) Condominium is an ownership form, not an architectural style.
   (D) Condominiums cannot be rented.

10. The money for making FHA loans is provided by
    (A) qualified lending institutions
    (B) the Department of Housing and Urban Development
    (C) the Federal Housing Administration
    (D) the Federal Savings and Loan Insurance Corporation

11. License law forbids
    (A) soliciting for listings before one is licensed
    (B) collecting a commission from more than one party to a transaction
    (C) showing property to other licensees
    (D) the purchase by a broker of property that she has listed

12. The term REALTOR®
    (A) is a registered trademark
    (B) refers to anyone who has a real estate license
    (C) refers to anyone who sells real estate
    (D) none of the above

13. Complaints about housing discrimination may be brought
    (A) to the Secretary of Housing and Urban Development
    (B) directly to court
    (C) either A or B
    (D) neither A nor B

14. Which of the following is (are) ALWAYS exempt from real property taxes?
    (A) Income-producing property owned by a church
    (B) Government-owned property
    (C) Most restaurants
    (D) A private, for-profit school

15. Tenancy in severalty refers to
    (A) ownership by a married couple
    (B) ownership by one person
    (C) ownership by people who are related, but not married
    (D) ownership by unrelated people

16. For every contract of sale there must be
    (A) an offer and acceptance
    (B) a mortgage loan
    (C) a broker
    (D) good consideration

17. Real estate brokers can lose their licenses for which of the following?
    (A) Using moneys received as commissions to pay office help
    (B) Representing the buyer in a transaction
    (C) Refusing a listing
    (D) Paying a commission to a nonlicensed person

18. A broker must keep all earnest money deposits in
    (A) her office safe
    (B) her business checking account
    (C) an escrow or trust account
    (D) a savings account

19. Eminent domain is
    (A) the right of the government to take private property for public use
    (B) the extent to which state boundaries reach out to sea
    (C) an ancient form of ownership not common today
    (D) the right of the federal government to pass laws that supersede state law

20. Bernard signs a listing that guarantees the listing broker a commission payment if the sale is effected by any licensed agent. This is
    (A) an open listing   (C) an exclusive right to sell listing
    (B) an exclusive agency listing   (D) a net listing

21. Macrae negotiates with Ortez to list Ortez's property once Macrae is issued his real estate license. When the license is issued, Ortez signs a listing with Macrae.
    (A) The listing is valid.
    (B) The listing is invalid.
    (C) The listing is valid only at the listing price.
    (D) Macrae can collect only half the normal commission.

22. A licensee can lose his license for
    (A) selling properties quickly, at low prices
    (B) buying property for his own use from his principal
    (C) splitting a commission with another participating broker
    (D) none of the above

23. The major source of single-family home mortgage loan funds is
    (A) mortgage banks
    (B) commercial banks
    (C) savings and loan associations
    (D) the Federal National Mortgage Association (FNMA)

24. A conventional mortgage is
    (A) amortizing
    (B) guaranteed by FHA
    (C) not guaranteed by a government agency
    (D) approved by the VA

25. Among other things, the principal is obligated to
    (A) compensate the agent for her services
    (B) reimburse the agent for expenses incurred on behalf of the principal
    (C) both A and B
    (D) neither A and B

26. Which of the following is NOT required to have a real estate license?
    (A) The resident manager of an apartment project
    (B) The resident manager of an apartment project who, for a fee, sells a house across the street
    (C) A student who sells houses as part of a research project
    (D) All of the above

27. Recordation of a deed is the responsibility of the
    (A) grantor   (C) both A and B
    (B) grantee   (D) neither A nor B

Questions 28–31 refer to the Far Hills Estates diagram on page 346.

28. Which of following statements is (are) true?
    (A) Four lots in Block E have frontage on two streets.
    (B) Iron Road has more lots fronting on it than any of the other streets on the plat.
    (C) Both A and B
    (D) Neither A nor B

29. Which lot has the greatest footage on Wood Lane?
    (A) Lot 11, Block E   (C) Lot 1, Block L
    (B) Lot 12, Block E   (D) Lot 19, Block E

30. Which lot has the greatest depth?
    (A) Lot 4, Block L   (C) Lot 5, Block E
    (B) Lot 7, Block E   (D) Lot 16, Block E

31. Which of following statements is (are) true?
    (A) The lots on the westerly side of Dale Road should appear in Block F.
    (B) There is no indication of where to find a plat of the easterly side of Lambert Drive.
    (C) Both A and B
    (D) Neither A nor B

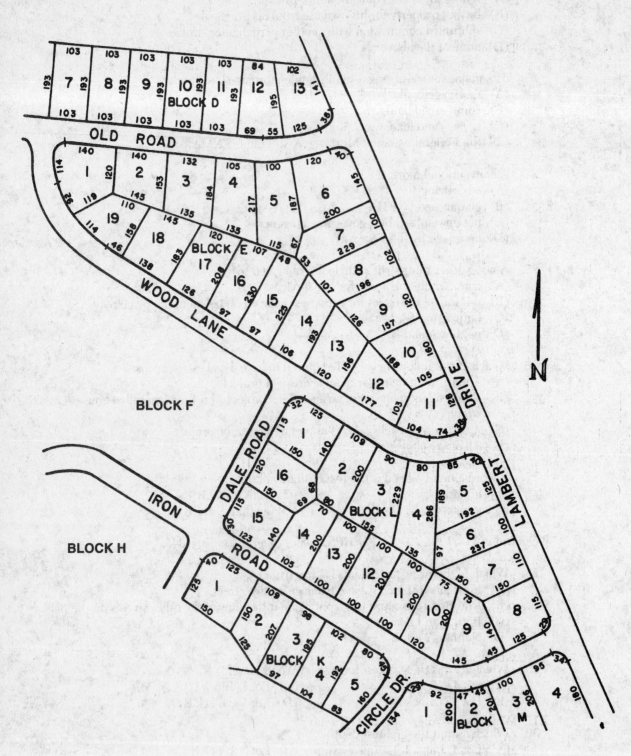

Far Hill Estates

32. The part of conveyance that defines or limits the quantity of the estate granted is
    (A) habendum
    (B) premises
    (C) equity
    (D) consideration

33. The Statute of Frauds
    (A) requires certain contracts to be in writing to be enforceable
    (B) requires a license to operate as broker or salesperson
    (C) regulates escrow accounts
    (D) regulates the estate owning real estate

34. A warranty deed protects the grantee against a loss by
    (A) casualty
    (B) defective title
    (C) both A and B
    (D) neither A nor B

35. The income approach to appraisal would be most suitable for
    (A) a newly opened subdivision
    (B) commercial and investment property
    (C) property heavily mortgaged
    (D) property heavily insured

36. Real estate is defined as
    (A) land and buildings
    (B) land and all permanent attachments to it
    (C) land and everything growing on it
    (D) land only

37. A second mortgage is
    (A) a lien on real estate that has a prior mortgage on it
    (B) the first mortgage recorded
    (C) always made by the seller
    (D) smaller in amount than a first mortgage

38. Depreciation can be caused by
    (A) physical deterioration
    (B) functional obsolescence
    (C) economic obsolescence
    (D) all of the above

39. Regulation Z applies to
    (A) all real estate salespersons and brokers
    (B) all retail stores
    (C) all wholesale establishments
    (D) none of the above

40. One discount point is equal to
    (A) 1% of the sales price
    (B) 1% of the interest rate
    (C) 1% of the loan amount
    (D) none of the above

41. Which of the following is NOT realty?
    (A) Fee simple estate
    (B) Leasehold for indefinite duration
    (C) Lumber
    (D) Life estate

42. A lease can state that the rent is to be paid in
    (A) labor
    (B) crops
    (C) cash
    (D) any of the above

43. A mortgaged property can be
   (A) sold without the consent of the mortgagee
   (B) conveyed by the grantor making a deed to the grantee
   (C) both A and B
   (D) neither A nor B

Questions 44 and 45 refer to the diagram below of a house and a lot.

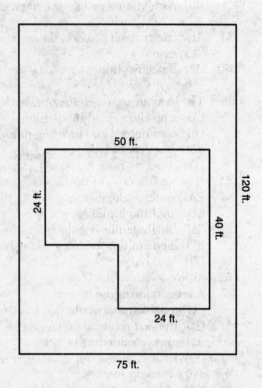

44. How many square feet are there in the house?
   (A) 384   (C) 1,584
   (B) 1,200   (D) 2,000

45. What percentage of the area of the lot is taken up by the house?
   (A) 13½%   (C) 22.2%
   (B) 17.6%   (D) 24.0%

46. Regulation Z covers
   (A) borrowing from relatives
   (B) borrowing by a business
   (C) real estate credit transactions
   (D) inheritances

47. A contract that gives someone the right but not the obligation to buy at a specified price within a specified time is
   (A) a contract of sale
   (B) an option
   (C) an agreement of sale
   (D) none of the above

48. Jones decides to divide his farm into lots for homes. Jones is a
    (A) subdivider
    (B) developer
    (C) farm divider
    (D) land architect

49. Which of the following may be an environmental hazard?
    (A) Argon gas
    (B) Lead-based paint
    (C) Copper wiring
    (D) Hard water

50. Mr. and Mrs. Smith decide to have a large screen porch enclosed to form a weatherproof den, with a fireplace. To do the construction work, they will hire a (an)
    (A) Architect
    (B) Developer
    (C) Contractor
    (D) Subdivider

51. The prohibitions of the 1968 Fair Housing Act apply to
    (A) multifamily dwellings of five or more units
    (B) multifamily dwellings of four or fewer units if the owner occupies one of the units
    (C) single-family dwellings
    (D) none of the above

52. Consideration that is of value only to the person who receives it is called
    (A) good consideration
    (B) near consideration
    (C) valuable consideration
    (D) no consideration

53. An easement in gross
    (A) covers an entire property and all parts of it
    (B) extends to one person only
    (C) extends to the general public
    (D) occurs when the public has used private land without hindrance for a certain period of time

54. A condominium homeowner's association may
    (A) require that certain owners sell their units and leave
    (B) assess fees for the upkeep of common property
    (C) practice discrimination, if it is done subtly
    (D) none of the above

55. If government takes private property it must
    (A) make just compensation for the property taken
    (B) require the property for a public use
    (C) both A and B
    (D) neither A nor B

56. The lot shown on page 350 sold for $78,300. What was the price per square foot?
    (A) $4.17
    (B) $3.56
    (C) $2.90
    (D) $2.45

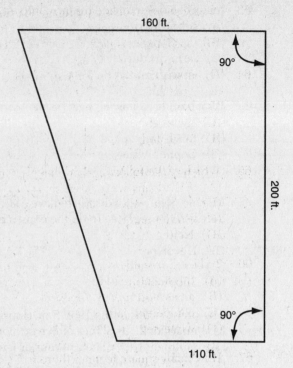

57. A millage rate of 84.5 mills is the same as
    (A) $84.50 per $1,000
    (B) 8.45%
    (C) both A and B
    (D) neither A nor B

58. A single-family house privately owned by an individual owning fewer than three such houses may be sold or rented without being subject to the provisions of the Fair Housing Act unless
    (A) a broker is used
    (B) discriminatory advertising is used
    (C) both A and B
    (D) neither A nor B

59. The transfer, by a tenant, of certain rights and obligations of an existing lease to another tenant is called
    (A) assignment of lease   (C) subletting
    (B) a release   (D) an eviction

60. A "contract for deed" is also known as
    (A) an installment land sales contract
    (B) a land contract
    (C) both A and B
    (D) neither A nor B

61. Nadel buys a new house costing $470,000. Land value is 15 percent of total price. The house contains 1733 sq. ft. What is the cost per square foot of the house alone (not including the land)?
    (A) $4.11   (C) $27.41
    (B) $23.05   (D) $31.80

62. An estoppel certificate is required when the
    (A) mortgage is sold to an investor   (C) property is being foreclosed
    (B) property is sold   (D) mortgage is assumed

63. An owner who seeks a mortgage loan and offers three properties as security will give
    (A) a blanket mortgage
    (B) an FHA mortgage
    (C) a conventional mortgage
    (D) a chattel mortgage

64. A contract that has no force or effect is said to be
    (A) voidable
    (B) void
    (C) avoided
    (D) voidiated

65. Which of the following statements is (are) false?
    (A) FHA loans are insured loans.
    (B) VA loans are guaranteed loans.
    (C) Both A and B
    (D) Neither A nor B

66. To be enforceable, a sales agreement must have
    (A) the signature of the wife of a married seller
    (B) an earnest money deposit
    (C) competent parties
    (D) witnesses

67. How many square feet are there in 1¼ acres?
    (A) 10,890
    (B) 44,649
    (C) 54,450
    (D 152,460

68. Under Regulation Z, borrowers must be informed in writing of
    (A) the annual percentage rate
    (B) the total dollar amount of the finance charge
    (C) both A and B
    (D) neither A nor B

69. An item of personalty that is affixed to realty so as to be used as a part of it is
    (A) a fixture
    (B) a chattel
    (C) personal property
    (D) encumbered

70. The requirement that all parties to a contract have an understanding of the conditions and stipulations of the agreement is
    (A) consenting realty
    (B) a proper offer
    (C) good and valuable consideration
    (D) mutual agreement

71. A deed of conveyance must be signed by
    (A) the grantee and the grantor
    (B) only by the grantor
    (C) both A and B
    (D) neither A nor B

72. In the application of the income approach to appraising, which of the following statements is true?
    (A) The higher the capitalization rate, the lower the appraised value.
    (B) The higher the capitalization rate, the higher the appraised value.
    (C) The present value is equal to future income.
    (D) None of the above

73. Jackson's will left to Mrs. Jackson the right to use, occupy, and enjoy Jackson's real estate until her death. At that time the real estate will become the property of their children. Mrs. Jackson is a
    (A) remainderman
    (B) life tenant
    (C) joint tenant
    (D) tenant in common

74. To prove his right to a commission, the broker must show
    (A) that he was licensed throughout the transaction
    (B) that he had a contract of employment
    (C) that he was the "efficient and procuring cause" of the sale
    (D) all of the above

75. Contracts made by a minor are
    (A) enforceable at all times
    (B) void
    (C) voidable by either party
    (D) voidable only by the minor

76. Mr. Beans owns land worth $5,000; Mr. Pork owns a house worth $30,000, subject to a $20,000 mortgage, which Beans will assume. For a fair trade,
    (A) pork should pay $5,000 cash in addition
    (B) beans should pay $5,000 cash in addition
    (C) they may trade properties evenly
    (D) none of the above

77. From the standpoint of the grantor, which of the following types of deed creates the least liability?
    (A) Special warranty
    (B) General warranty
    (C) Bargain and sale
    (D) Quit claim

78. The lending of money at a rate of interest above the legal rate is
    (A) speculating
    (B) usury
    (C) both A and B
    (D) neither A nor B

79. A licensee's license must be
    (A) carried in her wallet at all times
    (B) posted in a public place in the broker's office
    (C) kept on the wall at the licensee's home
    (D) kept on the wall at the Real Estate Commission

80. The parties to a deed are the
    (A) vendor and vendee
    (B) grantor and grantee
    (C) offeror and offeree
    (D) acceptor and acceptee

81. A person must be licensed if he is to sell
    (A) his home
    (B) property belonging to an estate for which he is executor
    (C) property belonging to other clients who pay him a commission
    (D) property that he has inherited

82. Which of the following is NOT an appraisal approach?
    (A) Cost
    (B) Sales comparison
    (C) Income
    (D) Trade

83. The most comprehensive ownership of land at law is known as
   (A) estate for years   (C) fee simple
   (B) life estate   (D) defeasible title

84. Each of the following pairs of words or phrases describes the same extent of land EXCEPT
   (A) 1 acre—43,560 square feet
   (B) 1 mile—5,280 feet
   (C) 1 square mile—460 acres
   (D) 1 section—640 acres

85. In order to sell property, one must
   (A) have a realtor's license
   (B) belong to a realtor's association
   (C) hire only realtors
   (D) none of the above

86. Which of the following is correct?
   (A) A section is 1 square mile.
   (B) One square mile contains 840 acres.
   (C) One acre contains 640 sections.
   (D) A section is 2850 ft. on a side.

87. How many acres are in N½ NW¼ SE¼ of a given section?
   (A) 20   (C) 160
   (B) 40   (D) 180

88. Which of the following describes a section whose eastern boundary is 25 miles *west* of the principal meridian and whose northern boundary is 42 miles *north* of the base line?
   (A) Section 35, T7N, R5W   (C) Section 2, T7N, R5W
   (B) Section 35, T8N, R5W   (D) none of the above

89. How far must a rabbit hop in a straight line from the western boundary of NE¼, NW¼ to the eastern boundary of NE¼, NE¼ of the same section?
   (A) 0.5 mi.
   (B) 900 yd.
   (C) 3960 ft.
   (D) 14.667 acres

90. Which of the following contractual arrangements would be unenforceable?
   (A) A agrees to buy B's house.
   (B) A agrees with B that B shall steal money from C.
   (C) A agrees to find a buyer for B's car.
   (D) A agrees with B that B shall make restitution to C for money stolen by B.

91. The two parties to a lease contract are the
   (A) landlord and the serf   (C) lessor and the lessee
   (B) rentor and the rentee   (D) grantor and the grantee

92. When a person deliberately lies in order to mislead a fellow party to a contract, this act is
   (A) fraud
   (B) misrepresentation
   (C) legal if no third parties are involved
   (D) all right if the lie is not written into the contract

93. A contract that transfers possession but not ownership of property is
    (A) a special warranty deed   (C) an easement
    (B) an option   (D) a lease

94. Egbert owns a building in life estate. Upon Egbert's death, ownership of the building will go to Ethel. Ethel is a
    (A) remainderman   (C) common tenant
    (B) life tenant   (D) reversionary interest

95. A person owning an undivided interest in land with at least one other, and having the right of survivorship, is said to be a
    (A) tenant in common   (C) joint tenant
    (B) tenant at will   (D) tenant at sufferance

96. A person who has some rights to use land, but not all possessory rights, is said to have
    (A) an interest in land   (C) a life estate in land
    (B) an estate in land   (D)   a tenancy in common

97. Which of the following is NOT corporeal property?
    (A) Fee simple real estate   (C) Easement
    (B) Leasehold   (D) Fixture

98. A listing contract that says the broker will receive a commission no matter who sells the property is called
    (A) an open listing
    (B) a net listing
    (C) an exclusive agency listing
    (D) an exclusive right to sell listing

99. Which of the following best describes an installment or land contract?
    (A) A contract to buy land only
    (B) A mortgage on land
    (C) A means of conveying title immediately while the purchaser pays for the property
    (D) A method of selling real estate whereby the purchaser pays for the property in regular installments while the seller retains title to the property

100. Ms. Maloney has a 3-month option on 20 acres at $200 per acre. She may
    (A) buy the property for $4,000   (C) not buy the land
    (B) sell the option to another   (D) all of the above

Salesperson Examination 2

Answer the following questions. Use one of the answer forms at the back of the book. You have 2 hours and 30 minutes to complete this examination. Answer key is on page 430. Answers to arithmetic problems are on page 434.

1. The mortgagor's right to reestablish ownership after delinquency is known as
    (A) reestablishment   (C) equity of redemption
    (B) satisfaction   (D) acceleration

2. A broker must place funds belonging to others in
    (A) his office safe, to which only he knows the combination
    (B) a safety deposit box
    (C) an account maintained by the Real Estate Commission
    (D) a trust, or escrow, account

3. A licensee's license can be revoked for
   (A) closing a deal
   (B) intentionally misleading someone into signing a contract that she ordinarily would not sign
   (C) submitting a ridiculous offer to a seller
   (D) all of the above

4. Capitalization is a process used to
   (A) convert income stream into a lump sum capital value
   (B) determine cost
   (C) establish depreciation
   (D) determine potential future value

5. The number of square feet in 1 acre is
   (A) 64,000
   (B) 460
   (C) 440
   (D) 43,560

6. When changed surroundings cause an existing house to lose value, there is
   (A) physical deterioration
   (B) economic obsolescence
   (C) functional obsolescence
   (D) all of the above

7. An appraisal is
   (A) a forecast of value
   (B) an estimate of value
   (C) a prediction of value
   (D) a precise estimation of value

8. A lien for unpaid property taxes
   (A) can be sold at auction
   (B) takes priority over all other liens
   (C) cannot exist unless taxes are at least 36 months overdue
   (D) is a form of adverse possession

9. The prohibitions of the 1968 Fair Housing Act apply to privately owned housing when
   (A) a broker or other person engaged in selling or renting dwellings is used
   (B) discriminatory advertising is used
   (C) both A and B
   (D) neither A nor B

10. According to Regulation Z, to cancel a credit transaction the borrower must inform the lender, within 3 days,
    (A) by phone
    (B) in writing
    (C) both A and B
    (D) neither A nor B

11. A agrees to trade his car to B in exchange for a vacant lot that B owns.
    (A) This is a valid contractual agreement.
    (B) This is not a contract because no money changes hands.
    (C) This is not a contract because "unlike" items can't be traded.
    (D) This is not a valid contract because the car is titled in A's name.

12. A percentage lease requires the tenant to pay
    (A) a percentage of taxes and insurance
    (B) a percentage of net income as rent
    (C) a percentage of sales as rent
    (D) none of the above

13. A seller of real estate is also known as the
    (A) vendee
    (B) grantor
    (C) vendor
    (D) grantee

14. An estate at will is
    (A) a limited partnership
    (B) a tenancy of uncertain duration
    (C) an inheritance by will
    (D) a life tenancy

15. A hands B a deed with the intent to pass title and orally requests B not to record the deed until A dies. When is the deed valid?
    (A) Immediately   (C) When A dies
    (B) When B records the deed   (D) Never

16. A quitclaim deed conveys only the interest of the
    (A) guaranteed   (C) claimant
    (B) property   (D) grantor

17. A gross lease requires the tenant to pay rent based on
    (A) gross sales   (C) gross profit
    (B) net sales   (D) none of the above

18. The recording of a deed
    (A) passes the title
    (B) insures the title
    (C) guarantees the title
    (D) gives constructive notice of ownership

19. If the property is assessed at $60,000 and the millage rate is 32.5, the tax is
    (A) $19.50   (C) $1,950.00
    (B) $195.00   (D) $19,500.00

20. The law that requires most real estate contracts to be written to be enforceable is the
    (A) Statute of Limitations
    (B) Statute of Frauds
    (C) Statute of Written Real Estate Agreements
    (D) Law of Property

21. In the absence of an agreement to the contrary, the mortgage normally having priority will be the one that
    (A) is for the greatest amount
    (B) is a permanent mortgage
    (C) was recorded first
    (D) is a construction loan mortgage

22. A net listing is one
    (A) that requires the broker to seek a net price for the property
    (B) that is legal in all states
    (C) that most ethical brokers prefer to use
    (D) in which the broker's commission is the amount by which the sale price exceeds the agreed-upon net price the seller desires

23. Under Regulation Z, a borrower may have the right to cancel, within 3 days,
    (A) a second mortgage on his dwelling
    (B) a first mortgage loan used to purchase his dwelling
    (C) a home-improvement loan more than 1 year old
    (D) none of the above

24. Which of the following does not terminate an agency relationship?
    (A) Making an offer
    (B) Death of either party
    (C) Resignation of agent
    (D) Destruction of subject matter

25. The 1968 Fair Housing Act protects against housing discrimination on the basis of
    (A) race and color
    (B) race, color, and religion
    (C) race, color, religion, and national origin
    (D) race, color, religion, national origin, sex, familial status, and handicap

26. A person who dies leaving no will is said to have died
    (A) intestate   (C) unbequeathed
    (B) without heirs   (D) unwillingly

27. From the point of view of the grantee, the safest kind of deed that can be received is a
    (A) general warranty deed   (C) quitclaim or release deed
    (B) special warranty deed   (D) trustee's deed

28. What is NOT an essential element of a valid contract?
    (A) Offer and acceptance   (C) Lack of ambiguity
    (B) Capacity of participants (D) Legal objective

29. A freehold estate is
    (A) an estate acquired without paying anything
    (B) any leasehold
    (C) any estate wherein one may use the property as one wishes
    (D) an estate of uncertain duration

30. In order to do business, a licensee must
    (A) make proper application for a license
    (B) pass a licensing examination
    (C) have a license issued by the appropriate state agency
    (D) all of the above

31. When a loan is assumed on property that is sold,
    (A) the original borrower is relieved of further responsibility
    (B) the purchaser becomes liable for the debt
    (C) the purchaser must obtain a certificate of eligibility
    (D) all of the above

32. An estoppel certificate is often required when a
    (A) mortgage is sold to an investor
    (B) property is sold
    (C) property is being foreclosed
    (D) mortgage is assumed

33. Which of the following will not terminate a lease?
    (A) Performance   (C) Surrender
    (B) Breach   (D) Vacancy

Questions 34–35 refer to the diagram shown.

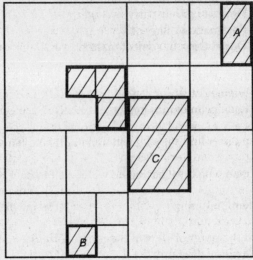

Section 20, T 14 S, R 16 W

34. Which of the following describes the shaded area marked *A*?
    (A) NE¼, NW¼, NE¼   (C) E½, NE¼
    (B) E¼, NE¼   (D) E½, NE¼, NE¼

35. How many acres are there in the shaded tract marked *A*?
    (A) 20   (C) 80
    (B) 40   (D) 160

36. A road is built through a section. It follows the line dividing E½, SE¼ from W½, SE¼ then follows the line dividing N½ from S½ until it reaches the western boundary of the section. How long is the part of the road inside the section?
    (A) 0.5 mi.   (C) 1 mi.
    (B) 0.75 mi.   (D) 1.25 mi.

37. A road is built along the northern boundary of SW¼, SE¼ of a given section. The road extends 66 ft. in width into the tract. How many acres in this tract are not covered by the road?
    (A) 27.81   (C) 38
    (B) 33   (D) 38.80

38. A broker's unlicensed secretary
    (A) may sell property providing he does it under the broker's direct supervision
    (B) may sell or negotiate deals so long as he does not leave the office
    (C) may refer interested clients to the broker or her employed licensees
    (D) all of the above

39. Discount points in FHA and VA loans are generally paid by the
    (A) lender   (C) seller
    (B) purchaser   (D) broker

40. Which of the following is NOT required of an agent with respect to his principal?
    (A) To be loyal
    (B) To act in person
    (C) To account for the agent's own personal finances
    (D) To act in the principal's best interests

41. Tenancy in severalty refers to
    (A) ownership by one person only
    (B) ownership by two persons only
    (C) ownership by at least three persons
    (D) a special form of joint ownership available only to married couples

42. A person who has permission to use land, but has no other rights, has
    (A) tenancy at sufferance   (C) license
    (B) tenancy in common   (D) fee simple estate

43. When tastes and standards cause an existing house to lose value, there is
    (A) physical deterioration   (C) functional obsolescence
    (B) economic obsolescence   (D) all of the above

44. A rule-of-thumb method for determining the price a wage earner can afford to pay for a home is to multiply her annual income by
    (A) 1½   (C) 4
    (B) 2½   (D) 6

45. A real estate license, once received,
    (A) remains in effect indefinitely
    (B) is good for a limited period of time
    (C) must be filed in county records
    (D) may be inherited by the holder's spouse

46. Which of the following is most accurately described as personal property?
    (A) A fixture   (C) An improvement
    (B) A chattel   (D) Realty

47. A real estate broker is a
    (A) general agent   (C) secret agent
    (B) special agent   (D) travel agent

48. A broker may use escrow moneys held on behalf of others
    (A) for collateral for business loans
    (B) for collateral for personal loans
    (C) for salary advances to licensees in his employ
    (D) none of the above

49. Which of the following forms of deeds has one or more guarantees of title?
    (A) Quitclaim   (C) Warranty
    (B) Executor's   (D) Special form

50. Which of the following should be disclosed to a prospective purchaser of a home?
    (A) Excessive levels of radon
    (B) Paint on exterior is over five years old
    (C) Current occupants of home are smokers
    (D) All of the above

51. The highest price a buyer is willing, but not compelled, to pay and the lowest price a seller is willing, but not compelled, to accept is
    (A) estimated value   (C) marginal value
    (B) economic value   (D) market value

52. To be valid, a deed need NOT necessarily be
    (A) signed   (C) sealed
    (B) written   (D) delivered

53. A person who receives title to land by virtue of having used and occupied it for a certain period of time, without actually paying the previous owner for it, receives title by
   (A) will
   (B) descent
   (C) alienation
   (D) adverse possession

54. A conventional mortgage is
   (A) amortizing
   (B) guaranteed by the FHA
   (C) not guaranteed by a government agency
   (D) approved by the VA

55. The party to whom a deed conveys real estate is the
   (A) grantee
   (B) grantor
   (C) beneficiary
   (D) recipient

56. Which is NOT considered a permanent attachment to land?
   (A) anything growing on it
   (B) fixtures
   (C) chattels
   (D) anything built on the land

57. The main appeal of VA mortgages to borrowers lies in
   (A) low interest rates
   (B) minimum down payments
   (C) unlimited mortgage ceiling
   (D) easy availability

58. For which reason is a deed recorded?
   (A) to insure certain title
   (B) to give notice to the world
   (C) to meet a state requirement
   (D) to save title insurance cost

59. Ownership of real property is transferred
   (A) when the grantor signs the deed
   (B) when the grantor's signature has been notarized
   (C) when the deed is delivered
   (D) when the correct documentary stamps are put on the deed and canceled

60. A valid contract of purchase or sale of real property must be signed by the
   (A) broker
   (B) agent and seller
   (C) seller only
   (D) buyer and seller

61. A sublease is a
   (A) lease made by a lessor
   (B) lease made by a lessee and a third party
   (C) lease for basement space
   (D) condition of property

62. "Hand money" paid upon the signing of an agreement of sale is called
   (A) an option
   (B) a recognizance
   (C) earnest money
   (D) a freehold estate

63. Market value appraisals assume that
   (A) the purchaser pays all cash (no mortgage financing)
   (B) FHA or VA financing is employed
   (C) the appraiser can determine the types of financing involved
   (D) the financing, if any, is on terms generally available in that area

64. A licensed salesperson
    (A) must work under the supervision of a broker
    (B) can collect commission payments only from his broker
    (C) must have his license held by his employing broker
    (D) all of the above

65. Jim sold a parcel of land for $164,450. He made a profit of 43 percent. What was his purchase price?
    (A) $82,755.00
    (B) $93,736.50
    (C) $115,000.00
    (D) $164,450.00

66. How many acres are contained in a rectangular tract of land measuring 1,700 ft. by 2,100 ft.?
    (A) 81.96
    (B) 92.91
    (C) 112.01
    (D) 115.00

67. An appraisal is
    (A) a forecast of value
    (B) a prediction of value
    (C) an estimate of value
    (D) a statement of exact value

68. The number of square feet in 1 acre is
    (A) 640
    (B) 45,630
    (C) 43,560
    (D) 53,460

69. How is the *gross rent multiplier* calculated?
    (A) Market value/market rental
    (B) Monthly payment/market rental
    (C) Market rental/market price
    (D) Sales price/market price

70. Laws that set minimum construction standards are
    (A) building codes
    (B) zoning codes
    (C) environmental laws
    (D) condemnation laws

71. Which of the following is NOT an appraisal approach?
    (A) Cost
    (B) Trade
    (C) Sales comparison
    (D) Income

72. Value is determined by
    (A) supply and demand
    (B) asking prices
    (C) interest rates
    (D) active brokers

73. Permission for land use not normally permitted by the zoning classification of the property is
    (A) a differential
    (B) a zone change
    (C) a variance
    (D) an egregement

74. Smith sells a tract of land 400 ft. by 665 ft. for $17,100. To the nearest dollar, what is the price per acre?
    (A) $2,800
    (B) $2,950
    (C) $3,117
    (D) $3,228

75. When changes in taste cause a neighborhood to become less desirable, there is
    (A) physical deterioration
    (B) functional obsolescence
    (C) economic obsolescence
    (D) all of the above

76. The income approach is generally most suitable for appraising
    (A) commercial and investment property
    (B) single-family homes
    (C) heavily mortgaged property
    (D) heavily insured property

Questions 77–79 concern the following situation:

Mr. Jones died, leaving Mrs. Jones the right to use, occupy, and enjoy his real estate until her death, at which time their son Willis would receive a fee simple estate in the real estate.

77. Mrs. Jones is a
   - (A) remainderman
   - (B) life tenant
   - (C) joint tenant
   - (D) tenant in common

78. Willis is a
   - (A) remainderman
   - (B) life tenant
   - (C) joint tenant
   - (D) tenant in common

79. Mrs. Jones has a
   - (A) fee simple estate in joint tenancy with Willis
   - (B) fee simple estate as tenant in common with Willis
   - (C) life estate
   - (D) reversionary interest

80. A freehold estate is
   - (A) an estate acquired without paying anything for it
   - (B) an estate always acquired by adverse possession
   - (C) an estate of uncertain duration
   - (D) any leasehold estate

81. A person who appears to own a piece of real estate, but actually does not, has
   - (A) good title
   - (B) recorded title
   - (C) constructive notice
   - (D) color of title

82. A real estate broker is
   - (A) a general agent
   - (B) an attorney-in-fact
   - (C) a special agent
   - (D) an agent provocateur

83. Contracts made by a minor are
   - (A) void
   - (B) voidable by the minor
   - (C) voidable by all parties
   - (D) voidable by adult parties

84. The parties to a deed are
   - (A) vendor and vendee
   - (B) testator and testatee
   - (C) grantor and grantee
   - (D) offeror and offeree

85. A quitclaim deed conveys only the interest of the
   - (A) grantor
   - (B) claimant
   - (C) quittor
   - (D) property

86. Which of the following will NOT terminate a lease?
   - (A) Breach
   - (B) Performance
   - (C) Vacancy
   - (D) Surrender

87. One discount point is equal to
   - (A) 1% of the sale price
   - (B) 1% of the loan amount
   - (C) 1% of the interest rate
   - (D) none of the above

88. Which of the following is NOT covered by title insurance?
   - (A) Forged deed
   - (B) Deed by incompetent
   - (C) Tornado damage
   - (D) Undisclosed heirs

89. Ownership of realty by one person is
    (A) tenancy in severalty
    (B) conjoint tenancy
    (C) tenancy by the entirety
    (D) tenancy sole

90. Green made an offer to purchase real estate from Blue. The offer gave Blue 7 days to consider it. Two days later, without hearing anything from Blue, Green found another property that he liked better. Green then wanted to withdraw his offer to Blue.
    (A) Green had to wait until the 7 days had passed.
    (B) Green was required to notify Blue of his desire to withdraw the offer, and to give Blue "reasonable time" to accept or reject it.
    (C) Green could withdraw the offer immediately.
    (D) none of the above

91. The secondary mortgage market is the market
    (A) for second mortgages
    (B) in which existing mortgages are bought and sold
    (C) in which junior mortgages are originated
    (D) for older, low-interest loan assumptions

92. A landowner leases her land to a lessee, who in turn leases the land to a sublessee. Who holds the *sandwich lease*?
    (A) Landowner
    (B) Lessee
    (C) Sublessee
    (D) None of the above

93. The covenant whereby a person warrants that he is the possessor and owner of property being conveyed is the covenant of
    (A) seizin
    (B) habendum
    (C) possession
    (D) further assurance

94. Title to land passes
    (A) on the date shown on the deed
    (B) upon recordation of the deed
    (C) when the deed is signed
    (D) upon delivery of the deed

95. Provisions for defeat of the mortgage are found in the____clause.
    (A) alienation
    (B) acceleration
    (C) foreclosure
    (D) defeasance

96. All mortgages are
    (A) due on sale
    (B) liens
    (C) recorded
    (D) none of the above

97. A fixture is
    (A) anything that cannot be removed from the real estate without leaving a hole
    (B) anything the property owner says is a fixture
    (C) anything necessary to the proper and efficient use of the real estate
    (D) none of the above

98. Byrd lives in an apartment owned by Lyon. The lease has expired, but Byrd has stayed on and continues to pay rent to Lyon. This is an example of tenancy
    (A) by remainder
    (B) at will
    (C) at suffrance
    (D) in common

99. Which of the following is NOT real estate?
    (A) A flagpole affixed to a house
    (B) A tomato crop not ready for harvest
    (C) A greenhouse
    (D) All of the above *are* real estate.

100. The law that requires that all transfers of ownership rights to real estate be in writing is the
    - (A) Statute of Frauds
    - (B) Statute of Limitations
    - (C) Parol Evidence Rule
    - (D) Statute of Liberties

Broker Examination 1

Answer the following questions. Use one of the answer forms at the back of the book. You have 2 hours and 30 minutes to complete this examination. Answer key is on page 431. Answers to arithmetic problems are on page 434.

1. Will openly occupied Ward's land for a period of time, without interference from Ward, and then received fee simple title to the land. This was an example of
    - (A) an easement in gross
    - (B) adverse possession
    - (C) estoppel
    - (D) subrogation

2. Max has Beth's power of attorney. Beth is called
    - (A) an agent in place
    - (B) a real estate broker
    - (C) a lawyer
    - (D) an attorney-in-fact

3. The right by which the state takes title to real estate for which no legal owner can be found is
    - (A) police power
    - (B) tenancy
    - (C) eminent domain
    - (D) escheat

4. Which of the following types of deeds has no warranty?
    - (A) executor's
    - (B) quitclaim
    - (C) general warranty
    - (D) trustee's

5. Louise does work on Joe's house, but is not paid. She may file a
    - (A) mechanic's lien
    - (B) satisfaction piece
    - (C) notice of foreclosure
    - (D) sheriff's auction

6. What is the cash-on-cash ratio for a property having a cash flow of $8,360 and an initial investor's cash equity of $76,000?
    - (A) 0.10%
    - (B) 0.105
    - (C) 0.11
    - (D) 0.12

7. What percent of 1 square mile is 96 acres?
    - (A) 21%
    - (B) 19.6%
    - (C) 15%
    - (D) 12%

8. Which claim is paid first at a foreclosure?
    - (A) Tax lien
    - (B) First mortgage
    - (C) Second mortgage
    - (D) Mechanic's lien

9. In an agency relationship, the principal is the
    - (A) seller
    - (B) buyer
    - (C) broker
    - (D) employer

10. In a lease contract, the landlord is the
    - (A) leasee
    - (B) leasor
    - (C) lessee
    - (D) lessor

11. If consideration has value only to the person receiving it, it is
    (A) personal consideration
    (B) good consideration
    (C) valuable consideration
    (D) good and valuable consideration

12. A lease that requires the landlord to pay operating expenses of the property is a_____ lease.
    (A) gross
    (B) flat
    (C) net
    (D) step

13. Taxes are due on June 1 of the year in which they are assessed. Tax rate is 41 mills. Assessed value is $53,250. If a sale of the property is closed on August 15, then at settlement (using the statutory year)
    (A) seller owes buyer $818.72
    (B) buyer owes seller $818.72
    (C) buyer owes seller $1,364.53
    (D) seller owes buyer $1,364.53

14. A properly done appraisal is
    (A) an authentication of value
    (B) an estimate of value
    (C) a prediction of value
    (D) a statement of exact value

15. If Murphy defaults on the payments to his mortgagee, under which clause may the lender demand immediate payment in full of the entire remaining loan balance?
    (A) Defeasance
    (B) Subrogation
    (C) Acceleration
    (D) Due-on-sale

16. Which of the following does NOT have the right of survivorship?
    (A) Joint tenant
    (B) Tenant in severalty
    (C) Tenant by the entirety
    (D) All of the above

17. An easement can be
    (A) the right to cross someone else's land to get to the road
    (B) a variety of fraud exclusive to real estate
    (C) the right to inherit if there is no will
    (D) none of the above

18. A broker's license is revoked. The broker's salespeople
    (A) also have their licenses revoked
    (B) may continue to operate the broker's business
    (C) may, upon proper application, transfer their licenses to another broker
    (D) must place their licenses on inactive status for a year

19. In an exclusive right-to-sell listing,
    (A) only one broker is authorized to act as the seller's agent
    (B) if the seller finds the buyer, the seller still must pay the broker a commission
    (C) the broker must use her best efforts to solicit offers
    (D) all of the above

20. Among the broker's functions, he may
    (A) accept an offer on behalf of the seller
    (B) solicit offers for the seller's listed property
    (C) try to negotiate better terms before submitting an offer
    (D) work to get the buyer the best possible price

21. Which of the following is an "improvement" to land?
    (A) Rezoning
    (B) Driveway
    (C) Orchard
    (D) All of the above

22. Which of the following is a nonfreehold estate?
    (A) Fee simple estate   (C) Life estate
    (B) Leasehold estate   (D) Dower estate

23. The rent for Sam's store is based at least in part upon Sam's gross business revenues. Sam's lease is a____lease.
    (A) reappraisal   (C) step
    (B) net   (D) percentage

24. What is usury?
    (A) Collecting more interest than that allowed by law
    (B) Building a structure that extends over someone else's land
    (C) Selling property for less than the asking price
    (D) Selling real estate without a license

25. Joe wants to build a patio 20 yd. by 20 ft. and 6 in. thick. How many cubic yards of concrete will he need?
    (A) 22.2   (C) 20.0
    (B) 40.0   (D) 400

26. The number of square feet in 1 acre is
    (A) 640   (C) 45,360
    (B) 43,560   (D) 53,460

27. How is the *gross rent multiplier* calculated?
    (A) Market value/market rental   (C) Market rental/market price
    (B) Monthly payment/market rental   (D) Sales price/market price

28. Minimum allowable construction standards are established by
    (A) building codes   (C) environmental laws
    (B) zoning codes   (D) condemnation laws

29. An allowed land use that is NOT normally permitted by the property's zoning classification is
    (A) a dispensation   (C) a variance
    (B) a zone change   (D) a restrictive covenant

30. Peeling paint and loose floorboards are examples of
    (A) physical deterioration   (C) economic obsolescence
    (B) functional obsolescence   (D) both A and B

31. The sales comparison approach is generally most suitable for appraising
    (A) commercial and investment property   (C) heavily mortgaged property
    (B) single-family homes   (D) heavily insured property

32. A feature of a freehold estate is that it
    (A) is acquired without paying anything for it
    (B) is always acquired by adverse possession
    (C) has uncertain duration
    (D) is any leasehold estate

33. A person who has the appearance of owning land, but does not own it, has
    (A) good title   (C) constructive notice
    (B) recorded title   (D) color of title

34. A contract entered into by a minor can be
   (A) void
   (B) voidable by the minor
   (C) voidable by all parties
   (D) voidable by adult parties

35. Which of the following will NOT terminate a lease?
   (A) Surrender
   (B) Performance
   (C) Vacancy
   (D) Breech

36. In mortgage lending, one discount point is equal to
   (A) 1% of the sale price
   (B) 1% of the loan amount
   (C) 1% of the interest rate
   (D) 1% of the commission

37. Hooper's offer to purchase Looper's real estate stated that the offer would become void if not accepted within 5 days. The day after the offer was made, having heard nothing from Looper, Hooper wanted to withdraw his offer
   (A) Hooper had to wait until the 5 days had passed.
   (B) Hooper was required to notify Looper of his desire to withdraw the offer, and to give Looper "reasonable time" to accept or reject it.
   (C) Hooper could withdraw the offer immediately.
   (D) None of the above

38. In a real estate transaction, title to land passes
   (A) on the date shown on the deed
   (B) upon recordation of the deed
   (C) upon notarization of the deed
   (D) upon delivery of the deed

39. A fixture is
   (A) anything that cannot be removed from the real estate without leaving a hole larger than 6 ins.
   (B) anything the seller says is a fixture
   (C) anything needed for the proper use of the real estate
   (D) none of the above

40. The law that requires that all transfers of ownership rights to real estate be in writing is the
   (A) contract act
   (B) statute of limitations
   (C) statute of recordation
   (D) statute of frauds

41. All of the following should be recorded EXCEPT
   (A) a deed of trust
   (B) a 20-year lease
   (C) an executor's deed
   (D) a contract of sale

42. In a typical mortgage loan transaction, the mortgagor is the
   (A) lender
   (B) borrower
   (C) appraiser
   (D) closing agent

43. A salesperson sold a property for $106,000. If the broker received 50 percent of the commission, and the salesperson's 60 percent share of that amount was $2,544, what was the commission rate charged on the sale?
   (A) 7%
   (B) 7.5%
   (C) 7.75%
   (D) 8%

44. An estate that any party can terminate at any time is an estate
   (A) for years
   (B) at will
   (C) in possession
   (D) leasehold entailed

45. A listing contract says that the seller receives $32,000, and the broker receives all of the purchase price over $32,000 as his commission. This is a(an)_____listing.
    (A) open
    (B) net
    (C) multiple
    (D) exclusive

46. Jones leases a building that is damaged by a storm. Under common law,
    (A) the lease is no longer enforceable
    (B) Jones needn't pay rent until the building is repaired
    (C) Jones must repair the building, but may deduct the cost from rent
    (D) Jones must continue to pay rent until the lease expires

47. In each locality, real estate brokerage commissions are determined by
    (A) the local board of REALTORS®
    (B) the laws of the state
    (C) the board of estimate
    (D) agreement between property owner and broker

48. A lot sold for $98 a front foot. If the lot was 132 ft. deep and had an area of 6,468 sq. ft., how much did the lot sell for?
    (A) $6,468
    (B) $5,771
    (C) $4,800
    (D) $3,900

49. Which of the following is required for "mutual agreement" in a contract?
    (A) Offer and acceptance
    (B) Proper consideration
    (C) Description of the land
    (D) Legal form

50. In Florida, a 6-month lease
    (A) must be in writing
    (B) need not be written
    (C) may not be in writing
    (D) ought not to be written

51. The expenses of settlement are
    (A) paid by the broker
    (B) paid by the seller
    (C) negotiated between buyer and seller
    (D) paid by the buyer

52. In Florida a primary source of revenue for local government is
    (A) income taxes
    (B) sales taxes
    (C) property taxes
    (D) severance taxes

53. The purpose of real estate licensing laws is to protect
    (A) salespersons
    (B) lawyers and legislators
    (C) developers
    (D) the general public

54. In Florida, an unlicensed person who collects a real estate commission is
    (A) subject to duress
    (B) guilty of a misdemeanor
    (C) guilty of a felony
    (D) inactivated

55. Salesperson Jones pockets an earnest money deposit and is found out. Jones's broker must
    (A) report the incident to the state real estate authorities
    (B) repay the money if Jones cannot do so
    (C) pay to defend Jones in court, if necessary
    (D) both A and B

56. Listed real estate should be advertised in the name of the
    (A) owner
    (B) salesperson
    (C) broker
    (D) closing agent

57. A 2.6-acre lot sold for $188,000. What was the price per square foot?
   (A) $1.19   (C) $1.66
   (B) $1.55   (D) $1.82

58. Hamilton's broker license is revoked by the real estate commission. Hamilton may
   (A) apply for a salesperson's license
   (B) appeal the revocation to the courts
   (C) wait 6 months and apply for reinstatement
   (D) continue to operate his business until his existing listings are sold or have expired

59. Commissions from the sale of real estate
   (A) must be divided equally between broker and salesperson
   (B) must be divided equally among all participating brokers
   (C) are not taxable income
   (D) none of the above

60. Which is the superior lien?
   (A) Tax lien   (C) Junior mortgage
   (B) First mortgage   (D) Mechanic's lien

61. A tenancy in severalty exists when
   (A) one person owns real estate
   (B) husband and wife own real estate together
   (C) any related persons own real estate together
   (D) none of the above

62. Which of the following is not a test of a fixture?
   (A) Manner of attachment   (C) Cost of the item
   (B) Intent of the person who put it there   (D) Custom in the community

63. During the life of the life tenant, the remainderman has
   (A) an easement in gross   (C) a fee simple estate
   (B) a reversionary interest   (D) a renewing leasehold estate

64. At settlement, the seller paid the buyer $351.00 toward the annual tax bill of $972.00. If taxes are assessed for the calendar year and must be paid by July 15, what was the date of the settlement?
   (A) May 10   (C) July 15
   (B) August 20   (D) Can't be determined

65. When parties to a contract agree to amend the contract, the document they prepare and sign is called a
   (A) deed amendment   (C) novation
   (B) satisfaction piece   (D) relinquishment

66. What kind of estate is received if the deed states that the grantor grants to the grantee "and his heirs and assigns forever"?
   (A) Fee simple   (C) Life estate
   (B) Leasehold   (D) Nonfreehold

67. A deed that conveys only the interest of the grantor is a
   (A) general warranty deed   (C) quitclaim deed
   (B) bargain and sale deed   (D) special warranty deed

68. A real estate license should be
    (A) carried in the licensee's wallet
    (B) posted at the Real Estate Commission
    (C) posted in a public place in the broker's office
    (D) posted in the licensee's home

69. The usefulness of the cost approach in appraisal may be limited if the subject property is
    (A) a new structure   (C) in an inactive market
    (B) functionally obsolescent   (D) proposed construction

70. A tenant paid rent at the beginning of the month; the property sold in the middle of the month. To prorate rent at settlement, you would
    (A) credit the buyer   (C) both A and B
    (B) credit the seller   (D) neither A nor B

71. Which of the following is considered a "finance charge" for the purposes of Regulation Z?
    (A) Title insurance fee   (C) Monthly payment
    (B) Deed preparation fee   (D) None of the above

72. A person who is employed by a broker to rent property, but not to sell it,
    (A) must be licensed   (C) must have a special rent-only license
    (B) need not be licensed   (D) must be a licensed broker

73. The process whereby a person may have her real estate sold to pay a debt or claim is called
    (A) lien   (C) covenant
    (B) foreclosure   (D) defeasance

74. A person who owns an undivided interest in real estate with at least one other person, and has the right of survivorship, is called a
    (A) tenant in severalty   (C) tenant in common
    (B) life tenant   (D) joint tenant

75. Which is NOT considered real estate?
    (A) Fixtures   (C) Chattels
    (B) Trees   (D) Sidewalk

76. A person who dies and leaves no will is said to have died
    (A) without heirs   (C) unbequeathed
    (B) intestate   (D) unherited

77. A broker must keep funds entrusted to her, but belonging to others, in
    (A) an office safe to which only she has the combination
    (B) a savings account in the name of the person whose money it is
    (C) a trust or escrow account
    (D) a special account managed by the state

78. When a party to a contract has deliberately lied in order to mislead the other party(ies) into agreeing to the contract, this action is an example of
    (A) fraud   (C) duress
    (B) misrepresentation   (D) defeasance

79. If a party to a contract acts so as to make performance under the contract impossible, this action is an example of
    (A) discharge of contract   (C) abandonment of contract
    (B) performance of contract   (D) breach of contract

80. A minor may be bound by the courts to contracts for
   (A) personal property
   (B) realty only
   (C) necessaries
   (D) rent

81. Edgar purchases a house costing $77,500. The loan requires a 15% down payment, an origination fee of 0.75%, 2.25 points discount, and a 0.5% PMI fee. How much money does Edgar need for these expenses?
   (A) $7,750
   (B) $9,665.25
   (C) $13,930.63
   (D) $14,337.50

82. A makes an offer to buy B's real estate. B makes a counteroffer to A.
   (A) A is bound by his original offer.
   (B) A must accept the counteroffer.
   (C) A's original offer no longer exists.
   (D) A may not counteroffer back to B.

83. A contract of sale of real estate must be signed by
   (A) buyer and seller
   (B) broker, buyer, and seller
   (C) buyer only
   (D) broker only

84. In a contract of sale, the seller is the
   (A) grantor
   (B) vendee
   (C) grantee
   (D) vendor

85. Which of the following statements is true?
   (A) To be valid, a contract of sale must be signed by the broker, if a broker assists in the transaction.
   (B) A corporation may be a party to a contract of sale.
   (C) A contract of sale need not be written if it is closed within 1 year.
   (D) A person who is an attorney-in-fact must also be an attorney-at-law.

86. Which of the following must be included in a deed?
   (A) Proper description of the real estate
   (B) Street address, if the real estate is a house
   (C) Area of the land ("more or less")
   (D) All of the above

87. A deed is recorded
   (A) to give public notice
   (B) to insure title
   (C) to satisfy the law
   (D) to avoid extra taxes

88. The part of a deed that defines or limits the quantity of estate granted is the
   (A) habendum
   (B) premises
   (C) equity
   (D) consideration

89. A final payment larger than the intermediate payments to a note is called
   (A) an escalator
   (B) an amortization
   (C) a balloon
   (D) a reappraisal

90. The interest rate on a loan is 11.5%. The interest for the month of July was $456.41. What was the loan balance at the beginning of July?
   (A) $55,173
   (B) $51,394
   (C) $47,625
   (D) $45,641

91. A conventional mortgage loan is
   (A) self-amortizing
   (B) not government insured/guaranteed
   (C) approved by the FHA
   (D) uninsurable

92. The mortgage with the highest priority is usually the one
    (A) with the highest unpaid balance
    (B) with the highest original loan amount
    (C) with the highest interest rate
    (D) that was recorded first

93. The seller of real estate takes a note secured by a mortgage on the real estate as partial payment. The mortgage is
    (A) sale financed
    (B) a purchase-income mortgage
    (C) a secondary mortgage
    (D) a first lien

94. An *ad valorem* tax is based on
    (A) the taxpayer's income
    (B) the sale price of the article taxed
    (C) the size and/or weight of the article
    (D) the value of the article taxed

95. A person who is too young to be held to a contract is called
    (A) minority-impaired
    (B) youthful
    (C) unavailable in law
    (D) incompetent

96. A contract in which rights to use and occupy real estate are transferred for a specified period of time is
    (A) a deed
    (B) an easement
    (C) a life estate
    (D) a lease

Questions 97 and 98 refer to the diagram shown.

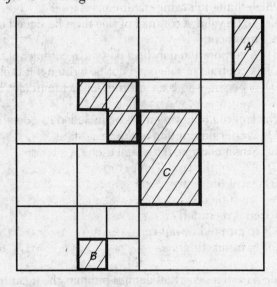

Section 20, T 14 S, R 16 W

97. Which of the following describes the shaded tract marked *B*?
    (A) SE¼, SW¼, SE¼
    (B) SW¼, SE¼, SW¼
    (C) SE¼, SW¼, NE¼
    (D) S¼, SE¼, S¼

98. What is the area of the shaded tract marked *B*?
    (A) 5 acres
    (B) 10 acres
    (C) 20 acres
    (D) 40 acres

99. A man owns SW¼, SW¼ of a section. He purchases the remainder of SW¼. By what percentage has he increased his holding of acreage?
    (A) 100%
    (B) 200%
    (C) 300%
    (D) 400%

100. Helen Smith purchases S½, NW¼, NE¼ of a section. What *percentage* of the total area of the section has she purchased?
(A) 1⁷/₁₆%
(B) 3⅛%
(C) 5%
(D) 31¼%

Broker Examination 2

Answer the following questions. Use one of the answer forms at the back of the book. You have 2 hours and 30 minutes to complete this examination. Answer key is on page 431. Answers to arithmetic problems are on page 435.

1. Jack wants to buy a house costing $111,500. The loan requires a down payment of $17,250, plus 1.5 percent origination fee, 2 points discount, and an 0.75 percent PMI fee. How much money does he need for these expenses?
(A) $17,250
(B) $19,665.25
(C) $21,988.75
(D) $21,255.63

2. The interest rate on a loan is 10.5 percent. The interest for the month of April was $496.56. What was the loan balance at the beginning of April?
(A) $49,656
(B) $56,750
(C) $60,000
(D) $62,500

3. Usury is defined as
(A) selling listed property for less than the seller's asking price
(B) selling real estate without a license
(C) collecting more interest than is allowed by law
(D) acquiring an easement by adverse possession

4. Ms. Simpson's broker license is revoked by the real estate commission. Ms. Simpson may
(A) apply for a salesperson's license
(B) appeal the revocation to the courts
(C) wait 6 months and apply for reinstatement
(D) continue to work her existing listings

5. Real estate commission payments
(A) must be divided equally among all participating brokers
(B) must be paid directly to the salesperson
(C) must be divided equally between broker and salesperson
(D) none of the above

6. Which is the superior lien in the event of foreclosure?
(A) Tax lien
(B) First mortgage
(C) Junior mortgage
(D) Home equity loan

7. A tenancy in severalty exists when
(A) husband and wife own real estate together
(B) any related persons own real estate together
(C) one person owns real estate
(D) the tenant has the right to sublet

8. Which one of the following is not a test of a fixture?
(A) Manner of attachment
(B) Intent of the person who put it there
(C) Time of attachment
(D) Custom in the community

9. Angel wants to build a driveway 70 ft. by 12. ft. and 5 in. thick. How many cubic yards of concrete will he need?
   (A) 9.6
   (B) 11.8
   (C) 13
   (D) 84

10. So long as the life tenant is alive, the remainderman has
    (A) an easement in gross
    (B) a reversionary interest
    (C) a fee simple estate
    (D) a renewing leasehold estate

11. A deed conveying only the grantor's interest is
    (A) a general warranty deed
    (B) an absolute deed
    (C) a quitclaim deed
    (D) a special warranty deed

12. A real estate license should be
    (A) posted in the licensee's home
    (B) carried in the licensee's car
    (C) posted at the Real Estate Commission
    (D) posted in a public place in the broker's office

13. The usefulness of the cost approach in appraisal may be limited if the subject property is
    (A) a new building
    (B) functionally obsolescent
    (C) in an inactive market
    (D) under construction

14. A landlord receives rent at the beginning of the month. The property is sold 10 days later. To prorate rent at settlement, you should
    (A) credit the buyer
    (B) credit the seller
    (C) both A and B
    (D) neither A nor B

15. Which of the following is considered a "finance charge" for purposes of Regulation Z?
    (A) Title insurance fee
    (B) Deed preparation fee
    (C) Monthly payment
    (D) Prepaid interest

16. Which method of advertising do real estate brokers use the most?
    (A) Radio and TV
    (B) Magazines
    (C) Newspapers
    (D) Billboards

17. Which of the following is a nonfreehold estate?
    (A) Fee simple estate
    (B) Leasehold estate
    (C) Life estate
    (D) Qualified fee simple

18. A lease that spells out specific increases in rent during the term of the lease is a____lease.
    (A) reappraisal
    (B) net
    (C) step
    (D) percentage

19. A clause in a percentage lease that allows the lessor to cancel the lease if the lessee's revenues are not at least a minimum amount is a____clause.
    (A) nonperformance
    (B) net
    (C) defeasance
    (D) recapture

20. Zoning laws are usually NOT enacted by____government.
    (A) federal
    (B) state
    (C) county
    (D) city

21. A court appoints a(an)____to settle and manage the estate of a person who dies intestate.
    (A) a trustee
    (B) an executor
    (C) an administrator
    (D) an attorney-in-fact

22. A lot 59 ft. 6 in. wide contains 535.5 sq. yd. How deep is the lot?
    (A) 5.33 rods
    (B) 88 ft.
    (C) 27 yd.
    (D) 0.03 mi.

23. A broker's license is suspended for 6 months. Salespersons whose licenses are held by this broker
    (A) may apply to transfer their licenses to another broker
    (B) must place their licenses on inactive status for 6 months
    (C) also lose their licenses for 6 months
    (D) may continue to operate the broker's business

24. The largest "bundle of rights" to real estate is a____estate.
    (A) remainder
    (B) fee simple
    (C) life
    (D) homestead

25. One of broker Mack's salespeople sold a house for $82,000. Mack received 48% of the commission and paid his salesperson 55% of that amount. How much did Mack keep, if the commission rate was 7%?
    (A) $1,239.84
    (B) $1,515.36
    (C) $2,583.00
    (D) $3,157.00

26. A 1.6-acre lot sold for $25,100. What was the price per square foot?
    (A) $3.61
    (B) $0.36
    (C) $1.88
    (D) $2.29

27. A broker who receives two offers on the same property at the same time should
    (A) reject both offers
    (B) submit both offers to the property owner
    (C) submit the better offer while trying to improve the other one
    (D) submit the better offer and reject the other one

28. As the seller's agent a broker may
    (A) reject an offer on behalf of the seller
    (B) work to get the buyer the best possible price
    (C) solicit offers for the seller's listed property
    (D) try to negotiate better terms before submitting an offer

29. Which of the following is not an "improvement" to land?
    (A) Building
    (B) Sidewalk
    (C) Corn crop
    (D) Flower bed

30. Unlicensed persons who receive shares of real estate commission payments may be in violation of
    (A) federal law
    (B) license law
    (C) zoning law
    (D) common law

31. A person who is employed by a broker to rent property, but not to sell it,
    (A) must be licensed
    (B) need not be licensed
    (C) must have a special rent-only license
    (D) must be a licensed broker

32. Which of the following statements is true?
    (A) A person who is an attorney-in-fact must also be an attorney-at-law.
    (B) To be valid, a contract of sale must be signed by the broker.
    (C) A corporation may be a party to a contract of sale.
    (D) A contract of sale need not be written if it is closed within 1 year.

33. Which of the following must be included in a deed?
    (A) Street address, if the real estate is a house
    (B) Area of the land ("more or less")
    (C) Proper description of land and improvements
    (D) Proper description of land

34. A deed is recorded
    (A) to give public notice
    (B) to insure title
    (C) to satisfy the law
    (D) to avoid extra taxes

35. The clause that defines or limits the quantity of estate granted in a deed is the
    (A) habendum
    (B) premises
    (C) addendum
    (D) consideration

36. In a mortgage, the contract specifies payments of $200 a month, and a final payment of $6,000 at the end of 30 years. The final payment is called
    (A) an escalator
    (B) an amortization
    (C) a balloon
    (D) a parachute

37. The process by which real estate is sold to pay debts or claims is known as
    (A) lien
    (B) foreclosure
    (C) covenant
    (D) defeasance

38. A person who owns an undivided interest in real estate with at least one other person, without the right of survivorship, is called a
    (A) tenant in severalty
    (B) life tenant
    (C) tenant in common
    (D) joint tenant

39. Brokers often hold funds belonging to others. They must keep these funds in
    (A) an office safe to which only the broker has the combination
    (B) a savings account in the name of the person whose money it is
    (C) a trust or escrow account
    (D) a special account managed by the state

40. When a party to a contract unintentionally misleads the other party(ies) into agreeing to the contract, this action is an example of
    (A) fraud
    (B) misrepresentation
    (C) duress
    (D) defeasance

41. If a party to a contract is responsible for making performance under it impossible, this action is an example of
    (A) specific performance
    (B) breach of contract
    (C) abandonment of contract
    (D) nonperformance of contract

42. At settlement, the buyer took over the seller's 1-year property insurance policy, which had been purchased on February 1 for $324.00. If the seller was credited for $63.00 at settlement, what was the settlement date?
    (A) May 10
    (B) November 20
    (C) July 19
    (D) Can't be determined

43. A minor may be bound by the courts to contracts for
    (A) personalty only
    (B) realty only
    (C) rent only
    (D) necessaries

MODEL EXAMINATIONS / **377**

44. Sally makes a counteroffer in response to Joe's offer to buy her lot.
    (A) Joe may not counteroffer back to Sally.
    (B) Joe is bound by his original offer.
    (C) Joe must accept the counteroffer as is, reject it, or let it expire.
    (D) If Joe makes a counteroffer, Sally may accept Joe's original offer.

45. A contract of sale of real estate must be signed by
    (A) buyer only
    (B) broker, buyer, and seller
    (C) buyer and seller
    (D) broker only

46. In a quitclaim, the seller is the
    (A) grantor
    (B) vendee
    (C) grantee
    (D) vendor

47. If a property has more than one mortgage on it, the one with the highest priority is usually the one that
    (A) has the highest interest rate
    (B) was recorded first
    (C) has the highest unpaid balance
    (D) has the highest original loan amount

48. The seller of real estate takes a note secured by a mortgage on the real estate as partial payment. The mortgage is
    (A) sale financed
    (B) a purchase-money mortgage
    (C) a secondary mortgage
    (D) a first lien

49. The market value of a house is $86,000. If property is assessed at 35% of market value and the annual tax rate is 42 mills, how much is the tax?
    (A) $1,264.20
    (B) $2,102.40
    (C) $3,511.00
    (D) $3,612.00

Questions 50–53 refer to the following situation:

May buys a house from Ray. The price is $77,900. May gets a VA loan for 90 percent of the purchase price. The loan discount is 2.5 points. The broker's commission on the sale is 6 percent. The contract interest rate on the VA loan is 9.75 percent.

50. What is the dollar amount of the discount?
    (A) $759.53
    (B) $1,182.20
    (C) $1,752.75
    (D) $1,947.50

51. What is the lender's effective rate of return on the loan?
    (A) 12.25%
    (B) 7.25%
    (C) 10.0625%
    (D) 9.6225%

52. Who pays the discount on the VA loan?
    (A) May
    (B) Ray
    (C) The broker
    (D) The VA

53. To whom is the discount paid?
    (A) The broker
    (B) The lender
    (C) The VA
    (D) May

54. An *ad valorem* tax is based on
    (A) size and/or weight of article taxed
    (B) value of article taxed
    (C) taxpayer's income
    (D) sale price of article taxed

55. Whenever all parties agree to the terms of a contract, there has been
    (A) reality of consent   (C) consideration
    (B) legality of object   (D) competency

Questions 56–61 refer to the diagram shown.

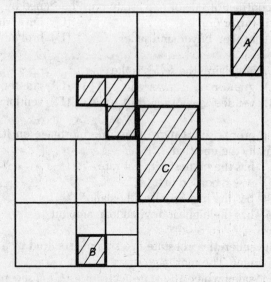

Section 20, T 14 S, R 16 W

56. Which of the following describes the irregular shaded area marked *C*?
    (A) NW¼, SE¼ *and* S½, SW¼, NE¼ *and* SE¼, SE¼, NW¼ *and* N½, SE¼, NW¼
    (B) NW¼, SE¼ *and* S½, SW¼, NE¼ *and* E½, SE¼, NW¼ *and* NW¼, SE¼, NW¼
    (C) both A and B
    (D) neither A nor B

57. What is the area of the irregular shaded area marked *C*?
    (A) 80 acres
    (B) 0.125 sq. mi.
    (C) 0.25 sq. mi.
    (D) 90 acres

58. What is the area of the portion of the irregular shaded tract marked *C* that is located in NW quarter of the section?
    (A) 20 acres   (C) 40 acres
    (B) 30 acres   (D) 80 acres

59. How far is the *center* of the illustrated section from the base line?
    (A) 86½ mi. north   (C) 24½ mi. south
    (B) 87½ mi. south   (D) 23½ mi. north

60. How far is the *center* of the illustrated section from the principal meridian?
    (A) 65½ mi. east   (C) 17½ mi. west
    (B) 65½ mi. west   (D) none of the above

61. If you travel exactly 4 miles due south from the center of the illustrated section, what section will you be in?
    (A) Section 5, T15S, R16W   (C) Section 8, T15S, R16W
    (B) Section 5, T14S, R17W   (D) Section 32, T14S, R16W

62. What is the cash-on-cash ratio for a property that has a cash flow of $32,300 and an initial investor's cash equity of $222,750?
    (A) 7.05% (C) 0.145
    (B) 0.0705 (D) 0.113

63. What percent of a square mile is a lot 1,085 ft. by 900 ft.?
    (A) 28.5% (C) 3.5%
    (B) 18.494% (D) 1.57%

64. Max has a 6-month lease that says the rent is $100 per week. The lease does not say when the rent shall be paid. When does Max have to pay?
    (A) At the end of each month (C) At the end of the lease period
    (B) At the beginning of each month (D) At the end of each week

65. Cortez got fee simple title to land that had belonged to Leone by using and occupying it openly for a certain time, unknown to and unmolested by Leone. This is an example of
    (A) estoppel (C) an easement in gross
    (B) subrogation (D) adverse possession

66. Baker gives Able his power of attorney. Able is called
    (A) an agent in place (C) a lawyer
    (B) a real estate broker (D) an attorney-in-fact

67. The right by which the state takes title to real estate for which no legal owner can be found is called
    (A) police power (C) eminent domain
    (B) tenancy (D) escheat

68. Moe receives title to Zoe's real estate after Zoe dies without a will. Moe has received
    (A) title by descent (C) an easement
    (B) clouded title (D) legacy title

69. A parcel of land is 1,077 ft. by 607 ft. How many acres does it contain?
    (A) 14.9 (C) 13.22
    (B) 9.88 (D) More than 15

70. Of the following instruments, the one with no warranty is the
    (A) executor's deed (C) general warranty deed
    (B) quitclaim deed (D) trustee's deed

71. A worker who is not paid for work that improved real estate may file a
    (A) labor judgment (C) mechanic's lien
    (B) novation (D) lis pendens

72. When a property is foreclosed, which of the following claims takes first priority?
    (A) Mechanic's lien (C) General lien
    (B) Mortgage dated June 11, 1989 (D) Mortgage dated July 22, 1990

73. In an agency relationship, the employer is called the
    (A) seller (C) principal
    (B) agent (D) broker

74. If consideration in a deed has value only to the person receiving it, it is
    (A) no consideration (C) valuable consideration
    (B) good consideration (D) good and valuable consideration

75. A lease that does not require the tenant to pay any of the operating expenses of the property is a____lease.
    (A) gross
    (B) flat
    (C) net
    (D) step

76. Sam's contractor quotes "per square foot" costs of $51.10 for the first 1,600 sq. ft. of house, $42.25 for square footage over 1,600, $22.50 for basements, $29.20 for attached garages. Sam wants a 2,100 sq. ft., two-story house, with a basement, and a 420-sq. ft. attached garage. What price (to nearest $1,000) will the contractor quote for the entire job?
    (A) $127,000
    (B) $139,000
    (C) $146,000
    (D) $162,000

77. A house is valued at $81,225 for tax purposes. This is the
    (A) assessed value
    (B) appraised value
    (C) market value
    (D) replacement value

78. Simmy buys a house and gets a mortgage loan for $128,000 to pay for it. Simmy becomes a
    (A) vendor
    (B) mortgagor
    (C) lessee
    (D) mortgagee

79. A function of Regulation Z is to
    (A) determine discounts on VA loans
    (B) set maximum interest rates on mortgage loans
    (C) allow borrowers to repay loans ahead of time without penalty
    (D) require that borrowers be informed of the cost of credit

80. An investor purchased three lots. Lot A cost $11,000, lot B cost 2.5 times the cost of A, and lot C cost half the cost of B. She then sold lots A and B for 25 percent more than the cost of all three lots. If she then sold lot C for twice its cost, what was her total profit (to the nearest $100)?
    (A) $19,100
    (B) $26,800
    (C) $33,800
    (D) None of the above

81. Zach dies without a will. According to the laws of the state, Zelda receives title to Zack's real estate. Zelda has received
    (A) title by descent
    (B) clouded title
    (C) an easement
    (D) legacy title

82. A person may void a contract if it
    (A) was entered into under duress
    (B) was entered into with a minor
    (C) turned out to be a bad deal
    (D) all of the above

83. Which of the following real estate contracts can be unilateral?
    (A) A lease
    (B) A contract of sale
    (C) A mortgage
    (D) None of the above

84. Which of the following has no warranty?
    (A) Executor's deed
    (B) Quitclaim deed
    (C) General warranty deed
    (D) Trustee's deed

85. A worker who is not pai
    (A) suit for quiet title
    (B) lis pendens

86. When a property is foreclosed, whicl
    (A) Tax lien   (C
    (B) First mortgage   (D)

87. Which of the following is a specific lien?
    (A) A judgment
    (B) A mechanic's lien
    (C) A lease
    (D) None of the above

88. Real estate is
    (A) land and buildings
    (B) land and all permanent attachments to it
    (C) land only
    (D) land and everything growing on it

89. In an agency relationship, the employer is called the
    (A) seller   (C) principal
    (B) buyer   (D) broker

90. Real estate licenses, once received, are
    (A) valid indefinitely   (C) inheritable
    (B) filed in the county record office   (D) valid for a limited period only

91. In a lease contract, the tenant is the
    (A) lessee   (C) leasee
    (B) lessor   (D) leasor

92. Consideration that has value only to the person receiving it is
    (A) no consideration   (C) valuable consideration
    (B) good consideration   (D) good and valuable consideration

93. A general warranty deed protects the grantee against a loss by
    (A) casualty
    (B) defective title
    (C) defective materials
    (D) all of the above

94. A lease that requires the tenant to pay operating expenses of the property is a____lease.
    (A) gross   (C) net
    (B) flat   (D) step

95. The mortgagor's right to reestablish ownership after foreclosure is called
    (A) acceleration   (C) equity of redemption
    (B) resatisfaction right   (D) redemption provenance

96. Regulation Z
    (A) sets maximum interest rates on mortgage loans
    (B) determines discounts on VA loans
    (C) allows borrowers to repay loans ahead of time without penalty
    (D) requires that borrowers be informed of the cost of credit

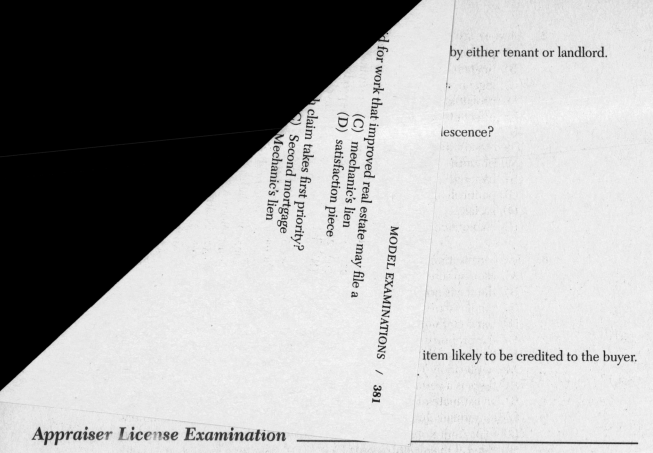

by either tenant or landlord.

escence?

for work that improved real estate may file a

(C) mechanic's lien
(D) satisfaction piece

claim takes first priority?
Second mortgage
Mechanic's lien

item likely to be credited to the buyer.

Appraiser License Examination

Directions: Select the choice, marked A, B, C, D, or E, that best answers the question or completes the thought. Mark your answers clearly on the answer sheet. You have 3 hours to complete this examination. Answers are on page 432; math solutions on page 436.

1. The present and future demand for a property and its absorption rate is considered in a
   (A) letter appraisal
   (B) market feasibility study
   (C) market segmentation
   (D) highest and best use analysis
   (E) transmittal letter

2. The appraiser's final value estimate should be based on
   (A) an average of three value indications obtained by the three approaches to value
   (B) a weighing of the reliability of the information analyzed in each of the three approaches to value
   (C) the average of the three closest comparable sales
   (D) the most sophisticated guess technique
   (E) adjustments for most recent indicators in the local market

3. The appropriate time adjustment is concluded to be an increase of 7 percent per year compounded. The time adjustment for a comparable sales property that sold for $240,000 two years ago is
   (A) −$34,776
   (B) −$33,600
   (C) −$16,800
   (D) +$33,600
   (E) +$34,776

4. The criteria for determining highest and best use include all of the following EXCEPT
   (A) physical possibility
   (B) financial feasibility
   (C) legal permissibility
   (D) probable use
   (E) effect on community welfare

5. The broad forces affecting value do NOT include
   (A) physical
   (B) life-style
   (C) political
   (D) social
   (E) economic

6. The certification of value section of an appraisal report states everything EXCEPT that
   (A) the appraiser has no interest in the property
   (B) the fee is not contingent upon any aspect of the report
   (C) the facts are correct to the best of the appraiser's knowledge
   (D) last year the property was appraised by another person
   (E) the property was personally inspected by the appraiser

7. One implication of competition and excess profit is that
   (A) there is a certain optimum combination of land, labor, capital, and entrepreneurship
   (B) an estimate of value should be based on future expectations
   (C) abnormally high profits cannot be expected to continue indefinitely
   (D) maximum value accrues to real estate when social and economic homogeneity are present in a neighborhood
   (E) the direct sales comparison approach becomes compelling

8. Cost indexes offered by standardized services are used to
   (A) derive units of comparison
   (B) catalog building components
   (C) estimate operating expenses
   (D) update past costs into current costs
   (E) estimate the local consumer price index

9. A demonstration narrative appraisal report
   (A) contains many items that are not considered in practice
   (B) is an appraisal report prepared for a client
   (C) contains all the items that might be used in practice
   (D) may be based on hypothetical or assumed data
   (E) should be prepared on a nontypical property to show appraisal expertise

10. In real estate a *submarket* is
    (A) a group of salespersons who deal mostly in the same type of property
    (B) a group of sales that occur at the same time
    (C) a group of similar properties in the same area
    (D) a small portion of the market of similar properties
    (E) an area where sandwiches on French bread are eaten

11. The fact that rents for equally desirable space tend to be set by the market reflects the principle of
    (A) balance
    (B) substitution
    (C) externalities
    (D) consistent use
    (E) conformity

12. The fee for an appraisal assignment is
    (A) based on a percentage of the final value estimate
    (B) agreed upon during the preliminary study stage
    (C) determined after the appraisal is completed
    (D) set by the fee schedule of the local board of REALTORS®
    (E) set by a fee scale from the Real Estate Commission

13. The last step in the appraisal process is to
    (A) write the report
    (B) reconcile all data
    (C) analyze the data
    (D) inspect the property
    (E) set the fee to be charged

14. The form in which a formal appraisal is presented is called
    (A) a presentation of value
    (B) an appraisal log
    (C) an appraisal report
    (D) a value certification
    (E) a narrative report

15. A formal appraisal report must include the
    (A) date of the value estimate
    (B) signature of the appraiser
    (C) identification of the property appraised
    (D) certification
    (E) all of the above

16. The highest and best use of land as if vacant forms part of the basis for
    (A) mortgage-equity analysis
    (B) a property rights adjustment
    (C) an operating expense estimate
    (D) the cost approach
    (E) the square footage approach

17. Identifying and studying submarkets of a larger market is called
    (A) market research
    (B) market survey
    (C) market agglomeration
    (D) market segmentation
    (E) market data

18. The identification and study of a pertinent market is called
    (A) market analysis
    (B) neighborhood review
    (C) property research
    (D) market reflection
    (E) market interaction

19. Which of the following is (are) important for good appraisal communication?
    (A) Word choice
    (B) Reading level
    (C) Grammatical correctness
    (D) Clarity
    (E) All of the above

20. All of the following are true EXCEPT
    (A) real property is a type of service
    (B) value is dependent on market conditions
    (C) a good or service has no value in exchange unless it possesses certain economic and legal characteristics
    (D) the price representing value is usually quoted in terms of money
    (E) real estate may be sold for all cash or financed

21. In estimating the market value of a comparable sale, an appraiser must consider all of the following EXCEPT
    (A) whether the transaction was made in cash, terms equivalent to cash, or other precisely revealed terms
    (B) whether the property had reasonable exposure in a competitive market
    (C) whether a fair sale was transacted, with neither the seller nor the buyer acting under duress
    (D) whether the replacement cost of the property corresponds to its market value
    (E) whether the seller was related to the buyer

22. In preparing an appraisal report, your analysis concludes that one of the approaches to value is not applicable to this particular case. You should
    (A) omit the approach altogether
    (B) base the approach on hypothetical data
    (C) state that the approach is not relevant
    (D) state that the approach is not applicable, explain the reasons for this contention, and provide supporting data
    (E) find another approach so as to include three approaches

23. In the cost approach the site is valued as if it were
    (A) vacant and available for development to its highest and best use
    (B) improved and suited for its intended use or development
    (C) developed and operating
    (D) attractively landscaped
    (E) without nearby utilities

24. *Investment value* is best described as
    (A) market price
    (B) market value
    (C) the cost of acquiring a competitive substitute property with the same utility
    (D) the present worth of anticipated future benefits to a certain entity
    (E) value in exchange

25. Location decisions involve analysis on which three levels?
    (A) General, specific, detailed
    (B) Country, state, community
    (C) Residential, commercial, industrial
    (D) Country, state, county
    (E) Region, neighborhood, site

26. The length of a tract of land along a street is called
    (A) depth
    (B) width
    (C) frontage
    (D) abutment
    (E) lineage

27. The most comprehensive type of appraisal report is
    (A) a form report
    (B) an oral report
    (C) a letter report
    (D) a narrative demonstration report
    (E) an unbiased report

28. The principle of____states that a buyer will not pay more for a site than for another equally desirable one:
    (A) anticipation
    (B) imbalance
    (C) substitution
    (D) balance
    (E) conformity

29. The principle of anticipation is
    (A) future oriented
    (B) past oriented
    (C) the "as of" date for an appraisal
    (D) the anticipated loan-to-value ratio for the subject property
    (E) similar to the principle of substitution

30. The principle of____states that value levels are sustained when the various elements in an economic or environmental mix are in equilibrium.
    (A) anticipation
    (B) equivalence
    (C) substitution
    (D) balance
    (E) highest and best use

31. Price and value are
    (A) not necessarily the same
    (B) synonymous
    (C) different, depending on financing terms
    (D) almost the same in an inactive market
    (E) interchangeable in a report

32. The purpose of a____is to analyze a property's potential for success.
    (A) feasibility study
    (B) marketability study
    (C) market segmentation study
    (D) appraisal report
    (E) need study

33. A use must be____to be considered as a possible alternative for highest and best use.
    (A) physically and legally possible and financially feasible
    (B) physically and legally possible
    (C) already in existence and legal
    (D) physically possible and appropriate
    (E) legal and profitable

34. An appraiser
    (A) determines price
    (B) defends value
    (C) estimates price
    (D) estimates value
    (E) determines value

35. The objective of the appraisal should be stated in the report because
    (A) the market needs it
    (B) it defines the problem and identifies the value sought
    (C) it identifies the function of the report
    (D) it absolves the appraiser of liability
    (E) there are too many definitions of market price

36. The value estimate provided in an appraisal
    (A) changes with the use to which it is put
    (B) changes with the function of the appraisal
    (C) remains the same regardless of use
    (D) depends upon the use or function of the appraisal
    (E) always reflects market value

37. Population increases____demand for housing.
    (A) depress the
    (B) are incapable of stimulating the
    (C) have no effect on the
    (D) are likely to create a
    (E) are determined by the

38. Environmental hazards that an appraiser must be conscious of include all of the following EXCEPT
    (A) asbestos
    (B) radon
    (C) Drano
    (D) urea formaldehyde
    (E) PCBs

39. In analyzing the economic environment and market area, it is best to
    (A) start at the general level and work down to the specific
    (B) start at the specific and work up to the general level
    (C) limit the analysis to the national level
    (D) limit the analysis to the local level
    (E) generally consider traffic flow

40. The first step in the appraisal process is to
    (A) define the problem
    (B) gather data
    (C) analyze data
    (D) determine the approaches to the value
    (E) make a final value estimate

41. Combining two or more sites in order to develop one site with a greater value than the individual sites have separately is called
    (A) assemblage
    (B) plottage
    (C) surplus land
    (D) excess land
    (E) highest and best use of land

42. Assemblage is
    (A) always reflected in the market value
    (B) the act of bringing two or more smaller lots into common ownership for use
    (C) inappropriate for parcels containing 10 or more acres
    (D) uneconomical
    (E) illegal

43. Typically, land is appraised by the
    (A) square foot
    (B) front foot
    (C) acre
    (D) all of the above
    (E) none of the above

44. It is____for an appraiser to receive or pay finder's or referral fees.
    (A) reasonable
    (B) unethical
    (C) necessary
    (D) customary
    (E) convenient

45. A sale between relatives is considered
    (A) an arm's length transaction
    (B) a purely comparable sale
    (C) an open market sale
    (D) a distorted sale
    (E) a good deal

46. What of the following is true about zoning?
    (A) It reflects the expectation that government will preserve property values.
    (B) It is based on the right of government to regulate for health, morals, welfare, and safety.
    (C) It is inappropriate for parcels with mixed uses.
    (D) It represents an effort to establish the land's highest and best use.
    (E) It represents the right to reuse property.

47. For an appraiser to use the assistance of another appraiser is
    (A) inconsiderate
    (B) unethical
    (C) illegal
    (D) ethical
    (E) questionable

48. It is____to provide a value range to a client who requests it and understands its meaning and use.
    (A) foolish
    (B) appropriate
    (C) unethical
    (D) approximate
    (E) difficult

49. Any recent sale of a subject property being appraised
    (A) should be considered confidential
    (B) cannot, under any circumstances, be considered in estimating the current market value of the property
    (C) should be discussed in the appraisal report
    (D) was not an arm's length sale
    (E) should be used as a comparable sale, though adjusted for its time and terms

50. The dimensions of a warehouse are customarily measured from
    (A) the roof line
    (B) the midpoint of the exterior walls
    (C) the inside of finished walls
    (D) the outside of finished walls
    (E) the foundation slab

51. The construction of a luxury home in a neighborhood almost completely developed with one- and two-bedroom apartments would
    (A) produce external obsolescence
    (B) be called an underimprovement
    (C) result in plottage value
    (D) result in neighborhood amenities
    (E) be reasonable or appropriate

52. The most detailed, complex, costly and time-consuming method of cost estimation is the
    (A) quantity survey
    (B) trade breakdown
    (C) comparative unit
    (D) unit in place
    (E) comparable unit

53. An improvement's remaining economic life
    (A) is its chronological age
    (B) is its effective age
    (C) is the period over which the improvements are expected to generate benefits
    (D) is effective age minus chronological age
    (E) is effective age plus chronological age

54. The cost approach is most applicable when the property being appraised
    (A) has old improvements
    (B) has relatively new improvements that represent the highest and best use of the land
    (C) suffers substantial functional obsolescence
    (D) is more costly than the surroundings
    (E) has many older features that make interesting reading in a report

55. Price per front foot is
    (A) a physical unit of comparison
    (B) not as accurate as price per acre
    (C) rarely used in residential site analysis
    (D) an accurate guide to site marketability
    (E) useful when there are few physical differences between sites

56. Which is the last step in reconciliation?
    (A) Identify which of the three approaches to use.
    (B) Apply the three approaches to the data collected.
    (C) Apply judgment to the data collected.
    (D) Review previous work and analysis.
    (E) Select a final estimate of value.

57. The highest and best use of a site is its
    (A) existing use
    (B) most probable use
    (C) immediate next use
    (D) synonymous with ordinary and necessary use
    (E) different from most probable use

58. Markets in residential real estate are
    (A) equivalent to those for securities
    (B) related to physical boundaries
    (C) local
    (D) physically obscure
    (E) found by courthouse sales

59. Inflation tends to increase the value of
    (A) fixed-income securities
    (B) mortgages
    (C) deeds in lieu of foreclosure
    (D) real estate
    (E) debts

60. Real estate markets
    (A) are international in scope
    (B) meet none of the criteria of a perfect market
    (C) are centralized in nature
    (D) consist of used property only
    (E) are well developed in former Communist countries

61. The subject property has 85 percent occupancy. What conclusion would you most likely draw if the typical occupancy rate in the area was 95 percent?
    (A) Advertising is average.
    (B) The rents are high.
    (C) The rents are low.
    (D) Management is good.
    (E) New construction will occur soon.

62. The fact that the value of a property tends to equal the cost of an equally desirable substitute is an example of the principle of
    (A) balance
    (B) substitution
    (C) contribution
    (D) diminishing returns
    (E) supply and demand

63. Population flow to different regions of the United States will change primarily because of
    (A) changing economic opportunities
    (B) environmental control legislation
    (C) rezoning legislation
    (D) state tax policies
    (E) air conditioning in the Sunbelt

64. When each alternative use requires the same capital investment, the use that maximizes the investment's____on a long-term basis is the highest and best use.
    (A) diversified portfolio
    (B) operating expenses
    (C) net operating income
    (D) potential gross income
    (E) occupancy rate

65. What would be the indicated value of a property that rented for $750 per month, using a monthly gross rent multiplier of 100, if the expenses attributable to the property were $115 per month?
    (A) $75,670
    (B) $75,000
    (C) $68,750
    (D) $61,125
    (E) $13,750

66. Which of the following criteria most completely defines "highest and best use"?
    (A) Physically possible, legally acceptable, and generating a higher present land value than any other use
    (B) Legally authorized, politically viable, and socially acceptable
    (C) Physically possible, comparable to other uses in the neighborhood, and legally authorized
    (D) Comparable to other local uses, physically possible, and generating a higher present land value than any other use
    (E) The tallest and most beautiful structure that can be placed on the land

67. The total income anticipated from income property operations after vacancy and collection allowances and operating expenses are deducted is
    (A) net operating income
    (B) before-tax cash flow
    (C) effective gross income
    (D) potential gross income
    (E) property residual income

68. Which principle of value best affirms that value is the present worth of expected future benefits?
    (A) Supply and demand
    (B) Balance
    (C) Substitution
    (D) Anticipation
    (E) Conformity

69. Which principle of value best affirms that the maximum value of property generally cannot exceed the cost of its replacement?
    (A) Increasing and decreasing returns
    (B) Supply and demand
    (C) Substitution
    (D) Balance
    (E) Anticipation

70. Which of the following would be classified as a tangible rather than an intangible amenity?
    (A) Pride of ownership
    (B) A sense of security
    (C) A free dishwasher
    (D) Work satisfaction
    (E) Clean air

71. Which type of property is subject to ad valorem taxation?
    (A) Property owned by a religious organization and used for a religious purpose
    (B) New industrial plants that state and local governments have induced, with tax exemption as an incentive, to locate within their jurisdictions
    (C) Commercial property with more than 50 percent nonprofit tenants
    (D) State colleges and universities
    (E) A state capitol

72. Compared with other assets, real estate is
    (A) immobile
    (B) expensive
    (C) long-lived
    (D) mortgagable
    (E) all of the above

73. All of the following are sources of comparable sales EXCEPT
    (A) public records
    (B) brokers
    (C) buyers and sellers
    (D) mortgage servicers
    (E) appraisers

74. An allowance for vacancy and collection loss is estimated as a percentage of
    (A) net operating income
    (B) before-tax cash flow
    (C) effective gross income
    (D) potential gross income
    (E) after-tax cash flow

75. The annual net operating income from an apartment is $11,000. If a capitalization rate of 11% is used, the indicated market value is
    (A) $126,000
    (B) $176,000
    (C) $100,000
    (D) $242,000
    (E) $2,420

76. Which of the following statements is true of a *gross lease*?
    (A) The tenant pays all operating expenses.
    (B) The landlord pays all operating expenses.
    (C) This lease is used only for commercial properties.
    (D) Rent rises with the cost of living.
    (E) This lease must be drafted by an attorney.

77. Natural or manmade features that affect a neighborhood and its geographic location are____influences.
    (A) social
    (B) economic
    (C) government
    (D) environmental
    (E) legal

78. The four broad forces influencing value are
    (A) utility, transferability, demand, and supply (scarcity)
    (B) governmental, economic, social, and political
    (C) supply, demand, location, and popular taste
    (D) governmental, economic, social and physical
    (E) police power, eminent domain, taxation, and escheat

79. The federal government is active in which of the following areas?
    (A) Housing and urban development
    (B) Environmental protection
    (C) Monetary and fiscal policy
    (D) Secondary mortgage market encouragement
    (E) All of the above

80. Population increases____demand for housing.
    (A) depress the
    (B) are capable of diminishing the
    (C) have no effect on the
    (D) can create a
    (E) are determined by the

81. In eminent domain, "just compensation" means
    (A) the fair market value of the property
    (B) the current market value plus compensation for anticipated future benefits
    (C) the market value when the property was bought by the current owner
    (D) the insurable value
    (E) none of the above

82. The right of government or quasi-government units to take private property for public use upon the payment of just compensation is
    (A) escheat
    (B) condemnation
    (C) eminent domain
    (D) estoppel
    (E) an unconstitutional practice

83. ____is the exercise of the right of government to take private property for public use.
    (A) condemnation
    (B) certified appraisal
    (C) immediate justice
    (D) land removal
    (E) both A and B

84. The fullest and most common type of estate in realty is
    (A) fee tail
    (B) mortgage
    (C) supra leasehold
    (D) community property
    (E) fee simple

85. An estate in severalty is ownership by
    (A) more than two parties
    (B) two parties
    (C) one or two parties
    (D) one party
    (E) two or more parties with right of survivorship

86. Which of the following is evidence of real estate ownership?
    (A) Title
    (B) Defaulted mortgage
    (C) Estate
    (D) Fee simple
    (E) Tenancy

87. The concept of value in exchange assumes that
    (A) supply does not affect market value
    (B) a commodity is traded in a marketplace, and for that reason prices may be measured objectively
    (C) value can be determined without exposure in a marketplace
    (D) the real estate appraiser can be held liable if the property does not sell in a reasonable time for the appraised value
    (E) the property value will support a reasonable mortgage debt

88. The definition of market value in appraisal does NOT include
    (A) payment in cash or equivalent
    (B) exposure in the market
    (C) informed parties
    (D) topography of the property
    (E) probable price

89. "Value in exchange" is most closely related to
    (A) value in use
    (B) market value
    (C) investment value
    (D) sentimental value
    (E) none of the above

Questions 90–93 are based on the information below:

A 100-unit apartment complex includes 40 one-bedroom units that rent for $950 and 60 two-bedroom units that rent for $1,150 monthly. The vacancy rate is 5 percent; miscellaneous income is $5,000 annually. Operating expenses amount to $400,000. The mortgage loan requires payments of $630,000 annually.

90. Potential gross income is
    (A) $1,289,000
    (B) $112,000
    (C) $107,000
    (D) $1,284,000

91. Effective gross income is
    (A) $1,224,800
    (B) $1,220,000
    (C) $824,800
    (D) $107,000

92. Net operating income is
    (A) $1,224,800
    (B) $824,800
    (C) $424,800
    (D) none of the above

93. Before-tax cash flow is
    (A) $1,030,000
    (B) $824,800
    (C) $194,800
    (D) none of the above

94. Which statement is FALSE?
    (A) Value in use may be lower than value in exchange.
    (B) Market price is the amount actually paid for a good or service, a historical fact from a particular transaction.
    (C) Cost represents the amount paid for the construction of a building or the amount paid for its acquisition.
    (D) Value in use may be far higher than value in exchange.
    (E) The appraiser must be professionally designated for the value to be accurate.

95. The three common types of legal description are
    (A) metes and bounds; recorded lot, block, and tract; and government rectangular survey
    (B) government rectangular survey, private survey, and house number
    (C) metes and bounds, acreage blocks, and government rectangular survey
    (D) land survey, building survey, and depreciation
    (E) short legal, average legal, and long legal

96. Valuation of property for real estate tax purposes results in
    (A) assessed value
    (B) appraisal
    (C) a special assessment
    (D) a millage rate
    (E) none of the above

97. ____can render existing supply obsolete and less valuable.
   (A) Inflation
   (B) Interest rates
   (C) Employment
   (D) Income levels
   (E) Changes in tastes and standards

98. One implication of competition and excess profit is that
   (A) a certain optimum combination of land, labor, capital, and entrepreneurship exists
   (B) an estimate of value should be based on future expectations
   (C) abnormally high profits cannot be expected to continue indefinitely
   (D) maximum value accrues to real estate when social and economic homogeneity is present in a neighborhood
   (E) the direct sales comparison approach becomes irrelevant

99. Because real estate markets deal with different desires and needs, they are said to be
   (A) fractionated
   (B) structured
   (C) segmented
   (D) submarketed
   (E) spacious

100. Demand for real estate clearly exists when
   (A) population and employment are on the rise
   (B) there is desire or need for space, plus available mortgage financing
   (C) there is desire or need for space, plus ability to pay
   (D) purchasing power increases
   (E) farm prices rise

Certified Residential Appraiser Examination

Directions: Select the choice, marked A, B, C, D, or E, that best answers the question or completes the thought. Mark your answers clearly on the answer sheet. You have 3 hours to complete this examination. Answers are on page 432; math solutions on page 436.

1. In economics, the four factors of production are
   (A) land, labor, capital, and improvements
   (B) land, labor, capital, and entrepreneurship
   (C) land, labor, capital, and money
   (D) land, improvements, labor, and materials
   (E) land, labor, site, and improvements

2. The law of supply and demand is
   (A) a basic economic principle
   (B) legislated by Congress
   (C) seldom used in the appraisal process
   (D) not applicable in the short term
   (E) all of the above

3. Which of the following is NOT an agent of production?
   (A) Land
   (B) Transportation
   (C) Labor
   (D) Capital
   (E) Entrepreneurship

4. Political forces affecting value may include
   (A) life-styles and living standards
   (B) topography
   (C) athletic levels and recreation facilities
   (D) government spending and taxation policy
   (E) primary registration and turnout

5. What are the two categories of tangible property?
   (A) Real property and personal property
   (B) Intangible property and real property
   (C) Real estate and intangible property
   (D) Legal and illegal investments
   (E) Open and shut transactions

6. Zoning is an exercise of the
   (A) equity courts
   (B) police powers
   (C) Environmental Protection Agency
   (D) right of condemnation
   (E) right of escheat

7. Which of the following types of property is subject to ad valorem taxation?
   (A) Property owned by a religious organization and used for a religious purpose
   (B) New industrial plants that state and local governments have induced, with tax exemption as an incentive, to locate within their jurisdictions
   (C) Commercial buildings leased in part by nonprofit foundations
   (D) State colleges and universities
   (E) A state capitol

8. A person owning less than the entire bundle of rights has
   (A) escheat
   (B) a fee simple title
   (C) a partial interest
   (D) personal property
   (E) a fee tail

9. A metes and bounds description begins and ends with the
   (A) street and house number
   (B) block number
   (C) point of beginning
   (D) grid coordinates
   (E) iron pin

10. A(n)____identifies a property in such a way that it CANNOT be confused with any other property.
    (A) coded map book
    (B) legal description
    (C) narrative appraisal
    (D) full city survey
    (E) engineering report

11. All of the following statements are true EXCEPT
    (A) real property is a type of service
    (B) value is dependent on market conditions
    (C) a good or service has no value in exchange unless it possesses certain economic and legal characteristics
    (D) the price representing value is usually quoted in terms of money
    (E) real estate may be sold for all cash or financing arranged

12. All of the following will affect the market value of a property EXCEPT
    (A) political factors
    (B) legal use restriction
    (C) acquisition cost to present owner
    (D) economic factors
    (E) social concerns

13. Market value is____the same as selling price.
    (A) always
    (B) never
    (C) sometimes
    (D) usually
    (E) none of the above

14. Price is
    (A) market value
    (B) most probable sales price
    (C) investment value
    (D) a historical fact
    (E) all of the above

15. Functional utility depends on
    (A) zoning
    (B) wear and tear on the structure
    (C) tastes and standards
    (D) age of the equipment
    (E) insurance requirements

16. *Value in use* is
    (A) subjective
    (B) objective
    (C) readily measurable
    (D) a market phenomenon
    (E) synonymous with market price

17. The value added to total property value by a particular component is an example of the principle of
    (A) substitution
    (B) anticipation
    (C) change
    (D) contribution
    (E) conformity

18. The concept that the value of a particular component is measured by the amount that its absence would detract from the value of the whole is
    (A) opportunity cost
    (B) substitution
    (C) competition
    (D) contribution
    (E) conformity

19. The market loss caused by depreciation in an older structure may be offset by all of the following EXCEPT
    (A) architectural interest
    (B) historical registration
    (C) strong demand relative to supply
    (D) strong supply relative to demand
    (E) renovation of the structure

20. Studying appraisal helps a person
    (A) to improve value estimation skills
    (B) to pass the real estate brokers' license examination
    (C) to understand other real estate courses
    (D) to communicate with appraisers
    (E) all of the above

21. A dramatic change in short-term demand for real estate in the local market is likely to im-
    mediately precipitate
    (A) construction
    (B) price changes
    (C) conversions
    (D) activity
    (E) no change in supply

22. The area and community analysis section of an appraisal report
    (A) should "sell" the community
    (B) should describe the community objectively
    (C) is a study by the state's industrial development commission
    (D) considers the negative aspects only
    (E) considers the positive aspects only

23. In analyzing the economic environment and market area, it is best to
    (A) start at the general level and work down to the specific
    (B) start at the specific and work up to the general level
    (C) limit the analysis to the national level
    (D) limit the analysis to the local level
    (E) generally consider traffic flow

24. Which of the following reports is usually NOT prepared by a real estate appraiser?
    (A) Marketability study
    (B) Economic study
    (C) Feasibility study
    (D) Transportation network study
    (E) Valuation study

25. An appraisal of a specific-purpose property for insurance purposes would depend most
    heavily on
    (A) book value
    (B) cost estimate
    (C) land value
    (D) highest and best use
    (E) specialty value

26. The first step in the appraisal process is to
    (A) define the problem to be solved
    (B) gather relevant data
    (C) analyze the data
    (D) inspect the property
    (E) set the fee to be charged

27. An appraisal is
    (A) an estimate of net realizable value
    (B) always concerned with the market value
    (C) a defensible estimate of market value
    (D) a precise statement of value
    (E) a broker's comparative sales analysis with further detail

28. The "as of" date in an appraisal report is
    (A) often the date of the last inspection
    (B) immaterial to the value estimate
    (C) the date on which the report is delivered
    (D) the date on which the property will be conveyed
    (E) the anticipated closing date

29. Sales data descriptions of an appraisal report contain
    (A) details about each comparable sale
    (B) an analysis of the data, using the value approaches
    (C) the investigation of market forces
    (D) analysis of the street each comparable property is on
    (E) zoning details

30. All of the following are ways to delineate a neighborhood EXCEPT
    (A) natural barriers
    (B) utility service
    (C) political boundaries
    (D) streets
    (E) income characteristics

31. All of the following are sources of comparable sales EXCEPT
    (A) public records
    (B) brokers
    (C) buyers and sellers
    (D) mortgage servicers
    (E) appraisers

32. Which of the following criteria most completely define "highest and best use"?
    (A) Legally authorized, politically viable, and socially acceptable.
    (B) Physically possible, comparable to other uses in the neighborhood, and legally authorized.
    (C) Physically possible, legally permissible, financially feasible, and generating a higher present land value than any other use.
    (D) Comparable to other uses in the neighborhood, physically possible, and generating a higher present land value than any other use.
    (E) The tallest and most beautiful structure that can be placed on land.

33. The three basic approaches used to estimate value are
    (A) use, exclusion, and disposition
    (B) cost, sales comparison, and use
    (C) cost, sales comparison, and market data
    (D) cost, sales comparison, and production
    (E) cost, sales comparison, and income capitalization

34. Units of comparison are used in
    (A) only the sales comparison approach
    (B) only the cost approach
    (C) only the income capitalization approach
    (D) A, B, and C
    (E) the appraisal of special-purpose properties only

35. Final value estimates should be rounded to reflect the
    (A) absence of good data
    (B) property's location
    (C) fact that a selling price will probably be a round number
    (D) lack of precision associated with an opinion
    (E) high value of real estate

36. When reconciling the adjusted sales prices of comparables, the greatest emphasis should be given to
    (A) the average
    (B) the median
    (C) the mode
    (D) the mean of A, B, and C
    (E) none of the above

37. Which of the following forms of appraisal report is NOT recommended?
    (A) Completely filled-in institutional form
    (B) Telephone conversation
    (C) Letter report
    (D) Long narrative report
    (E) Demonstration

38. Which of the following approaches would probably be given the most weight in appraising a large office building?
    (A) Reproduction cost
    (B) Subdivision development
    (C) Replacement cost
    (D) Income capitalization
    (E) Market absorption

39. The form in which a formal appraisal is presented is called
    (A) a presentation of value
    (B) an appraisal log
    (C) an appraisal report
    (D) a value certification
    (E) a narrative report

40. The form of an appraisal report
    (A) has no influence on the appraisal process
    (B) is the same, regardless of the problem
    (C) is set by the amount of the fee
    (D) is determined by the appraiser
    (E) determines the appraisal framework

41. The effective age and the useful life of a building represent judgments made by the
    (A) appraiser
    (B) property owner
    (C) tax assessor
    (D) buyer
    (E) insurer

42. The period over which existing improvements are expected to continue to contribute to property value is their
    (A) effective age
    (B) remaining economic life
    (C) remaining physical life
    (D) period of diminishing returns
    (E) chronological age

43. For a building, *effective age* is best defined as
    (A) the average age of the roof
    (B) the actual age divided by the age-life
    (C) the age of other property in equivalent condition and utility
    (D) the chronological age of the building
    (E) the period over which the building may be effectively used

44. The *utility* of real estate is its
    (A) attractiveness to the trained observer
    (B) longevity
    (C) capacity to satisfy human needs and desires
    (D) effective demand
    (E) remaining economic life

45. In appraising a residence, adjustments are NOT made to the comparable property for
    (A) age
    (B) lot value
    (C) assessed valuation
    (D) terms of sale
    (E) size

46. When a site has improvements on it, the highest and best use
    (A) is not definable
    (B) is its existing use
    (C) is its potential use
    (D) depends on whether or not the existing use is changeable
    (E) may be different from its existing use

47. To be considered as a comparable, a property
    (A) must have been sold within the past 5 years
    (B) must be competitive with the subject
    (C) must have been sold by an open-market transaction
    (D) must be a similar color
    (E) Both B and C

48. The direct sales comparison approach is better than the income or cost approach because
    (A) fewer comparable properties are required, so it is easier to outline the results to clients
    (B) there are fewer mathematical calculations, so there is less chance of mathematical errors
    (C) the market for real estate is slow to change
    (D) it is always easier to obtain data for the direct sales comparison approach
    (E) none of the above is true

49. The appraisal of an established 20-year-old motel on a road with numerous competitive motels would most likely be based on the
    (A) square foot area of improvements
    (B) number of units
    (C) reproduction cost
    (D) gross rent multiplier
    (E) occupancy rate

50. In applying gross rent multiplier analysis to the subject property, the appraiser would use the
    (A) market rental
    (B) actual rent being paid
    (C) rent currently asked by the owner
    (D) rent offered by a potential tenant
    (E) rent listed in advertising the property

Questions 51–56 are based on the following information:

Factor	Subject	Comparable 1	Comparable 2	Comparable 3
Price		$270,000	$265,500	$261,000
Living area (sq. ft.)	1,500	1,600	1,450	1,400
Condition	Good	Fair	Excellent	Good
Garage	One-car	Two-car	One-car	Two-car
Time of sale	Now	Last year	Last year	This year

Adjusted Sales Price: Prices have been rising by 5 percent per year in the area for this type of property.

Other Adjustments: Each square foot of livable area is judged to be worth $90; condition grades are fair, good, and excellent, with each difference in condition grade worth 5 percent; a two-car garage is judged to be worth $4,500 more than a one-car garage.

51. What is the size adjustment for Comparable 1?
    (A) +$4,500
    (B) −$4,500
    (C)   0
    (D) +$9,000
    (E) −$9,000

52. What is the size adjustment for Comparable 2?
    (A) +$4,500
    (B) −$4,500
    (C)   0
    (D) +$9,000
    (E) −$9,000

53. What is the condition adjustment for Comparable 1?
    (A)   0
    (B) +$13,500
    (C) −$13,500
    (D) +$27,000
    (E) −$27,000

54. What is the condition adjustment for Comparable 2?
    (A)   0
    (B) +$13,275
    (C) −$13,275
    (D) +$26,550
    (E) −$26,550

55. What is the garage adjustment for Comparable 2?
    (A)   0
    (B) +$4,500
    (C) −$4,500
    (D) +$9,000
    (E) −$9,000

56. What is the garage adjustment for Comparable 3?
    (A)   0
    (B) +$4,500
    (C) −$4,500
    (D) +$9,000
    (E) −$9,000

57. In estimating the market value of a comparable sale, an appraiser must consider all of the following EXCEPT
   (A) whether the transaction was made in cash, terms equivalent to cash, or other precisely revealed terms
   (B) whether the property had reasonable exposure in a competitive market
   (C) whether a fair sale was transacted, with neither the seller nor the buyer acting under duress
   (D) whether the replacement cost of the property corresponds to its market value
   (E) whether the seller was related to the buyer

58. The terms of financing, whether good or bad,
   (A) have no effect on the market price
   (B) have no effect on the market value
   (C) have no effect on affordability
   (D) depend on fiscal and monetary policy
   (E) should be ignored when adjusting comparables

59. Adjustments for the property rights conveyed, financing, conditions of sale, date of sale, and location are often made to the____of the comparable property.
   (A) unit price
   (B) actual sales price
   (C) price per square foot
   (D) gross income multiplier
   (E) cash equivalent value

60. Cumulative percentage adjustments may be used
   (A) when the characteristics are interdependent
   (B) when the characteristics are independent
   (C) when dollar figures are available
   (D) when unimproved properties are being appraised
   (E) under no circumstances

61. The best unit of comparison for vacant land is
   (A) the square foot
   (B) the total lot
   (C) a combination of square foot and front foot units
   (D) the linear foot
   (E) the unit considered important by the market

62. You are asked to appraise a vacant building lot. The neighborhood is about 75% built up. Most lots in the area are from 55 to 65 ft. wide; the lot under appraisal is 60 ft. Comparable sales indicate that lots are selling at $120 to $150 per front foot. What is a good estimate of the price range for this lot?
   (A) $9,000–$11,000
   (B) $7,200–$9,000
   (C) $5,400–$6,750
   (D) $6,600–$7,600
   (E) $6,600–$11,250

63. In appraising a residential property by the cost approach, the appraiser considers the
   (A) sales prices of comparable properties
   (B) depreciation of the land
   (C) depreciation of improvements
   (D) potential for new competition
   (E) potential misuse of this approach

64. In the cost approach,____is deducted after estimating the cost to reproduce an existing structure.
   (A) land cost
   (B) cost to maturity
   (C) depreciation
   (D) cash equivalence
   (E) personal property value

65. External or economic obsolescence can be caused by all of the following EXCEPT
   (A) economic factors
   (B) political factors
   (C) social factors
   (D) factors within the property
   (E) legal factors

66. Economic obsolescence in a residence does NOT result from
   (A) an outdated kitchen
   (B) construction of a freeway near the property
   (C) the presence of an earthquake fault nearby
   (D) building restrictions in the community
   (E) factors external to the subject property itself

67. Reproduction or replacement cost includes all of the following EXCEPT
   (A) direct or hard costs
   (B) indirect or soft costs
   (C) entrepreneurial profit
   (D) fixed and variable expenses of operations
   (E) elevator shafts

68. In analyzing obsolescence, the test of curability of a component in a building is whether the cost to cure is no greater than the
   (A) expected increase in value
   (B) reproduction cost new
   (C) replacement cost
   (D) installation cost
   (E) economic life of the new component

69. Which of the following is NOT a type of depreciation?
   (A) Entrepreneurial loss
   (B) External obsolescence
   (C) Physical deterioration
   (D) Functional obsolescence
   (E) Economic obsolescence

70. Estimation of accrued depreciation and obsolescence does NOT involve
   (A) physical deterioration
   (B) economic obsolescence
   (C) financial structure
   (D) functional obsolescence
   (E) wear and tear

71. In appraisal, accrued depreciation is really an estimate of
   (A) physical deterioration
   (B) diminished utility
   (C) book depreciation
   (D) capital recovery
   (E) sinking fund factor

72. The cost approach is NOT useful for
    (A) checking value approaches
    (B) appraising institutional or special-use properties
    (C) estimating the value of new property
    (D) appraising older homes in an active market
    (E) insurance appraisals

Questions 73–75 are based on the following information:

An appraiser noted the following about a rental home:

needs exterior paint	$750 cost to cure
needs new water heater	$250 cost to cure
has one bath in market for two	$4,000 capitalized rent loss
has poor floor plan	$2,500 capitalized rent loss
is located next to a convenience store	$1,200 capitalized rent loss

73. How much is curable physical deterioration?
    (A) $250
    (B) $750
    (C) $4,000
    (D) $2,500
    (E) None of the above

74. How much is functional obsolescence?
    (A) $250
    (B) $1,000
    (C) $6,500
    (D) $7,700
    (E) None of the above

75. How much is environmental obsolescence?
    (A) $250
    (B) $750
    (C) $1,200
    (D) $2,500
    (E) $4,000

76. *Cash-on-cash return* is
    (A) the annual cash flow divided by the equity investment
    (B) an internal rate of return that represents annual income and all gains or losses pro-rated to an effective annual amount
    (C) a percentage or decimal rate that, when divided into a periodic income amount, offers a lump-sum capital value for income
    (D) a value that does not change with time
    (E) none of the above

77. Which report is usually NOT prepared by a real estate appraiser?
    (A) Marketability study
    (B) Economic study
    (C) Feasibility study
    (D) Mineral valuation study
    (E) Highest and best use

Questions 78–81 are based on the information below.

You are appraising a 40-acre tract of unimproved land. The size is zoned for single-family residential use. All utilities are available along the street on which the land fronts. The engineers who will plat the proposed subdivision told you that 20 percent of the land area will be used for streets and sidewalks. Zoning will permit four lots per acre of net developable land after deducting streets. Research indicates that lots similar to those that will be available on the subject land will sell for $18,000 each and that the entire tract can be developed and sold in 1 year. You find that 40 percent of the sale price of each lot must be allocated to selling cost, overhead, contingencies, carrying cost, and developer's profit, and that 2,000 feet of streets (including water, storm sewer, and sanitary sewer lines) must be installed at a cost of $80 per foot.

78. What is the number of lots to be developed?
    (A) 40
    (B) 128
    (C) 80
    (D) 88
    (E) 32

79. What is the gross amount that will be realized from the sale of all the lots?
    (A) $720,000
    (B) $2,304,000
    (C) $1,440,000
    (D) $1,584,000
    (E) $576,000

80. What is the cost of installing streets, water, and sewer lines?
    (A) $16,000
    (B) $32,000
    (C) $64,000
    (D) $160,000
    (E) None of the above

81. What is the amount of selling cost, overhead, contingencies, carrying cost and developer's profit?
    (A) $921,600
    (B) $576,000
    (C) $288,000
    (D) $633,600
    (E) None of the above

82. Which of the following forms of appraisal report is NOT recommended?
    (A) Completely filled-in institutional form
    (B) Telephone conversation
    (C) Letter report
    (D) Long narrative report
    (E) Demonstration

83. The term *vertical interests* does NOT refer to rights to
    (A) subsurface mineral extraction
    (B) the construction of railroad tunnels
    (C) the use and regulation of air space
    (D) subdivision and development
    (E) the construction of buildings over railroad yards

84. Inflation tends to increase the value of
    (A) fixed-income securities
    (B) mortgages
    (C) deeds in lieu of foreclosure
    (D) tangible long-lived investments
    (E) debts

85. With an amortized mortgage loan,
    (A) interest only is paid until maturity
    (B) some principal is repaid with each payment
    (C) the entire principal is repaid before maturity
    (D) equal amounts of principal are repaid each period
    (E) there is a balloon payment at maturity

Questions 86–89 are based on the following information:

A building contains 50 one-bedroom units and 150 two-bedroom units. The one-bedroom units rent for $550 monthly; two-bedroom are $675. The vacancy rate is 7 percent; operating expenses are estimated at 40 percent of effective gross income. There is $2,000 annual income from vending machines.

86. Potential gross income is
    (A) $64,375
    (B) $1,547,000
    (C) $1,545,000
    (D) $717,425
    (E) none of the above

87. Effective gross income is
    (A) $64,375
    (B) $1,547,000
    (C) $1,545,000
    (D) $1,438,850
    (E) none of the above

88. Net operating income is
    (A) $64,375
    (B) $268,970
    (C) $863,310
    (D) $719,425
    (E) none of the above

89. Operating expenses are
    (A) $1,545,000
    (B) $54,075
    (C) $2,000
    (D) $719,425
    (E) $575,540

90. In one step of the land residual technique, the building capitalization rate is applied to the known building value to estimate the
    (A) highest and best use of the site
    (B) cost of the building
    (C) income needed to support the land
    (D) net operating income needed to support the building
    (E) land value

91. The basic formula for property valuation via income capitalization is
    (A) $V = IR$
    (B) $V = I/R$
    (C) $V = R/I$
    (D) $V = SP/GR$
    (E) $V = I/F$

92. All of the following lease provisions are advantageous to the lessee EXCEPT
    (A) an escape clause
    (B) a renewal option
    (C) a purchase option
    (D) an escalation clause
    (E) none of the above

93. When each alternative use requires the same capital investment, the use that maximizes the investment's_____on a long-term basis is the highest and best use.
    (A) diversified portfolio
    (B) operating expenses
    (C) net operating income
    (D) potential gross income
    (E) occupancy rate

94. Land purchased for $50,000 cash appreciates at the rate of 15 percent compounded annually. About how much is the land worth after 5 years? Disregard taxes, insurance, and selling expenses.
    (A) $100,000
    (B) $87,500
    (C) $57,500
    (D) $37,500
    (E) $7,500

95. A land speculator expects that a certain 100-acre tract can be sold to a subdivider 4 years from now for $10,000 per acre. If holding and selling costs are disregarded, what cash price today (rounded to the nearest $1,000) would allow the speculator to realize a 15 percent compounded annual rate of return on the entire tract?
    (A) $572,000
    (B) $5,000
    (C) $600,000
    (D) $6,000
    (E) None of the above

96. Gross income multipliers are generally considered part of
    (A) the cost approach
    (B) the direct sales comparison approach
    (C) the income capitalization approach
    (D) the insurance approach
    (E) none of the above

97. Use of a gross rent multiplier is valid when the subject and comparable properties have similar
    (A) potential gross incomes
    (B) effective gross incomes
    (C) net operating incomes
    (D) operating expense ratios
    (E) cash flows

98. Time-distance relationships between a site and all relevant origins and destinations are called
    (A) access roads
    (B) transit facilities
    (C) ingress and egress
    (D) linkages
    (E) synergies

99. The land on which a 10-year-old house is located is valued at $128,000, and the reproduction cost of the dwelling is $92,000. Straight-line depreciation is 2 percent per year, applied to the building only. If there is no other obsolescence, what is the indicated value of the property?
    (A) $196,000
    (B) $201,600
    (C) $217,000
    (D) $217,700
    (E) $220,000

100. An allowance for vacancy and collection loss is estimated as a percentage of
    (A) net operating income
    (B) before-tax cash flow
    (C) effective gross income
    (D) potential gross income
    (E) after-tax cash flow

Certified General Appraiser Examination

Directions: Select the choice, marked A, B, C, D, or E, that best answers the question or completes the thought. Mark your answers clearly on the answer sheet. You have 3 hours to complete this examination. Answers are on page 432; math solutions on page 437.

1. Effective gross income is income after an allowance for
    (A) depreciation
    (B) operating expenses
    (C) cash expenditures
    (D) both A and B
    (E) none of the above

2. In discounted cash flow analysis, the reversion to be received at the end of the holding period is
    (A) a separate cash flow
    (B) an annuity in arrears
    (C) an ordinary annuity
    (D) a percentage of annual income
    (E) an amount to be capitalized in perpetuity

3. To earn 12 percent annual cash return on a cash investment, what should you pay for a property that earns $4,000 per month and has operating expenses of $1,250 per month?
    (A) $150,000
    (B) $275,000
    (C) $229,166
    (D) $333,333
    (E) $400,000

4. In selecting an overall capitalization rate for an income-producing property, the appraiser will consider all of the following EXCEPT
   (A) return on invested capital
   (B) risk factors
   (C) return of invested capital
   (D) the interest rate on the existing loan, which was arranged last year
   (E) the interest rate prevailing in the market

Questions 5–8 are based on the following information:

A 200-unit apartment complex includes 80 one-bedroom units that rent for $475 and 120 two-bedroom units that rent for $575 monthly. The vacancy rate is 5 percent; miscellaneous income is $5,000 annually. Operating expenses amount to $400,000. The mortgage loan requires annual payments of $630,000.

5. Potential gross income is
   (A) $1,289,000
   (B) $1,284,000
   (C) $112,000
   (D) $107,000
   (E) none of the above

6. Effective gross income is
   (A) $1,224,800
   (B) $1,220,000
   (C) $824,800
   (D) $107,000
   (E) none of the above

7. Net operating income is
   (A) $1,224,800
   (B) $1,220,000
   (C) $824,800
   (D) $424,800
   (E) none of the above

8. Before-tax cash flow is
   (A) $1,030,000
   (B) $824,800
   (C) $424,800
   (D) $194,800
   (E) none of the above

9. To obtain the present value of a series of incomes, a(n)_____rate is applied.
   (A) discount
   (B) income
   (C) overall capitalization
   (D) equity capitalization
   (E) stated

10. A fast-food chain could buy the building and land necessary for a new outlet for $200,000. Instead, an investor bought the property for this amount and leased it for $2,000 per month over a 20-year term. Rent is payable at the end of each month. What yield to maturity is implied by the lease, assuming that, at the end of 20 years, the property is still worth about $200,000?
    (A) 8%
    (B) 10%
    (C) 12%
    (D) 14%
    (E) 15%

11. When market rent is less than contract rent, the difference is known as
    (A) overage rent
    (B) excess rent
    (C) percentage rent
    (D) gross rent
    (E) slippage rent

12. If a particular buyer requires a recapture of the building portion of the purchase price in 25 years, what is the indicated recapture rate for the building, assuming straight-line recapture?
    (A) 0.25%
    (B) 2%
    (C) 4%
    (D) 20%
    (E) 25%

13. In a high-rise, 100-unit apartment building there is a basement laundry area that brings in $100 monthly from the concessionaire. The laundry income is
    (A) included, as miscellaneous income, in potential gross income
    (B) included, as other income, in effective gross income
    (C) deducted from effective gross income
    (D) added to before-tax cash flow
    (E) distributed to the maintenance workers

14. A forecast using discounted cash flow analysis would include
    (A) income, vacancy, and operating expenses
    (B) an economic analysis
    (C) reversion at the end of the holding period
    (D) discounting expected future cash flows to a present value
    (E) all of the above

15. In discounted cash flow analysis, the reversion to be received at the end of the holding period is
    (A) a separate cash flow
    (B) an annuity in arrears
    (C) an ordinary annuity
    (D) a percentage of annual income
    (E) an amount to be capitalized in perpetuity

16. A $1,000,000 property will have a 70 percent loan at a 12 percent annual mortgage constant. What must the net operating income be to produce a 15 percent cash-on-cash return?
    (A) $150,000
    (B) $90,000
    (C) $129,000
    (D) $75,000
    (E) $750,000

17. Income capitalization is the term used to describe the process of estimating the value of income property by studying expected future income. This process
    (A) converts the net income of a property into its equivalent capital value
    (B) reflects the time value of money by reducing or discounting future income to its present worth
    (C) focuses on the present worth of future benefits
    (D) uses market interest rates
    (E) all of the above

18. To earn 12% on your investment, what should you pay for a property that earns $6,000 per month and has operating expenses of $1,250 per month?
    (A) $475,000
    (B) $150,000
    (C) $229,166
    (D) $333,333
    (E) $400,000

19. The land development method is used to estimate the value of vacant acreage that is ready to be subdivided. This method requires
    (A) the study of current sales of subdivided lots
    (B) the projection of land development costs
    (C) RTC approval
    (D) both A and B
    (E) none of the above

20. A technique of income capitalization in which the analyst need not distinguish interest rates from capital recovery rates, but that is most useful for comparable income properties, is
    (A) direct capitalization
    (B) building residual
    (C) land residual
    (D) bank of investment
    (E) internal rate of return

21. A mortgage is
    (A) a gift from the mortgagee
    (B) a transfer of real estate to a financial institution
    (C) any loan
    (D) a pledge of real estate as collateral for a loan
    (E) a cloud on the title to real estate

22. The portion of the loan payment for recapture of the investment capital in a mortgage is
    (A) principal, interest, taxes, and insurance
    (B) principal reduction or amortization
    (C) interest and principal payment
    (D) negative amortization
    (E) mortgage banking

23. An appraisal is
    (A) an establishment of value
    (B) a prediction of sales price
    (C) a mathematically precise forecast of value
    (D) an estimate of rental levels
    (E) an estimate of value

24. An appraiser
    (A) determines value
    (B) determines price
    (C) estimates value
    (D) measures price
    (E) forecasts price

25. An appraiser
    (A) determines rent rates
    (B) sets value
    (C) suggests financing
    (D) estimates value
    (E) inspects electrical, mechanical, and plumbing for working condition

26. The_____establishes the market conditions prevailing when the appraisal is made.
    (A) statement of limitations
    (B) statement of conclusions
    (C) introductory note
    (D) transmittal letter
    (E) date of the value estimate

27. Analysis of a location involves which three levels?
    (A) General, specific, detailed
    (B) Country, state, community
    (C) Residential, commercial, industrial
    (D) Country, state, county
    (E) Region, neighborhood, site

28. Market data are used
    (A) in the direct sales comparison approach
    (B) in the income approach
    (C) in the cost approach
    (D) in statistical analysis
    (E) all of the above

29. The cost approach is most applicable when the subject property
    (A) has new improvements that represent the highest and best use
    (B) is in an active local market for similar properties
    (C) produces a positive cash flow
    (D) is in an area where many comparable properties have recently been sold
    (E) exhibits a great deal of functional obsolescence

30. In preparing an appraisal report, your analysis concludes that one of the approaches to value is not applicable to this particular case. You should therefore
    (A) omit the approach altogether
    (B) base the approach on hypothetical data
    (C) state that the approach is not relevant
    (D) state that the approach is not applicable, explain the reasons for this contention, and provide supporting data
    (E) find another approach so as to include three approaches

31. Reconciliation involves
    (A) averaging the unadjusted sales prices of comparables
    (B) recalculating all data
    (C) averaging all estimates derived, weighting each according to its importance
    (D) placing primary emphasis on the estimate deemed most reliable
    (E) averaging estimates from the three approaches, giving each equal weight

32. Cost and market value are more likely to be almost the same when properties are
    (A) new
    (B) old
    (C) depreciated
    (D) syndicated
    (E) appraised

33. In appraisal, reconciliation is
    (A) an estimate of value
    (B) one of the three approaches used in estimating value
    (C) a process of reevaluation that leads to the final value estimate
    (D) an assurance of checkbook accuracy
    (E) a process that is similar to correlation in statistics

34. The essential elements of an appraisal report
    (A) usually follow the valuation or appraisal process
    (B) vary with the type of report
    (C) depend on the client's needs
    (D) depend on the fee charged
    (E) depend on the number of comparables located

35. A demonstration narrative appraisal report
    (A) contains many items that are not included in the usual report
    (B) is an appraisal report prepared for a fussy client
    (C) contains all the items that may be used in practice and is generally the most detailed report
    (D) may be based on hypothetical or assumed data
    (E) should be prepared on a nontypical property to show appraisal expertise

36. A parcel of land that is improved to the point of being ready to be built upon is called
    (A) realty
    (B) land
    (C) a site
    (D) terrain
    (E) a location

37. Before performing a site inspection, an appraiser should
    (A) gather basic information about the site
    (B) know the reasons for the site inspection
    (C) have a map or drawing of the site
    (D) have writing materials for taking notes
    (E) all of the above

38. Environmental hazards that an appraiser must be conscious of include all of the following EXCEPT
    (A) asbestos
    (B) radon
    (C) Drano
    (D) urea formaldehyde
    (E) dry cleaning chemicals

39. The term that denotes the attractiveness and usefulness of a property is
    (A) price estimate
    (B) highest and best use
    (C) location
    (D) functional utility
    (E) value in use

40. Combining two or more sites in order to develop one site with a greater value than the individual sites have separately is called
    (A) assemblage
    (B) plottage
    (C) surplus land
    (D) excess land
    (E) highest and best use of land

41. In the cost approach, the valuation of land involves the principle of
    (A) conformity
    (B) contribution
    (C) highest and best use
    (D) marginal productivity
    (E) variable proportions

42. The highest and best use of land is the reasonable use
    (A) to which land is currently being put
    (B) to which land can be put without adverse effect over the short term
    (C) to which land can most profitably be put over the short term
    (D) to which land can most profitably be put over the long term
    (E) whereby land will become agriculturally productive

43. The direct sales comparison approach should be used
    (A) without exception
    (B) on residential properties only
    (C) on residential and income properties
    (D) in all cases where comparable sales are available
    (E) on vacant land

44. The direct sales comparison approach involves
    (A) analyzing sales
    (B) comparing properties that have recently been sold to a subject property
    (C) analyzing market rentals
    (D) both A and B
    (E) none of the above

45. If the monthly rental for the subject property is $575 and the gross rent multiplier is 127, what estimate of value is indicated?
    (A) $74,750
    (B) $75,000
    (C) $72,925
    (D) $73,125
    (E) $73,000

46. The direct sales comparison approach
    (A) uses the replacement cost of improvements, added to a comparable vacant land value
    (B) uses data on recent sales of comparable properties
    (C) uses the income-producing capability of the property
    (D) involves multiple listing service data
    (E) requires at least three comparable sales for application

47. What is the indicated value of a property that rents for $750 per month, using a monthly gross rent multiplier of 110, if the expenses attributable to the property are $125 per month?
    (A) $75,670
    (B) $82,500
    (C) $68,750
    (D) $61,125
    (E) $13,750

48. A 7-year-old residence is currently valued at $216,000. What was its original value if it has appreciated by 60% since it was built?
    (A) $81,000
    (B) $113,400
    (C) $135,000
    (D) $345,600
    (E) None of the above

49. For residential property, market value appraisals assume that
    (A) the purchaser pays all cash; no money is borrowed
    (B) an FHA or VA mortgage is used
    (C) a purchase money mortgage is considered
    (D) the value estimate is based on no special financing
    (E) the seller pays no more than five points

50. In considering comparable sales in direct sales comparison appraisal,
    (A) the seller's motivation is significant
    (B) the date of sale is significant
    (C) the proximity of the properties is most important
    (D) both A and B
    (E) none of the above

Questions 51–53 are based on the following information:

Seven comparables have been found for a single-family dwelling being appraised and gross rent multipliers calculated from the sales prices as follows:

Comparable	GRM
1	125
2	125
3	127
4	127
5	127
6	128
7	130

51. What is the mean GRM?
    (A) 125
    (B) 126
    (C) 127
    (D) 128
    (E) 130

52. What is the median GRM?
    (A) 125
    (B) 126
    (C) 127
    (D) 128
    (E) 130

53. What is the mode for the GRMs?
    (A) 125
    (B) 126
    (C) 127
    (D) 128
    (E) 130

54. Land prices are analyzed and adjusted in the sales comparison process. These adjustments may involve
    (A) adding or subtracting lump-sum amounts
    (B) adding or subtracting percentages
    (C) accumulating percentages
    (D) using several units of comparison
    (E) any of the above

55. The adjustment process in the direct sales comparison technique involves
    (A) identifying the similarities between properties and adjusting the sales prices
    (B) analyzing the comparables and adjusting the prices for similarities
    (C) identifying the significant differences between the subject and comparable properties and adjusting the sales prices of the comparables for differences
    (D) locating competitive properties and ranking them in the order of desirability
    (E) adjusting the subject to be like the comparables

56. In the cost approach, the site is valued as if it were
    (A) vacant and available for development to its highest and best use
    (B) improved and suited for its intended use or development
    (C) developed and operating
    (D) attractively landscaped
    (E) lacking nearby utilities

57. The direct sales comparison approach is especially suitable for appraising land zoned for which of the following types of use?
    (A) Single-family residential
    (B) Commercial
    (C) Industrial
    (D) Multifamily residential
    (E) Any of the above

58. All of the following are accepted classifications of accrued depreciation for appraisal purposes EXCEPT
    (A) functional obsolescence
    (B) economic obsolescence
    (C) accounting allocation
    (D) physical deterioration
    (E) external obsolescence

59. Accrued depreciation can be defined in appraisal terms as
    (A) an increase in value from inflationary gains
    (B) a total loss in value from all causes
    (C) diminished utility from trade imbalance
    (D) competitive pressures
    (E) functional form changes

60. The cost estimates used in appraisal typically reflect
    (A) wholesale costs
    (B) current cost levels
    (C) typical costs to build a building like this subject
    (D) the actual historic cost of the building being appraised
    (E) both B and C

61. Cost indexes are used to
    (A) derive units of comparison
    (B) catalog building components
    (C) estimate operating expenses
    (D) update past costs into current costs
    (E) estimate the local consumer price index

62. The most detailed, time-consuming, and costly method of estimating cost new is
    (A) unit of comparison
    (B) quantity survey
    (C) trade breakdown
    (D) unit-in-place
    (E) segregated cost

63. In calculating depreciation, a limitation of the age-life method is that it
    (A) tends to ignore physical deterioration
    (B) cannot be used with estimates of cost new
    (C) is based on replacement cost rather than reproduction cost
    (D) tends to ignore functional and economic obsolescence
    (E) is difficult to compute

64. Two baths are required to serve a three-bedroom house if
    (A) the appraiser believes they are necessary
    (B) the selling price is more than $225,000
    (C) two baths are demanded by a typical purchaser of a three-bedroom house in the given market
    (D) four or more persons will live in the house
    (E) one of the bedrooms is at the opposite end of the house from the other two

65. Which is the most precise yet least used cost estimation method?
    (A) Index method
    (B) Quantity survey method
    (C) Comparative square foot method
    (D) Unit-in-place method
    (E) Segregated cost method

66. A defect is considered curable if
    (A) major structural alterations are not required
    (B) the cost of the cure represents more than 25% of the remaining utility
    (C) the cost to cure the condition is less than or equal to the anticipated addition to value
    (D) the cost to cure increases the remaining economic life of the improvement
    (E) the cure is in conformity with building codes

67. External or economic obsolescence is normally NOT
    (A) curable by the owner, the landlord, or the tenant
    (B) discovered during the neighborhood analysis portion of appraisal
    (C) evident in both land and buildings
    (D) caused by forces outside the property
    (E) also called environmental obsolescence

68. A house built in 1965 and appraised in 1994 would have
    (A) a useful life of 29 years
    (B) a chronological age of 29 years
    (C) an effective age of 29 years
    (D) an economic age of 29 years
    (E) a 29-year-old replacement cost

69. In one step of the land residual technique, the building capitalization rate is applied to the known building value to estimate the
    (A) highest and best use of the site
    (B) cost of the building
    (C) income needed to support the land
    (D) net operating income needed to support the building
    (E) land value

70. An example of partial interest is
    (A) a life estate
    (B) a leasehold estate
    (C) a lengthy attention span
    (D) a short attention span
    (E) both A and B

71. A condominium is
    (A) a type of mortgage on real estate
    (B) a building like a cooperative
    (C) a legal concept of ownership
    (D) a zero-lot-line house
    (E) a style of housing

72. Clarity and accuracy contribute to the
    (A) quality of an appraisal
    (B) quantity of evidence
    (C) appraisal fee
    (D) final value estimate
    (E) appearance of the report

73. If an appraiser is asked to undertake an assignment on a property type with which she has no previous experience and is otherwise unfamiliar, she should
    (A) refuse the assignment
    (B) accept the assignment, thereby expanding her abilities, but reduce the fee
    (C) ask the client to hire another appraiser to help her
    (D) associate herself with another appraiser experienced in this type of assignment and inform the client of this fact
    (E) get the necessary computer software to solve the problem

74. Real estate markets are composed of
    (A) buyers only
    (B) sellers only
    (C) types of property
    (D) buyers and sellers
    (E) appraisers and counselors

75. Real estate supply factors include
    (A) the current housing supply
    (B) new construction activity
    (C) tax depreciation allowances
    (D) both A and B
    (E) none of the above

76. The mortgage constant is a function of all of the following EXCEPT
    (A) the term of the loan
    (B) the borrower's income level
    (C) the interest rate
    (D) the term of amortization
    (E) It is a function of all of the above.

77. The benefit(s) forgone from a project that cannot be built is (are) called
    (A) anticipation
    (B) substitution
    (C) opportunity cost
    (D) surplus productivity
    (E) marginal cost

78. The debt coverage ratio
    (A) is federally approved for residential valuation
    (B) can be applied uniformly to all properties
    (C) is the most equitable method of determining a cap rate
    (D) indicates the safety of the loan
    (E) is generally less than 1.00

79. The____is a key safety factor for the lender.
    (A) maturity term
    (B) sales price
    (C) loan-to-value ratio
    (D) age of the improvements
    (E) land value

80. A parcel of land is sold for $115,000. If it appreciated at 12% per year, and the seller held it for four years, how much did the seller pay for it (disregard taxes, selling costs, etc.)?
    (A) $60,000
    (B) $101,000
    (C) $73,000
    (D) $62,500
    (E) $81,700

81. A 30-year-old building with an effective age of 20 years has a total life expectancy of 50 years. How much depreciation has occurred?
    (A) 10%
    (B) 20%
    (C) 40%
    (D) 60%
    (E) None of the above

82. A plot of land, 100 ft. × 200 ft., along an interstate freeway, is situated 12 miles north of the central business district of a city with a population approaching 1 million. Which of the following would be the highest and best use of the land?
    (A) Service station
    (B) Convenience store
    (C) Two-story office building
    (D) Medical office building
    (E) There is not enough information to make a determination.

83. A $2 million shopping center is purchased with a 75% loan-to-value ratio mortgage, payable monthly over 25 years at 12% interest. It generates $205,000 annual net operating income. The land is considered to be worth $500,000; the balance of cost is represented by land improvements. What is the improvement ratio?
    (A) 25%
    (B) 50%
    (C) 75%
    (D) 100%
    (E) None of the above

84. The adjustment for below-market-rate financing may provide an estimate of
    (A) market price
    (B) cash equivalence
    (C) property price
    (D) creative financing
    (E) replacement cost

85. Land or site appraisals assist in
    (A) the sale and purchase of land
    (B) land development
    (C) ad valorem and income tax situations
    (D) all of the above
    (E) none of the above

86. Overall rate of return is
    (A) the annual net operating income divided by the purchase price
    (B) annual income and all gains or losses prorated to an effective annual amount minus an internal rate of return
    (C) a percentage or decimal rate that, when divided into a periodic income amount, offers a lump-sum capital value for the income
    (D) an income that is unchanging with time
    (E) none of the above

87. All of the following are used in the valuation of income-producing property EXCEPT
    (A) rental rates
    (B) operating expenses
    (C) income taxes
    (D) net leasable area
    (E) vacancy and collection allowance

88. A $1 million property will have a 75% loan at a 12% annual mortgage constant. What must the net operating income be to produce a 15% cash-on-cash return?
    (A) $75,000
    (B) $90,000
    (C) $127,500
    (D) $150,000
    (E) $750,000

89. If a particular buyer requires a recapture of the building portion of the purchase price in 25 years, what is the indicated recapture rate for the building, assuming straight-line capture?
    (A) 0.25%
    (B) 2%
    (C) 4%
    (D) 20%
    (E) 25%

90. In a high-rise 100-unit apartment building there is a basement laundry area that brings in $100 monthly from the concessionaire. The laundry income is
    (A) included, as miscellaneous income, in potential gross income
    (B) included, as other income, in effective gross income
    (C) deducted from effective gross income
    (D) added to before-tax cash flow
    (E) distributed to the maintenance workers

91. In an appraisal of income property, which of the following items should be excluded from the expense statement?
    (A) Mortgage loan interest payments
    (B) Ordinary and necessary current expenses
    (C) Projected replacement reserve
    (D) Management fees
    (E) Advertising expenses

Questions 92–95 are based on the following information:

A building contains 25 one-bedroom units and 75 two-bedroom units. The one-bedroom units rent for $550 monthly; two-bedrooms are $675. The vacancy rate is 7%; operating expenses are estimated at 40% of effective gross income. There is $1,000 annual income from vending machines.

92. Potential gross income is
    (A) $773,500
    (B) $772,500
    (C) $719,425
    (D) $64,375
    (E) none of the above

93. Effective gross income is
    (A) $773,500
    (B) $772,500
    (C) $719,425
    (D) $64,375
    (E) none of the above

94. Net operating income is
    (A) $64,375
    (B) $286,970
    (C) $431,655
    (D) $719,425
    (E) none of the above

95. Operating expenses are
    (A) $1,000
    (B) $54,075
    (C) $287,770
    (D) $719,425
    (E) none of the above

96. Which approach involves an investigation of the rent schedules of the subject property and the comparables?
    (A) Cost approach
    (B) Just compensation evaluation
    (C) Income approach
    (D) Comparable rent approach
    (E) All of the above

97. Property free and clear of indebtedness is offered for sale. The property is net-net leased (the tenant pays all operating expenses) for $90,000 per year under a 30-year lease. Rent is payable annually at the end of each year. The building cost $850,000, including a developer's profit and risk allowance; the land cost $100,000, and its value is well established by comparable sales. It is estimated that the building will be worth only about half its current cost at the end of the lease term, and that the land will remain constant in value over that period. A 10% discount rate is considered appropriate. Using the building residual technique estimate the value of the building.
    (A) Between $250,000 and $300,000
    (B) Between $300,000 and $750,000
    (C) Between $750,000 and $1,000,000
    (D) Between $1,000,000 and $1,500,000
    (E) Not within any of the above ranges

98. Which of the following statements is true of a *gross lease*?
    (A) The tenant pays all operating expenses.
    (B) The landlord pays all operating expenses.
    (C) This lease is used only for commercial properties.
    (D) Rent rises with the cost of living.
    (E) This lease must be drafted by an attorney.

99. Land purchased for $100,000 cash appreciates at the rate of 15%, compounded annually. About how much is the land worth after 5 years? Disregard taxes, insurance, and selling expenses.
    (A) $200,000
    (B) $175,000
    (C) $115,000
    (D) $75,000
    (E) $15,000

100. An allowance for vacancy and collection loss is estimated as a percentage of
    (A) net operating income
    (B) before-tax cash flow
    (C) effective gross income
    (D) potential gross income
    (E) after-tax cash flow

Chapter 25/*Supplemental Examinations: Contracts and Settlement Statements*

The examinations in this chapter are designed to meet the special requirements of broker applicants.

Supplemental Examinations 1 and 2 concern listing and sales contracts, respectively. Supplemental Examination 3 considers settlement statements. Knowledge of these is required of broker applicants. You will read a narrative, which will give you the information needed to fill out the blank settlement sheet provided. Then you are asked to answer questions. A correctly filled-out settlement statement is included in the answer key to this examination.

Supplemental Examination 1 _____

(Answer keys are on page 433; arithmetic problems are explained on page 438.)

Listing Contract

LISTING CONTRACT NARRATIVE

On June 16, 1996, you contact Mr. Sydney Purvis, whose two-story brick house has a "For Sale by Owner" sign in front. The house has 2510 sq. feet of space, with four bedrooms (one downstairs) and three baths (one downstairs). It is federal colonial in style. The address is 8811 Quagmire Place, being Lot 18, Block G, Quagmire Estates Addition, Benedictine County, New York. You have done some checking and know that Mr. Purvis has bought a new home. The house he is selling is 12 years old and has natural gas heat and hot water, central air conditioning, no basement, a breakfast area in the kitchen, a 98 ft. × 155 ft. lot, an entrance foyer and a center hall plan, and an attic with pull-down stairs. It is assessed for $26,550, and the tax rate is 88 mills. Mr. Purvis is moving in a week, so a prospective buyer can be offered immediate possession.

The next morning you call Mr. Purvis at his home (555-1116) and get no answer, so you call his office (555-2822) and he agrees to see you immediately to sign a listing agreement. At that time you find out that his current mortgage loan is not assumable, and that he will include all appliances (refrigerator, dishwasher, and dryer). He prefers to show the home only by appointment and will give you a key to keep handy at your office. Nearby schools are Dennis Elementary, DePalma Junior High, Moray High School, and St. Francis Parochial. You and Mr. Purvis agree on a 90-day listing at $112,500, with a 7½% commission, and your broker signs it.

QUESTIONS ON LISTING CONTRACT

1. This contract is
   (A) an exclusive right to sell listing
   (B) an exclusive agency listing
   (C) an open listing
   (D) a net listing

2. If the property is sold at the listed price, the broker's commission will be
   (A) $3,270.00
   (B) $6,360.00
   (C) $8,437.50
   (D) $8,800.00

3. This listing will expire on
   (A) September 15, 1996
   (B) September 16, 1996
   (C) September 17, 1996
   (D) September 18, 1996

4. The annual tax bill on the property is
   (A) $233.64
   (B) $2,336.40
   (C) $2,398.00
   (D) $4,796.00

5. The date of the listing is
   (A) June 16, 1996
   (B) June 17, 1996
   (C) June 18, 1996
   (D) September 15, 1996

6. Which of the following is *false*?
   (A) The parochial school is St. Francis.
   (B) The home has three bathrooms.
   (C) The house has four bedrooms.
   (D) The house is Spanish colonial in style.

7. Which of the following is *true*?
   (A) The home will be shown only by appointment.
   (B) The key to the home is under the doormat.
   (C) Both A and B
   (D) Neither A nor B

8. Which of the following is *true*?
   (A) The home is assessed for $26,550.
   (B) The kitchen has a breakfast area.
   (C) Both A and B
   (D) Neither A nor B

9. Which of the following telephone numbers can be used to contact the seller?
   (A) 555-1717
   (B) 555-2282
   (C) 555-1116
   (D) none of the above

10. Which of the following is *false*?
    (A) The lot size is 98 ft. × 155 ft.
    (B) The house is 21 years old.
    (C) The home has natural gas heat.
    (D) All of the above

11. Which of the following is *false*?
    (A) Immediate possession is possible.
    (B) The listing price is $112,500.
    (C) The home has 2510 sq. ft.
    (D) The owner's home telephone number is 555-2822.

12. Which of the following is *true*?
    (A) The home is in Benedictine County.
    (B) The address is 8811 Quagmire Place.
    (C) The home telephone number is 555-1116.
    (D) All of the above

13. The home is Lot____of Block____of Quagmire Estates Subdivision.
    (A) 17, F
    (B) 18, G
    (C) 16, G
    (D) 18, F

14. Which features does the house have?
    (A) Four bedrooms
    (B) Central air conditioning
    (C) Both A and B
    (D) Neither A nor B

15. Which of the following is *true*?
    (A) The tax rate is 88 mills.
    (B) The home has four bedrooms on the second floor.
    (C) The house has 1½ baths on each floor.
    (D) The house is 15 years old.

Supplemental Examination 2

(Answers are on page 433; arithmetic problems are explained on page 438.)

Contract of Sale

CONTRACT OF SALE NARRATIVE

On August 14, 1996, you show the home belonging to Sydney Purvis to a prospective purchaser, Ms. Miriam Stein.

Three days later Ms. Stein informs you that she wishes to offer $106,000 for the house, subject to getting a mortgage loan for at least 80 percent of the sale price, with a term of 30 years and at the currently prevailing rate of interest. Closing will be at the broker's office no later than September 18, 1996. Ms. Stein leaves her personal check for $2,000 as a deposit. Mr. Purvis will receive all cash at the closing, from the proceeds of Ms. Stein's loan, her deposit, and additional cash necessary to make up the purchase price.

The next day your broker draws up the contract and Mr. Purvis and Ms. Stein sign it.

QUESTIONS ON CONTRACT OF SALE

1. The broker's commission will be
   (A) $5,400.00
   (B) $7,900.00
   (C) $7,950.00
   (D) $8,332.21

2. The purchaser requires a loan of at least
   (A) $86,800
   (B) $84,800
   (C) $80,000
   (D) $77,852.21

3. The contract allows how many days until closing?
   (A) 29
   (B) 30
   (C) 31
   (D) 32

4. After allowing for the deposit she has made and a mortgage loan of 80 percent of the purchase price, how much additional cash must the purchaser pay at closing?
   (A) $21,200
   (B) $19,200
   (C) $20,200
   (D) $18,200

5. The date of the contract is
   (A) August 14, 1996
   (B) August 17, 1996
   (C) August 18, 1996
   (D) August 20, 1996

6. The deposit paid by the buyer is
   (A) $2,000, paid by check
   (B) $2,000, paid in cash
   (C) $2,500, paid by check
   (D) There is no deposit.

7. The parties to the contract are
   (A) Mr. Purvis (the seller) and your broker
   (B) Ms. Stein (the buyer) and you (the salesperson)
   (C) Mr. Purvis (the seller) and Ms. Stein (the buyer)
   (D) your broker and you (the salesperson)

8. The purchaser's loan must
   (A) be at an interest rate of 9%
   (B) be for a term of 30 years
   (C) be for 90% of the purchase price
   (D) The purchaser will pay all cash; there is no loan.

9. In this deal,
   (A) the purchase price is $106,000
   (B) the buyer will assume the seller's mortgage loan
   (C) closing will be on or before November 11, 1996
   (D) the buyer will make a down payment of $10,600

10. The closing
   (A) will be at the broker's office
   (B) will be no later than September 18, 1996
   (C) both A and B
   (D) neither A nor B

Supplemental Examination 3

(Answers are on page 433; arithmetic problems are explained on page 439.)

Settlement Statement

SETTLEMENT STATEMENT NARRATIVE

On September 18, 1996, you close a sale between Sydney Purvis (seller) and Miriam Stein (buyer). The sale price is $106,000, and your commission is 7½% of the sale price. Ms. Stein receives a mortgage loan for 80 percent of the sale price and has paid a deposit of $2,000.00. The property is assessed at $26,550.00, and the tax rate is 88 mills. Taxes are on a calendar-year basis but must be paid by June 15 each year. Ms. Stein will assume a 3-year fire insurance policy, which Mr. Purvis took out on October 22, 1994, paying the full 3-year premium of $888.75 at that time. Mr. Purvis's existing mortgage loan of $32,331.70 will be paid off at closing from the proceeds of the sale.

Mr. Purvis must pay attorney fees of $175.00, a deed preparation fee of $80.00, and miscellaneous fees of $356.55. Ms. Stein must pay attorney fees of $325.00, an appraisal fee of $100.00, a mortgage insurance premium of 2½% of the loan amount, and a title insurance premium of 0.85% of the purchase price.

Fill out the accompanying settlement statement worksheet on page 429 according to the information given above. From it, answer the questions below.

QUESTIONS ON SETTLEMENT STATEMENT

Answer the questions *only* by referring to the settlement statement sheet you have filled out. Do *not* refer to the narrative.

1. The buyer will owe what amount of cash at closing?
   (A) $26,821.21   (C) $6,898.98
   (B) $21,777.07   (D) $23,631.39

2. The seller will receive what amount of cash at closing?
   - (A) $66,092.14
   - (B) $16,465.55
   - (C) $63,170.20
   - (D) $68,907.11

3. With regard to the property taxes, which of the following is *true*?
   - (A) The prorated amount is $661.98.
   - (B) The seller pays $661.98 to the buyer.
   - (C) The prorated amount is $2,336.40.
   - (D) The prorated amount is $1,674.42 and is paid by buyer to seller.

4. The buyer's mortgage insurance premium is
   - (A) $1,297.50
   - (B) $887.50
   - (C) $2,120.00
   - (D) $2,650.00

5. The buyer's title insurance premium is
   - (A) $397.80
   - (B) $720.80
   - (C) $801.00
   - (D) $901.00

6. The buyer's loan will be
   - (A) $88,400
   - (B) $84,800
   - (C) $44,200
   - (D) $90,000

7. The broker's commission is
   - (A) $6,002
   - (B) $6,650
   - (C) $7,250
   - (D) $7,950

8. With regard to the prorated insurance policy, which of the following is *true*?
   - (A) The prorated amount is $565.34.
   - (B) The seller pays this amount to the buyer.
   - (C) Both A and B
   - (D) Neither A nor B

9. The purchaser's earnest money deposit being held by the broker until closing is shown as a
   - (A) credit to the purchaser
   - (B) debit to the seller
   - (C) credit to the seller
   - (D) debit to the broker

10. The seller will pay a broker's commission. The commission is shown as
    - (A) a credit to the seller
    - (B) a debit to the seller
    - (C) a debit to the buyer
    - (D) both A and C

11. The buyer will pay for an appraisal and title insurance at closing. These items are shown as
    - (A) a credit to the buyer
    - (B) a debit to the buyer
    - (C) a credit to the seller
    - (D) both A and C

12. The buyer will take over the unexpired portion of the seller's insurance policy, for which the seller has paid the full premium. The unexpired premium is a
    - (A) debit to the buyer
    - (B) credit to the seller
    - (C) both A and B
    - (D) neither A nor B

13. The mortgage insurance premium is a
    (A) credit to the seller
    (B) credit to the buyer
    (C) debit to the seller
    (D) debit to the buyer

14. The purchase price is
    (A) shown on seller's statement as a debit
    (B) shown on seller's statement as a credit
    (C) not shown on seller's statement
    (D) shown on seller's statement as both credit and debit

15. The payoff of the existing mortgage is
    (A) a credit to the buyer
    (B) a credit to the seller
    (C) a debit to the seller
    (D) none of the above

SETTLEMENT STATEMENT WORKSHEET

SETTLEMENT DATE:	BUYER'S STATEMENT		SELLER'S STATEMENT	
	DEBIT	CREDIT	DEBIT	CREDIT

Chapter 26/Answer Keys and Explanations

Following are answer keys to all the model examinations in Chapter 24 and 25. Also included is the settlement statement worksheet for Supplemental Examination 3.

A final section contains explanations of all the arithmetic questions in all the examinations.

Salesperson Examination 1

1. A	21. B	41. C	61. B	81. C
2. B	22. D	42. D	62. A	82. D
3. C	23. C	43. C	63. A	83. C
4. D	24. C	44. C	64. B	84. C
5. D	25. C	45. B	65. D	85. D
6. A	26. A	46. C	66. C	86. A
7. C	27. B	47. B	67. C	87. A
8. B	28. B	48. A	68. C	88. C
9. C	29. A	49. B	69. A	89. C
10. A	30. A	50. C	70. D	90. B
11. A	31. B	51. A	71. B	91. C
12. A	32. A	52. A	72. A	92. A
13. C	33. A	53. B	73. B	93. D
14. B	34. B	54. B	74. D	94. A
15. B	35. B	55. C	75. D	95. C
16. A	36. B	56. C	76. B	96. A
17. D	37. A	57. C	77. D	97. C
18. C	38. D	58. C	78. B	98. D
19. A	39. D	59. C	79. B	99. D
20. B	40. C	60. C	80. B	100. D

Salesperson Examination 2

1. C	16. D	31. B	46. B	61. B
2. D	17. D	32. A	47. B	62. C
3. B	18. D	33. D	48. D	63. D
4. A	19. C	34. D	49. C	64. D
5. D	20. B	35. A	50. A	65. C
6. B	21. C	36. D	51. D	66. A
7. B	22. D	37. C	52. C	67. C
8. B	23. A	38. C	53. D	68. C
9. C	24. A	39. C	54. C	69. A
10. B	25. D	40. C	55. A	70. A
11. A	26. A	41. A	56. C	71. B
12. C	27. A	42. C	57. B	72. A
13. C	28. C	43. C	58. B	73. C
14. B	29. D	44. B	59. C	74. A
15. A	30. D	45. B	60. D	75. B

76. A	81. D	86. C	91. B	96. D
77. B	82. C	87. B	92. B	97. D
78. A	83. B	88. C	93. A	98. B
79. C	84. C	89. A	94. D	99. B
80. C	85. A	90. C	95. D	100. A

Broker Examination 1

1. B	21. B	41. D	61. A	81. C
2. D	22. B	42. B	62. C	82. C
3. D	23. D	43. D	63. B	83. A
4. B	24. A	44. B	64. A	84. D
5. A	25. A	45. B	65. C	85. B
6. C	26. B	46. D	66. A	86. A
7. C	27. A	47. D	67. C	87. A
8. A	28. A	48. C	68. C	88. A
9. D	29. C	49. A	69. B	89. C
10. D	30. A	50. B	70. A	90. C
11. B	31. B	51. C	71. D	91. B
12. A	32. C	52. C	72. A	92. D
13. B	33. D	53. D	73. B	93. B
14. B	34. B	54. B	74. D	94. D
15. C	35. C	55. B	75. C	95. D
16. B	36. B	56. C	76. B	96. D
17. A	37. C	57. C	77. C	97. C
18. C	38. D	58. B	78. A	98. B
19. D	39. D	59. D	79. D	99. A
20. B	40. D	60. A	80. C	100. B

Broker Examination 2

1. D	21. C	41. B	61. C	81. A
2. B	22. C	42. B	62. C	82. A
3. C	23. A	43. D	63. C	83. D
4. B	24. B	44. C	64. D	84. B
5. D	25. A	45. C	65. D	85. C
6. A	26. B	46. A	66. D	86. A
7. C	27. B	47. B	67. D	87. B
8. C	28. C	48. B	68. A	88. B
9. C	29. C	49. A	69. D	89. C
10. B	30. B	50. C	70. B	90. D
11. C	31. A	51. C	71. C	91. A
12. D	32. C	52. B	72. A	92. B
13. B	33. D	53. B	73. C	93. B
14. A	34. A	54. B	74. B	94. C
15. D	35. A	55. A	75. A	95. C
16. C	36. C	56. C	76. B	96. D
17. B	37. B	57. D	77. A	97. A
18. C	38. C	58. B	78. B	98. C
19. D	39. C	59. B	79. D	99. B
20. A	40. B	60. D°	80. B	100. D

°The correct answer to #60 is 100½ miles *west*.

Appraiser License Examination

1. B	21. D	41. B	61. B	81. A
2. B	22. D	42. B	62. B	82. C
3. E	23. A	43. D	63. A	83. A
4. E	24. D	44. B	64. C	84. E
5. B	25. E	45. D	65. B	85. D
6. D	26. C	46. B	66. A	86. A
7. C	27. D	47. D	67. A	87. B
8. D	28. C	48. B	68. D	88. D
9. C	29. A	49. C	69. C	89. B
10. C	30. D	50. D	70. C	90. D
11. B	31. A	51. A	71. C	91. A
12. B	32. A	52. A	72. E	92. B
13. A	33. A	53. C	73. D	93. C
14. C	34. D	54. B	74. D	94. E
15. E	35. B	55. A	75. C	95. A
16. D	36. C	56. E	76. B	96. A
17. D	37. D	57. B	77. D	97. E
18. A	38. C	58. C	78. D	98. C
19. E	39. A	59. D	79. E	99. C
20. A	40. A	60. B	80. D	100. C

Certified Residential Appraiser Examination

1. B	21. B	41. A	61. E	81. A
2. A	22. B	42. B	62. B	82. B
3. B	23. A	43. C	63. C	83. D
4. D	24. D	44. C	64. C	84. D
5. A	25. B	45. C	65. D	85. B
6. B	26. A	46. E	66. A	86. C
7. C	27. C	47. E	67. D	87. D
8. C	28. A	48. E	68. A	88. C
9. C	29. A	49. B	69. A	89. E
10. B	30. B	50. A	70. C	90. D
11. A	31. D	51. E	71. B	91. B
12. C	32. C	52. A	72. D	92. D
13. C	33. E	53. B	73. E	93. C
14. D	34. D	54. C	74. C	94. A
15. C	35. D	55. A	75. C	95. A
16. A	36. E	56. C	76. A	96. B
17. D	37. B	57. D	77. D	97. D
18. D	38. D	58. B	78. B	98. D
19. D	39. C	59. B	79. B	99. B
20. E	40. A	60. A	80. D	100. D

Certified General Appraiser Examination

1. E	10. C	19. D	28. E	37. E
2. A	11. B	20. A	29. A	38. C
3. B	12. C	21. D	30. D	39. D
4. D	13. B	22. B	31. D	40. B
5. B	14. E	23. E	32. A	41. C
6. A	15. A	24. C	33. C	42. D
7. C	16. C	25. D	34. A	43. D
8. D	17. E	26. E	35. C	44. D
9. A	18. A	27. E	36. C	45. E

46. **B**	57. **E**	68. **B**	79. **C**	90. **B**
47. **B**	58. **C**	69. **D**	80. **C**	91. **A**
48. **C**	59. **B**	70. **E**	81. **C**	92. **B**
49. **D**	60. **E**	71. **C**	82. **E**	93. **C**
50. **D**	61. **D**	72. **A**	83. **C**	94. **C**
51. **C**	62. **B**	73. **D**	84. **B**	95. **C**
52. **C**	63. **D**	74. **D**	85. **D**	96. **C**
53. **C**	64. **C**	75. **D**	86. **A**	97. **C**
54. **E**	65. **B**	76. **B**	87. **C**	98. **B**
55. **C**	66. **C**	77. **C**	88. **C**	99. **A**
56. **A**	67. **A**	78. **D**	89. **C**	100. **D**

Supplemental Examinations

1—LISTING CONTRACT QUESTIONS

1. **A**	4. **B**	7. **A**	10. **B**	13. **B**
2. **C**	5. **B**	8. **C**	11. **D**	14. **C**
3. **A**	6. **D**	9. **C**	12. **D**	15. **A**

2—CONTRACT OF SALE QUESTIONS

1. **C**	3. **C**	5. **C**	7. **C**	9. **A**
2. **B**	4. **B**	6. **A**	8. **B**	10. **C**

3—SETTLEMENT STATEMENT QUESTIONS

1. **D**	4. **C**	7. **D**	10. **B**	13. **D**
2. **A**	5. **D**	8. **D**	11. **B**	14. **B**
3. **A**	6. **B**	9. **A**	12. **C**	15. **C**

Answer Explanations—Arithmetic Questions

SALESPERSON EXAMINATION 1

6. The tax is based on 100% of the appraised value of $250,000. City tax is 10 mills, or 1%, so

$250,000 × 0.01 = $2,500 city tax

County tax is 8 mills, or 0.8%, so

$250,000 × 0.008 = $2,000 county tax

44. The house is a combination of two rectangles: one is 50 ft. × 24 ft. (1,200 sq. ft.) and the other, smaller part jutting out to the bottom is 24 ft. × 16 ft. (384 sq. ft.). You get the 16 ft. measurement by subtracting the 24 ft. of the short side of the house from the 40 ft. of the long side.

1,200 sq. ft. + 384 sq. ft. = 1,584 sq. ft.

45. The lot is 120 ft. × 75 ft. = 9,000 sq. ft. The area taken by the house is

1,584 sq. ft. ÷ 9,000 sq. ft. = 0.176 = 17.6%

56. This figure is a trapezoid. The top (T) and bottom (B) are of unequal lengths, while the height (H) does not change. The formula for this figure is

Area = ½ × (T + B) × H

The area of the lot, then, is

½ × (110 ft. + 160 ft.) × 200 ft.

= ½ × 270 ft. × 200 ft. = 27,000 sq. ft.

If the lot is sold for $78,300.00, the price per square foot is

$78,300.00 ÷ 27,000.00 = $2.90

61. First find the value of the house alone. Land is 15% of the total value, which means that the house is 85% of the total (100% − 15% = 85%). Then the house is worth

0.85 × $47,000 = $39,950

If the house has 1,733 sq. ft., the cost per square foot is

$39,950 ÷ 1,733 sq. ft.

= $23.05251, which rounds to $23.05.

67. One acre contains 43,560 sq. ft., so
$$1\tfrac{1}{4} \times 43{,}560 \text{ sq. ft.} = 54{,}450 \text{ sq. ft.}$$

SALESPERSON EXAMINATION 2

19. The millage rate of 32.5 is 3.25%, so tax on $60,000 is
$$0.0325 \times \$60{,}000 = \$1{,}950$$

65. If Jim made a profit of 43%, then he sold the land for 143% of its purchase price. The purchase price was
$$\$164{,}450 \div 1.43 = \$115{,}000$$

66. Area = 1,700 ft. × 2,100 ft. = 3,570,000 sq. ft.
$$3{,}570{,}000 \text{ sq. ft.} \div 43{,}560 \text{ sq. ft.} =$$
$$81.96 \text{ acres}$$

74. Area = 400 ft. × 665 ft. = 266,000 sq. ft.
266,000 sq. ft. ÷ 43,560 sq. ft. = 6.1065 acres
$17,100.00 ÷ 6.1065 acres = $2,800.29, or
$2,800 per acre

BROKER EXAMINATION 1

6. Cash-on-cash ratio is annual cash return received, divided by the cash spent (original equity) to acquire the investment.
$$\$8{,}360 \div \$76{,}000 = 0.11$$

7. Because 1 sq. mi. contains 640 acres,
$$96 \div 640 = 0.15, \text{ or } 15\%$$

13. The sale closed August 15, but the taxes were due on June 1. Therefore, the taxes have already been paid by the seller. So *buyer pays seller* at closing, to reimburse the taxes already paid.
Assessed value is $53,250; tax rate is 41 mills (which is 4.1%, or 0.041). So the year's tax is 53,250 × 0.041 = $2,183.25
Seller owned property for exactly 7½ mo. (January through July, and half of August). So buyer owes seller the taxes for the remaining 4.5 mo. of the year that the buyer will own the property. One month's taxes amount to $2,183.25 ÷ 12 = $181.9375; 4.5 × $181.9375 = $818.719, or (rounded) $818.72 that buyer owes seller.

25. Because 20 yd. is 20 × 3 = 60 ft., the area of the patio is 60 × 20 = 1,200 sq. ft. The patio is 6 in., or ½ ft., thick. Then 1,200 × 0.5 = 600 cu. ft., the *volume* of the patio. One cubic yard is 3 × 3 × 3 = 27 cu. ft. Therefore, Joe will need
$$600 \div 27 = 22.22, \text{ or (rounded)}$$
$$22.2 \text{ cu. yd. of concrete}$$

43. First we find the amount of the total commission. Salesperson's share of $2,544 was 60% of the total the firm received. $2,544 ÷ 0.6 = $4,240 for the firm's share, which was 50% of the total. $4,240 ÷ 0.5 = $8,480 total commission.
Because the house sold for $106,000,
$$\$8{,}480 \div \$106{,}000 = 0.08, \text{ or } 8\%$$

48. We have to determine the number of front feet in the lot, and multiply that number by $98 to determine the price the lot sold for.
6,468 ÷ 132 = 49 front ft. 49 × 98
= $4,802, or $4,800 rounded

57. $188,000 ÷ 2.6 acres = $72,307.69 per acre
$72,307.69 ÷ 43,560 = $1.65997,
or $1.66 rounded

64. We have to determine how long the seller owned the property. We know he owned it at the beginning of the year. We calculate time from his tax payment, and then figure from January 1 to determine the date of settlement. Remember: the settlement date is considered a day that the *seller* owned the property. The total tax bill is $972. $972 ÷ 12 = $81 per month
$$\$81 \div 30 = \$2.70 \text{ per day}$$
First we determine how many *whole months* the seller owned the property by dividing his share of taxes ($351) by the monthly tax share of $81; $351 ÷ $81 = 4.33333. Thus, the seller owned the property for 4 whole months (January through April) and part of May, the month in which settlement must have occurred. Now we subtract the 4 whole months worth of taxes from the seller's share; 4 × $81 = $324, and $351 − $324 = $27. So the seller also owned the property for $27 "worth" of May. $27 ÷ $2.70 = 10 of May's 31 days (statutory year). Thus, the closing had to be on May 10.

81. We have to calculate the down payment, the origination fee, the discount, and the PMI fee and then add all of these to determine the answer.
Down payment is 15%; $77,500 × 0.15 = $11,625 down payment
Origination fee, discount, and PMI fee all are calculated as part of the *loan amount* (not the sales price). The loan will be the sales price less the down payment, or $77,500 − $11,625 = $65,875 loan amount.
Origination fee (0.75%) is $65,875 × 0.0075 = $494.06
Discount (2.25%) is $65,875 × 0.0225 = $1,482.19 (rounded)

PMI fee (0.5%, or ½%) is $65,875 × 0.005 = $329.38 (rounded)

$$\$11,625 + \$494.06 + \$1,482.19 + \$329.38 = \$13,930.63$$

90. We have to calculate the monthly interest rate, because we are given a monthly interest payment; 11.5% ÷ 12 = 0.95833% = 0.0095833. The interest payment of $468.75 is 0.95833% of the loan amount.

456.41 ÷ 0.0095833 = $47,625 rounded

BROKER EXAMINATION 2

1. We know the down payment and must calculate the origination fee, the discount, and the PMI fee and then add all of these to determine the answer.

   Origination fee, discount, and PMI fee all are calculated as part of the *loan amount* (not the sales price). The loan will be the sales price less the down payment, or $111,500 − $17,250 = $94,250 loan amount

   Origination fee (1.5%) is $94,250 × 0.015 = $1,413.75

   Discount (2%) is $94,250 × 0.02 = $1,885.00
   PMI fee (0.75%) is $94,250 × 0.0075 = $706.88 (rounded)

   $$\$17,250 + \$1,413.75 + \$1,885.00 + \$706.88 = \$21,255.63$$

2. We have to calculate the monthly interest rate, because we are given a monthly interest payment; 10.5% ÷ 12 = 0.875% = 0.00875. The interest payment of $496.56 is 0.875% of the loan amount.

   496.56 ÷ 0.00875 = $56,750 rounded

9. The area of the driveway is 70 ft. × 12 ft. = 840 sq. ft. The driveway is 5 in., or ⁵⁄₁₂ ft., thick; 5 ÷ 12 = 0.41667 ft. thick. Then 840 × 0.41667 = 350 cu. ft. (rounded), the *volume* of the driveway. Because 1 cu. yd. is 3 × 3 × 3 = 27 cu. ft., Joe will need

   350 ÷ 27 = 12.96, or (rounded)
   13 cu. yd. of concrete.

22. Because 59 ft. 6 in. = 59.5 ft. and 535.5 sq. yd. = 535.5 × 9 = 4,819.5 sq. ft., we have 4,819.5 ÷ 59.5 = 81 ft. of depth. This answer is not one of the choices. However, three of the answers are expressed in measures other than feet: 0.03 mi. is 0.03 × 5,280 = 158.4 ft.; 5.33 rods is 5.33 × 16.5 = 87.95 ft. Both of these choices are incorrect. However, 27 yd. is 27 × 3 = 81 ft., which is correct.

25. The commission was 7%; $82,000 × 0.07 = $5,740 total commission. Mack's 48% share is $5,740 × 0.48 = $2,755.20; 55% of that was paid to the salesperson, leaving 1 − 0.55 = 0.45 or 45% for Mack.

   $2,755.20 × 0.45 = $1,239.84

26. Because 1.6 acres is 1.6 × 43,560 = 69,696 sq. ft.,

   $25,100 ÷ 69,696 = 0.3601,
   or $0.36 rounded

42. We have to determine how long the seller owned the property, and then figure from February 1 (the day the insurance policy was purchased) to determine the date of settlement. Remember, the settlement date is considered a day that the *seller* owned the property.

   The total bill was $324; $324 ÷ 12 = $27 per month, and $27 ÷ 30 = $0.90 per day.

   First we determine how many *whole months* of the policy year the buyer owned the property. We divide her share of the policy cost ($63) by the monthly share of $27; $63 ÷ $27 = 2.33333. Thus, the buyer owned the property for 2 whole months and part (0.3333) of a third; 0.3333 × 30 = 10 more days. The policy expires January 31, so the buyer's 2 full months are December and January. Since she had already owned the policy for 10 days at the beginning of December, the settlement must have occurred in November. 30 − 10 = 20 of November.

49. Assessed value is 35% of $86,000; 0.35 × $86,000 = $30,100. Since 42 mills is 4.2%, 0.042 × $30,100 = $1,264.20

50. The discount is based on the *loan amount*. The loan is 90% of $77,900; 0.9 × $77,900 = $70,110. The discount is 2.5 points, or 2.5%. 0.025 × $70,110 = $1,752.75

51. For every 1 point discount paid, we increase the *effective* rate of return to the lender by ⅛%, or 0.125%. The contract interest rate is 9.75%, and there are 2.5 points; 2.5 × 0.1255 = 0.3125%, which we add to the contract rate.

   9.75% + 0.3125% = 10.0625%

62. Cash-on-cash ratio is the annual cash return received, divided by the cash spent (original equity) to acquire the investment.

   $32,300 ÷ $222,750 = 0.145 rounded

63. There are $1,085 \times 900 = 976,500$ sq. ft. in the lot. Because 1 sq. mi. contains $5,280 \times 5,280 = 27,878,400$ sq. ft.,
$$976,500 \div 27,878,400 = 0.035,$$
or 3.5% rounded

69. The area is $1,077 \times 607 = 653,739$ sq. ft., and $653,739 \times 43,560 = 15.0078$ acres. The only acceptable answer, therefore, is "more than 15."

76. This problem isn't difficult, but it requires several calculations. It is wise to leave time-consuming problems such as this one until after you have answered the simpler questions.
We have to calculate the cost of the house, basement, and garage and then add them together.
House: First 1,600 sq. ft. cost $\$51.10 \times 1,600 = \$81,760$. There are $2,100 - 1,600 = 500$ additional sq. ft. to pay for. $500 \times \$42.25 = \$21,225$ additional. $\$81,760 + \$21,225 = \$102,885$ for the house.
Basement: Note that this is a two-story house. Therefore, the basement will be only *half* the area of the house, or $2,100 \div 2 = 1,050$ sq. ft.; $1,050 \times \$22.50 = \$23,625$ for the basement.
Garage: $420 \times \$29.20 = \$12,264$
$$\$102,885 + \$23,625 + \$12,264$$
$= \$138,774$, or \$139,000 to the nearest \$1,000

80. First we calculate the cost of the lots. We know A costs \$11,000. B costs 2.5 times that amount; $2.5 \times \$11,000 = \$27,500$. C costs half the price of B; $\$27,500 \div 2 = \$13,750$. So $\$11,000 + \$27,500 + \$13,750 = \$52,250$, the cost of all three lots.
A and B were sold for 25% more than this amount, or 125% of this amount, or $1.25 \times \$52,250 = \$65,312.50$. C was sold for twice its cost; $\$13,750 \times 2 = \$27,500$.
Thus, $\$65,312.50 + \$27,500 = \$92,812.50$, the amount all three lots sold for. $\$92,812.50 - \$52,250 = \$40,562.50$. However, this is not one of the answer choices. Therefore, "none of the above" is correct.

APPRAISER LICENSE EXAMINATION

3. $1.07 \times 1.07 = 1.1449$, which is 14.49 percent increase. Then
$$0.1449 \times \$240,000 = \$34,776$$

65. The expenses don't matter, since GRM applies to gross rental, without regard for expenses. Therefore, value = rent × GRM, or
$$\$750 \times 100 = \$75,000$$

75. Value = NOI / rate:
$$\$11,000 \div 0.11 = \$100,000$$

90. Monthly rents: $40 \times \$950 = \$38,000$; $60 \times \$1,150 = \$69,000$; $\$69,000 + \$38,000 = \$107,000$.
Potential annual gross income = $\$107,000 \times 12 = \$1,284,000$

91. Effective gross income is potential gross income plus miscellaneous income, less vacancy. Vacancy is 5 percent of potential gross rent: $\$1,284,000 \times 0.05 = \$64,200$ vacancy
$$\$1,284,000 + \$5,000 - \$64,200$$
$$= \$1,224,800$$

92. NOI is effective gross less operating expenses:
$$NOI = \$1,224,800 - \$400,000 = \$824,800$$

93. Before-tax cash flow is NOI less mortgage servicing:
$$\$824,800 - \$630,000 = \$194,800$$

CERTIFIED RESIDENTIAL APPRAISER EXAMINATION

51. Comp 1 is 100 sq. ft. larger than subject, so adjustment will be negative: -100 sq. ft. at \$90:
$$100 \times \$90 = -\$9,000$$

52. Comp 2 is 50 sq. ft. smaller than subject, so adjustment will be positive: $+50$ sq. ft. at \$90:
$$+50 \times \$90 = +\$4,500$$

53. Comp 1 is one condition grade worse than subject, so adjustment ($+5$ percent) will be positive:
$$\$270,000 \times +0.05 = +\$13,500$$

54. Comp 2 is one condition grade better than subject, so adjustment (-5 percent) will be negative:
$$\$265,500 \times -0.05 = -\$13,275$$

55. Comp 2 and subject have same garage situation, so no adjustment is made.

56. Comp 3 has 2-car garage, subject has 1-car, so adjustment is negative: $-\$4,500$.

62. Subject is 60 feet wide, front footage comps are \$120 to \$150 per front foot. $\$120 \times 60 = \$7,200$.
$$\$150 \times 60 = \$9,000, \text{ so } \$7,200 \text{ to } \$9,000$$
is indicated range.

73. Exterior paint ($750) and water heater ($250) are the items of curable physical deterioration; they add up to $1,000. No answer of $1,000 is given, so the correct answer is "none of the above."

74. Functional obsolescence items are one bath ($4,000) and poor floor plan ($2,500); these add up to $6,500.

75. Location next to convenience store ($1,200) is the only environmental item given.

78. 20 percent of the land can't be built upon which leaves 80 percent that can:
$$0.8 \times 40 = 32 \text{ developable acres.}$$
Zoning allows 4 lots per developable acre:
$$4 \times 32 = 128 \text{ lots allowed}$$

79. At an average price of $18,000, the 128 lots will gross $2,304,000.
$$\$18,000 \times 128 = \$2,304,000$$

80. Cost of installing 2,000 feet of streets, etc., at $80 per foot:
$$2,000 \times \$80 = \$160,000$$

81. These expenses amount to 40 percent of total sales: $2,304,000 × 0.4 = $921,600

86. Monthly rents: 50 × $550 = $27,500; 150 × $675 = $101,250; $27,500 + $101,250 = $128,750
Potential annual gross income = $128,750 × 12 = $1,545,000

87. Effective gross income is potential gross income plus miscellaneous income, less vacancy.
Vacancy is 7 percent of potential gross rent:
$1,545,000 × 0.07 = $108,150 vacancy
$$\$1,545,000 + \$2,000 - \$108,150$$
$$= \$1,438,850$$

88. NOI is effective gross less operating expenses, which are 40 percent of effective gross, so NOI is 60 percent of effective gross:
$$\text{NOI} = \$1,438,850 \times 0.6 = \$863,310$$

89. Operating expenses are 40 percent of NOI:
$$\$1,438,850 \times 0.4 = \$575,540$$

94. $(1.15)^5 \times \$50,000 = 1.15 \times 1.15 \times 1.15 \times 1.15 \times 1.15 \times \$50,000 = 2.011 \times \$50,000$, or $100,000 rounded.

95. Expected sale price in 4 years: 100 acres × $10,000/acre = $1,000,000. Today's value would be $1,000,000/(1.15)^4$; $(1.15)^4 = 1.15 \times 1.15 \times 1.15 \times 1.15 = 1.749$.
$$\$1,000,000 \div 1.749 = \$571,753, \text{ or}$$
$$\$572,000 \text{ rounded}$$

99. Building has depreciated 2 percent a year for 10 years, or 20 percent total; thus it's worth 80 percent of reproduction cost: $92,000 × 0.8 = $73,600. Add $128,000 land value to get answer of $201,600.

CERTIFIED GENERAL APPRAISER EXAMINATION

3. Cash return per month: $4,000 − $1,250 = $2,750; $2,750 × 12 = $33,000 per year.
$$\$33,000 \div 0.12 = \$275,000$$

5. Monthly rents: 80 × $475 = $38,000; 120 × $575 = $69,000; $38,000 + $69,000 = $107,000.
Potential annual gross income =
$$\$107,000 \times 12 = \$1,284,000$$

6. Effective gross income is potential gross income plus miscellaneous income, less vacancy.
Vacancy is 5 percent of potential gross rent:
$1,284,000 × 0.05 = $64,200 vacancy
$$\$1,284,000 + \$5,000 - \$64,200$$
$$= \$1,224,800$$

7. NOI is effective gross less operating expenses:
$$\text{NOI} = \$1,224,800 - \$400,000 = \$824,800$$

8. Before-tax cash flow is NOI less mortgage servicing:
$$\$824,800 - \$630,000 = \$194,800$$

10. Since it is assumed that the property will keep its value of $200,000 for the entire 20 years, use simple capitalization. Annual rent is $24,000; value is $200,000:
$$\$24,000 \div \$200,000 = 0.12, \text{ or } 12\%$$

12. Recapture rate is 100%/25 years = 4% per year.

16. Property is worth $1,000,000. A 70 percent loan is $700,000, which leaves $300,000 equity. A 12 percent constant applied to the loan is $700,000 × 0.12 = $84,000. A 15 percent cash-on-cash return to the $300,000 equity is $300,000 × 0.15 = $45,000. The mortgage constant payment + cash on cash return = NOI, so
$$\text{NOI} = \$84,000 + \$45,000 = \$129,000$$

18. Monthly NOI is $6,000 − $1,250 = $4,750.
Annual NOI is $4,750 × 12 = $57,000.
$57,000 ÷ 0.12 = $475,000 value

45. Value = rent × GRM:
$575 × 127 = $73,025, or $73,000 rounded

47. When using GRM, you ignore expenses, so
don't pay any attention to the $125 monthly
expenses. Just use the monthly rent of $750.
Value = rent × GRM:
$750 × 110 = $82,500

48. The residence is now worth 160 percent of
what is was worth when it was built:
$216,000 ÷ 1.6 = $135,000

51. To find the mean, add the seven GRMs, divide by 7:

$$(125 + 125 + 127 + 127 + 127 + 128 + 130) ÷ 7 = 889 ÷ 7 = 127$$

52. The GRMs are already arranged in order; the
median is the one in the middle (the fourth):
127.

53. The mode is the value that appears most
often. Since 127 appears three times
(more than any other GRM value), the mode
is 127.

80. Purchase price will be $115,000/(1.12)^4.
$(1.12)^4 = 1.12 × 1.12 × 1.12 × 1.12 = 1.574$.
$115,000 ÷ 1.574 = $73,084
= $73,000 rounded

81. Effective depreciation is figured for 20 out of a
total of 50 years, or 20/50 = 0.4 = 40%

83. You are given more information than you
need. Improvement ratio is value of improve-
ments/total property value. Since total value
is $2,000,000 and land is worth $500,000, improvements are worth $1,500,000.
$1,500,000 ÷ $2,000,000 = 0.75 = 75%

88. Loan is 75 percent of value: $1,000,000 ×
0.75 = $750,000. 12 percent constant:
$750,000 × 0.12 = $90,000. There is $250,000
of equity, for which 15 percent cash-on-cash is
desired: $250,000 × 0.15 = $37,500.
NOI will have to be mortgage payment + desired cash return:
$37,500 + $90,000 = $127,500

89. Recapture rate is 100% / 25 years = 4% per
year.

92. Monthly rents: 25 × $550 = $13,750; 75 ×
$675 = $50,625; $13,750 + $50,625 =
$64,375.
Potential annual gross income =
$64,375 × 12 = $772,500

93. Effective gross income is potential gross income plus miscellaneous income, less vacancy.
Vacancy is 7 percent of potential gross rent:
$772,500 × 0.07 = $54,075 vacancy
$772,500 + $1,000 − $54,075 = $719,425

94. NOI is effective gross less operating expenses, which are 40 percent of effective
gross.
NOI is 60 percent of effective gross:
$719,425 × 0.6 = $431,655

95. Operating expenses are 40 percent of NOI:
$719,425 × 0.4 = $287,770

97. Land value is $100,000; 10 percent of that
($10,000) is return to land, so $90,000 −
$10,000 = $80,000 is the return to the building. This implies a value of a little less than
$800,000 for the income over 30 years
($80,000/0.1), *plus* the present value of a re-
version of about $400,000, which wouldn't be
very much. The range $750,000 to
$1,000,000 clearly is correct.

99. Value will be $(1.15)^5$ × $100,000 = 2.011 ×
$100,000 = $201,100 = $200,000 rounded.

SUPPLEMENTAL EXAMINATION 1

2. The commission is 7½% of $112,500.00.
0.075 × $112,500.00 = $8,437.50

4. The tax rate is 88 mills (8.8%) on $26,550.00.
0.088 × $26,550.00 = $2,336.40

SUPPLEMENTAL EXAMINATION 2

1. The commission is 7½% of $106,000.00.
0.075 × $106,000.00 = $7,950.00

2. The mortgage loan is at least 80% of the
price.
0.8 × $52,000= $41,600

4. Cash that the buyer must provide is $106,000
− $84,800 = $21,200. Since she already has
paid $2,000 in earnest money, she must pay
an additional $19,200 at closing.

SUPPLEMENTAL EXAMINATION 3

3. The annual property taxes are $2,336.40 (see question 4, Supplemental Examination 1). The closing date is September 18, and the seller has already paid the full year's tax bill. The buyer will own the house for the remaining 12 days of September and the three months of October, November, and December.

   $2,336.40 \div 12 = $194.70 taxes per month
   $194.70 \div 30 = $6.49 taxes per day
   3 months @ $194.70 = $584.10
   12 days @ $6.49 = $\underline{77.88}$

   Total tax proration $661.98, paid by buyer to seller

4. The mortgage insurance premium is 2½% of the mortgage amount. The mortgage is 80% of $106,000.00
   $0.8 \times $106,000 = $84,800$
   $0.025 \times $84,800 = $2,120$

5. The title insurance premium is 0.85% of the sale price.
   $0.0085 \times $106,000 = 901

6. The buyer's loan will be $0.8 \times $106,000 = $84,800.

7. The broker's commission is $0.075 \times $106,000 = $7,950.

8. The 3-year premium is $888.75, which is $296.25 annually, $24.6875 monthly, and $0.8229 daily. The policy expires on October 21, 1997, leaving the buyer with 1 year, 1 month, and 3 days of insurance.

1 year	$296.25
1 month	24.6875
3 days @ 0.8229	$\underline{2.4687}$
Total prorated amount	$323.41
paid by buyer to seller	

   Neither answer is correct.

SETTLEMENT STATEMENT WORKSHEET

SETTLEMENT DATE: 9/18/96	BUYER'S STATEMENT		SELLER'S STATEMENT	
	DEBIT	CREDIT	DEBIT	CREDIT
SALE PRICE	212,000.00			212,000.00
BROKER'S COMMISSION			15,900.00	
MORTGAGE LOAN PROCEEDS		169,600.00		
DEPOSIT		2,000.00		
PRORATED TAXES	661.98			661.98
PRORATED INSURANCE	323.41			323.41
ATTORNEY FEES	325.00		175.00	
DEED PREPARATION FEE			80.00	
MISCELLANEOUS FEES			356.55	
APPRAISAL FEE	100.00			
MORTGAGE INSURANCE	4,240.00			
TITLE INSURANCE	901.00			
MORTGAGE LOAN PAYOFF			32,331.70	
SUBTOTALS	218,551.39	171,600.00	48,843.25	212,985.39
DUE FROM BUYER		46,951.39		
DUE TO SELLER			164,142.14	
	218,551.39	218,551.39	212,985.39	212,985.39

Answer Sheets

SALESPERSON EXAMINATION 1

NAME_____ SESSION_____ AM ☐   PM ☐
   LAST   FIRST   MIDDLE   Enter your
SOC. SEC. # _____ / _____ / _____   IDENT.   EXAM CODE # _____
                                               NUMBER
DATE_____   BOOK# _____
PLACE
OF EXAM_____ SALESMAN ☐ BROKER ☐ ____   :0: :1: :2: :3: :4:   :5: :6: :7: :8: :9:
TITLE   :0: :1: :2: :3: :4:   :5: :6: :7: :8: :9:
OF EXAM_____   :0: :1: :2: :3: :4:   :5: :6: :7: :8: :9:
     IMPORTANT: IN MARKING YOUR ANSWERS   —   :0: :1: :2: :3: :4:   :5: :6: :7: :8: :9:
        FILL IN ANSWER BOX COMPLETELY

		4 :A: :B: :C: :D:	8 :A: :B: :C: :D:	12 :A: :B: :C: :D:
1 :A: :B: :C: :D:	5 :A: :B: :C: :D:	9 :A: :B: :C: :D:	13 :A: :B: :C: :D:
2 :A: :B: :C: :D:	6 :A: :B: :C: :D:	10 :A: :B: :C: :D:	14 :A: :B: :C: :D:
3 :A: :B: :C: :D:	7 :A: :B: :C: :D:	11 :A: :B: :C: :D:	15 :A: :B: :C: :D:
		19 :A: :B: :C: :D:	23 :A: :B: :C: :D:	27 :A: :B: :C: :D:
16 :A: :B: :C: :D:	20 :A: :B: :C: :D:	24 :A: :B: :C: :D:	28 :A: :B: :C: :D:
17 :A: :B: :C: :D:	21 :A: :B: :C: :D:	25 :A: :B: :C: :D:	29 :A: :B: :C: :D:
18 :A: :B: :C: :D:	22 :A: :B: :C: :D:	26 :A: :B: :C: :D:	30 :A: :B: :C: :D:
		34 :A: :B: :C: :D:	38 :A: :B: :C: :D:	42 :A: :B: :C: :D:
31 :A: :B: :C: :D:	35 :A: :B: :C: :D:	39 :A: :B: :C: :D:	43 :A: :B: :C: :D:
32 :A: :B: :C: :D:	36 :A: :B: :C: :D:	40 :A: :B: :C: :D:	44 :A: :B: :C: :D:
33 :A: :B: :C: :D:	37 :A: :B: :C: :D:	41 :A: :B: :C: :D:	45 :A: :B: :C: :D:
		49 :A: :B: :C: :D:	53 :A: :B: :C: :D:	57 :A: :B: :C: :D:
46 :A: :B: :C: :D:	50 :A: :B: :C: :D:	54 :A: :B: :C: :D:	58 :A: :B: :C: :D:
47 :A: :B: :C: :D:	51 :A: :B: :C: :D:	55 :A: :B: :C: :D:	59 :A: :B: :C: :D:
48 :A: :B: :C: :D:	52 :A: :B: :C: :D:	56 :A: :B: :C: :D:	60 :A: :B: :C: :D:
		64 :A: :B: :C: :D:	68 :A: :B: :C: :D:	72 :A: :B: :C: :D:
61 :A: :B: :C: :D:	65 :A: :B: :C: :D:	69 :A: :B: :C: :D:	73 :A: :B: :C: :D:
62 :A: :B: :C: :D:	66 :A: :B: :C: :D:	70 :A: :B: :C: :D:	74 :A: :B: :C: :D:
63 :A: :B: :C: :D:	67 :A: :B: :C: :D:	71 :A: :B: :C: :D:	75 :A: :B: :C: :D:
		79 :A: :B: :C: :D:	83 :A: :B: :C: :D:	87 :A: :B: :C: :D:
76 :A: :B: :C: :D:	80 :A: :B: :C: :D:	84 :A: :B: :C: :D:	88 :A: :B: :C: :D:
77 :A: :B: :C: :D:	81 :A: :B: :C: :D:	85 :A: :B: :C: :D:	89 :A: :B: :C: :D:
78 :A: :B: :C: :D:	82 :A: :B: :C: :D:	86 :A: :B: :C: :D:	90 :A: :B: :C: :D:
		94 :A: :B: :C: :D:	98 :A: :B: :C: :D:	
91 :A: :B: :C: :D:	95 :A: :B: :C: :D:	99 :A: :B: :C: :D:	
92 :A: :B: :C: :D:	96 :A: :B: :C: :D:	100 :A: :B: :C: :D:	
93 :A: :B: :C: :D:	97 :A: :B: :C: :D:		

SALESPERSON EXAMINATION 2

NAME_____
LAST   FIRST   MIDDLE

SOC. SEC. #_____/_____/_____

DATE_____

PLACE
OF EXAM_____ SALESMAN ☐ BROKER ☐

TITLE
OF EXAM_____

**IMPORTANT: IN MARKING YOUR ANSWERS
FILL IN ANSWER BOX COMPLETELY**

Enter your
IDENT.
NUMBER

SESSION   AM ☐   PM ☐

EXAM CODE #_____

BOOK#_____

1 :A: :B: :C: :D:	4 :A: :B: :C: :D:	8 :A: :B: :C: :D:	12 :A: :B: :C: :D:
2 :A: :B: :C: :D:	5 :A: :B: :C: :D:	9 :A: :B: :C: :D:	13 :A: :B: :C: :D:
3 :A: :B: :C: :D:	6 :A: :B: :C: :D:	10 :A: :B: :C: :D:	14 :A: :B: :C: :D:
	7 :A: :B: :C: :D:	11 :A: :B: :C: :D:	15 :A: :B: :C: :D:
16 :A: :B: :C: :D:	19 :A: :B: :C: :D:	23 :A: :B: :C: :D:	27 :A: :B: :C: :D:
17 :A: :B: :C: :D:	20 :A: :B: :C: :D:	24 :A: :B: :C: :D:	28 :A: :B: :C: :D:
18 :A: :B: :C: :D:	21 :A: :B: :C: :D:	25 :A: :B: :C: :D:	29 :A: :B: :C: :D:
	22 :A: :B: :C: :D:	26 :A: :B: :C: :D:	30 :A: :B: :C: :D:
31 :A: :B: :C: :D:	34 :A: :B: :C: :D:	38 :A: :B: :C: :D:	42 :A: :B: :C: :D:
32 :A: :B: :C: :D:	35 :A: :B: :C: :D:	39 :A: :B: :C: :D:	43 :A: :B: :C: :D:
33 :A: :B: :C: :D:	36 :A: :B: :C: :D:	40 :A: :B: :C: :D:	44 :A: :B: :C: :D:
	37 :A: :B: :C: :D:	41 :A: :B: :C: :D:	45 :A: :B: :C: :D:
46 :A: :B: :C: :D:	49 :A: :B: :C: :D:	53 :A: :B: :C: :D:	57 :A: :B: :C: :D:
47 :A: :B: :C: :D:	50 :A: :B: :C: :D:	54 :A: :B: :C: :D:	58 :A: :B: :C: :D:
48 :A: :B: :C: :D:	51 :A: :B: :C: :D:	55 :A: :B: :C: :D:	59 :A: :B: :C: :D:
	52 :A: :B: :C: :D:	56 :A: :B: :C: :D:	60 :A: :B: :C: :D:
61 :A: :B: :C: :D:	64 :A: :B: :C: :D:	68 :A: :B: :C: :D:	72 :A: :B: :C: :D:
62 :A: :B: :C: :D:	65 :A: :B: :C: :D:	69 :A: :B: :C: :D:	73 :A: :B: :C: :D:
63 :A: :B: :C: :D:	66 :A: :B: :C: :D:	70 :A: :B: :C: :D:	74 :A: :B: :C: :D:
	67 :A: :B: :C: :D:	71 :A: :B: :C: :D:	75 :A: :B: :C: :D:
76 :A: :B: :C: :D:	79 :A: :B: :C: :D:	83 :A: :B: :C: :D:	87 :A: :B: :C: :D:
77 :A: :B: :C: :D:	80 :A: :B: :C: :D:	84 :A: :B: :C: :D:	88 :A: :B: :C: :D:
78 :A: :B: :C: :D:	81 :A: :B: :C: :D:	85 :A: :B: :C: :D:	89 :A: :B: :C: :D:
	82 :A: :B: :C: :D:	86 :A: :B: :C: :D:	90 :A: :B: :C: :D:
91 :A: :B: :C: :D:	94 :A: :B: :C: :D:	98 :A: :B: :C: :D:	
92 :A: :B: :C: :D:	95 :A: :B: :C: :D:	99 :A: :B: :C: :D:	
93 :A: :B: :C: :D:	96 :A: :B: :C: :D:	100 :A: :B: :C: :D:	
	97 :A: :B: :C: :D:		

BROKER EXAMINATION 1

NAME_____ SESSION   AM ☐   PM ☐
        LAST   FIRST   MIDDLE
SOC. SEC. # _____ / _____ / _____   Enter your   EXAM CODE # _____
                                                 IDENT.
DATE_____   NUMBER   BOOK# _____
PLACE
OF EXAM_____ SALESMAN ☐ BROKER ☐
TITLE
OF EXAM_____
        IMPORTANT: IN MARKING YOUR ANSWERS
        FILL IN ANSWER BOX COMPLETELY

:0:	:1:	:2:	:3:	:4:		:5:	:6:	:7:	:8:	:9:
:0:	:1:	:2:	:3:	:4:		:5:	:6:	:7:	:8:	:9:
:0:	:1:	:2:	:3:	:4:		:5:	:6:	:7:	:8:	:9:
:0:	:1:	:2:	:3:	:4:		:5:	:6:	:7:	:8:	:9:

1 :A: :B: :C: :D:	4 :A: :B: :C: :D:	8 :A: :B: :C: :D:	12 :A: :B: :C: :D:
2 :A: :B: :C: :D:	5 :A: :B: :C: :D:	9 :A: :B: :C: :D:	13 :A: :B: :C: :D:
3 :A: :B: :C: :D:	6 :A: :B: :C: :D:	10 :A: :B: :C: :D:	14 :A: :B: :C: :D:
	7 :A: :B: :C: :D:	11 :A: :B: :C: :D:	15 :A: :B: :C: :D:
16 :A: :B: :C: :D:	19 :A: :B: :C: :D:	23 :A: :B: :C: :D:	27 :A: :B: :C: :D:
17 :A: :B: :C: :D:	20 :A: :B: :C: :D:	24 :A: :B: :C: :D:	28 :A: :B: :C: :D:
18 :A: :B: :C: :D:	21 :A: :B: :C: :D:	25 :A: :B: :C: :D:	29 :A: :B: :C: :D:
	22 :A: :B: :C: :D:	26 :A: :B: :C: :D:	30 :A: :B: :C: :D:
31 :A: :B: :C: :D:	34 :A: :B: :C: :D:	38 :A: :B: :C: :D:	42 :A: :B: :C: :D:
32 :A: :B: :C: :D:	35 :A: :B: :C: :D:	39 :A: :B: :C: :D:	43 :A: :B: :C: :D:
33 :A: :B: :C: :D:	36 :A: :B: :C: :D:	40 :A: :B: :C: :D:	44 :A: :B: :C: :D:
	37 :A: :B: :C: :D:	41 :A: :B: :C: :D:	45 :A: :B: :C: :D:
46 :A: :B: :C: :D:	49 :A: :B: :C: :D:	53 :A: :B: :C: :D:	57 :A: :B: :C: :D:
47 :A: :B: :C: :D:	50 :A: :B: :C: :D:	54 :A: :B: :C: :D:	58 :A: :B: :C: :D:
48 :A: :B: :C: :D:	51 :A: :B: :C: :D:	55 :A: :B: :C: :D:	59 :A: :B: :C: :D:
	52 :A: :B: :C: :D:	56 :A: :B: :C: :D:	60 :A: :B: :C: :D:
61 :A: :B: :C: :D:	64 :A: :B: :C: :D:	68 :A: :B: :C: :D:	72 :A: :B: :C: :D:
62 :A: :B: :C: :D:	65 :A: :B: :C: :D:	69 :A: :B: :C: :D:	73 :A: :B: :C: :D:
63 :A: :B: :C: :D:	66 :A: :B: :C: :D:	70 :A: :B: :C: :D:	74 :A: :B: :C: :D:
	67 :A: :B: :C: :D:	71 :A: :B: :C: :D:	75 :A: :B: :C: :D:
76 :A: :B: :C: :D:	79 :A: :B: :C: :D:	83 :A: :B: :C: :D:	87 :A: :B: :C: :D:
77 :A: :B: :C: :D:	80 :A: :B: :C: :D:	84 :A: :B: :C: :D:	88 :A: :B: :C: :D:
78 :A: :B: :C: :D:	81 :A: :B: :C: :D:	85 :A: :B: :C: :D:	89 :A: :B: :C: :D:
	82 :A: :B: :C: :D:	86 :A: :B: :C: :D:	90 :A: :B: :C: :D:
91 :A: :B: :C: :D:	94 :A: :B: :C: :D:	98 :A: :B: :C: :D:	
92 :A: :B: :C: :D:	95 :A: :B: :C: :D:	99 :A: :B: :C: :D:	
93 :A: :B: :C: :D:	96 :A: :B: :C: :D:	100 :A: :B: :C: :D:	
	97 :A: :B: :C: :D:		

BROKER EXAMINATION 2

NAME_____
LAST   FIRST   MIDDLE

SOC. SEC. # _____ / _____ / _____

DATE_____

PLACE
OF EXAM_____ SALESMAN ☐ BROKER ☐ _____

TITLE
OF EXAM_____

**IMPORTANT: IN MARKING YOUR ANSWERS
FILL IN ANSWER BOX COMPLETELY**

SESSION   AM ☐   PM ☐

Enter your IDENT. NUMBER

EXAM CODE #_____

BOOK# _____

1 :A: :B: :C: :D:
2 :A: :B: :C: :D:
3 :A: :B: :C: :D:
4 :A: :B: :C: :D:
5 :A: :B: :C: :D:
6 :A: :B: :C: :D:
7 :A: :B: :C: :D:
8 :A: :B: :C: :D:
9 :A: :B: :C: :D:
10 :A: :B: :C: :D:
11 :A: :B: :C: :D:
12 :A: :B: :C: :D:
13 :A: :B: :C: :D:
14 :A: :B: :C: :D:
15 :A: :B: :C: :D:
16 :A: :B: :C: :D:
17 :A: :B: :C: :D:
18 :A: :B: :C: :D:
19 :A: :B: :C: :D:
20 :A: :B: :C: :D:
21 :A: :B: :C: :D:
22 :A: :B: :C: :D:
23 :A: :B: :C: :D:
24 :A: :B: :C: :D:
25 :A: :B: :C: :D:
26 :A: :B: :C: :D:
27 :A: :B: :C: :D:
28 :A: :B: :C: :D:
29 :A: :B: :C: :D:
30 :A: :B: :C: :D:
31 :A: :B: :C: :D:
32 :A: :B: :C: :D:
33 :A: :B: :C: :D:
34 :A: :B: :C: :D:
35 :A: :B: :C: :D:
36 :A: :B: :C: :D:
37 :A: :B: :C: :D:
38 :A: :B: :C: :D:
39 :A: :B: :C: :D:
40 :A: :B: :C: :D:
41 :A: :B: :C: :D:
42 :A: :B: :C: :D:
43 :A: :B: :C: :D:
44 :A: :B: :C: :D:
45 :A: :B: :C: :D:
46 :A: :B: :C: :D:
47 :A: :B: :C: :D:
48 :A: :B: :C: :D:
49 :A: :B: :C: :D:
50 :A: :B: :C: :D:
51 :A: :B: :C: :D:
52 :A: :B: :C: :D:
53 :A: :B: :C: :D:
54 :A: :B: :C: :D:
55 :A: :B: :C: :D:
56 :A: :B: :C: :D:
57 :A: :B: :C: :D:
58 :A: :B: :C: :D:
59 :A: :B: :C: :D:
60 :A: :B: :C: :D:
61 :A: :B: :C: :D:
62 :A: :B: :C: :D:
63 :A: :B: :C: :D:
64 :A: :B: :C: :D:
65 :A: :B: :C: :D:
66 :A: :B: :C: :D:
67 :A: :B: :C: :D:
68 :A: :B: :C: :D:
69 :A: :B: :C: :D:
70 :A: :B: :C: :D:
71 :A: :B: :C: :D:
72 :A: :B: :C: :D:
73 :A: :B: :C: :D:
74 :A: :B: :C: :D:
75 :A: :B: :C: :D:
76 :A: :B: :C: :D:
77 :A: :B: :C: :D:
78 :A: :B: :C: :D:
79 :A: :B: :C: :D:
80 :A: :B: :C: :D:
81 :A: :B: :C: :D:
82 :A: :B: :C: :D:
83 :A: :B: :C: :D:
84 :A: :B: :C: :D:
85 :A: :B: :C: :D:
86 :A: :B: :C: :D:
87 :A: :B: :C: :D:
88 :A: :B: :C: :D:
89 :A: :B: :C: :D:
90 :A: :B: :C: :D:
91 :A: :B: :C: :D:
92 :A: :B: :C: :D:
93 :A: :B: :C: :D:
94 :A: :B: :C: :D:
95 :A: :B: :C: :D:
96 :A: :B: :C: :D:
97 :A: :B: :C: :D:
98 :A: :B: :C: :D:
99 :A: :B: :C: :D:
100 :A: :B: :C: :D:

APPRAISER LICENSE EXAMINATION

NAME_____

LAST   FIRST   MIDDLE   Enter your IDENT. NUMBER

SESSION _____   AM ☐   PM ☐

SOC. SEC. # _____/_____/_____

EXAM CODE # _____

DATE _____

PLACE OF EXAM _____ SALESMAN ☐ BROKER ☐

BOOK# _____

TITLE OF EXAM _____

IMPORTANT: IN MARKING YOUR ANSWERS
FILL IN ANSWER BOX COMPLETELY

1 :A: :B: :C: :D: :E:	4 :A: :B: :C: :D: :E:	8 :A: :B: :C: :D: :E:	12 :A: :B: :C: :D: :E:
1 :A: :B: :C: :D: :E:	5 :A: :B: :C: :D: :E:	9 :A: :B: :C: :D: :E:	13 :A: :B: :C: :D: :E:
2 :A: :B: :C: :D: :E:	6 :A: :B: :C: :D: :E:	10 :A: :B: :C: :D: :E:	14 :A: :B: :C: :D: :E:
3 :A: :B: :C: :D: :E:	7 :A: :B: :C: :D: :E:	11 :A: :B: :C: :D: :E:	15 :A: :B: :C: :D: :E:
16 :A: :B: :C: :D: :E:	19 :A: :B: :C: :D: :E:	23 :A: :B: :C: :D: :E:	27 :A: :B: :C: :D: :E:
17 :A: :B: :C: :D: :E:	20 :A: :B: :C: :D: :E:	24 :A: :B: :C: :D: :E:	28 :A: :B: :C: :D: :E:
18 :A: :B: :C: :D: :E:	21 :A: :B: :C: :D: :E:	25 :A: :B: :C: :D: :E:	29 :A: :B: :C: :D: :E:
	22 :A: :B: :C: :D: :E:	26 :A: :B: :C: :D: :E:	30 :A: :B: :C: :D: :E:
31 :A: :B: :C: :D: :E:	34 :A: :B: :C: :D: :E:	38 :A: :B: :C: :D: :E:	42 :A: :B: :C: :D: :E:
32 :A: :B: :C: :D: :E:	35 :A: :B: :C: :D: :E:	39 :A: :B: :C: :D: :E:	43 :A: :B: :C: :D: :E:
33 :A: :B: :C: :D: :E:	36 :A: :B: :C: :D: :E:	40 :A: :B: :C: :D: :E:	44 :A: :B: :C: :D: :E:
	37 :A: :B: :C: :D: :E:	41 :A: :B: :C: :D: :E:	45 :A: :B: :C: :D: :E:
46 :A: :B: :C: :D: :E:	49 :A: :B: :C: :D: :E:	53 :A: :B: :C: :D: :E:	57 :A: :B: :C: :D: :E:
47 :A: :B: :C: :D: :E:	50 :A: :B: :C: :D: :E:	54 :A: :B: :C: :D: :E:	58 :A: :B: :C: :D: :E:
48 :A: :B: :C: :D: :E:	51 :A: :B: :C: :D: :E:	55 :A: :B: :C: :D: :E:	59 :A: :B: :C: :D: :E:
	52 :A: :B: :C: :D: :E:	56 :A: :B: :C: :D: :E:	60 :A: :B: :C: :D: :E:
61 :A: :B: :C: :D: :E:	64 :A: :B: :C: :D: :E:	68 :A: :B: :C: :D: :E:	72 :A: :B: :C: :D: :E:
62 :A: :B: :C: :D: :E:	65 :A: :B: :C: :D: :E:	69 :A: :B: :C: :D: :E:	73 :A: :B: :C: :D: :E:
63 :A: :B: :C: :D: :E:	66 :A: :B: :C: :D: :E:	70 :A: :B: :C: :D: :E:	74 :A: :B: :C: :D: :E:
	67 :A: :B: :C: :D: :E:	71 :A: :B: :C: :D: :E:	75 :A: :B: :C: :D: :E:
76 :A: :B: :C: :D: :E:	79 :A: :B: :C: :D: :E:	83 :A: :B: :C: :D: :E:	87 :A: :B: :C: :D: :E:
77 :A: :B: :C: :D: :E:	80 :A: :B: :C: :D: :E:	84 :A: :B: :C: :D: :E:	88 :A: :B: :C: :D: :E:
78 :A: :B: :C: :D: :E:	81 :A: :B: :C: :D: :E:	85 :A: :B: :C: :D: :E:	89 :A: :B: :C: :D: :E:
	82 :A: :B: :C: :D: :E:	86 :A: :B: :C: :D: :E:	90 :A: :B: :C: :D: :E:
91 :A: :B: :C: :D: :E:	94 :A: :B: :C: :D: :E:	98 :A: :B: :C: :D: :E:	
92 :A: :B: :C: :D: :E:	95 :A: :B: :C: :D: :E:	99 :A: :B: :C: :D: :E:	
93 :A: :B: :C: :D: :E:	96 :A: :B: :C: :D: :E:	100 :A: :B: :C: :D: :E:	
	97 :A: :B: :C: :D: :E:		

CERTIFIED RESIDENTIAL APPRAISER EXAMINATION

NAME_____   SESSION   AM ☐   PM ☐
     LAST   FIRST   MIDDLE

SOC. SEC. #_____/_____/_____   Enter your IDENT. NUMBER   EXAM CODE #_____

DATE_____   BOOK#_____

PLACE OF EXAM_____ SALESMAN ☐ BROKER ☐

TITLE OF EXAM_____

IMPORTANT: IN MARKING YOUR ANSWERS
FILL IN ANSWER BOX COMPLETELY

1 :A: :B: :C: :D: :E:	4 :A: :B: :C: :D: :E:	8 :A: :B: :C: :D: :E:	12 :A: :B: :C: :D: :E:
2 :A: :B: :C: :D: :E:	5 :A: :B: :C: :D: :E:	9 :A: :B: :C: :D: :E:	13 :A: :B: :C: :D: :E:
3 :A: :B: :C: :D: :E:	6 :A: :B: :C: :D: :E:	10 :A: :B: :C: :D: :E:	14 :A: :B: :C: :D: :E:
	7 :A: :B: :C: :D: :E:	11 :A: :B: :C: :D: :E:	15 :A: :B: :C: :D: :E:
16 :A: :B: :C: :D: :E:	19 :A: :B: :C: :D: :E:	23 :A: :B: :C: :D: :E:	27 :A: :B: :C: :D: :E:
17 :A: :B: :C: :D: :E:	20 :A: :B: :C: :D: :E:	24 :A: :B: :C: :D: :E:	28 :A: :B: :C: :D: :E:
18 :A: :B: :C: :D: :E:	21 :A: :B: :C: :D: :E:	25 :A: :B: :C: :D: :E:	29 :A: :B: :C: :D: :E:
	22 :A: :B: :C: :D: :E:	26 :A: :B: :C: :D: :E:	30 :A: :B: :C: :D: :E:
31 :A: :B: :C: :D: :E:	34 :A: :B: :C: :D: :E:	38 :A: :B: :C: :D: :E:	42 :A: :B: :C: :D: :E:
32 :A: :B: :C: :D: :E:	35 :A: :B: :C: :D: :E:	39 :A: :B: :C: :D: :E:	43 :A: :B: :C: :D: :E:
33 :A: :B: :C: :D: :E:	36 :A: :B: :C: :D: :E:	40 :A: :B: :C: :D: :E:	44 :A: :B: :C: :D: :E:
	37 :A: :B: :C: :D: :E:	41 :A: :B: :C: :D: :E:	45 :A: :B: :C: :D: :E:
46 :A: :B: :C: :D: :E:	49 :A: :B: :C: :D: :E:	53 :A: :B: :C: :D: :E:	57 :A: :B: :C: :D: :E:
47 :A: :B: :C: :D: :E:	50 :A: :B: :C: :D: :E:	54 :A: :B: :C: :D: :E:	58 :A: :B: :C: :D: :E:
48 :A: :B: :C: :D: :E:	51 :A: :B: :C: :D: :E:	55 :A: :B: :C: :D: :E:	59 :A: :B: :C: :D: :E:
	52 :A: :B: :C: :D: :E:	56 :A: :B: :C: :D: :E:	60 :A: :B: :C: :D: :E:
61 :A: :B: :C: :D: :E:	64 :A: :B: :C: :D: :E:	68 :A: :B: :C: :D: :E:	72 :A: :B: :C: :D: :E:
62 :A: :B: :C: :D: :E:	65 :A: :B: :C: :D: :E:	69 :A: :B: :C: :D: :E:	73 :A: :B: :C: :D: :E:
63 :A: :B: :C: :D: :E:	66 :A: :B: :C: :D: :E:	70 :A: :B: :C: :D: :E:	74 :A: :B: :C: :D: :E:
	67 :A: :B: :C: :D: :E:	71 :A: :B: :C: :D: :E:	75 :A: :B: :C: :D: :E:
76 :A: :B: :C: :D: :E:	79 :A: :B: :C: :D: :E:	83 :A: :B: :C: :D: :E:	87 :A: :B: :C: :D: :E:
77 :A: :B: :C: :D: :E:	80 :A: :B: :C: :D: :E:	84 :A: :B: :C: :D: :E:	88 :A: :B: :C: :D: :E:
78 :A: :B: :C: :D: :E:	81 :A: :B: :C: :D: :E:	85 :A: :B: :C: :D: :E:	89 :A: :B: :C: :D: :E:
	82 :A: :B: :C: :D: :E:	86 :A: :B: :C: :D: :E:	90 :A: :B: :C: :D: :E:
91 :A: :B: :C: :D: :E:	94 :A: :B: :C: :D: :E:	98 :A: :B: :C: :D: :E:	
92 :A: :B: :C: :D: :E:	95 :A: :B: :C: :D: :E:	99 :A: :B: :C: :D: :E:	
93 :A: :B: :C: :D: :E:	96 :A: :B: :C: :D: :E:	100 :A: :B: :C: :D: :E:	
	97 :A: :B: :C: :D: :E:		

CERTIFIED GENERAL APPRAISER EXAMINATION

NAME _____
LAST   FIRST   MIDDLE

SOC. SEC. # _____ / _____ / _____

DATE _____

PLACE
OF EXAM _____ SALESMAN ☐ BROKER ☐

TITLE
OF EXAM _____

**IMPORTANT: IN MARKING YOUR ANSWERS
FILL IN ANSWER BOX COMPLETELY**

Enter your IDENT. NUMBER

SESSION   AM ☐   PM ☐

EXAM CODE # _____

BOOK# _____

1 A B C D E
2 A B C D E
3 A B C D E
4 A B C D E
5 A B C D E
6 A B C D E
7 A B C D E
8 A B C D E
9 A B C D E
10 A B C D E
11 A B C D E
12 A B C D E
13 A B C D E
14 A B C D E
15 A B C D E
16 A B C D E
17 A B C D E
18 A B C D E
19 A B C D E
20 A B C D E
21 A B C D E
22 A B C D E
23 A B C D E
24 A B C D E
25 A B C D E
26 A B C D E
27 A B C D E
28 A B C D E
29 A B C D E
30 A B C D E
31 A B C D E
32 A B C D E
33 A B C D E
34 A B C D E
35 A B C D E
36 A B C D E
37 A B C D E
38 A B C D E
39 A B C D E
40 A B C D E
41 A B C D E
42 A B C D E
43 A B C D E
44 A B C D E
45 A B C D E
46 A B C D E
47 A B C D E
48 A B C D E
49 A B C D E
50 A B C D E
51 A B C D E
52 A B C D E
53 A B C D E
54 A B C D E
55 A B C D E
56 A B C D E
57 A B C D E
58 A B C D E
59 A B C D E
60 A B C D E
61 A B C D E
62 A B C D E
63 A B C D E
64 A B C D E
65 A B C D E
66 A B C D E
67 A B C D E
68 A B C D E
69 A B C D E
70 A B C D E
71 A B C D E
72 A B C D E
73 A B C D E
74 A B C D E
75 A B C D E
76 A B C D E
77 A B C D E
78 A B C D E
79 A B C D E
80 A B C D E
81 A B C D E
82 A B C D E
83 A B C D E
84 A B C D E
85 A B C D E
86 A B C D E
87 A B C D E
88 A B C D E
89 A B C D E
90 A B C D E
91 A B C D E
92 A B C D E
93 A B C D E
94 A B C D E
95 A B C D E
96 A B C D E
97 A B C D E
98 A B C D E
99 A B C D E
100 A B C D E

SUPPLEMENTAL EXAMINATION 1

NAME_____ SESSION _____ AM ☐ PM ☐
LAST   FIRST   MIDDLE

SOC. SEC. # _____ / _____ / _____   Enter your IDENT. NUMBER   EXAM CODE # _____

DATE _____

PLACE OF EXAM _____ SALESMAN ☐ BROKER ☐   BOOK# _____

TITLE OF EXAM _____

IMPORTANT: IN MARKING YOUR ANSWERS FILL IN ANSWER BOX COMPLETELY

1	:A: :B: :C: :D: :E:	4	:A: :B: :C: :D: :E:	8	:A: :B: :C: :D: :E:	12	:A: :B: :C: :D: :E:
2	:A: :B: :C: :D: :E:	5	:A: :B: :C: :D: :E:	9	:A: :B: :C: :D: :E:	13	:A: :B: :C: :D: :E:
3	:A: :B: :C: :D: :E:	6	:A: :B: :C: :D: :E:	10	:A: :B: :C: :D: :E:	14	:A: :B: :C: :D: :E:
		7	:A: :B: :C: :D: :E:	11	:A: :B: :C: :D: :E:	15	:A: :B: :C: :D: :E:

SUPPLEMENTAL EXAMINATION 2

NAME_____ SESSION _____ AM ☐ PM ☐
LAST   FIRST   MIDDLE

SOC. SEC. # _____ / _____ / _____   Enter your IDENT. NUMBER   EXAM CODE # _____

DATE _____

PLACE OF EXAM _____ SALESMAN ☐ BROKER ☐   BOOK# _____

TITLE OF EXAM _____

IMPORTANT: IN MARKING YOUR ANSWERS FILL IN ANSWER BOX COMPLETELY

1	:A: :B: :C: :D: :E:	4	:A: :B: :C: :D: :E:	8	:A: :B: :C: :D: :E:
2	:A: :B: :C: :D: :E:	5	:A: :B: :C: :D: :E:	9	:A: :B: :C: :D: :E:
3	:A: :B: :C: :D: :E:	6	:A: :B: :C: :D: :E:	10	:A: :B: :C: :D: :E:
		7	:A: :B: :C: :D: :E:		

SUPPLEMENTAL EXAMINATION 3

NAME_____ SESSION _____ AM ☐ PM ☐
LAST   FIRST   MIDDLE

SOC. SEC. # _____ / _____ / _____   Enter your IDENT. NUMBER   EXAM CODE # _____

DATE _____

PLACE OF EXAM _____ SALESMAN ☐ BROKER ☐   BOOK# _____

TITLE OF EXAM _____

IMPORTANT: IN MARKING YOUR ANSWERS FILL IN ANSWER BOX COMPLETELY

1	:A: :B: :C: :D: :E:	4	:A: :B: :C: :D: :E:	8	:A: :B: :C: :D: :E:	12	:A: :B: :C: :D: :E:
2	:A: :B: :C: :D: :E:	5	:A: :B: :C: :D: :E:	9	:A: :B: :C: :D: :E:	13	:A: :B: :C: :D: :E:
3	:A: :B: :C: :D: :E:	6	:A: :B: :C: :D: :E:	10	:A: :B: :C: :D: :E:	14	:A: :B: :C: :D: :E:
		7	:A: :B: :C: :D: :E:	11	:A: :B: :C: :D: :E:	15	:A: :B: :C: :D: :E:

More selected BARRON'S titles:

BARRON'S ACCOUNTING HANDBOOK, 3RD ED.
Joel G. Siegel and Jae K. Shim
Provides accounting rules, guidelines, formulas and techniques, etc., to help students and
business professionals work out accounting problems.
Hardcover, $35.00, Canada $48.95/ISBN 0-7641-5282-3, 880 pages

REAL ESTATE HANDBOOK, 5TH ED.
Jack P. Friedman and Jack C. Harris
A dictionary/reference for everyone in real estate. Defines approximately 2000 legal,
financial, and architectural terms.
Hardcover, $35.00, Canada $49.00/ ISBN 0-7641-5263-7, approx. 780 pages

HOW TO PREPARE FOR THE REAL ESTATE LICENSING
EXAMS: SALESPERSON, BROKER, APPRAISER, 6TH ED.
Bruce Lindeman and Jack P. Friedman
Reviews current exam topics and features updated model exams and supplemental exams,
all with explained answers.
Paperback, $14.95, Canada $21.00/ISBN 0-7641-0773-9, 340 pages

BARRON'S FINANCE AND INVESTMENT HANDBOOK, 6TH ED.
John Downes and Jordan Elliot Goodman
This hard-working handbook of essential information defines more than 3000 key terms,
and explores 30 basic investment opportunities. The investment information is thoroughly
up-to-date.
Hardcover, $39.95, Canada $55.95/ISBN 0-7641-5554-7, 1408 pages

FINANCIAL TABLES FOR MONEY MANAGEMENT
Stephen S. Solomon, Dr. Clifford Marshall, Martin Pepper, Jack P. Friedman, and Jack C. Harris
Pocket-sized handbooks of interest and investment rate tables used easily by average
investors and mortgage holders.

Each book: Paperback.
Adjustable Rate Mortgages, 3rd Ed., $8.95, Canada $12.95/0-7641-2454-4, 288 pp.
Canadian Mortgage Payments, 3rd Ed., Canada $8.95/0-7641-2374-2, 336 pp.
Mortgage Payments, 3rd Ed., $7.95, Canada $11.50/0-7641-1801-3, 336 pp.
Real Estate Loans, 3rd Ed., $7.95, Canada $11.50/0-7641-1800-5, 350 pp.

Books may be purchased at your bookstore or by mail from Barron's. Enclose check or money order for
total amount plus sales tax where applicable and 18% for postage and handling (minimum charge $5.95).
NY State, New Jersey, Michigan, and California residents add sales tax. Prices subject to change without
notice.

 Barron's Educational Series, Inc.
250 Wireless Blvd., Hauppauge, NY 11788
In Canada: Georgetown Book Warehouse
34 Armstrong Ave., Georgetown, Ontario L7G 4R9
www.barronseduc.com

(#11) R9/04